EAGLE AGAINST THE SUN

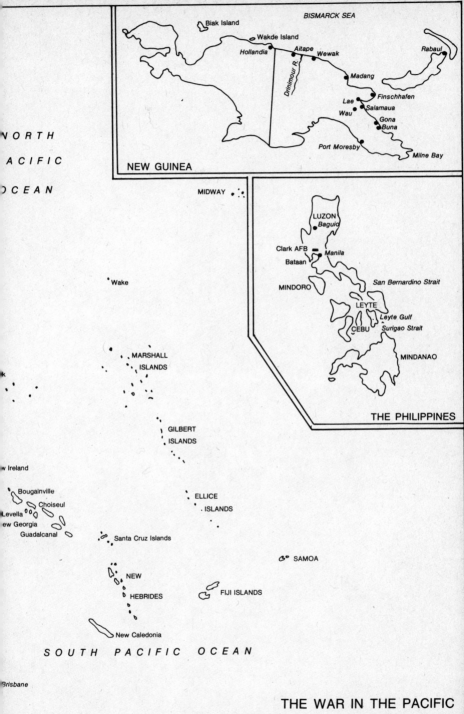

NORTH

ACIFIC

OCEAN

BISMARCK SEA

Biak Island

Wakde Island

Hollandia

Aitape

Wewak

Rabaul

Madang

Drinimour R.

Finschhafen

Lae

Salamaua

Wau

Gona

Buna

Port Moresby

Milne Bay

NEW GUINEA

MIDWAY

LUZON

Baguio

Clark AFB

Manila

Bataan

Wake

MINDORO

San Bernardino Strait

LEYTE

Leyte Gulf

CEBU

Surigao Strait

MINDANAO

THE PHILIPPINES

MARSHALL

ISLANDS

GILBERT

ISLANDS

w Ireland

Bougainville

Choiseul

Levella

ELLICE

ew Georgia

ISLANDS

Guadalcanal

Santa Cruz Islands

SAMOA

NEW

HEBRIDES

FIJI ISLANDS

New Caledonia

SOUTH PACIFIC OCEAN

Brisbane

THE WAR IN THE PACIFIC
1941-1945

The American War with Japan

EAGLE AGAINST THE SUN

Ronald H. Spector

Vintage Books
A Division of Random House
New York

First Vintage Books Edition, November 1985

Library of Congress Cataloging in Publication Data

Spector, Ronald H., 1943–
Eagle against the sun.

Bibliography: p.
Includes index.
1. World War, 1914–1918—Campaigns
—Pacific Area.
2. World War, 1939–1945—United States.
3. World War, 1939–1945—Japan.
4. United States—History—1933–1945
5. Japan—History—1912 –1945.   I. Title.
D767.S69   1985b   940.54′26   85–40140
ISBN 0–394–74101–3 (pbk.)

To the memory of my father,
David D. Spector

Contents

Acknowledgments

The late Professor Louis Morton, editor of the "Wars of the United States" series, selected me to write this volume and approved the initial outline shortly before his death. Although he did not live to see the completed work, it is my hope that the end product would not disappoint him.

Many of my colleagues at the Center of Military History, although at times skeptical that the experience of the war with Japan could be meaningfully encompassed within one volume, were kind enough to read and comment on portions of the manuscript. They include Robert W. Coakley, Stanley Falk, Charles MacDonald, Morris J. MacGregor, and Robert Ross Smith. Bernard Nalty of the office of the Chief of Air Force History read a portion of the manuscript and also assisted me in locating relevant Air Force records. John Toland generously gave me access to his extensive notes and files used in the preparation of his prize-winning book, *The Rising Sun.*

Michael Howard and the late Richard Storry discussed the book with me during my brief visit to Oxford in 1978 and Professor Howard kindly read a portion of the first draft. My old friends Stephen Peltz and Sadao Asada read parts of the manuscript dealing with Japanese plans and policies. Professor Robert Love of the U.S. Naval Academy read parts of the manuscript and shared with me his unparalleled knowledge of Pacific strategy and World War II Navy politics and personalities. Mr. John Hammond Moore kindly allowed me to use a prepublication draft of his excellent book on G.I.s in Australia, *Down Under War.* Alexander S. Cochran shared with me the results of his wideranging research in the cryptographic records, the results of which have since been published in the *Revue d'histoire de la deuxieme guerre mondiale.* Thomas C. Hone gave me the benefit of his extensive knowledge of technology and naval policy in the interwar years. Alan R. Millett took time from his own demanding research to give the entire manuscript a thorough reading, as did Peter J. O'Connell, who also helped with the early planning and organization of the book.

The late Charles Romanus introduced me to research in the records of the China-Burma-India theater when I was a young journeyman in the Center of Military History. Although the present results may not have met his exacting standards, I could not have had a better guide.

Like many other researchers in the complex and voluminous records of World War II, I have benefited immensely from the knowledge and experience of archivists at various government repositories. At the Naval Historical Center Operational Archives, Dr. Dean Allard, who has been an unfailing help since my graduate days, put his formidable knowledge of World War II at my disposal. I am also grateful to Geri Judkins and Martha Crowley of the Operational Archives Branch and to Mary Wolfskill of the Library of Congress. The Naval and old military records branch and the modern military records branch of the National Archives are staffed by men and women whose collective knowledge of World War II and its records is probably unmatched anywhere in the country. I am especially grateful to William Cunliffe, Terry Hammett, Timothy Nenninger, Edward Reese, and John E. Taylor for their invaluable assistance. I am also grateful to Sally Marks of the Civil and Diplomatic branch of the National Archives, for her patience and prompt assistance with my many requests.

Mrs. Helene Masson-Bruno cheerfully and patiently typed the many drafts and revisions while also acting as perceptive first-line critic and copy-editor. I am also grateful to my editors at The Free Press—Barbara Chernow, Joyce Seltzer, and Eileen DeWald—who patiently saw the book through its lengthy gestation. Finally, I would like to thank my wife Dianne and my sons Daniel and Jonathan, who have had to live with this book for nine long years. The opinions expressed in this book are mine and should not be construed as those of any of the above-mentioned individuals or of any agency of the U.S. government.

Introduction

The war between the United States and Japan was in many ways a unique and unprecedented conflict—the first, and probably the last, to be waged on such a scale and upon such a stage. It began with a stunning display of air power by the Japanese and ended with the most deadly air raids in history by the Americans. As a naval war, it was unparalleled. More battles were waged at sea and more warships sunk than in all other twentieth century naval campaigns combined. The land campaigns were more limited in size than those in Europe. Nevertheless, in China, the Philippines, and Okinawa they approached the Italian and North African campaigns in scale, if not in duration. Never before had such great armies been projected across hundreds, even thousands of miles of ocean to land on hostile shores, supported only by air cover and warships. And never before had planes and ships achieved such a degree of coordination and power.

The Japanese-American war was the most momentous event in the history of East Asia in half a century. It radically altered the course which the two great Asian powers, Japan and China, had followed for the last three decades and brought an abrupt end to the pattern of Western political dominance in Asian affairs. Until the 1940s, the European nations and their American offspring appeared destined to control or manipulate the countries of Asia indefinitely, with Japan eagerly following in their footsteps in Manchuria and north China. The war decisively changed this state of affairs. The subject peoples of Asia witnessed the sweeping defeat of the western powers at the hands of the Japanese. Many received arms and military training and took the first steps toward independence under Japan's hegemony. By the time the colonial powers returned, under the umbrella of the victorious British and Americans, to reclaim their former possessions, they found a rapidly maturing nationalism which would shortly sweep away the last vestiges of western rule more decisively than the most powerful Japanese army.

In his classic, *The Island War,* Major Frank Hough observed "probably no man who served . . . in the Pacific will read this book without feeling that his outfit has been slighted. And he will be right!" * In attempting to condense the complex and multidimensional story of that immense conflict into a single volume, I have been obliged to cover an even broader range of subjects and thus to slight not only units and individuals, but entire battles and campaigns as well as significant social and political events. For such omissions I can only beg the reader's indulgence on a greater scale than that granted Maj. Hough.

This is primarily an interpretive work. It relies heavily upon the work of American, British, and Australian official historians as well as the many fine monographs, battle studies, biographies, and memoirs which have appeared in the four decades since the war. However, in the case of controversial or little-explored aspects of the war, I have based my account as far as possible on primary sources, particularly those which were not available to official historians—cryptographic records, oral history memoirs, and important private collections such as the Ernest J. King papers.

In keeping with the overall approach of the Wars of the United States series, I have emphasized the subjects of policy, strategy, and operations—especially the latter two. However, I have also attempted to give the reader some sense of what the war was like for the men and women who fought it, and to provide an idea of their reactions to the strange and sometimes inhospitable lands in which they found themselves. The story is told primarily from the American point of view. The scope and emphasis is thus different from that of other general works such as John Toland's *The Rising Sun,* which approaches the war from the Japanese viewpoint, or Basil Collier's

* Frank O. Hough, *The Island War* (Philadelphia: J. B. Lippincott Company, 1947), p. vii.

The War in the Far East and John Costello's *The Pacific War,* which present a British perspective.

Though my own perspective is from the American side, I have benefitted from recently declassified British material in the Public Record Office, from translations of Japanese documents and histories available in Washington-area archives, and from English-language works by Japanese scholars.

The conduct and politics of the war with Japan have sparked surprisingly few controversies, the two great exceptions being the attack on Pearl Harbor and the use of atomic bombs against Hiroshima and Nagasaki. Each of these subjects, especially the former, have inspired a mountain of writing so immense as to dwarf the total literature devoted to all other aspects of the conflict. In this book, I have endeavored to show that many other aspects of the war are worth close examination, even reexamination.

Most discussions of American strategy in the war treat the two-pronged advance across the Pacific by Nimitz and MacArthur as a sensible compromise solution to the problem of bringing about the speedy defeat of Japan. I suggest here that the adoption of this course of action was due less to strategic wisdom than to the army and navy's reluctance to entrust their forces to the command of an officer of the rival service, together with the almost insolvable problem of what to do with a popular hero like MacArthur, who—despite his defeat in the Philippines—had emerged as a towering American public figure. The establishment of two theaters and two routes of advance in the Pacific neatly solved these bureaucratic and public relations problems. The two advances were also intended to be mutually supporting, yet they might well have led to disaster had the Japanese taken greater advantage of their opportunities—as they almost did during the Bougainville-Empress Augusta Bay operation in 1943 and the Biak campaign in 1944.

The major problem involved in defeating Japan proved to be less a matter of choosing the correct strategy than of breaking the logistical bottlenecks—devising means of getting critical items, whether amphibious craft, cargo ships, fighter planes, engineer battalions, or transport aircraft—to the right portions of the battlefronts on time and in sufficient numbers. Many of the debates about strategy within the councils of the Joint Chiefs of Staff and between the Americans and British were, in essence, debates about the allocation of resources.

Similarly, the contest for resources often determined the course of action of American military leaders. King and MacArthur's separate proposals in the spring and summer of 1942 for an offensive in the South Pacific aimed at Rabaul can be best understood as a bid on their part to stake out early claims on whatever resources might become available to the Allies in 1942 by the quick opening of a new fighting front in the Pacific. The Guadalcanal campaign, which grew out of these proposals, itself developed into a protracted fight for resources between the services as well as a protracted struggle on the battlefield. In the Tarawa campaign also, as I argue later, Nimitz's need for haste led him to risk a landing when unfavorable tides might be expected: this was due not only to the need to keep the Japanese off-balance, but also to King's concern to "get the Central Pacific drive under way so that the British could not hedge" on their recent agreement at the Quebec Conference to devote greater resources to the Pacific.

Resources were significant in another way as well: the Pacific War was in many respects a war of attrition. After the recent conflict in Vietnam, it has become almost a tautology to say that the U.S. cannot win a war of attrition. Yet this was essentially the kind of war the U.S. waged against Japan after mid-1942. Following the Battle of Midway, United States forces did not confront a major Japanese fleet until mid-1944. They did not engage even a medium-size Japanese army until the end of 1944. Yet by that time Japan had been effectively defeated. Her supply lines had been severed by American submarines, her air power had been dissipated in costly air battles over the Solomons and New Guinea, Rabaul and Truk; and her cruiser and destroyer forces had been worn down in countless night clashes in the Solomons. That war of attrition—and the even more deadly attrition by submarines and heavy bombing in 1944–45—finally spelled Japan's defeat.

The leadership of the Pacific War has recently been subject to reexamination by a number of scholars. Most notably, General Douglas MacArthur, popularly regarded as the hero and strategic genius of the war against Japan, has been subjected to searching reexamination. Scholars such as D. Clayton James and Carol M. Petillo have questioned MacArthur's conduct and judgment in a number of key episodes of his career as a theater commander. In addition, the recent discovery of the diaries of Dwight D. Eisenhower has shown that Ike's attitude toward his former chief, far from being worshipful, was often one of angry impatience and skepticism.

My own view of MacArthur is that, despite his undoubted qualities of leadership, he was unsuited by temperament, character, and judgment for the positions of high command which he occupied throughout the war. This was most clearly demonstrated in the Philippine debacle and the bloody campaigns in Papua. Both were attributable—at least in part—to MacArthur's errors of judgment and his refusal to face reality. He demonstrated these failings in success as well as in adversity, as witness his mismanagement of the northern Luzon campaign near the end of the war.

Other commanders, of course, made serious errors of judgment in the war, most notably Admiral Yamamoto at Midway, Admiral Spruance at the Battle of the Philippine Sea and Admiral Halsey at Leyte Gulf. Yet MacArthur stands alone in his refusal to confront or even acknowledge the consequences of his actions. It is impossible to imagine MacArthur saying, as Lieutenant General Joseph Stilwell did after the Allied defeat in Burma, "I say we got a hell of a beating. . . ." Stilwell had misjudged—and would continue to misjudge—the willingness and capability of the Chinese government to wage war, but he did not seek, as MacArthur consistently did, to pass the blame to subordinates, the Allies, or Washington.

No history of the Pacific War can fail to show the vital role played by intelligence in that conflict. The recent declassification of records relating to communications intelligence activities during World War II has made available a flood of new material on the subject. Some of this information, I believe, appears for the first time in this book. These newly declassified records demonstrate the contributions of code-breaking to the Allied victory, yet they also demonstrate its limitations. Thus, I have tried to show how vital messages concerning the Japanese landings in Papua and Admiral Mikawa's devastating night attack on the American naval forces in the Battle of Savo Island were intercepted and read by U.S. intelligence. Unfortunately, they were of no practical value. In the first case they were not believed; in the second case the message was "broken" too late. Similarly, Lieutenant General Walter Krueger ignored the excellent cryptographic intelligence available to him in 1944 about Japanese operations on Leyte in the area of Ormoc. The result was that his forces had to fight a bloody slugging match in rugged mountains astride the route to the town.

The sudden, awful end of the war in the radioactive ruins of Hiroshima and Nagasaki has obscured the less spectacular horrors which both sides had inflicted on each other by 1945. The conduct of the Japanese military forces in Southeast Asia and China and their treatment of prisoners of war is well known. Less obvious are the thousands of other deaths from famine and disease caused by the crushing demands of the locust-like Japanese war machine upon the fragile agricultural economies of the countries it occupied.

Americans usually assume that the unrestricted submarine campaigns and the incendiary air raids on Japanese cities were measures of expediency and desperation, adopted only after the war had begun and the implacable nature of the foe had been demonstrated. In fact, as I show, the U.S. Navy's plans and preparations to wage unrestricted submarine warfare were made months *before* Pearl Harbor, and American military experts had been discussing the possibility of incendiary raids on Japanese cities since 1919.

The reader will probably come to share the conclusion of the distinguished Japanese scholar Asada Sadao: the war "dehumanized both victor and vanquished alike," * and, in the course of the desperate struggle, Americans came to abandon some of the principles which they had long upheld. A nation which had entered the First World War in large part out of opposition to unrestricted submarine warfare deliberately chose to wage such warfare from the opening day of World War II. Similarly, American opposition to the Japanese conquest of China rested largely on revulsion against the Japanese use of air power on civilian targets. Yet the United States itself initiated an unprecedented campaign of aerial bombardment against Japan.

* Asada Sadao, "Japanese Perceptions of the A-Bomb Decision 1945–1980," in Joe C. Dixon, ed., *The American Military and the Far East* (Washington: G.P.O., 1980), p. 216.

Prelude: Pearl Harbor, December 7, 1941

They came in from the north over the blue-green hills of Kahuku Point on Oahu. In steady waves, 181 Japanese fighters, dive-bombers, and torpedo planes—the most modern, highly trained and deadly naval air force in the world—roared across the island toward their targets. It was 7:40 A.M., the morning of December 7, 1941.

The Japanese planes were deployed in four groups; and headed south toward the Pacific Fleet base at Pearl Harbor and the nearby air bases at Ewa, Hickam Field, and Kaneohe. Inside the crowded anchorage of Pearl Harbor were ninety-six ships of the Pacific Fleet under Admiral Husband E. Kimmel.

The fleet had been in Hawaii since May 1940, acting as a putative deterrent to Japanese aggression against British or Dutch possessions in Southeast Asia.[1] Admiral James O. Richardson, who then commanded the Pacific Fleet, thought this was a harebrained idea. He pointed out that in the event of war, the fleet would have to return to the U.S. West Coast anyway. Only by doing so could its crews attain full war strength. The logistical, repair, and training facilities at Pearl Harbor were inferior to those on the West Coast, and prolonged absence from their families in the western states had affected the morale of his men adversely.[2] As for the Japanese, they undoubtedly knew about the unreadiness of the fleet and were unlikely to be deterred by its presence.[3] Richardson was so vociferous in his objections that he was relieved of command at the end of one year and replaced by Admiral Kimmel. The ships remained at Pearl Harbor.

On this particular Sunday morning, all of the battleships of the Pacific Fleet except *Colorado*—which was in dry dock on the West Coast—were at Pearl Harbor. The carriers *Lexington* and *Enterprise,* with their escorting cruisers and destroyers, were at sea: they were delivering aircraft to Wake and Midway Islands. On the airfields near Pearl Harbor, almost four hundred army, navy and Marine Corps planes were parked: wing-tip to wing-tip—as protection against sabotage.

Although Japanese-American relations had been in crisis for several months, no special measures had been taken to prepare for the outbreak of hostilities. Since June 1940 Hawaii had had three major alerts and numerous air-raid and anti-submarine drills. At least as far back as 1936, American war plans had discussed the possibility of a surprise air raid against Pearl Harbor. In March 1941 an army aviator, Major General Frederick L. Martin, and a naval airman, Rear Admiral Patrick N. L. Bellinger, had completed a report on the defense of Hawaii. It specifically pointed out that a surprise attack from the air was "the most likely and dangerous form of attack" against the fleet base on Oahu. Another report—by the Hawaiian air force staff in August 1941—even conjectured that the Japanese might employ up to six carriers in such an attack, and that it would probably be delivered in the early morning.[4] Yet in Hawaii no one, as of December 1941, actually believed it could happen. Hawaii was the strongest American base in the Pacific. Army Chief of Staff General George C. Marshall described it to President Roosevelt in May 1941 as

". . . the strongest fortress in the world. . . . Enemy carriers, naval escorts and transports will begin to come under air attack at a distance of approximately 750 miles. This attack will increase in intensity until within 200 miles of the objective, the enemy forces will be subject to all types of bombardment closely supported by our most modern pursuit. . . . An invader would face more than 35,000 troops backed by coast defense guns and anti-aircraft artillery."[5]

However frequently army and navy leaders discussed the possibility of a Japanese attack, in the final analysis it appeared unlikely, almost fantastic.[6]

The feeling that Hawaii was probably immune from attack was reinforced during the autumn of 1941 by constant intelligence reports, news, and rumors concerning Japanese preparations to move against British and Dutch possessions in Southeast Asia and against the Philippines. Few believed that Japan could or would undertake a simultaneous attack against Pearl Harbor. Besides, as Admiral Richardson had bluntly pointed out, there was no need for them to do so. The Pacific Fleet, although formidable on paper, was in no shape to contest Japanese moves in the western Pacific. Recalled Captain Vincent R. Murphy, Admiral Kimmel's assistant war plans officer,

> I thought it would be utterly stupid for the Japanese to attack the United States at Pearl Harbor. We could not have materially affected their control of the waters they wanted to control whether or not the battleships were sunk at Pearl Harbor. . . . I did not believe we could move the United States Fleet to the Western Pacific until such time as the material condition of the ships was improved, especially with regard to anti-aircraft and until such time as the Pacific Fleet was materially reinforced." [7]

Admiral Kimmel and Lieutenant General Walter C. Short, commanding general of the Hawaiian Department, thus felt justified in devoting most of their efforts to training; but planes or ships used for training could not at the same time be used for scouting enemy raiders—or held on alert to repel an attack.

On the morning of the seventh, the only scouting planes in the air were a few Catalina Flying Boats on routine antisubmarine patrol to the west of Oahu.[8] None of the dozens of army and navy fighters were on alert, and the army's antiaircraft gunners had not been issued live ammunition.[9]

A radar warning system had been set up in August, but it was still operating on a part-time basis. The Signal Corps, which was responsible for training, was reluctant to relinquish control of this system to the Army Air Corps, which was responsible for full-time operations. The part-time schedule which had been arranged called for the radar sets to operate between 4:00 and 7:00 A.M. On this particular morning, however, the radar station at Opana, near Kahuku Point, had not closed down exactly as scheduled and, at 7:02 A.M., the operator detected the attacking Japanese planes about 137 miles north of Oahu. He promptly telephoned the Army Aircraft Warning Service Information Center at Oahu. The duty officer, Lieutenant Kermit Tyler, believed that the aircraft picked up on the Opana radar were a flight of B-17s due to arrive from the mainland—he told the radar operator not to "worry about it." [10]

His mistake was understandable; the information center had no liaison personnel from the navy, Marine Corps, or Army Bomber Command regularly assigned to it. That morning, Tyler and a switchboard operator were the only people in the center. Lieutenant Tyler was a fighter pilot with no previous experience as a controller or with an air-warning system.[11]

At the Harbor Control Post in the operations office of the Fourteenth Naval District, Navy Lieutenant Harold Kaminski faced a somewhat similar problem. At 6:53 A.M., he had received a message from the USS *Ward*, the duty destroyer patrolling off the entrance to Pearl Harbor. The *Ward* had attacked a submarine operating in an area where no submarine had any business to be. Like Lieutenant Tyler, Kaminski was alone with a single telephone operator in his command post. Moreover, he had standing orders to contact over half-a-dozen other command posts and headquarters by telephone in the event of trouble.

Shortly before 7:00 A.M., Kaminski started dialing. He reached the chief of staff, who requested confirmation from the *Ward* and referred the matter to Admiral Kimmel and to Admiral C. C. Bloch, Commandant of the Fourteenth Naval District. Bloch, like Kimmel, decided to wait for confirmation from the *Ward*.[12]

Twelve thousand feet above Oahu, Commander Fuchida Mitsuo stared down at the American battleships moored together in groups of two off Ford Island. " 'I had seen all German warships assembled in Kiel harbor,' " he later recalled. " 'I have also seen the French battleships in Brest. And finally, I have seen our own warships assembled for review before the Emperor, but I have never seen ships, even in the deepest peace, anchored at a distance less than 500 to 1,000 yards from each other. . . . this picture down there was hard to comprehend.' "[13] At 7:53 Fuchida radioed back to the waiting Japanese task force: "Tora, Tora, Tora"—the code word indicating that surprise had been achieved.

The Japanese dive-bombers and fighters peeled off to attack the air bases, while the torpedo planes, along with dive-bombers and high-level bombers, concentrated on the battleships. Aboard the battleship *West Virginia,* Ensign Roland Brooks, the officer of the deck, mistook the first bomb blast for an internal explosion aboard one of the neighboring ships and instantly gave the order "Away Fire and Rescue Party!" Of all the mistakes on that day, this one alone had fortunate consequences, for Ensign Brooks's alarm started the *West Virginia's* crew running for their stations before the first bombs and torpedos hit the ship. Although severely damaged, the *West Virginia* suffered relatively few casualties. Hit below the water-line, she avoided capsizing by skillful damage control, and settled right side up on the shallow bottom.[14]

Other ships were not so lucky. The battleship *Arizona* was buried under a rain of bombs, one of which penetrated the forecastle and detonated the forward magazine. More than 80 percent of her crew of over 1,500 men were killed or drowned. The *Oklahoma* was hit by three torpedoes almost simultaneously and rapidly capsized, taking with her over 400 of her crew. The *California,* which had her water-tight doors "unbuttoned," for an anticipated inspection, was hit by two torpedoes at the beginning of the attack. "Her bulkheads were so leaky the water entering the great gash [made by these hits] could not be isolated." [15]

In almost all ships, many key officers were ashore for the weekend. In the incredible noise and confusion, the flames of burning oil, and the dull crash of bombs, it was the junior officers, young reserve lieutenants and ensigns, many of them only a few months out of college or the naval academy, who carried most of the burden of command. Ensign J. K. Taussig, a "Navy brat," got the *Nevada* under way in forty-five minutes—a task which normally required two and one-half hours and the assistance of four tugboats. Commanded by Lieutenant Commander Francis J. Thomas, a middle-aged reservist, her antiaircraft guns directed by Ensign Taussig and a second ensign, the *Nevada* steamed majestically down the channel and later beached herself near the southern end of Ford Island.[16]

While the Pacific Fleet anchorage was under attack, other Japanese planes bombed and strafed the nearby navy, army, and Marine Corps air bases. Three squadrons of Catalina Flying Boats from the navy seaplane base at Kaneohe Bay were almost totally destroyed in two successive waves of Japanese dive-bombing attacks.[17] At the principal Army Air Corps fields—Bellows, Wheeler, and Hickam—the closely parked planes would have required a minimum of four hours to be ready for takeoff.[18] Within a few minutes, fighters and dive-bombers had knocked out most of the army planes and severely damaged the hangar facilities. The Marine Corps air station at Ewa suffered the same fate. All but two of the dozen Wildcat fighters were destroyed, and Japanese fighters roamed the area freely—shooting up barracks, hangars, and other targets of opportunity.

When the attacks were at their height, the twelve B-17s from the mainland which Lieutenant Tyler had thought Opana was tracking on its radar appeared over Hickam Field. To save weight on the long flight, the big bombers carried no ammunition and their guns were not mounted. Low on fuel, sniped at by Japanese fighters and by nervous American antiaircraft gunners, the B-17 pilots nevertheless managed to land their planes on the wreckage-strewn airfield.

There was a short lull in the battle around eight-thirty, as the first wave of Japanese attackers departed. The defenders took advantage of this brief respite to improvise additional defenses. When the second wave—eighty dive-bombers, fifty-four high-level bombers, and thirty-six fighters—arrived around nine, they were given a hot reception. Six fighters and fourteen dive-bombers of this second group of attackers were lost to antiaircraft fire—more than double the number shot down in the initial onslaught.

The second attack concentrated on the least-damaged ships. The battleship *Pennsylvania*, which was in dry dock, was hit by a bomb which caused minor damage. But two destroyers in the same dock, *Cassin* and *Downes*, were almost totally destroyed. In a nearby floating dock, the destroyer *Shaw*'s bow was blown off by a bomb.

By ten o'clock the second wave of attackers had departed, leaving behind six battleships sunk or sinking; two other battleships, three destroyers, and three cruisers damaged. Almost 3,600 men had been killed or wounded.[19] Columns of black smoke, hundreds of feet high, hung over the fleet anchorage. Burning oil covered parts of the harbor as salvage teams worked frantically to free men still trapped in the hulls of sunken ships.

At the airfields, work crews fought fires and struggled to clear away enough of the wreckage to permit takeoffs and landings. One hundred eighty planes had been destroyed and 128 others damaged. At Ewa Marine Air Station and the naval air station at Kaneohe, not a single plane was in condition to fly. Late in the morning a handful of army and navy planes flew off from Hickam field to look for the Japanese task force, which had long since safely withdrawn to the north.

In Washington that afternoon, President Franklin D. Roosevelt met with his military advisors amid reports of Japanese attacks on Guam, Wake, and Hong Kong, as well as against Singapore and other parts of Southeast Asia. Present at the meeting were Secretary of State Cordell Hull, Navy Secretary Frank Knox, Secretary of War Henry L. Stimson, and the two military service chiefs. The president read them a draft message to Congress asking for a declaration of war against Japan.

Around noon the next day, millions of Americans gathered by their radios to listen to the president's six-minute address to the Congress: "Yesterday, December 7, 1941, a date which will live in infamy, the United States was suddenly and deliberately attacked by naval and air forces of the Empire of Japan." Less than an hour later Congress, with one dissenting vote, approved the declaration of war against Japan.

In Tokyo, the Imperial Rescript announcing the beginning of hostilities was read over the radio by the prime minister, General Tojo Hideki. Then came a Japanese martial song, "Umi Yukaba." It included the lines:

Across the sea, corpses in the water
Across the mountain, corpses in the field.

It was an appropriate overture to the bloody forty-four month war which had now begun.

NOTES

1. Admiral H. R. Stark to Admiral J. O. Richardson, May 27, 1940 in U.S. Congress, Joint Committee on *Pearl Harbor Hearings,* Part 1, p. 262.
2. Memo, Richardson to Secretary of the Navy, 12 September, 1940, *Pearl Harbor Hearings,* Part 4, pp. 955–57.
3. James O. Richardson, *On the Treadmill to Pearl Harbor: The Memoirs of Admiral J. O. Richardson USN* (Washington: G.P.O., 1973) p. 330.
4. *Pearl Harbor Hearings,* Part 24, p. 351; Part 14, pp. 1022–26.
5. Forrest C. Pogue, *George C. Marshall: Ordeal and Hope 1939–1942* (New York: Viking, 1966) p. 173.
6. Gordon W. Prange, *At Dawn We Slept: The Untold Story of Pearl Harbor* (New York: McGraw-Hill, 1981) p. 188.
7. *Pearl Harbor Hearings,* Part 26, p. 207.
8. Roberta Wohlstetter, *Pearl Harbor: Warning and Decision* (Stanford: Stanford University Press, 1962) p. 131.
9. Wohlstetter, *Pearl Harbor,* p. 9.
10. Walter Lord, *Day of Infamy* (New York: Henry Holt and Company, 1957) pp. 47–49.
11. *Pearl Harbor Hearings,* Part 22, p. 223.
12. *Pearl Harbor Hearings,* Part 33, p. 1305.
13. Quoted in A. J. Barker, *Pearl Harbor* (New York: Ballantine Books, 1969) p. 95.
14. Samuel Elliott Morison, *History of United States Naval Operations in World War II,* Vol. 3, *The Rising Sun in the Pacific 1931–April 1942* (Boston: Little, Brown and Company, 1948) pp. 103–7.

15. Morison, ibid., p. 135.

16. Lord, *Day of Infamy*, p. 116.

17. Morison, *The Rising Sun*, p. 122.

18. Wesley Frank Craven and James Lea Cate, eds., *The Army Air Forces in World War II*, Vol. 1, *Plans and Early Operations* (Chicago: University of Chicago Press, 1948) p. 198.

19. Casualty figures from Louis Morton, *U.S. Army in World War II: The War in the Pacific, Strategy and Command: The First Two Years* (Washington, D.C.: Department of Army, 1962)

ONE

States of Mind: American

The failures and successes at Pearl Harbor, as well as those in the coming years of the Pacific War, were to a considerable extent determined by the attitudes, hopes, fears, and plans developed by the Japanese and American armed forces during the three decades before December 7, 1941. Few wars in American history had been so long anticipated, so long planned for. Yet the plans themselves played a minor role compared to the beliefs and calculations behind them in shaping the course of the conflict just begun.

● ●

In the 1920s and '30s, most Americans hoped and believed that the United States would avoid involvement in foreign wars—would indeed, avoid foreign entanglements of any sort. Suspicion of the military was widespread, along with a growing conviction that American participation in World War I had been a disastrous mistake brought about by the efforts of Wall Street, the international arms cartel, and British propaganda. Disarmament was welcomed so long as it involved no foreign commitments, but participation in collective security efforts, such as those of the League of Nations, was not.

After the First World War, the army suffered most from parochialism, poverty, and neglect among the armed services. Throughout the 1920s and the early '30s, the strength of the army hovered at around 135,000 men.[1] Beginning in 1936, the army was gradually built up to 268,000 in 1940; it then rapidly expanded to almost one and a half-million during 1940 and 1941. However, in 1939, at the renewed outbreak of European war, the army could still field only about 190,000 men: fifty thousand in the outlying U.S. possessions and 140,000 scattered among 130 posts and stations in the United States. Six of the nine infantry divisions were in reality merely understrength brigades, while the two cavalry divisions had a total strength of less than 2,500 men.[2] Future Chief of Staff George Marshall once found himself commanding a "battalion" which numbered 200 men, less than the size of a company in some European armies.[3] Only three divisions were anywhere near their full war strength.

By the late 1930s, the U.S. Army's weapons and equipment, so long neglected, were in an advanced stage of decay. In 1936 the Army General Staff noted that, in the event of mobilization, the troops mustered during the first thirty days "can be supplied with required equipment from storage or procurement except for airplanes, tanks, combat cars, scout cars, anti-aircraft guns, searchlights, anti-aircraft fire-control equipment and .50 calibre machine guns." [4]

A modest program of rearmament got under way in the late 1930s. By the beginning of World War II, however, the average infantryman was still armed with the 1903 Springfield rifle, although a new type of semiautomatic rifle, the M-1 (or Garand) was on order. The standard artillery piece was still the modified French 75 millimeter gun—which American commanders had declared inadequate as early as 1918.[5] An army officer who took an advanced artillery course in the 1930s recalled that "they were back in the period of at least World War I, if not the Spanish-American War."[6]

In 1939 less than 2 percent of the military budget was allocated to research and development. The entire R & D program amounted to about one-twentieth the cost of a contemporary battleship—less than one four-hundredth of what it cost to develop the atomic bomb. The American army between the two wars was almost as far from the army of atomic bombs, proximity fuses, electronic countermeasures, and radar as it was from the Continentals who fought at Yorktown 175 years earlier. It was a tight-knit, hard-drinking, hard-bitten, long-service army: an army of inspections and close-order drill, and of long evenings over drinks at the officers' club. An army where success at football or boxing could be as important to a man's career as success in maneuvers.[7]

In the "old army," enlisted men served between four and five years before they could hope for promotion beyond PFC. Highschool graduates were rare; outright illiterates were common. Of regular enlisted men in the army prior to Pearl Harbor, over 75 percent had failed to complete highschool and 41 percent had never been to highschool at all. Most of the noncommissioned officers had seen twenty or more years of service.[8] Like Sergeant Worden in James Jones's *From Here to Eternity,* they were equally at home on the drill field, in a barroom scrap, or threading their way through the labyrinth of army paperwork.[9]

During the interwar period, the army was a sort of "gentleman's club for its officers."[10] Most of the "club's" members "were personally acquainted, and they associated mainly with each other. Army posts were often located in isolated or sparsely populated areas—but even when this was not the case, there was little interaction between the officer corps and the larger community. One officer recalled that his only contact with civilians consisted of attending horseshows, playing polo against civilian teams, and dating young women from civilian families.[11] In the peacetime army, the main enemies were boredom and debt. Army pay had not increased since 1920: many of the younger officers had to struggle to make ends meet. The answer to such problems was often liquor. There are no reliable figures on alcohol consumption in the services between the wars, but the incidence of overindulgence was probably high.[12]

A less destructive form of escape—at least from boredom—was athletics, a pastime indulged in by all ranks with a single-mindedness and intensity devoted to few other aspects of army life. Whether it was the annual Army-Navy Game or an intraregimental boxing match, a man's fitness report or even promotion could ride on his success as a coach, trainer, or competitor in organized sports. A welcome relief from the tedium of peacetime service, big-time athletics were nevertheless costly and often interfered with normal training, absorbing the time of key personnel.[13]

For officers as well as for enlisted men, promotion was glacially slow. "When I entered the service [in 1924]," recalled one officer, "I had it figured out that if I completed thirty years, I could retire as a lieutenant colonel." Thirteen years was the normal interval between attaining the rank of first lieutenant and promotion to captain, and some remained captains for seventeen years. An army manpower expert later estimated that had it not been for World War II, the entire West Point Class of 1917 would have retired as majors with thirty years' service.[14] Normally an officer attained the rank of colonel at fifty-nine: major generals had at most one to two years' service

ahead of them before they reached the mandatory retirement age.[15]
In 1941 the four top field commanders—Lieutenant General Hugh
Drum, Lieutenant General John L. Dewitt, Lieutenant General Walter Krueger, and Lieutenant General Ben Lear—were all veterans
of the Spanish-American War.[16] The consequences of such a system
are well illustrated by the experience of George C. Marshall, one
of the most brilliant staff officers of World War I. A personal favorite
of, and former aide to General John J. Pershing, Marshall had been
a temporary lieutenant colonel during World War I, but after the
armistice he had been dropped to his old rank of captain and served
ten years as a major. He did not reach the rank of brigadier general
until 1936, when he was 56 years old.[17] For other officers, less brilliant
or determined or lucky than Marshall, this system bred mental stagna-
tion, reverence for routine, parochialism—and indifference. When
the rapid expansion of the army in 1940 and 1941 catapulted these
officers into positions of great responsibility and high command, many
shook off the lethargy of the interwar years. Some did not, however,
and proved unequal to the complex, deadly demands of modern
war.[18]

Insofar as the old army had ideas about future conflicts, they dealt
mainly with questions of mobilization and expansion in the event
of war.[19] The experience of World War I largely determined the
views of army planners, who thought primarily in terms of a single-
theater war. In such a war, the chief of staff would become the
commanding general of a GHQ formed in Washington; he would
then move to the actual theater of war, leaving a residual staff behind
in the capital.[20]

As to who the likely enemy might be, army strategists had few
notions. They recognized Japan as a possible menace—but with more
annoyance than interest. As Forrest Pogue observes, the struggle
to keep alive the interest of officers who saw little chance for promotion, to make do with penurious budgets, and simultaneously to cope
with obsolescent weapons and equipment left little time "to think
in terms of world problems or possible American collaboration in
international conflict."[21] In any case, no foreign power seemed as
menacing to the army in the interwar period as did rivalry from
the navy and the Army Air Corps.

● ●

"The Air Service," observed an Air Corps general, "or rather
the air effort of the United States since we entered the World War,

has probably been the most investigated activity ever carried on by the Government." [22] Between 1919 and 1935, no less than fifteen different special government boards and committees had been convened to study the proper function and organization of military aviation in the national defense.[23] What little attention the general public gave to military matters was mostly focussed on the spectacular developments in aviation.

Army aviators had emerged from World War I to find themselves at the low end of the postwar pecking order. The air service was rapidly reduced in size from 20,000 officers on Armistice Day to about 200 one year later.[24] Air service officers found themselves to be junior to other officers who had entered the army at the same time, but who had been commissioned earlier because of the longer training period for aviators. In addition, many pilots were former enlisted men who had been commissioned in the final months of the war.[25] Since these officers were obliged to compete for promotions with all other army officers, their lack of seniority was a distinct disadvantage. Finally, the flyers resented the monopoly of the army's high command positions by what they saw as hidebound West Pointers.

Convinced that they were practitioners of a wholly new type of warfare, resentful of their low place on the army ladder, the aviators naturally sought a rearrangement of the traditional military status quo. "Only by securing a considerable measure of autonomy," observes the official air force history, "could the air service formulate its air combat doctrine, develop appropriate equipment and direct its forces in battle," [26] and, it may be added, only in this manner could Air Corps officers hope to attain positions of responsibility and high command. Thus inspired by a complex mixture of vision and careerism, the army aviators set out to win the nation's support for aerial warfare and a separate air arm.

The leader of the militant flyers, the most colorful and controversial military figure of the interwar period, was Brigadier General William "Billy" Mitchell, who had commanded the air forces of the A.E.F. in France.[27] Returning to the United States in 1919, Mitchell embarked on a determined campaign to convince the public "that aerial warfare now ranked with naval and ground warfare in importance." [28] Like the European theorists Hugh Trenchard and Guilio Douhet, Mitchell was already thinking in terms of strategic bombing, of destroying the enemy's "vital centers"—his large cities and industrial areas—by massive air bombardment. Yet he was aware that the American public would oppose such a radical, not to say immoral, doctrine of offensive warfare. Instead Mitchell shrewdly emphasized the contributions which airpower could make to America's defenses.

Specifically, he declared that aviation was capable of replacing both the navy and the army's coastal artillery in America's defense. In a series of highly publicized bombing tests against the former German battleship *Ostfriesland* and the old American battleships *Alabama, Virginia,* and *New Jersey,* Mitchell's army aviators demonstrated that bombing planes could indeed sink heavily protected men-of-war.[29]

The reaction was predictable. Admirals decried the "artificiality" of the tests; Mitchell declared that "the problem of the destruction of seacraft by air forces has been solved and is finished. . . . Aircraft now in existence can find and destroy all classes of seacraft under war conditions with a negligible loss."[30] Mitchell's claims—for the time being—were almost as absurd as those of the admirals. His planes could not "find and sink" any warship they chose in the seas off the coast. As Mitchell's biographer observes: "The proper navigational equipment to guide aircraft out of sight of land did not [yet] exist. . . . [Mitchell] and his crews could not have operated over water without the navigational and rescue support of a string of destroyers acting as markers to the target."[31] In 1931 nine planes of the Army Air Corps conducted a four-hour search for an aged navy transport, the *Mt. Shasta,* as part of a military exercise, but failed to find it. In a second attempt, the planes found the ship but scored only one direct hit out of forty-nine bombs dropped.[32]

Undeterred, Mitchell continued his campaign for "air power" with articles and provocative announcements. Banished to Fort Sam Houston in Texas, he finally went too far, giving his many enemies in the War and Navy Departments the chance they had been waiting for. In September 1925 he responded to the news of two recent naval aviation disasters by denouncing the "incompetency, criminal negligence, and almost treasonable administration of the National Defense by the Navy and War Departments." Two weeks later, Mitchell was summoned before a court-martial to answer charges of conduct prejudicial to good order and military discipline and "conduct of a nature to bring discredit upon the military service."

The trial was a sensation, and served briefly to focus public attention on the question of military aviation. Interest quickly faded after Mitchell's inevitable conviction and retirement from the service. However much the public might thrill to the daring feats of the aviators and delight in Mitchell's blunt criticism of "the brass hats," they could perceive no compelling reason to undertake the drastic and expensive reorientation of defense policy which the general advocated.

Far from the realm of congressional hearings and Sunday supplements, however, a dedicated band of officers at the Air Corps Tactical School labored to translate Mitchell's ideas into a workable system of warfare. Practical pilots as well as theorists, the young captains and majors who served as instructors at the tactical school in the late 1920s and 1930s welcomed the writings of Mitchell and European advocates of airpower like B. H. Liddell Hart and Guilio Douhet for their publicity value. Yet they were acutely aware of the large number of questions concerning the employment of aviation which remained unanswered in the wake of World War I.[33]

The doctrine developed by the Air Corps Tactical School was outwardly much like the writings of Mitchell: air forces *must* be employed offensively against the "vital centers" of the enemy. The only realistic means of defense against air attack was counterattack. Initial operations to destroy the enemy's air force on the ground would be of greatest importance. "No nation can afford to decline the role of aggressor and sacrifice the opportunity of attacking an enemy that may be unprepared."[34]

Yet, the practical implications of these pronouncements had still to be worked out. First of all there was the problem of target selection, since even the largest air force could not bomb everything. In addition, a means had to be found for ensuring a reasonable proportion of hits on the target; finally, a practical long-range bomber had to be developed to carry out such missions.

By the late 1930s the theorists of the Air Corps Tactical School were confident that they were well on the way toward solving all of these problems. The concept of "precision bombing" which emerged from their experiments was in some ways a characteristically American idea, combining as it did faith in technology, lingering humanitarian concerns, and a taste for clean, decisive solutions in wartime. Instead of indiscriminate night bombings of large areas, precision bombing called for careful selection of targets by thorough analysis of the enemy's economy and war machinery.

The new Norden bombsight promised astounding accuracy from high altitudes. By 1935 Army Air Corps bombers were placing their bombs within 200 feet of the target from almost three miles up.[35] This type of pinpoint accuracy of course demanded daytime visibility conditions which, in turn, demanded high altitude for protection against antiaircraft fire.

Fortunately, the B-10 and B-12—the new twin-engine, all-metal bombers which came into service in the early 1930s—seemed likely to fulfill these requirements. With a top speed of over 200 miles an hour, the new bombers were almost as fast as contemporary fighters and had a range of almost 1,000 miles. But even more formidable weapons were on the horizon. In 1935, the Boeing Aircraft Corporation produced a four-engine bomber, the B-17, which represented a striking qualitative advance over previously available aircraft. The B-17 had a top speed of over 250 MPH, a range of more than 2,000 miles, and a battery of machine guns to protect it against attacking fighters. By 1936 the first thirteen B-17s were on order for the Army Air Corps.

With planes such as the B-17, Air Corps theorists were more confident than ever that "no known agency can frustrate accomplishment of the bombardment mission." [36] As Lieutenant Kenneth N. Walker, a young instructor at the Air Corps Tactical School explained, "a defensive formation of bomber planes, properly flown, can accomplish its mission "unsupported by friendly pursuit." [37]

One aviation officer who emphatically disagreed was Major Claire Lee Chennault, head of the Pursuit Section at the Air Corps Tactical School. Chennault argued that the new bombers appeared invincible mainly because existing American fighters were obsolescent. With high-performance, single-seat interceptors, an effective early-warning system, and centralized fighter control, pursuit would represent a formidable obstacle to any attacking air force. Even obsolescent fighters could provide an effective defense if backed by an adequate early-warning and control system. [38]

Although Chennault's arguments were to prove prophetic, his was an almost solitary voice in the 1930s. More representative was General Oscar Westover, who observed that the "modern trend of thought is that high speed and otherwise high performance bombardment aircraft, together with reconnaissance planes of superior speed and range will suffice for the defense of the country." [39] "With the retirement of Chennault in 1937," observes the official air force history, "there remained no powerful voice in the Air Corps to speak for fighters." [40]

If fighters were despised, attack planes—light bombers and fighter-bombers for close air support of ground operations—were almost ignored. Air Corps officers allowed that such aircraft might prove useful in disrupting railways and other lines of communications but argued that, "Because of relative invulnerability of dispersed ground troops, aviation should not be used against dispersed ground troops except in vital situations." [41]

The Air Corps' role in attacking hostile fleets at sea, the question which had sparked the Mitchell controversies, remained unsettled, although it had long ceased to be a *cause célèbre*. Army aviators coveted the coastal defense role because it represented a truly independent mission which would justify the creation of a separate service. Naval aviators however, doggedly refused to concede that any aspect of combat operations over the sea should be entrusted to any but the navy's hands. Throughout the 1920s and 1930s, the army and navy attempted in vain to delineate appropriate responsibilities for offshore patrolling and air combat.[42] The precise roles and missions of each service were still so unclear that on the day of the Pearl Harbor attack, neither the army nor the navy commanders in Hawaii were completely sure who was responsible for what in regard to air defense and reconnaissance.

Despite all these false starts and exaggerated expectations, the Air Corps officers were fundamentally right: air power was to prove the decisive element in the Pacific War. Unfortunately, they were often fundamentally wrong about the ways in which air power would be applied.

By the eve of Pearl Harbor, Mitchell's disciples had accomplished much. In 1935 the War Department had a semi-autonomous GHQ air force, and all air combat units were responsible to a single commanding general, who reported directly to the chief of staff in peace and to the theater commander in war. With the appointment of General George C. Marshall as chief of staff, the position of chief of the Air Corps was further enhanced, and airmen were placed in key positions throughout the War Department.[43]

Despite these advances, the Army Air Corps was still smaller in numbers of men than the field artillery in 1939. By February 1941 it had less than 500 combat planes, including only 50 B-17s.[44] The latest fighter aircraft, the P-40B, just then coming into production, was to prove inferior to the latest Japanese fighters one year later. Despite the claims of the air enthusiasts and the impressive achievements of the new aircraft, most Americans in 1941 still looked to the navy as the "first line of defense" against Japan.

● ●

On the eve of World War II the United States Navy was still a remarkably homogeneous organization. Like the characters in Richard McKenna's *The Sons of Martha,* most of the enlisted men were long-service personnel who found navy life superior to unemployment. During the depression the reenlistment rate climbed to around 90 percent; applicants so outnumbered available openings that only one out of every eighteen aspirants was accepted.[45]

Virtually all the officers were graduates of the naval academy at Annapolis. In the army, in 1941, neither Chief of Staff George C. Marshall nor the top four field commanders were graduates of West Point; in the navy by contrast, all important commands were held by Annapolis men. With the great expansion of the navy after Pearl Harbor, reserve officers sometimes attained responsible commands in aviation or in amphibious forces, but command of all major combatant vessels, task forces, and fleets remained the exclusive privilege of the Annapolis graduates.[46] Indeed, almost all top naval commanders of World War II, including William F. Halsey, Harold Stark, Chester Nimitz, Raymond Spruance, Richmond K. Turner, Thomas C. Kinkaid, Frank Jack Fletcher, John H. Towers, Husband E. Kimmel, Aubrey Fitch, Robert Ghormley, and Wilson Brown had been midshipmen together at the academy between 1901 and 1905.[47]

The naval academy from which these officers had graduated was parochial, spartan, intellectually sterile, and pedagogically backward. In 1923 the Board of Visitors to the Naval Academy had observed that a " 'sound symmetrical general education is lacking.' " The academy's curriculum was " 'incapable of supplying even the fundamental training in the physical sciences,' "[48] while the humanities were thrown together in a single academic department which the midshipmen eloquently referred to as "bull." Another Board of Visitors' report called attention to the " 'unspoken willingness' " of the academy's staff " 'to use subjects of instruction as a means of discipline.' "[49]

It seems unlikely that the leaders of the naval academy were greatly troubled by this type of criticism. The academy was intended not so much to stimulate the intellect as to mold character. "Character is the big thing," declared Admiral Thomas C. Hart; "it is presence and personality and looks, it is qualities of mind, but particularly . . . guts, all of that is in it." Successful midshipmen were expected to develop qualities of reliability, leadership, integrity, good judgement, loyalty to the service and to each other.[50] It was this last that was especially stressed. Midshipmen left Annapolis with a lively regard for the reputation and standing of their service—and even more concern for their own reputation *in* the service.

As far as the naval officer had ideas about warfare, they were mainly those about "seapower" developed by Alfred Thayer Mahan and his collaborators at the Naval War College before the turn of the century. Mahan emphasized concentrated fleets of battleships which could fight for and win "command of the sea," that is, the ability to use the sea while denying its use to the enemy. "Command of the sea" would normally be attained by the defeat of the enemy's fleet in a decisive battle, after which the enemy's coast and ports would be subject to blockade and perhaps invasion. The idea of the one big battle which would decide the war at sea was at the core of most of the navy's strategic thinking between the wars. This was how the war with Spain and the Russo-Japanese War had been decided, and it might have been the way in which the First World War would have been decided had the Germans not "escaped" at the Battle of Jutland.

"The chief strategic function of the fleet is the creation of situations that will bring about decisive battle," Commander Richmond Kelly Turner told the Naval War College class of 1937, "and to provide sufficient battle power to bring about the defeat of the enemy." [51] For this reason, the battles of Jutland and Trafalgar were endlessly refought on the war-game boards of the Naval War College. [52] For this reason, the interwar navy remained, despite advances in aviation and undersea warfare, primarily a battleship navy. During the 1920s more than 80 percent of the Annapolis midshipmen first went to sea in battleships. [53] Command of a battleship was almost a prerequisite for attaining admiral's rank.

Big guns, big ships, the big battle—these dominated navy thinking in the interwar period. Aircraft and torpedoes were important, but they were distinctly secondary weapons. Cruisers and destroyers were discussed mainly in connection with attack and defense of the battle line. In war games at the Naval War College, torpedoes were assumed to have a maximum range of 17,000 yards at twenty-six knots or 6,000 yards at forty-six knots. [54] This at a time when the Japanese were perfecting a torpedo with a maximum range of 22,000 yards at forty-nine knots. Japanese heavy cruisers carried a full battery of torpedo tubes; American heavy cruisers carried none.

The navy's research and development program was much better financed than the army's, yet it was far from opulent. Each navy bureau had its own R & D program, with the General Board of the navy serving as a kind of court of last resort when serious disputes arose over the design characteristics of new ships. [55] Important advances were made in acoustics, radar, and marine engineering, but development was uneven. The United States Navy had the best submarines in the world but the worst torpedoes; it pioneered in the development of dive-bombing, but failed to develop an effective medium-range antiaircraft gun to meet such attacks.[56] The newest battleships were fast and well protected, but had only sixteen-inch guns against the eighteen-inch counterparts of the Japanese.

The navy entered the 1920s a far richer and more powerful service than either the army or the fledgling Air Corps; nevertheless, it was beset by threats and troubles. On one flank were the disarmament advocates who threatened the navy's hopes for a fleet "second to none"; on the other stood the air power enthusiasts who aimed to deprive the service of many of its time-honored responsibilities. The great disarmament treaties of the interwar period—the five-power disarmament treaty signed at the Washington Conference in 1922, and the London naval treaty of 1930—put an upper limit on naval building in the category of battleships, cruisers, destroyers, and carriers, and established ratios between the great naval powers. Capital ships, carriers, and cruisers were also subject to limitations as to tonnage and armament. At the Washington Conference, the United States was granted equality in capital ship tonnage with Great Britain and a 40 percent superiority over Japan. The London treaty added limitations on the number and type of cruisers which could be built by the three great naval powers and set the ratios in this category at 10 : 10 : 7 for Great Britain, the United States, and Japan, respectively. Naval officers protested loudly and persistently against these arrangements: the Washington treaties, for example, obliged the United States to scrap some of its latest battleships and battle cruisers and the London treaty allowed foreign diplomats to determine American warship characteristics.[57] But the most dangerous aspect of the treaties from the naval point of view was the provision of the Five Power Washington Treaty which forbade further fortifications or military bases in the Pacific island possessions of Britain, France, the United States, and Japan. The navy had always believed it was imperative to have major bases on the island of Guam, in the Mariannas, and in the Philippines in order to carry on a successful war against Japan. Yet now these areas could not be developed, and their existing facilities were completely inadequate to support major fleet operations.

Despite these misgivings, the navy learned to live with the disarmament treaties. Two of the "scrapped" battle cruisers were converted into the giant aircraft carriers *Lexington* and *Saratoga;* the oldest remaining battleships were converted to burn oil instead of coal; and all but the latest battleships had their turrets modified so that the main batteries could be elevated to thirty degrees, thus increasing the effective range of the guns. Congress also authorized construction of eighteen modern cruisers, although some were not laid down until the end of the 1920s.

The treaty restrictions nevertheless exacted their toll. American warship designs were obliged to conform to the tonnage restrictions of the Washington and London agreements. Cruisers, for example, could not exceed 10,000 tons displacement—although a ship of this size would have to sacrifice speed and armor protection to obtain the fuel economy necessary for operations in the western Pacific in a war with Japan. Thus the heavy cruisers of the *Pensacola, Northhampton,* and *Indianapolis* classes had great range, but their armament and armor were inferior to their Japanese counterparts. The navy could have had more formidable ships by abandoning the requirement to carry the war into Japanese waters. But this in turn would have meant forfeiting the navy's principal justification for appropriations—the need to prepare for a future war against Japan in defense of the Philippines and of other American interests in eastern Asia.[58]

Then came the Great Depression. President Hoover's response was to cut government spending, especially spending on the armed forces. Vessels were laid up, naval personnel was reduced. The older battleships had their complements reduced as much as sixty percent, and Congress clearly indicated that it had little intention of approving the new construction necessary even to reach the modest limits set by the London treaty.[59]

With the inauguration of President Franklin Roosevelt, the navy's fortunes took a decided turn for the better. The new President had been an assistant secretary of the navy; he was an amateur yachtsman and a collector of ship models. He considered the navy his special province: he personally chose the flag officers for the top command and staff positions in the service. Under Roosevelt, naval appropriations rose every year. As Waldo Heinrichs observes, "The Roosevelt Navy was a growth enterprise. It felt it required managers and policy that would avoid costly errors, keep naval opinion together, prevent public brawls, and make the most of the favoring winds in the executive and legislative branches." [60]

This approach is well illustrated in the navy's handling of the other major "threat" of the interwar period: that emanating from the air-power enthusiasts. The challenge posed by Mitchell and his followers in the early twenties was both real and unprecedented. Not only did Mitchell lay claim to the traditional naval function of first line of defense; he even proposed that the air service be provided with aircraft carriers on the grounds that these were, properly considered, "aircraft transports" rather than warships! [61]

While Mitchell's pronouncements outraged many in the navy, there was one group of officers in that service who found them extremely useful. These were the naval aviators. Like their army counterparts, the navy pilots were relatively junior officers fighting for recognition of their specialty. They resented the control exercised over them by nonflying senior officers. Unlike the army aviators, however, the naval officers did not seek independence or autonomy but merely equality with more traditional navy officers. Under the leadership of the brilliant and imaginative Rear Admiral William A. Moffett, chief of the Bureau of Aeronautics during most of 1921 to 1933, the aviators accomplished many of their goals.

Moffett was a regular line officer, a graduate of the naval academy with much service at sea.[62] He reassured navy conservatives by his oft-repeated statements that "naval aviation . . . must go to sea on the backs of the fleet." [63] At the same time, he shared Mitchell's talent for publicity and conducted a well-conceived public relations campaign designed to sell the American people on the importance of naval aviation.[64]

In 1926 Congress passed legislation requiring that all commanding officers of aircraft carriers, seaplane tenders, and naval air stations be qualified aviators. This legislation produced a sudden flocking of middle-aged captains and commanders, anxious to qualify for the new commands, to the aviation training centers. Captains Ernest J. King and William F. Halsey, for example, learned to fly in their mid–forties and –fifties, respectively. The younger pilots who had been with aviation from its early days naturally resented these latecomers, but their presence gave added weight to naval aviation in the upper ranks of the navy.[65]

By the early 1930s the navy was experimenting with independent operations by aircraft carriers. By the end of the decade, naval aviators were eager to cut the carriers loose from the slow, ponderous battle line in favor of independent multicarrier operations, but this was too radical a departure from naval orthodoxy to be readily accepted.[66] For most naval officers, the airplane's chief function was scouting for, and protecting, the battle line. As late as 1939, a Naval War College pamphlet issued to its students rejected "the idea that aviation alone can achieve decisive results against well-organized military or naval forces." In a naval battle, the destruction of the enemy's carriers would give our fleet the "advantage of concealing its movements and knowing where the enemy is," but would not in itself be decisive. The pamphlet also warned that "the destruction of land air bases is a far more difficult task than the destruction of floating air bases [i.e. carriers]." [67]

Aside from its own conservatism, there were good reasons for the navy's doubts about aviation's military potential. Technological uncertainties abounded in the 1930s. The only sure way to resolve these uncertainties was through extensive experimentation and experience with various types of carriers and aircraft—but treaty limitations and tight budgets severely restricted the number of aircraft and carriers available. A further handicap was posed by the long period required to build a carrier and thoroughly test its capabilities. The first American warship built as an aircraft carrier from the keel up, the *Ranger,* was designed before much had been learned from the operations of the *Saratoga* and *Lexington,* while the *Ranger's* successor ships—the *Yorktown* and *Enterprise*—had had to be designed before the former ship was even launched.[68]

Naval aircraft were improving rapidly during the late 1930s; they had performed impressively in maneuvers, but they had also proven to be highly dependent on good weather and visibility. Their carriers, meanwhile, had proved highly vulnerable to both surface and air attack. Tactics that were to prove decisive in the air–sea battles of the 1940s appeared impossible with the aircraft available in the 1930s. "There was just not enough evidence [before 1941] that aircraft carriers had become the dominant ship type" to convince most of the navy's senior command to abandon the battleship as the basis of the combat fleet.[69]

Moreover, aviation was not the only area of naval warfare experiencing rapid technological progress. By the mid-1930s for example, studies by the Bureau of Construction and Repair had demonstrated that a new type of twenty-eight-knot battleship could be built within the existing treaty displacement limit of 35,000 tons without sacrificing either firepower or protection. This meant that future cruisers and destroyers, in order to screen the battleforce would have to be even *faster.* As with the carriers, the navy required time to take advantage of any lessons learned by the design and construction of the new, fast battleships. In the late 1930s, Chief of Naval Operations Admiral William H. Standley actually vetoed a General Board recom-

mendation to begin construction of more battleships because not
enough experience had yet been gained with the *North Carolina* and
Washington, the first U.S. battleships to be laid down since 1920.[70]
Still, cruisers and destroyers were developing rapidly even within
the limits of the disarmament treaties; by the early 1930s they were
being fitted with central fire-direction gear earlier available only to
battleships.

The navy's answer to its technological difficulties was the "balanced
fleet," in which no one kind of warship or mode of warfare would
have undue predominance. Although an expensive, and perhaps too
conservative, policy, in the late 1930s the balanced fleet seemed
the only sensible course to steer between the technological and other
uncertainties which loomed on all sides as the world drifted toward
war.[71]

● ●

Of all the U.S. combat services, the Marine Corps emerged from
World War I in the most precarious and discouraging position, but
in the end its response was the most creative.

The Marine Corps had existed for a century and a half as the
navy's poor stepsister, without important tasks or clear doctrine. In
the nineteenth century it had been common for failing or delinquent
midshipmen at the naval academy to be offered commissions in the
Marine Corps. When Midshipman John A. Lejeune wished to enter
the Marine Corps after graduating from Annapolis, he was discouraged by the academy authorities because he stood too high in the
class; eventually he had to use congressional influence to get his
Marine Corps commission.[72] Marines served aboard ship as gun crews
and landing parties (and to intimidate the crew) and ashore as a
kind of "colonial infantry" in Central America and the Caribbean
during the days when Theodore Roosevelt wielded the big stick
and Woodrow Wilson was teaching the Latins "to elect good men."
But the days of such heavyhanded peacekeeping were clearly waning
by the late 1920s.

The Marine Corps emerged from the World War with its prestige
greatly enhanced by the performance of its Fourth Brigade, which
served as part of one of the AEF's most famous divisions. Its well-
publicized exploits at Belleau Wood, Soissons, and Mont Blanc, and
its vigorous recruiting drive at home had made the Marine Corps
popular with the American public and earned it the lasting enmity
of many army generals who saw the marines' publicity triumphs as
belittling to the army.[73]

Nevertheless, it seemed to many in the economy-minded 1920s, both inside and outside the service, that the days of this venerable corps might be numbered. Across the Atlantic, the Royal Marines—the original model for the U.S. Marine Corps—had suffered a drastic budget cut and had been stripped of most of its supporting arms, including the highly regarded Royal Marine Artillery.

At the end of the 1920s, a secret study by the army staff suggested that the army could well assume most of the Marine Corps functions. The chief of naval operations reportedly concurred in this idea, "recognizing that by shifting the Marines [to the army], the Navy could save money." [74]

The Hoover administration, always interested in saving money, also greeted the plan with enthusiasm. Between 1929 and 1933, Hoover imposed a 24.4 percent manpower cut on the Marine Corps, as compared to 5.6 percent for the navy and none for the army. In December 1932 Hoover proposed even more drastic cuts; they were tied to planned withdrawals from Latin America which would have reduced the Marine Corps from a high of 18,000 in 1931, to a strength of only 13,600 men. This reduction was so serious that it would have forced the closing of the marines' boot camp at Parris Island. The Marine Corps responded with an impressive public relations campaign. Retired army and Marine Corps generals were mobilized to "speak for the Corps," and influential Congressmen like Carl Vinson, Melvin J. Maas, and Fiorello La Guardia threw their weight behind restoring the cuts. In a showdown vote, the House Appropriations Committee voted down Hoover's proposed cuts and held the strength of the corps at a little over 15,000 men.[75]

The corps had been "saved"—but all concerned realized that it had been a close call. Something more was needed beside the recollection of gallant services in past wars to justify the continued existence of the marines. In a way their problem was the precise opposite of the Air Corps. The airmen had new missions and new weapons, but lacked an organization. The marines had an organization, but neither a clearly defined mission nor radically new weapons.

As early as 1919 Major General John A. Lejeune, the commandant of the Marine Corps, had realized that the marines required a new mission. The mission he chose—and which the marines were to develop to a degree of effectiveness unknown in foreign armies—was the amphibious assault: a landing by seaborne troops on hostile shores against active enemy opposition.

To the minds of many interwar military leaders, the marines might as well have proposed to land on the moon. Amphibious warfare was a little-known and much-despised form of war before World War II. The last great amphibious operations, the Anglo-French attacks against Turkey at Gallipoli in 1915, had ended in bloody failure. After Gallipoli, few military men saw any future for amphibious operations. An Army Command and General Staff School text proclaimed that "descents upon a hostile coast, if opposed, have a very small chance of success," [76] and Navy Captain W. S. Pye observed that "the chances for success of an invasion by forces transported overseas are becoming smaller and smaller." Even Commodore Sir Roger Keyes, who had been second in command of the naval forces at Gallipoli, spoke of "the folly of attempting to storm a defended beach in daylight." [77]

Despite these dour pronouncements, there were excellent reasons for the marines to specialize in amphibious warfare. They already possessed an organization known as the "Advanced Base Force"—later called the "Marine Corps Expeditionary Force"—for the establishment and defense of outlying bases. Since Japan was the most likely future antagonist of the United States, bases for attack and to defend the line of communications in the Pacific would be an obvious necessity.

Most of all, the state of interservice politics made amphibious warfare a natural choice for the marines. As Brigadier General Rufus M. Lane, Adjutant and Inspector General of the Marine Corps, observed in 1923, the corps could safely concentrate on amphibious work because the navy would never spare its ships' crews for such activities, and the army would never allocate units to be trained with the navy.[78] In addition, since the Marine Corps was part of the naval service, amphibious operations carried out by the corps would neatly avoid the unpleasant necessity for interservice cooperation so distasteful to everyone.

So Lejeune set to work. In 1920, the Advanced Base Force was reorganized to emphasize offensive landing operations rather than simply the defense of bases already held. At the same time, the Marine Corps Schools complex at Quantico, Virginia, began to examine the problems of amphibious warfare.[79] In 1921 Major Earl H. Ellis, a Marine Corps officer who had served on the staff of the Naval War College, developed a paper on amphibious strategy in a Japanese-American war. The paper was officially adopted by General Lejeune and subsequently "became the keystone of strategic plans for a Pacific War so far as the Corps was concerned. . . ." [80] Ellis recognized that the seizure of bases in the Pacific would require assaults against heavily defended beachheads; his studies of the logistics, manpower, tactics and equipment required for such assaults were to prove amazingly accurate.

In the early twenties small-scale landing exercises were held in the Caribbean. They were perhaps best characterized by Marine Brigadier General Eli K. Cole's two-word description: "chaos reigned." Yet the navy and marines were learning: although duties in the Far East and Latin America prevented any more amphibious exercises until 1931, the study of amphibious warfare continued. In 1929 the Joint Army-Navy Board issued a directive in which it was tacitly acknowledged that the marines' role within the military establishment was to act as an amphibious assault force.[81]

With the withdrawal of the last marine units from Latin America in 1933, the development of amphibious warfare began in earnest. The Fleet Marine Force—two small, brigade-sized bodies of marines—was established at Quantico and San Diego; it was designed as an integral part of the U.S. fleet under the tactical control of the latter's commander in chief. The following year the Marine Corps Schools produced a "Tentative Manual for Landing Operations," which was to serve as the foundation for all American amphibious doctrine in World War II.

The "Tentative Manual" was as much a catalogue of problems which would have to be solved in an amphibious assault as a guide to its execution. An amphibious assault force would have to rely on the guns of its supporting ships as a substitute for normal field artillery. Yet warships carried limited supplies of ammunition; naval shells were unsuitable for use against land targets; and naval guns had flatter trajectories than land-based artillery. The landing forces would need adequate air support—but no one yet knew anything about aerial support of troops in an amphibious attack. Finally, no adequate vehicle was available to convey the attacking troops from their ships to the shore. The ordinary type of ship's boats were useless even in moderate surf. They could not be beached high enough for swift debarcation, nor could they back off the beach once they were there.

A host of problems involving supply, communications, and command and control were only vaguely understood, but they would have to be solved before this new mode of warfare could be successfully practised. Yet, as Russell F. Weigley observes: "Simply by defining the specific problems into which amphibious problems divided themselves, the Marine Corps made it evident that the problems most likely were not insoluble." [82] On the eve of Pearl Harbor, some of the problems had been solved—but many had not. The solutions had to be worked out later on the bloody beaches of the central Pacific.

● ●

The United States entered the war with four more-or-less independent armed services, each with its own organizational goals, interests, and dogmas. Each service was led by officers committed to these organizational views and hopes. The same officers were also committed to an ever-present, strong though disciplined, careerism. In the conflict soon to begin, these ideas and preconceptions underwent unprecedented stress and testing. How successful these officers were in modifying, or in some cases transcending, their service outlook and careerism would, in large measure, determine their success in the Pacific War.

NOTES

1. The highest figure between 1922 and 1935 was 141,618 in 1924; the lowest figure was 133,949 in 1927. For more detailed data see Mark S. Watson, *U.S. Army in World War II: The War Department: Chief of Staff: Prewar Plans and Preparations* (Washington, D.C.: Historical Division, United States Army, 1950), p. 16.

2. Russell F. Weigley, *History of the United States Army* (New York: Macmillan and Company, 1967), p. 419.

3. Watson, *Chief of Staff*, p. 26.

4. Weigley, *History of the United States Army*, p. 403.

5. Ibid., pp. 414, 419.

6. "Conversation between General Robert E. Wood and Lt. Col. William Marens Jr.," U.S. Army Military History Research Collection, Carlisle, Pa.

7. Watson, *Chief of Staff*, p. 32; Reminiscences of Hanson W. Baldwin, U.S. Naval Historical Foundation, Oral History Collection, Naval Historical Center, Washington, D.C., p. 152.

8. Samuel Stauffer et al., *The American Soldier: Adjustment to Army Life*, pp. 142, 158–59; Wood interview, Part 2, p. 14.

9. "Conversations between Gen. Clyde D. Eddleman and Lt. Col. L. G. Smith and Lt. Col. M. G. Swindler," Debriefing Program, U.S. Army Military History Research Collection (hereafter "Eddleman interview").

10. Russell H. Weigley, "The Role of the War Department and the Army" in Dorothy Borg and Shumpei Okamoto, eds., *Pearl Harbor as History* (New York: Columbia University Press, 1973), p. 115.

11. Conversation between General Ralph E. Haines Jr. and Captain William J. Hudson, Section 1, p. 17, Senior Officer Debriefing Program, U.S. Army Military History Institute, Carlisle, Pa.

12. George H. Decker interview, Senior Officer Debriefing Program, U.S. Army Military History Institute. On this point, see reminiscences of General Wood, pp. 38–39 and General Eddleman, cited above. In the Philippines high-quality scotch sold for about a dollar a bottle and beer was available for about a penny a mug.

13. Hanson W. Baldwin interview, p. 152.

14. George H. Decker interview, Part 1; "Address by M. Gen. Melvin Zais to U.S. Army Sergeant Majors Conference, 4 December 1967," Zais Papers, U.S. Army Military History Research Collection.

15. D. Clayton James, *The Years of MacArthur,* Vol. 1, *1880–1941* (Boston: Houghton Mifflin Company, 1970) p. 453.

16. Pogue, *Ordeal and Hope,* p. 84.

17. On the vicissitudes of Marshall's interwar career, see Forrest C. Pogue, *George C. Marshall: The Education of a General 1880–1939* (New York: Viking, 1964), pp. 221–317.

18. On the inability of many officers to measure up, see Pogue, *Ordeal and Hope,* pp. 92–94.

19. Weigley, *History of the United States Army,* p. 409.

20. Watson, *Chief of Staff,* p. 2.

21. Pogue, *Ordeal and Hope,* p. 47.

22. Quoted in H. H. Arnold, *Global Mission* (New York: Harper and Row, 1949), p. 964.

23. *Final Report of the War Department Special Committee on Army Air Corps* (Washington: GPO, 1934), p. 61.

24. Alfred F. Hurley, *Billy Mitchell: Crusader for Air Power* (Bloomington: Indiana University Press, 1975), p. 41.

25. Hurley, *Mitchell,* p. 84; Craven and Cate, eds., *The Army Air Forces in World War II,* Vol. 1, *Plans and Early Operations January 1939 to August 1942* (Chicago: University of Chicago Press, 1948), p. 19.

26. Craven and Cate, ibid.

27. The most scholarly and balanced account of Mitchell's ideas is Alfred Hurley's, *Billy Mitchell.* Burke Davis, *The Billy Mitchell Affair* (New York: Random House, 1967) was the first book based on the newly opened court-martial transcript. Other, more partisan biographies, are Roger Burlingham, *General Billy Mitchell* (New York: McGraw Hill, 1952) and Isaac Don Levine, *Mitchell, Pioneer of Airpower* (New York: Duell, Sloan and Pearce, 1958).

28. Hurley, *Mitchell,* p. 42.

29. Burke Davis, *The Billy Mitchell Affair,* p. 118. For details of these tests (from the navy's viewpoint) see Archibald D. Turnbull and Clifford L. Lord, *History of United States Naval Aviation* (New Haven: Yale University Press, 1949), pp. 193–202.

30. Davis, *The Billy Mitchell Affair,* p. 200.

31. Hurley, *Mitchell*, p. 69.

32. *From the Wright Brothers to the Astronauts: The Memoirs of Major General Benjamin D. Foulouis* (New York: McGraw Hill, 1968), pp. 215–219. An excellent discussion of Air Corps efforts to establish an independent mission by assuming responsibility for the defense of the coast against seaborne attack may be found in John F. Shiner, "The Air Corps, The Navy and Coast Defense 1919–1941," *Military Affairs,* October 1981, pp. 113–120.

33. Haywood Hansel, *The Air Plan That Defeated Hitler* (privately published, 1972), p. 8; Thomas H. Greer, *The Development of Air Doctrine 1917–1941: USAF Historical Studies, No. 89* (USAF History Division, Research Studies Institute, September 1955), pp. 19, 30, 50–51, and passim.

34. Greer, *Development of Air Doctrine,* p. 51.

35. Arnold, *Global Mission,* p. 150.

36. Craven and Cate, *Plans and Early Operations,* pp. 63–65.

37. Robert F. Futrell, *Ideas, Concepts, Doctrine: A History of Basic Thinking in the Air Force* (Montgomery: Air University, 1968), p. 37.

38. Futrell, *Ideas, Concepts, Doctrine,* p. 43; Greer, *Development of Air Doctrine,* pp. 59–62.

39. Craven and Cate, *Plans and Early Operations,* pp. 64–65.

40. Greer, *Development of Air Doctrine,* p. 82.

41. Futrell, *Ideas, Concepts, Doctrine,* p. 44.

42. Shiner, "The Air Corps, the Navy and Coast Defense," pp. 114–119.

43. Pogue, *Ordeal and Hope,* p. 49.

44. George C. Marshall to Admiral Harold L. Stark, 7 February 1941, *Pearl Harbor Hearings,* Part 3, pp. 1064–65.

45. John R. M. Wilson, "Herbert Hoover and the Armed Forces," (Ph.D. diss., Northwestern University, 1970) p. 37. There is no comprehensive history of the navy comparable to Weigley's *History of the United States Army.* By far the most important and provocative works on the interwar navy are the articles by Thomas C. Hone cited below. Excellent discussions of aspects of the naval history of the period may be found in the article by Waldo Heinrichs cited below and in the articles on "Robert E. Coontz" by Lawrence H. Douglas, "Edward W. Eberle" by Richard W. Turk, "Charles F. Hughes" by William R. Braisted, "William V. Pratt" by Craig L. Symonds, "William H. Standley" by John C. Walter, "William D. Leahy" by John Major, and "Harold R. Stark" by B. Mitchell Simpson III in Robert W. Love, ed., *The Chiefs of Naval Operations* (Annapolis: Naval Institute Press, 1980). Less detailed but equally thought-provoking are Philip T. Rosen, "The Treaty Navy 1919–1937" and John Major, "The Navy Plans for War, 1937–1941," in Kenneth J. Hagan, ed., *In Peace and War* (Westport, Conn.: Greenwood Press, 1978).

46. In the Fifth Fleet, for example, during the invasion of the Marshalls in early 1944, Annapolis men commanded all battleships, fast carriers, cruisers, destroyer squadrons, and task forces. Reservists commanded a portion of the transports, destroyer escorts, and minesweepers. Samuel Eliot Morison, *The Aleutians, Gilberts, and Marshalls: History of U.S. Naval Operations in World War II* (Boston: Little Brown and Company, 1951), Appendix 3, pp. 343–351.

47. E. B. Potter, *Nimitz* (Annapolis: U.S. Naval Institute, 1976), p. 52.

48. David Rosenberg, "Arleigh Burke and Officer Development in the Inter-War Navy," *Pacific Historical Review* 44 (November 1975), p. 509.

49. Peter Karsten, *The Naval Aristocracy: The Golden Age of Annapolis and the Emergence of Modern American Navalism* (New York: The Free Press, 1972), p. 41.

50. Reminiscences of Admiral Thomas C. Hart, U.S. Naval Historical Foundation, Oral History Collection, pp. 65, 25–46; Rosenberg, "Arleigh Burke," p. 507.

51. Turner, "The Strategic Employment of the Fleet," 28 October 1937, Record Group 4, Box 44, Naval Historical Collection, U.S. Naval War College, Newport, Rhode Island.

52. For a discussion of the influence of Jutland on strategic thinking in the interwar navy, see Russell F. Weigley, *The American Way of War: A History of United States Military Strategy and Policy* (New York: Macmillan, 1973), pp. 93–94. See also General Thomas T. Handy's oral history interview, U.S. Army Military History Research Collection, p. 44. Michael T. Vlahos has calculated that the War College refought the Battle of Jutland fifty times, but argues that these were not so much realistic simulations as "symbolic moral examples of greatness and decline . . . a dramatic encounter in which the moral qualities of each opponent cry for open evaluation." Michael Vlahos, *The Blue Sword: The Naval War College and the American Mission 1919–1941* (Newport: Naval War College Press, 1980), pp. 149–150.

53. Rosenberg, "Arleigh Burke," p. 509.

54. "Cruisers and Destroyers in a General Action," U.S. Naval War College pamphlet, June 1937, Naval Historical Collection, Record Group 4, pp. 118–19.

55. Thomas C. Hone and Mark David Mandeles, "Managerial Style in the Interwar Navy: A Reappraisal," *Naval War College Review*, September-October 1980, p. 95. Hone and Mandeles argue that this system of decentralized management and organized conflict among administrative units may be more conducive to innovation than highly centralized direction.

56. Ibid., p. 96.

57. For a good discussion of navy reaction to the treaties see Gerald E. Wheeler, *Admiral William Veazie Pratt U.S. Navy: A Sailor's Life* (Washington, D.C.: Naval History Division, 1974), pp. 177–88, 302–9.

58. Thomas C. Hone, "Spending Patterns of the United States Navy 1921–1941," *Armed Forces and Society,* Vol. 8 (Spring 1982), pp. 445–46 and passim.

59. Wheeler, *William Veazie Pratt,* p. 214.

60. James O. Richardson, *On the Treadmill to Pearl Harbor: The Memories of Admiral J. O. Richardson* (Washington, D.C.: Naval History Division, 1973), p. 3; Waldo H. Heinrichs, Jr., "The Role of the U.S. Navy" in Borg and Okamoto, eds. *Pearl Harbor As History,* pp. 199, 201.

61. Hurley, *Mitchell,* pp. 44–45, 49.

62. Gerald E. Wheeler, "Mitchell, Moffett, and Air Power," *The Airpower Historian* Vol. 8 (April 1961), p. 80.

63. Edward Arpee, From *Frigates to Flattops: The Story of the Life and Achievements of Rear Admiral William Adger Moffett U.S.N.* (Lake Forrest, Ill: Privately printed, 1953).

64. Wheeler, "Mitchell, Moffett, and Airpower," p. 85.

65. Clark G. Reynolds, *The Fast Carriers: The Forging of an Air Navy* (New York: McGraw-Hill, 1968), p. 16.

66. Ibid., pp. 19–20; Heinrichs, "Role of the Navy," p. 201.

67. "The Employment of Aviation in Naval Warfare," 14 December 1939, Naval Historical Collection, Record Group 4, No. 2175, Box 47.

68. Charles C. Melhorn, *Two Block Fox: The Rise of the Aircraft Carrier 1911–1929* (Annapolis: U.S. Naval Institute, 1974), p. 3; Hone and Mandeles, "Managerial Style," pp. 90–91; Hone, "Spending Patterns," pp. 445–6.

69. Clifford L. Lord, "History of Naval Aviation 1898–1939, Part VI," unpublished manuscript, Naval Historical Center, Washington, D.C., pp. 1193–99; Charles Melhorn, *Two Block Fox*, pp. 3–26; Hone and Mandeles, "Managerial Style," pp. 90, 95–96.

70. John C. Walter, "William Harrison Standley" in Robert W. Love, ed., *The Chiefs of Naval Operations*, p. 95.

71. Hone and Mandeles, "Managerial Style in the Interwar Navy," pp. 91–92, 96–97.

72. Robert D. Heinl, *Soldiers of the Sea* (Annapolis: Naval Institute Press, 1962), p. 316; Allan R. Millett, *Semper Fidelis: The History of the United States Marine Corps* (New York: MacMillan, 1980), p. 111.

73. Ibid., pp. 317–18.

74. "Memo, Amalgamation of the Marine Corps," 8 May 1931, Simonds Papers, Library of Congress, cited in John R.M. Wilson "Herbert Hoover and the Armed Forces," p. 74.

75. Heinl, *Soldiers of the Sea*, p. 296.

76. Colonel William K. Naylor, *Principles of Strategy with Historical Illustrations* (Fort Leavenworth: General Service Schools, 1921), p. 335.

77. W. S. Pye, "Joint Army-Navy Operations," *U.S. Naval Institute Proceedings* 51 (February 1925); Keyes quoted in Jeter A. Isely and Philip A. Crowl, *The U.S. Marines and Amphibious Warfare* (Princeton: Princeton University Press, 1951), p. 21.

78. Isely and Crowl, *The U.S. Marines and Amphibious Warfare*, p. 27.

79. Ibid., p. 26.

80. Heinl, *Soldiers of the Sea*, p. 253; Isely and Crowl, *The U.S. Marines and Amphibious Warfare*, p. 26.

81. Isely and Crowl, ibid., pp. 31, 28.

82. Weigley, *The American Way of War*, p. 264.

TWO

States of Mind: Japanese

The Japanese army and navy were the product of diverse European and American influences—from the German General Staff to the British Royal Navy to the histories of Alfred Thayer Mahan. On the eve of World War II, they shared with their western models a common set of strategic concepts, a characteristic professional myopia, and a technological conservatism which had been only mildly shaken by the events of World War I.

In their relation to Japan's political structure, however, the armed forces were unique. By tradition and—after 1936—by law, the ministers of the army and navy were chosen from among their respective senior officers on active duty. Both the army and the navy, by refusing to name a minister, could prevent the formation of a cabinet of which they disapproved; by withdrawing their minister, they could force the dissolution of an existing government. In addition to these very considerable powers, the military also claimed "the right of supreme command," according to which the chiefs of the Army and Navy General Staffs were independent of the government, directly responsible to the Emperor in matters vital to the national defense. As a corollary, the service chiefs had direct access to the Emperor on military or strategic matters.

The Imperial Japanese Army and Navy believed that they occupied a special place in the unique and superior Japanese "national polity," or *kokutai*. They claimed a special relationship with the Emperor, who was the embodiment of the *kokutai,* and whose "Imperial Rescript to Soldiers and Sailors" predated the constitution.[1]

The social and educational background of the Japanese officer of the twenties and thirties tended strongly to reinforce these assumptions. By the late twenties, almost a third of the army's officers came from lower middle-class backgrounds.[2] These sons of petty landowners and small shopkeepers felt far less assured of their place in the social hierarchy than did the aristocratic lords of the Choshu and Satsuma clans who had dominated the army high command before World War I: they were thus all the more ready to embrace ideas which reassured them about their unique role in the nation. Some 25 to 30 percent of the officer corps had attended official military preparatory schools (*rikugun yonen gakko*) where, from the age of twelve or thirteen, they had "been immersed in preparing for a military career . . . in surroundings totally isolated from ordinary society."[3] Their education stressed the "mission" of the army officer and his special place in society.

The army's roots in Japan's traditional rural society were broad and deep. Not only were the majority of its younger officers drawn from this segment of society, but the villages of Japan were bound to the army by an entire network of civic and patriotic societies. Organizations such as the Imperial Military Reserve Association, the Youth Association, and the National Defense Woman's Association had representatives and chapters in every rural community; the National Defense Woman's Association alone had over 4,000 branches. Through their varied activities, youth training centers, community relief projects, military drills, and social gatherings, these organizations strengthened the ties of sentiment and tradition between the army and its rural base.[4]

Their backgrounds shaped by rural conservatism and the rarified teachings of the cadet schools, army officers looked askance at the new ideas of party government, labor reform, academic freedom, and disarmament which were beginning to take hold in the more sophisticated urban segments of Japanese society. Every diplomatic, political or economic setback of the 1920s, every scandal or abuse, was associated in the minds of army officers "with the deplored tendencies of the day, the liberal and left-wing thought prevalent in the universities, the impact of modern Western books, music and social customs."[5]

Although the Japanese army of the 1920s and early 1930s might appear monolithic to an outsider, it was in fact riddled with factions and cliques. The officer corps was divided between a small elite group composed of graduates of the Army War College, who held the choicest command and staff assignments, and the great majority of officers destined for more mundane careers.[6] Clan rivalries (*hanbatsu*), although not so virulent as in Meiji times, were still very much alive. Even more divisive was the desire of staff officers like Colonel (later General) Nagata Tetsuzan and Colonel Ishiwara Kanji to prepare the military for "total war." Such mobilization would involve the mechanization and rationalization of the army and the establishment of large-scale economic planning to harness all the resources of the nation to the national defense effort.[7] The more traditionalist officers were dismayed by this tendency to stress "materialistic" factors at the expense of the traditional "spiritual factors," the "imperial way," "the Japanese spirit"—the soul of the Japanese state, which had given the army its valor and aggressiveness. Officers who held to this more conservative view were usually referred to as the *Kodo-ha,* or Imperial Way faction. Finally, many younger officers had begun to flirt with various super-patriotic and militarist political ideas and movements, many of which advocated the "reconstruction" and purification of Japan through an army-directed reformation.

The shattering impact of the Great Depression—especially the widespread poverty and near-starvation in rural areas—served only to deepen the younger officers' conviction that radical action would be needed to save Japanese society. Middle-level officers—colonels, lieutenant colonels and majors—exercised an extraordinary influence in the Japanese army. This was due in part to the tendency of commanders to rely heavily upon their staff officers.[8] In part it was a result of the growing spirit of *gekokujō*—a kind of loyal insubordination, in which subordinates took matters into their own hands to achieve some higher good. By the end of the twenties, many middle-level officers were convinced that only overseas expansion could solve Japan's social and economic ills. That conviction was shared by quite a few of their superiors in the higher ranks of the army.

In September 1931 middle-grade officers of the Kwantung Army, the Japanese military force in Manchuria, with the tacit approval of some of their superiors (on the spot and in Tokyo), manufactured an "incident" on the South Manchuria Railway near Mukden. Within hours a full-scale Japanese attack on Manchuria was underway. While the cabinet in Tokyo vacillated and debated, the Kwantung Army gobbled up Manchuria in a few months, establishing the puppet state of Manchukuo as an "independent" nation under Japanese protection by September 1932. The government at home found itself powerless to restrain the army; in the end, it attempted to justify the military's actions to the world.

The world, or at least the League of Nations, was unconvinced. In 1933 the League adopted the report of the Lytton Commission, which had visited Manchuria. This amounted to a strong vote of censure upon Japan, which thereupon withdrew from the League.

The conquest of Manchuria did not produce the economic miracle which army extremists had expected, but this failed to dampen the ardor of the zealots. Their goals were vague, but they always pursued them with passionate fanaticism. The aims of the extremists included the purging of corruption in government and business through army control of the machinery of state; the institution of some sort of state socialism; military expansion in Asia; and a tougher policy toward the great powers. In March and October 1931, the high command and the police discovered plans for a coup, but the conspirators went unpunished except for transfers to other commands. The next year, nationalist fanatics assassinated the finance minister; on May 15 a party of naval officers and army cadets assassinated Premier Inukai Tsuyoshi, who had opposed the army's actions in Manchuria.

Many of the officers involved in these outrages were let off with reprimands or token punishments, while the actual perpetrators were tried in a series of sensational trials. These the rightists turned into public forums to air their views. Patriotic sentiment was aroused. One hundred ten thousand petitions for clemency were received by the presiding judges. One group of petitioners, "to show their good faith, enclosed their own little fingers pickled in a jar of alcohol." [9] None of the conspirators was executed: and in a few years, all had been paroled.

The years of plotting and assassinations reached a climax in February 1936. Officers of the First Division, stationed in Tokyo, staged a revolt against the government and rival factions of the army. Government buildings were occupied; troops broke into the homes of the prime minister, the lord privy seal, the finance minister, the inspector-general of military training, and other important officials. The finance minister, the inspector-general, and former Prime Minister Admiral Saito Makoto were assassinated; others had narrow escapes. The rebels published a manifesto in the newspapers and called for a new government.

Many army leaders were inclined to temporize with the rebels, but the Emperor stood firm. Backed by his confidential adviser, Prince

Saionji Kinmochi who had himself narrowly escaped assassination—and by the navy, the Emperor refused to consider any changes in the government, insisting that the rebels should be suppressed immediately. Loyal soldiers and sailors were brought to the capital, where they surrounded the rebel units. Leaflets ordering surrender were dropped on the rebel positions.

In three days, the rebellion had collapsed and most of the ringleaders were in custody. This time there were no sensational show trials and no cover-ups. The leaders of the rebellion were quietly tried and executed, together with a handful of civilian right-wing ideologists they had long been associated with. The army high command relentlessly exploited the fear and uneasiness caused by the attempted coup to establish its supremacy throughout the ruling establishment. The army at home and in Manchuria was thoroughly purged; officers associated with the *Kodo-ha* faction were forced into retirement or transferred to unimportant posts. The more hardheaded, pragmatic generals were now firmly in power; henceforth they could use the threat of further right-wing upheavals to extract whatever they wished from the badly shaken civilian ministers of the government. It was these men who were to guide the Imperial Japanese Army throughout the Pacific War.

Despite the militarism and bellicosity of its leaders, the army was singularly ill prepared for modern warfare, especially for the type of modern warfare it was destined to fight against the United States. Alone among the armies of the great powers, the Japanese army had never experienced at first hand the full power of modern weaponry of the sort used on the European fronts in World War I.[10] Japanese army doctrine continued to stress "the superiority of spiritual factors"—loyalty, faith in victory, aggressiveness and fighting spirit—over material ones in warfare. The army's successes against superior forces in the Sino-Japanese War of 1894–1895 and the Russo-Japanese War of 1904–1905 gave its leaders confidence that their unique Japanese fighting spirit would ensure victory even against nominally stronger enemies. Army cadets were taught that "offense was the best tactic under any circumstances without regard to cost." [11] In August 1939 Japanese troops clashed with Soviet units in the Nomonhan region, a disputed border area in the southeastern corner of Manchuria. In short but bloody fighting, the Soviets used their superior artillery, armor, and mechanized forces to inflict crippling losses on the Japanese. Yet Imperial Army leaders refused to learn any lessons from the Nomonhan defeat; they focussed instead on the brilliant German victories in Poland during the same months,[12] victories made possible by the very type of organization, methods, and material the Japanese army disdained.

Japanese ground units were designed primarily for operations against the Soviet Union. Warfare in Asiatic Russia meant fighting in severe cold in sparsely populated areas at the end of long supply lines. The large-scale logistical organizations created for such operations were not easily adapted for warfare on small tropical islands.[13]

Likewise, the constant demands of operations in Manchuria, and later in China, resulted in a shortage of qualified instructors to train the rapidly expanding army. Training exercises and maneuvers also had to be curtailed in size, and tactical training for combat in tropical areas was "very poor and of little use." Few troops had any training or experience in amphibious warfare.[14]

Before the outbreak of World War II, the army high command wasted little thought on England or the United States. While large numbers of officers visited Germany and the Soviet Union each year as attachés or on study tours, few were ever sent to England or the United States. When an American officer suggested to Ishiwara Kanji that he visit the United States on his way home from two years' study in Germany, the future Japanese staff planner replied, "The only occasion on which I plan to visit the United States is when I arrive there as chief of the Japanese forces of occupation." [15] English was not even taught in the army's military colleges. The Anglo-American powers were thought to be too weak militarily and too divided domestically to pose a serious threat to Japanese ambitions.[16] In any case, war with the United States or Britain was regarded as primarily a naval problem.

The Japanese navy was both less xenophobic and politically less influential than the Japanese army. Naval officers prided themselves on their "cosmopolitan" outlook—many had served or studied in England, Germany, or the United States—and on their detached, "scientific" approach to problems. Naval statesmen like Admiral Kato Tomosaburo, Saito Makoto, and Yonai Mitsumasa had the breadth of outlook and experience required to serve as ambassadors or cabinet ministers after retirement. Significantly, it was a retired admiral, Nomura Kichisaburo, who represented Japan in the final, last-ditch effort to reach a settlement with the United States in the months before Pearl Harbor.

Yet the navy—like the army—was racked by factional and bureaucratic rivalries. Probably the most significant division was between the Navy Ministry and the Naval General Staff. The two organizations were entirely separate. The ministry was responsible for the naval budget, ship construction, weapons procurement, personnel, relations with the Diet and the cabinet, and broad matters of naval policy. The general staff directed the operations of the fleet and the preparation of war plans. Until the 1920s, the Navy Ministry, under the leadership of powerful ministers like Admiral Yamamoto Gombei and Admiral Kato Tomosaburo, had played the predominant role in naval affairs, while the Naval General Staff occupied a distinctly secondary position.[17] Officers of the General Staff resented this inferior status; during the 1920s and 1930s, they made increasingly successful efforts to reverse the situation. The Washington Conference accentuated and gave focus to this endemic rivalry. Those admirals who favored continued cooperation with the Anglo-American powers and who supported the Washington disarmament agreements were to be found principally in the Navy Ministry; the opponents of the Washington treaty system principally in the Naval General Staff.[18]

The leader of the anti-treaty group (or the "Fleet Faction," as it was often known) was Admiral Kato Kanji, Vice-Chief of the Naval General Staff, who had been a naval adviser at Washington. An inveterate enemy of the disarmament treaties and an admirer of Germany, Kato argued that the 6:10 ratio in capital ships fixed at Washington was insufficient to ensure a successful defense against an American naval offensive.

Kato's supporters in the fleet and navy staff took an extremely narrow and mechanistic view of questions concerning naval strategy. Military writers had long held the maxim that an attacking force needed to be at least 50 percent stronger than the defending force. Interpreting this literally, Japanese strategists argued that a 6:10 ratio was unacceptable, since it would give the United States a 67 percent margin of superiority, whereas a 7:10 ratio would redress this margin to 43 percent.[19]

The idea of a 70 percent ratio "sufficient to defend but insufficient to attack" had been part of Japanese naval thinking since the turn of the century. "Reinforced by further strategic studies, war games, maneuvers in the Pacific, and the object lessons of the First World War, the notion of a 70 percent ratio had become a firmly established consensus within the Navy by the time of the Washington Conference. Indeed, it grew into an axiomatic conviction, even an obsession that dominated Japanese naval policy, strategic planning, and building program throughout the 1920s and up to Pearl Harbor." [20]

Proponents of the Washington treaty like Admiral Yamanashi Katsunoshin, Kato Tomasaburo, and Vice Admiral Hori Teikichi ridiculed the idea that an increase of 10 percent in the naval ratio would enable the Japanese fleet to defeat the U.S. or Britain. Far more important, they argued, was the Americans' ability to construct vessels rapidly after the outbreak of war, together with their vast industrial superiority.[21]

These officers—and other "moderates" like Admirals Yonai Mitsumasa, Yamamoto Isoroku, and Inoue Shigeyoshi—were not closet pacifists.[22] They looked forward to, and worked for, Japan's growth into one of the world's great powers, the predominant nation in Asia. They opposed naval rivalry with the U.S. not out of opposition to a large fleet, but because the reckless navalism of the Fleet Faction was likely to bring Japan into collision with stronger powers before she was fully ready for such a contest. Yamamoto Isoroku summed up these views in a letter to a younger officer in 1934. There was

. . . an immeasurable difference [between] Japan's strength now compared with the time of the Washington Conference, and I feel keenly that the time has come for this mighty empire rising in the east to devote itself, with all due circumspection, to advancing its own fortunes. The example afforded before the Great War by Germany—which if only it had exercised forebearance for another five or ten years would by now be unrivaled in Europe—suggests that the task facing us now is to build up our strength calmly and with circumspection." [23]

Kato Tomasaburo, Yonai, Yamamoto, and other moderates were just as devoted as the Fleet Faction to the "advancement of Japan's fortunes," but their calls for "circumspection" and "forebearance" were lost on their less subtle colleagues in the Naval General Staff and the fleet.

Despite vociferous protests, however, most Japanese naval leaders were not wholly displeased with the Washington agreements. For one thing, they allowed Japan to construct unlimited numbers of cruisers, destroyers, and submarines; they also halted the fortification of American bases in the western Pacific, which the far-sighted Admiral Kato Tomosaburo had all along regarded as more crucial than haggling over ratios.[24] Moreover, the United States displayed no inclination during the twenties to bring its fleet up to treaty strength. Still, few naval leaders—outside the handful of moderates in the Navy Ministry—were prepared to tolerate any further limitations. Yet that was precisely what the British and Americans demanded at the London Naval Conference of 1930.

At London the United States insisted that the 6:10 ratio established for capital ships be extended to cruisers as well. The Japanese believed that they would need at least a 7:10 ratio in this class to safeguard their superiority in East Asian waters. In the end, the two countries reached a compromise called the Reed-Matsudaira formula, whereby the 6:10 formula was accepted in principle but the United States agreed not to build beyond a 7:10 ratio until the next disarmament conference, scheduled for 1936.

Kato Kanji and the Fleet Faction attacked the London disarmament agreements as dangerous to security, humiliating, and a violation of the Navy General Staff's right of supreme command. A major domestic political battle broke out over the ratification of the treaty. Moderate admirals of the "Treaty Faction" supported Prime Minister Hamaguchi Osachi, whose party won a smashing victory at the polls; the treaty was subsequently accepted by the Diet.[25] This proved to be the last victory for the proponents of arms limitation and cooperation with the Western democracies.

In November 1930 Hamaguchi was shot by a fanatic from one of the ultranationalist patriotic societies. Even before his death, the storm of criticism over the London agreements had obliged his government to promise larger naval appropriations and to replace those navy leaders most prominently associated with the treaty. Moving quickly to consolidate its position, the Fleet Faction prevailed upon Prince Fushimi Hiroyasu—a member of the royal family whose nationalism greatly exceeded his intelligence—to become chief of the Naval General Staff. During what Asada Sadao has characterized as "his long and undistinguished career," Fushimi amply served the purposes of the extremists in the Fleet Faction.[26]

The faction next took steps to enhance the authority of the Naval General Staff at the expense of the Navy Ministry. Just as the army had played on the panic produced by the February Mutiny to consolidate its position, so the Fleet Faction took advantage of the fear of extremism engendered by the rise of ultranationalist groups—in which young naval officers played a prominent part—to press its own demands.

Under incessant prodding from Prince Fushimi and Kato Kanji, the navy minister, Admiral Osumi Mineo, carried out a purge of the senior admirals associated with the disarmament treaty: men like Yamanashi and Hori were forced into early retirement. Henceforth the middle-grade officers of the Naval General Staff, the planners and section chiefs—younger disciples of Kato Kanji—were to play an increasingly powerful role in shaping naval policy.[27]

Though the navy leaders had succeeded in cowing the civilian government, they still faced stiff opposition from the army for appropriations. Army strategists argued that Japan's ground forces had to be rapidly expanded to meet the threat of Soviet Russia. At the same time, expansion had to continue in northern China to secure the Empire's southern flank and to protect Manchukuo.[28]

Navy planners realized that if they went along completely with the army's program of expansion, there would be little room for large naval appropriations. The navy proposed instead that Japan adopt a policy of advance into the "South Seas" or the "Southern Region"—the navy's term for French Indochina, the Dutch East Indies, Malaya, and the mandated islands of the Pacific. An advance in this region would bring Japan essential resources, especially oil; it would, of course, also require an expansion of the navy.[29] Admiral Oikawa Kojirō succinctly summoned up the reasons behind the navy's proposals: "The southern advance will result in England and the United States being our opponents and a northern advance means a collision with Russia." [30]

The army agreed that an advance into the "South Seas" was highly desirable, but argued that the Russian threat must be dealt with first. The navy conceded that Russia was a menace, but insisted that the "southern advance" ought to take precedence: the army should avoid provoking the Russians until the aims of the advance were achieved.

In the end, both the army and the navy got their way—with disastrous consequences. In August 1936, the cabinet adopted a document entitled "Fundamental Principles of National Policy." By its terms the government undertook both " 'the securing of a firm diplomatic and defensive position on the East Asiatic Continent' " and " 'the extension of national influence to the South Seas.' " The advance to the South Seas was to be accomplished " 'gradually and by peaceful means,' " and in the north " 'extreme caution will be exercised to avoiding causing trouble with the Soviet Union.' " At the same time, the army and navy were both to be expanded. The army was to be built up to " 'a strength to resist the forces the Soviet Union can employ in the Far East,' " and the navy was " 'to be brought to a level sufficient to secure command of the Western Pacific against the U.S. Navy.' " [31] This very tall order required an increase of ten divisions and additional air squadrons in the army and an addition to the navy of two battleships, seven carriers, and twenty destroyers.[32]

The program represented by the "Fundamental Principles of National Policy" not only saddled Japan with an immense arms race, but produced a set of dangerous, provocative, and ultimately competing foreign policies. Expansion in China, confrontation with Russia, and penetration of the South Seas were bound to result in collision with one or more of the great powers.

Events in China soon revealed just how dangerously open-ended the new policy could be. According to the "Fundamental Principles of National Policy," China was to be asked to join a tripartite pact with Japan and Manchukuo against Russia and to allow the conversion of its five northern provinces into a buffer zone under Japanese protection.[33] But China proved surprisingly stubborn. Political and economic pressure failed to move her into the Japanese orbit. There were new incidents; in July 1937 full-scale war erupted between Japan and China.

The Sino-Japanese War (or the "China Incident," as the Japanese persisted in calling it) dragged on into 1938, into 1939, 1940 and 1941—despite smashing Japanese victories and declarations that the Chinese were finally beaten; despite moral condemnation from the West and half-hearted attempts to uphold the principle of the Open Door. The war, together with the navy's continuing desire for an advance to the south, set Japan on a collision course with England and the United States. The navy, which had invented the drive to the south and the crusade against Western imperialism as a device to secure more naval building, now found itself called upon to make good on its own propaganda.

● ●

Whatever the differences in its social and political position, the Japanese navy was a faithful mirror image of its American opponent in strategy. Japanese naval officers, too, had inhaled deeply the heady, if somewhat musty, fumes of Mahan's classic brew of imperialism and saltwater. Mahan had been translated into Japanese well before the turn of the century; the master's works were required reading at navy schools and colleges. The "father of Japanese naval strategy," Akiyama Saneyuki, had served as an observer aboard Admiral Sampson's flagship in the Spanish-American War, and had himself talked with Mahan; he introduced the same types of staff planning and table-top maneuvers to the Japanese Naval War College as the Americans employed at Newport.[34]

Mahan's emphasis on the climactic battle for "command of the seas" seemed confirmed for the Japanese by their own experiences in the wars with China (1894–1895) and Russia (1904–1905). In the former, the Japanese fleet under Admiral Ito had destroyed the principal Chinese fleet in the Battle of the Yangtze. Similarly, in the war against Russia, the Japanese had defeated the Russian Far East fleet in the Battle of the Yellow Sea and then had annihilated a second Russian naval force sent from Europe in the famous battle of Tsushima. Japanese strategists were confident that future naval wars would be decided in the same manner. The Imperial Navy's operations manual, the *Kaisen Yoh-murei,* declared that " 'Battle is the sole means of victory. So everything should satisfy what the battle demands.' " [35]

In the first decade of the twentieth century, Akiyama, Sato Tetsu-taro ("The Japanese Mahan"), and Suzuki Kantaro had mapped out the basic contours of Japanese naval strategy. A blend of Mahan's doctrines and traditional Chinese and Japanese military concepts, their thinking emphasized the subjugation of the enemy through maneuver, strategy, and attrition, rather than by strict quantitative superiority.[36]

The navy's basic plan for war against the United States dated from around 1907, when tensions between the two nations had risen due to American discrimination against Japanese immigrants. Like the American "Orange Plan," it was more a blueprint for a campaign than for a sustained naval war. At the outset of the hypothetical war, the Japanese planned to seize control of the Philippines and Guam. This would force the American fleet to cross the Pacific to rescue its possessions. The Japanese would intercept the American fleet in the seas near Japan and destroy it in a decisive battle—just as they had destroyed the Russian fleet at Tsushima after its long voyage from Europe. The Japanese, fighting near their home bases and with an "early-warning line" in the vicinity of the Bonins, would be able to choose the most advantageous time and place to strike the American fleet, already worn down by its long journey.[37]

After World War I and the signing of the Washington treaty, this plan was revised to take into account Japan's acquisition of the former German islands in the central Pacific and the inferiority of the Japanese battlefleet imposed by that treaty. The new Japanese campaign plan had two parts: the attrition stage and the decisive battle stage.

At the outbreak of war, Japanese submarines would position themselves off the United States coast. From there they would shadow the American fleet as it made its way across the Pacific and attack it with torpedoes. As the Americans came within range of the Japanese-held mandated islands, land and carrier-based planes would join the attack. The decisive battle stage would begin as the American fleet approached the Philippines. The advance body of Japanese cruisers and destroyers, supported by fast battleships, would carry out a torpedo attack on the enemy at night. The following day, the Japanese battle fleet would engage the remaining American forces—presumably weakened seriously by the repeated torpedo and aircraft attacks, and destroy them.[38]

To ensure the success of these plans, the Japanese naval strategists counted upon three factors: the superior toughness, morale, and fighting spirit of their men—the unique "Japanese spirit" which had won the day against the larger forces of China and Russia; incessant drill and training; and the development of new and superior weapons.

In the 1930s the Japanese navy led the world in the development of torpedoes and torpedo carriers. By 1933 the Japanese had perfected a twenty-four-inch, completely oxygen-fueled torpedo with a maximum range of twenty-four miles at thirty-nine knots or twelve miles at forty-nine knots, and an extremely powerful warhead. By contrast, the best American torpedoes in 1941 were twenty-one-inch models with a range of about 4,500 yards.[39] To deliver these deadly weapons, the Japanese developed a formidable array of warships. All Japanese heavy cruisers were equipped with torpedo tubes (their American counterparts were not). Japanese cruisers were very fast and well-armed, though lightly protected. The destroyers Japan built in the early thirties were probably the most advanced in the world, and the Imperial Navy's larger "I"-type submarines had a cruising radius of over 10,000 miles.

Although the Japanese produced many innovative warship designs, they often attempted to pack too much armament, speed, and protection into the limited dimensions of their ships. In design matters, the Naval General Staff arrogantly overrode the objections of Admiral Hiraga Yuzuru, chief of the Naval Construction Bureau. When the "light cruisers" of the *Mogami* class were completed in 1935, for example, with a main armament of no less than fifteen 6.1-inch guns on a displacement of only 8,500 tons, it was found that the hull was too light to bear the weight of the guns, so the ships had to be drastically modified. Likewise, many Japanese destroyers and torpedo boats were so heavily armed that they proved unstable in bad weather. In 1934, the newly commissioned torpedo boat *Tomatsuru* foundered in a storm; in 1935 so many destroyers of the *Fubuki* class were damaged in a typhoon that the whole class had to be reconstructed.[40]

These powerful cruisers and destroyers had been designed to deliver the torpedo attacks against the American battle fleet contemplated in the Japanese war plans. For that purpose, they were relentlessly drilled and maneuvered under the worst possible conditions. The fleet's yearly training cycle began in December and continued with few pauses until the end of October. Japanese sailors quipped that the navy's calendar consisted entirely of week days. Exercises and maneuvers were frequently held in the stormy northern waters near the Kurile Islands to toughen the men and preserve secrecy. Special emphasis was placed upon training for night fighting; for this purpose, the Imperial Navy had developed special range finders, binoculars, and illumination devices.[41] Maneuvers and exercises were carried out at high speed at night, by ships lacking radar or other electronic devices, and disastrous collisions were far from rare. Yet the navy persisted in its efforts to bring commanders and crews to a high state of proficiency for night fighting. Although the decisive surface battle with the American fleet never took place, the awesome superiority of the Japanese navy in night fighting and torpedo warfare proved a great source of calamity to the Allied navies in the narrow waters of the Dutch East Indies and the Solomon Islands.

The most formidable weapon in the Imperial Navy's arsenal ultimately proved to be not ships but airplanes. To deliver long-range attacks against American ships, the Japanese had developed the Type 95 (Nell) long-range torpedo bomber with a range of almost 1,300 miles.[42] In the war against China, these planes flew the first transoceanic bombing missions—from Taiwan and Kyushu to Shanghai.

Like the United States, Japan had converted two of its capital ships (the *Akagi* and *Kaga*) into aircraft carriers after the Washington Conference. The Japanese also practised dive-bombing and developed a number of very effective carrier aircraft. Their "Kate" torpedo bomber was generally superior to American types, and their "Claude" fighter, developed in 1935, was the first carrier-based monoplane fighter. But the most formidable Japanese carrier plane was the redoubtable "Zero." Entering service in 1940, the Zero fighter represented a giant step in the development of naval aircraft. It was the first carrier-based fighter to equal or surpass the performance of the best contemporary land-based fighters; it was superior to *any* fighter in the United States Army or Navy at the outbreak of the war.[43] Yet the Zero had serious weaknesses: its superior speed, climb, firepower, and maneuverability had been purchased at the price of protection. Unlike contemporary American aircraft, it lacked armor and self-sealing fuel tanks, and its light construction made it extremely vulnerable. These weaknesses were to prove fatal later in the war as Allied airmen learned appropriate tactics against Zeros and began to receive improved fighters of their own.

Like its planes, the Japanese navy's pilots were among the best in the world. Many had had years of experience flying combat over China. By 1941 these pilots had received over 300 hours of flying experience before joining their first tactical unit; those who participated in the Pearl Harbor attack averaged about 800 hours each.[44] Yet lack of a large-scale pilot training program to provide replacements for these experienced aviators proved a serious source of weakness later in the war.

However effective their destroyers, torpedoes and aircraft, the Japanese senior admirals were too faithful students of Mahan to put their faith for ultimate victory in any weapon except the battleship. Japanese strategists knew that they would always be outnumbered by the capital ships of Britain and the United States, but they hoped to compensate for this inferiority by building ships that were qualitatively superior to their foreign counterparts. In 1931, the Navy successfully tested an eighteen-inch gun firing a projectile 30 percent more powerful than the largest shells used by foreign warships.[45]

In 1937 secret construction began on two battleships with a standard displacement of 64,000 tons, armed with nine eighteen-inch guns and protected by a 25.5-inch armor belt. The *Yamato* and *Musashi* were the largest and most powerful battleships ever built up to that time. They were designed to withstand the largest shells, bombs, and torpedoes and to outrange and outfight any foreign battleship. To match the *Yamato*, the United States would have had to build ships so large that they could not pass through the locks of the Panama Canal. The Japanese were confident that by that time, the Imperial Navy would have even greater superships.[46] By the outbreak of war with the United States, Japan had two ships of the *Yamato* type nearly completed and a third under construction.

Although the majority of the Naval General Staff continued to adhere faithfully to the big battleships–decisive battle school of thought, one group of officers, those connected with naval aviation, offered a qualified dissent. They argued that some of the money being spent on the super-battleships could better be spent on aircraft and aviation equipment.[47] As the quality of their aircraft improved, and their planes proved themselves over China, the aviators became increasingly assertive.

The basic Japanese war plan assigned to the carriers the task of launching torpedo plane attacks against the approaching American fleet. Once the battle was joined, the Japanese carrier planes were to concentrate on wrecking the flight decks of the American carriers so that they would be unable to launch scouting planes.[48] To the battleship admirals, scouting was still the airplane's most important function.

The aviators rejected this secondary role and argued that carrier-borne aircraft could be made a decisive offensive weapon.[49] While they never won over the naval high command to this point of view, the airmen had made important gains by the end of the 1930s. The First Air Fleet, composed of the six largest and fastest carriers, had been formed as a separate battle force in the spring of 1941; formations of four or more large aircraft carriers were now recognized as new and powerful tactical units.[50]

In the area of antisubmarine warfare, the Japanese navy was woefully unprepared. Indeed, Japanese admirals seemed hardly aware that the problem existed. "As a Japanese naval officer, I spent nearly half my career on the sea," recalled a retired admiral after the war, "but I never saw exercises dealing with warfare either against or in defense of maritime communication lines." [51] Japanese submarines, in accordance with the principle of interceptive operations, were intended to lie in wait for the enemy battle fleet, shadow it, and attack it with torpedoes. Japanese strategists mistakenly "took it for granted that the role played by American submarines would be about the same as that of her own submarine forces." [52] In addition, these strategists vastly underestimated the capabilities of the American submarine forces, assuming that Americans were inherently unsuited to the physical and mental strain of prolonged submarine duty.[53]

One strategist, Vice Admiral Inoue Shigeyoshi, head of the Naval Affairs Bureau of the Navy Ministry, was a brilliant, iconoclastic, and somewhat eccentric officer. He urged the navy to junk its plans for "the decisive battle," and prepare instead for protracted air- and amphibious warfare in the central Pacific, use its submarines to attack enemy commerce, and build larger numbers of escort vessels to keep its own lines of communications open.[54] These ideas made no impression on the Naval General Staff. Inoue was kept on the sideline until 1944, when he was asked to join Admiral Yonai as navy vice-minister in trying to salvage the wreckage of the Japanese war effort.[55]

Few Japanese admirals were as far-sighted as Inoue. A careful student of the Japanese navy has concluded that the service lacked first-rate leadership at the high command level. Many Japanese officers, after the rigorous, almost savage training and competition at the naval academy at Etajima, appeared to "burn out," both physically and intellectually. They made little effort to keep up with professional developments; they lacked imagination and flexibility.[56] The "purge" of Treaty Faction admirals in the early 1930s only aggravated the problem by removing some of the ablest leaders.

Still preparing for "the decisive battle" in the western Pacific, hypnotized by the gigantic batteries of the "unsinkable" *Yamato,* their faith secure in the unconquerable "Japanese spirit," the Japanese navy drifted toward war.[57]

● ●

Ostensibly to establish unity of command, the Imperial General Headquarters had been created in 1937. The ministers of war and navy, and the heads of the Army and Navy General Staffs, with their principal assistants, all belonged to the Headquarters, which met about twice a week on the grounds of the Imperial Palace. Operational control of forces in the field remained, however, with the general staffs, acting through the Army Section and the Navy Section of the Headquarters. These sections were not even located in the same building. Thus, on the eve of Pearl Harbor, the Japanese army and navy were still separate-but-equal entities, each with its own air force, each jealously guarding its interests against the rival service.[58]

Where joint action of the services was essential, "central agreements" were reached between the army and navy, but "by far the greater number of orders and directives issued by the Central Authorities were independent Army or Navy actions." [59] If the army and navy could not agree on a joint undertaking, the operation had to be postponed or even abandoned. When they did agree, the army and navy commanders concerned were not usually placed under a joint command, but were instructed to "cooperate" under the terms of the Central Agreement.

As the armed forces assumed an ever more important part in the making of policy, an arrangement known as the "Liaison Conference" was established to coordinate the action of the cabinet and the high command. The members of the Liaison Conference were the service chiefs, the army and navy ministers, the prime minister and the minister of foreign affairs. The Liaison Conference usually met twice a week in a small meeting room of the Imperial Palace to discuss such topics as war plans, important diplomatic measures, and the allocation of national resources.[60]

Although the Liaison Conference had no formal legal status, the
character of its membership soon made it the most important policy-
making organ of the Japanese government. When exceptionally important questions were to be discussed, the meetings of the Liaison
Conference were attended by the Emperor. Such meetings were referred to as "Conferences in the Imperial Presence." The Emperor
would sit in silence on a raised dias at the head of a long table
while generals or cabinet ministers delivered formal presentations.
The president of the Privy Council represented the Emperor in ques-
tioning the speakers. The Emperor himself rarely spoke but when
he did, his pronouncements always had a strong impact on his ministers and advisors.

NOTES

1. On the concept of *kokutai* and the army's special relationship to the nation,
   see Richard Smethhurst, *A Social Basis for Pre-War Japanese Militarism* (Berkeley:
   University of California Press, 1974), p. 164 and passim; and Richard Storry,
   The Double Patriots: A Study of Japanese Nationalism (Boston: Houghton Mifflin
   Company, 1957), pp. 3–7.

2. Storry, *Double Patriots,* p. 43.

3. Fujiwara Akira, "The Role of the Japanese Army," in Dorothy Borg and Shumpei Okamoto eds., *Pearl Harbor as History: Japanese-American Relations 1931–
   1941* (New York: Columbia University Press, 1973), p. 92.

4. Smethhurst, *Social Basis for Japanese Militarism,* passim.

5. Storry, *Double Patriots,* pp. 59–60.

6. James B. Crowley, *Japan's Quest for Autonomy: National Security and Foreign Policy*
   (Princeton: Princeton University Press, 1966), p. 383 and passim; Leonard
   A. Humphreys, "Crisis and Reaction: The Japanese Army in the 'Liberal' Twen-
   ties," *Armed Forces and Society* 5 (Fall 1978), pp. 79–81.

7. Crowley, *Japan's Quest for Autonomy,* pp. 88–91. On the bizarre life and hard
   times of Ishiwara Kanji, one of the most vocal advocates of total war planning,
   see Mark R. Peattie, *Ishiwara Kanji and Japan's Confrontation With the West*
   (Princeton: Princeton University Press, 1975), pp. 186–216.

8. This point is discussed more fully in Fujiwara Akira, "The Role of the Japanese
   Army," pp. 193–94.

9. Toland, *The Rising Sun,* p. 11.

10. Alvin Coox and Saburo Hayashi, *Kogun: The Japanese Army in the Pacific War*
    (Quantico, Virginia: Marine Corps Association, 1959), p. 16; Humphreys, "Cri-
    sis and Reaction," pp. 173–77.

11. Fujiwara, "The Role of the Japanese Army," pp. 192–93.

12. Coox and Hayashi, *Kogun,* p. 16.

13. Ibid., p. 26.

14. *History of Imperial General Headquarters, Army Section,* Japanese Monograph No. 45; HQ U.S. Army, Japan, pp. 22–23. Copy in U.S. Army Center of Military History.

15. Peattie, *Ishiwara Kanji,* p. 80.

16. Stephen E. Pelz, *Race to Pearl Harbor; The Failure of the Second London Naval Conference and the Onset of World War II* (Cambridge: Harvard University Press, 1974), p. 18.

17. Ian T. M. Gow: "Political Involvement of the Japanese Naval General Staff"; Paper presented at U.S. Naval Academy Naval History Symposium, Annapolis, Maryland 1–2 October 1981.

18. Asada Sadao, "The Japanese Navy and the United States" in Borg and Okamoto, eds., *Pearl Harbor as History,* pp. 726–27.

19. Mitsuo Fuchida and Masatake Okumiya, *Midway: The Battle That Doomed Japan* (New York: Ballantine Books, 1955), p. 27; Yokoi Toshiyuki, "Thoughts on Japan's Naval Defeat," *U.S. Naval Institute Proceedings* 86 (10 October 1960), p. 71; Hiroyuki Agawa, *The Reluctant Admiral: Yamamoto and the Imperial Navy* (Tokyo: Kodansha, 1979) pp. 29–32.

20. Asada, "Japanese Admirals and the Politics of Naval Limitation: Kato Tomosaburo vs. Kato Kanji," in Gerald Jordan, ed., *Naval Warfare in the Twentieth Century* (London: Croom Helm, 1978) pp. 146–48.

21. Agawa, *The Reluctant Admiral,* pp. 32–33.

22. For contrasting assessments of the "moderates," see Pelz, *Race to Pearl Harbor,* pp. 214–15 and Arthur Marder, *Old Friends, New Enemies* (Oxford: Oxford University Press, 1981), pp. 107–8. Yamamoto's label as a moderate is at best questionable; although personally close to men of the "Treaty Faction" like Hori Teikichi, he strongly opposed the treaty signed at London in 1930. As Asada observes, "Even taking into account his assigned duty as a naval advisor, Yamamoto's record in London is at variance with his reputation as a leader of the treaty faction." Asada Sadao, "The Imperial Japanese Navy and the Politics of Naval Limitation 1918–1930," unpublished paper, 1983, p. 52.

23. Yamamoto to Miwa Yoshitake, 10 November 1934, reproduced in Agawa, *The Reluctant Admiral,* pp. 37–38.

24. Ibid., p. 149.

25. Pelz, *Race to Pearl Harbor,* pp. 14–15.

26. Asada, "Japanese Navy and the United States," p. 230.

27. Ibid.

28. The discussion which follows is based primarily on Pelz, *Race to Pearl Harbor,* pp. 168–76.

29. "Political Strategy Prior to the Outbreak of War," Part 1, p. 10, Japanese Monograph No. 144, prepared for HQ, Army Forces, Far East, Military History Section. Copy in U.S. Army Center of Military History.

30. Commander, Third Fleet (Oikawa) to Navy Minister, 27 March 1936, quoted in Pelz, *Race to Pearl Harbor,* p. 176.

31. "Political Strategy Prior to the Outbreak of War," Part 1, Appendix 1, pp. i–iv.

32. "New Diplomatic Policy" 7 August 1936 *Gendai shi shiryō*, Vol. 7, pp. 36–65, cited in Pelz, *Race to Pearl Harbor*, p. 176. See also "Political Strategy Prior to Outbreak of War," Part 1.

33. Pelz, *Race to Pearl Harbor*, pp. 172–73.

34. Mark R. Peattie, "Akiyama Saneyuki and the Emergence of Modern Japanese Naval Doctrine," *U.S. Naval Institute Proceedings*, Vol. 103, January 1977, pp. 62–65.

35. Quoted in Yokoi Toshiyuki, "Thoughts on Japan's Naval Defeat," *U.S. Naval Institute Proceedings*, 86 (October 1960), p. 71.

36. Peattie, "Akiyama Saneyuki," p. 67.

37. Sadao Seno, "Chess Game With No Checkmate: Admiral Inoue and the Pacific War," *Naval War College Review*, January-February 1974, pp. 27–28.

38. Pelz, *Race to Pearl Harbor*, pp. 35–39, is an especially fine and vivid discussion of this plan. See also Sadao Seno, "Chess Game With No Checkmate," pp. 27–28 and Morison, *The Rising Sun*, p. 82.

39. Morison, *The Rising Sun*, p. 7.

40. Sadao, "Chess Game," p. 37; Admiral Hiraga, whose surname meant "concede" objected so often and so vigorously that the navy staff officers nicknamed him "Yuzurazu" (never concede).

41. Marder, *Old Friends, New Enemies*, pp. 292–95; Morison, *Rising Sun*, pp. 23–25; Yokoi, "Thoughts on Japanese Naval Defeat," p. 72.

42. Japanese planes were named for the year (of the Japanese calendar) in which they entered service. To avoid confusion, the American identification names, e.g. "Kate," "Nell," will be used here.

43. Marder, *Old Friends, New Enemies*, pp. 307–8.

44. Ibid., p. 305.

45. Pelz, *Race to Pearl Harbor*, p. 32; Matsumoto Kitaro and Chihaya Masatake, "Design and Construction of the *Yamato* and *Musashi*," *U.S. Naval Institute Proceedings* 79 (October 1953), pp. 1101–1107.

46. Matsumoto and Chihaya, "Design of the *Yamamoto*," p. 1104.

47. Sadao, "Chess Game," p. 29.

48. Pelz, *Race to Pearl Harbor*, p. 36.

49. Reynolds, *The Fast Carriers*, pp. 5–7.

50. Ibid., p. 6.

51. Yokoi, "Thoughts on Japan's Naval Defeat," p. 73.

52. Carl Boyd, "The Japanese Submarine Force and the Legacy of Doctrine Developed between the Wars," in *Selected Papers from the Citadel Conference on War and Diplomacy 1978* (Charleston, S.C.: Citadel Press, 1979), p. 27.

53. Oi Atsushi, "Why Japan's Anti-Submarine Warfare Failed," *U.S. Naval Institute Proceedings* 78 (June 1952), p. 588.

54. Asada, "The Japanese Navy and the United States," p. 235.

55. The best discussion of Inoue's ideas, based on Japanese sources and personal interviews with the Admiral, is Seno Sadao, "Chess Game with no Checkmate," cited above.

56. Marder, *Old Friends, New Enemies,* pp. 95, 285–86.

57. By the standards of their time, the admirals were probably justified in believing these ships to be "unsinkable." The *Musashi* was only sunk after successive waves of Allied planes had hit her with twenty torpedoes and more than two dozen bombs, far more damage than a battleship would be likely to suffer in a Jutland-style fleet action. See Matsumoto and Chihaya, "Design of the *Yamato,*" p. 364.

58. Louis Morton, *Strategy and Command,* p. 235.

59. "History of Imperial General Headquarters, Army Section," p. 3.

60. Ibid., p. 10.

THREE

Orange

General Leonard Wood, chief of staff of the United States Army, hero of the Apache campaign, former commander of the Rough Riders, former governor general of Moro Province in the Philippines, was in an angry mood. On this particular day in 1913, he had just lost a battle with Admiral George Dewey—and Wood was not used to losing battles. The battle in question had raged for almost ten years and concerned the site for a major naval base in the Philippines.

This was a vital question, not only for the defense of the Philippines, but for all of United States naval policy in the Pacific. In any war with Japan—which, after 1905, was the only possible United States enemy in Asia—the Philippines would almost certainly be attacked. The navy would have to cross the Pacific in order to defend them, but it would need bases along the way and in the archipelago itself. It was 7,000 miles from the West Coast to Manila; from Hawaii to Manila was almost 5,000 miles. The navy would need bases for refueling and repairs at Hawaii, at the American-owned island of Guam in the Marianas, and in the Philippines. That was why the naval base was so important. It would have to be in a strong, well-defended location, for it was estimated that it would take the battle fleet a minimum of three to four months to cross the Pacific, relieve the troops in the Philippines, and engage the Japanese forces.

The navy favored Olongapo, on Subic Bay, northwest of Manila, from which the Americans could attack the flank of an invading fleet headed for Manila. Olongapo was hard to defend against a land attack, but at the turn of the century, when the most likely enemies were considered to be Germany or Russia, this did not seem a serious problem. It was assumed that an attack by those powers would be primarily by sea. After 1905 when Japan became the potential antagonist, Olongapo looked hopeless. The army declared it could not be defended from the land side—and proposed Manila Bay instead. The navy, headed by Admiral Dewey, clung stubbornly to Olongapo, refusing to have the fleet "bottled up" in Manila Bay.

The dispute dragged on for years without resolution. The navy chose Pearl Harbor as the site for its major base while toying with the idea of making Guam its forward operating base in the western Pacific. In the meantime the army had built powerful defensive works to defend the entrance to Manila Bay; the navy, however, had no first-class base in the islands, and the army had too few troops for a really effective defense. Congress, with fine impartiality, refused to appropriate money for a naval base—whether in Guam or the Philippines.[1]

At the close of World War I, Manila was well fortified but had no fleet base; Guam was defenseless; and Hawaii had Pearl Harbor— 5,000 miles from the expected scene of action. At the same time, Japan had acquired a broad trusteeship over the former German island possessions in the central Pacific, the Marianas, the Marshalls, and the Carolines, all of which she had captured during the war. These island chains stood directly astride the American route to the Philippines. Japanese control of these islands, and the provisions of the Washington treaties (which prohibited further fortifications in some of the Pacific possessions of the great powers) so altered the strategic picture as to call for fundamental changes in American plans for a possible war with Japan.

The so-called "Orange Plan" for war with Japan was one of a number of contingency war plans developed by the United States before World War I. They were often referred to as "color plans" because the hypothetical enemies were each assigned a color: red for Great Britain, black for Germany, green for Mexico, orange for Japan. The plans were developed under the auspices of the Joint Army and Navy Board, which had been established by the secretaries of war and navy in the summer of 1903 to consider all matters referred to it by the service secretaries requiring interservice cooperation.[2] The board was made up of four high-ranking officers each from the army and the navy, with Admiral George Dewey acting as president.

After a promising start, the board angered President Theodore Roosevelt over its manifest inability to agree on a site for a Pacific base. It infuriated Woodrow Wilson by its insistence on what he considered provocative and warlike preparations during a diplomatic crisis with Japan in 1913.[3] By the First World War, the board had "virtually disappeared."[4]

After the war, however, the Joint Board was revived and greatly strengthened. It remained an advisory body, but it now had a permanent staff: a Joint Planning Committee of officers from the army and navy War Plans Divisions. The board was empowered to consider questions on its own initiative, without waiting for referral by one of the service secretaries.

This revitalized Joint Board had the task of bringing the Orange Plan into line with the realities of the postwar world. By the time the board began its formal deliberations, navy planners had already concluded that in any war against Japan, the Philippines were doomed. The Japanese could overwhelm the defenders long before the United States fleet could reach the scene. Japan could transport 50,000–60,000 men to the Philippines in the first week of the war. In the second week she could transport another 100,000. Within the first month a total of about 300,000 Japanese soldiers could be in the Philippines. The American garrison in the islands consisted of about 11,000 men plus 6,000 members of the paramilitary Philippine Constabulary, supported by twenty airplanes.[5] The only sensible mission for the defenders, then, was to hold out as long as possible.

So the Philippines could not be effectively defended—but who was to tell the American people? Who was going to say that war with Japan would require, in the words of General Leonard Wood, "the abandonment of American posts, American soldiers, an American fleet, American citizens in the Far East?" Wood, now Governor General of the Philippines, warned that such a course would "have a disintegrating and demoralizing effect upon our people." He did not know—any more than the Joint Board—how the Philippines could be saved against the overwhelming military superiority of Japan. Nevertheless, Wood confidently assumed that the planners would come up with something. They should "keep alive the problem and work it out."[6]

So the pattern was set. The revised Orange Plan, officially adopted in 1924, made no mention of the predictable plight of the Philippines. Instead, it bravely asserted that at the outbreak of hostilities the United States would conduct an "offensive war primarily naval in character," aimed at the establishment "at the earliest possible date" of American seapower superior in strength to that of Japan in the western Pacific. The Philippine garrison was to hold Manila Bay as a base for the navy until superior American seapower arrived.[7]

This pattern repeated itself over the next twelve years. Each time the Orange Plan was reconsidered navy—or, more often, army—officers pointed out that " 'to carry out the present Orange Plan . . . would be literally an act of madness.' " [8] Yet the Joint Board shrank before the psychological and political implications of writing off the Philippines; it always reaffirmed that Manila Bay would be held, and that the United States would take the offensive in the western Pacific.

Although the Orange Plan was never formally abandoned, its objectives were progressively reduced. In 1935, the navy added a provision for capture of islands in the Marshalls and Carolines and their development as bases before the fleet proceeded to the Philippines. This implied a recognition that the advance across the Pacific might take years rather than months. Along the same lines, the mission of the Philippine garrison was changed in 1936 from holding all of Manila Bay to holding its entrances.[9]

At the Naval War College, a generation of officers debated, tested, and refined, war with Orange. One hundred twenty-seven times—in chart maneuvers and board games—the American fleet crossed the Pacific to do battle with its Japanese opponent. How much useful knowledge was distilled from these games is still a matter of debate. Admiral Nimitz insisted that "the courses were so thorough that nothing that happened in the Pacific War was strange or unexpected." [10] One historian of the war college agrees, declaring that the war games were "prophetic . . . the oracle of victory," while Kennedy, an equally knowledgeable analyst, finds that the studies were "impeded by insufficient data for realistic war games, avoidance of alliance problems, and disproportionate emphasis on tactics." [11]

Whatever the case, the war college exercises did inject a certain realistic sense of the nasty problems posed by a war in the Pacific into both tactical and strategic thinking. "Sharp, bloody, and confused, the Orange tactical problems often seemed to mirror in grim reality the coming war." [12] Bits and pieces of future campaigns in the Marshalls, the Marianas, and the Philippines emerged—albeit incompletely and in a confused form—from the deliberations and experiments at Newport and at the navy's War Plans Division and the General Board of the Navy in Washington.

By 1937 army and navy leaders were deadlocked over the whole question of a future war with Japan. General Stanley D. Embick was now chief of the army's War Plans Division. As a captain he had helped plan the defenses of Manila Bay in 1907. As a colonel in the General Staff after World War I, he had opposed the 1924 Orange Plan; and as commander of the Corregidor fortress, he had written the critique labelling Orange an "act of madness." [13] Embick believed that in case of war with Japan, the United States should withdraw behind its "natural strategic peacetime frontier in the Pacific: the line Alaska-Oahu-Panama." [14] This would place the United States in an almost invulnerable defensive position. [15]

The navy did not find this new approach appealing. Orange had always been *their* war: an "offensive war, primarily naval in character." Naval officers were schooled in the tradition of Mahan, which held that "war once declared must be waged offensively, aggressively. The enemy must not be fended off but beaten down." [16] The very concepts of offensive and defensive were different for the army and the navy. In land warfare, defensive war usually called for different tactics than offensive war. In naval warfare, there was little difference at the tactical level between the two. A ship is both a defensive and offensive weapon. A war which was strategically defensive in character would still be fought at sea in the same manner as a war which was strategically offensive—only the scope and objectives would be different. [17]

Now the army planners proposed to confine the navy to patrolling a defensive line in the mid-Pacific. Such a reduced and circumscribed mission was clearly unacceptable from the point of view of the navy's prestige, morale, and mission. The army saw its primary function as the defense of the continental United States, and it had hardly enough strength for this task. But the navy, with the world's largest battle fleet, could not well confine itself to guarding the army's defensive perimeter. [18]

Unable to find a strategy acceptable to both services, the Joint Board turned the problem over to General Embick and Rear Admiral James O. Richardson, the navy's chief planner, with instructions to work out a compromise. Like most compromises, the new Orange Plan—which finally emerged from their deliberations and was subsequently approved by the Joint Board early in 1938—avoided most of the important issues. The new plan provided for an initial defensive phase or "position of readiness" along the lines suggested by the army; at the same time, army and navy forces would prepare to take the offensive, first against the Japanese mandates and eventually westward towards the Philippines. As for the latter islands, they were to be defended at Manila, but no mention was made of their reinforcement or relief.[19]

It was at this point that the realities of the international situation finally began to influence the abstract calculations of the strategists. Hitler had annexed Austria in March 1938, intimidated the British and French at Munich in September, and gobbled up the remains of Czechoslovakia in March 1939. France and Britain concluded a defensive alliance with Poland, while Hitler signed a "non-aggression pact" with the Soviet Union. The possibility that the United States and Japan might contend in splendid isolation appeared less and less likely as the possibility of war in Europe reached near certainty. Thus, in the summer of 1939 the Joint Planning Board began work on a new series of war plans dealing with the contingency of war between the United States and a coalition of enemies.

These new plans, the "Rainbow" series, were based on five hypothetical war situations. Rainbow 1 was a plan for a defensive war to protect the United States and the Western Hemisphere north of ten degrees S latitude. In such a war, the United States was assumed to be without major allies. Rainbow 2 assumed that the United States would be allied with Britain and France. This would permit an immediate American offensive in the Pacific. Rainbow 3 was a repetition of the Orange Plan, with the proviso that hemispheric defense would first be secured, as provided in Rainbow 1. Rainbow 4 was based on the same assumptions as Rainbow 1 but extended the American mission to include the defense of the entire Western Hemisphere. Rainbow 5, destined to become the basis for American strategy in World War II, assumed that the United States was allied with Britain and France and provided for offensive operations by American forces in Europe, Africa or both.[20]

The variety of situations and strategies envisioned in the Rainbow plans epitomized American leaders' confusion and uncertainty as Europe drifted into war.

● ●

On the first day of September 1939, the president was awakened by a trans-Atlantic phone call at 3:00 A.M. It was William C. Bullitt, the American ambassador in France. After the conclusion of the Versailles peace conference he had told reporters that he was "going to lie on the beach on the Riviera and watch the world go to hell!" Now Bullitt sounded tense and worried. " 'Mr. President, several German divisions are deep in Polish territory . . . There are reports of bombers over the city of Warsaw.' " Roosevelt was silent for a moment. " 'Well, Bill' " he finally replied, " 'it has come at last. God help us all.' " [21]

Few Americans took so somber a view as the president. The war might be long, but few doubted that the Allies would win in the end. A Gallup poll in mid-September revealed that 82 percent of those queried expected an Allied victory. Military experts like George Fielding Elliott and Hanson W. Baldwin assured readers of popular magazines and Sunday supplements that the Germans would exhaust themselves against the fortifications of France and Belgium.[22]

Then, in the spring of 1940, these opinions abruptly changed. Hitler unleashed his divisions against the low countries on May 10. Holland capitulated in five days. By May 15 five German armored divisions had crossed the Meuse and were sweeping north around the vaunted Maginot Line, headed toward the English channel. Belgium surrendered at the end of May, and the British began to withdraw their troops from the Continent at Dunkirk. On June 10 Italy entered the war on the side of Germany; on June 16 Marshal Henri Philippe Petain replaced Paul Reynaud as premier of France. Petain signed an armistice with Germany June 22, and with Italy two days later.

Americans were stunned. In forty days, the Germans had done what they had been unable to do in four years in World War I. Now only Britain stood between the United States and the Axis— but her survival appeared doubtful. Army strategists reminded the president that the South American countries had large German communities and that Dakar, in French West Africa, was only 1,600 miles from the New World.[23]

After the initial surprise came virtual panic. Congress, which a few weeks before had been reluctant to approve a $2 billion appropriation for defense, now quickly voted appropriations totalling $10.5 billion. The National Guard was mobilized, the first peacetime draft in history was approved, and the army's General Staff started to plan a buildup that would ultimately bring its forces to almost nine million men. In the White House, the president's advisers talked of building a 50,000-plane air force, although there were as yet neither pilots nor technicians available for such a huge air armada.

The General Board of the navy warned that the United States would have to build warships "to the utmost capacity of existing facilities" in order to meet the new threat in the Atlantic and to keep pace with Japan in the Pacific. This time Congress listened. In June it appropriated $4 billion for additional naval construction beyond that already authorized; in July it voted over $1.3 billion more. It took only two months for Congress to authorize funds for almost double the number of ships it had approved during the entire prewar period.[24]

The frantic rearmament was inspired, at least in part, by the fear that America might soon face the Axis powers alone. In such a situation, the United States could do little in the Pacific and would be hard put to defend the Atlantic frontier if the French or British fleets fell to the Germans. These apprehensions were spelled out in the so-called "Strong Memorandum" of June 1940, drafted by the army's War Plans Division under the direction of Brigadier General George V. Strong. The memorandum took stock of the nation's limited military means and the perils confronting her, predicted an "early defeat" for Britain and France, and called for immediate mobilization for hemispheric defense, the termination of military aid to the Allies, and a purely defensive posture in the Pacific.[25]

President Roosevelt was far less ready to write off Great Britain: he directed the military strategists to base their plans on the assumption that Great Britain would remain in the war and would continue to receive at least some types of aid. Nor was the president willing to order a full peacetime mobilization in the midst of an election campaign, but on the need for strengthening U.S. forces in the Pacific there was little argument.

The president also took another step which, while little related to strategic planning, was to have immense consequences for the armed forces. In June 1940, he appointed two prominent Republicans, Frank Knox, a Chicago newspaper publisher, and Henry L. Stimson, a Wall Street lawyer and former secretary of war and secretary of state, to head the Navy and War Departments. Both men were in their 70s: Knox had been a Rough Rider in Cuba and Stimson had been secretary of war under Taft. Both were outspoken internationalists. Stimson had made a speech at Yale University—one of the citadels of isolationism—in the spring of 1940. On that occasion he called for compulsory military training and all-out aid to Britain, protected by American warships. "Thank God you are not in the government," telegraphed one of his listeners. A few weeks later, Stimson was sworn in as secretary of war.[26] The installation of Knox and Stimson, together with the appointment, the previous fall, of General George C. Marshall as army chief of staff and Admiral Harold Stark as chief of naval operations, gave the armed forces an exceptionally able team of leaders to face the months of crisis ahead.

• •

If the sweeping German victories in Europe had impressed the United States, their effect upon the Japanese was even more marked. France and the Netherlands were defeated; their colonies in the Far East were weak and almost unprotected. The British were engaged in a desperate battle for survival. Under these circumstances, Japan's leaders saw a chance to finally choke off the aid reaching China from the outside and to assure herself a monopoly of Southeast Asia's important natural resources, such as oil, tin, and rubber. Almost immediately, the Japanese began to exert strong pressure on the French government at Vichy and on the British to remove their garrisons from the international settlements in China; they were also urged to close off the flow of aid to China from Burma and French Indochina. The Dutch government of the Netherlands Indies (modern Indonesia) was reminded that Japan had a special interest in the colony's oil.[27]

These moves were not enough to satisfy the grandiose ambitions of the Japanese army and navy, however. In July 1940 the war minister, General Hata Shunroku, gave the premier, Admiral Yonai Mitsumasa, some "important advice." The important advice, which Yonai quickly followed, was to resign, making room for the army's handpicked successor, Prince Konoye Fumimaro. Konoye was an aristocrat-politician of considerable intelligence and experience, but he was also weak, irresolute, and unable to stand up to pressures of the military. His foreign minister, Matsuoka Yosuke, was perhaps best described by another cabinet minister who, after listening to one of Matsuoka's harangues, turned to his colleagues and observed "the foreign minister is crazy, isn't he?" [28]

The Konoye government lost little time in taking advantage of what the military referred to as "present opportunity." In September, the French authorities in Indochina were intimidated into allowing Japan to establish military bases in the northern part of the colony and to move troops through the area in operations against China. At the same time, negotiations went forward with Berlin for a German alliance and with Moscow for a non-aggression pact with Russia. It was clear that when these arrangements were completed, the remainder of Southeast Asia would lie open to the Japanese. The British could do little, the French and Dutch even less. Only the United States appeared in a position to challenge Japanese expansion.

The policy of the American government towards Japan, ever since the "China Incident" began, had been "firm but conciliatory." The United States would not willingly agree to an abridgement of any of its rights and interests in China and would refuse to recognize Japan's conquests in the Far East. On the other hand, it would do nothing which might provoke Japan or cause an incident. The United States would neither condone nor actively oppose Japan's actions.

This "policy of inaction and nonprovocation," conceived by President Roosevelt and carried out mainly by Secretary of State Cordell Hull, was designed to avoid serious crisis with Japan.[29] In practice, the policy usually took the form of Hull's lecturing the Japanese on the "principles of good behavior" and deploring Japan's frequent lapses from them, while avoiding any positive action. Such a course seemed satisfactory to Roosevelt and his advisers. It had less appeal to Americans in China, who often found themselves bullied, or even physically abused, by the conquering Japanese. It did not appeal either to the public, which could observe the establishment of Japan's "New Order" in newsreels and picture magazines portraying the "Rape of Nanking" and the bombing of Canton. American newspapers carried such headlines as "20 CITIES HIT BY JAP AIR RAIDS/ 2000 CIVILIANS STRUCK DOWN IN CANTON ATTACK/ CHILDREN HUNT KIN IN CHINESE RUINS." [30] Moviegoers could watch Paul Muni, Louise Rainer, and other Hollywood Chinese peasants stoically enduring the hardships of war in films such as *The Good Earth.*

Yet, while the public had immense sympathy for China, neither it nor the government was ready to contemplate war with Japan. This was graphically demonstrated when the U.S. gunboat *Panay,* patrolling the Yangtze River, was deliberately sunk by Japanese bombers in December 1937. The incident provoked momentary anger in the United States, but when Japan profusely apologized and agreed to pay an indemnity, the incident was quickly forgotten. The late 1930s were the heyday of isolationism in the United States: citizens were far more interested in discussing the Ludlow amendment, which would have required a nationwide referendum before a declaration of war; most people wanted a further strengthening of the Neutrality Acts. The *Panay* incident did have one concrete result, however. In December 1937, Captain Royal E. Ingersoll, chief of the Navy's War Plans Division, was sent to London to discuss—informally—plans for cooperation with the Royal Navy in case of war with Japan.[31]

The outbreak of war in Europe and Japan's new ambitions in Southeast Asia alarmed American leaders and led to more forceful efforts to restrain Japan. In July 1939 the United States had terminated its thirty-year-old commercial treaty with Japan. This gave Washington a free hand to limit or cut off exports to Japan. Furthermore, in April 1940 the Pacific Fleet was ordered to remain indefinitely in Hawaii. After the fall of France and the installation of the Konoye government in Japan came an American embargo on the sale of high-grade scrap iron and aviation gasoline to Japan. When the Japanese moved into northern Indochina, the embargo was extended to include all scrap metal placing a serious strain on Japanese heavy industry.

Japan's response was the Tripartite Pact, an alliance between Germany, Italy, and Japan in which Japan recognized "the leadership of Germany and Italy in the establishment of a new order in Europe," and Germany and Italy recognized Japan's new order in "Greater East Asia." The three countries pledged to assist each other if any one of them were "attacked by a power at present not involved in the European War.[32] Since the Soviet Union was specifically excluded from the terms of the pact, there could be little doubt the alliance was aimed at the United States.

The Japanese army had favored an alliance with the Axis since the Germans had first proposed one in 1938; its leaders believed that such a move would cause the British and Americans to abandon their support for China and accept a settlement of the "China Incident" on Japanese terms. The navy's leadership, comprising Admiral Yonai Mitsumasa as navy minister (subsequently Prime Minister until July 1940), Vice Admiral Yamamoto Isoroku as his vice-minister, and Naval Affairs Bureau chief Vice Admiral Inoue Shigeyoshi, had been as firmly opposed to the proposed alliance as the army had been in favor of it. They feared such an agreement would inevitably lead to war with both Britain and the U.S., with the navy facing hopeless odds against the two strongest naval powers. They also recognized that the Imperial Navy, and indeed the entire Japanese economy, were dependent on imports of raw materials from the United States.[33]

As pressure for the conclusion of the pact from the army and its right-wing supporters increased, Yonai and Yamamoto became a target for extremist attacks and threats. The atmosphere appeared so threatening that tanks and machine guns were installed at the Navy Ministry. Yamamoto, in particular, received so many threatening letters and demands for his resignation that employees at the ministry began to exchange the half-serious warning, "Whatever you do don't accept a lift in the vice-minister's car." A reward of 100,000 yen was reportedly offered for his assassination.[34]

Yonai's successor, Admiral Yoshida Zengo, continued to oppose the pact until he suffered a nervous collapse brought on by stress and overwork, but most of the other leaders of the Navy Ministry and virtually all the Naval General Staff had finally been persuaded to agree to, or at least acquiesce in, the pact. Many younger officers in the Navy Ministry and naval staff were pro-German and others found persuasive Matsuoka's argument that an Axis alliance would deter the U.S. In addition Navy leaders were concerned that their bitter quarrel with the army might lead to a coup or to civil war. Army support was also essential to pursue the navy's aims of southern expansion and a rapid fleet buildup.[35]

As the United States and Japan gradually moved toward a confrontation in the Pacific, American army and navy leaders became increasingly anxious about the lack of any definite agreement in the United States—much less between the United States and Britain—on a clearcut line of strategy to be followed in the event of war with the Axis powers. President Roosevelt had been less than fully responsive to the army's Strong memorandum in June; by the following November, with the presidential election over, it was the navy's turn to try. In a memorandum to the president, which was to become one of the best-known documents of World War II, Admiral Harold Stark pointed out that the United States faced four major alternatives: (a) to concentrate mainly on hemispheric defense; (b) to prepare for an all-out offensive in the Pacific while remaining on the defensive in the Atlantic; (c) to make an equal effort in both areas; (d) to prepare for a strong offensive in the Atlantic while remaining on the defensive in the Pacific.

Stark was certain that paragraph (d), or "Dog" in the military alphabet, was the right course for the United States. The British were making their desperate effort in Europe and the United States was already assisting them as much as possible. Germany was a stronger and nearer military menace than Japan; an effort against the Nazi forces would be the best defense of the Western Hemisphere. As for the Pacific, Stark favored a strictly defensive strategy, although he foresaw that a limited offensive might have to be undertaken.[36] In keeping with these recommendations, Stark urged the president to authorize the American service chiefs to begin secret and formal talks with their British counterparts. The British had been urging such a meeting since the spring of 1940.[37]

"Plan Dog," as Stark's memo came to be called, represented a sharp reversal of the navy's traditional preoccupation with Japan, as reflected in the Orange Plan. Yet, as Admiral Richardson observed, Orange had always been more of a budget plan than a fighting plan. Now the navy found itself with an unbalanced and unprepared battle fleet at Hawaii and a real and growing menace in the Atlantic. The Lend-Lease Act was on the horizon; convoys would most likely be next. Under these conditions, the navy was more than prepared to accept Stark's reasoning.

To the army, however, the navy's abrupt endorsement of old army arguments seemed too good to be true. Colonel J. W. Anderson, chief of the War Plans Division, commented suspiciously that the Dog memorandum was a navy ploy to commit the United States to " 'an unlimited war in the Atlantic plus, at the minimum, a limited objective war in the Pacific.' "[38] Stark angrily retorted that the army was reading his memo backwards. General Marshall eventually acquieced to Plan Dog, which was subsequently approved by the Joint Board and the secretaries of war and navy.[39]

When the British and American staff meetings convened in January 1941, the military chiefs quickly agreed, in the spirit of the Stark memo, that Europe was the vital theater and that Germany and Italy must be defeated first. They also understood the need to safeguard the Western Hemisphere. On the question of the Far East, however, there was less agreement. The British had far more to lose in the East than did the United States. British Malaya, British Borneo, and Burma—all lay within easy striking distance of Japan. Beyond them lay the even bigger prizes of Australia, New Zealand, and India.

The key to the defense of East Asia, the British believed, was the fortified naval base of Singapore—"the Gibraltar of the East"— as it was dramatically but inaccurately called. The fortress guarded the sea lanes from the Indian Ocean through the Malay straits to Australia and New Zealand. Since the spring of 1940, British leaders had urged the United States to send a portion of its naval forces to Singapore. They had no success. Marshall, Stark, and their associates doubted the strategic value of Singapore. They knew that the base was inadequately garrisoned, that it was within range of Japanese planes based in Indochina, and that the Singapore dockyard lacked the personnel, spare parts, and machine tools to repair large warships.[40] American navy leaders proposed instead the defense of the Far East by offensive action against Japanese positions in the Marshalls and the Carolines, thus drawing off enemy forces from Southeast Asia.[41]

In any case, the Americans agreed that the main effort must be in the Atlantic, not in the Far East. Above all, the strategists were unwilling to spend American blood and treasure simply to defend Britain's Asian empire. As the Joint Board instructions to the U.S. representatives at the British-American staff talks warned, "We can not afford, nor do we need, to entrust our national future to British direction. . . . The proposals of the British representatives will have been drawn up with chief regard to the support of the British Commonwealth. Never absent from their minds are their post-war interests, commercial and military." [42]

In the end, the United States agreed to transfer a portion of its fleet to the Atlantic. This would allow the British to send a number of their ships to Singapore. United States planners began to draw up operational plans based on Plan Dog and the British-American staff conversations. Yet although the American and British military leaders had agreed upon a basic strategy for war with Japan, this strategy remained contingent upon American entry into the war: the United States had still made no commitment to go to war, nor even indicated when, or under what circumstances, she would do so. This continuing uncertainty about what the U.S. would do should Japan strike, even more than disagreements about naval moves or dispositions, had a crippling effect on British and American war planning in the Far East.[43]

By this point the Japanese had come to realize that the United States was not to be intimidated by the Tripartite Pact. Japan sent a new Ambassador to the United States in February 1941. Admiral Nomura Kishisaburo was a moderate, favorably inclined toward the U.S. Early in March he and Secretary of State Hull began a series of desultory conversations which dragged on into summer. Neither man had anything really new to offer, and some historians believe the talks may have done more harm than good by obscuring how far apart in policy the two countries actually were.[44] Meanwhile, the peripatetic Matsuoka concluded a non-agression pact with the Soviet Union in April 1941.

Matsuoka's pact became a bad joke just two months later, when Hitler unexpectedly launched a massive attack on Russia. Although most Japanese leaders were surprised and angry at Hitler's failure to consult them, some army officers toyed with the idea of taking advantage of Russia's discomfiture to finish off their old opponent to the north. Other army leaders, however, were more inclined to listen to navy arguments that Japan should continue her advance into Southeast Asia. This would provide Japan with the resources she needed and give her the advanced bases to build an impregnable position.

By the end of June, the navy's arguments had persuaded the other members of the government.[45] On July 21, the Vichy government, after appealing unsuccessfully to both the United States and the Germans for help, signed another agreement with the Japanese. France retained her "sovereignty" and control of the civil government in Indochina, but 50,000 Japanese troops occupied the country. Japanese warships moved into Cam Ranh Bay and Japanese planes were based at airfields in southern Indochina. The Japanese were now within easy striking distance of Malaya, the Philippines, and the Netherlands Indies.

President Roosevelt's response was an executive order freezing all Japanese funds and assets in the United States. Roosevelt did not intend, with this order, to back Japan into a corner but that was its ultimate effect. The order meant that the shipment of any goods to Japan would require an export license, but the president's plan was to allow a limited amount of oil and gas to be exported under this arrangement so as to forestall a crisis. He failed to make his intentions clear either to the Japanese or to his own subordinates. While Roosevelt was absent at a secret meeting with Churchill, government officials, acting in accord with what they believed was the aim of the freezing order, rejected all applications for exports of gas and oil to Japan. By the time the president learned of this, it was too late to back down. To grant the licenses now might be taken by Japan as a sign of weakness.[46] Thus the effect of the order was that Japan could not obtain the crucial supplies of American oil and other strategic commodities which she needed to keep her war machine operating.

At the same time as he issued the freezing order, the president called the Army of the Philippine Commonwealth into the service of the United States. General Douglas MacArthur, a hero of World War I and former army chief of staff who had been serving as military adviser to the Philippine government, was recalled to active service as commanding general of a new organization: "U.S. Army Forces, Far East," consisting of the Philippine Army and all United States Army units in the islands.

NOTES

1. The foregoing discussion is based primarily on William R. Braisted, *The United States Navy in the Pacific 1897–1909* (Austin: University of Texas Press, 1958), 253–62; and Braisted, *The United States Navy in the Pacific 1909–1922* (Austin: University of Texas Press, 1970) pp. 30–36, 58–77, 135–40, 147–49; Louis Morton, "The Origins of Pacific Strategy" *Marine Corps Gazette*, August 1957; Ronald Spector, *Admiral of the New Empire: The Life and Career of George Dewey* (Baton Rouge: LSU Press, 1974), pp. 162–71, 182–86.

2. Vernon E. Davis, "The History of the Joint Chiefs of Staff in World War II: Organizational Development: Vol. 1, Origins of the Joint and Combined Chiefs of Staff" (Historical Division, Joint Secretariat JCS, 1972), pp. 5–7; MS copy in National Archives, Washington, D.C.

3. Braisted, *United States Navy in Pacific 1909–1922*, pp. 138–40; Spector, *Admiral of the New Empire;* Davis, *Origins of the Joint and Combined Chiefs of Staff,* pp. 7–10.

4. Davis, *Origins of the Joint and Combined Chiefs of Staff,* p. 11.

5. Louis Morton, "War Plan Orange: Evolution of a Strategy," *World Politics* 11 (January 1959), pp. 228–30.

6. Ibid., p. 229.

7. Joint Army-Navy Basic War Plan Orange, March 12, 1924, Record Group 94, National Archives, Washington, D.C.

8. The quotation is of General Stanley D. Embrick, commander of the Corregidor garrison in 1933, cited in Morton, "War Plan Orange," p. 237.

9. Grace P. Hayes, "The Joint Chiefs of Staff and the War Against Japan" (History Division JCS, MS copy in National Archives) pp. 4–5.

10. Michel Vlahos, *The Blue Sword: The Naval War College and the American Mission 1919–1941* (Washington, D.C.: GPO, 1980), pp. 143, 119.

11. Ibid., pp. 119, 151; Kennedy, "The Naval War College," p. 353.

12. Vlahos, *The Blue Sword,* p. 151.

13. Henry G. Morgan, "Planning the Defeat of Japan: A Study of Total War Strategy," unpublished MS prepared for Office Chief of Military History, p. 16. MS copy in U.S. Army Center of Military History, Washington, D.C.

14. Memo, Embick to CG, Philippine Dept., April 19, 1933, on "U.S. Policy in the Philippines." MS copy in U.S. Army Center of Military History, Washington, D.C.

15. Morton, "War Plan Orange," p. 245.

16. Gerald E. Wheeler, *Prelude to Pearl Harbor: The U.S. Navy and the Far East* (Columbia, Mo.: University of Missouri Press, 1963), pp. 82–83.

17. Morgan, "Planning the Defeat of Japan," p. 186.

18. Ibid., p. 186.

19. Morton, *Strategy and Command, p. 42.*

20. Ibid., pp. 50–55.

21. Quoted in John E. Wiltz, *From Isolation to War* (New York: Crowell, 1968).

22. William L. Langer and S. Everett Gleason, *The Challenge to Isolation: The World Crisis of 1937–1940 and American Foreign Policy* (New York: Harper and Row, 1964) p. 269.

23. Pogue, *Ordeal and Hope,* p. 55.

24. Pelz, *Race to Pearl Harbor,* p. 210.

25. Morton, *Strategy and Command,* pp. 76–77; Weigley, "Role of the War Department and the Army," p. 179.

26. Elting Morison, *Turmoil and Tradition: A Study of the Life and Times of Henry L. Stimson* (New York: Atheneum Publishers, 1964), p. 294.

27. James W. Morley, ed., *The Fateful Choice: Japan's Advance into Southeast Asia 1939–1941: Selected Translations from Taiheiyo senso e no michi kaisen gaiko shi [Japan's Road to the Pacific War]* (New York: Columbia University Press, 1980), pp. 125–208.

28. Robert J. C. Buton, *Tojo and the Coming of the War* (Princeton: Princeton University Press, 1961), pp. 139, 208.

29. Robert Dallek, *Franklin D. Roosevelt and American Foreign Policy 1932–1945* (New York: Oxford University Press, 1979) pp. 76–77 and passim.

30. *Chicago Tribune,* September 24, 1937. Cited in Ernest R. May, "U.S. Press Coverage of Japan 1931–1941" in Borg and Shumpei, *Pearl Harbor as History,* p. 523.

31. Morton, *Strategy and Command,* p. 68.

32. Authorized English version as published by the German Government, reproduced in William L. Langer and S. Everett Gleason, *The Undeclared War 1940–1941* (New York: Harper and Row, 1953), pp. 30–31.

33. Marder, *Old Friends, New Enemies,* pp. 99–114; Agawa, *The Reluctant Admiral,* pp. 157–60 and passim.

34. Agawa, *The Reluctant Admiral,* pp. 100, 129–31, 144, 160–63.

35. Marder, *Old Friends, New Enemies,* pp. 123–26.

36. For a detailed discussion of Stark's "Plan Dog" memo, see Morton, *Strategy and Command,* pp. 81–84; Watson, *Pre-War Plans,* pp. 170–73; and John Major, "Harold Raynsford Stark" in Love, *Chiefs of Naval Operations,* pp. 124–25.

37. Langer and Gleason, *The Undeclared War,* p. 222.

38. Morgan, "Planning the Defeat of Japan," p. 47.

38. Morgan, "Planning the Defeat of Japan," p. 47.

39. Weigley, "Role of the War Department and the Army," pp. 179–80; Morton, *Strategy and Command*, p. 84; Pogue, *Ordeal and Hope*, pp. 126–27.

40. Morison, *Rising Sun*, pp. 50–51; Tracy B. Kittredge, "U.S.-British Naval Cooperation 1940–1945," unpublished MS, pp. 347–350, copy in Naval Historical Center, Washington, D.C.

41. James R. Leutze, *Bargaining for Supremacy* (Chapell Hill: University North Carolina Press, 1977) pp. 240–46; Marder, *Old Friends, New Enemies*, pp. 191–95.

42. Morton, *Strategy and Command*, p. 80; Kittredge, "U.S.-British Naval Cooperation," p. 332.

43. Marder, *Old Friends, New Enemies*, pp. 200–1.

44. Cf. Charles E. Neu, *The Troubled Encounter: The United States and Japan* (New York: John Wiley and Sons, 1975) pp. 177–78.

45. Pelz, *Race to Pearl Harbor*, pp. 220–21; Morley, *The Fateful Choice*, pp. 234–37.

46. Dallek, *Roosevelt and American Foreign Policy*, pp. 274–75.

FOUR

Some Last Minute Changes

The recall of General MacArthur was intended, at least in part, as a psychological gesture to impress the Japanese and Filipinos with the seriousness of the situation. Yet the general's appointment was to have more of a psychological effect on the War Department than on Tokyo or Manila. MacArthur could be an able and inspiring leader, but he was also vainglorious and ambitious. One of the army's best-known leaders, the son of a Civil War hero, he had graduated first in his class at West Point and had served with distinction in World War I, being decorated for bravery several times. He ended the war as the youngest American general to command a division. Reporters—and Secretary of War Newton Baker—often referred to him as the army's best frontline general. He also became well known for his eccentric dress (MacArthur always carried a riding crop at the front), his frequent conflicts with superiors, and his unstinting quest for publicity—all of which remained characteristic of him throughout his career.[1]

Returning to the U.S., MacArthur became superintendent of West Point and chief of staff of the army in 1930. In July 1932, he personally directed the army's brutal eviction from Washington of World War I veterans—the so-called Bonus Army—who had come in the depths of the depression to lobby Congress for early payment of their service pensions. Following his retirement as chief of staff, he had spent three frustrating years as Field Marshal of the impoverished,

under-manned and ill-trained Army of the Philippine Commonwealth.[2] By 1940 President Manuel Quezon was thinking about relieving his old friend MacArthur and toyed with the idea of "neutralization" for the Philippines in the event of a Japanese-American
conflict.[3]

Subsequent events in the Far East ended thoughts of neutralization,
while Roosevelt's mobilization of the Philippine Army provided
American pay and equipment for the Filipino soldier. Yet MacArthur
was unlikely to be satisfied with this. Convinced of his own destiny,
he was unwilling to serve merely as the commander of a doomed
outpost in the Pacific. MacArthur argued persuasively that the Philippines could be successfully defended without altering the basic strategic arrangements already worked out in the Rainbow Plans and British–American talks. In a letter to the War Department, he pointed
out that with the mobilization of the Philippine Army, he would
soon have ten Filipino divisions in addition to the American units
under his command, making a grand total of almost 200,000 men.[4]

Visions of martial grandeur arose before the general as he contemplated this impressive paper army. He could, he assured Washington,
undertake an effective defense of all the islands rather than cling
futilely to the defense of Manila Bay, as contemplated in the Orange
Plan. MacArthur planned to meet the main enemy attacks on the
beaches and fling the invaders back into the sea. There was to be
"no withdrawal from beach positions. The beaches were to be held
at all costs."[5]

The revised plan for the defense of the islands was in keeping
with MacArthur's habit of bold, aggressive leadership. It was also
impossible to carry out. The ten Filipino divisions which were gradually being mobilized, one regiment at a time, were impressive in
numbers only. Most of the men called up had received no training
whatsoever. Those few who had been trained for a few months as
Philippine Army reservists had learnt, according to one American
general, only two things: " 'one, when an officer appeared, to yell
attention in a loud voice, jump up and salute, the other to demand
3 meals per day.' "[6]

Training programs were hastily established for the Filipino units.
However, these did not get under way until the fall of 1941, and
many Filipino soldiers went into action in December without ever
having fired their rifles. The rifles themselves were mainly obsolescent
Springfields and Enfields. Many units lacked such essential items of
equipment as steel helmets, entrenching tools, raincoats, blankets,

mosquito netting, and even proper shoes.[7] Combat support units were if anything worse off. In the artillery "most of the men had never fired a 75-mm gun and many had never seen one fired." The Thirty-First Division discovered that the commanding officer of its signal company, "who was to be division signal officer, was unable to establish radio contact with units a mile away in the same camp." [8] With these half-trained, half-equipped Philippine divisions, plus one United States Army division, MacArthur proposed to meet the attack of the Japanese army, hardened and experienced by five years of war in China.

That MacArthur's plan was utterly unrealistic seems obvious in hindsight. It was not so obvious in 1941. MacArthur was one of the most experienced senior officers in the army; he was believed to know the Philippines—and the Filipinos—better than any other American officer. More important, MacArthur was telling Stimson and Marshall something that they wanted to believe. No one had ever really felt comfortable with the assumption, implicit in the latest war plans, that the Philippines would simply be sacrificed to the Japanese.

Now MacArthur was suggesting that they could be held—if he were given the proper support from Washington. In August, Colonel Leonard T. Gerow, chief of the War Plans Division, pointed out to Marshall that with American war production moving into high gear and more weapons and equipment becoming available, it would be possible for the first time to make tanks, planes, antiaircraft artillery, and other modern equipment available to strengthen Philippine defenses. Marshall and Stimson quickly agreed. "I have directed," wrote General Marshall to MacArthur in September, "that United States Army Forces in the Philippines be placed in the highest priority for equipment, including authorized defense reserves for fifty thousand men." [9] Within a short time, a steady flow of modern military weapons and equipment of all types—including modern antiaircraft guns, radar, 105-mm howitzers, and the new M-1 (Garand) rifle— were en route or earmarked for the Philippines.[10]

Among the most important reinforcements for the islands was a force of B-17 heavy bombers. By 1941 the air corps had unbounded confidence in the new "Flying Fortress." British reports on their performance under lease in Europe confirmed this confidence.[11] With its great range, the B-17 could strike invading fleets far out at sea, while its ability to bomb accurately at high altitudes would enable it to evade antiaircraft fire. Air force officers described it as the "best bombardment aircraft in existence, particularly for coastal defense." [12] General Arnold, chief of staff of the Army Air Corps, planned to station more than 300 B-17s in the islands. Not only were the B-17s expected to make an invasion difficult; because of their potential for long-range bombardment they were expected to play a role in offensive operations against the Japanese as well. The B-17s, exulted Stimson, now gave the United States the opportunity to "get back into the Islands in a way it hadn't been able to for twenty years." Early in October, a study by the War Plans Division concluded that "American air and ground units now available or scheduled for dispatch to the Philippine Islands in the near future have changed the entire picture in the Asiatic area." [13]

The War Department's belief that the Philippines could be successfully defended appeared reasonable enough *if* sufficient time were available to complete the reinforcement program and the training of the Philippine Army. By early December 1941, however, the training program was barely underway. Many essential weapons and items of equipment had not yet arrived and only thirty-five B-17s were in the islands. MacArthur and his staff were confident that war would not begin before April 1942, when he expected his preparations to be completed. In late November, he assured High Commissioner Francis B. Sayre that the Japanese would not attack before spring.[14] What was worse, MacArthur insisted on putting his more ambitious defense plan into effect immediately, even though his forces would not be prepared or equipped to carry it out for several months.

While Washington rushed reinforcements to the Philippines, the Japanese debated their next move. The American freeze order caused shock and consternation in Tokyo. Cut off from vital supplies of oil and other raw materials, Japan had barely enough resources for two years of war. The Japanese navy estimated that it had enough oil for only eighteen months of operations under war conditions.[15] The Japanese were left with two alternatives: they could seek a settlement with the United States which would lead to the lifting of the embargo, or they could continue the "southern advance" by seizing Malaya and the Dutch East Indies. This latter course would give them access to the raw materials they needed, but it would almost certainly precipitate war with the United States. To break the deadlock, Premier Konoye proposed a secret personal meeting with President Roosevelt.

Many Japanese army and navy leaders had already decided that war was inevitable. Even before the American oil embargo was announced, Admiral Nagano Osami, chief of the Naval Staff, was telling colleagues that " 'there is no choice left but to fight and break the iron chains strangling Japan,' " [16] while the army warned that any settlement with the United States would be unacceptable if it required a withdrawal of troops from China. Nevertheless, the military were willing to allow Konoe to meet with Roosevelt "so long as the premier was firmly resolved to go to war with the United States in the event the president 'did not interpret correctly the Emperor's true intentions.' " [17] At the same time, the general staffs began their planning for war.

In the spring of 1940 Japan's navy had conducted large-scale map exercises involving a Japanese seizure of the Dutch East Indies. This was the only occasion before the outbreak of war that such exercises were conducted—and the results were far from reassuring. Any attack on the East Indies would ultimately result in war with the United States: a protracted war, in which Japanese "chances of winning would be nil." Although these conclusions were duly reported to the navy minister and the chief of staff, the navy failed to make them known to Japanese political leaders, or even to the army.[18]

Now, in the summer and autumn of 1941, army and navy strategists considered four alternatives: (1) to seize the Dutch East Indies first, then the Philippines and Malaya; (2) to advance step by step from the Philippines to Borneo, Java, Sumatra, and Malaya; (3) to begin with Malaya and then advance in reversed order to the Philippines, thus delaying an attack on American territory; (4) to attack Malaya and the Philippines simultaneously, followed by a quick seizure of the Dutch East Indies.[19] The last course of action was the most difficult. It raised complicated problems of coordination and timing and entailed a dangerous dispersal of forces—but it was the only plan on which both army and navy could agree, and so it was adopted.[20]

This decision was typical of the Japanese approach to decision making. Compromises which would enable the services to give an appearance of unanimity were sought more eagerly than hard analysis. "When agreement was fairly unanimous, it was easier to join the group than to cause trouble. . . . Had anyone attempted to probe deeply, he would have been told not to quibble. . . . Hence as a general rule no one said anything even when assailed by doubts." [21] As one of the leading army planners complained many years after the war, the Army

did not worry about the Pacific Ocean. We were confident of the Navy's ability to hold back the United States fleet. . . . Why didn't they tell us they weren't so confident! We trusted them; they didn't come out and warn us of their limitations. . . . We Japanese have a tendency not to push matters too far. So we assumed they could hold off the United States fleet. This was never discussed openly in higher-level meetings and even in our low-level meetings. *They* [the Navy] *were not open enough!* [emphasis in original].[22]

Whatever the army believed, the navy could hardly oppose war with the United States and Britain and still expect to retain its claim to priority allocation of money, industrial output, and scarce resources. Like the United States Navy, the Imperial Japanese Navy had used the danger of a war in the Pacific as a budgetary and bureaucratic weapon. Unlike the United States Navy, however, it could not conveniently shift its stance. The Japanese admirals were trapped by their own rhetoric.[23]

Considerations of time also reinforced the feeling among army and navy planners that there was no turning back. Not only were Japan's oil reserves being steadily depleted, but the type of operations envisioned by the planners could only be carried out during certain seasons of the year. After the end of December, for example, weather and tide conditions would make landings in Malaya or the Philippines extremely difficult.

In mid-August Secretary of State Cordell Hull replied to Konoe's bid for a summit conference by observing that it would be necessary to reach agreement on some of the outstanding issues between the two countries prior to such a meeting. By this time, Japanese army and navy leaders were pressing for a decision on war with the United States. On September 3 a liaison conference agreed that "if by the early part of October there is still no prospect of being able to obtain our demands, we shall immediately decide to open hostilities against the United States, Great Britain and the Netherlands."[24] Negotiations with the United States were to continue, but they would now go hand in hand with military preparations. In keeping with the strategists' preoccupations, a definite time limit was set for the negotiations so as not to forestall the possibility of successful military action.

When the army and navy chiefs of staff appeared before the Emperor to explain the decisions of the liaison conference, they found His Majesty skeptical. "Had not the Army promised in 1937 that the China Incident would be settled in a month?" asked the Emperor—yet fighting was still raging four years later. Army General Sugiyama attempted to argue that there was a great difference between war in China with its vast hinterland and attacks on the islands and peninsulas of the Pacific and Southeast Asia. " 'If you call the

Chinese hinterland vast, would you not describe the Pacific as even more immense?' " queried His Majesty.

At this point, the Chief of Naval General Staff Nagano stepped in to explain that the military considered the current state of Japan's relations with the U.S. comparable to a patient slowly dying of a lingering disease. An operation might prove immediately fatal, but if successful it might save the patient's life. The military was anxious for a diplomatic solution; but should this prove impossible, an "operation" might be necessary.[25]

Nagano's analogy evidently failed to impress the Emperor. At the Imperial Conference held on September 6 to ratify the new policy, His Majesty unexpectedly broke his traditional silence during such meetings to read a poem on the theme of peace composed by his grandfather, the Emperor Meiji, and to express his hopes for peace in his own time. The military chiefs hastened to assure him that every effort would be made to come to a diplomatic agreement, with war to be chosen only as a last resort.[26]

● ●

At sea, in the gray stormy waters of the North Pacific, Admiral Yamamoto Isoroku bleakly contemplated the growing prospect of war with the United States. He had never had much faith in the strategy and plans of the Naval General Staff, perhaps because he had never had much faith in the men who made them.[27] His outspoken opposition to the Tripartite Pact and the pro-Axis faction had continued even after August 1939, when Yonai finally—to save him from assassination—sent him to sea as commander of the Combined Fleet.[28]

Unlike the confident planners in the naval staff sections, Yamamoto had extensive first-hand knowledge of the United States. He had few illusions about the course which an American-Japanese war might take.[29] In late September, Yamamoto himself went to see Nagano in Tokyo, attempting to dissuade him from pursuing the September 5 decision to begin war preparations; Nagano would not listen.[30]

If Yamamoto could do nothing about the decision for war, he could at least change the plans for such a war, plans which he believed would result in certain defeat. Yamamoto argued that the traditional Japanese naval strategy, to lie in wait for the American battle fleet and "ambush" it in the central or south Pacific, was ineffective and dangerous, especially since, according to the latest plan, major elements of the Japanese fleets would be needed to protect the operations against Malaya and the Philippines. Such a strategy left the initiative in American hands. The United States might delay its offensive until it had built up overwhelming strength, or it might take advantage of the dispersion of part of the Japanese fleet in Southeast Asia to strike quickly from Pearl Harbor at the poorly defended Japanese mandates in the central Pacific.[31] The only way to resolve this problem was to eliminate the threat of the American Pacific Fleet. The Japanese navy could not well carry out a conventional assault on the formidable base at Pearl Harbor, but Yamamoto believed another way might be found.

Yamamoto's conclusions arose logically from his respect for, and knowledge of, the United States. He had studied English at Harvard in the 1920s and traveled extensively in the United States, returning there a few years later as naval attaché.[32] Far better than his colleagues in the naval staff, Yamamoto understood the latent power of his prospective opponent. Only extraordinary measures had any chance of success in such a contest. In a letter to the navy minister, he acknowledged the risks of his plan but pointed out that the basic idea of going to war against America, Britain, and China "after four years of exhausting operations in China with the possibility of fighting Russia also to be kept in mind" was far more risky and illogical. ' "If,' " he continued, " 'in the face of such odds we decide to go to war—or rather are forced to do so by the trend of events—I . . . can see little hope of success in any ordinary strategy.' " [33]

For some months Admiral Yamamoto had been studying the idea of a surprise air attack on Pearl Harbor. The precise origins of this plan remain obscure.[34] As early as 1936 the Japanese Naval War College had produced a paper on "Strategy and Tactics in Operations Against the United States" which suggested a surprise attack on Hawaii. Among those who participated in the War College study was Captain Kuroshima Kameto, who was now Yamamoto's operations officer. Yamamoto had also been impressed by the performance of the navy's torpedo bombers during fleet maneuvers in the spring of 1940.[35]

Early in 1941 Yamamoto wrote privately to his old friend Rear Admiral Ōnishi Takejiro, chief of staff of the Eleventh Air Fleet, outlining his idea for an air attack on Pearl Harbor. Ōnishi was a respected aviator and staff officer, but not closely associated with Naval General Staff thinking. He turned for advice on Yamamoto's proposal to Commander Genda Minoru, one of the most brilliant "Young Turks" of naval aviation in Japan. Within six weeks, Ōnishi and Genda were ready with an assessment. The operation would be risky and difficult. It could only succeed through surprise—but it could be done.[36]

Shortly after receiving Ōnishi's assessment, Yamamoto directed the staff of the newly formed First Air Fleet to prepare an operational plan for the Pearl Harbor operation. Vice Admiral Nagumo Chūichi, commander of the First Air Fleet, was a courageous fighter and an expert in torpedo warfare, but his knowledge of aviation was small. He turned the planning over to his chief of staff, Admiral Kusaka Ryūnosuke, an experienced carrier commander, and to his senior assistants: Commanders Genda and Oishi Tamotsu.[37]

Kusaka had no sooner inherited the Ōnishi-Genda study than he proceeded to pick it to pieces. His critique was so devastating that Admiral Ōnishi himself began to have his doubts. In September Kusaka persuaded Ōnishi to go with him to Yamamoto and tell the commander in chief that his plan could not succeed.

Shortly before noon at the end of September 1940, Kusaka and Ōnishi were standing stiffly near the table of the admiral's dining room aboard Yamamoto's flagship, the *Nagato*. The battleship's band was assembled one deck above the admiral's quarters, instruments at the ready. At precisely 11:50 A.M., the band began to play; at 11:55, Yamamoto's staff and guests sat down at the table. On the stroke of noon, the commander in Chief walked down the narrow passageway and entered the dining room. The band struck up a march; the officers bowed while sitting. Then the admiral was seated and the band began a more subdued luncheon concert.[38]

After lunch, Ōnishi and Kusaka explained their objections to the Pearl Harbor Plan. Ōnishi, as chief of staff of the Eleventh Air Fleet— the navy's principal land-based air strike force—was worried that his command might be unable to carry out its mission against the Philippines and Malaya without support from at least some of the carriers which Yamamoto proposed to use in the Hawaii operation. Yamamoto's staff countered that the Eleventh Air Fleet had enough planes to do the job on its own.

Kusaka's objections were more general in nature: the course of discussion frequently became heated. Kusaka called Yamamoto "an amateur naval strategist" and criticized his ideas as a dangerous gamble. " 'I like games of chance,' " replied the commander in chief; " 'you have told me that the operation was a gamble, so I shall carry it out.' " After further discussion and argument, Yamamoto closed the meeting. He ordered that planning and preparations should continue. Accompanying Kusaka to the gangplank, Yamamoto patted him on the shoulder and said quietly: " 'What you recommended was understandable but I have resolved to carry out the Pearl Harbor attack no matter what the cost. So please do your best to develop the plan from now on. I will place all the details of the project in your hands.' " [39]

By the end of September Genda and Oishi, working under Kusaka's direction, had a plan ready for Yamamoto to present to the Naval General Staff. This plan called for a massive air strike by four of the six large carriers in the First Air Fleet—Yamamoto later threw in all six—utilizing both torpedo planes and bombers.

There were two major difficulties: to achieve success, it was necessary to devise an effective weapon for sinking battleships in the shallow anchorage at Pearl Harbor. To achieve surprise, it was necessary for the attacking carriers and their escorts to approach within two hundred miles of Hawaii without being discovered. To minimize the chance of meeting foreign vessels on the way, Kusaka and Genda selected a route of approach far to the north of the usual shipping routes, beginning in the Kurile Islands, passing far north of Midway and then turning almost due south for Hawaii. In October 1941 the Japanese liner *Taiyo Maru* made this journey and did not sight a single ship.[40]

To solve the problem of attacking the fleet, Japanese scientists and technicians labored to perfect a torpedo which would be effective in the forty-foot depth of Pearl Harbor. An ordinary torpedo would simply plunge to the bottom but by September, the navy had developed a new type of stabilizing device which allowed for extremely shallow runs. To get at ships which could not be reached by torpedoes, the navy began converting sixteen-inch armor-piercing naval shells into aerial bombs to be delivered by high-level and dive-bombers.[41]

The Naval General Staff was less than enthusiastic about the Pearl Harbor scheme. It pointed out that the essential surprise element could easily be lost by a chance meeting with a foreign ship or plane; that the ships of the attack force would have to refuel at sea in the stormy waters of the North Pacific; and that Yamamoto would be gambling the entire first-line carrier striking force on a single operation, one which might well prove futile if the American fleet happened to be absent from Pearl Harbor. In a war game played at the Naval War College, the attacking force was discovered by the Americans and suffered two carriers sunk and one damaged. In a second game, played with the same umpires and a new set of dice, the attackers suffered less damage and successfully sank part of the American fleet.[42]

Although these results were far from conclusive, Yamamoto continued to insist on the Pearl Harbor plan, even threatening to resign if it were not approved. In October 1941 Admiral Nagano gave his reluctant consent. Preparations went ahead to launch the Pearl Harbor operation.

While the Combined Fleet practiced for the Pearl Harbor raid, time was rapidly running out for opponents of war in Tokyo. Army and navy leaders pressed for war by early November, before weather conditions made operations too difficult. On October 16 Konoe resigned; his successor was the war minister, General Tojo Hideki.

Tojo was determined to end the agonizing uncertainty by achieving either a diplomatic agreement or a decision for war. On November 5 an Imperial Conference agreed that if no satisfactory agreement with the United States had been achieved by December, Japan would go to war. At the same time, the Japanese government would attempt to persuade Italy and Germany to join the conflict against the United States.

At Imperial General Headquarters, final preparations were made for war. The Japanese planned to seize and occupy a vast area, including all of Southeast Asia they did not already hold—Burma, Siam, Malaya, the Philippines, and the Dutch East Indies. Japan would occupy the American island outposts of Guam and Wake; she would also destroy or at least neutralize the Pacific Fleet at Pearl Harbor. On the first day of the war the Philippines and Malaya were to be hit by air attacks, followed soon after by invasion. Simultaneously, troops would occupy British Borneo and Hong Kong. Once the Philippines—and the Malay peninsula, with its important fortress of Singapore—had been taken, the conquest of Burma and the Dutch East Indies would follow.[43]

To execute this vast plan, the Japanese had available only some 2,000 combat planes: about 700 army and 1,300 navy. Most of the army's forces were required to garrison China, Korea, and Japan, and to keep watch on Russia. Only about eleven divisions—about a fifth of those in service—could be spared for the southern campaigns.[44] The Japanese navy was slightly superior to the combined American, British, and Dutch naval forces in the Pacific, but its major striking force (the six big carriers) would be tied up in the raid against Pearl Harbor.

Nevertheless, the Japanese were confident of success. They knew that the military forces of the Allies, while formidable on paper, were scattered over a wide area; and that much of their equipment, including the majority of their aircraft, were obsolescent. The Japanese expected to move rapidly in swift, far-reaching attacks supported by their superior air power. Speed was the key to catching the enemy off balance and then defeating him in detail. Speed was also essential to complete the conquest of Southeast Asia before the end of winter in case the Soviet Union should decide to attack in the spring: an earlier response was unlikely in view of the severe winter in Manchuria (the Japanese puppet-state Manchukuo). Severe weather conditions could also be expected in Southeast Asia, however, where the northeast monsoon would make landing operations difficult after December. For the conquest of the Philippines, the Japanese alloted 50 days; for Malaya, 100 days; and for the Dutch East Indies, 150 days.[45]

Japan's decision to attack Pearl Harbor has been criticized in retrospect. Samuel Eliot Morison and others point out that the Japanese neglected to attack the critically important repair shops and fuel storage facilities at Pearl Harbor; that they missed the Pacific Fleet's carriers; and that the sneak attack, coming without declaration of war, united the country as nothing else could have in a terrible resolve to fight to the finish. Far better, they argue, for Japan to have retained her traditional naval strategy of allowing the American Fleet to come to her. Morison points out that the U.S. fleet would have taken at least six to nine months to fight its way through the Marshalls and Carolines, even with sufficient auxiliaries and destroyer protection. This would have given the Japanese ample time to complete their conquests in Southeast Asia.[46]

In response to Morison Admiral Fukudome Shigeru presents the following argument: by using the traditional interception strategy the Japanese navy could not possibly have inflicted greater damage on the American navy than it did, in fact, inflict at Pearl Harbor on the first day of the war. The Pearl Harbor attack delayed the American advance in the central Pacific, Fukudome maintains, not for six to nine months but for almost two years.[47]

Fukudome's point is of course well taken. The Pearl Harbor attack did achieve the traditional aim of Japanese strategy—to cripple the American battle fleet; moreover, it did so decisively and at little cost to the attackers. Yet the loss of so many aging battleships did not delay the start of an American offensive nearly so much as did the shortage of aircraft carriers (of which never more than four were available in the Pacific at any time before late 1943), amphibious shipping, and destroyers. A more effective way to delay a U.S. advance would have been to wreck the logistic facilities at Pearl Harbor, forcing the fleet to operate from the West Coast!

Following the Pearl Harbor strikes, Genda had urged Nagumo to remain in the area so as to locate and sink the two American carriers which had been absent from Pearl Harbor, and to deliver additional attacks against the dockyards and fuel tanks on Oahu. But Nagumo and his chief of staff, Admiral Kusaka, were astounded and elated at having kept their forces intact; they were in no mood for further gambles. They reasoned that the attack had more than achieved its hoped-for results and that a second assault would be far riskier, since the location of the American carriers was still unknown and the Pearl Harbor defenses were fully alerted. Besides, Nagumo's carriers were urgently needed in support of the main Japanese offensives into Southeast Asia. Nagumo therefore never seriously considered a second attack despite Genda's strenuous efforts at persuasion.[48]

Yamamoto might have ordered Nagumo to strike again, and several of his staff officers advised him to do so. Yet, to reverse Nagumo's decision would be to inflict "a stinging loss of face [upon him] before his whole command." [49] In addition, Yamamoto did not know all of the details of the situation facing Nagumo's force. For those reasons, no countermanding orders came from Combined Fleet.

In hindsight, Japan's great mistake was not so much to attack Pearl Harbor as it was to attack the United States at all. Had she avoided American possessions and concentrated on the British and Dutch, Roosevelt would have found it awkward trying to win support for a war in defense of distant European colonies in Asia, rather than leading a righteous crusade to avenge Pearl Harbor. With the information available to them, however, the Japanese views were reasonable enough. The Germans still appeared a good bet to win in Europe—in any case, the European war was bound to keep the United States occupied for some time to come. Japanese strategists did not believe that the United States could vigorously fight and win a war on two fronts simultaneously. Neither, in 1941, did American strategists.

•   •

In Washington, Ambassador Nomura placed the final Japanese proposals before the American government. The first, labeled Plan "A," repeated all the old Japanese conditions for a settlement in the Far

East and had no chance of success. The second, Plan "B," was a kind of interim agreement, a modus vivendi: Japan would cease her expansion in Southeast Asia and promise to eventually evacuate Indochina if the United States would reopen trade and stop providing military aid to China.

The State Department rejected Plan B as well as Plan A; but Secretary of State Hull and the president considered proposing an American counterpart to the Japanese offer of a modus vivendi. Such a temporary solution would have given the army and navy vital time to prepare themselves; it would have allowed the reinforcement of the Philippines to be completed. In the event, vigorous protests from the Chinese government and expressions of concern from the British, Dutch, and Australians led Roosevelt to abandon the idea.[50] Instead, the United States submitted a lengthy ten-point proposal for a comprehensive settlement in the Far East. Intended mainly to keep the record straight, the proposal called for complete evacuation of China and Indochina and abandonment of the puppet regime in Manchuria. The Japanese, as expected, rejected the proposal; on December 4 a Conference in the Presence of the Emperor agreed to commence hostilities on December 7.

Since late in 1940 American cryptoanalysts had been able to read the most secure Japanese diplomatic codes. The president and his advisers were consequently aware that there was little hope of an agreement with Japan and that the Island Empire was preparing for war in the immediate future. On November 27 Hull wrote to Stimson: "I have washed my hands of it and [the situation] is now in the hands of you and Knox, the Army and Navy."[51]

One day before, the Pearl Harbor task force had left its bleak, windblown anchorage on the southern coast of Etorofu in the Kurile Islands and headed east into the gray, fog-shrouded seas. Far to the south, Japanese submarines were leaving the Marshall Islands to take station off Hawaii. Their mission was to pick off any warships attempting to enter or leave Pearl Harbor. Six of the submarines also carried two-man midget submarines, intended to sneak into the harbor and torpedo ships at anchor.

At first Yamamoto had vigorously objected to the submarines. He believed—correctly—that their presence might give away the attack, but the submarine ambush had been a part of the traditional Japanese war plan for so long that Naval General Staff refused to discard it. The more conservative admirals "expected that more damage would be inflicted by submarine attacks than by air."[52]

In Washington President Roosevelt met with Secretary Hull, General Marshall, Admiral Stark, and the service secretaries at noon on November 28. Secretary of War Stimson brought with him a report that a large Japanese expeditionary force had sailed from Shanghai headed south. As Stimson recorded in his diary: "It was now the opinion of everyone that if this expedition was allowed to get around the southern point of Indochina and to go off and land in the Gulf of Siam, either at Bangkok or further, it would be a terrific blow at all of the three powers: Britain at Singapore, the Netherlands, and ourselves in the Philippines." Roosevelt and the cabinet secretaries agreed that the president should address a personal appeal for peace to the Emperor of Japan. He would also deliver a special message to Congress warning of the menace posed by the latest Japanese moves: he would, in effect, publicly warn "Japan that we can not permit her to take any further steps of aggression against any of the countries in the Southwestern Pacific including China." [53]

Ominous reports and warnings continued to pour into Washington. On November 30 intelligence experts decrypted a message from Tokyo to the Japanese ambassador in Berlin, instructing him to tell the Nazi leaders that "there is extreme danger that war may suddenly break out between the Anglo-Saxon nations and Japan through some clash of arms. . . . This war may come quicker than anyone dreams." [54] American consulates in Southeast Asia and British and Dutch intelligence continued to report Japanese troop buildups in Formosa and Indochina. Twenty-one transports were reported in Cam Ranh Bay.

For many months the British and Dutch had sought assurances of military support in the event of a Japanese attack on their Asian territories. American leaders had always declined to make a definite commitment because they feared adverse public opinion should word of any such secret understanding leak out. In any case, such a prior commitment would not be binding since, under the U.S. Constitution, only Congress could declare war on Japan. Naval commanders of the three powers had held a number of talks concerning actions and strategy to be pursued in case of war, but no agreement had been reached. When American, Dutch, and British officers met at Singapore and drew up a report on measures to be taken by the three navies, it was promptly disapproved by Washington, together with the attendent operational plans (called PLENAPS). The continuing uncertainty as to what the United States might do was a crippling handicap to planning and preparations among the would-be allies. [55]

Finally—in December 1941—Roosevelt told the British ambassador, Lord Halifax, that if Japan moved against British or Dutch territory, "we should obviously all be together." Two days later, he explicitly declared to Halifax that he was speaking of "armed support" in regard to a Japanese attack on Malaya, the Indies, or even Thailand.[56]

The president had evidently decided that the situation was so grave as to justify a definite commitment. He and his advisers were confident that Congress and the public would support his request for a declaration of war in the event Japan moved on Southeast Asia.[57] Yet Roosevelt was by no means certain that the Japanese had irrevocably decided on war. On December 6 he told Halifax of his hopes that an appeal to the Emperor might still avert war.

In any case, more information on Japanese activities was urgently needed. In late November the commander of the U.S. Asiatic Fleet, Rear Admiral Thomas C. Hart, had on his own initiative ordered his Catalina patrol bombers to reconnoiter Cam Ranh Bay, the anchorage of the Japanese convoys in Indochinese waters.[58] On November 30 the Navy Department itself ordered such a reconnaissance and cautioned that the planes were "to observe only. They must not approach so as to appear to be attacking but must defend themselves." [59]

The following day Hart received one of the strangest and most controversial messages of the war. Beginning with the phrase, "President directs that the following be done as soon as possible," the message instructed Hart to charter three small vessels to be employed as a "defensive information patrol." The three vessels were to take station off the Indochina coast, one just south of Tonkin Gulf between Hainan Island and Hue, another off southern Annam between Cam Ranh Bay and Cape St. Jacques, and the third off the Camau peninsula where the Gulf of Siam joined the South China Sea. Armed with a small gun or two and commanded by a U.S. naval officer with mixed Filipino-American crew, the little ships were to patrol precisely in the path of any likely Japanese invasion force. However, only one vessel—formerly the admiral's yacht, *Isabel*—was ready in time; she patrolled off Cam Ranh Bay, where she was observed but not attacked by Japanese planes. *Isabel* was recalled on December 5 and returned safely to Manila.[60]

Roosevelt's instructions to Hart remain the subject of controversy. Rear Admiral Kemp Tolley, who commanded one of the three vessels, has argued that Roosevelt was attempting to provoke an incident

like that of the *Panay* in order to ensure U.S. entry into war should
Japan attack the British or Dutch. Admiral Hart and his biographer,
James Leutze, incline to support such a view. Indeed Leutze goes
further and suggests the possibility that "Washington was using him
[Hart] without keeping him fully informed and utilizing the Asiatic
Fleet as bait to provoke the Japanese into attacking the U.S." Other
authorities, such as Samuel Eliot Morison and Stanley Falk, have
dismissed any notion of such devious motives and emphasize instead
how necessary reconnaissance was to keep Washington informed;
they point out that the patrol areas of at least two of the vessels
were outside the areas which could be covered by Hart's planes.
American B-17s were in fact ordered to carry out equally risky reconnaissance of the Japanese Pacific islands and Taiwan. In any case, it
is hard to reconcile the president's hope to avoid war, as he expressed
it to Halifax, with a desire to create another *Panay* incident. Had
such an incident been Roosevelt's main objective, it is hard to see
why Hart's patrol bombers would not have sufficed.[61]

On December 6 the president's appeal to the Emperor was dispatched to the American embassy in Tokyo. By this time, the Pearl
Harbor striking force had turned south for its final run to Oahu.
In Formosa and Indochina, planes were being readied for attacks
against the Philippines and Malaya. Japanese convoys had passed
the Camau peninsula at the southern tip of Indochina and were nearing Siam. A small task force stood off Guam; a larger force was
standing by at Kwajalein in the Marshall Islands, prepared to attack
Wake Island.

Early that morning, Admiral Nagumo, aboard the flagship *Akagi,*
had received a final report from the Japanese consulate at Hawaii,
relayed from Tokyo. The consul reported nine battleships (there
were actually eight) and a large number of smaller warships in the
harbor—but all three carriers were absent.[62]

Nagumo, never strong for the Pearl Harbor project, was dismayed
to learn that the carriers were gone. He discussed the message with
his staff. Perhaps the attack should be abandoned? Genda, Kusaka
and the fleet intelligence officer all urged him to continue. Nine
battleships, Kusaka argued, ought to be worth at least three carriers.
Nagumo decided to go ahead.[63]

At 6.00 A.M. the following morning, the *Akagi* and five other
carriers of the First Air Fleet turned east into the wind. Waves broke
across the bows of the escorting destroyers and the larger ships rolled
gently in the heavy seas. Twenty minutes later a triangular flag with

a white circle on a red background was hoisted to the top of the flagship's mainmast, then swiftly lowered. The first Zero fighter rolled down the deck of the *Akagi* and climbed slowly into the early morning sky. War had come to the Pacific.

NOTES

1. Carol Morris Petillo, *Douglas MacArthur: The Philippine Years* (Bloomington, Ind.: Indiana University Press, 1981) pp. 118–20.

2. Louis Morton, *The Fall of the Philippines* (Washington, D.C.: Office of the Chief of Military History, Department of the Army, 1953) pp. 15–16. For MacArthur's experience as advisor to the Philippine army, see D. Clayton James, *The Years of MacArthur*, vol. 1:*1880–1940* (Boston: Houghton Mifflin Company, 1970) pp. 524–31, 536–42, and Petillo, *Douglas MacArthur*, pp. 173–97.

3. James, *Years of MacArthur, Vol. 1*, pp. 537–38; Petillo, *Douglas MacArthur*, pp. 194–97.

4. Morton, *Fall of the Philippines*, pp. 65–69.

5. Ibid., p. 69.

6. Quoted in James, *Years of MacArthur Vol. 1*, p. 600.

7. Ibid., p. 599–602; Morton, *Fall of the Philippines*, pp. 27–29.

8. Morton, *Fall of the Philippines*, p. 30.

9. Ibid., p. 33.

10. Watson, *Chief of Staff: Pre-War Plans and Preparations*, pp. 436–38, 440.

11. Henry L. Stimson and McGeorge Bundy, *On Active Service in Peace and War* (New York: Harper and Row, 1948), p. 388.

12. Arnold, *Global Mission*, p. 157; Craven & Cate, *Plans and Early Operations*, p. 63.

13. Watson, *Pre-War Plans and Preparations*, pp. 445–46; Pogue, *Ordeal and Hope*, p. 186.

14. Francis B. Sayre, *Glad Adventure* (New York: Macmillan, 1957), p. 221.

15. Butow, *Tojo*, pp. 236–37.

16. Pelz, *Race to Pearl Harbor*, pp. 223–24; Asada, "Japanese Navy and the United States," p. 254.

17. Butow, *Tojo*, p. 244.

18. Tsunoda Jun, "The Navy's Role in Southern Strategy" in James W. Morley, ed., *The Fateful Choice* (New York: Columbia University press, 1980) pp. 245–46, 252.

19. Louis Morton, "Japan's Decision for War" in Kent Roberts Greenfield, ed., *Command Decisions*, p. 116.

20. In addition to sources cited above, useful discussions of Japanese military planning may be found in Hattori Takushiro, *Complete History of the Greater East Asia War*, 4 vols. (Tokyo: Masu, 1953) [Manuscript English trans. in U.S. Army Center of Military History] Vol. 2, pp. 1–25; Stanley Falk, "Japanese

Strategy in World War II," *Military Review*, June 1962, pp. 70–74; "History of Imperial General Headquarters, Army Section," rev. ed., Japanese Monograph No. 45, HQ, U.S. Army Japan, ACS G-3, pp. 12–57. Copy in U.S. Army Center of Military History, Washington, D.C.

21. Butow, *Tojo*, p. 315.

22. Colonel Kumao Imoto in interview with John Toland, March 1968; Toland Interview Collection.

23. Asada, "The Japanese Navy and the United States" in Borg, ed., *Pearl Harbor*, p. 253; Tsunoda Jun, "Navy's Role in Southern Strategy," pp. 252, 259, 260.

24. Butow, *Tojo*, p. 250. Butow's translation differs from that given in several other versions, which translate the last phrase as "get ready for hostilities"; see *Pearl Harbor Hearings*, Part 20, pp. 4022–23, and Morton, "Japan's Decision," fn. 20.

25. Ibid., pp. 255–57.

26. Ibid., pp. 258–59.

27. Agawa, *Reluctant Admiral*, pp. 44–45.

28. Asada, "Japanese Navy," p. 247; Toland, *The Rising Sun*, p. 149; Agawa, *Reluctant Admiral*, pp. 154–67.

29. Agawa, *Reluctant Admiral*, pp. 20–22, 138–89.

30. Asada, "Japanese Navy," p. 255.

31. Robert E. Ward, "The Inside Story of the Pearl Harbor Plan," *U.S. Naval Institute Proceedings*, 79 (December 1951), p. 1274; Vice Adm. Shigeru Fukudome, "Hawaii Operation," *U.S. Naval Institute Proceedings*, 81 (December 1953), p. 1317.

32. Agawa, *Reluctant Admiral*, pp. 79, 83–84. Yamamoto reportedly advised younger officers stationed in the U.S. to read a biography of Lincoln to better understand the country, and to skip meals so as to have more funds for travel to see various states.

33. Yamamoto to Shimada Shigetaro, 24 October 1941, cited in Prange, *At Dawn We Slept*, pp. 301–2.

34. Tsunodo Jun and Uchida Kazutomi, "The Pearl Harbor Attack: Admiral Yamamoto's Fundamental Concept," *Naval War College Review* 31 (Fall 1978), pp. 83–88.

35. Asada, "Japanese Navy," pp. 237–8; Omi Heijiro, "The Combined Fleet and My Memories of the Navy," 1966, p. 3; Private translation for John Toland, Toland Interview Collection; Fukudome, "Hawaii Operation," p. 1317.

36. Ward, "Pearl Harbor Plan," p. 1272; Fukudome, "Hawaii Operation," p. 1318; Prange, *At Dawn We Slept*, pp. 18–20.

37. Toland interview with Admiral Kusaka Ryunosuke, July 1, 1969, Toland Interview Collection; Toland, *Rising Sun*, pp. 177–179.

38. Fukudome, "Hawaii Operation," p. 1318; Toland, *Rising Sun*, p. 155. The description of Yamamoto's luncheon is from Toland's second interview with Omi Heijiro, January 17, 1969, Toland Interview Collection.

39. Quotations from Prange, *At Dawn We Slept*, pp. 261–263.

40. Ibid., pp. 218–219, 227; Lord, *Day of Infamy*, p. 15.

41. Ward, "Pearl Harbor Plan," p. 1280.

42. Ibid., p. 1274; Fukudome, "Hawaii Operation," pp. 1318–1819; Toland, interview no. 1 with Commander Miyo.

43. "History of Imperial General Headquarters, Army Section," p. 50; Wohlstetter, *Pearl Harbor,* p. 340.

44. Morton, "Japan's Decision for War," p. 111.

45. Stanley L. Falk, *Seventy Days to Singapore* (New York: G. P. Putnam's Sons, 1975), pp. 22–24, 27–28.

46. Morison, *Rising Sun,* pp. 125–26, 129–32; for the views of American naval officers, see Prange, *At Dawn We Slept,* pp. 549–50.

47. Fukudome, "Hawaii Operations," p. 1328.

48. Prange, *At Dawn We Slept,* pp. 542–46.

49. Ibid., p. 548.

50. In *The Pacific War* (New York: Rawson Wade, 1981), John Costello argues that Roosevelt's decision to abandon the idea of a modus vivendi was because he had received an "explosive piece of intelligence. . . . a positive war warning [which] must have been quite specific, absolutely believable and from a trusted source. . . ." He speculates that this intelligence must have come from Churchill, and was probably a copy of Yamamoto's "Combined Fleet Operation Order No. 1," which contained the broad outline of Japanese strategy for war with the U.S., Britain, and the Netherlands. Costello reports finding a copy of the plan "in recently declassified records" (*Pacific War,* pp. 626–637). He believes this document was in British hands by November 26, and that at least part of its contents was passed on to the Americans. Whether or not the President received a "piece of explosive intelligence," it is highly unlikely it was Combined Fleet Operation Order No. 1. The copy of that document found by Costello in the records is copy No. 145 of 700 copies. An identical document bearing *this same serial number* did, in fact, fall into American hands—but not until April 1945, when it was recovered from the Japanese cruiser *Nachi.* It was subsequently published as an exhibit in the records of the Congressional enquiry into the Pearl Harbor attack (*Pearl Harbor Hearings* Part 13, pp. 431–438). For further discussion of this question see Stanley Falk, "Pearl Harbor: What Did We Know," *Army,* May 1982.

51. Stimson Diary entry for November 27, *Pearl Harbor Attack,* Part 2, p. 5434.

52. Ward, "Pearl Harbor Plan," p. 1282; Lord, *Day of Infamy,* p. 27; Fukudome, "Hawaii Operation," p. 1326.

53. Stimson Diary entry for November 28, *Pearl Harbor Attack,* Part 4, pp. 5435, 5439.

54. *Pearl Harbor Hearings,* Part 12, p. 204.

55. On these discussions, see Marder, *Old Friends, New Enemies,* pp. 216–19 and passim; also the two studies by James R. Leutze, *Bargaining for Supremacy,* Chapters 10 and 11, and *A Different Kind of Victory,* Chapters 7 and 8.

56. Sir Llewellyn Woodward, *British Foreign Policy in World War II* (London: H. M. Stationary Office 1962), pp. 186–187; Raymond A. Esthus, "President Roosevelt's Commitment to Britain to Intervene in a Pacific War," *Mississippi Valley Historical Review* 50 (June 1963), pp. 33–36.

57. Esthus, "President Roosevelt's Commitment to Britain," pp. 36–37.

58. Leutze, *A Different Kind of Victory,* p. 222; Kemp Tolley, *Cruise of the Lana Kai* (Annapolis: U.S. Naval Institute, 1973), pp. 265–67.

59. Message, OPNAV to CINCAF, 30 November 1941, copy in Asiatic Fleet Records, Naval Historical Center.

60. OPNAV to CINCAF, 1 December 1941, copy in Naval Historical Center; Leutze, *A Different Kind of Victory,* pp. 222–24.

61. Tolley, *Cruise of the Lana Kai,* pp. 264–80 and passim; Leutze, *A Different Kind of Victory,* pp. 226–28; Morison, *The Rising Sun,* p. 57; Falk, *Seventy Days to Singapore,* p. 62. Prange, *At Dawn We Slept,* p. 461.

62. Wohlstetter, *Pearl Harbor,* pp. 375–76.

63. Mitsuo Fuchida, "I led the Attack on Pearl Harbor," *U.S. Naval Institute Proceedings,* 78 (September 1952), p. 944.

FIVE

The Issue Is in Doubt

At eleven o'clock on the evening of December 7, Treasury Secretary Henry Morganthau returned from the White House to brief his senior assistants. "It is just unexplainable," Morganthau exclaimed; "[it is] much worse than anyone realizes. . . . Knox feels something terrible. . . . Stimson kept mumbling that all the planes were in one place. . . . They have the whole fleet in one place . . . the whole fleet in this little Pearl Harbor base. They will never be able to explain it." [1]

Morgenthau's words proved literally true. Over the course of the next decade, the question of how the Pearl Harbor disaster could have occurred was endlessly discussed and debated. The discussion usually took the form of an attempt to discover the individual or individuals "responsible" for the catastrophe.

In the immediate aftermath of the debacle, most Americans were convinced that Admiral Kimmel and General Short were primarily to blame. Rumors circulated "that Army and Navy commanders were at odds, that most of the troops and crewmen were drunk, and that no effort had been made to carry out orders from Washington." [2] A commission of inquiry headed by Supreme Court Justice Owen J. Roberts reported in January 1942 that the two commanders were guilty of dereliction of duty for failing to take "appropriate measures of defense required by the imminence of hostilities" and to consult and cooperate on such measures.[3] Kimmel and Short had already been relieved and were subsequently retired from the service.

The Roberts inquiry was followed by six more administrative investigations. Finally, an exhaustive congressional investigation produced thirty-nine thick volumes of testimony and documents. These subsequent investigations, while they did not exonerate Kimmel and Short, demonstrated that Washington officials also shared some responsibility for the defeat. For example, the War Department had been informed by General Short at the end of November, 1941, that he had alerted his forces "to prevent sabotage"—yet the department failed to warn him that it wished him to be prepared for other possible dangers as well.[4]

Kimmel and Short lacked the capability to decipher and read Japanese diplomatic code as American intelligence analysts were doing in Washington; they would later claim that the War and Navy Departments failed to pass on to them a number of important intercepts that would have alerted them to the threat their commands faced. Most notably, the Navy Department failed to pass on to Kimmel an intercepted message of September 1941 from Tokyo to the Japanese consul at Honolulu, ordering him to divide the waters of Pearl Harbor into five sub-areas. He was to report regularly on the number, type, and movements of ships in these areas.[5] Colonel Rufus Bratton, head of the Far East Section of Army Intelligence, considered the message significant, for it indicated that "the Japanese were showing unusual interest in the port at Honolulu." High-level officials in the army and navy, however, saw no importance in the message; it was passed on by Naval Intelligence in a routine manner to the Asiatic Fleet—but not to Hawaii.[6] Neither this message nor any other single piece of information would have offered clear warning of an attack on Pearl Harbor, and there is no way of knowing what Hawaiian commanders might have done had they received such information. Yet, as Gordon Prange points out, "evaluation and dissemination of just such information were functions of the Army and Navy staffs in Washington. They failed to evaluate properly and they did not disseminate to the parties of primary interest—Kimmel and Short." [7]

A final warning never reached the Pearl Harbor commanders at all because of fumblings and oversights in Washington. In the early morning of December 7 (Washington time), Naval Intelligence had intercepted and read the last part of a long fourteen-part Japanese reply to Secretary of State Hull's proposals. This final section of the Japanese reply announced that Tokyo was breaking off any further negotiations. Army Intelligence intercepted another message at the same time, instructing Ambassador Nomura to submit the entire fourteen-part document to the State Department at 1:00 P.M. Washington time on Sunday, December 7. Again it was Colonel Bratton who grasped the significance of the message. He was struck by the fact that it was to be delivered on a Sunday and that Tokyo had, for the first time, specified a precise hour. The colonel was convinced that the delivery time was intended to coincide with a Japanese attack on some American installation in the Far East, probably the Philippines. He did not consider Pearl Harbor because he assumed the fleet had gone to sea in accordance with long-standing war plans.[8]

Bratton frantically attempted to reach Chief of Staff Marshall and his assistants but was unable to reach the general for almost an hour because Marshall had gone for his Sunday morning horseback ride. When Bratton finally saw the chief of staff—some two and one-half hours after receiving the intercepts—he explained the significance of the 1:00 o'clock delivery time. The chief of staff immediately drafted a message to army commanders in the Pacific:

> The Japanese are presenting at 1 P.M. Eastern Standard Time today what amounts to an ultimatum. Also they are under orders to destroy their code machine immediately. Just what significance the hour set may have we do not know but be on the alert accordingly.[9]

Marshall queried Admiral Stark, who by now had also seen the Japanese intercepts, whether he wished navy commanders included in the warning message. The chief of naval operations asked that "Inform Navy" be added to the message. He also offered the use of navy wireless communications to send the message, but Marshall declined. Instead, the despatch was sent in code by commercial telegraph because, unknown to Marshall, the army's signal communications were temporarily unable to contact Hawaii. The message, which had failed to receive a "Priority" marking, finally reached General Short's headquarters shortly after the Japanese attack was completed.[10]

Some "revisionist" historians have argued that President Roosevelt and his close associates in the cabinet (Hull, Stimson, and Knox) deliberately exposed the fleet to destruction at Pearl Harbor in order to ensure support for America's entry into World War II. Authors such as Charles C. Tansill, Charles A. Beard, Robert Theobald, and Harry Elmer Barnes claim that since the U.S. was reading the Japanese code, Washington must have known in advance of the attack, and that Roosevelt consciously withheld vital information from the Hawaiian commanders. It was his purpose, they maintain, to keep the fleet in harbor and thus vulnerable to attack.[11]

Although revisionists are convinced that Roosevelt purposely kept Short and Kimmel in the dark, it might as plausibly be argued that both of them conspired to ignore Washington's repeated warnings. On November 24, 1941, the chief of naval operations had warned Pacific commanders that "a surprise aggressive movement [by Japan] in any direction . . . is a possibility" Three days later he had sent an even more strongly worded message: "This dispatch is to be considered a war warning. Negotiations with Japan . . . have ceased and an aggressive move by Japan is expected within the next few days." The following day, army commanders were similarly warned of "hostile action possible at any moment." One week later, Washington informed Kimmel that the Japanese diplomatic and consular posts in Hong Kong, Manila, Washington, and London were destroying their secret code equipment.[12]

The fact was that Kimmel and Short *were* alert to the possibility of imminent war with Japan. They simply did not expect it to begin at Pearl Harbor. Despite repeated fleet exercises, war games, studies, plans and discussions concerning the danger of surprise air attack, despite repeated surprise alerts and drills, the fact remained that American army and navy leaders at the highest levels simply could not *really* believe that a surprise air attack on the fleet would actually take place. In the most exhaustive study of Pearl Harbor, Gordon Prange singles out this fundamental disbelief as the root of the whole tragedy.[13]

Among the mass of secret Japanese messages which were being intercepted and decoded in Washington there were signs that pointed towards Pearl Harbor, but many others seemed to indicate an attack on the Philippines and Singapore—or even against the Soviet Union. As Roberta Wohlstetter, a perceptive student of the Pearl Harbor debacle observes: "We failed to anticipate Pearl Harbor not for want of the relevant materials but because of a plethora of irrelevant ones. . . . There is a difference between having a signal available somewhere in the heap of irrelevances and perceiving it as a warning, and there is also a difference between perceiving it as a warning and acting on it." [14]

Kimmel and Short, along with the vast majority of American military leaders, expected war to begin in the Far East and saw sabotage as the chief threat to Hawaii. Of course they were also unaware that the Japanese had perfected a torpedo that would be effective in the shallow waters of Pearl Harbor; moreover, they had received numerous urgent warnings from Washington in the past which had resulted only in false alarms. Finally, relations between the services was such that army and navy had only the vaguest notion of the defensive readiness and capabilities of the other.

The debate on Pearl Harbor took a new turn in 1982 with the publication of John Toland's book, *Infamy.* Toland is a respected historian whose previous book on the war with Japan had won a Pulitzer Prize. In *Infamy,* Toland presents what he considers new evidence that Roosevelt and a small group of advisors—including Stimson, Knox, and Marshall—had, by December 4, unambiguous information indicating that Japanese carriers were headed eastward toward Hawaii.[15] This information included Japanese radio signals picked up by American radio operators aboard the liner *Lurline* and by communications experts in the Twelfth Naval District, San Francisco. Both groups had concluded that the signals came from a Japanese naval force north-northwest of Hawaii. They had each reported their findings to intelligence authorities; at least in the case of the communications experts in Twelfth Naval District, they "felt assured that not only O.N.I. [Office of Naval Intelligence], but the President would be promptly informed." [16] Toland also reports that Dutch codebreakers in the Netherlands Indies had intercepted a Japanese consular message to Bangkok which told of plans for attacks against Hawaii, the Philippines, Malaya, and Siam. The Dutch turned this information over to Brigadier General Elliot Thorpe, the senior American military observer, who in turn gave it to the American consul in Batavia. The consul's message, as later published in *Foreign Relations of the United States 1941,* makes no mention of Hawaii.[17] Yet Thorpe claimed that he had sent a message to Washington—through the U.S. naval attaché—which *did* warn of such an attack.[18]

Having received such warnings, Toland argues, "Roosevelt and a small group of advisers were faced with three options. They could announce to the world word of the approaching *Kido Butai* [Nagumo's striking force]; this would indubitably have forced the Japanese to turn back." They could alert Kimmel and Short, but "once discovered out of range, Kido Butai would have turned back," for "if Kimmel, Short, and others had been privy to the secret they might possibly have reacted in such a way as to reveal to the Japanese that their attack plan was known." Finally, they could keep the Hawaiian commanders in ignorance "to insure that the Japanese would launch their attack." [19]

Most other students of the Pearl Harbor attack have criticized Toland's thesis severely. David Kahn, a well-known authority on the history of intelligence, questions the reliability of Toland's evidence. Kahn points out that the Japanese Pearl Harbor striking force maintained complete radio silence from the time it left its base in the Kuriles; it never transmitted any messages, even on low-power ship-to-ship channels. Toland's informants had, in all probability, picked up naval transmissions originating from Japan and nearby waters. "Shipboard direction finding was then notoriously unreliable with a likely error of easily 11 to 20 degrees in a bearing," enough to throw off the calculations of the *Lurline* radio men. Kahn also points out that the U.S. Navy's entire network of intercept posts in the Pacific—from the Aleutians through Hawaii, Midway, Samoa, Guam, and the Philippines—were making every effort to locate the missing carriers. "It is less probable that the Navy's experienced monitors missed [the signals] than that the two men mistook whatever they heard for the transmission of warships headed for Hawaii." [20]

Even assuming that Toland's description of the various warnings to Washington are correct, and assuming further that all reached the White House, it is still pertinent to repeat Roberta Wohlstetter's point: the mere presence of accurate information among a mass of inaccurate or misleading information is no guarantee that the accurate information will be recognized and acted upon. In the last weeks of peace, Washington was full of rumors and reports of Japanese schemes and maneuvers. Why a report from a radio operator aboard a merchant ship, a relatively low-ranking navy intelligence analyst and an army general in distant Batavia should have instantly set alarm bells ringing throughout the War and Navy Department is hard to understand.

Finally, there is the question of why Roosevelt and his senior advisers would have wished to keep Kimmel and Stark in ignorance of the impending attack. Even assuming that they desired, above all else, to bring the country into war with Japan, why could they not warn the fleet and make the first battle a victory? Toland's answer is that "once discovered out of range (the Japanese) would have turned back." Harry Elmer Barnes made the same argument, declaring that "it appeared necessary to prevent Hawaiian commanders from taking any offensive action which would deter the Japanese from attacking Pearl Harbor, which of necessity had to be a surprise attack." [21] However, neither writer offers any evidence that Roosevelt knew what Admiral Nagumo's orders were for such a contingency.

In fact the Japanese striking force, if discovered prior to launching their attack, would *not* have turned back. The Japanese hoped to achieve surprise, but they were not counting on it. Admiral Nagumo and his staff half expected to have to fight their way in. This, after all, is what had befallen the strike force in one of the tabletop war games.[22] Moreover, the discovery of a large Japanese fleet a few hundred miles from America's principal naval base would in itself have been sufficient *casus belli*, regardless of whether the Japanese actually attacked or not.

If Roosevelt and his advisors did know of the impending Pearl Harbor attack by December 4, it is hard to explain the chief executive's remarks to the British ambassador, Lord Halifax, on that same day. The president, who had promised Halifax a few days before that the U.S. would go to war with Japan if the latter attacked British and Dutch possessions in the Far East, declared that he had not given up hope for a temporary settlement with Japan and planned to appeal directly to the Emperor.[23] Later, on December 6, Roosevelt turned down a request from Australia that he issue a strong warning to Japan because he wished to await the outcome of his appeal to the Emperor.[24]

In any case, the Pearl Harbor disaster was not simply the result of American errors of omission and commission. A good deal was also owed to the immense care and skill with which the Japanese planned and organized their attack and to the conceptual daring of the plan itself—which perhaps only Yamamoto, the great gambler, could have pushed through to success. Yamamoto was willing to trust in luck and the Japanese certainly enjoyed a full measure of luck in the Pearl Harbor operation: from the favorable weather enjoyed by the attackers to the fortuitous foul-ups by the Americans in handling the radar sightings and submarine contacts, to the long series of misunderstandings and missed guesses by Washington and the Hawaiian commanders.

Devastating surprise attacks against forces who have received ample warning are far from rare in warfare. It was to happen again in the Philippines, hours after the attack on Pearl Harbor,* and it had happened to Stalin the previous spring. More recently, American

* See below, p. 106 ff.

forces in Vietnam were taken unawares by North Vietnamese and
Viet Cong forces in the Tet offensive of 1968, and the Israeli armed
forces were surprised by the Egyptians and Syrians in 1973. Americans and Israelis alike suffered unexpected onslaughts despite the
fact that both had received excellent intelligence about enemy preparations.

In recent years a whole field of scholarly enquiry has grown up
around the investigation of intelligence and warning.[25] Studies in
this field have found that advance warning of attack is rarely altogether absent, but that "response necessarily lags behind warning."
The warning indicators are often ambiguous and scattered; hesitation
or indecision by the leaders of the country being attacked can fatally
delay an effective response; purposeful deception by the attacker
can contribute to the victim's uncertainty; and the weeks or months
of crisis which usually precede the outbreak of war, with their atten-
dant false alarms, "desensitize observers to the danger of imminent
war." [26] Surprise attacks have therefore enjoyed a large degree of
success even though the victims often had substantial information
pointing to an impending offensive by their opponents. Pearl Harbor,
then, was a far from unique and inexplicable phenomenon: it was
one example of a class of events sadly familiar to students of warfare.

● ●

Looking back from the vantage point of the sixties and seventies,
it appeared to many writers that the outcome of the war with Japan
was a foregone conclusion. The Japanese were hopelessly outclassed.
Pitted against the immense industrial capacity of the United States,
it was only a matter of time before they were forced to capitulate.
In fact the war was a useful exercise for the American army and
navy, allowing them to expand, to flex their muscles, and to prepare
themselves for the cold war era.

That was the view from recent decades. In December of 1941,
the situation appeared quite different. A feeling akin to panic gripped
the country. After Pearl Harbor, the feeling was that anything might
happen. San Francisco had three air-raid alerts on the first night of
the war. The following morning, Major General John L. Dewitt,
commander of the Fourth Army and of West Coast defenses, assured
reporters that "death and destruction are likely to come to this city
at any moment." Enemy planes had been spotted over the city that
night, he declared. "They were tracked out to sea. Why bombs were
not dropped, I do not know. . . . I don't think there's any doubt

the planes came from a carrier." While the West Coast trembled before the menace of a non-existent carrier, Mayor Fiorello La Guardia of New York warned that the East Coast might also be vulnerable to attack. "It was an extreme crisis and anything could be expected." In Hawaii a dog on an Oahu Beach was even reported to be "barking in Morse code to Japanese sub offshore." [27]

The belief that anything might be expected was not confined to the public. In a paper prepared for the president in late December, the Joint Army-Navy Board credited the Japanese with the ability to "undertake devastating raids" on Alaska, Hawaii, the West Coast, and the Panama Canal. In Europe the planners feared that the Germans would invade Spain, Portugal, and French North- and West Africa.[28] A submarine commander who had fought through the unsuccessful campaigns against the Japanese in the Philippines and Netherlands Indies advised a friend that the U.S. could have no hope of holding Hawaii; it "would be better to conserve our resources for the defense of California." [29]

Nervously, the chief of naval operations informed Admiral Kimmel that Japanese attacks on Midway, Maui, and Hawaii were expected in the near future; he urged the admiral not to base any ships larger than submarines at Pearl Harbor until its defenses were strengthened. Kimmel replied that most of the salvageable warships were at the bottom of the harbor. They could not be sent to the West Coast: the fleet would stay at Pearl.[30]

In the western Pacific, where the real war was beginning, the Japanese moved rapidly to complete the first phase of their plan. Within a few hours of the Pearl Harbor attack, Japanese task forces headed for Guam and for Wake Island. Guam fell quickly. At Wake Island, however, the Japanese received their first unpleasant surprise of the war.

A present-day visitor to Wake Island may find it hard to believe that a battle was fought there. The atoll is tiny, only about 2,600 acres of sand and coral, and absolutely flat. No part of the three long, narrow islands which compose the V-shaped atoll is more than 1,100 yards from the sea—which appears, at times, about to swamp them.

In 1941, however, Wake figured importantly in American military plans as a way station for aircraft on their way to the Philippines and as a base for reconnaissance into the Japanese-held Marshall Islands. Since the beginning of that year, more than eleven hundred construction workers had been transforming Wake from an isolated

overnight stop for the trans-Pacific Pan-Am Clipper flying boats
into an important military base. On Wake, the largest island, a 5,000-
foot runway had been built. On Peale Island, which formed the
right-hand tip of the "V," a seaplane base was under construction.
On Wilkes Island, at the opposite end of the "V," plans called for
a submarine base, although no work had yet been done.

In December 1941 the island, under Navy Commander Winfield
Scott Cunningham, was defended by a detachment of the First Marine
Defense Battalion, about 450 men under Major James P. S. Dever-
eux, and a marine fighter squadron, VMF-211, under Major Paul
A. Putnam. The Defense Battalion was so understrength that only
six of the twelve antiaircraft guns could be manned at one time.
There was no radar at all for fire control or early-warning purposes.[31]

The fighter squadron had twelve F4F-3 Wildcats. Although these
fighters were already out of date, they were still completely new
to the pilots of VMF-211, who had just received them—the protective
bunkers for the planes had not been completed when the first Japanese
bombers struck at noon on December 8, 1941.

Except for defenseless Guam, Wake was the American base nearest
to the Japanese home islands; only 600 miles separated it from Japan's
strongholds in the Marshalls. Japanese war plans called for the early
capture of the atoll; this mission was assigned to Vice Admiral Inoue
Shigeyoshi's Fourth Fleet, which was responsible for the defense of
the Japanese-held island chains in the southwest and central Pacific.
Planes from Inoue's base at Kwajalein were already on their way
to Wake by the time the bombs began to fall at Pearl Harbor.

Fighters from Wake were on patrol as the Japanese bombers approached, but missed them in the squally weather: most of the remaining Wildcats were destroyed on the ground, along with much of
the aviation gasoline stored near the field. Subsequent air raids destroyed the hospital and the fire control instruments on some of
the coastal defense guns—but the guns themselves were very much
intact, as the Japanese learned when they made their first attempt
to land on December 11, 1941.

The Japanese invasion force, 450 men loaded into transports and
old destroyers, escorted by three light cruisers and six more destroyers, arrived off Wake in the early morning. Carefully waiting until
the ships had closed to about 5,000 yards, the five-inch batteries
on Wake and Wilkes opened a devastating fire against the Japanese.
Four five-inch shells ripped into the light cruiser *Yubari;* she turned
away in a dense cloud of smoke. Off Wilkes Island the destroyer
Hayate was literally blown out of the water by three salvoes from

Battery "L." As the *Hayate* disappeared beneath the waves, the gunners at the battery broke into a spontaneous cheer. Platoon Sergeant Henry Bedell quickly returned them to reality: " 'Knock it off, you bastards, and get back on the guns!' " roared Bedell in a voice that carried above all the noise of battle. " 'What d'ye think this is, a ball game?' " [32]

Within half an hour, battery "L" had scored hits on another destroyer and a transport, forcing them to retire. At the same time, Battery "B" on Peale Island was engaged in a furious duel with three Japanese destroyers. Japanese shells knocked out the battery's communication system and disabled one of the guns, but the marines continued to fire with the remaining gun, scoring hits on two of the destroyers. The Japanese broke off the action and fled.

The four surviving Wildcat fighters, which had been held in reserve for this moment, pursued the fleeing Japanese, sank a destroyer, damaged two light cruisers, and set a transport on fire. The Wildcats, however, were damaged by antiaircraft fire and rough landings; only three remained fit to fly.

News of the successful defense of Wake electrified an American public frustrated and discouraged by the news of one Allied defeat after another in Malaya, the Philippines and the Pacific. "MARINES KEEP WAKE," screamed the headlines. The *Washington Post* compared it to the gallant, hopeless stand at the Alamo. A story repeated everywhere told of how, when asked by radio what they needed, the beleaguered marines had replied: "Send us more Japs!" (It was not until after the war that this message was shown to be a myth.)

On the tiny atoll, the marines did not find the slogan "Send us more Japs!" as inspiring as did their fellow countrymen. After December 11, Wake was bombed every day but one, and although casualties were not as heavy as in the first raid, the steady pounding took its toll on the nerves of the tired defenders. Many of the civilian construction workers had scattered in panic to uninhabited parts of the island after the first bombings, but at least three hundred, led by the redoubtable construction superintendent, Dan Teters, a hardbitten veteran of World War I, worked round-the-clock with the marines, digging foxholes and bomb shelters, filling sandbags, clearing rubble, and helping in the mess and at the makeshift field hospital. Ground crews and mechanics of VMF-211 kept one or two planes flying by heroic improvisation and by cannibalizing parts from wrecks of the others, but by December 22 all the Wildcats had been shot down or crashed.

Meanwhile, in Hawaii, Admiral Husband E. Kimmel was completing plans for the relief of Wake. Kimmel had long regarded Wake as a valuable lure to draw out the Japanese fleet for battle. Even with most of his battleships out of action, Kimmel believed that a portion of the Japanese fleet could be ambushed at Wake.[33] The admiral committed all three of his aircraft carriers, *Lexington, Saratoga,* and *Enterprise,* to the operation. A task force built around the *Saratoga* was to make the actual relief attempt, while the *Lexington* and *Enterprise* task forces carried out diversionary raids and stood by in support.

The operation was dogged by delay and hesitation from the start. The marine reinforcements, loaded in the seaplane tender *Tangier,* along with the rest of the task force, were delayed two days at Pearl Harbor waiting for the *Saratoga,* which had been rerouted because of a submarine scare. The task force finally sailed on December 16 under Rear Admiral Frank Jack Fletcher, who had never commanded carriers before. Because the force would probably have to fuel en route, the entire fleet could make only thirteen knots, the top speed of its accompanying oiler.

Back at Pearl Harbor, Vice Admiral William S. Pye had temporarily replaced Admiral Kimmel as commander of the Pacific Fleet. A new commander, Admiral Chester W. Nimitz, was on his way from the East Coast. In the meantime, Pye had been informed by Washington that both the chief of naval operations and the secretary of the navy considered Wake "a liability, not an asset." He also knew that the Japanese could marshal stronger naval forces in the Pacific than could the United States. Under these circumstances, Pye decided to order the *Lexington* task force, under Vice Admiral Wilson E. Brown, to join Fletcher in the relief of Wake. This entailed a further delay so that Brown could move within supporting range. Pye also cautioned Fletcher to fuel before entering the possible battle zone.[34] Admiral Fletcher took so much time to fuel in the rough seas that he was still about 600 miles from Wake on December 23, when its marine defenders reported a second Japanese landing.

The second Japanese expedition was considerably stronger than the first: it included four heavy cruisers and about 2,000 troops. The *Soryu* and the *Hiryu,* two carriers detached from the returning Pearl Harbor armada, provided distant support with air strikes against Wake. Prudently keeping beyond range of the Marine shore batteries, the Japanese forces shelled Wake from the sea while about 1,000 men—in landing barges and two patrol boats—landed on Wilkes Island and the southern shore of Wake itself. Many of the defenders were tied down manning the five-inch guns and the machine-gun positions, so that Major Devereux had a total of only about eighty-five men available as infantry to oppose the Japanese. On Wilkes, the situation was much the same, but here the entire Japanese force concentrated on attacking a single three-inch gun position. This enabled the Wilkes Island commander, Captain Wesley McC. Pratt, to gather a number of men from other gun positions and launch a surprise assault on the Japanese massed around the three-inch battery. Although outnumbered five to one, the marines' assault was so audacious and unexpected that the Japanese panicked and were wiped out piecemeal. On Wake the Japanese were not so obliging as to concentrate their forces in one area. By dawn, the enemy was well established ashore and most of the marine positions were surrounded. The island was ringed by more than a dozen men-of-war, and Japanese carrier planes from the *Soryu* and *Hiryu* pounded the defenses.

While these events were transpiring, Admiral Fletcher's forces were still laboring through heavy seas almost 450 miles away. Meanwhile, Admiral Pye and his chief of staff, Rear Admiral Milo F. Draemel, were increasingly having second thoughts about Wake. A seaplane had recently flown in from the island, piloted by two ensigns carrying despatches from Cunningham and Devereux. "We talked to these two pilots, both of them very, very young and inexperienced," recalled an officer on Pye's staff; "the main word I remember hearing in their replies was 'grim, grim, grim.' " [35] The reports evidently had a marked effect on Pye and Draemel.

In the early morning of December 22 (December 23 at Wake), Commander Cunningham informed Pacific Fleet Headquarters: "Enemy Apparently Landing." Captain Charles H. McMorris, the Pacific Fleet's operations officer, immediately summoned Pye and Draemel; together the three men discussed the despatch and argued over what steps to take. [36] They had reached no agreement when, two hours later, Cunningham sent a second message: "The Enemy is on the Island. The Issue is in Doubt." This was enough for Admiral Pye. At 9:00 A.M., he ordered Fletcher to return to Pearl Harbor. At that moment the Japanese transports and escorting vessels were lying at anchor off Wake "with no apparent measures for security against surface attack" and out of range of their supporting carriers. [37] An air or surface attack by Fletcher's forces could have wreaked havoc on the unprepared transports and destroyers as well as on the Japanese ashore. But Fletcher was already on his way back to Pearl.

At 0700, Commander Cunningham informed Major Devereux that no relief could be expected. "Isn't any help coming?" asked Devereux. "No," replied Cunningham. "There are no friendly ships within twenty-four hours."

"Not even submarines?"

"Not even them."

A few moments later, Cunningham made the inevitable decision, and Major Devereux, accompanied by a sergeant carrying a white rag lashed to a mop handle, went to meet the Japanese.

It is hard to quarrel with Samuel Eliot Morison's observation that "the failure to relieve Wake resulted from poor seamanship and a want of decisive action." [38] Yet there is no doubt that Washington also played a large role in the debacle. Admiral Kimmel bore a measure of responsibility for the Pearl Harbor disaster, so relieving him of his post could certainly be justified. But the decision of the president and navy secretary to remove him even before the arrival of Admiral Nimitz, and to appoint Pye as a sort of interim commander, was surely ill-advised. Kimmel's removal sealed the fate of Wake.

The capture of Wake and Guam gave Japan absolute control of the line of communications across the Central Pacific. The Philippines were now isolated and the Japanese attack on the islands, so long contemplated with dread by American strategists, was about to begin.

● ●

A few days before the war an American reporter in Manila observed that "if the Japs come down here they'll be playing in the big leagues for the first time in their lives." Actually, it was the "old army" which would be playing in the big leagues for the first and only time in the Pacific War. The army divisions of 1942 and 1943, which were to fight their way along the back of New Guinea and up the Solomons ladder, were new men: draftees, reservists, products of "basic training," and the new Officer Candidate Schools. It was still the "old army"—albeit leavened a bit with reservists, National Guardsmen, and even some draftees—which received the first shock of war in the Philippines. It was an army of polo ponies and long golf games, of cheap domestic help, and shopping trips to Shanghai and Hong Kong. At the Army and Navy Club, officers gathered each year on the lawn to listen to the Army-Navy football game during the early hours of the morning. When Army made a touchdown, a mule would be ceremoneously paraded around the lawn. When Navy scored, a goat was similarly honored.

The backbone of the old army in the Philippines was the Philippine

Scouts, Filipinos enlisted as regulars in special units of the United States Army and commanded by American officers. Tough, experienced and well-trained, many of the scouts had seen twenty or even thirty years' service. But like all American units in the islands, they were understrength and lacked important items of equipment.

At two-thirty on the morning of December 8, the Asiatic Fleet headquarters in downtown Manila intercepted a message from Hawaii: "Air raid on Pearl Harbor. This is no drill." Within an hour General MacArthur and his principal commanders knew that war had come. By five General Lewis Brereton, MacArthur's air commander, was at the commanding general's headquarters, pressing for permission to send his B-17s against Japanese bases in Formosa. General Richard K. Sutherland, MacArthur's autocratic chief of staff, refused to allow Brereton to see MacArthur. The general was busy. Brereton then requested permission to carry out a raid on Formosa. Sutherland told him to go ahead with preparations but to wait for word from MacArthur before undertaking offensive operations.[39]

Two hours later, Brereton, having alerted his bomber commanders to prepare for a mission, went again to MacArthur's headquarters but was still unable to see the commander in chief; he was told by Sutherland to stand by for orders. By ten—having still received no word—Brereton telephoned MacArthur's headquarters and spoke with Sutherland. To no avail. From this point on the story becomes confused, but at some time between ten and eleven, Brereton apparently received the long-sought directive, either from MacArthur or Sutherland, to go ahead with a bombing raid against Formosa: by 11:20 A.M., orders for such an attack had been sent by teletype to Clark Field and the bombers were being armed and fueled for their mission.[40]

Brereton's bombers were still on the ground at 12:20 that afternoon when the first Japanese planes from Formosa, fifty-four bombers and thirty-six new Zero fighters, attacked Clark Field. Two squadrons of B-17s and a squadron of P-40s were totally destroyed. At Iba airfield, forty miles west of Clark, a second formation of Japanese planes caught a squadron of P-40s just returning from a patrol, destroyed all but two of them, then went on to wreck the air base.[41]

This catastrophe, which deprived MacArthur of almost half of his best aircraft on the first day of the war, has never been adequately explained. Army and air force historians attempted to piece the story together after the war, but with little success. Few reliable records survived and the principals—Sutherland, Brereton, and MacArthur—

flatly contradicted each other.[42] General Brereton blamed Sutherland and—indirectly—MacArthur for delaying the proposed air attack on Formosa. Sutherland in turn blamed Brereton for not moving his bombers south to Del Monte airfield in Mindanao, where they would have been safely out of range. MacArthur had ordered the move some days before, but Brereton had so far moved only about half his squadrons: the southern airfield was not completely ready and additional bombers, expected to arrive shortly from the United States, were to be based there. An additional factor which delayed launching the bomber attack was a lack of adequate photo reconnaissance information about Formosa. Brereton claimed that MacArthur had forbidden any prewar reconnaissance of the island, while Sutherland later cited the need to wait for reconnaissance as one reason for delaying the start of the bombing mission.[43]

That the bombers and fighters were caught on the ground seems even more inexplicable. Several officers assert that advance warnings were sent to Clark Field; others assert just as emphatically that no advance warning was received. Even the question of whether the aircraft were adequately dispersed is shrouded in confusion.[44] MacArthur washed his hands of all responsibility in his postwar writings and pronouncements. The man who eagerly sought the mission of "conducting strong offensive air operations" in November 1941 [45] declared in 1946 that "our air forces in the Philippines, containing many antiquated models, were hardly more than a token force. . . . They were hopelessly outnumbered and never had a chance of winning." [46]

Actually, MacArthur had had the strongest American air forces outside the United States: 277 planes, including 35 heavy bombers and about 100 modern fighters.[47] But the Japanese had almost twice as many planes, a superior type of fighter, and more experienced pilots. Moreover the Japanese had achieved a major "technological surprise" by modifying the engines and the fuel mix of their Zero fighters so that they could accompany the bombers on the long flight to Clark Field.[48] The American P-40s lacked such range, and what Brereton's unescorted B-17s might have accomplished in a daylight attack on the well-protected Japanese bases on Formosa is open to serious question.

By December 22, when the main Japanese landings on Luzon began, MacArthur's air force had been reduced to a handful of fighters and a few surviving B-17s. The navy yard at Cavite in Manila Bay was devastated by an air raid; all naval forces, with the exception of some patrol bombers, gunboats, and motor torpedo boats ("PTs") were sent south to join British and Dutch forces in the Netherlands Indies.

Lieutenant General Homma Masaharu, an amateur playwright who had served as an observer with the British army in World War I, commanded the Fourteenth Army. Its assignment was to conquer the Philippines. Homma's command comprised only two divisions, the Sixteenth and the Forty-eighth, together with support and service units; he was scheduled to loose the Forty-eighth Division for operations in the south in fifty days, by which time he was expected to have completed the conquest of Luzon.

After preliminary landings in the extreme southern and northern parts of Luzon, Homma's forces began their main push on December 22 along Lingayen Gulf, northeast of Manila near the Philippine summer capital of Baguio. The two Philippine army divisions guarding the 120-mile Lingayen coast offered some resistance, but in general, the weather proved more of an obstacle to the Japanese than the poorly-trained, ill-equipped Filipino troops who, on their first day of combat, found themselves up against strafing planes, tanks, dive-bombers, and artillery.

Lieutenant General Jonathan M. Wainwright, who commanded the North Luzon Force, threw in the Twenty-sixth Cavalry, a tough, well-trained regiment of Philippine Scouts, to stiffen the resistance. But the scouts lacked their organic artillery and many of their armored cars, while the handful of tanks which should have cooperated with them were not even under Wainwright's command but that of a separate tank group commander. Under these circumstances, the Twenty-sixth Cavalry could do little more than cover the retreat of the two Filipino divisions as they fell back before the advancing Japanese.[49] At the village of Binalonan the Twenty-sixth Cavalry, now reduced to about 450 men, and lacking antitank weapons, detained a Japanese armored column for over two hours. This allowed Wainwright's disorganized divisions to withdraw across the Agno River, the first defensible obstacle on the road south to Manila.[50]

Wainwright, a cavalryman of the old school who felt more comfortable commanding from his horse "Little Boy" than from behind a desk, now proposed that he be given the Philippine Division, a crack unit composed entirely of American regulars and Philippine Scouts, to mount a counterattack.[51] But the harsh light of reality had finally begun to dawn in MacArthur's headquarters. "Viewing the broken, fleeing North Luzon Force, [MacArthur] realized that his cherished plan of defeating an attempt to advance toward Manila from the north was not now possible."[52]

In the early morning hours of December 24, word went out to all field commanders that the old War Plan Orange (WPO-3) was in effect. Manila was declared an open city and the government of the Philippines moved with MacArthur's headquarters to the island fortress of Corregidor at the entrance to Manila Bay. While orders for WPO-3 were being issued a second, smaller Japanese force—about 7,000 men counting support troops—landed at Lamon Bay southwest of Manila and began pushing their way east through rugged terrain and against gradually stiffening resistance.

MacArthur's forces were now in a precarious situation. They would have to execute a long retreat under fire into the Bataan Peninsula, as called for in WPO-3, while delaying long enough to permit Bataan to be stocked with supplies and equipment.[53] Wainwright's men, spread out along the Agno River line, would have to retreat an average distance of 150 miles.[54] His retiring troops were to occupy five successive defensive positions, labelled D-1, D-2, D-3, D-4, and D-5. These positions were to be defended just long enough to force the enemy to stop and deploy for a major attack. The troops would then pull out for the next defensive line. At the D-5 line Wainwright would have to hold long enough to cover the withdrawal of the South Luzon Force under Brigadier General Albert M. Jones, which was to come north from the Lamon Bay area and then westward across the vital Calumpit bridges spanning the Pampanga River and then south into Bataan.

Had the Japanese pressed Wainwright hard and employed their air forces more skillfully, they might have turned the withdrawal into a rout. But General Homma was under orders to capture Manila. Japanese plans had made no provision for a retreat to Bataan; they had assumed that MacArthur's forces would fight their big battle to defend the capital.[55] As it was, through a combination of luck, speed, and the stubborn gallantry of many small units, Wainwright and Jones made good their escape into Bataan.

Yet, although the bravery of his Filipino and American troops and Japanese mistakes could somewhat improve the tactical situation, they could do little to alter the effects of MacArthur's ill-conceived scheme on the United States forces' logistical system. Under MacArthur's plan for defending all of Luzon, supplies and equipment had been moved to forward areas near the beaches instead of to Bataan as they would have been under the old Orange plans. Now these same supplies had to be hurriedly transferred to Bataan. Through heroic efforts, MacArthur's staff managed to move some of the supplies from the Manila Bay area across to Bataan and Corregidor, but much had to be abandoned when the city was evacuated on December 31.

In the forward areas, the situation was even worse. Supply troops and civilian workers, caught up by fear of the advancing Japanese, fled their posts. Railway workers deserted in large numbers. Drivers of the few trucks available sometimes made a headlong dash for Bataan—without freight. The important supply base at Fort Stotsenburg was, in the circumspect words of the official army historian, "evacuated long before the approach of enemy forces." Critics later charged that only a fraction of its supplies ever reached Bataan.[56]

The situation was further complicated by Filipino laws and regulations forbidding the movement of rice and other foods from one province to another. MacArthur and Philippine President Manuel Quezon insisted on enforcing these prohibitions. As a result, invaluable stocks of food were lost, including about 10 million tons of rice at the government depot at Cabanatuan.

By the end of the first week, the defenders of Bataan were already on half rations, about 2,000 calories a day, less than half the normal requirement for an active man. There was no fresh meat or fruit and only limited amounts of onions, cereals, and canned fruit. There was about enough rice to last twenty days. The Twenty-sixth Cavalry had to shoot and eat their horses. Philippine water buffaloes were hunted and slaughtered, although their meat was sometimes so tough as to be inedible.[57] Medical supplies, especially certain types of drugs, were in critically short supply. Most of the Filipino troops had worn out their shoes on the withdrawal to Bataan and were practically barefoot. They also lacked raincoats, blankets, mosquito netting, and even underwear.

The consequences of this shortage of supplies was soon evident everywhere on Bataan: malaria, scurvy, beriberi and dysentery quickly made their appearance. By early March the number of hospital admissions for malaria alone ran to about 500 a day.[58] "If we had had something in our bellies, some hope that we could expect help from the United States, things might have been a little more endurable," wrote Wainwright. "But our perpetual hunger, the steaming heat by day and night, the terrible malaria and the moans of the wounded were terribly hard on the men." [59]

On January 9 General MacArthur boarded a PT boat for his first and, so far as is known, only visit to the beleaguered defenders of Bataan. The main American line, called "the main battle position," stretched across the center of the peninsula from the village of Mabating, on Manila Bay, to the town of Mauban on the South China

Sea. The twenty-mile line was divided in two by a high mountain, Mount Natib, near the center of the line. The western part of the line, between Mount Natib and the South China Sea, was held by Wainwright's I Corps. It consisted of three Philippine divisions, the First, Thirty-first, and Ninety-first and the battered Twenty-sixth Cavalry, together with supporting artillery. The II Corps, under Major General George M. Parker, was made up of the Eleventh, Twenty-first, Forty-first, and Fifty-first Philippine Armies and a regiment of Philippine Scouts, the Fifty-seventh Infantry; these forces defended the eastern sector, from Mt. Natib to the bay. Eight miles behind the main battle position, a second or "rear battle position" was being hastily prepared along a line stretching across the peninsula between the towns of Bagac and Orion. Located here were the Philippine Division (minus the Fifty-seventh Infantry), the tanks, and more artillery. The southern tip of the peninsula, called "the service command area," held the supply and service troops.

MacArthur spent about ten hours inspecting the battle positions on Bataan and conferring with his commanders. He expressed concern about the fact that the American line did not extend to the heights of Mount Natib, but most of his commanders believed the jagged peaks and deep ravines of the extinct volcano would be impassable: they merely sent out patrols to cover the gap. Returning to Corregidor that evening, MacArthur assured President Quezon that "he could hold Bataan and Corregidor for several months; the morale of our forces was high, there was no reason for immediate worry." [60] At the time the general was thus reassuring President Quezon, Japanese troops had already launched an attack on Parker's Second Corps.

On January 2, the day his troops entered Manila, General Homma received word that Imperial General Headquarters had taken away his best division, the Forty-eighth, and ordered it to the Dutch East Indies. In its place Homma received the Sixty-fifth Brigade, an occupation force of overage, overweight veterans "absolutely unfit for combat duty." [61] General Homma was not greatly worried. He believed he was now engaged in nothing more than mopping-up operations against a beaten and disorganized enemy. After a brief stand, he expected the Americans and Filipinos to retreat to Marivelles near the tip of the Bataan peninsula, then pull out for Corregidor. He ordered General Nara Akira, commander of the Sixty-fifth Brigade, to advance down the coastal highway paralleling Manila and attack Parker's forces.[62]

Hindered by the difficult terrain, by a lack of reliable maps, and by devastating American artillery fire, the Sixty-fifth Brigade made little progress against Parker's defenses on the east side of the line. Stubborn defense and aggressive American counter attacks forced Nara to shift his forces west, probing for a weak spot in the American lines.

A poorly coordinated thrust by the 51st Division on the American's left flank gave him his opportunity. One regiment of the division advanced so rapidly that it pushed ahead of the units on its right and left, thereby creating a dangerous bulge in the American line. The Japanese attacked both sides of the bulge; the regiment gave way. Soon the whole 51st Division had disintegrated and Parker's corps was in danger of being outflanked. Repeated counter-attacks by the Philippine Division failed to restore the line.

On the other side of the peninsula, a Japanese battalion, crossing the supposedly impassable peaks of Mt. Natib between the American corps, emerged behind Wainwright's line and took up a blocking position on the only road connecting the I Corps with the southern peninsula. Repeated attacks by greatly superior American forces failed to dislodge the Japanese. Wainwright's troops were forced to fall back along the beach, abandoning most of their artillery. By this time, MacArthur's headquarters, realizing the seriousness of the situation, had ordered Parker to withdraw as well. By January 26 the American and Filipino defenders stood on their final line of defense, the Bagac-Orion line. Watching the withdrawal, an American officer noted that "the men had a blank stare in their eyes, and their faces, covered with beards, lacked any semblance of expression." [63]

In the midst of the battle, MacArthur had sent a message to his troops on Bataan which was later the subject of much bitterness and ridicule. The message read, in part:

> Help is on the way from the United States. Thousands of troops and hundreds of planes are being dispatched. The exact time of arrival of reinforcements is unknown as they will have to fight their way through . . . it is imperative our troops hold until these reinforcements arrive.
>
> No further retreat is possible. We have more troops on Bataan than the Japanese have thrown against us. Our supplies are ample. A determined defense will defeat the enemy's attack. [64]

This declaration has since been castigated as cruel and misleading. In a sense it was. Yet MacArthur had some basis for his optimism in the messages he was receiving from Washington. On December 28 a Navy Department communique announced that the navy was "following an intensive and well-planned campaign against Japanese forces which will result in positive assistance to the defense of the

Philippines." General Marshall wrote to MacArthur on January 4 that "Our great hope is that the rapid development of overwhelming air power will cut the Japanese communications south of Borneo and permit an assault in the southern Philippines. . . . Every day of time you gain is vital to the concentration of the overwhelming power necessary to our purpose." [65]

Yet the relief of the Philippines was not in fact being planned, for the very good reason that such an operation was impossible. As early as January 3, Army planners had advised Marshall that an expedition to relieve the Philippines would require at least 1,500 aircraft of various types, seven to nine battleships, five to seven carriers, fifty destroyers, and sixty submarines with the necessary auxiliaries. Even if such a massive effort could be mounted in time, it would "constitute an entirely unjustifiable diversion of forces from the principal theater—the Atlantic." [66]

General Marshall, Secretary Stimson and the president accepted the logic of this argument, but they could not bring themselves to accept its consequences. They continued to hope that somehow a way might be found to save the Philippines—or at least to stave off defeat. The thought that the United States, which through the years had held the Philippines on the assumption that it was protecting them, might now have to abandon them to the Japanese, and that thousands of American soldiers, including many friends and acquaintances of the men in the War Department, might be lost, was a hard one to bear.

Something might have been accomplished during the first few days of the war if a determined effort had been made to rush immediate reinforcements to the Philippines before the Japanese were firmly established. MacArthur urged that the navy convoy to him supply ships which had been diverted to Australia; he also called for a carrier raid on Japan. The navy, however, still reeling from the effects of Pearl Harbor, was not willing to risk its few remaining ships, especially the irreplaceable carriers, in any such risky venture. An advanced base was established in Australia to forward supplies and reinforcements to MacArthur, but getting them to the Philippines proved an almost impossible task.[67]

In desperation, the War Department decided to employ blockade runners to try to take in the much-needed supplies. " 'Use your funds without stint,' " Marshall instructed the American commander in Australia. " 'Colonel Chamberlin has a credit of ten million dollars of Chief of Staff's funds. . . . Arrange for advance payments, partial payments for unsuccessful efforts and large bonuses for actual delivery. . . . Organize groups of bold and resourceful men, dispatch them with funds by plane . . . to buy food and charter vessels for service. . . . Only indomitable determination and pertinacity will succeed and success must be ours.' " [68]

In January Marshall despatched General Patrick J. Hurley—a fiery Oklahoma politican and former secretary of war who was one of MacArthur's staunchest admirers—on a special mission to Australia to cut red tape and speed the delivery of supplies to MacArthur. But after a few weeks, even the indomitable Hurley had to admit that " 'we were out-shipped, out-planed, out-manned and out-gunned by the Japanese.' " [69]

A handful of blockade runners did succeed in breaking through to the southern Philippines, but only a small proportion of their cargo could be brought by fast interisland ships to Corregidor and Bataan. Submarines were more successful; they continued to deliver supplies to the Philippines up to the final weeks of the campaign, but there were only a few of them available and their cargo capacity was ridiculously small. The total of submarine deliveries equalled only enough food to provide one meal for two-thirds of the men on Bataan.[70]

Increasingly isolated on Corregidor, MacArthur and his staff grew progressively more bitter and resentful at Washington's seeming abandonment of the Philippines. Philippine President Quezon, already in poor health, was desperately worried and depressed by reports of Japanese atrocities in Manila; messages from Washington detailing plans to evacuate the Filipino leader in order to form a government in exile darkened his gloom still more. This mood of resentment and desperation formed the backdrop for one of the strangest episodes of the Pacific War: the confidential transfer of large sums of money to General MacArthur and certain members of his staff by the Filipino Government in February 1942.

On January 3, 1942, Quezon issued an executive order expressing the gratitude of the Filipino people to MacArthur and his staff for " 'their magnificent defense' " of the islands and offering " 'recompense and reward for their achievements.' " [71] First brought to light by Carol Petillo in 1979, the executive order was accompanied by the award, in mid-February, of $500,000 to MacArthur, $75,000 to Sutherland, $45,000 to his Deputy Chief of Staff Richard J. Marshall, and $20,000 to his aide Sidney L. Huff.[72]

Petillo explains Quezon's strange action as an attempt to bind MacArthur still closer to the Philippines; the Philippine president believed that the general would use his influence to ensure the relief—

or at least the liberation—of the islands and to ease the sufferings of the Filipino people. During the struggle for Bataan, notes Petillo, "much needed food was often left in local provinces, further diminishing the scant USAFFE stores in Bataan. In addition, bombing schedules were often revised on the advice of the Commonwealth President." MacArthur's actions in these cases have usually been explained in terms of his devotion to the Filipino people and their leader. Petillo suggests that "perhaps MacArthur's personal ties and devotion were reinforced by the half-million dollars given him by Quezon." [73]

From Quezon's point of view, the award of money was a natural and necessary action to reinforce MacArthur's—and American—support of the Philippines in their hour of trial. Seen within the context of the Filipino concept of reciprocal personal obligations and loyalties, his action was unexceptionable, even laudable. MacArthur's motives for accepting the gift, however, must remain a matter of conjecture. Even more puzzling is the fact that Roosevelt, Stimson, and Marshall were apparently aware of the transaction, and allowed it to go forward. Perhaps, as Petillo suggests, they agreed with Marshall's deputy chief of war plans, Dwight D. Eisenhower, a former assistant to MacArthur, that the latter was "losing his nerve" and had to be kept fighting by any means.[74]

On Bataan, the Japanese as well as the Americans were nearing the point of exhaustion. The Sixty-fifth Brigade had lost about 1,500 casualties out of a total of 6,500 officers and men. Yet Homma persisted in his effort to crack the defenses of Bataan. As MacArthur's troops took up their new positions on the Bagac-Orion line, Homma launched a number of small amphibious assaults against "the points," narrow fingers of land jutting out from the southwest tip of the Bataan peninsula far behind the main defense line. Here the Japanese were met by a heterogeneous force of service troops, grounded airmen, sailors, and Philippine constabulary, most of whom had had no infantry training. The sailors impressed the Japanese as "a new type of suicide squad" who "would attempt to draw Japanese fire by sitting down, talking loudly and lighting cigarettes," but they nevertheless managed to contain the invaders long enough for a regiment of Philippine Scouts to arrive and push the Japanese back into the sea.[75]

While the "Battle of the Points" was raging, a Japanese regiment was able to slip behind the American lines. The Japanese then split into two groups and formed two "pockets" behind Wainwright's corps. It took almost three weeks of hard fighting to wipe out these pockets and a Japanese relief column which was attempting to reach them.

By early February, Homma's Fourteenth Army was thoroughly exhausted, suffering from malaria, beriberi, and dysentery; it had been greatly weakened by the heavy losses it suffered in the battles of the last month. The Japanese had no choice but to call a halt and send for reinforcements. MacArthur's forces might have counter-attacked with advantage, but they too were in poor shape. So a lull settled over the thick jungles of Bataan while Homma waited for reinforcements and the Americans and Filipinos waited for MacArthur to "reach downward and pull the rabbit out of the hat." [76]

At this point, MacArthur might justifiably have been relieved. As the distinguished Australian historian Gavin Long observes, "MacArthur's leadership in the Philippines had fallen short of what might have been expected from a soldier of such wide experience." [77] Like Kimmel and Short, but with less excuse, he had allowed his air force to be crippled by surprise attacks on the first day of the war. His ill-conceived and grandiose plan to defend the entire archipelago had resulted in confusion and near disaster; it helped to produce the acute supply shortage which was sapping the strength of the Bataan forces. His grandiloquent pronouncements, together with his strange refusal to visit the front, hurt morale and shook the confidence of his men.

While some troops in Bataan maintained their faith in MacArthur, others contemptuously sang of "Dugout Doug" in a devastating ballad which proclaimed that

Dugout Doug's not timid, he's just cautious, not afraid;
He's protecting carefully the stars that Franklin made.
Four-star generals are as rare as good food on Bataan;
And his troops go starving on.[78]

Yet MacArthur was not relieved. Indeed, he had become a hero—even a legend—in the United States. The press published breathless accounts of the exploits of "The Lion of Luzon." The respected columnist, Walter Lippmann, wrote of his "vast and profound conceptions." Honorary degrees were showered upon him. Babies were named for him. The National Father's Day Committee named him "Number One Father of 1942." In March 1942 the President announced the award of the Congressional Medal of Honor to MacArthur for, among other achievements, "the heroic conduct of defensive and offensive operations on the Bataan Peninsula." [79]

MacArthur's great stature in the United States was in part due
to his own highly efficient public relations organization. Most of
the war news from the Philippines which the American public read
came from MacArthur's communiques and press releases. Of 142
communiques released by his headquarters between December and
March 109 mentioned only one individual: MacArthur. "When an
action was described, it was 'MacArthur's right flanks on Bataan'
or 'MacArthur's men.' The communiques . . . omitted the names
of combat units, commanders and individuals who had performed
exceptional exploits." [80]

Yet it was not simply self-promotion that accounted for MacArthur's fame. The American public was starved for good news. As
Eisenhower shrewdly observed, "The public has built itself a hero
out of its own imagination." [81] With Allied forces in defeat and disar-
ray almost everywhere, Roosevelt, Stimson, and Marshall seized on
the MacArthur myth and used it unsparingly to prop up sagging
morale. It was in fact General Marshall and the president who devised
the plan to award MacArthur the Medal of Honor.

Obviously, a general of MacArthur s stature could not be left to
perish on Luzon. Since the beginning of February, Marshall and his
staff had been discussing ways and means of extricating MacArthur
from his doomed command in the Philippines. At first, MacArthur
refused to consider suggestions that he be evacuated. Finally, on
February 22, Marshall sent a direct order to MacArthur from the
president, instructing the general to leave the islands to take command
of a new American force in Australia. The general was allowed to
choose the best "psychological moment" for his departure.[82]

Eisenhower, who had worked closely with MacArthur in the Philippines during the late 1930s, had serious doubts about the plan. After
being told by the President's military aide, Brigadier General Edwin
"Pa" Watson, that the hero of Bataan was "worth five army corps,"
Eisenhower confided to his diary that he was "dubious about the
thing. I cannot help believing that we are disturbed by editorials
and reacting to 'public opinion' rather than military logic. . . .
[MacArthur] is doing a good job where he is. Bataan is made to
order for him. It's in the public eye; it has made him a public hero;
it has all the essentials of drama. . . . If brought out, public opinion
will force him into a position where his love of the limelight may
ruin him." [83]

In the Philippines, the exhausted Americans and Filipinos also
took a more critical view of MacArthur's action. "Who had the right

to say that 20,000 Americans should be sentenced without their consent and for no fault of their own to an enterprise that would involve
for them endless suffering, cruel handicap, death or a hopeless future
. . . ?" wrote General William E. Brougher, who commanded the
Eleventh Division on Bataan. " 'A foul trick of deception has been
played on a large group of Americans by a commander in chief
and small staff who are now eating steak and eggs in Australia. God
damn them!' " [84]

NOTES

1. John Morton Blum, *From the Morganthau Diaries: Years of War 1941–1945* (Boston: Houghton Mifflin Company, 1967), p. 1.
2. Pogue, *Ordeal and Hope,* p. 435.
3. *Pearl Harbor Hearings,* Part 39, pp. 20–21.
4. Pogue, *Ordeal and Hope,* pp. 211–12.
5. *Pearl Harbor Hearings,* Part 12, p. 261.
6. The most thorough discussion of this so-called "bomb plot message" is in Prange,
   At Dawn We Slept, pp. 248–53.
7. Ibid., p. 253.
8. *Pearl Harbor Hearings,* Part 9, pp. 4516–529, 4534, 4548; Part 3, p. 1114.
9. Pogue, *Ordeal and Hope,* pp. 227–29.
10. Ibid., p. 230.
11. Charles C. Tansill, *Back Door to War: The Roosevelt Foreign Policy, 1933–41* (Chi-
    cago: Henry Regnery, 1952); Charles A. Beard, *President Roosevelt and the Coming
    of The War 1941* (New Haven: Yale University Press, 1948); Robert A. Theo-
    bald, *The Final Secret of Pearl Harbor* (New York: Devin-Adair, 1954); Harry
    Elmer Barnes, *Perpetual War for Perpetual Peace* (New York, 1953).
12. *Pearl Harbor Hearings,* Part 14, pp. 1404–06, 1409.
13. Prange, *At Dawn We Slept,* p. 736.
14. Wohlstetter, *Pearl Harbor: Warning and Decision,* pp. 387–88.
15. John Toland, *Infamy: Pearl Harbor and Its Aftermath* (Garden City, N.J.: Double-
    day and Company, 1982) pp. 317–19 and passim.
16. Ibid., pp. 276–81.
17. *Foreign Relations of the United States 1941,* Vol. 4, p. 713.
18. Toland, *Infamy,* pp. 281–82.
19. Ibid., p. 319.
20. David Kahn, "Did FDR Invite the Pearl Harbor Attack?" *New York Review
    of Books,* May 27, 1982, pp. 34–37.
21. Barnes, "Pearl Harbor After a Quarter Century," quoted in Prange, *At Dawn
    We Slept,* p. 841.
22. Prange, *At Dawn We Slept,* pp. 227–30, 373–76 and passim.

23. Sir Llewellyn Woodward, *British Foreign Policy in the Second World War* (London: HMSO, 1962) pp. 187–88.

24. *Pearl Harbor Hearings*, Part II, pp. 5163–66.

25. Roberta Wohlstetter was a pioneer in this field. For representative recent studies, see Steve Chan, "The Intelligence of Stupidity: Understanding Failures in Strategic Warning," *American Political Science Review* 73, (March 1979); Richard K. Betts, ed., *Surprise and Defense* (Washington: The Brookings Institution, 1981); Ammon Sella, "Barbarosa: Surprise Attack and Communication," *Journal of Contemporary History*, July 13, 1978; and Avi Shlaim, "Failures in National Intelligence Estimates: The Case of the Yom Kippur War," *World Politics* 28 (April 1976).

26. Richard Betts, "Surprise Despite Warning: Why Sudden Attacks Succeed," *Political Science Quarterly*, pp. 553, 557.

27. Richard R. Lingeman, *Don't You Know There's a War On?: The American Home Front 1941–1945* (New York: G. P. Putnam's Sons, 1970), p. 27; the barking-dog story is recounted in Prange, *At Dawn We Slept*, p. 569.

28. Pogue, *Ordeal and Hope*, p. 391.

29. W. J. Holmes, *Double-Edged Secrets* (Annapolis: Naval Institute Press, 1979), p. 95.

30. Grace P. Hayes, The War Against Japan, vol. 1, Pearl Harbor to Trident," pp. 46–48; Morison, *The Rising Sun*, p. 219.

31. Unless otherwise noted, this account of the struggle for Wake is based on R. D. Heinl, Jr., *The Defense of Wake* (Washington: Historical Section, USMC, 1947). A fine popular account is Duane Schultz, *Wake Island: The Heroic Gallant Fight* (New York: St. Martin's Press, 1978).

32. Morison, *The Rising Sun*, p. 232.

33. Major General Omar T. Pfeiffer, Oral History Transcript, p. 177, Marine Corps Historical Center.

34. John B. Lundstrom, *The First South Pacific Campaign: Pacific Fleet Strategy, December 1941–June 1942* (Annapolis: Naval Institute Press, 1976) p. 17.

35. Pfeiffer, Oral History Transcript, p. 178.

36. Schultz, *Wake Island*, p. 144.

37. Morison, *The Rising Sun*, pp. 253–54; Heinl, *Defense of Wake*, p. 39.

38. Morison, *The Rising Sun*, pp. 254–55.

39. Morton, *Fall of the Philippines*, p. 81; D. Clayton James, *The Years of MacArthur, vol. 2: 1941–1945* (Boston: Houghton Mifflin Company, 1975) p. 7.

40. Morton, *Fall of the Philippines*, pp. 80–82.

41. Morton, ibid., pp. 85–87; James, *The Years of MacArthur*, pp. 4–5; Allison Ind, *Bataan: The Judgment Seat* (New York: Macmillan, 1944), pp. 96–101; Shimada Koichi, "Japanese Naval Air Operations in the Philippine Invasion," *Naval Institute Proceedings*, Vol. 81 (January 1955).

42. In addition to the sources cited above, see Craven and Cate, *Army Air Forces in World War II*, Vol. 1, pp. 200–209; Walter Edmonds, "What Happened at Clark Field" *The Atlantic*, July 1951, pp. 20–33; and Lewis H. Brereton, *The Brereton Diaries* (New York: William Morrow and Company, 1946) pp. 36–45.

43. Morton, *Fall of the Philippines*, pp. 82–83.

44. Ibid., pp. 84–86.

45. Ibid., p. 67.

46. Quoted in James, *Years of MacArthur*, p. 12.

47. Morton, *Fall of the Philippines*, p. 62. The Japanese had almost twice as many planes on Formosa but many of their Army planes lacked the range to reach Manila.

48. Shimada Koichi, "Japanese Naval Air Operations," pp. 4–9.

49. Morton, *Fall of the Philippines*, pp. 128–237; W. E. Chandler, "26th Cavalry (PS) Battles to Glory," Part 1, *Armored Cavalry Journal*, March-April 1947, pp. 13–15.

50. Chandler, "The 26th Cavalry (PS) Battles to Glory," Part 2, *Armored Cavalry Journal*, May-June 1947, pp. 9–10; Jonathan M. Wainwright, *General Wainwright's Story* (Garden City, N.Y.: Doubleday and Company, 1946) pp. 38–39.

51. Wainwright, *General Wainwright's Story*, pp. 35–36; Ernest B. Miller, *Bataan Uncensored* (Long Prairie, Minn.: Hart, 1949).

52. Colonel James V. Collier, quoted in Morton, *Fall of the Philippines*, p. 163.

53. Morton, "The Decision to Withdraw to Bataan," in Kent Roberts Greenfield, ed., *Command Decisions* (Washington, D.C.: GPO, 1959), p. 162.

54. Wainwright, *General Wainwright's Story*, p. 37.

55. Morton, *Fall of the Philippines*, pp. 51–59.

56. Miller, *Bataan Uncensored*, p. 1 and passim; Morton, *Fall of the Philippines*, p. 179.

57. Morton, *Fall of the Philippines*, pp. 256–57; Wainwright, *General Wainwright's Story*, p. 53.

58. Morton, *Fall of the Philippines*, pp. 375–79.

59. Wainwright, *General Wainwright's Story*, p. 53.

60. Manuel Quezon, *The Good Fight* (New York: Appleton Century, 1946) p. 53.

61. "14th Army Operations" Japanese Monograph No. 6, Vol. 1, p. 19; copy in U.S. Army Center of Military History.

62. Toland interview no. 1 with General Akira Nara, Toland Interview Collection.

63. Morton, *Fall of the Philippines*, pp. 261–63, 293–94.

64. Ltr. USAFFE to all Unit Commanders, 15 January 1942, sub: "Msg from Gen. MacArthur." A copy of this message is in Louis Morton files, U.S. Army Center of Military History.

65. James, *Years of MacArthur*, pp. 50–51.

66. Ibid., pp. 65–68; Baldwin, *Battles Lost and Won* (New York: Harper and Row, 1966) pp. 130–31; Toland, *Rising Sun*, p. 300.

67. Morton, *Strategy and Command*, pp. 187–91; Hayes, "War Against Japan," Part 1, pp. 40–45; James, *Years of MacArthur*, pp. 22–23. MacArthur's proposal for a carrier raid made sense strategically. The Doolittle raid on Tokyo in April did have a marked psychological effect on the Japanese. But in December the navy had neither the confidence nor the carrier operations experience to carry out such a raid.

68. Quoted in Morton, *Fall of the Philippines,* pp. 391–92.

69. Quoted in Pogue, *Ordeal and Hope,* pp. 244–46.

70. Morton, *Fall of the Philippines,* p. 400.

71. Quoted in Carol Morris Petillo, *Douglas MacArthur: The Philippine Years* (Bloomington, Ind.: Indiana University Press, 1981), p. 205.

72. Carol Morris Petillo, "Douglas MacArthur and Manuel Quezon: A Note on an Imperial Bond," *Pacific Historical Review* 48 (February 1979), pp. 107–17.

73. Petillo, *Douglas MacArthur: The Philippine Years,* pp. 207–9.

74. Ibid., p. 211.

75. Morison, *The Rising Sun,* pp. 199–201; Morton, *Fall of the Philippines,* pp. 301–26.

76. James, *Years of MacArthur,* p. 68.

77. Gavin Long, *MacArthur as Military Commander* (London: B. T. Batsford Ltd., 1969), p. 81.

78. James, *Years of MacArthur,* pp. 64–67.

79. Ibid., pp. 131–34.

80. Ibid., pp. 89–90.

81. Robert H. Ferrell, ed., *The Eisenhower Diaries* (New York: W. W. Norton and Company, 1981), p. 51.

82. Pogue, *Ordeal and Hope,* pp. 247–51.

83. Ferrell, ed., *The Eisenhower Diaries,* p. 49.

84. Quoted in James, *Years of MacArthur,* pp. 127–28.

SIX

The Short, Unhappy Life of
ABDACOM

On December 12th Prime Minister Winston Churchill, together with the British chiefs of staff, embarked for the United States on the battleship *Duke of York*. Everywhere in East Asia, British possessions were under heavy attack. Yet Churchill felt only exaltation. The invincible coalition against the Axis, which he had labored so long to build, was now a reality. "No American will think it wrong of me if I proclaim"—he later wrote—"that to have the United States at our side was to me the greatest joy. . . . Hitler's fate was sealed. Mussolini's fate was sealed. As for the Japanese, they would be ground to powder. All the rest was merely the proper application of overwhelming force." [1] The embattled British had only one fear—that American leaders, under pressure from Japanese attacks in the Far East, might wish to alter the strategy agreed upon before the war and concentrate first on the war in the Pacific.

They were quickly reassured. In Churchill's meetings and discussions with Roosevelt and his advisers at the end of December—known as the ARCADIA Conference—the president and the American chiefs of staff reaffirmed their commitment to the "Germany First" strategy. At ARCADIA the two powers reaffirmed that " 'the Atlantic and European area was considered to be the decisive theater" and that "only the minimum of force necessary for the safeguarding of vital interests in other theaters should be diverted from operations against Germany.' " [2] In the months to come, the "minimum of force" proved far greater and the "vital interests" more extensive than at first believed, but the basic principle remained.

During the conference the Americans were impressed by the efficiency and close coordination of the British high command. The British chiefs of staff met with the prime minister at least once a day, and their activities were fully coordinated with other agencies of the British war government. The British Chiefs of Staff Committee—consisting of the heads of the services and the prime minister's chief staff officer—was responsible, under the immediate supervision of the prime minister, for the higher direction of the war. Their tight, smoothly functioning organization assured unity of command.

The Americans had no such effective machinery of high command. The chief of staff of the army and the chief of naval operations were the heads of two autonomous services; they did not constitute a corporate body like the Chiefs of Staff Committee. The only organization for interservice cooperation, the Joint Board, was not intended to provide close integration of the services or unity of command; it was merely regarded as a means of achieving "sufficient coordination to allow the services to continue to operate autonomously in all major essentials." [3]

Even before the ARCADIA Conference this system was beginning to show signs of strain. In the immediate aftermath of Pearl Harbor, both services had rushed to speed reinforcements to Hawaii without any attempt at coordination; they had tripped over each other like school children trying to squeeze out the door of a classroom. The army quickly had two ships loaded with supplies, troops, and aircraft, but complained that the navy refused to escort them to Hawaii. The navy retorted that the army knew nothing about convoys and refused to spare additional escorts for only two ships. The navy urged the army to send all its uncommitted antiaircraft units to Pearl Harbor; the army replied that the West Coast and the Panama Canal would also have to be protected; and so the interservice fumbling and bumbling continued. [4]

The ARCADIA Conference made a change in the old system even more imperative than before. At formal meetings the Americans found themselves wholly outclassed by the well-oiled British staff machinery. The British had come to the conference with an entire agenda of proposals ready. Their chiefs were always well informed and well prepared, while the Americans often found themselves in the dark about what commitments or arrangements the president might have made in his talks with Churchill. The American military leaders suspected, not without reason, that the British regarded the U.S. simply as a gigantic pool of weapons and manpower "for campaigns tailored to suit [their] interests." They were worried and annoyed by Roosevelt's habit of making off-the-cuff proposals and agreements without consulting or informing them.[5]

The Allies had agreed at ARCADIA to establish a unified British-American high command located in Washington. It was to be called the Combined Chiefs of Staff, composed of the British Chiefs of Staff Committee or their Washington representatives and the "U.S. Chiefs of Staff." The latter group included General Arnold, head of the Army Air Corps, and Admiral Ernest J. King, Commander of the U.S. Fleet, in addition to Marshall and Stark. The Americans rapidly began to evolve an interservice high command system of their own called the Joint Chiefs of Staff in order to match the elaborate but smooth-running system of committees and secretariats which supported the British chiefs.

The membership of the Joint Chiefs of Staff, which remained unchanged after March 1942, consisted of General Marshall, General Arnold, and Admiral King. Admiral Stark had departed to become commander of U.S. naval forces in Europe. His place was taken by Admiral William D. Leahy, a former chief of naval operations; Leahy served as chairman of the Joint Chiefs and as the president's personal representative to the service chiefs. His appointment retained the balance of two navy and two army officers as Joint Chiefs and gave the chiefs a direct line of communication to the president. In addition, it forestalled the danger that Roosevelt might succumb to the rising popular demand that "the Hero of the Philippines," General MacArthur, be brought to Washington as overall supreme military commander.[6]

Marshall and King were usually the dominant influences in JCS discussions. These two did most of the talking, while Admiral Leahy guided the discussions and occasionally quashed lines of argument he disagreed with. General Arnold normally said little except in discussion of matters related to aviation. One of King's top assistants recalled that King and Arnold did not get along very well and that the army chief of staff often disagreed with the navy chief. Yet heated arguments were usually avoided. "King knew he had to get along. That was the compelling influence on all of them. They knew they had to get along." [7]

The JCS was supported by a network of permanent and ad hoc interservice committees. The most important of these was the Joint

Staff Planners, composed of the senior planning officers of the army and navy or their deputies; this group had broad responsibilities for policy, strategy, and operations. Much of the actual planning work was performed by two other committees: the Joint Strategic Survey Committee, which was responsible for long-range strategy, and the Joint War Plans Committee, which dealt with immediate operational planning.

At the same time both the services underwent important internal reorganization. The War Department was transformed from a loose confederation of agencies and bureaus into a tightly organized body capable of both extensive planning and rapid execution of war measures. In place of the sixty-odd organizations which reported directly to the chief of staff before the war, Marshall created three field commands outside the War Department: Army Ground Forces, Army Air Forces, and Army Service Forces. Army Ground Forces, under General Leslie J. McNair, was responsible for the administration, organization, and training of combat troops. Army Air Forces, under Arnold, had similar responsibilities for aviation personnel; it also controlled the development and procurement of aviation equipment. Army Service Forces represented a gigantic new organization under General Brehon B. Somervell; it handled supply, procurement, communications, and a myriad of "housekeeping" items.[8]

To plan and direct operations, Marshall gutted the old General Staff sections to create instead a unified Operations Division (OPD). A kind of General Staff within the General Staff, the OPD had responsibility for the planning, control, and coordination of all operations. It was, as one historian has observed, the army's "Washington Command Post."[9]

The navy's organization was necessarily different from the army's since, with the departure of Admiral Stark, Admiral King had become both chief of naval operations (CNO) and commander in chief of the U.S. Fleet. Summoned to Washington to assume the post of commander in chief of the U.S. Fleet after Admiral Kimmel's relief, King was a vigorous, aggressive leader whose masterful performance as head of the Atlantic Fleet during 1941 had won him the respect and admiration of Knox and Roosevelt. An old friend and associate of Admiral Stark, he had—even before the latter's departure—assumed the leading role in shaping the navy's approach to grand strategy.[10] Arrogant, aloof and suspicious, a "sundowner," or strict disciplinarian, King inspired respect in many but affection in few.[11] His admirers professed to see in him a brilliant strategist. To be sure, in sheer intellect he far overmatched his JCS colleagues, but his outlook was so strongly shaped by his intense and narrow devotion to navy interests that he was seldom able to take a detached view of any strategic problem.

As commander in chief U.S. Fleet (COMINCH) as well as chief of naval operations, King had, in effect, two staffs. The Office of Chief of Naval Operations, headed by a vice-chief of naval operations, was responsible for training, shore establishments, personnel, logistics, and general housekeeping, while the U.S. Fleet Staff, headed by the deputy commander in chief, U.S. Fleet, planned and directed operations. The nerve centers of the Fleet Staff were the Operations Division and the Plans Division. The Plans Division, initially headed by Rear Admiral Richmond Kelly Turner and later by Admiral Charles E. Cooke, handled both operational and long-range planning, while the Operations Division exercised general control over all fleet task forces and naval air elements.

Whatever his failings in interpersonal relations, King was a superb administrator and a determined foe of bureaucratization. His Fleet Staff was kept purposely small and officers were constantly rotated in from sea duty, then rotated out again in a year or so—before they could acquire what King balefully referred to as "the Washington mentality." [12]

• •

While the most far-reaching actions of the ARCADIA Conference reaffirmed the Germany-first strategy and established the machinery for a binational high command, the most immediate problem was to counter Japanese attacks in Southeast Asia and the Pacific.

The advancing Japanese confronted heterogeneous units of the Dutch, British, Australian, and American armed forces scattered over several thousand miles, from Burma to Western New Guinea. At the urging of General Marshall, the conferees at ARCADIA agreed to establish a single unified command for the area, to be called ABDACOM for American, British, Dutch, and Australian Command. The ABDACOM area took in Burma, Malaya, the Dutch East Indies, Western New Guinea, Northwest Australia and, nominally, the Philippines. Within a few months, all of these territories—except Australia—fell to the Japanese.

Neither the Americans nor the British were particularly anxious to nominate one of their nationals for the honor of commanding ABDACOM. The Americans believed a British commander would serve to reassure London that due attention would be paid to the defense of British possessions in Southeast Asia, while the British sourly observed that the Americans wished to have a foreigner to blame for the inevitable disasters in that theater.[13]

General Marshall was well aware that the chances for a successful defense of the ABDACOM area were slim, but he regarded its creation as an important step in establishing the principle of unity of command in all theaters. The eventual choice to command ABDACOM was General Sir Archibald Wavell, a man who had already conducted more than his share of desperate battles in near hopeless circumstances. Wavell was probably not informed that he was being sacrificed on the altar of the principle, "unity of command"; but that he was going to be sacrificed was readily apparent. When, on January 10, 1942, he arrived at Batavia on the island of Java, the days of European domination in Southeast Asia were fast drawing to a close.

The Japanese master plan, despite its complexity, despite its dangerous dispersal of ships and armies over thousands of miles, despite its demands on the Empire's slender resources, was succeeding beyond even the most optimistic hopes of Imperial General Headquarters. In the first days of the war, the British battleship *Prince of Wales* and the battle cruiser *Repulse,* which had been sent out to the Far East with great fanfare shortly before Pearl Harbor, had been sunk by Japanese aircraft off the coast of Malaya while vainly searching for an enemy convoy. "It means that from Africa eastwards to America through the Indian Ocean and the Pacific, we have lost control of the sea," wrote the chief of the Imperial General Staff, General Sir Alan Brooke, upon hearing the news.[14]

Hong Kong fell on Christmas Day after a spirited but hopeless defense by its garrison of British regulars, Canadian militia, and civilian volunteers. British Borneo was occupied a few days later. The Japanese controlled the Celebes Sea between the East Indies and the Philippines; they dominated the Makassar Strait leading south to Java as well. While the attacks were under way against Hong Kong, the Philippines and Borneo, larger Japanese forces moved by land from Indochina through Siam's Kra Isthmus into Malaya. Similar numbers were transported by sea across the Gulf of Siam to land on the northern coast of Malaya and just north of the Siamese border.

The Japanese army had never fought in tropical jungle terrain like Malaya before. Its battle experience had all been on the vastly different terrain of China and Manchuria. Yet the Japanese soldier proved himself a remarkable jungle fighter. Combining reckless frontal attacks with skillful flanking movements from the sea and through supposedly impassable jungle, the Japanese pushed the British down the Malay peninsula to within a hundred miles of Singapore. The British and Commonwealth troops actually outnumbered the Japanese nearly two to one, but they had no tanks and only a handful of outdated aircraft.

Things were proceeding so well for the Japanese that Imperial General Headquarters, at Field Marshal Terauchi's recommendation, actually advanced the schedule for the conquest of the Dutch East Indies. This would deprive the Allies of time to regroup and reinforce their troops; it would also make possible an earlier redeployment of Japanese troops to Manchuria, where the threat of a Soviet attack in the spring was still considered very real.[15]

Despite these ominous developments, Allied commanders were rather optimistic about their chances of stopping the Japanese. Wavell expressed confidence that the British could hold at least Singapore as well as Burma. In the Dutch East Indies Vice Admiral Conrad E. H. Helfrich, who commanded the Dutch naval forces, was optimistic about what the Allied cruisers and destroyers could do against Japanese invasion convoys. Admiral Thomas C. Hart, who had been designated commander of ABDACOM naval forces, did not share this general optimism.

So far the war had been mostly a bad dream for Hart. His Asiatic Fleet had been bombed out of Manila Bay in the first days of the war. Hart himself had had to come south in a submarine when MacArthur abruptly abandoned Manila at the end of December.[16] The Asiatic Fleet was small and ageing. Not much was expected of it—but its achievements so far had fallen short of even that. MacArthur and the War Department complained bitterly about what they saw as the navy's lack of support for MacArthur's forces. " 'Hart [in a conversation with General MacArthur] took the usual defeatist position that the Philippines were doomed,' " recorded Secretary Stimson in his diary.[17]

Hart was far from a defeatist, but he had few tools to do the immense job expected of him. The most potent element of the Asiatic Fleet were twenty-nine submarines, many of the latest design. Like the Air Corps' B-17s, the submarines had been expected to make life very difficult for a Japanese invasion force approaching the Philippines.[18] In fact, they achieved even less than the bombers. None of the eight separate landings made by the Japanese in the Philippines was impeded or even threatened by the American submarines. During December, Asiatic Fleet submarines made a total of forty-five separate attacks on enemy shipping, expending a total of ninety-six torpedoes to sink three freighters. The submarine *Sargo* made six separate attacks on Japanese convoys leaving Cam Ranh Bay in Indochina, expending thirteen torpedoes—without a single success.[19]

There were many reasons for the disappointing performance of the subs. Despite prior warnings, the force was poorly deployed to resist invasion. Captains and crews were untrained and inexperienced at long-range extended patrols, and the tactics employed were excessively cautious and conservative. Commanders were advised to be sparing of torpedoes and to avoid risking their boats unnecessarily.[20] " 'Don't try to go out there and win the Congressional Medal of Honor in one day' " a division commander instructed his skippers. " 'The submarines are all we have left. Your crews are more valuable than anything else. Bring them back.' " [21]

A few commanders proved themselves only too willing to follow these instructions. Men who had been perfectly satisfactory as peacetime officers sometimes lacked the combination of nerve, judgement, and calculated recklessness needed in a successful submarine commander.[22] The most important factor in the failure of the submarine effort, however, was the fact that their primary weapon, the torpedo, was defective. The Mark-14 torpedoes carried by American submarines at the beginning of the war tended to run deeper than the depth set for them, causing the torpedoes to run under the target. Even when the Mark-14 did score a hit, it often failed to explode because of defects in the detonating mechanism.[23] These defects remained undetected for many months. It was to be many months before American submarines became a factor of decisive importance in the Pacific War.

With the submarine failure fresh in mind, and having had firsthand exposure to the power of the Japanese war machine, Hart could not share the general optimism. He pointed out that the Japanese would have control of the air, so that Allied surface ships would have to operate under constant threat of air attack and under the eyes of Japanese reconnaissance planes. As for the submarine forces, "They had not yet broken up any of the enemy's amphibious expeditions." [24] The weeks ahead were to demonstrate the full significance of Hart's warnings.

ABDACOM was a strange, hybrid command. Hart—an American—commanded the naval forces, while a Dutch officer, Lieutenant

General Hein ter Poorten, was in charge of ground forces and Britain's Air Chief Marshall Sir Richard E. C. Pierce commanded the air contingents. Vice Admiral Conrad E. H. Helfrich, commander in chief of the Royal Netherlands East Indian Navy and minister of the navy, was not included in this arrangement, yet Hart was obligated to work with him in regard to matters concerning the Dutch navy. Helfrich resented Hart and believed that a Dutch commander would be far more qualified to direct the naval defense of the Indies. The relationship between the two men was seldom an easy one.[25]

With the exception of the Americans, who had no territory to protect, the ABDACOM commanders spent a good deal more time worrying about the security of their own colonies than about a coordinated defense of the area. The Americans and Australians were mainly concerned about the southwest Pacific and the approaches to Australia. Wavell appeared to Hart and other non-British officers to be preoccupied with the defense of Malaya. He apparently wished to employ the naval forces in protecting convoys to Singapore; the formation of an offensive striking force was a low priority for him. His frequent absence from ABDACOM headquarters to inspect defenses at Rangoon and Singapore reinforced this impression.[26]

Many of ABDACOM's ships were still on convoy duty on January 21, when the Japanese moved to occupy the rich oil fields of Borneo near the town of Balikpapan. The only ships available to oppose them—two American light cruisers, *Marblehead* and *Boise,* with four destroyers under Rear Admiral W. A. Glassford—were at Kupang Bay on the island of Timor, southeast of Borneo.

When he received word of the Japanese landings at Balikpapan, Glassford immediately sailed for Borneo. *Marblehead* was having engine trouble and *Boise* struck a rock, which sent her limping back to Java for repairs. But the four destroyers, hardy veterans of World War I, steamed on alone into Makassar Strait and the first American naval battle of the war.

Two hours after midnight on the morning of January 24, sailors in the blacked-out destroyers could see the shapes of the Japanese convoy at anchor, silhouetted against the fires of Balikpapan's burning oil fields. Still undetected, the destroyers roared in at twenty-seven knots and launched torpedoes. The transport *Sumanoura Maru* exploded in a roar that shook the harbor.

Ignoring the enemy escorts—which were dashing wildly about searching for submarines—the destroyers doubled back and launched more torpedoes; the transports *Tatsukami Maru* and *Kuretake Maru* and a large patrol boat all fell victim to the attackers. Still unscathed but without more torpedoes, the destroyers made another pass, firing their five-inch guns at targets of opportunity, then retired south toward Java. Four Japanese transports and a patrol boat had been sunk. Many more would probably have gone to the bottom except for the inexperience of the American destroyer men and the same type of defective torpedoes which plagued the submarines.[27]

The battle off Balikpapan was a gratifying success, but it failed to halt the Japanese advance or even slow it down. Subsequent efforts by the combined Dutch, American, and British naval forces were less successful. An attempt to strike at Japanese troops invading the southern Celebes was frustrated by heavy air attacks, which knocked the *Marblehead* out of the campaign and deprived the *Houston* of her after eight-inch gun turret. In Badung Strait off the Island of Bali, a night raid against a handful of Japanese ships by three Dutch cruisers and a dozen Dutch and American destroyers was fended off by just two Japanese destroyers. The long months of training by the Japanese navy in night fighting now began to pay off. The Japanese held the attackers at bay and even sank a Dutch destroyer. "As a result of this battle," notes a Japanese participant with classic understatement, "the Japanese Navy gained great confidence in its ability to fight night engagements."[28]

The Japanese continued their inexorable advance toward Java. On February 15 Singapore, considered by many an impregnable fortress, capitulated. On the nineteenth the Japanese completed their occupation of Bali. On the same day carrier planes from Admiral Nagumo's Pearl Harbor force staged a devastating attack on the port of Darwin in northwest Australia, sinking close to a dozen ships and wrecking the town. This severed the main link between Java and Australia.

By now, Wavell was advising the Combined Chiefs that further protection of the Netherlands East Indies was probably hopeless. The Dutch, of course, heatedly disagreed. They insisted that Java must be defended to the last. They were also becoming very uneasy about a foreigner in charge of their naval defenses and blamed Hart for their meager successes at sea. The real problem was Admiral K.W.F.M. Doorman, who held the top sea command. Doorman had missed several good opportunities—such as Badung Strait—because of excessive caution and conservatism. But he was Dutch, and could not very well be relieved.[29]

So Doorman stayed and Admiral Hart was recalled to the U.S. "for reasons of health"; he was succeeded by Admiral Helfrich. Even though Hart could be sacrificed to Dutch sensibilities, there was no denying the logic of Wavell's arguments about the futility of defending the East Indies. On February 25 the Combined Chiefs of Staff agreed that Wavell should close out his headquarters and turn over command of ABDA—from which Burma had already been withdrawn—to the Dutch.[30] Most of the British and American air units left with Wavell, but the ships of the Asiatic Fleet remained behind for the final defense of Java.

On the morning of February 24, American patrol planes and submarines sighted large Japanese convoys in Karimata Channel, between Borneo and Sumatra near the island of Bawean in the Java Sea. With the combined striking force of two Dutch, one American, and two British cruisers and about a dozen destroyers, Admiral Doorman sortied from Surabaya to intercept the convoys. The crews of Doorman's ships were exhausted from two nights of fruitless searching for the enemy, and *Houston's* after turret was still inoperative. In the late afternoon of February 27, Doorman's force sighted the Japanese: two heavy and two light cruisers with sixteen destroyers, covering a large convoy. For an hour the two fleets exchanged salvos at long range. The Japanese enjoyed the advantage of spotter planes to direct their gunfire, but their shooting was nevertheless poor. Finally, an armor-piercing shell from one of the Japanese cruisers hit the British cruiser *Exeter,* causing her to loose speed and fall off to the left. This threw the whole Allied battle line into confusion and made them prime targets for the long-range torpedoes of the Japanese. The Dutch destroyer *Kortenaer* was hit and sunk in this way, but skillful screening by other destroyers kept the Japanese from finishing off the *Exeter;* she limped back to Surabaya escorted by a Dutch destroyer.[31]

Admiral Doorman now reformed his forces and ordered his remaining destroyers, four old American World War I types, to counterattack with torpedoes. The Americans launched their torpedoes at 10,000 yards and did no harm to the enemy, but they did manage to knock out the destroyer *Asagumo* with gunfire.[32] Then, having expended all their torpedoes, the four destroyers also headed east to Surabaya.

In the growing darkness Admiral Doorman, with his four remaining cruisers, attempted to sneak by the screening Japanese warships and strike the convoy. Japanese aircraft kept him under observation with calcium flares, however, and at eleven he was again intercepted by the Japanese cruisers and destroyers. After an initial exchange of gunfire, the Japanese launched torpedoes. Once again the painstaking Japanese attention to night training and their superiority in torpedo warfare paid great dividends. At a range of over 8,000 yards, the Allied flagship *De Ruyter* and a second Dutch cruiser, the *Java*, were fatally damaged by torpedoes. The remaining cruisers, the *Houston* and HMS *Perth*, managed to break off the action and get through to Batavia. In the battle of the Java Sea, the Allies had lost two cruisers and four destroyers: they had delayed the Japanese invasion of Java by exactly one day.

After this, the fate of the Netherlands Indies was a foregone conclusion. Most of the handful of remaining Allied warships were sunk while attempting to escape to the Indian Ocean. Ironically, two of these ships, the Australian cruiser *Perth* and the American cruiser *Houston,* while attempting to make their escape, ran into a portion of the Japanese invasion force which Doorman had vainly sought a few days before. In a wild night battle against hopeless odds, the two cruisers managed to sink or damage more than half a dozen Japanese ships before going down with colors still flying. By the time the *Houston* sank, her crew had exhausted her ammunition and were firing illumination rounds at the enemy.[33] Japanese forces had landed in strength on Java by March 1. Batavia fell the next day, and one week later the remaining Dutch defenders surrendered. The short unhappy life of ABDACOM was at an end.

Now only the American forces in the Philippines still disputed the Japanese advance in the southwest Pacific and their fighting days were clearly numbered. On April 3 General Homma politely suggested that the defenders of Bataan and Corregidor follow the sensible example of "the defenders of Hong Kong, Singapore, and Netherlands East Indies, in the acceptance of an honorable defeat." [34] The Americans did not deign to reply.

When he left Corregidor for Australia, General MacArthur had intended to continue in direct command of the forces in the Philippines from his base in Australia. General Wainwright was to command the forces on Luzon, while units on Mindanao and in the Visayan Islands in the southern Philippines would be under separate commands. All would report to MacArthur through an advanced echelon on Corregidor.[35] It may be doubted whether this cumbersome arrangement could ever have worked in practice. In the event, it was never tried. The president and the War Department, ignorant of MacArthur's intentions, designated General Wainwright as the new commander of all U.S. forces in the Philippines.

In late March Wainwright informed MacArthur that " 'rations for troops on Bataan have been reduced to approximately 1,000 calories

which, according to the surgeon, is barely sufficient to sustain life
without physical activity.' " [36] At the same time, General Homma
had been heavily reinforced with replacements for his badly depleted
units by an entire new division, the 14th, and elements of another,
the 21st. In addition, strong artillery and air elements, now available
after the campaigns against Singapore and Hong Kong, were rushed
to the Philippines.[37]

When the Japanese opened a new offensive on April 3, the result
was never in doubt. The Filipino and American defenders, wracked
by disease and weakened by hunger, simply collapsed. General Parker's Second Corps, holding the east side of the Bagac-Orion line,
was quickly routed. The I Corps began a retreat to protect its open
flank. In the midst of the chaos and disintegration came another
ringing message from MacArthur ordering the Luzon forces to carry
out a general counterattack toward the town of Olongapo on the
east coast of the Bataan peninsula. The supplies seized at this base,
MacArthur observed, would help rectify the food shortage.[38]

At the time that MacArthur was directing this dramatic reposte,
approximately 80 percent of the front line troops had malaria, 75
percent suffered from dysentery, and about 35 percent had beriberi.[39]
Brigadier General Funk, chief of staff to Major General Edward P.
King, commander of the Luzon, forces, came to Corregidor to explain
the situation. The Luzon Force, he told Wainwright, might soon
have to surrender. Wainwright read him MacArthur's order: the
Luzon Force would attack. " 'General,' " Funk replied wearily, " 'you
know of course what the situation is over there. You know what
the outcome will be.' " " 'I do,' " Wainwright replied. " 'I understand
the situation. God help you all over there.' " [40]

That night, April 8, King conferred by telephone with his corps
commanders, who confirmed that the end was near. After carefully
reviewing the tactical situation with his staff, General King concluded
that his force could no longer even hope to delay the enemy appreci-
ably, let alone stop his advance. At midnight, General King announced that he had decided to surrender. " 'I have not communi-
cated with General Wainwright,' " he told his staff, " 'because I do
not want him to be compelled to assume any part of the responsibility.' " [41]

Now only Corregidor and its satellite islands remained between
the Japanese and final mastery of Luzon. As long as the fortified
islands remained in American hands, the Japanese would be denied
access to Manila Bay and the use of its excellent harbor, although

by this time Japanese conquests had progressed so far that this was only a minor inconvenience.

The defenses of Corregidor and the other islands were formidable, but they were designed primarily as a defense against attack by sea. Most of the ammunition was of the armor-piercing type—intended to penetrate the heavy armor of warships. When fired against land targets, these shells would often bury themselves deep in the sand. Many of the heavy gun batteries were mounted in open pits or behind concrete barbettes; they were vulnerable, however, to high-angle fire or attacks from the air. Corregidor's headquarters, hospital, communications center, and storage areas were located underground in the island's famous Malinta Tunnel. They were safe from bombardment but the tunnel itself—crowded with technicians, casualties, refugees, and the remnants of numerous headquarters and service organizations—was hot, humid, and badly ventilated. The island's water supply was insufficient to support the number of people crowded onto it; the power plant, also inadequate, was exposed to enemy fire.

The Japanese wasted little time before moving against Corregidor. With the high ground at the southern tip of Bataan under their control, the attackers assembled almost a hundred artillery pieces on the high cliffs and began an intense shelling of Corregidor.[42] The bombardment continued for over three weeks. Shelling usually began at dawn and continued, with a lull during the early afternoon, until about midnight. Japanese air raids added to the din and destruction. Most of the guns on Corregidor, the fire control equipment, and the communications were gradually destroyed. Parts of the island were literally blown into the sea. A group of Filipinos was buried alive when an overhanging cliff collapsed and sealed the entrance to the cave in which they had taken shelter.[43]

All the while General Homma, increasingly distraught and nervous under intense pressure from Imperial General Headquarters, waited impatiently for the final assault on Corregidor. Finally, on May 6, the Japanese were ready. They attacked near the narrow tail of the island on the north shore. The two assault battalions involved were late in starting, so their landing boats were soon lost in the darkness. Caught by an unexpectedly strong tide, they made their landings "on the wrong beach and in the wrong order."[44]

The Fourth Marine Regiment, brought to Manila from China by Admiral Hart in the last days of peace, was waiting on shore. In the weeks since the fall of Bataan the regiment had been fleshed out with several hundred sailors, Philippine Scouts, artillerymen, and army service troops. Most of these reinforcements had no infantry training—but they were learning fast. Approaching the shore in bright moonlight, the Japanese Second Battalion came under murderous fire from the surviving American artillery and smaller beach defense guns. At point-blank range, the Japanese boats were blown to bits. Less than half of the attackers lived long enough to reach land.

The First Battalion also suffered heavily. All the same, it managed to establish a beachhead, then advance west to capture a ridge in the center of the narrow neck of the island, formerly occupied by "Battery Denver" of the Corregidor artillery. Repeated counterattacks against the Denver position failed to dislodge the invaders; around six in the morning, the defenders pulled back to a line further west.

Meanwhile the Japanese consolidated their position and pounded the Americans with artillery. By morning they had brought some light artillery and a few tanks ashore; these caused havoc among the defenders. By ten-thirty the Americans had pulled back to within a few dozen yards from the Malinta Tunnel. A new Japanese attack was expected in a few hours. All reserves had been commited; most of the artillery was out of action; the garrison's water supply was sufficient only for a few more days; and ammunition was almost exhausted.

The Japanese were low on ammunition, too, and short of boats—but the Americans could not know this. At ten o'clock General Wainwright sent a last message to Washington: " 'Please say to the nation that my troops and I have accomplished all that is humanly possible and that we have upheld the best traditions of the United States and its Army. . . . With profound regret and with continued pride in my gallant troops I go to meet the Japanese commander.' " [45] "Corregidor surrendered last night," Eisenhower glumly recorded in his diary. "Poor Wainwright! He did the fighting in the Philippine Islands. Another got such glory as the public could find in the operation. . . . MacArthur's tirades to which TJ and I so often listened in Manila would now sound as silly to the public as they did to us. But he's a hero! Yah." [46]

After the war, armchair strategists and Roosevelt-haters would fume over "the sacrifice of the Philippines" and their gallant defenders by Washington pencil pushers. Yet the Philippines had been doomed for at least twenty years by America's inability to project naval power into the western Pacific. This would have been the case even without the Pearl Harbor debacle. After Pearl Harbor, the fleet could not even make a credible feint. MacArthur and his apologists always insisted that "our Navy . . . might well have cut through the Japanese blockade. . . . A serious naval effort might well have saved the Philippines and halted the Japanese drive to the south and east." [47] In their naïveté about naval affairs, MacArthur and his associates totalled up the surviving paper strength of the navy, including ships in the Atlantic and under repair, and concluded it was sufficient to relieve the Philippines. Yet what would have been required was not simply a fleet to "cut its way through," but a massive and continuous convoy effort through hundreds of miles of enemy-held waters in the teeth of superior air power. Such an effort would have meant the postponement of all operations in other theaters and would probably have failed in any case.

While the Philippines were doomed in any event, the responsibility for the specific form and substance of the American defeat must be laid at the door of MacArthur. If it is true, as his biographer insists, that "his presence was the primary reason why the resistance . . . was successful for so long," [48] it is equally true that his presence in the Philippines gave rise to the exaggerated hopes, the ridiculous overestimate of the Philippine army's capabilities, and the muddled planning. The troops on Luzon would have been defeated in any case, but without MacArthur they might have been defeated without being racked by disease and tortured by slow starvation.

If MacArthur must bear the primary responsibility for the debacle, it is nonetheless true that neither the navy nor the air force contributed much—beyond further disasters—at the time. The heavy bomber was to prove a weapon of great power later in the war but, as Hanson Baldwin observes, in 1941 the Americans had yet to discover "that air power to be effective against surface power had to be used in massive numbers and with great skill." [49] The same could be said of the navy's use of submarines.

MacArthur's apologists later claimed that the prolonged defense of the Philippines "disrupted the Japanese timetable" and delayed their operations against Australia, New Guinea, and the Solomons.[50] In retrospect, this appears to be nonsense: the Japanese had no immediate plans for an invasion of Australia; their operations against New Guinea and the Solomons, not to mention the ABDACOM area, were not delayed in the least by the Philippine campaign.[51]

The importance of the Philippine battle was more psychological and moral than military. Only in the Philippines had the Japanese drive been stalled. Only there, in the battle of the Points, had their amphibious attacks been pushed back into the sea. As a former Japanese general staff officer explained to John Toland, "Tokyo was concerned that [the successful resistance on Bataan was] giving the world the impression Japan was bogged down in the Philippines." [52]

Gavin Long sourly observed that " 'it cost a far stronger Japanese army as many days of actual combat to take Malaya and Singapore as it cost Homma to take Bataan and Corregidor.' " [53] In the war years, no one made such abstract calculations. The psychological and political repercussions of the two campaigns were quite different. The Malayan debacle left the British shocked and bitter; her colonial and commonwealth partners felt demoralized and betrayed. The defense of the Philippines, on the other hand, gave an enormous lift to American morale and will to win. The "battling bastards of Bataan," "the Rock," MacArthur's dramatic escape, the heroic doctors and nurses of Corregidor—all became part of American folklore. President Roosevelt was exaggerating only a little when he asserted in one of his last messages to Wainwright that " 'you and your devoted followers have become the living symbol of our war aims and the guarantee of victory.' " [54]

NOTES

1. Winston S. Churchill, *The Second World War*, Vol. 3: *The Grand Alliance* (New York: Bantam Books, 1962), p. 511.

2. Grace P. Hayes, "Pearl Harbor to Trident," p. 53.

3. Davis, *Origin of the Joint and Combined Chiefs of Staff*, pp. 95–96; 28–29.

4. Hayes, "Pearl Harbor to Trident," p. 35.

5. Pogue, *Ordeal and Hope*, p. 264–65.

6. Robert W. Love Jr., "Ernest Joseph King," in Love, ed., *Chiefs of Naval Operations*, p. 147.

7. "Reminiscences of Admiral Richard L. Conolly," Naval Historical Foundation, Oral History Collection, pp. 375–76.

8. James E. Hewes, *From Root to McNamara: Army Organization and Administration 1900–1963* (Washington, D.C.: Center of Military History, 1975) pp. 67–70; Pogue, *Ordeal and Hope*, pp. 41–47.

9. Ray S. Cline, *Washington Command Post: The Operations Division*, (Washington, D.C.: Office of the Chief of Military History, 1951).

10. Robert W. Love, Jr., "Ernest Joseph King," in Love, ed., *Chiefs of Naval Operations*, pp. 140–44; a recent biography of King is Thomas B. Buell, *Master of Seapower* (Boston: Little, Brown and Company, 1980); King's own recollections may be found in Ernest J. King and Walter M. Whitehill, *Fleet Admiral King: A Naval Record* (New York: W. W. Norton and Company, 1952).

11. E. B. Potter, *Nimitz* (Annapolis: Naval Institute Press, 1976), p. 32.

12. Ernest J. King and Walter M. Whitehill, *Fleet Admiral King: A Naval Record* (New York: W. W. Norton and Company, 1952), pp. 357–59.

13. On the establishment of ABDACOM, see Pogue, *Ordeal and Hope,* pp. 275–82; Morton, *Strategy and Command,* pp. 160–64; and Arthur Bryant, *The Turn of the Tide, 1939–1943* (Garden City, N.Y.: Doubleday, 1957), pp. 235–37.

14. Bryant, *Turn of the Tide,* p. 226.

15. *History of Imperial General Headquarters, Army Section,* Revised Edition, Japanese Monograph No. 45, Headquarters U.S. Army Japan, copy in U.S. Army Center of Military History.

16. Leutze, *A Different Kind of Victory,* pp. 245–49.

17. Cited in ibid., p. 240.

18. Morison, *The Rising Sun,* p. 153.

19. Clay Blair, Jr., *Silent Victory: The U.S. Submarine War Against Japan* (New York: J. B. Lippincott Company, 1975), p. 132.

20. Ibid., pp. 132–34; Thomas C. Hart, "Narrative of Events, Asiatic Fleet, Leading Up to War and From 3 December 1941 to 15 February 1942," copy in Naval Historical Center, p. 68.

21. Blair, *Silent Victory,* p. 108.

22. Ibid., p. 176.

23. Ibid., pp. 249–54 and passim. Few historians would be prepared to accept Blair's conclusion that "intelligently employed, with a workable torpedo, submarines might have entirely prevented the Japanese invasion of the Philippines and the Netherlands East Indies." German submarines with effective equipment, good coordination, and excellent, experienced skippers were unable to prevent the Allied invasions of North Africa, Italy, and Normandy. Yet there is no doubt that they might well have exerted an important influence on the campaign; see Blair, pp. xvii–xviii.

24. Hart, "Narrative of Events, Asiatic Fleet," p. 54.

25. Leutze, *A Different Kind of Victory,* pp. 256–57, 267–69.

26. Hart, "Narrative of Events," pp. 61–62.

27. Morison, *The Rising Sun,* pp. 284–91; "Naval Operations in the Invasion of the Netherlands East Indies," Japanese Monograph No. 101, Historical Section, G-2 Far East Command, copy in C.M.H., pp. 78–80; Paul S. Dull, *A Battle History of the Imperial Japanese Navy* (Annapolis: U.S. Naval Institute, 1978), pp. 67–68.

28. "Naval Operations in the Invasion of the Netherlands East Indies," p. 91.

29. Morison, *The Rising Sun,* pp. 305–306, 321–26; Hart, "Narrative," p. 75; Hayes, "Pearl Harbor to Trident," pp. 94–95; Leutze, *A Different Kind of Victory,* pp. 278–82.

30. Hayes, "Pearl Harbor to Trident," pp. 111–17.

31. "Naval Operations in the Invasion of the Netherlands East Indies," p. 38; Dull, *The Imperial Japanese Navy,* pp. 79–86.

32. Van Oosten believes that the *Asagumo*'s hits actually came from the British cruiser *Exeter* and the Dutch destroyer *Witt de With,* and that they were received prior to the torpedo attack by the American destroyers: *Battle of the Java Sea,* p. 51.

33. Van Oosten, *Battle of the Java Sea*, pp. 59–60; Morison, *Rising Sun*, pp. 367–69.

34. Morton, *Strategy and Command*, p. 265.

35. Ibid., pp. 195–96.

36. John Jacob Beck, *MacArthur and Wainwright: The Sacrifice of the Philippines* (Albuquerque: University of New Mexico Press, 1974), p. 180.

37. Morton, *Fall of the Philippines*, pp. 413–14.

38. Ibid., p. 450.

39. Beck, *MacArthur and Wainwright*, p. 188.

40. Ibid; Wainwright, *General Wainwright's Story*, p. 79.

41. Morton, *Fall of the Philippines*, pp. 457–58.

42. Ibid., pp. 536–41; Hanson W. Baldwin, "The Rock: The Fall of Corregidor," in *Battles Lost and Won: Great Campaigns of World War II* (New York: Harper & Row, 1966), pp. 139–43; Baldwin puts the number of Japanese guns at perhaps 200: see p. 141.

43. Morton, *Fall of the Philippines*, p. 533.

44. Ibid., p. 555.

45. Wainwright, *General Wainwright's Story*, pp. 122–23.

46. Ferrell, *The Eisenhower Diaries*, p. 54; "T. J." is Captain T. J. Davis, who served as MacArthur's aide and as administrative officer for MacArthur's training mission to the Philippines in the late 1930s.

47. Douglas MacArthur, *Reminiscences*, p. 121.

48. James, *Years of MacArthur*, p. 153.

49. Baldwin, "The Rock," p. 153.

50. Charles A. Willoughby and John Chamberlain, *MacArthur 1941–1945* (New York: McGraw-Hill, 1954) pp. 2–3.

51. Morton, *Fall of the Philippines*, p. 584; James, *Years of MacArthur*, p. 151–52.

52. John Toland interview with Major Kumao Imoto, Toland Interview Collection.

53. Cited in James, *Years of MacArthur*, p. 152.

54. Wainwright, *General Wainwright's Story*, p. 82.

SEVEN

"The Vital Flank"

With the heart of the southwest Pacific and southeast Asia now in Japanese hands, Washington strategists surveyed the wreckage and turned their attention to safeguarding what President Roosevelt called the two "vital flanks" in the battle with Japan: India, China, and Burma on the west, and Australia on the east. India and Southeast Asia would continue to be a British responsibility, while the Pacific would be primarily an American concern. Australia and New Zealand possessed considerable military and naval forces, but these were mainly occupied in the local defense of those countries. The Americans alone possessed the resources to mount a wide-ranging counteroffensive against the Japanese advance.[1]

On March 9th, as the last Dutch forces on Java capitulated, Roosevelt proposed in a personal message to Churchill that the United States and Britain divide the world into three general areas. "The whole of the operational responsibility for the Pacific area will rest on the United States," with an American officer under the direction of the Joint Chiefs of Staff in overall command. The British would have similar authority and duties in a "middle area" stretching from Singapore across the Indian Ocean to the Persian Gulf, the Red Sea, and the Mediterranean. The European and Atlantic segment would be a combined U.S.–British responsibility under the immediate direction of the Combined Chiefs of Staff. The JCS would also control and coordinate overall strategy and allocate resources for the other two areas.[2]

The British readily agreed to this arrangement, but the Australian and New Zealand governments were unhappy about a plan which left them with no voice in overall Pacific strategy. " 'I cannot believe,' " wrote the Australian foreign minister, " 'that if this situation has been fully appreciated by the British Chiefs of Staff, they will be content to leave the matter in the hands of the U.S. Chiefs of Staff to deal with as they think fit.' "[3]

That, however, was precisely what the Joint Chiefs of Staff intended. The Pacific War was going to be an exclusive project of the army and navy, with as little interference by outsiders as possible. Coordination of strategy with the Dutch, Australians, Chinese, and other allies would take forever and might hamstring operations.[4] Yet, while the U.S. did in fact gain undisputed freedom to shape grand strategy for the Pacific War, this did not extend to control over the allocation of such scarce Allied resources as planes, merchant shipping, and amphibious craft. This remained a lively subject of contention between the British and Americans for some time to come.

To mollify the smaller powers, a "Pacific War Council," with representatives from Australia, Britain, Canada, China, the Netherlands, New Zealand, and—later—the Free French, was set up in Washington. The council was a consultative body which "would discuss broad questions relating to the war effort." The Joint Chiefs of Staff agreed that the Pacific War Council was a useful device for allowing the member nations "to let off steam, but not such as would in any way affect the United States in its military decisions."[5] Appropriately enough, the council held its first meeting on April Fools' Day, 1942.

So certain were the Joint Chiefs of Staff of American preeminence in the Pacific that command arrangements for that region had actually been established before the British gave their formal approval to the worldwide allocation of spheres of responsibility. The Pacific had traditionally been a special preserve of the navy; the army might have agreed to keep it that way had the strategy of concentrating on the war with Germany been immediately carried out. Yet despite agreement in principle on "Germany first," the critical situation in the Pacific and the need to safeguard Australia—one of the two "vital flanks"—led initially to the allocation of large forces to the Pacific.

To guard the Australian flank and its routes of communication nearly 80,000 troops sailed for the southwest Pacific between January and the end of March, 1942. This was nearly four times the number departing for Europe during the same period. A total of 290,000 Army troops were scheduled for deployment to the Pacific by the end of 1942.[6] Along with them went hundreds of Army Air Forces warplanes for the defense of Australia, New Zealand, and the islands of the South Pacific along the "lifeline" to those countries. Thus the Pacific was far from a minor theater for the army. In addition, the leaders of Australia expected—and had been promised—that their country would form the nucleus for a major Allied command. While they were willing enough to entrust an American with the leadership of such a command, it was doubtful that they would accept a naval officer with headquarters in distant Hawaii as supreme commander.

Above all, there was the presence in the Pacific of General Douglas MacArthur. MacArthur was by this time a hero of towering stature, a man who had to be employed in some task commensurate with his supposed greatness.[7] Indeed, Republican politicians and publicists were already calling for his appointment as supreme commander of the entire army and navy.[8] The navy did not share this general admiration for MacArthur and, in any case, would never have entrusted the fleet to a general unschooled in the mysteries of seapower. Add to this the fact that MacArthur was much senior to any admiral who might be appointed, and the matter was settled. Against all common sense, against the dictates of military doctrine, against the essence of Roosevelt's message to Churchill, the Pacific was divided into two theaters.

MacArthur was appointed commander in chief of the Southwest Pacific Area: Australia, the Philippines, the Solomons, New Guinea, the Bismarck Archipelago, Borneo, and all of the Netherlands Indies except the large island of Sumatra. The navy was given the remainder of the Pacific Ocean except for the coastal waters of Central and South America. This vast navy domain was designated Pacific Ocean Areas; it was entrusted to Admiral Chester W. Nimitz, who also retained his position as commander of the Pacific Fleet. The Pacific Ocean Areas theater was divided into three subordinate commands: the North, Central, and South Pacific Areas. Admiral Nimitz commanded the North and Central Pacific Areas directly, while Vice Admiral Robert L. Ghormley was appointed commander of the South Pacific Area.

MacArthur and Nimitz each received his orders from the head of his respective service, acting for the Joint Chiefs of Staff, who had the final say on matters of strategy. This meant that overall direction of operations in the Pacific was in the hands of a committee, and that below the level of that committee, there was no single authority to make decisions for the Pacific theater.

The traditional elements of careerism and doctrinal differences within the armed forces had combined to produce a monstrosity. As Louis Morton observes in the Army's official history, the command arrangements in the Pacific "led to duplication of effort and keen competition for the limited supplies of ships, landing craft and airplanes, and it placed on the Joint Chiefs the heavy burden of decision in many matters that could well have been resolved by lesser officials." [9]

Even more disastrously, future operations in the Pacific—requiring close coordination of all arms, aircraft, amphibious forces, army and navy—were placed in the straitjacket of control by old-fashioned means. In the case of Nimitz's Pacific Theater this meant a traditional navy-style staff. MacArthur's Southwest Pacific Theater command was structured along only slightly less traditional army lines. As early as March 1942, Captain Richmond Kelly Turner, one of the navy's chief planners, was warning that MacArthur would probably " 'use his naval forces and air forces in the wrong manner, since he has shown clear unfamiliarity with proper naval and air functions.' " [10] The accusation by one service that another service was misusing its peculiar weapons system or its forces was to be a characteristic of the Pacific War—a characteristic produced at least in part by the peculiar command arrangements created by the Joint Chiefs in 1942.

Although the directives to both MacArthur and Nimitz included instructions to prepare for offensive operations, it appeared that the two commanders would be fully occupied simply trying to stop the Japanese. Only Nimitz, who still had the remnants of the Pacific Fleet—which was being reinforced by naval forces from the Atlantic—was in a position to take even limited offensive action against the Japanese.

Admiral Chester W. Nimitz had the reputation of being able to do much with little, a quality he would need in his new assignment. As commander in chief of the Pacific Fleet (CINCPACFLT, or more usually CINCPAC) as well as commander of the Pacific Ocean Areas, he had not only theater responsibility (like MacArthur) but also operational control of almost all naval forces in the Pacific, except for a small force allocated to MacArthur. There were other contrasts between the two theater commanders, as well. While MacArthur was a forceful and colorful personality, a man of dramatic gestures and rhetoric, Nimitz was soft-spoken and relaxed, a team player, a leader by example rather than exhortation. "The admiral was frequently the despair of his public relations men," wrote correspondent Robert Sherrod; "it simply was not in him to make sweeping statements or to give out colorful interviews." [11] An officer recalled that during tense moments, while awaiting word of the outcome of important operations or battles, Nimitz would joke with his staff "while he calmly practised on his pistol range or tossed ringers with horseshoes just outside his office." By contrast, at such moments MacArthur "would as a rule sit stonily in his chair, chewing on the stem of a corncob pipe." [12]

There were contrasts as well in the two men's relations with Washington. According to one of King's biographers, Thomas Buell, the Chief of Naval Operations "never entirely trusted Nimitz's judgement," believing him too susceptible to bad advice and too ready to compromise with the Army. Throughout the war, King held frequent personal meetings with Nimitz, usually in San Francisco or Hawaii. By contrast, Marshall saw army theater commanders in Europe infrequently, and MacArthur only once. King's numerous conferences with Nimitz may indeed "indicate the extent of King's anxiety to keep Nimitz under his thumb"; they may also have reflected King's special interest in directing Pacific strategy.[13]

Nimitz and MacArthur differed radically in style of command. Whereas Nimitz came to Pearl Harbor virtually alone, retaining many of the members of Kimmel's staff, MacArthur brought with him from the Philippines a group of loyal and deferential—critics said sycophantic—subordinates who served as his key staff officers and assistants throughout the war. In the course of his campaigns MacArthur later developed other close personal relationships, with General Robert Eichelberger, Admiral Thomas Kinkaid, General George C. Kenney—even to some extent with Admiral Halsey—but the ascendency of "the Bataan gang" was never challenged.

Most commanders in time of war endeavor to obtain operational commands for their most capable staff officers. This was the practice followed by King and Nimitz and by General Marshall, who chose his chief planner, Eisenhower, to command the North African invasion in 1942. Yet MacArthur did not adhere to this custom. He kept his top staff officers at headquarters, normally located far to the rear; their contacts with the fighting fronts were usually infrequent.[14]

Nimitz arrived at Pearl Harbor in a navy flying boat on Christmas morning, 1941. As a whaleboat carried him from his plane across the harbor to the dock, the admiral could see a number of small craft moving about the harbor searching for the bodies of sailors. Corpses were still rising to the surface from the sunken battleships.[15]

Disregarding Admiral King's idea that he ought to "rid Pearl Harbor of pessimists and defeatists," Nimitz brought to Hawaii only a flag secretary; he asked most of the old Pacific Fleet staff to serve under him.[16] Some of the most able officers of the navy were saved from professional oblivion in this way; many of them, like Captain Charles "Soc" MacMorris and Commander Edwin T. Layton, were to play a distinguished part in the Pacific War.

The Pearl Harbor disaster obliged the Navy to shelve its ambitious plans—embodied in Rainbow 5—for attacks on the Japanese-controlled Marshall and Caroline Islands and the large Japanese base at Truk. Instead, the remnants of the Pacific Fleet were ordered to guard Hawaii and its approaches, including Midway and Johnston Islands, and to keep open the line of communications through the island chains of the South Pacific to Australia. To protect this line, the Joint Chiefs of Staff were sending reinforcements to Samoa and other islands along the Oahu-Samoa-Fiji route.

Army strategists, headed by Brigadier General Dwight Eisenhower, chief of the War Plans Division, were worried. They feared that the large numbers of troops and planes being sent to garrison the islands on the way to Australia and New Zealand could develop into a dangerous drain on army resources, resources which could be better employed in Europe. " 'The Navy wants to take all the islands in the Pacific—have them held by Army troops to become bases for Army pursuit and bombers,' " warned Eisenhower; " 'Then! The Navy will have a safe place to sail its vessels.' " [17] Army planners would have been even more disturbed had they known that Admiral King was already looking toward an early start for an offensive in the South Pacific.[18]

The Pacific Fleet before Pearl Harbor had been organized into a Battle Force and Scouting Force (much like the British Fleet at the Battle of Jutland). The fleet was now reorganized in task forces; each such task force had a large, fast aircraft carrier as its center. There were four task forces, each of which had an accompanying screen of cruisers and destroyers. Scouting was left to aircraft and submarines. There were also about a half-dozen operational battleships, three of which had been transferred from the Atlantic. But the battleships were a good ten knots slower than the carriers, and so could not operate with them. Nimitz had insufficient cruisers, destroyers, and aircraft to screen the battleships; he also had too few tankers to fuel them. So they were relegated to patrol and escort duties between California and Hawaii. Thus the battle fleet, which had been the center of navy thinking and planning for over thirty years, quietly disappeared. Its place was taken by a new weapon: the carrier task force.

In 1941 and 1942 the carrier was a new and untried weapon, a weapon of expediency.[19] Up to that time, aircraft carriers had been employed principally to attack the enemy's battleships or to protect one's own. Neither the Japanese nor the Americans quite realized that naval warfare was entering a new phase, one in which the sea-borne aircraft of the two navies would contest for supremacy, with all other forces in a supporting role.

At the outset of the war, the Japanese carrier forces were probably the finest naval weapon in the world. Their Zero fighter was superior to anything in the Allied air forces, their carrier-based torpedo bombers were effective and deadly, and all were manned by expert veterans, many of whom had fought in China. When the war began, the average Japanese pilot had accumulated about 700 hours of flight time before completing training—more than twice that of American carrier pilots. The American carriers were somewhat larger than their Japanese counterparts and carried more planes, but American naval aircraft were generally inferior to Japanese. The standard navy fighter, the Grumman Wildcat, was no match for the Zero in a one-to-one fight; the Douglas Devastator torpedo plane was so slow and unmaneuverable as to be "utterly useless in fast carrier battles." [20]

"It was a terrific blow to us, all our pilots particularly, to find that the Japanese Zero was a better airplane than anything we had," recalled Admiral Arleigh Burke.[21] A handful of navy aviators led by Lieutenant Commander James Thach had perfected a defensive fighter tactic called the "Thach weave" to meet the challenge of the Zero. The new tactic helped to nullify some of the Zero's superior performance, but required considerable experience and practice to carry out.[22]

Of the carrier planes with which the navy began the war, only the rugged Douglas Dauntless dive-bomber was to prove an effective weapon. Dive-bombing, in which the attacking plane released its bombs at the end of a steep, high-speed dive—a technique pioneered by the Americans—was to account for most of the damage inflicted on Japanese ships during the early months of the war.

American flyers were less experienced than their Japanese opponents, but the U.S. Navy rotated experienced pilots between combat and training duties, thus providing a permanent nucleus of veteran instructors. The Japanese kept their best pilots flying combat until they were annihilated. Late in starting and lacking experienced instructors, the Japanese wartime program for replacing its combat pilots never really accomplished its goals.

For protection against attacking aircraft, Japanese carriers tended to rely heavily on their own excellent fighters. The Americans put somewhat more stress on maneuver. For this reason, they favored operating their carriers in separate task forces where maneuverability would be better.[24] No one was very sure in early 1942 what carriers ought to do. When Task Forces 16 and 17 departed for the Battle of Midway at the end of May 1942, "each operated under its own cruising instructions, which were not necessarily the same." [25] More importantly, most of the senior naval commanders at the time of Pearl Harbor knew little about carriers or aviation. Admirals like Frank Jack Fletcher and Wilson E. Brown, who were to command many of the carrier operations in the early months of the war, had almost no previous experience in this type of warfare.

●　●

Despite heavy responsibilities and slim resources, neither King nor Nimitz intended to carry on a passive defense. With King's active encouragement, Nimitz began to plan almost at once for carrier raids against the Japanese-held Gilbert and Marshall islands as a device to take pressure off the Allies in ABDA and forestall further advances in the Pacific. To send carriers against heavily defended land bases was, in 1942, still considered too risky unless surprise could be achieved as at Pearl Harbor. So Nimitz found himself opposed by many of the senior officers at Pearl Harbor, including most of the air officers. At this point Vice Admiral William F. Halsey, who commanded one of the carrier task forces and was the senior carrier admiral, intervened to support Nimitz: indeed, he offered to lead the attack.

At the end of January 1942, after escorting reinforcements to Samoa, Admiral Halsey's Task Force 8, built around the carrier *Enterprise,* raided Japanese bases at Kwajalein, Wotje, and Taroa in the northern Marshall Islands. At the same time, Task Force 17, under Rear Admiral Frank Jack Fletcher, in the carrier *Yorktown,* struck targets in the southern Marshalls. The raids did little damage and had no effect on the progress of the Japanese offensive, but they served to raise morale and gave the carrier air groups valuable practice.

On February 24 Halsey's forces, now renamed Task Force 16, were back again, this time with a raid on Wake Island. Another force, under Vice Admiral Wilson E. Brown in the carrier *Lexington*, was sent far to the south to attack Rabaul, on the island of New Britain northeast of New Guinea, which the Japanese had recently captured and were converting into a major base.

When Brown's Task Force 11 was still 500 miles from Rabaul, he was spotted by Japanese patrol planes. In the ensuing air battle, Japanese bombers—attacking at long range without fighter escort— were almost wiped out by the *Lexington's* fighters, which sustained only light losses. Brown temporarily retired, sending word to Pearl that it would be wise to have an additional carrier join him for the attack against Rabaul. Accordingly, Admiral Fletcher's *Yorktown* task force was sent south to join Brown in a second attempt against Rabaul.

But by this time word had come of more attractive targets nearer at hand. On March 8 Japanese forces landed at the villages of Lae and Salamaua on Huon Gulf in the narrow Papuan peninsula of eastern New Guinea. Advised of this development, Brown immediately set course for New Guinea. Steaming into the Gulf of Papua on the opposite shore of the peninsula, Brown sent over a hundred aircraft from the *Yorktown* and *Lexington* across the towering Owen Stanley Mountains on the morning of March 10.

The obsolete Devastator torpedo planes from the *Lexington,* underpowered and carrying huge torpedoes, were unable to clear the highest ridge line of the Owen Stanleys. Lieutenant Commander James Brett, leader of the torpedo group, climbed and climbed; still he found himself below the ridge and had to turn away. Then Brett, a former glider pilot, noticed the sun reflecting on the mountains and recalled that this often created thermal updrafts of air. Signaling his squadrons to follow, Brett circled his plane in the updraft and was gently swept over the ridge by rising air currents. Swooping down on the Japanese shipping in Huon Gulf, the Devastators executed a skillful torpedo attack but, like the submariners, the pilots discovered their torpedoes to be faulty. "You could see streaks of torpedoes going right to the side of these cruisers and nothing happened," recalled one pilot. "Some obviously hit the cruisers and didn't explode. I saw one or two go right on underneath, come out the other side and bury themselves in the bank on the shore." [26]

The dive-bombers were more successful. The surprised Japanese at Lae and Salamaua lost two large transports and two other vessels, while nine other ships, including a light cruiser and two destroyers, were damaged. It was the most important American naval success of the war to date and came as a nasty shock to the Japanese.[27] To Vice Admiral Inoue Shigeyoshi, commanding the New Guinea operations, the lesson of the air attack was clear: to complete the conquest of New Guinea, he would need the protection of aircraft carriers.[28]

Yet carriers were as scarce a resource in the Japanese as in the American navy, and there were other contenders for their use. Since early January Japanese strategists had been debating what to do next. As it became evident that all of Japan's initial objectives would be easily achieved, the army and navy began to search for new worlds to conquer. The army did not have to look far. Its eyes were riveted on the Soviet Union. But for the navy there were a number of options to be considered. Initially the Naval General Staff favored an attack on Australia, which they feared might be built up into a major Allied base from which a counteroffensive could be launched. The army took one look at the Australian proposal, at the long supply lines, immense distances, and the manpower required, and "absolutely refused to agree to the operations." [29] The army's solution to the threat posed by the Allied buildup in Australia was to capture Port Moresby in southeastern New Guinea, from which the Japanese could attack northern Australia and check any Allied advance from that direction. The army was prepared to launch an overland attack against Port Moresby at an early date.[30]

Responding to the army's counterproposal, the Naval General Staff put forward a compromise plan for the isolation of Australia through the progressive occupation of strategic points in New Guinea, New Caledonia, the Fiji Islands, and Samoa. The occupation of Lae and Salamaua had been the first step in this new program. Before further steps could be taken, however, Admiral Yamamoto and his staff intervened.

Because of Yamamoto's immense prestige, the staff of his Combined Fleet, although nominally subordinate to Imperial General Headquarters, exercised great influence in the determination of strategy. The Combined Fleet staff had also initially considered moving against Australia, but decided instead to plan for an attack on Hawaii. However, the planners soon concluded that Hawaii was too distant, too well defended, and too large for a fleet attack to have a good chance of success.

Another possibility was an offensive westward into the Indian Ocean to Ceylon and then on toward a possible linkup with German forces in the Middle East or southern Russia. Like the Australian plan, the western offensive would require cooperation by the army; once again the army demurred. The Germans also evinced little interest in cooperation. The navy had to settle for a major raid into the Indian Ocean by the carrier striking force.[31]

On March 26, 1942, Admiral Nagumo—with five large carriers, four fast battleships, three cruisers, and nine destroyers fresh from the conquest of the East Indies—left the Celebes Islands near Borneo and passed through the Straits of Malacca into the Indian Ocean. Around the same time, another force under Vice Admiral Ozawa, consisting of a small aircraft carrier, six cruisers, and eight destroyers, sailed from Malaya to attack shipping in the Bay of Bengal.

The raid was a complete success. For a week, Nagumo's task force roamed the Indian Ocean virtually unchallenged by the British, whose Royal Navy had held undisputed sway there for a hundred and fifty years. The main British bases at Colombo and Trincomalee in Ceylon were bombed by Nagumo's carrier planes, while Ozawa's force sank almost a hundred thousand tons of shipping in the Bay of Bengal in just five days.[32] The British Eastern Fleet under Admiral Sir James Somerville, which had only two modern carriers with less than a hundred aircraft, avoided a confrontation with the Japanese, but the heavy cruisers *Dorsetshire* and *Cornwall* and the small carrier *Hermes*, which had been at Ceylon at the time of the air raids, were sunk by Nagumo's planes. The rest of the Eastern Fleet eventually withdrew to East Africa.

While Nagumo's carriers were in the Indian Ocean, the debate on Japanese strategy continued. Admiral Yamamoto and the Combined Fleet staff now favored an attack on the island of Midway, 1100 miles west of Hawaii. An attack on Midway would almost certainly draw out the American fleet, affording the Japanese the opportunity of destroying it in a decisive battle. Even if the Americans refused battle, Midway would be a valuable addition to Japan's defensive perimeter of island bases.[33]

On April 2 Commander Watanabe Yasuji took the Midway plan to Tokyo and dropped it in the laps of the Naval General Staff, which was already preparing for the New Guinea–New Caledonia–Fiji operations. The Naval General Staff heatedly opposed the Midway idea at first. Commander Miyo Tatsukichi, the air officer of Operations Section, complained that the Combined Fleet was planning to fight its big battle practically in the enemy's backyard. At Midway the Americans would have the support of land-based planes as well as long-range bombers from Hawaii, while the Japanese would be far beyond the support of land-based airplanes. After Pearl Harbor, there was little chance the U.S. forces could be surprised again. Even if Midway were captured, the Americans could always take it back later. Supplying Japanese forces on the island across hundreds of miles of ocean, within easy range of Hawaii-based submarines and aircraft, would be a nightmare. If the object was to draw out the U.S. fleet, New Caledonia was a more valuable piece of real estate than Midway—and it had the advantage of being further from the U.S.[34]

Nevertheless, Naval General Staff was in a poor position to oppose Combined Fleet's wishes. The chief of the Naval Staff, Admiral Nagano, believed that since operations had gone smoothly so far, there was no reason to question the plans of the Combined Fleet. Nagano's deputy, Vice Admiral Ito Seiichi, and Rear Admiral Fukudome Shigeru, head of the Operations Section, had both served as chief of staff to Admiral Yamamoto; they were reluctant to oppose their old leader.[35] When Watanabe insisted that the staff telephone Admiral Yamamoto to get his opinion, opposition to the Midway plan collapsed.[36] According to some accounts, Nagumo and many of his commanders and staff officers opposed the idea of an assault on Midway. One of his carrier captains reportedly called it "an impossible and pointless operation." [37] Yet Nagumo, still smarting from criticism of his failure to follow up on the Pearl Harbor attack, was not disposed to argue.

The Naval General Staff dragged its feet on preparations for the Midway operation, claiming that the needed material could not be assembled; it proposed that the date of the attack—which Combined Fleet planned to launch in early June—be postponed about three weeks. Army headquarters also had doubts, fearing that the Midway operation would lead inevitably to a campaign to capture the Hawaiian islands. Then, on April 18, an event occured which put an end to all debate.

On April 1, sixteen Army Air Force B-25 medium bombers were lifted by crane from the pier at Alameda Naval Air Station, California, onto the deck of the new aircraft carrier *Hornet,* which had just come through the Panama Canal from the Atlantic. The *Hornet* sailed west for a rendezvous with Admiral Halsey's *Enterprise* task force and one of the most unusual and dramatic operations of the war. The army bombers, with their superior fuel capacity, were intended to be launched from the *Hornet* five hundred miles away from Japan; they were to bomb Tokyo and then continue on, landing at friendly air bases in China.

President Roosevelt had frequently expressed his desire to see the Japanese home islands bombed; Britain's Air Chief Marshal Sir Charles Portal had suggested a carrier raid on Japan to General Arnold at ARCADIA.[38] Arnold thought the suggestion impractical. But a few days later Admiral King's operations officer, Captain Francis S. Low, suggested a plan for such a raid. It would use army bombers, launched from carriers outside the range of Japanese fighters. With King's approval, Low and Captain Donald B. Duncan, King's air officer, prepared a detailed proposal. They submitted it to Arnold in mid-January. The air force chief, who was already thinking of operating bombers from aircraft carriers in connection with a projected invasion of North Africa, readily agreed.[39] Arnold assigned Lieutenant Colonel James H. Doolittle, a distinguished aviator and aeronautical engineer, to head the mission. Doolittle quickly selected the B-25 as the most suitable aircraft. This operation, for which a Naval War College study after the war could find "no serious strategical reason" other than to raise Allied morale, was nevertheless to have momentous consequences.[40]

The army air crews had trained for a month in Florida, practicing the extremely short takeoffs that would be needed to fly from the *Hornet,* but when the task force sailed, none of the pilots had had the opportunity to take off from the deck of a carrier.[41] Nor did they learn what their mission would be until the *Hornet* was well out at sea. On April 13, the *Hornet* and its escort of two cruisers and four destroyers rendezvoused with Halsey's Task Force sixteen north of Midway, then headed west through heavy seas toward Japan.

Admiral Yamamoto, anticipating that the Americans might try a carrier raid on Japan, had established a picketboat line extending over a thousand-mile front some six to seven hundred miles east of Japan.[42] Early in the morning of April 18, the *Enterprise's* radar picked up one of these picketboats. Halsey altered course, but a few hours later the dawn search flight and fighter patrol sighted another picketboat. Again the task force changed course, but it sighted a third vessel at 20,000 yards an hour later.

By this time it was obvious that the chance for surprise had been lost. Halsey's force comprised half the carrier strength of the Pacific Fleet; it could not be risked against air strikes from Japan. Although the task force was still 650 miles from Japan, the bombers would have to be launched at once. This also meant that the attack on Tokyo, originally planned to take place at night, would now have to take place during daylight; the B-25s, forced to fly 150 miles further to reach Japan, would have only a slight chance of landing at airfields in China.

At seven in the morning the *Hornet* turned into the wind to launch the bombers. The ship was rolling violently and green seas were breaking over the bow as Colonel Doolittle's heavily loaded B-25 rolled down the carrier's deck and climbed laboriously into the air. The rest of the squadron followed. Most of the planes roared down the deck at too great a speed, pulled up, climbed sharply in a near stall, then struggled to nose down again. To the army pilots, blissfully ignorant of the hazards of carrier launchings, "the takeoffs seemed natural and without difficulty." [43]

In Tokyo the Japanese were just completing an air-raid drill when the first American planes appeared. Sweeping in on the city at treetop level, the first two bombers released their bomb loads and swung away unscathed. Twenty minutes later the remaining planes reached the city; they met occasionally heavy but inaccurate antiaircraft fire. Because many of the planes had been off course, the attackers closed on the city from the south, north and east, greatly adding to Japanese confusion. A handful of Japanese fighters rose to intercept, but did little damage. Fifteen of the sixteen planes managed to reach China. With their fuel exhausted, they crash-landed or were abandoned in the air by their crews. The other plane—the sixteenth—landed in Russia and was interned. Of the eighty men who had carried out this first raid on Tokyo, seventy-one survived. [44]

The damage actually inflicted by the raid was small, but its psychological effect on the Japanese was all that might have been desired. The army and navy had failed in their duty to safeguard the homeland and the Emperor from attack. Admiral Yamamoto regarded the raid as a mortifying personal defeat. All opposition to the Midway operation on the part of the Naval General Staff abruptly ceased. Admiral Inoue was notified that his operations against New Guinea and the Solomon Islands would be moved up to occur in early May. Since most of the carrier striking force would be training and refitting for the Midway operation, only two carriers, the *Shokaku* and *Zuikaku,* were alloted to the South Seas operations.

For Admiral Inoue, this was only the latest in a long series of frustrations. Ever since January he had been attempting to convince Imperial General Headquarters of the need to seize eastern New Guinea and the Solomon Islands in order to protect the Japanese bases at Rabaul and Truk and to choke off the flow of Allied supplies

to Australia. Along with Yamamoto, Inoue was one of the most
air-minded admirals but it was land-based air power, not carrier-based
air power, that obsessed him. Only by controlling an interlocking
network of island air bases, he believed, could the defense of the
Empire's far flung perimeter in the Pacific be assured.[45]

In January Inoue's forces, supported by the Combined Fleet, had
seized Rabaul on New Britain and converted it into a major base.
Inoue's next objective was Port Moresby, an important Australian
base on the south coast of Papua, the narrow eastern neck of New
Guinea. In Japanese hands Port Moresby could serve as a base for
reconnaissance and air strikes into the Coral Sea and northern Australia; it would also provide a link to air bases in the Dutch East Indies.
In Allied hands, however, Port Moresby could serve as a base for
bombing attacks against Rabaul and Truk.[46]

Combined Fleet had issued orders for the move south against New
Guinea at the end of January, but Inoue had encountered a number
of unexpected obstacles. First, the destructive American air raid on
his invasion force off Lae and Salamaua had obliged him to request
carrier support before undertaking further advances. Next, preparations for the Midway operation had seriously cut into the size of
his support; finally, the Doolittle raid and the consequent speedup
in preparations for Midway had obliged him to push up his own
timetable.

Now at last, at the end of April, all was ready. Inoue's forces
for the MO, or Port Moresby operation, comprised the MO Invasion
Force under Rear Admiral Goto Aritomo. It was divided into three
groups: the Main Force, composed of four heavy cruisers, a destroyer,
and the small carrier *Shoho;* the Port Moresby Invasion Force, made
up of the troop transports for the landing; and a Support Group
made up of a large seaplane carrier, two light cruisers, and some
auxiliaries. A small force of transports, destroyers, and auxiliaries
under Rear Admiral Shima Kiyohide was assigned to capture the
island of Tulagi in the Solomons in order to deny the Allies a vantage
point for scouting into the eastern approaches to the Coral Sea. The
Support Group planned to establish a seaplane base at Tulagi. Covering the entire operation was a "Striking Force" under Rear Admiral
Takeo Takagi. It consisted of two carriers, *Shokaku* and *Zuikaku,*
both veterans of the Pearl Harbor operation and the Indian Ocean
raid, accompanied by two heavy cruisers and six destroyers.

The Japanese plan was to seize Tulagi first, on May 3, to guard
the left flank of the invasion. The Port Moresby Invasion Force would

sail the next day. The Striking Force, after covering the Tulagi landings, would continue down the eastern side of the Solomons, then swing around the eastern tip of the island chain and head west into the Coral Sea in order to protect the Port Moresby Force against attack from the south or east. Simultaneously, the Support Group would occupy the island of Deboyne, just off the east coast of New Guinea. From there seaplanes could scout for the Port Moresby convoy and cover its movements.

The Allies would probably fight for Port Moresby, but since two American carriers had been reported in the raid on Tokyo, the Japanese did not believe that they would face much opposition. Besides, the Japanese expected to have the advantage of surprise. Allied forces rushing west or north in reaction to the attack on Port Moresby could be picked off by the Striking Force, lurking in ambush far to the east.[47]

Yet there were to be some big surprises in the MO operation not foreseen in the Japanese plan. Six thousand miles away, in a dingy, windowless cellar beneath the Fourteenth Naval District Administration building, a handful of sailors and officers puzzled over the Japanese movements in the South Pacific. Since September 1940 the Office of Naval Intelligence had been reading parts of the Japanese navy's most widely used operational code, called JN-25. At the same time Naval Intelligence was able to track the location and movement of Japanese warships through a process called radio traffic analysis. Traffic analysts did not read enemy messages; they studied the location, volume, and pattern of these messages. Together, cryptoanalysis (code-breaking) and traffic analysis gave the Office of the Naval Intelligence valuable clues about Japanese activities and intentions.

In the weeks before the Pearl Harbor attack, this system had all but broken down because of the extraordinary precautions of the Japanese. On November 1, the Japanese Navy changed all the call signs of its ship and shore installations. One month later it changed them again, thus temporarily throwing off the traffic analysts. The JN-25 code was modified, making it impossible to read any Japanese messages for the time being.[48] By April, however, "Station Hypo," the code-breaking and traffic analysis facility at Pearl Harbor, together with similar facilities in Washington and Australia, had regained all the lost ground. Their success was due in large part to a long delay by the Japanese in completing the regular periodic distribution of new codes and ciphers to many of the far flung headquarters, ships, and bases of their now much expanded empire. This delay in turn meant that units and headquarters without new code or cipher material were obliged to continue using older ones—giving American code-breakers extra time and additional familiar material to work on.[49] The code-breakers could seldom read more than ten or fifteen percent of most messages but this, together with the results of traffic analysis, was enough to justify a high degree of confidence in the guesses made about Japanese intentions.[50]

By mid-April Pacific Fleet intelligence knew that the Japanese were preparing for an offensive in the South Pacific and that Port Moresby would be the objective. Decrypted messages and traffic analysis placed three aircraft carriers enroute to Rabaul for operations in the Australia area. Intercepted messages to the MO Fleet, MO Occupation Force, and MO Attack Force convinced analysts that MO was the designation for Port Moresby.[51]

Nimitz wasted no time. The carrier *Lexington* was sent from Pearl Harbor to join the *Yorktown* force already in the Coral Sea under Rear Admiral Frank Jack Fletcher. The Pacific Fleet's battleships, which had been patrolling in the eastern Pacific, were sent back to the West Coast, thus freeing much-needed tankers and destroyers to support the carriers. From Australia, General MacArthur sent a small force of Australian and American cruisers and destroyers, under Australian Rear Admiral J. G. Crace, to join Fletcher. On April 25 Halsey's task force returned to Pearl Harbor from its raid against Tokyo and, after a short refit, it too rushed south to the Coral Sea, although it was unlikely that Halsey could complete the thirty-five hundred-mile voyage in time to be useful.

What Nimitz expected to find in the Coral Sea is unclear. Perhaps, as most historians believe, he was making a desperate attempt to stem the Japanese advance.[52] Perhaps, as one recent writer has suggested, he was confidently seeking a showdown with the Japanese carrier fleet. In any case, Nimitz believed that " 'our superior personnel in resourcefulness and initiative and the undoubted superiority of much of our equipment' " would give the Americans an edge in the coming battle.[53]

Although Port Moresby was squarely in General MacArthur's Southwest Pacific Theater, Admiral Fletcher's ships belonged to the Pacific Fleet and remained under Nimitz's command. MacArthur, however, commanded all the land-based aircraft in Australia and New Guinea. Thus MacArthur was called upon to provide support for naval operations over which he had no control, while Nimitz and Fletcher were dependent on support from the land-based planes over which they had no control. Scarcely a week after it had been established, the divided command for the Pacific was already causing problems.

MacArthur's air forces, commanded by Lieutenant General George Brett, were formidable on paper, but many of the air crews and their equipment were worn out from fighting in the Dutch East Indies. Other pilots were newly arrived and inexperienced. Many of the planes of the Royal Australian Air Force were also worn out or obsolescent. Of Brett's 500-odd aircraft, only about 200 were operational. These concentrated on raids against Rabaul and on searches of the Solomon Sea, the area off the coast of northeast Australia. Large sections of the central and eastern parts of the Coral Sea and the eastern Solomons were not searched at all.[54]

On May 1 the *Lexington's* task force under Rear Admiral Aubrey W. Fitch joined Fletcher; both task forces began refueling from their accompanying oilers, an extremely slow process which consumed most of the next two days. On the evening of May 2, Fletcher, anxious over enemy movements reported by Brett's planes decided to take the *Yorktown* and the ships which had completed fueling into the center of the Coral Sea to conduct air searches. The *Lexington* group was to finish refueling and rendezvous with him next day at a point further east where Admiral Crace's force, coming from Australia, would join him as well.

The next afternoon Fletcher received word of the Japanese landings at Tulagi. Rushing north with the *Yorktown* force, he launched three air strikes against the Tulagi invasion force. Admiral Takagi's carrier striking force—which should have provided air cover for Tulagi—was far away, having been delayed by ferrying aircraft to Rabaul and by refueling.[55] There were no Japanese planes in the air when Fletcher's dive bombers roared down on Admiral Shima's minesweepers, transports, and destroyers off Tulagi.

The pilots returned to their carriers in a jubilant mood to report cruisers, destroyers, and transports sunk. In fact, Japanese losses were confined to a destroyer, two patrol boats, and a transport, with a second transport badly damaged. This was a small success indeed for the number of bombs and torpedoes expended, but enough to send the remnants of the Tulagi force steaming hurriedly back to Rabaul.[56]

Rejoining Fitch and Crace, Fletcher headed northwest to intercept the Port Moresby invasion force. From intelligence reports and air sightings, the admiral believed that the invaders would come through the Jomard Passage, a narrow seaway through the network of reefs, shallows, and straits which jutted out into the Coral Sea from the eastern tip of New Guinea. Fletcher expected the Japanese to appear on about the seventh or eighth of May. He had little information about the enemy carriers but assumed they would be covering the flanks of the convoy.

In fact, Takagi's two big carriers, *Shokaku* and *Zuikaku,* were actually behind—that is, to the northeast—of Fletcher's force, having rounded the Solomon Islands according to plan on the sixth of May. Assuming correctly that Fletcher was to the west of him, waiting to attack the invasion convoy, Admiral Takagi decided to proceed in that direction; but first he decided to search to the south and east to make sure no American forces were waiting in ambush behind *him.*

At dawn on the seventh, the skies over the Coral Sea were thick with search planes, both Japanese and American. The carrier forces were looking for each other, while Japanese bombers and seaplanes from Rabaul and Tulagi and Allied bombers from Australia joined in the hunt. Around half past seven, a Japanese search plane reported a carrier and a cruiser almost due south of the Japanese striking force. Some eighty-odd planes roared off to attack, but they found only the American oiler *Neosho* and the destroyer *Sims,* which had been ordered by Fletcher to a supposedly safe rendezvous in the south. Those ships had been mistaken by the Japanese search plane for a carrier and a cruiser. After vainly searching for the nonexistent carrier, the Japanese planes attacked the *Neosho* and *Sims,* sinking the destroyer and crippling the tanker.

While this was happening Fletcher was busy searching for the Japanese. At sunrise on the morning of the seventh, Fletcher had detached Admiral Crace's force of three cruisers and two destroyers, ordering them to stand off the Jomard Passage and intercept any Japanese shipping that might come through the narrow pass. Less than two hours later, one of Fletcher's planes sighted Admiral Marumo's Kuninovi's Support Group of two old light cruisers and some gunboats, but incorrectly reported it as two carriers and four heavy cruisers. The *Lexington* and *Yorktown* immediately launched their planes against the supposed carriers. Thus, both the American and Japanese carrier commanders had hurled their air groups against the wrong targets.

On this day the Americans were luckier than their foes, however. One of the *Lexington's* bombers, on its way to attack Marumo's antique fleet, spotted the carrier *Shoho* and the other ships of Admiral Goto's Covering Group. All ninety-three American planes peeled off to attack the *Shoho,* which was blasted out of the water by bombs and torpedoes. The Americans lost only three planes.

Fletcher had recovered his planes and was ready to launch a second strike by midafternoon, but he decided to wait until the other Japanese carriers were located. The Japanese meanwhile had completely lost track of Fletcher and were busily bombing Crace's force with land-based planes from Rabaul. Without air cover, but maneuvering brilliantly, Crace's ships dodged the successive air attacks—including one by three U.S. Army B-17s, which mistook them for Japanese.

Meanwhile Admiral Takagi, his planes having returned from their attack on the *Neosho* and *Sims,* decided to launch a late afternoon strike on Crace's force, which he mistakenly assumed to include the American carriers. Searching unsuccessfully for Crace, the twenty-seven Japanese bombers had a harrowing ordeal. Picked up by the *Lexington's* radar, they were ambushed by American fighters, suffering nine losses. In the darkness and bad weather, several Japanese planes mistook the American carriers for their own and were shot down while attempting to land. Others crashed in the sea; less than a dozen returned safely to their carriers.[57]

The next morning the two carrier forces searched for and found each other. Planes from the *Yorktown* and *Lexington,* attacking repeatedly, damaged the carrier *Shokaku* but not fatally. *Zuikaku,* a few miles away, was hidden by a rain squall. The attack on the *Shokaku* demonstrated that the "undoubted superiority" of American pilots and planes, confidently alluded to by Nimitz, was mostly wishful thinking. The American torpedo planes, older and slower than their Japanese counterparts, launched their torpedoes from too far away; all missed their targets or failed to explode. The torpedoes themselves were so slow at long range that the Japanese ships could actually outrun them.[58]

The *Yorktown* and *Lexington* had come under attack by planes from *Zuikaku* and *Shokaku* in the meantime. The two American carriers had only fifteen fighters for their protective screen or "combat air patrol," and these were poorly handled by the *Lexington* fighter direction officer. Only two planes were able to intercept the Japanese attack group before it reached the carriers; they were kept away from the bombers and torpedo planes by Japanese fighters.[59] To supplement the fighters, the Americans sent up some of their dive-bombers to intercept the slower Japanese torpedo planes, but this was a hopeless task.

Hardly bothered by these efforts, the seventy Japanese planes bore down on the American carriers, dropping their deadly loads of bombs and torpedoes. The *Lexington* received two torpedo hits on her port side and a bomb hit on her main deck. The *Yorktown,* smaller and handier than the *Lexington,* managed to dodge all the torpedoes. She was hit by a bomb which penetrated to her fourth deck. The resultant fires were soon brought under control.

The Japanese pilots returned to their carriers to report both American carriers "sunk." Actually, the *Yorktown* had been only lightly damaged and the *Lexington,* although more heavily hurt, was still able to steam at twenty-five knots and to conduct flight operations. An hour after the Japanese attack ended, most of the damage aboard the *Lexington* had been temporarily repaired and fires put out, but at 12:47 gasoline released by one of the torpedo hits ignited, and a violent explosion rocked the ship. Two hours later, a second internal explosion caused the fires already burning in the ship to rage out of control. Late that afternoon, the *Lexington* was abandoned; one of the escorting destroyers sank her.

The loss of the *Lexington* drastically changed the odds in the Coral Sea. Admiral Fletcher now had only a single carrier and about forty aircraft. He knew that at least one of the Japanese carriers remained in the fight and he had received reports that an additional carrier might have joined the Japanese task force since the battle.[60] Fletcher decided to withdraw, a decision confirmed by orders from Nimitz a few hours later.

The Japanese were in no position to take advantage of Fletcher's retirement. The *Shokaku* had been damaged so badly that she had to head back to Truk for repairs. Allied intelligence reports of a third carrier were in error. Admiral Takagi's Striking Force was left with only one carrier, the *Zuikaku;* it was undamaged, but it was low on fuel and had fewer than forty operational aircraft. From Rabaul Admiral Inoue decided that a single carrier with half an air group was insufficient to provide air cover for the Port Moresby invasion in the face of the Allied land-based aircraft still active in New Guinea and Australia.[61] The attack on Port Moresby was postponed—as it turned out, forever.

The Japanese believed that they had gained another in their long string of victories and, in a sense, they were correct, for the sinking of the *Lexington* and *Neosho* more than balanced the loss of the little *Shoho* and the handful of small ships sunk at Tulagi. On the other hand, the Port Moresby invasion had been turned back, never to be attempted again by sea. The *Shokaku* and *Zuikaku* had lost so many aircraft and crews at Coral Sea that they could not be ready in time for the Midway operation, thus cutting the strength of the Combined Fleet carrier striking force by one third. The "vital flank" remained secure.

NOTES

1. Morton, *Strategy and Command*, p. 241.

2. Francis L. Loewenheim, Harold D. Langley and Manfred Jonas, eds., *Roosevelt and Churchill: Their Secret Wartime Correspondence* (New York: E. P. Dutton, 1975) pp. 189–90; Hayes, "Pearl Harbor to Trident," pp. 127–28.

3. Quoted in Michael Howard, *Grand Strategy*, Vol. 4 (London: H.M.S.O., 1972) p. 77.

4. Hayes, "Pearl Harbor to Trident," pp. 130–131; Robert E. Sherwood, *Roosevelt and Hopkins* (New York: Grosset and Dunlap, 1950), p. 515. An excellent discussion of Australia's unsuccessful efforts to influence grand strategy in the Pacific may be found in D. M. Horner, *High Command: Australia and Allied Strategy 1939–1945* (Canberra: Australian War Memorial, 1982) pp. 256–57, 262. At the end of 1943, Prime Minister Curtin complained that he " 'had never seen any reports on the background of higher strategy.' " (p. 237).

5. Hayes, "Pearl Harbor to Trident," p. 131; "Summary of Status With Respect to Spheres of Strategic Responsibility," 30 March 1942, Ernest J. King Papers, Double Zero Files.

6. Maurice Matloff and Edwin M. Snell, *Strategic Planning for Coalition Warfare 1941–1942* (Washington, D.C.: Office of the Chief of Military History, 1953) pp. 149, 162–64.

7. Pogue, *Ordeal and Hope*, pp. 373–75.

8. James, *The Years of MacArthur 1941–1945*, p. 139.

9. Morton, *Strategy and Command*. See also Richard Leighton and Robert W. Coakley, *Global Logistics and Strategy 1940–1943* (Washington, D.C.: GPO, 1955), pp. 390–393.

10. Memo, Turner to Admiral E. J. King, 19 March 1942, cited in Hayes, "Pearl Harbor to Trident," p. 141.

11. Robert Sherrod, *On to Westward: War in the Central Pacific* (New York: Duel Sloan and Pearce, 1945) p. 234.

12. Charles A. Lockwood and Hans C. Adamson, *Battles of the Philippine Sea* (New York: Duell, Sloan, and Peares, 1967) p. 7.

13. Thomas B. Buell, *Master of Sea Power* (Boston: Little, Brown and Company, 1980) p. 361.

14. James, *Years of MacArthur*, pp. 80–81, 195, 594–95.

15. Potter, *Nimitz*, p. 16.

16. Morison, *The Rising Sun*, p. 256.

17. Matloff and Snell, *Strategic Planning for Coalition Warfare 1941–1942*, p. 154.

18. Love, "Ernest Joseph King," p. 149.

19. Reynolds, *The Fast Carriers*, p. 22; James H. Belote and William M. Belote, *Titans of the Seas* (New York: Harper and Row, 1975) pp. 17–31.

20. Reynolds, *The Fast Carriers*, p. 30.

21. "Reminiscences of Adm. Arleigh Burke," U.S. Navy Oral History Collection, interview no. 5, p. 383.

22. "Reminiscences of Adm. James Thach, U.S. Navy Oral History Collection, interview no. 2, p. 146.

23. Okumiya and Horikoshi, *Zero*, pp. 35–36.

24. U.S. Naval War College, "The Battle of Midway—Strategical and Tactical Analysis," pp. 91–93 and passim. Unpublished manuscript.

25. Ibid., p. 48.

26. "Reminiscences of Adm. James Thach," interview no. 2, pp. 202–4, 206.

27. Lundstrom, *First South Pacific Campaign*, p. 38; Morison, *The Rising Sun*, 387–389.

28. *Reports of General MacArthur: Japanese Operations in the Southwest Pacific Area II Part 1*, p. 131.

29. *Reports of General MacArthur*, Vol. 2, Part 1, p. 132.

30. Paul S. Dull, *A Battle History of the Imperial Japanese Navy* (Annapolis: Naval Institute, 1978), p. 139.

31. Mitsuo Fuchida and Masatake Okumiya, *Midway: The Battle That Doomed Japan* (Annapolis: Naval Institute, 1955) pp. 56–58; Lundstrom, *First South Pacific Campaign*, pp. 42–43.

32. S. W. Roskill, *The War At Sea* Vol. 2, *The Period of Balance* (London: H.M.S.O., 1956) pp. 24–30.

33. Fuchida and Okumiya, *Midway*, pp. 58–63.

34. Ibid., pp. 62–63; Toland interview with Commander Miyo Tatsukichi, 14 October 1967, Toland Interview Collection.

35. Toland interview with Commander Miyo Tatsukichi.

36. Fuchida and Okumiya, *Midway*, p. 64.

37. Agawa, *The Reluctant Admiral*, pp. 308–9.

38. Arnold, *Global Mission*, pp. 276–77, 298.

39. Carrol V. Glines, *Doolittle's Tokyo Raiders* (New York: Arno Press, 1980) pp. 9–19.

40. U.S. Naval War College, *The Battle of the Coral Sea: Strategical and Tactical Analysis*, p. 2, unpublished manuscript; Morton, *Strategy and Command*, p. 269.

41. This account of the raid is based on a manuscript history entitled "Tokyo Raid," written by S. L. A. Marshall for the War Department Historical Staff. Copy in Center of Military History.

42. Fuchida and Okumiya, *Midway*, p. 68.

43. S. L. A. Marshall, "Tokyo Raid," p. 26.

44. Eight men were captured in Japanese-controlled China and one crewman was killed while bailing out. An excellent collection of first-hand accounts by airmen

who took part in the mission may be found in Glines, *Doolittle's Tokyo Raiders,* pp. 127–312.

45. Lundstrom, *First South Pacific Campaign,* p. 23.

46. Ibid., pp. 24–25.

47. Ibid., pp. 72–73; Morison, *Coral Sea,* pp. 10–12; Naval War College, *Battle of the Coral Sea,* pp. 16–17.

48. Blair, *Silent Victory,* p. 70; Potter, *Nimitz,* pp. 63–65; Holmes, *Double-Edged Secrets,* pp. 53–54, 58–59, 65–68.

49. Ronald Lewin, *The American Magic: Codes, Ciphers, and the Defeat of Japan* (New York: Farrar, Straus, and Giroux, 1982) pp. 88–89.

50. Ibid; John B. Lundstrom, *The First South Pacific Campaign,* pp. 75–77.

51. Examples of decrypted messages may be found in SRN-001-SEN 2, 114 "Translations of Japanese Navy Messages, Japanese Naval Forces," R.G. 457, National Archives. The researcher should be aware that it is normally impossible to tell the precise date that messages were decrypted and who was apprised of their contents.

52. Potter, *Nimitz,* pp. 66–67; Samuel Eliot Morison, *Coral Sea, Midway and Submarine Actions, May 1942–August 1942* (Boston: Little, Brown and Company, 1980), p. 16.

53. Lundstrom, *First Southwest Pacific Campaign,* pp. 86–87.

54. U.S. Naval War College, *Battle of the Coral Sea,* pp. 24–26.

55. Lundstrom, *First Southwest Pacific Campaign,* pp. 98–99.

56. Dull, *The Imperial Japanese Navy,* p. 127.

57. Morison, *Coral Sea,* pp. 43–44, gives Japanese losses as about twenty with only six or seven recovered. Lundstrom, *First South Pacific Campaign,* p. 109, says only nine were lost. The Japanese carriers had to turn on their searchlights to guide their planes home.

58. Morison, *Coral Sea,* p. 51.

59. U.S. Naval War College, *Battle of the Coral Sea,* p. 91.

60. Ibid., p. 101.

61. Lundstrom, *First South Pacific Campaign,* p. 112.

EIGHT

From Midway to Massacre Valley

The Coral Sea battle did not unduly disturb Yamamoto and his planners. The postponement of the Port Moresby operation was annoying but unimportant. More significant was the fact that the *Shokaku* and *Zuikaku* would be unavailable for the Midway operation, but the Japanese believed that both American carriers had been sunk or crippled at Coral Sea. The four remaining carriers in the Japanese striking force should be more than enough to do the job. [1]

One week before, in war games aboard the Combined Fleet flagship *Yamato*, all the principal tasks in the Midway operation had been rehearsed with little difficulty. Yamamoto's chief of staff, Rear Admiral Ukagi Matome, saw to that by arbitrarily cancelling or revising adverse rulings of the games' umpires. [2] Japanese naval officers were so confident of success that they brought back aboard ship many personal belongings such as cameras, pictures, games, which had been put ashore for safekeeping at the time of Pearl Harbor. [3] Admiral Nagumo's intelligence estimate observed that the Americans had lost heavily in "frequent defeats" and "lack the will to fight." [4]

The Japanese forces for the Midway operation, comprising most of the Japanese navy. were divided into sixteen different groups of warships, all working to a complex plan devised by Captain Kuroshima Kameto, Yamamoto's senior operations officer. The onslaught would begin with an air attack by planes from the two light carriers of Vice Admiral Hosogaya Boshiro's Northern Area Force on Dutch Harbor in the Aleutians, far to the north of Midway. The air attack would be followed by the occupation of Attu and Kiska at the western end of the island chain. The strike at the Aleutians was intended to neutralize any American air power there and provide a diversion from the main event, the assault on Midway. Backing up the Aleutians attack would be four battleships of Vice Admiral Takasu Shiro's Aleutians Screening Force.

Midway island would be hit the next day by the four big carriers of Admiral Nagumo's striking force, coming from the northwest. The day after that, Vice Admiral Kondo Nobutake's Second Fleet, comprising two battleships, a small aircraft carrier, and half a dozen heavy cruisers, would move with the invasion convoy up from the southwest to capture Midway. Yamamoto, with the "Main Body" built around the three most powerful battleships, and including a small carrier, would take position three hundred miles to the west of Nagumo and Kondo, awaiting the expected counterattack by the U.S. fleet. [5]

Historians have criticized Yamamoto for spreading his forces all over the northern Pacific. Had the Japanese aligned their forces differently, they might have had eight carriers instead of four opposing the American carrier task forces at Midway. Although three of the Japanese carriers were small "light carrier" types, Yamamoto would still have held a decisive advantage. Yet any graduate of the Japanese staff system or war college of the 1930s, and probably their American counterparts as well, would have been thoroughly at home with the existing plan. Yamamoto's dispositions were designed to engage the American fleet no matter from which direction it came. He would do this in the time-honored way. Cordons of submarines would be thrown across the likely avenues of approach from Pearl Harbor to scout and to snipe at the enemy. Then the carriers of Nagumo's or Hosagaya's force, depending on the direction of the approach, would strike at the Americans; finally, the Japanese battle line would weigh in to strike the decisive blow. [7] Since the Midway attack was expected to come as a surprise, the Japanese assumed that they would have ample time to complete the conquest of Midway before the enemy fleet arrived on the scene. As two leading Japanese students of the battle observed, Yamamoto's whole plan "rested on the obsolete concept. . . . that battleships rather than carriers constituted the main strength of the fleet." [8]

By way of contrast, Nimitz's battleships had long been relegated to patrolling the West Coast; at the time of Midway five of them were in San Francisco harbor with orders to "defend it against air attack." [9] Thus, warships which had a few months before been the backbone of the fleet were now assigned to harbor defense. Yet Yamamoto's battleships, most of which were as old as their American counterparts, were still preparing for a Japanese version of the battle of Jutland. This was less because the Americans were more progressive than because lack of oilers and destroyers left Nimitz no choice but to leave the battlewagons close to home.

Since time was short and many of the forces for the Midway operation were already at sea, Combined Fleet sent the entire complex operations order for the Midway attack by radio. A new edition of the Japanese naval code was scheduled to go into effect on April 1, but difficulties in distributing the codebooks forced postponement of the change until May 1. Then the hurried preparations for Midway forced postponement again until June 1.

That was a bonanza for American cryptanalysts.* In Hawaii and Australia the American codebreakers recovered almost 90 percent of this long and complex message. By the last week of May they knew the date, place, and time of the operation, as well as the composition of the Japanese forces involved.[10]

At first, the American high command was hard to convince. Admiral King's staff in Washington, looking at many of the same intercepted messages, wondered whether the Japanese were not actually preparing for another offensive in the South Pacific. (They were, but only *after* Midway.)[11] Many of Nimitz's strategists found it hard to believe that the Japanese would use practically their whole navy to capture the tiny atoll of Midway and two icebound islands in the Aleutians.[12] By mid-May, however, all American commanders were convinced that the target would be Midway. Reinforcements were rushed to the island and the carrier task forces were hurriedly recalled from the South Pacific to Pearl Harbor.

The *Yorktown* arrived on May 22, still damaged from the Coral Sea battle; she immediately went into dry dock. Before the dock had completely drained, Admiral Nimitz and the navy's technical experts were sloshing around on the bottom, tiny figures dwarfed by the huge smoke-blackened hull of the carrier. A brief inspection showed that the damage was extensive. Ninety days was a reasonable estimate for repairs. " 'We must have this ship back in three days' ", Nimitz told the shipyard technicians.

Shipyard workers labored around the clock to make temporary repairs to the *Yorktown*. Shipfitters and welders worked in the smoke and 120-degree heat inside the hull, while electricians and mechanics

---

* American codebreaking efforts are discussed in more detail in Chapter 20.

swarmed over the superstructure. On the morning of the twenty-ninth, the *Yorktown,* with many yard workmen still aboard, cleared the dry dock and headed out into the stream. The next day she was on her way to Midway.[13]

The *Hornet* and *Enterprise* had already refueled and departed Pearl Harbor. Unfortunately their commander, Admiral Halsey—the most experienced and respected carrier commander in the fleet—was ashore, hospitalized with a skin infection. Nimitz, on Halsey's recommendation, appointed Rear Admiral Raymond A. Spruance in his place. Admiral Frank Jack Fletcher acted as overall commander of the carrier forces.

While Halsey had become almost a folk hero since Pearl Harbor, Spruance was an unknown quantity. He was a non-aviator, a member of "the gun club," whose greatest ambition had been to command a battleship. Where Halsey was friendly, informal, warm, and enthusiastic, Spruance had a reputation as a cold fish. Aboard his former flagship he had even taken his meals alone. Cool, remote, unflappable, he inspired respect rather than love. Spruance tirelessly picked the brains of his staff for information and ideas about carrier warfare. Captain Miles E. Browning, his chief of staff inherited from Halsey, was a mine of information—but he was also erratic, emotionally unstable, and a sloppy administrator. The staff itself was a casual, slipshod organization of brilliant individualists which caused Spruance plenty of headaches during the ensuing action.[14]

For the coming battle Nimitz instructed his commanders to take position northeast of Midway, out of range of Japanese search planes. Midway-based search planes could do the Americans' scouting, while the carriers remained safely out of sight.

The Japanese steamed toward Midway unaware that they were sailing into a trap. On the voyage out, the radio intelligence unit aboard Yamamoto's flagship picked up unusually large amounts of radio traffic originating from Hawaii: this seemed to suggest that the Americans were up to something. The Japanese had scheduled an aerial reconnaissance of Pearl Harbor by long-range flying boats to check on this possibility, but the planes would have to refuel from submarines at French Frigate Shoals, tiny islets five hundred miles west of Hawaii. When the Japanese submarines arrived, they found the anchorage already occupied by an American seaplane tender. The reconnaissance had to be called off. Another Japanese submarine patrolling the waters around Midway reported unusual activity and around-the-clock work on the island. None of this information was passed on by Yamamoto to Nagumo, because to do so would mean breaking radio silence.[15] So far as Nagumo knew, the enemy fleet was still at its berths in Pearl Harbor.

On Midway, the Americans were completing their furious preparations for defense. From the crowded island, navy PBY Catalina Flying Boats—slow, unmaneuverable, but with good range and endurance—and Army Air Force B-17 bombers took off daily to search for the Japanese. A submarine picket line was also established west of the island.

At nine o'clock on the morning of June 3, one of the Flying Boat pilots sighted a row of gray smudges on the horizon. It was the transports and destroyers of the Midway Occupation Force. The pilot, Ensign Jack Reid, handed his binoculars to his copilot and asked " 'Do you see what I see?' " " 'You're damn right I do' " [16] was the reply. B-17s and torpedo-carrying Catalinas attacked the transports later that day, but scored only a minor hit on an oiler.

Nagumo's carriers, many miles to the northeast of the invasion convoy, were still hidden by bad weather; they had not been seen, but the convoy's discovery removed the last lingering doubt that the Japanese were heading for Midway. At Pearl Harbor and aboard the American carriers, there were feelings of relief and exhilaration, combined with lingering anxiety about the whereabouts of the Japanese striking force.

Still unaware that an American fleet was lying in wait for him, Nagumo began launching his planes for an attack on Midway early on the morning of June 4. As a precaution, only about half of the planes available were allocated for the Midway strike. The rest remained aboard the carriers, spotted for an immediate attack against any enemy ships which might appear. A limited search was also undertaken by scout planes from the escorting cruisers of the task force but one of these planes, from the cruiser *Tone,* was late in starting. This small delay was to have fateful consequences.

Shortly after the Midway attack wave had been launched, Midway search planes finally located Nagumo's carriers. At the same time, a PBY noticed a large formation of planes heading for Midway and flashed a warning. The American carriers turned southwest to close with the Japanese carriers; Midway flew off all its attack aircraft to hit the same target.

Midway was fully alerted and ready when the Japanese planes appeared, but the antiquated marine fighters which rose to intercept them did little damage to the attackers and suffered heavy losses. Japanese bombers knocked out the marines' command post and mess, and damaged storehouses and fuel storage facilities, but they failed to do any really critical damage. Casualties were low, the airfield was intact, and most gun positions were undamaged. American anti-aircraft fire was heavy and accurate, taking a heavy toll of the attacking Japanese.

Thirty-eight Japanese planes were lost in the Midway strike and about thirty others were too heavily damaged to fly again, a loss of over 60 percent.[17] After these losses, Nagumo had fewer operable planes than the three U.S. carriers stalking him—and considerably fewer than the combined U.S. air strength on Midway and at sea. The Japanese commander now had occasion to sorely miss the carriers assigned by Yamamoto to the Aleutians attack, the two small carriers with the Second Fleet, and the battleships so many miles away.

Surveying the island from his bomber, the Japanese strike commander radioed back to Nagumo: " 'There is need for a second attack.' " At the time the admiral received this message, his own carriers were under attack from the first of the Midway-based aircraft, six torpedo planes and four Army B-26 bombers, also armed with torpedoes. The attack was easily broken up by Japanese fighters, which shot down all but three of the American planes, but the admiral needed little convincing that Midway was still dangerous. To prepare a second strike against Midway would mean rearming the torpedo planes with bombs and changing the dive-bombers' loads from armor-piercing to high-explosive bombs, a job which might take at least an hour. Yet Nagumo's scouting planes had been out for over two hours and had found no American ships in the area. An hour's delay seemed a safe enough chance to take. At 7:15 A.M. he ordered the change.

As the Japanese torpedo planes and dive-bombers were being rearmed, the scout plane of the cruiser *Tone,* which had been late beginning her search, sent back disquieting news. At 7:28 this plane reported "ten ships, apparently enemy, bearing 10 degrees . . . ." This message was the first indication Nagumo had received that American ships were in the area. If the newly discovered fleet included carriers, the Japanese would be at a serious disadvantage: caught in the midst of rearming, with the Midway striking force returning planes now expected within the hour. Nagumo ordered the rearming of the planes for the second Midway strike to be halted. He sent an urgent message to the *Tone*'s scout plane: " 'Ascertain ship types and maintain contact.' "

While they waited anxiously for a reply, the Japanese were repeatedly attacked by additional Midway-based planes. Sixteen Marine Corps dive-bombers of VMSB-241, commanded by Major Lofton

Henderson appeared first. Many of the pilots had never before flown the new Douglas Dauntless bombers which had just arrived at Midway. So inexperienced were they that Major Henderson decided to lead the squadron in a long, shallow glide-bombing attack on the Japanese carriers—an even more dangerous mode of attack than the steep high-speed dive but one requiring less skill. Japanese fighters and antiaircraft guns took a heavy toll of the bombers. Half of the planes, including that of Major Henderson, were lost. Again no hits were scored on the carriers.

A few minutes later, a formation of fifteen Army B-17s under Lieutenant Colonel Walter C. Sweeny was more fortunate. Their high altitude and formidable defensive armament saved them from losses at the hands of Japanese fighters, but they too failed to score any hits. A formation of old and slow Marine Corps Vindicator dive-bombers which followed the B-17s was unable to penetrate the Japanese fighter screen; it veered off to attack the escorting battleship *Haruna.* Again, no hits—but only one of the Vindicators was lost.

While Nagumo's striking force was beating off the Midway planes, its flagship received a reply from the *Tone* scout: " 'Enemy ships are five cruisers and five destroyers.' " Ten minutes later came a further message which caused consternation on the bridge of the *Akagi:* " 'Enemy force accompanied by what appears to be an aircraft carrier bringing up the rear.' " Rear Admiral Yamaguchi Tamon, commanding the *Soryu* and *Hiryu* of Carrier Division Two, signaled the flagship: " 'Consider it advisable to launch attack force immediately.' " [18] The *Soryu* and *Hiryu* had three dozen dive-bombers armed and ready to go. A number of torpedo planes, which had been rearmed with bombs, were spotted on the decks of the *Kaga* and *Akagi;* but these planes would have to proceed without fighter escort since all available fighters had already been committed to beating off the American air attacks.

Admiral Nagumo decided to wait. He would first recover the Midway attack force planes which were now returning; then he would rearm and reorganize his forces for a balanced attack on the American fleet.[19] By this decision, Nagumo doomed his force to destruction. He had good reasons, however, for deciding as he did. The scouting reports from the *Tone* plane had been vague and spoke of only one American carrier. Besides, he had just witnessed a vivid demonstration of what could happen to bombers which tried to attack without fighter cover. It seemed more sensible to wait. The Americans so far had certainly proved no real problem in the air.

To the northwest of the Japanese, Admiral Spruance, leading Task Force 16, was reaching an exactly opposite conclusion. Spruance's optimum point for launching an attack was about 100 miles from the Japanese carriers' reported position. At this distance, his short-legged planes would have ample time to find the Japanese, maneuver, and return.

Spruance, however, " 'wanted to hit the Japanese carriers as early as possible with all the air strength he had available for this purpose' "; he therefore launched his attack some two hours earlier—at the dangerously long range of over 150 miles.[20] This was almost the extreme range for many of his planes; but Spruance reasoned that if the strike were despatched early it had a good chance of surprising the Japanese while recovering their Midway attack force. So he decided to throw his entire striking force—sixty-eight dive-bombers, thirty torpedo planes, and twenty fighters—at the enemy, retaining only a few fighters to cover his task force. By eight the attacking planes on their way.

Admiral Fletcher received word of Spruance's strike but did not launch his air strike until ninety minutes later in case additional Japanese carriers might be reported. He probably remembered how a faulty scouting report at the Battle of the Coral Sea had led him to waste his striking force on the small carrier *Shoho,* while the big Japanese carriers went unmolested. Finally, at 8:30, he decided to launch half of his dive-bombers and all of his torpedo planes, along with a few fighters, while holding back the rest of the aircraft to deal with whatever might develop.

After recovering his Midway attack force, Nagumo had retired to the northeast in order to open the range between himself and the American carriers while his planes were rearmed and refueled. This abrupt change of course made the Americans' problem more difficult. Inexperienced in coordinating attacks, departing at different times, flying at various speeds and altitudes, the planes of Spruance's striking force soon became separated and attacked the Japanese piecemeal.

Arriving at the estimated Japanese position, Spruance's planes found it empty and had to search for the enemy. The *Hornet*'s fighters and dive-bombers never did find the carriers: they had to return empty-handed when their fuel ran low. *Hornet*'s Torpedo Squadron Eight, led by Commander John C. Waldron, managed to locate the Japanese; it attacked alone and was totally destroyed. Not a single plane survived the relentless attacks of the Japanese Zeros and the carrier's antiaircraft fire. A similar fate befell the *Enterprise*'s torpedo squadron under Lieutenant Commander Eugene E. Lindsey: it lost ten of its fourteen planes. Neither squadron scored any hits.

The *Yorktown*'s planes managed to stay together reasonably well and had less trouble finding the Japanese. Although starting later, they reached the target at about the same time as the *Enterprise*'s planes, which had had to search longer for it. But the *Yorktown*'s torpedo planes, attacking first, also failed to damage the enemy ships. Only two of the twelve aircraft survived.

Trying to cover the torpedo planes, Commander James Thach, leader of the *Yorktown*'s fighters, saw a plane near him burst into flames. "Zeros were coming in on us in a stream from astern. Then I saw a second large group streaming right past us on to the torpedo planes. The air was just like a beehive. . . " Using their special tactic, "the Thach weave," the outnumbered fighters fought on doggedly against the Zeros. But simple logic told Thach that with the Zeros' superior performance and overwhelming numbers, he could not hope to survive for long. "Then I saw this glint in the sun and it just looked like a beautiful silver waterfall; these dive bombers coming down. I could see them very well because that was the direction of the Zeros too. They weren't anywhere near the altitude the dive bombers were. I'd never seen such superb dive bombing." [21]

The battle with the torpedo planes had fully occupied the Japanese fighter pilots. Like the rest of the Japanese navy, they considered the torpedo plane the most deadly carrier weapon, and, in Japanese hands, it was. So the Zeros had swarmed down on the American torpedo bombers at low altitude, barely above deck level. There were virtually no Japanese fighters left to interfere when the dive-bombers of the *Yorktown* and *Enterprise* came screaming down on the Japanese carriers, whose decks were crowded with planes, bombs, and fuel.

Two minutes after the last torpedo plane attacks, three of the *Enterprise*'s dive-bombers loosed their bombs on the flagship *Akagi* at about 2,500 feet. The first bomb was a near miss, but the other two exploded on the flight deck and in the hangar, detonating bombs and torpedoes being used to rearm the Japanese planes. In a few minutes the flagship was enveloped in flames.

The *Kaga* took four bombs, which blew her island superstructure to bits and started other explosions among the munitions and bombs on the flight deck. The blasts killed most of the personnel on the bridge and also destroyed the fire-fighting water pumps. Flames spread rapidly through the ship, trapping most of the engineering crew in the engine room. The *Soryu* was hit by a bomb which struck just in front of the forward elevator, flinging the elevator against the island bridge. Two more bombs exploded among the munitions on the flight and hanger decks, engulfing them in sheets of flame. Within twenty minutes the *Soryu* was a blazing wreck and had to be abandoned. The *Akagi* and *Kaga* did not sink until evening but it was soon clear that they were beyond salvage.[22]

Only the *Hiryu*, which had become separated from the others in the wild maneuvering to avoid the successive American air attacks, had escaped unscathed. At eleven she launched two waves of dive-bomber and torpedo plane attacks against the *Yorktown*. It was the last time that Japan's veteran air aces would fly against American carriers and, in this last sortie, they did well. Pushing home their attack through American fighters and antiaircraft fire, they dropped three bombs on the *Yorktown*. This was followed by two torpedoes from the second wave of attackers, which caused the *Yorktown*'s commander to order "Abandon Ship!"

But this was the end of the pilots who had wreaked havoc with the Allies from Pearl Harbor to the Bay of Bengal. Only a dozen-odd planes survived to return to the *Hiryu*. Three hours later dive-bombers from the *Enterprise* (ten of the twenty-four dive-bombers in this strike were from *Yorktown* air groups which had had to land on the *Enterprise*) found the *Hiryu* and left her in sinking condition.

By this time night was falling. Fletcher, whose task force was without a carrier, had virtually handed over command to Spruance. The Americans believed they had scored an important success but the whereabouts and intentions of the rest of the Japanese fleet remained unknown. One thing was certain: the Japanese still enjoyed an overwhelming superiority in gun power to the Americans. In any engagement after dark, that superiority would be decisive. Spruance decided to retire temporarily to the east and then head west again after midnight.

This was just as well, for by the evening powerful Japanese forces were converging on the American task force. Admiral Yamamoto had not given up hope of capturing Midway; he was coming south to rendezvous with Nagumo and with the battleships and cruisers of Admiral Kondo's Midway Invasion Force, which had come racing up from the southwest. On Yamamoto's orders, Kondo had already detached four of his heavy cruisers—the largest and fastest in the Japanese navy—commanded by Vice Admiral Takeo Kurita. Their mission was to carry out a night bombardment of Midway. At 7:15 P.M. Nagumo's force, which still included two battleships, was only about 100 miles from Spruance. Kondo was about 150 miles further, and Kurita was 250 miles from Midway.[23]

Spruance's temporary retirement to the east, however, put a night battle out of the question. By the early morning of June 5, Admiral Yamamoto must have realized this. By then he knew that the *Hiryu* had been knocked out. The two carriers of Admiral Kakuta Kakuji's Second Carrier Striking Force were far to the north delivering an air strike on Dutch Harbor in the Aleutians, and could not reach the scene of the battle until about June 8.[24] At three o'clock on the morning of the fifth, Yamamoto ordered a general retirement.

Admiral Kurita's cruisers were less than a hundred miles from Midway when they received Yamamoto's order. A few minutes later the cruisers sighted the American submarine *Tambor,* which was patrolling west of Midway. Kurita ordered a high-speed turn to port to evade the submarine; but *Mogami,* last in line, failed to get the signal and ran into *Mikuma,* the next ship ahead. The following day reconnaissance planes from the *Enterprise* spotted the two damaged cruisers limping west at about twelve knots. Bombers from the *Enterprise* and *Hornet* promptly sank the *Mikuma* and damaged the *Mogami* so badly that she was out of the war for a year.[25]

The rest of the Japanese fleet was now far out of range of the Americans and Spruance was running low on fuel. Moreover, if he continued westward, he would soon be within range of Japanese land-based planes on Wake. On the evening of the sixth, Task Force 16 turned back for Pearl Harbor.

The Battle of Midway had ended in a devastating defeat for Japan: four carriers and the most experienced pilots had been lost, a heavy cruiser sunk, and another damaged—against one carrier and a destroyer lost by the United States. In a sense the Japanese had defeated themselves through carelessness, overconfidence, and faulty disposition of forces. Their carrier air groups were far more effective than their American counterparts but most of them had been blasted while still on the decks of their carriers, before their superior skill and experience could be brought to bear.

For their part, the Americans still had much to learn. The test of battle had demonstrated that the staff Spruance inherited from Halsey, although probably the most experienced of any in carrier operations, was yet unequal to the complexities of this new type of warfare.

After the first attack on the Japanese carriers, the staff had not informed the returning pilots about the task force's changes of position. As a result many planes became lost and ran out of fuel before they could find their carriers.[26] Later that day the staff of the flagship *Enterprise* failed to relay vital information to the *Hornet,* so that the latter was late in launching her planes for the second attack against *Hiryu.* In the words of Spruance's biographer, "The staff became progressively more confused and disoriented as the battle progressed, unable to cope with the need for disciplined planning and the coordinated task force operations." [27] It required many months and many new faces before such deficiencies could be remedied.

The Midway battle was a victory whose full implications were not understood until long afterward. It was known, of course, that four of the largest Japanese carriers had been sunk—but it was hard to believe that a handful of dive-bombers from the *Yorktown* and *Enterprise* had done all the damage. The Army Air Force's heavy bombers based on Midway had flown a total of fifty-five sorties against the Japanese fleet and dropped 184,000 pounds of bombs. Navy and Marine Corps bombers and torpedo planes from Midway dropped over 50,000 pounds more, as well as seventeen torpedoes. Surely, it seemed, they must have hit *something.* [28]

In the first weeks after Midway, the Army Air Force claimed and was accorded an equal share of credit for the success. On June 12 a front-page story in the *New York Times* described how "Army Fliers Blasted Two Fleets Off Midway"; the paper commented editorially that the battle demonstrated "what land-based air power can do to naval and air power attacking from the open sea." [29] In reality, what it had done was almost nothing. Except for some minor damage to an oiler, some strafing hits, and a heroic crash-dive on a Japanese cruiser by one of the Marine dive bombers, the land-based aircraft had done no damage at all to the Japanese fleet. Not one of the dozens of bombs dropped had struck home. But this was not understood until much later; for a long time Midway was regarded as a salutory lesson in the dangers of sending aircraft carriers to challenge land-based planes.[30] Yet it was not the operational but the strategic implications of Midway which would preoccupy American leaders during the summer of 1942.

For the Japanese, Midway was an ill-conceived, sloppily executed operation. Yet Yamamoto had had the right idea: Unless Japan could inflict a shattering defeat on the U.S. early in the war, she would gradually be ground down by steadily growing American military power. The Japanese still had sufficient forces after Midway to again take the initiative for another try at the U.S. fleet. Instead they reverted to the defensive and allowed themselves to be drawn into a battle of attrition in the Solomons.

• •

The Japanese had salvaged one success from the Midway debacle. The two bare and unpopulated islands of Kiska and Attu in the Bering Sea, halfway between Alaska and Siberia at the extreme western end of the Aleutian chain, had been occupied by Vice Admiral Hosogaya Boshiro's task force. This was the only part of the Midway operation which had gone according to plan.

Hosagaya's carriers had twice raided Dutch Harbor on Unalaska, the principal American base in the Aleutians, doing only slight damage and suffering few losses. On their way back from one of the raids, four Zeros peeled off to attack an American patrol plane. One of the Zeros, hit by the patrol plane's machine guns, crash-landed on Akutan Island where it was recovered almost completely intact by the U.S. Navy and shipped to the U.S. for study. In less than eighteen months American engineers, studying and testing the captured Zero, would produce their own deadlier version: the F6F Hellcat.[31]

The weather was so bad in the Aleutians that it was over a week before reconnaissance planes discovered the Japanese on Kiska and Attu. There was a brief flurry of excitement. Reinforcements were rushed to Alaska; the Joint Chiefs of Staff speculated that the Aleutian attack might be part of a Japanese thrust into Siberia.[32]

The top military leaders in the Aleutians—Rear Admiral Robert A. Theobald, Commander North Pacific Area under Admiral Nimitz, Lieutenant General John L. Dewitt, commander of the army's Western Defense Command and his principal subordinate, Major General Simon Bolivar Buckner, Jr., commander of the Alaskan Defense Command—all urged an early offensive aimed at retaking Attu and Kiska. After a few weeks, however, Washington decided that there were more important areas than the Aleutians. Although their strategic position seemed impressive on a map, their year-round weather was so severe—with winds so high, storms so frequent, fog so persistent, terrain so forbidding—that they would have made a very unfavorable area for a major military effort. General Marshall knew this and therefore consistently cut the ambitious proposals coming out of the north down to modest size.[33]

It was not until the spring of 1943 that forces could be collected for an assault against the islands. In the meantime Theobald and Buckner could only bomb Attu and Kiska—when their planes could find them.[34] The war between the two American commanders was much livelier. The two were supposed to "cooperate," but both were strong-willed, opinionated egoists. One high-ranking naval officer referred to the complete lack of coordination between army and navy as "one of the worst managed affairs I have ever seen."[35]

Theobald's small task force attempted two bombardments of Kiska. In the first attempt they failed to locate the island in the fog; in the second they missed the Japanese installations and churned up an impressive hole in the tundra. Buckner complained that Theobald was "as tender of his [ships'] bottoms as a teen-age girl." The admiral replied in kind.[36] In December 1942 the navy replaced Theobald with Rear Admiral Thomas C. Kinkaid, veteran of battles in the South Pacific, who promptly clamped a tight blockade on the approaches to Attu and Kiska. A Japanese attempt to run reinforcements into Attu through this blockade led to one of the few daylight naval engagements between surface forces of the Pacific War.

Rear Admiral Charles H. McMorris, commanding Kinkaid's principal naval force—the light cruiser *Richmond,* heavy cruiser *Salt Lake City,* and four destroyers—encountered Vice Admiral Hosagaya's fleet escorting two fast merchant ships carrying reinforcements to Attu on March 26. Although Hosagaya had nearly twice as many cruisers, both faster and better armed, McMorris decided to fight. For an hour the *Salt Lake City* dueled at long range with the two Japanese heavy cruisers *Nachi* and *Maya. Nachi* was hit a number of times, but the Japanese warships were able to lead the Americans away from the merchantmen.

The shock generated by the *Salt Lake City*'s gunfire eventually damaged her own hydraulic steering system so that she could turn only with great difficulty. McMorris's destroyers laid a smoke screen for the stricken ship and the Americans turned due south in order to swing around the Japanese and head for home. Just as the turn to the south was completed, the *Salt Lake City* received a hit. Icy water poured into the after engine room and the ship took a five degree list to port. A mistake in damage control caused another loss of power, and the ship went dead in the water.

With the Japanese closing in, McMorris ordered a torpedo attack by his destroyers. They had a long way to go before they could get within range, and the Japanese filled the waters between them with eight-inch shells. Then, amazingly, the Japanese fleet turned away toward the west. Hosagaya was breaking off the action.

The Japanese navy never forgave him for that. His excuses—that his ammunition and fuel were low and that he momentarily expected an American air attack—were impatiently dismissed. He was relieved of his command and consigned to the naval reserve. McMorris returned a hero in the *Salt Lake City,* which had gotten under way soon after the Japanese withdrew. The Battle of the Komandorski Islands, as it came to be called, was the kind of battle American naval officers had been thinking of and planning for since Jutland: a long-range daylight gunnery duel. McMorris's little fleet had shown what the U.S. Navy could do in that kind of battle; unfortunately, such battles were becoming rare.

At the beginning of 1943 the Combined Chiefs agreed at Casablanca that the U.S. would conduct a holding action in the Aleutians while major forces were committed elsewhere in the Pacific. Kinkaid came back with a proposal to capture Attu, the less heavily defended of the islands held by the Japanese. An assault on Attu, he argued, could be accomplished with forces already in Alaska. The Joint Chiefs agreed and set D-Day for Operation LANDGRAB for May 7, 1943.[37] Air Corps bombers, aided by a spell of good weather, pounded Attu and Kiska for weeks before the attack. Admiral Nimitz sent an escort carrier and three old battleships, *Pennsylvania, Idaho,* and *Nevada,* to beef up the naval support. Bad weather delayed the landings until May 11. The Americans had overwhelming superiority both at sea and in the air; the assault troops outnumbered the Japanese defenders almost five to one.

Troops of the Seventh Division, under Major General Albert E. Brown, went ashore at two widely separate points, at Holtz Bay on the northeast end of the island, and at Massacre Bay on the southeast end. A troop of scouts landed at a small inlet northwest of Holtz Bay called Beach Scarlet. All forces landed unopposed. The advance soon bogged down nonetheless.

Fierce, chilling winds roared across the barren, spongy tundra where American troops trudged through snow or slippery mud. From high points on Attu's jagged hills the outnumbered Japanese poured down a deadly fire with rifles, mortars, and machine guns, while the Americans' view of the enemy on the heights was often obscured by fog.

In Massacre Valley, the southern force was pinned down at a narrow pass, with the Japanese holding the high ground on three sides. Repeated attacks up the pass in the next few days failed to dislodge them. From offshore the battleships blasted away at the mountains until their ammunition was exhausted, but the Japanese held.

Kinkaid and De Witt, impatient with General Brown's lack of apparent progress and his requests for reinforcements, decided to replace him with Brigadier General Eugene M. Landrum. Like many later American commanders relieved in the midst of battle, Brown was replaced just as his troops were achieving their first success.[38] On May 16 American forces in the northeast, around Holtz Bay, aided by furious naval bombardment and frequent air attacks, drove the Japanese from the high ground which separated the two arms of the bay and emerged to the rear of the enemy forces defending the pass at Massacre Valley on the south.

The American forces to the north and south linked up the following day as the Japanese retreated toward the extreme northeast tip of Attu. Ten days later, as the Americans closed in on the final Japanese positions on a small pocket of flat ground near the sea, the enemy commander, Colonel Yamasake Yasuyo, launched a surprise night attack with his remaining 800 men; some of them had no ammunition, only bayonets fixed to empty rifles. Yamasake hoped to bypass the American positions on the high ground under cover of darkness, then seize their supplies and guns to the rear.

Aided by darkness and fog, the Japanese swept through one company of the 32nd Infantry and overran a medical station at the base of a jagged ridge called Engineer Hill. At the top of the hill engineers, medics, clerks, and other rear area personnel formed an improvised perimeter under the leadership of Brigadier General Archibald Arnold, the divisional artillery commander.

Arnold's men lobbed grenades at the charging Japanese, then met them with bullets and bayonets, driving them back. A handful of Japanese broke through but were mowed down by a thirty-seven-millimeter gun which had just been brought up by the engineers. Further piecemeal efforts also failed. By the close of the day Yamasaki's force had been wiped out.

Ten weeks later, on August 15, an armada of nearly a hundred ships, including two battleships and five cruisers, converged on Kiska. It had been the target of continuous bombing raids since the beginning of July. Thirty-five thousand troops embarked for the invasion; but the Japanese had already gone, pulled out on the last day of July by a naval task force under cover of thick fog.

In proportion to the forces engaged, the Attu invasion was one of the costliest island campaigns of the Second World War. As in other such bloodlettings, the services learned lessons that would serve them in good stead later. But unlike Tarawa and Iwo Jima, the military logic behind the Attu campaign was at best questionable. Like China the Aleutians appeared to be a road that might prove a shortcut to Japan. Like China they proved, in the end, a road which led nowhere.

NOTES

1. Walter Lord, *Incredible Victory* (New York: Harper and Row, 1967), p. 11; Fuchida and Okumiya, *Midway*, pp. 98–100.

2. Fuchida and Okumiya, *Midway*, pp. 90–91.

3. Lord, *Incredible Victory*, p. 12.

4. Naval War College, *Midway*, p. 12; Morison, *Coral Sea, Midway*, p. 79.

5. Fuchida and Okumiya, *Midway*, pp. 82–85; Morison, *Coral Sea, Midway*, pp. 76–78.

6. Morison, *Coral Sea, Midway*, p. 77; Dull, *Imperial Japanese Navy*, p. 144.

7. Fuchida and Okumiya, *Midway*, pp. 84–85.

8. Ibid., p. 93.

9. Naval War College, *Midway*, p. 66.

10. David Kahn, *The Codebreakers: The Story of Secret Writing* (New York: Macmillan and Co., 1967), pp. 568–70.

11. Lundstrom, *First South Pacific Campaign*, pp. 160–61.

12. Potter, *Nimitz*, p. 83.

13. Lord, *Incredible Victory*, pp. 36–39.

14. Buell, *Quiet Warrior*, p. 126.

15. Fuchida and Okumiya, *Midway*, pp. 110–11; Toland, *The Rising Sun*, pp. 327–28.

16. Lord, *Incredible Victory*, p. 66.

17. Dull, *Imperial Japanese Navy*, p. 144.

18. Fuchida and Okumiya, *Midway*, p. 150.

19. Ibid.

20. Letter, Spruance to Vice Admiral E. P. Forrestal, n.d., cited in Buell, *Quiet Warrior*, p. 460. Most accounts of the Battle of Midway credit Miles Browning with persuading Spruance to launch the early attack. In his biography of Spruance, however, Buell marshalls convincing evidence to demonstrate that Spruance intended from the first to launch at the earliest possible moment and that Browning had little to do with it: *Quiet Warrior*, pp. 459–61.

21. Reminiscences of Vice Admiral James E. Thach, pp. 245–52.

22. Dull, *Imperial Japanese Navy*, pp. 159–64.

23. Fuchida and Okumiya, *Midway*, p. 184.

24. Ibid., p. 183; Morison, *Coral Sea, Midway*, p. 139.

25. Morison, *Coral Sea, Midway,* pp. 148–50.

26. Buell, *Quiet Warrior,* p. 134–35.

27. Ibid., p. 139.

28. Naval War College, *Midway,* p. 125.

29. *New York Times,* June 9, 1942.

30. Morison, *Coral Sea, Midway,* p. 159; idem, *Aleutians, Gilberts and Marshalls,* p. 85.

31. Brian Garfield, *The Thousand Mile War* (New York: Doubleday and Co., 1969), pp. 41–42.

32. Stetson Conn, Rose C. Engelman, and Byron Fairchild, *Guarding the United States and Its Outposts* (Washington, D.C.: Office of the Chief of Military History, 1964), p. 264.

33. Morton, *Strategy and Command,* p. 429.

34. Craven and Cate, *Army Air Forces in World War II,* Vol. 4, *The Pacific: Guadalcanal to Saipan* (Chicago: University of Chicago Press, 1950), pp. 375–76.

35. Letter, Rear Admiral J. W. Reeves, Jr., to R. Admiral C. S. Freeman, 13 June 1942; copy in King Papers, Double Zero files.

36. Garfield, *Thousand Mile War,* p. 121.

37. Craven and Cate, *Guadalcanal to Saipan,* p. 378.

38. The best discussion of the faulty communications, personal friction, and misperception which led to Brown's relief may be found in Garfield, *Thousand Mile War,* pp. 230–33, 235, 317–18.

NINE

Routes to Rabaul

It was just after one in the morning. Lieutenant R. E. Schaeffer, USNR, wiped the rain out of his eyes for what seemed the hundredth time as he cautiously steered his small motorized surfboat through the dark waters off Florida Island in the British Solomons. Behind Schaeffer chugged three heavily loaded amphibian tractors from the transport *President Adams.* The odd procession was headed for the tiny islet of Gavutu, where marines had landed the previous morning. Schaeffer was the ship's dentist—but the *President Adams* was so short of officers that he also commanded one of her boat divisions.

Steering by compass alone, Schaeffer completely missed Gavutu; he had to turn back and try again. Straining his eyes into the rain and darkness, he vainly sought the strip of beach where the marines were impatiently awaiting the food, water, and ammunition in his tractors. Three times the surfboat grounded and had to be towed off by the tractors. Suddenly a burst of small arms and machine-gun fire greeted the little fleet as it approached the beach at Gavutu. As he hurriedly took cover, Schaeffer could hear shouts in English from the shore and an answering stream of curses from his sailors. He had found the marines.[1]

Schaeffer's adventure went largely unrecorded in the history books. Yet its combination of improvisation, bravery, luck, and confusion typified the operation of which it was a part: the first American offensive in the Pacific, on a jungle-covered island called Guadalcanal.

Guadalcanal and the Solomons were no part of American war plans at the time of Pearl Harbor. What attracted the strategists' attention to them was the Japanese South Pacific advance, threatening the Allied line of communications with Australia. As early as March 1942 Admiral King had urged an offensive drive from bases in the New Hebrides through the Solomon Islands and along the New Guinea coast to the Bismarck Archipelago.[2]

Following the American success at Midway, General MacArthur too weighed in with his own plan for an offensive aimed at the great Japanese base at Rabaul on the northeast tip of New Britain Island, just east of New Guinea. In messages to Washington, MacArthur outlined a lightning campaign calling for the seizure of Rabaul in less than three weeks. To perform this piece of legerdemain, however, MacArthur would need a division of troops trained for amphibious assault. Since Rabaul was outside the range of land-based Allied fighter planes, he would also need a navy task force with two aircraft carriers.[3]

The navy readily agreed with MacArthur's plan for an offensive against Rabaul but it was not eager to turn over any of its precious carriers for the sort of dash at Rabaul which he proposed, one that would bring them into the narrow, poorly charted waters of the Solomon Sea close to Japanese aerodromes.[4] It would be far better, argued Admiral King and his chief planner, Admiral Charles E. Cooke, to advance more gradually toward Rabaul: through the Solomons and New Guinea, capturing the enemy's bases along the way. Such an operation, primarily amphibious in character, would naturally be under naval command, that is, under Nimitz and not MacArthur. MacArthur saw no difficulty with the step-by-step approach suggested by the navy. He declared that he had had that in mind all along, but insisted that since the operations contemplated lay within his theater, he must command.[5]

The argument over command rocked the Joint Chiefs of Staff for almost a week. At one point King warned Marshall that he would direct Nimitz to go ahead with the operation " 'even if no support of army forces in the southwest Pacific is made available,' " while MacArthur declared that the navy's obstinacy was part of a long-time plot to bring about " 'the complete absorption of the national defense function by the Navy, the Army being relegated to merely base, training, garrisoning, and supply purposes.' "[6]

Finally a solution was thrashed out in a series of meetings between

King and Marshall. The planned offensive was divided into three separate phases or "tasks." Task One, an attack on the island of Tulagi in the southern Solomons, would be under the control of Admiral Nimitz. For this purpose the boundaries of Nimitz's theater would be moved one degree west so as to encompass the island objective. Task Two involved an advance along the northeast coast of New Guinea together with a simultaneous advance up the Solomons chain, while Task Three comprised the final assault on Rabaul. The latter two "tasks" would be under General MacArthur's command, but the Joint Chiefs would determine the composition of forces and the timing for each task.[7]

Because the Japanese were rapidly consolidating their position in the southern Solomons, Task One would have to be launched as soon as possible. The formal directive was issued by the Joint Chiefs of Staff on July 2, 1942; the operation, code-named WATCH-TOWER, was set to begin August 1. When intelligence reports showed that the Japanese had begun to build an airfield on the large island of Guadalcanal, next to Tulagi, that island too was added to the list of objectives.

Far away in New Zealand Rear Admiral Robert L. Ghormley who, as Commander South Pacific Forces under Admiral Nimitz, would be in overall charge of Task One, viewed Washington's strategic decisions with grave misgivings. Recently arrived from a tour as senior naval observer in London, he had probably been chosen for his new post because of his skill as a diplomat. Such skill would be a useful asset for a commander who would have to deal with the proud, hypersensitive Free French in New Caledonia and a worried New Zealand Government in Auckland. Ghormley also seemed right for the job because of his acquaintance with the president, whom he had served as naval liaison officer.[8] His chief of staff, Rear Admiral Daniel J. Callaghan, had been the president's naval aide.

When Ghormley learned in late June of the impending operation, his amphibious assault force, the First Marine Division, was still at sea on its way to New Zealand. Its most experienced regiment, the Seventh Marines, had been sent to Samoa in April. The division was not combat-loaded. Its commander, Major General Alexander A. Vandegrift, had been assured by Admiral King that he need not expect a combat mission before 1943.[9] Almost nothing was known of Guadalcanal, Tulagi, and the Solomons beyond scattered reports from coastwatchers and a few old records in Australia.

Flying to Melbourne to confer with MacArthur on July 8, Ghormley's doubts were amply reinforced by the general's own pessimism. Together they dispatched a message to Washington calling attention to their lack of sufficient planes, ships, materiel, and port facilities to undertake WATCHTOWER. They urged postponement.[10] The MacArthur-Ghormley message was received in Washington with all the welcome of a whiskey advertisement at a temperance meeting. Admiral Cooke, King's chief planner, was especially caustic about MacArthur's abrupt change from breezy confidence that he could storm Rabaul itself to hesitancy about the much more limited WATCHTOWER operation. Perhaps, suggested Cooke, MacArthur's change in attitude was due to the fact that he was now confronted with " 'the concrete aspects of the problem.' " [11]

Cooke was probably underestimating MacArthur. The general must have known all along that he could not launch a quick campaign against Rabaul, even given all the troops and warships he had asked for. His "plan" for the Rabaul operation was simply a bid for scarce resources to be used in his theater. In this sense it was little different from King's own proposals for an offensive in the South Pacific. Such an offensive would ensure "the creation of an active fighting constituency in the Pacific with a rightful call on American resources before the Allies undertook major operations against Germany." [12] It was this contest for resources which dominated—and to a large extent continued to dominate—American decision making in the war against Japan. "They were fighting for men and supplies," recalled a Marine officer who served with the Joint Chiefs of Staff at this time. "The money was insignificant. You could get all the money you wanted but there were just so much supplies in the U.S." [13] For King, as for MacArthur, a major campaign in the South Pacific represented a bureaucratic success—but King, like MacArthur, was soon to be discomfited by the "concrete aspects of the problem"

The Joint Chiefs answered the MacArthur-Ghormley message with a terse order to get on with the job, but they did agree to postpone D-Day until August 7. Both King and Nimitz expected Ghormley to command WATCHTOWER in person. Unfortunately, they had not bothered to explain this to Ghormley. His directives from Nimitz and King were sufficiently ambiguous to allow him to conclude that he was to exercise only broad general command and not direct operational command of the actual invasion. When the transports carrying the marines sailed with their escorts from Wellington, New Zealand, Ghormley remained ashore at his new headquarters in Nouméa.[14]

● ●

While Ghormley worried over Task One, MacArthur's staff in Australia began to plan measures to support Task Two. The first step would be construction of a major airbase near Buna Government Station, on the north coast of the Papua peninsula which formed the long narrow "tail" of New Guinea. The airfield would support operations against the Japanese strongholds at Lae and Salamaua, which were further to the west along the same coast.

Brigadier General Robert H. Van Volkenburgh was placed in charge of the move to Buna, which was scheduled for August 10. On July 17, however, Van Volkenburgh learned that a large concentration of Japanese shipping had been spotted at Rabaul and that smaller boats loaded with troops had been sighted at sea. Van Volkenburgh concluded that the Japanese must be headed for Buna. He frantically telephoned MacArthur's headquarters, urging that troops be rushed to Buna by sea and air to forestall the Japanese.

In addition to Van Volkenburgh's reports, MacArthur's headquarters had received earlier warnings of a Japanese move on Buna. The navy's codebreaking unit in the Philippines ("CAST"), under Commander Rudolph Fabian, had been evacuated from beleaguered Corregidor by submarine along with its "Purple Machine" and had been reestablished as "Belconnen" with headquarters in Melbourne alongside the Intelligence Division of the Royal Australian Navy.[15] It was also closely linked to the U.S. Navy's other code-breaking activities in Hawaii and Washington. As early as May 18 Belconnen intercepted a Japanese message which discussed a land route to be established between Port Moresby and the north coast of the Papuan peninsula. Further intercepts confirmed the likelihood of a Japanese overland attack. Wilfrid J. Holmes, who served with navy code-breakers in Hawaii, recalls that early in July his unit was able to recover almost the entire text of a Japanese message (probably in a minor or superseded code) which gave definite information about an attack on Port Moresby to begin with a landing at Buna on July 21.[16] There is no evidence in General Sutherland's office files, however, that either MacArthur or his chief of staff ever saw this decrypt.[17]

MacArthur's staff had little time for these alarms and rumors in any case. The commander in chief was in the midst of moving his headquarters from Melbourne to Brisbane. There was no reason to think the Japanese were headed for Buna, General Sutherland told Van Volkenburgh. Colonel Charles A. Willoughby, MacArthur's intelligence officer, had indeed noted the Japanese buildup in the Rabaul area but had discounted the possibility of a move against Port Moresby and Buna.[18] Besides, hasty deployment to Buna of a portion of the occupation force might trigger a Japanese reaction.[19]

General MacArthur left Melbourne for his new headquarters aboard a special train on July 21. Behind MacArthur's maroon-colored coach, built for the Prince of Wales's visit to Australia and still bearing the royal crest, were two flatcars. The first carried MacArthur's limousine, gleaming in the afternoon sun; the second bore General Sutherland's slightly less grand Cadillac. As the train rolled into Brisbane early the next morning, Signal Corps men were waiting with an urgent message: the Japanese had landed at Buna.[20]

The Japanese forces, 16,000 men of General Horii Tomitaro's elite South Seas Detachment, quickly consolidated their position on the coast and struck out across the Owen Stanley Mountains for Port Moresby, the prize that had eluded them in the Battle of the Coral Sea. Between Buna and Port Moresby lay some of the most rugged, forbidding terrain on earth. Jagged mountain peaks rising to a height of over 13,000 feet, steep gorges, turbulent rivers and streams, all covered by thick jungle, dominate the interior of the Papuan peninsula. The rainfall is heavy and, in some seasons, almost continuous. A single overland route connected Port Moresby with Buna: the Kokoda trail, a primitive track of slippery mud and rock. In places it was almost vertical, in other places it was so narrow only a single man could pass at a time.

It was the sort of terrain that would have challenged even the most enthusiastic outdoorsman. But the Australian, Japanese, and American soldiers were not enthusiastic outdoorsmen. They were loaded down with up to seventy pounds of gear in the steaming heat of the low-lying jungle and swamps or the chilling cold of the higher mountain passes, plagued by malaria, dysentery, and a particularly virulent form of typhus; they were usually short of food, always near exhaustion. " 'There are mists creeping over the trees all day and sometimes you can't see your hand in front of your face under cover of the jungle,' " reported one Australian soldier. " 'Most of our chaps haven't seen a Jap! You don't see the Jap who gets you!' " Seventy-five percent of the troops fighting on the Kokoda trail had never seen a single Japanese soldier.[21]

Australian forces along the trail, badly outnumbered, fought a stubborn retiring action against Horii's advancing forces. By mid-September, they stood on the Imita Range in the southern foothills of the

Owen Stanleys, the last defensible barrier before Port Moresby.[22]

The Japanese advance caused amazement and consternation at General MacArthur's headquarters. Having been assured (quite erroneously) by his staff that the Australians outnumbered the Japanese on the Kokoda trail, MacArthur could only conclude that "the Australians won't fight." [23] Superficial inspections of "the front" by Sutherland and his staff served to reinforce the commander in chief's misgivings.[24] As the Japanese advance continued, MacArthur's headquarters became almost panic-stricken: this looked like Malaya all over again! General H. H. Arnold, visiting MacArthur on an inspection tour in early September, was surprised to see his "hands twitch and tremble—shell shocked". Arnold departed with the impression that "the Australian is not a bushman; he is not a field soldier. He is nothing but a city slum dweller." [25] An officer on MacArthur's staff told Admiral Nimitz that New Guinea was "gone." Prime Minister John Curtis "won't let the Americans do anything in New Guinea because of the political effect it might have" and the Australians themselves "won't fight. This war has been a series of disasters and withdrawals for them and now they have the habit." [26]

While MacArthur's staff wrung their hands, the Australians were winning one of the first Allied land victories of the war at Milne Bay on the eastern tip of the Papuan peninsula. Here Australian troops and American combat engineers, battling in the pouring rain and in terrain so muddy that even tanks bogged down in it, stopped a Japanese invasion intended to serve as the second prong of the movement against Port Moresby.[27]

MacArthur, unimpressed with the success at Milne Bay, sent Australian General Thomas Blamey, Commander, Allied Land Forces, Southwest Pacific, up to New Guinea to "vitalize" the Australian forces there. Yet events in the Solomons had already begun to "devitalize" the Japanese in a way which would prove decisive.

•　　•

Off the tiny island of Koro in the Fijis, the Guadalcanal invasion fleet came together on July 25 for the first time: seventy-six warships and auxiliaries from Australia, from Pearl Harbor, from New Zealand, from as far away as San Diego. Three of the navy's four remaining carriers were there, together with a brand new battleship and a division of cruisers from the Royal Australian Navy under Rear

Admiral V. A. C. Crutchley. Vice Admiral Frank Jack Fletcher, the
victor of the Coral Sea and Midway, was in tactical command. Rear
Admiral Richmond Kelly Turner, fresh from Washington where he
had been one of Admiral King's top strategists, commanded the
Amphibious Force South Pacific—the transports and cargo ships carrying the First Marine Division (reinforced by a regiment from the
Second Marine Division and other units) and their gear.

The principal commanders came aboard Fletcher's flagship *Saratoga*
the following day to discuss the impending operation. Fletcher was
openly skeptical about the undertaking. He implied that Turner—
and the rest of King's armchair strategists in Washington who had
planned it—had had no real fighting experience. Turner responded
in kind. His chief of staff, Captain Peyton, " 'was amazed and disturbed by the way these two admirals talked to each other. I had
never heard anything like it.' " [28]

Fletcher was most concerned about taking his precious carriers
within range of Japanese air bases and carriers. The carriers represented three-quarters of the navy's fighting strength in that category
and no replacements could be expected for the next nine months.
Two days was all the time that Fletcher believed he could keep his
carriers in an exposed position supporting the landings. The navy
had come a long way from Nimitz's confident observation that "because of the superiority of our personnel and equipment" the U.S.
could afford to accept adverse odds in battle with the Japanese.
Fletcher had seen what Japanese pilots could do at Coral Sea and
Midway.

Turner and Marine Commander Vandegrift vehemently protested
the decision to pull out after two days, pointing out that it would
take a minimum of four days to get all the troops and their equipment
ashore, but Fletcher refused to budge. Ghormley might have resolved
the impasse, but he was far away at Noumea. So Fletcher's decision
stood. After a brief rehearsal at Koro, which Vandegrift later described as "a complete bust," the fleet sailed for Guadalcanal.

On that island, and on neighboring Tulagi, the Japanese defenders
remained unaware of the American approach almost until the moment
high explosive shells from Crutchley's cruisers and destroyers came
roaring down on them like freight trains. The few Japanese on Guadalcanal, mostly construction troops, fled into the jungle. But on
Tulagi and the neighboring islets of Gavutu and Tanambogo the
marines encountered stiff, although brief, resistance. All three islands,

as well as the nearly completed airfield on Guadalcanal, were in American hands by the end of the second day, August 8.

By that time Admiral Fletcher was growing increasingly nervous about possible threats to his carriers from the large number of enemy planes he believed to be in the area. The whereabouts of the four Japanese carriers which had survived Midway were also unknown. At six in the evening of the eighth, Fletcher decided he could wait no longer. He radioed Admiral Ghormley:

> Fighter strength reduced from 99 to 78. In view of large number of enemy torpedo planes and bombers in this area, I recommend the immediate withdrawal of my carriers. Request tankers be sent forward immediately as fuel running low. [29]

Then, without waiting for a reply, he immediately set course for home.

Admiral Turner, with the transports off Guadalcanal, was amazed and angered by Fletcher's withdrawal twelve hours earlier than planned. He considered it little better than desertion, and most historians have agreed with him.[30] Samuel Eliot Morison points out that Fletcher's seventy-eight fighters were still more than the Americans had had at the beginning of the Midway battle, his ships had sufficient fuel for several days more, and "his force could have remained in the area with no more severe consequence than sunburn." [31]

At about the same time that Fletcher was sending his request to withdraw, MacArthur's headquarters at Brisbane was receiving a disquieting report from New Guinea. An Australian search plane, flying out of Milne Bay at 10:30 in the morning, had sighted Japanese warships heading south from Rabaul. Instead of breaking radio silence to report this important information, the pilot waited until after he had returned from his mission and had his afternoon tea. The report did not reach the forces at Guadalcanal until about seven that evening.

Those Japanese ships—which the Australian described as three cruisers, three destroyers, and two seaplane tenders or gunboats— were in fact five heavy cruisers, two light cruisers, and a destroyer, all under Vice Admiral Mikawa Gunichi, commander of the Eighth Fleet. Mikawa expected that the American ships at Guadalcanal would outnumber his, but he had a well-justified faith in Japanese night-fighting abilities. Although his eight ships had never fought or even steamed together before, he believed that if they could approach under cover of darkness they could break through the enemy's screen

Tugs and barges fight fires raging aboard the battleship *West Virginia* at Pearl Harbor. Eighteen U.S. warships, including eight battleships, were sunk or seriously damaged in the Japanese surprise attack on December 7, 1941, and 2400 men were killed. The supply and repair facilities at Pearl Harbor, however, were left undamaged—a major error on the part of the Japanese. All but two of the battleships were subsequently salvaged and rejoined the fleet during 1943 and 1944. *U.S. Navy*

Army Chief of Staff General George C. Marshall with Secretary of War Henry Stimson in 1942. The two formed one of the most effective partnerships in the history of the War Department. *U.S. Army*

American and Filipino troops, already showing the effects of malnutrition and disease, stand formation during the battle for Bataan in January 1942. Shortages of food and medicine were to play a large role in the American defeat in the Philippines. *U.S. Marine Corps*

Five-inch guns of *U.S.S. Northampton* bombard an island in Maloelap atoll in the Marshalls in February 1942. These early raids did little damage but gave the Navy much needed combat experience, expecially in carrier operations.

General James Doolittle's B-25B bombers crowded onto the flight deck of the *Hornet* en route to the raid on Tokyo in April 1942. Although the raid made little difference in the overall military situation, it boosted morale in the U.S. and reenforced Yamamoto's determination to carry out the Midway operation. *U.S. Navy*

Hornet's torpedo squadron 8, shortly before the Battle of Midway. Ensign George Gay (circled) was the only member of the squadron to survive the battle. Losses among torpedo plane squadrons of all three American carriers were heavy but their determined attacks distracted Japanese fighters and allowed American dive bombers to deliver their fatal blows. *U.S. Navy*

The wreckage of a Japanese type 97 "Kate" torpedo bomber floats near the U.S. fleet following Nagumo's final air attack in the Battle of Midway. The loss of four large carriers and many of their most skilled pilots in the battle was a devastating blow to the Japanese. *U.S. Navy*

General MacArthur with some of his top commanders in New Britain in 1943. To MacArthur's left are V. Adm. Thomas Kincaid, Maj. Gen. Ennis C. White-head, and Marine Maj. Gen. William H. Rupertus. To his right is Lt. Gen. Walter Krueger. The capture of Arawe and of Cape Gloucester on New Britain at the end of 1943 were part of the MacArthur-Halsey CARTWHEEL operation to isolate Rabaul. *U.S. Army*

Admiral Halsey (in pith helmet) talks with Marines on Bougainville during an inspection tour. To his left is Maj. Gen. Roy Geiger, who later commanded the Marines on Okinawa. *U.S. Navy*

A soldier in New Georgia cautiously checks out a Japanese pillbox typical of those which gave Americans problems all through the war. This one survived bombing and shelling intact. *U.S. Army*

A Japanese eight-inch naval gun on Tarawa. Guns like these, and smaller pieces, survived naval shelling to wreak havoc among the American landing forces. *U.S. Navy*

Marines capture a pill box sheltering a light machine gun. Marine in right foreground wears recently introduced camouflaged battle dress; the helmet became emblematic of marines in the Pacific. *U.S. Marine Corps*

A Grumman "Avenger" torpedo plane readies for takeoff aboard the carrier *Enterprise*. Sign boards relay last minute information to pilots. *U.S. Navy*

Douglas Dauntless dive bombers aboard the carrier *U.S.S. Yorktown*. Fast carrier operations made possible the rapid advance of the U.S. campaign in the Central Pacific. *U.S. Navy*

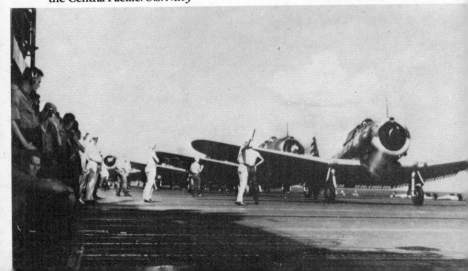

A bomb explodes alongside the *Enterprise* during the Battle of Santa Cruz Islands in October 1942. The *Enterprise*, completed in 1938, fought in almost all the great campaigns of the Pacific War. For a time, in late 1942, she was the only large U.S. aircraft carrier left in the Western Pacific. *U.S. Navy*

Grumman F6F Hellcat, designed specifically to outperform the Zero, proved to be the best carrier-borne fighter of the war. *U.S. Navy*

of warships and sink his transports.[32] Delaying near the island of Bougainville until late afternoon to avoid Allied search planes, Mikawa turned his ships toward Guadalcanal and sped down the narrow channel or "Slot" through the Solomon Islands at twenty-four knots.

Aboard Turner's flagship the admiral was conferring with General Vandegrift and Admiral Crutchley about what action to take in view of Fletcher's precipitous withdrawal. During the meeting Turner received a copy of the Australian sighting report, which was now eight and a half hours old. Turner had already received two warnings, based on radio intercepts by Nimitz's headquarters, that Mikawa's force was at sea,[33] but this in itself told him nothing of enemy intentions. Earlier that day, CINCPAC intelligence had intercepted a message from Mikawa stating his intention to rendezvous with his force near Bougainville and proceed to Guadalcanal for operations against an enemy convoy. Unfortunately for the Americans, this vital message was not decrypted until August 23.[34]

The two seaplane tenders mentioned in the Australian report suggested to Turner that the Japanese were headed for Santa Isabel Island, 155 miles from Guadalcanal, a good spot for a seaplane base. The reported strength of the force—three cruisers and three destroyers—its course, and its low speed, all seemed to confirm this estimate. Besides, if the Japanese were headed down the Slot, they ought to have been spotted by Rear Admiral John S. McCain's land-based search planes from New Caledonia, the Fijis, and the Santa Cruz Islands. But bad weather had grounded many of McCain's B-17s and Catalinas, a fact not reported to Turner until midnight. Under the circumstances, Turner and Crutchley assumed that the Japanese force was setting up for a seaplane strike the next day, not for a surface attack at night.[35] By this time Mikawa was less than five hours from Guadalcanal.

Five Allied heavy cruisers and five destroyers patrolled the western entrance to the sound between Florida and Guadalcanal, where Turner's transports were anchored. Crutchley's flagship, the cruiser *Australia,* was absent, carrying the admiral to his meeting with Turner. The remaining ships were divided into a "northern" and "southern" force in order to cover the two channels into the sound, which ran north and south of the small island of Savo. Further out, two destroyers equipped with radar, *Blue* and *Ralph Talbot,* patrolled the approaches to Savo.

None of these vessels sighted Mikawa's squadron as it swept down from the northwest and entered the sound south of Savo around one-thirty in the morning. The first ship to spot the Japanese was the destroyer *Patterson*, which broadcast a warning just as the entire area was suddenly and brilliantly illuminated by star shells and salvoes from the Japanese guns. The Australian cruiser *Canberra*, hit by two torpedoes and more than two-dozen shells, was left dead in the water, aflame and sinking.

The Japanese column then swung left around Savo, heading for the northern force and putting a torpedo into the cruiser *Chicago* on its way. Although the battle had been on for some five minutes, the ships of the northern force were still unaware of what was happening; the Allied ships to the south had been unable or too busy to warn them. As the Japanese bore down on the northern force's three cruisers—the *Astoria*, *Quincy* and *Vincennes*—the heavy cruiser *Aoba* snapped open her searchlight and illuminated the *Quincy*, whose guns were still trained fore and aft. Taken by surprise, the American cruisers were able to fire only a few salvoes. One hit by the cruiser *Quincy* wiped out the staff chartroom aboard Mikawa's flagship *Chokai*, but soon all three cruisers had been overwhelmed by the hail of shell from the Japanese.

On the *Chokai*'s bridge, Mikawa surveyed the devastation caused by his attack and pondered his next move. All of his ships had expended their torpedoes and the admiral's charts had gone up in smoke. He was tempted to press on and attack the transports, but his ships had become scattered in the confused night fighting and it would take at least two hours to sort them out. By then it would be almost dawn and his ships would be exposed to air attack by the American carriers he believed were still in the area.[36] At 2:20 the Admiral made his decision: the *Chokai* signalled "all ships withdraw." Twenty minutes later the Japanese were racing back up the Slot at thirty knots.

Behind them they left four Allied cruisers sunk or sinking and two destroyers and another cruiser damaged. It was the worst American naval defeat since 1812. Admiral Fletcher's carrier planes might have caught Mikawa retiring up the Slot the next morning, but his task force was already far to the south, having received Ghormley's permission to retire during the early hours of August 9. A small measure of revenge was exacted the following day, however, when the heavy cruiser *Kako*, returning to Kavieng after the battle, was torpedoed and sunk by the old American submarine S-44. This marked the first time a major Japanese warship had been sunk by a U.S. submarine.[37]

Despite the fact that his cruiser covering force had been practically wiped out in the Battle of Savo Island, Turner elected to continue unloading until noon on the ninth, enabling the marines to bring ashore a few more essential items. Yet when Turner's ships disappeared over the horizon the leathernecks' supply situation was far from opulent. They lacked radar, radio equipment, barbed wire, and construction equipment; moreover, they had only about four days' supply of ammunition. During the first six weeks the marines were limited to two very spare meals a day.

Among the marines "there was a lot of talk about Bataan." [38] "We had no idea what was going to happen," recalled one Marine officer; "we were all wondering where our planes were. The Navy had left, their carriers had left. We didn't have a thing there.[39] " 'It was about this time,' " recalled a veteran sergeant, " 'that the men began to knock off a lot of their letter writing.' " [40] "It was very galling to us to sit on Guadalcanal and listen to the radio at night," recalled Clifton B. Cates, who commanded the First Marines; "we would sit there and listen to these people make a statement, well, they *hoped* we could hold Guadalcanal. One Army Air Forces general even said it was foolish to try." [41]

Despite all this, Vandegrift had one priceless asset: the airstrip on Guadalcanal, which the marines had named Henderson Field, after Major Lofton Henderson who had led the Marine dive-bombers at the Battle of Midway. This field, which had been nearly finished by the Japanese, was rushed to completion utilizing captured equipment. On August 15 four fast destroyer-transports slipped into Guadalcanal with aviation gasoline, bombs, and a party of aircraft technicians. Five days later the first planes arrived: nineteen fighters and twelve dive-bombers flown in from the escort carrier *Long Island*. Control of the air over Guadalcanal gave the Americans a decisive advantage in the weeks of hard fighting which lay ahead.

The Japanese were slow to react to the American seizure of Guadalcanal. Their army was preoccupied with its offensive in New Guinea and had little interest in the Solomons. Until the American invasion, the Japanese army was not even aware that the navy was building an airfield on Guadalcanal. The Army General Staff, which had never been informed about the full extent of the navy's losses at Midway, expected no American offensive until the latter half of 1943. The army believed that the Americans were merely conducting a large-scale raid, and the apparent abandonment of the Marines on Guadalcanal following the Savo Island battle simply reinforced their confidence.[42] The Americans left on the island, Imperial General Headquarters reported, totalled about 2,000 men; their "morale was low"; and many were attempting to escape to Tulagi.[43] Recapture of the island should not prove difficult, but because of the airfield it should be undertaken without delay.[44]

The Seventeenth Army, commanded by Lieutenant General Hyakutaka Harukichi, with headquarters at Rabaul, was given the responsibility for clearing the Americans off Guadalcanal. Hyakutaka collected about 6,000 troops for the operation. Long before they could all be transported to the island, however, his advanced force—a 1,000-man combat team known as the Ichiki Force after its commander Colonel Ichiki Kiyono—had landed at Taivu to the east of Henderson field on August 18. From there it launched an ill-conceived attack on the marine perimeter along the Ilu River and was practically annihilated.[45]

"We have the bull by the tail and the bull doesn't like it," wrote Admiral Ghormley to Nimitz four days after the marines landed on Guadalcanal and Tulagi. He expected that the Japanese would soon "try to land an expedition against our positions in the Tulagi area and I want [our] carriers to hit their ships which carry that expedition toward their objective." [46] The Japanese move Ghormley anticipated got under way a few days after the Ilu River fight: on August 23 the Japanese attempted to run in more troops in a convoy covered by ships of the Combined Fleet.

Intelligence reports pointing to a big Japanese operation in the Solomons brought Admiral Fletcher's carriers hurrying up from the south. On August 24 they exchanged blows with the Japanese striking force in the Battle of the Eastern Solomons. The Japanese aim was to sink Fletcher's carriers while providing protection for their convoy of reinforcements. The big carriers *Shokaku* and *Zuikaku* would engage the American fleet while a detachment of heavy cruisers and the light carrier *Ryujo* attacked Henderson Field. American scouting planes discovered the *Ryujo* group first and Fletcher threw most of his planes into an attack on that small carrier, which was sunk.[47] This left Vice Admiral Kondo Nobutake's two big carriers *Shokaku* and *Zuikaku* unmolested. They flung their entire complement of bombers and torpedo planes at Fletcher's carriers; one of Kondo's attack groups failed to find the Americans, however, and the other scored three hits on the carrier *Enterprise* but failed to sink her.[48]

Both carrier forces now retired, but the Japanese troops for Guadalcanal were still at sea in the transport *Kinryu Maru,* escorted by the destroyers of Rear Admiral Tanaka Raizo's Reinforcement Force—dubbed "The Tokyo Express" by the marines. On the morning of August 25, marine dive-bombers from Henderson Field found Tanaka's force, put a bomb through Tanaka's flagship *Jintsu*, and reduced the *Kinryu Maru* to a wreck. A destroyer closed with the transport to take off her crew and the troops. Just then a squadron of B-17s from Espiritu Santo appeared. These high-level bombers were justly famous for making few hits at sea, but this time they were lucky. Three bombs hit the Japanese destroyer, sending her to the bottom and forcing Tanaka to retreat back up the Slot.[49]

A pattern of action now ensued which was to continue for the next two months. Both sides attempted to supply and reinforce their forces on Guadalcanal. American control of Henderson Field enabled the Americans to dominate the sea around the island during daylight hours but the Japanese, despite occasional painful losses, managed to run in troops and supplies via Tanaka's Tokyo Express under cover of darkness. After delivering their reinforcements, the warships of the Tokyo Express usually bombarded Henderson Field, making life miserable for the marines and sometimes forcing the curtailment of air operations by damage to aircraft or ground facilities. Japanese attempts to interfere with American reinforcements and American attempts to derail the Tokyo Express often resulted in major air and naval battles.

To the Americans and Japanese on Guadalcanal, it may at times have seemed as if the opposing troops were simply skirmishing with each other and that the real enemy was the jungle. Thick tropical rain forest covered most of the island, a fantastic tangle of vines, creepers, ferns, roots, and giant hardwoods; this reduced overland movement to a mile or two a day—and visibility to a few yards. The jungle was the domain of giant ants, three-inch wasps, spiders, leeches, and above all, the malarial mosquito, which often inflicted more casualties than the enemy. The constant dampness and humidity produced fungus and skin infections in abundance, while the smallest lapse in sanitation was likely to produce a virulent form of dysentery that rendered men too weak to move. The marines lived in tents or muddy dugouts and ate canned C-rations or dehydrated meats and vegetables, supplemented by captured Japanese rice. Few ate well—but their diet was rich and varied compared to the Japanese, who were sometimes reduced to eating coconuts, roots, and moss.[50]

Primitive living, the poor condition of the airfield, a lack of spare parts, shortages of fuel and ammunition, and intermittent night bombardments by the Japanese made flying from Henderson a nightmare for the pilots of Marine Brigadier General Roy S. Geiger's "Cactus Air Force." (Cactus was the Allied code-name for Guadalcanal.) Of the dive-bomber pilots in Marine Air Group Twenty-three, the first to operate from Guadalcanal, "only one would eventually be able to walk to the plane that carried him away from Henderson Field." [51]

Thirty days was estimated as about the maximum a flyer could spend on Guadalcanal and still be physically and psychologically able to fly.[52] The planes were used up even faster: at times Geiger had less than a dozen operational aircraft to throw against the Japanese. But a steady flow of reinforcements—supplemented by navy planes from sunk or disabled carriers and some Army Air Force fighters—kept the Cactus Air Force in business.

Marine Wildcat fighters were no match for Zeros; the Army Air Force P-40s were even worse. In altitude, rate of climb, and maneuverability they were simply not in the same league. Yet the Japanese had problems too. Their Zeros, fighting at the end of a long flight from Rabaul, could remain over the target only a few minutes; they were further handicapped by having to carry belly fuel tanks. Employing hit-and-run tactics similar to those of General Chennault in China, the American flyers were able to run up an impressive score against Japanese raiders.

At the end of August Tanaka's Tokyo Express, taking advantage of the dark moonless nights, was able to bring in almost 6,000 men under the command of Major General Kawaguchi Kiyotake. By this time the Japanese high command had begun to take Guadalcanal seriously. General Horii's forces in New Guinea were halted almost within sight of Port Moresby: their orders were to dig in and prepare to hold Kokoda and Buna. Reinforcements intended for Papua were diverted to Guadalcanal, which had now become "the pivotal point of operational guidance." [53]

General Kawaguchi's orders were to reconnoiter the airfield and determine whether it was possible to attack it with his present strength or whether reinforcements were needed. Without bothering to reconnoiter, Kawaguchi decided to attack. The battle that ensued was one of the crucial battles of the Guadalcanal campaign.

Attacking from the south of Henderson Field, Kawaguchi's troops attempted to overrun and outflank the marine perimeter on a low ridge about 1,000 yards from the airstrip. The position, which soon received the appropriate label "Bloody Ridge," was defended by men of the elite Raider and Parachute battalions under Lieutenant

Colonel Merritt Edson. Twelve times during the night of September 13 Kawaguchi's men, supported by heavy mortar fire, hurled themselves against the marine lines, shouting banzais and occasionally "Marine You Die!" in passable English.[54] The marines answered with obscenities and a hail of automatic weapons fire. Marine howitzers dropped shells on the attacking Japanese as close as 200 yards from the defenders' lines.

Slowly, Edson's companies pulled back to the final knoll of the ridge. There they held. The last Japanese charges ended in bloody failure; daybreak saw the ridge littered with corpses. Subsequent attacks against the marines' right flank west of the airfield were easily repulsed. The broken remnants of the Kawaguchi force staggered back into the jungle. There were no marine units strong enough to pursue them.[55] One-fifth of all the Marines engaged were killed or wounded. Of Kawaguchi's men, less than half survived.

News of Kawaguchi's defeat only redoubled Japanese determination to destroy the Americans on Guadalcanal. From the Dutch East Indies, from New Guinea, from China, and even from Japan troops were fed into the pipeline to reinforce the island.[56] Admiral Yamamoto committed the Combined Fleet to cover them.

While the Japanese were building up their forces, General Vandegrift's strength on the island remained relatively constant until September 14, when Admiral Turner sailed from Espiritu Santo in command of a convoy carrying the Seventh Marine Regiment. Boldly pushing through in the face of threatened air and submarine attacks, Turner landed his troops intact with all their weapons and equipment on the eighteenth. He returned unscathed, although the carrier *Wasp*, part of the task force which covered Turner's convoy, was sunk by a submarine.

During the next few weeks the Japanese continued to run in reinforcements until, on October 9, General Hyakutake himself arrived on Guadalcanal to direct the offensive. Admiral Ghormley's army commander, Major General Millard F. Harmon, feared that the Japanese would soon be strong enough to overrun the marines and capture the airfield if reinforcements continued at their present inadequate rate. Harmon urged Admiral Ghormley to send additional American troops to Guadalcanal as soon as possible. Ghormley and Admiral Turner were reluctant to commit still more troops because these might be needed for the occupation of Ndeni, an island in the Santa Cruz group about 330 miles south of Guadalcanal. The occupation of this island had been included as part of the original WATCH-

TOWER operation; its purpose was to secure the Allied line of communications to the Solomons and provide an intermediate air base for planes on their way from the south up to Henderson Field. The Ndeni operation had been repeatedly postponed but was still on the books. Harmon argued that the situation at Guadalcanal was so critical that any operations elsewhere would be a dangerous diversion.[57] Ghormley refused to cancel Ndeni as Harmon urged, but he did agree to send an army regimental combat team to shore up the defenses of Guadalcanal.

On October 9 the 164th Regiment of the Americal Division sailed from Nouméa for Guadalcanal aboard two of Turner's transports. The *Hornet* and a new fast battleship, *Washington,* provided backup, together with a force of cruisers and destroyers under Rear Admiral Norman Scott. In addition to protecting the transports, Scott hoped to derail the Tokyo Express on its regular night runs to Guadalcanal. For this purpose he had carefully trained his force in night fighting, had studied previous actions against the Japanese, and had carefully worked out plans for a night battle. On October 11 he got his chance.[58]

That afternoon American planes reported a Japanese force headed down the Slot toward Guadalcanal. This was a division of three heavy cruisers with two destroyers under Rear Admiral Goto Aritomo; it was covering two seaplane carriers and six destroyers carrying reinforcements and supplies for the Japanese forces on Guadalcanal. Scott took position just west of Savo Island, scene of the ill-fated battle in August, and waited. His two heavy cruisers, *San Francisco* and *Salt Lake City,* and two light cruisers, *Boise* and *Helena,* were in single column: three destroyers ahead and two more to the rear.

A half hour before midnight Scott ordered a reverse course to take the column back across the sound between Florida and Guadalcanal islands. The three destroyers at the head of the column were late getting the signal and had to swing wide left around the cruisers and pass rapidly along their right side in order to regain their place in the lead. Just as the column was beginning the turn to reverse its course, the *Helena* picked up a "blip" on her radar. This was Goto's force, less than twenty miles away. In a few minutes, the blip separated into three, heading toward the Americans at twenty knots. *Helena* tracked the contact for some ten minutes before reporting it to the flagship, which also made a radar contact a few minutes later.

What were these contacts? Friendly ships or enemy? The three lead destroyers were still passing along the right side of the cruiser column. Were they the cause of the blips? Scott decided to wait and make sure. But the *Helena* was sure: as soon as the Japanese ships became visible to the naked eye, she opened fire. Orange and yellow flashes momentarily lit up the night as the other American ships joined in.

On both sides there was considerable confusion. The Japanese were caught totally by surprise. Their heavy cruisers *Furutaka* and *Aoba* were badly mauled and the destroyer *Fubuki,* which at one point was the target of all four American cruisers, blew up and sank. Admiral Goto was concerned lest he be mistakenly firing on the Japanese supply force he was supposed to cover. Admiral Scott, too, feared that he was firing on his own ships—in his case the three destroyers on his right. Indeed, these ships were hit by some stray American shells. At one point Scott ordered a short cease-fire, which was ignored by some of his ships.

When the Americans resumed firing after Scott had checked on his destroyers, the Japanese had recovered sufficiently to beat a hasty retreat, covering their escape with heavy and accurate fire which damaged the cruiser *Boise,* almost sinking her. But the *Furutaka* was too far gone to make it home: it went down a few miles from Savo Island. The *Aoba* survived, but she was out of the war for several months, as was the *Boise.*

The Americans hailed this action, called the Battle of Cape Esperance, as a major victory. In a way it was. For the first time the Japanese had been bested in a night battle between surface ships with the odds even. Yet the U.S. Navy greatly overestimated the extent of Japanese losses. It also overlooked the fact that the Japanese had been surprised and thus failed to get off their normally deadly torpedo attack. Future battles would show that the Americans still had much to learn about night engagements at sea.

NOTES

1. Memorandum, Schaeffer to CO, *President Adams,* Sub.: Boat Operations at Gavutu, 11 August 1942, enclosure to Action Report, USS *President Adams* AP 38, 15 August 1942, Naval Historical Center, Washington, D.C.

2. Memorandum, King for President, 5 March 1942, Records of the Chief of Naval Operations, Double Zero Files, Naval Historical Center.

3. Morton, *Strategy and Command,* pp. 294–98.

4. Isely and Crowl, *U.S. Marines and Amphibious Warfare,* pp. 39–94.

5. Hayes, *Pearl Harbor to Trident,* p. 205.

6. Ibid., pp. 208–9.

7. Morton, *Strategy and Command,* pp. 301–2.

8. Samuel B. Griffith II, *The Battle for Guadalcanal* (Philadelphia: Lippincott, 1963), p. 9. Nimitz and King had both preferred Rear Admiral William S. Pye for the command. See "Implementation of Directives to Cin. C. Pacific Ocean Areas and Supreme Commander SW Pacific Area," 6 April 1942, Records of the Chief of Naval Operations, Double Zero Files, no. 132.

9. Griffith, *Guadalcanal,* pp. 23–24.

10. Ibid., p. 30–31; Morton, *Strategy and Command,* pp. 306–7.

11. Hayes, *Pearl Harbor to Trident,* pp. 212–13.

12. Robert W. Love, Jr., "Fighting a Global War," in Kenneth J. Hagan, ed., *In Peace and War: Interpretations of American Naval History* (Westport, Conn.: Greenwood Press, 1978), p. 275.

13. Lieutenant General Merwin H. Silverthorne, oral history interview, p. 265.

14. Dyer, *Amphibians Came to Conquer,* Vol. 1, pp. 303–5.

15. Lewin, *The American Magic,* p. 148.

16. Holmes, *Double-Edged Secrets,* pp. 118–19.

17. Richard K. Sutherland Papers, Modern Military Records Branch, National Archives.

18. Copies of Southwest Pacific Daily Intelligence Summaries may be found in Charles A. Willoughby Papers, Boxes 26–27, National Archives.

19. James, *Years of MacArthur,* pp. 191–92; Samuel Milner, *Victory in Papua* (Washington, D.C.: Office of the Chief of Military History, 1957), p. 53.

20. Lida Mayo, *Bloody Buna* (New York: Doubleday and Co., 1974), pp. 11–13.

21. George H. Johnston, *The Toughest Fighting in the World* (New York: Duell, Sloan, and Pearce 1943), pp. 127, 129.

22. Milner, *Victory in Papua,* pp. 71, 88–90, 95–99; *Reports of General MacArthur: Japanese Operations in the Southwest Pacific Area,* Vol. 2, Part 1, pp. 157–61; Dudley McCarthy, *Southwest Pacific Area: First Year: Kokoda to Wau* (Canberra: Australian War Memorial, 1959), pp. 108–46, 193–234.

23. Christopher Thorne, *Allies of a Kind,* p. 263; Milner, *Victory in Papua,* p. 91; McCarthy, *Southwest Pacific Area,* pp. 225, 234–35.

24. James, *Years of MacArthur,* p. 209.

25. Arnold Diaries, September 25–26, Henry H. Arnold Papers, Library of Congress.

26. "Notes on Conference at Palmyra Island, September 25, 1942," copy in King Papers, Double Zero File.

27. McCarthy, *Southwest Pacific Area,* pp. 155–82; Milner, *Victory in Papua,* pp. 81–84.

28. Quoted in Dyer, *Amphibians Came to Conquer,* Vol. 1, p. 301.

29. Dyer, *Amphibians Came to Conquer,* Vol. 1, p. 383.

30. Griffith, *Guadalcanal,* p. 57; Isely and Crowl, *U.S. Marines and Amphibious Warfare,* pp. 128–29.

31. Samuel Eliot Morison, *The Struggle for Guadalcanal, August 1942—February 1943* (Boston: Little, Brown and Co., 1950), p. 28.

32. Toland interview with Mikawa, Toland Interview Collection.

33. "Role of Communications Intelligence in the American-Japanese Naval War," Vol. 3, pp. 27–28, SRH 012, RG 457, National Archives.

34. Ibid., p. 36.

35. Dyer, *Amphibians Came to Conquer,* Vol. 1, pp. 360–72; Morison, *Struggle for Guadalcanal,* pp. 24–27.

36. Toland, interview with Mikawa, Toland Interview Collection; Morison, *Struggle for Guadalcanal,* p. 53.

37. Blair, *Silent Victory,* p. 273.

38. George MacMillan, *The Old Breed: A History of the First Marine Division in World War II* (Washington, D.C.: Infantry Journal Press, 1949), pp. 45–46.

39. Lieutenant General Edwin Pollock oral history interview, 1977, pp. 130–32, U.S. Marine Corps Historical Center.

40. MacMillan, *The Old Breed,* p. 46.

41. Clifton B. Cates oral history interview, p. 141.

42. Toland interview no. 2 with Colonel Imoto Kumao, Toland Interview Collection; Hattori Takushiro, *Dai Toa Senso Zenshi* (The Complete History of the Greater East Asia War) OCMH translation, Vol. 2, p. 16.

43. Hattori, *Dai Toa Senso Zenshi,* Vol. 2, p. 16.

44. Hattori, ibid., p. 17; Griffith, *Guadalcanal,* pp. 78–81; Morton, *Strategy and Command,* p. 327.

45. John Miller, Jr., *The United States Army in World War II: The War in the Pacific: Guadalcanal: The First Offensive* (Washington: GPO, 1949), pp. 95–99.

46. Letter, Ghormley to Nimitz, 11 August 1942, Serial 0051, copy in COMSOPAC File, King Papers.

47. Dull, *Imperial Japanese Navy,* pp. 207–12. Several authors—e.g., Morison as well as Belote and Belote, *Titans of the Seas,* pp. 120–22—suggest that the *Ryujo* may have been "bait" to lure Fletcher's planes away from the big Japanese carriers. Dull, however, could find no evidence in Japanese sources to support such a view. Dull, *The Imperial Japanese Navy,* p. 208.

48. Morison, *Struggle for Guadalcanal,* pp. 87–101.

49. Ibid., pp. 104–5.

50. Toland, *The Rising Sun,* p. 387; Miller, *Guadalcanal: The First Offensive,* p. 316.

51. Herbert Christian Merrillat, *Guadalcanal Remembered* (New York: Dodd, Mead and Co., 1982), p. 103.

52. Thomas G. Miller, Jr., *The Cactus Air Force* (New York: Harper and Row, 1969), p. 70.

53. Hattori, *Dai Toa Senso Zenshi,* p. 16; *History of Imperial General Headquarters, Army Section,* p. 104.

54. Herbert C. Merrillat, a Marine officer on Guadalcanal, wrote many years after: "I regard with skepticism attributions of English phrases to Japanese infantrymen, although I am guilty of having perpetuated some myself in wartime writings." He speculates that the marines may have misheard Japanese orders and battle cries. Merrillat, *Guadalcanal Remembered,* p. 140.

55. Griffith, *Battle for Guadalcanal,* pp. 116–21; Miller, *Guadalcanal: The First Offensive,* pp. 116–18.

56. Hattori, *Dai Toa Senso Zenshi,* p. 117.

57. Harmon to Admiral Ghormley, October 6, 1942, sub: Occupation of Ndeni, reproduced as "Appendix A" in Miller, *Guadalcanal;* Isely and Crowl, *U.S. Marines and Amphibious War,* pp. 153–55.

58. The following account is based primarily on Morison, *Struggle for Guadalcanal,* pp. 153–66.

TEN

Jungle Victories

On October 13, two days after the Battle of Cape Esperance, Admiral Richmond Kelly Turner led his transports safely into Guadalcanal. Three thousand men, together with all their jeeps, trucks, ammunition, and supplies, were landed by noon. Among the supplies were several hundred cases of candy bars "and by 9:00 A.M., trading was brisk on the beach. [Every marine] who could find an excuse to sneak down to Lunga hurried through the shadowy coconut groves toward this unexpected bonanza. Most were equipped with Japanese rifles, sabers, pistols, flags, helmets or officers' map cases. A Samurai sword that day went for three dozen large Hershey bars; a 'meat ball' flag—which Marines were now adept at manufacturing when supplies of originals ran low—was worth a dozen." [1]

The troops of the 164th Infantry were mostly former National Guardsmen from the Dakotas. On the average, the new men were almost ten years older than the marines, and they may have aged considerably more during their first two nights on Guadalcanal. [2] For on those two nights Henderson Field received its heaviest pounding. On the thirteenth, two battleships steamed into Iron Bottom Sound— the narrow stretch of water between Guadalcanal and neighboring Florida and Savo Islands—and during the night pumped over nine hundred rounds of fourteen-inch shell into the airfield, destroying or damaging half the aircraft and putting the main runway out of business for a week. "[It] was the most tremendous thing I've ever been through in all my life," recalled one Marine; "anybody who says a naval bombardment isn't worse than any artillery shelling is absolutely crazy. . . . There was one big bunker near our galley in the First Marines . . . a shell dropped right in the middle of it and practically everybody in the hole was killed. We tried to dig the men out but we saw it wasn't any use. . . ." [3] " 'It is almost beyond belief that we are still here, still alive, still waiting and still ready,' " wrote a war correspondent; " 'we keep notes with shaking hands. . . . The worst experience I've ever been through in my life. . . . It goes on hour after hour. I begin trembling.' " [4] The following two nights Japanese heavy cruisers poured in another 2,000 rounds of shell. Vandegrift signaled Ghormley: " 'Urgently necessary that this force receive maximum support of air and surface units.' " [5] Ghormley in turn warned Nimitz that the Japanese had started an all-out offensive and that his forces were " 'totally inadequate' " to stop them.[6]

● ●

By this time the campaign for Guadalcanal had become a critical battle in the bureaucratic and doctrinal war between the services. Admiral King consistently demanded more support for the Solomons operations, especially additional aircraft. At the same time, King was reluctant to fully disclose the seriousness of the situation there to his colleagues in the Joint Chiefs of Staff. "Admiral King was on a hot seat," a contemporary observer recalls; "he had been pressing for Guadalcanal right along. He had been the one who said 'go in even on a shoestring,' and these repercussions would not sit well with the American people." [7] So ignorant were army strategists of the actual situation on "Cactus" that a few days after the initial marine landings on Guadalcanal and Tulagi they proposed to get on with preparations for Task Two in the campaign against Rabaul.[8] Howls of protest from Ghormley and MacArthur soon put a stop to this line of thinking.[9]

Whatever the situation in the Solomons, General Arnold and the Army Air Force brass were determined to keep a tight ceiling on the number of planes sent to the South Pacific. All their attention was focused on the projected massive aerial bombardment of Germany from England which was to demonstrate at last that airpower, if given the opportunity, could win the war. As for the South Pacific, Arnold suspected that the navy, through "subterfuge and cunning . . . is trying to run a land war relying upon the Army, Air and

Marines to put it across" without risking its own major warships against the Japanese.[10] "The Navy wants to send in more and more planes apparently with the view of making that their main theater by employing most of our aircraft," Arnold confided to this diary; "Our policy is to build up aircraft against Germany . . . to demonstrate we can do things against Goering if we do not disperse all over the world." The Air Force chief recognized that "the Navy is hard pressed at Guadalcanal and does need a shot in the arm" but he believed "the best shot is getting new leaders who know and understand modern warfare; men who are aggressive and not afraid to fight their ships. So far, I'm afraid it's been the other way around." [11]

Arnold's views were reinforced by reports he was receiving from General Millard Harmon. Harmon believed that Ghormley and his navy subordinates simply did not understand airpower. They were slow to develop Henderson Field as a major air base and even slower to understand that control of the air around Guadalcanal would be the dominant element in the campaign. Harmon, too, believed that the navy had shown undue caution about risking its ships in support of Guadalcanal.[12]

The navy had some complaints of its own about the Army Air Forces. The army P-39 fighters were hopelessly outclassed in performance by the Zeros, but Arnold stubbornly refused to allocate any of the newer, better P-38 "Lightnings" to the South Pacific. The fast new twin-engine Lightnings were in great demand for duty in Europe and for the upcoming Allied invasion of North Africa, scheduled for November 1942. Air Force B-17 heavy bombers, with their rugged construction and heavy defensive armament, gave Japanese fighter pilots fits, but they were practically useless for hitting anything at sea. Between August and November, B-17s had dropped 828 bombs on some sixty enemy ships and sank only four. Air Force statistics showed the percentage of bomb hits on moving surface ships was about 1 percent.[13] As a reconnaissance plane and as a weapon for striking deep into enemy territory, the B-17 was proving itself a formidable instrument of war. As a means of attacking enemy fleets at sea—the mission claimed for it by air power enthusiasts in prewar days—it was sadly lacking.

Supplying and reinforcing Guadalcanal also gave the services plenty to argue about; yet all agreed that the logistics situation was a nightmare. No one in Washington had attempted to calculate how many men and how much equipment would be needed for the campaign.

Knowledge and appreciation of logistics, particularly in the navy, was rudimentary.[14] " 'I don't know what the hell this logistics is that Marshall is always talking about,' " Admiral King is supposed to have remarked during the first months of the war, " 'but I want some of it.' "[15]

In the entire South Pacific area there were no Allied ports nearer than New Zealand that had the docks, labor, and equipment to handle the mass of supplies needed to support operations at Guadalcanal. At Guadalcanal itself only one ship at a time could be unloaded by barges and lighters in the small harbor area. Air raids by the Japanese made these resupply operations even more time-consuming as well as dangerous. During September a supply ship could spend only six hours unloading during its two-day stop at Guadalcanal. The rest of the time was devoted to dodging bombs.[16] The nearest deep-water port with fully developed facilities was Nouméa, New Caledonia—some 900 miles away from Guadalcanal. Ships making the 6,400 mile voyage from San Francisco to New Caledonia were backed up for weeks there awaiting unloading or escort to the war zone. Partially unloaded ships remained in harbor for months while army and navy alike drew on them as floating warehouses. Since the Allies were facing a worldwide shipping shortage at this time, the situation at Nouméa kept Washington logistics planners tearing their hair.[17]

While Guadalcanal was a bureaucratic headache for navy officers in Washington, it was a solid, living nightmare to sailors in the South Pacific. Warships remained at sea for weeks, with only short intervals in port to take on fuel and supplies or make emergency repairs. Four hours on watch and four hours off, the unchanging sea and sky, fatigue, fear, frequent calls to battle stations—these were the ingredients of naval life during the struggle for Guadalcanal. Always present was the possibility of sudden, violent death: men blown apart by torpedoes or shells, men burned beyond recognition, drowned, mutilated, or simply missing. Some ships sank with virtually their entire crews. The destroyer *Jarvis* disappeared without a trace and was not accounted for until after the war; the destroyer *Barton* sank in less than two minutes; and the light cruiser *Juneau* blew up instantly after being hit by a torpedo, taking with her all but 10 of her 700 men. Fear, horror, fatigue, anxiety: that was Guadalcanal for the navy as well as for the fliers, marines, and army troops.

In mid-September, General Hap Arnold flew to the South Pacific to have a look for himself. His visit coincided with one by Admiral

Nimitz; the two conferred briefly at Nouméa. Though they disagreed on some important points, both Arnold and Nimitz came away from Nouméa with the conviction that a new commander was needed in the South Pacific.[18] Ghormley seemed unsure of himself and almost crushed by the burden of work and nervous strain. "He was really completely defeatist," recalled a newspaper man who visited Nouméa around this time. " 'He was almost despairing." [19] Arnold found that Ghormley had been so busy "he had not been able to leave his headquarters office on the ship for about a month . . . no man can sit continuously in a small office fighting a war . . . without suffering mentally, physically and nervously." [20]

On his return from the South Pacific, Admiral Nimitz called a meeting of his key staff members. All recommended that Ghormley be relieved.[21] Nimitz reluctantly agreed. Vice Admiral William F. Halsey, who was then en route to the South Pacific on an inspection tour, was ordered to assume command of the South Pacific theater immediately.

By this time Halsey had become a kind of legend in the navy. News of his appointment galvanized the tired and hard-pressed men on Guadalcanal and at sea. Halsey swept through Nouméa like a tornado. He bulldozed the French into giving him adequate headquarters space ashore and called a meeting of the principal commanders: Vandegrift, Harmon, and Turner. Much to Harmon's delight, he cancelled the Ndeni operation. By doing so, he "told all and sundry who came in contact with him that the major battle was 330 miles west northwest of the Santa Cruz Islands, on Guadalcanal." [22] To Vandegrift he gave the instruction: " 'Go on back. I'll promise you everything I've got.' " [23]

At the same time, in Washington, the Joint Chiefs of Staff received a terse directive from the president: "My anxiety about the Southwest Pacific is to make sure that every possible weapon gets into that area to hold Guadalcanal." [24] The Joint Chiefs replied that more aircraft, shipping, and an additional army division were already on their way to the South Pacific.[25]

● ●

By mid-October, the Japanese judged that they had built up sufficient strength on Guadalcanal for an all-out offensive. General Hyakutaka planned to capture Henderson Field in a three-pronged attack from the west and south, while powerful units of the Combined

Fleet stood by to polish off any American warships that attempted to interfere. After the airfield was taken, Combined Fleet carriers would fly in planes to help hold it.

The Second Division, under Lieutenant General Maruyama Masai, was to attack from the south, but it was late getting through the thick hilly jungle and into position. The offensive was postponed—and then postponed again. Word of the second postponement failed to reach Major General Sumiyoshi Tadashi: he launched his attack from the west along the Matanikau River, as originally scheduled, on October 23. Nine light tanks led an assault by a regiment of infantry—right into the muzzles of marine artillery already sighted in on their route of approach. The tanks were quickly knocked out; not a single Japanese reached the far bank of the river.[26]

Nevertheless, Sumiyoshi's debacle served to divert American attention from the southern flank of the airfield, where the main Japanese effort was shaping up unobserved by the marines. Indeed, one marine battalion had been withdrawn from that sector the day before Sumiyoshi's attack to strengthen the line on the Matanikau. The entire 4,000-yard perimeter south of the airfield was held by a single marine unit, the First Battalion, Seventh Marines, under Lieutenant Colonel Lewis "Chesty" Puller, already a legend in Marine Corps circles. To Puller's left were the newly arrived battalions of the 164th Infantry.

The Japanese attack came in pitch darkness and pouring rain near midnight on the twenty-third. Savage fights developed all along the perimeter as the Japanese sought to break through. A few positions were overrun but quickly recaptured. As the battle developed, elements of the 164th's reserve (the Third Battalion) were fed into the line to reinforce Puller's men. By morning the marines had discovered that the 164th was good for more than candy bars. The morning light revealed more than 1,000 Japanese bodies scattered around the American emplacements. U.S. losses were less than 200.[27]

The Japanese tried again the next night, but were beaten back. How many of their soldiers died in these two bloody nights will never be known. Estimates ran as high as 3,500. With them died also the last Japanese chance to capture Henderson Field, although this was far from clear at the time.

To the northeast of Guadalcanal, Vice Admiral Kondo Nobutake waited impatiently with his carriers and battleships for word that Henderson Field was in Japanese hands. Instead, he learned that an American task force was headed his way. On the twenty-sixth the two forces clashed in another carrier duel on the pattern of Midway and the Eastern Solomons. In this Battle of the Santa Cruz Islands the Americans lost the carrier *Hornet,* while the carrier *Enterprise* was damaged. The Japanese had two of their carriers, the *Zuiho* and *Shokaku,* badly knocked about. The Americans retired. Kondo still had two operational carriers, but he was harassed by land-based American aircraft and decided to pull out too. By now he knew that Maruyama's attack had failed, so his presence was superfluous anyway.

" 'We must be aware,' " wrote an officer at Imperial General Headquarters, " 'of the possibility that the struggle for Guadalcanal in the southeast area may develop into the decisive struggle between America and Japan.' " The failure to capture Henderson Field was discouraging; but the heavy losses which Kondo's naval forces claimed to have inflicted on the Americans seemed to promise good prospects for success in the future. Imperial Headquarters decided to send more reinforcements to Guadalcanal.[28]

Through the first days of November, Admiral Tanaka's ships brought in a steady trickle of supplies and men, while Combined Fleet got ready for the big move. An entire division and 3,000 naval landing troops, loaded into eleven high-speed transports, were to be landed near Tassafaronga. Meanwhile battleships and cruisers blasted Henderson Field to prevent any interference by the Cactus Air Force. Admiral Turner's transports were at Guadalcanal on November 12, bringing in another regiment of the Americal Division, when the Japanese bombardment force under Vice Admiral Abe Hiroaki was spotted coming down the Slot. Turner detached his cruiser-destroyer escort under Rear Admiral Daniel J. Callaghan to stop Abe.

Callaghan's five cruisers and eight destroyers tangled with Abe's force of two battleships, a light cruiser, and six destroyers in a confused night action east of Savo Island. As at the Battle of Cape Esperance, the American ships picked up the approaching Japanese on their radar but took too long before opening fire. By the time they did, sharp-eyed Japanese lookouts had spotted the cruiser *Atlanta* and quickly knocked her out with shells and torpedoes. The Americans concentrated on the battleships while taking fearful casualties from Japanese gunfire and torpedoes at ranges of only 2,000 to 3,000 yards. The destroyers were especially hard hit: three were promptly sunk and two were crippled. The cruiser *Portland* had her stern almost blown off; the *San Francisco* was damaged; Admiral Callaghan was killed. Yet the relentless American attack—sometimes at ranges so close he could not depress his big guns to hit the enemy—finally unnerved Admiral Abe. He ordered a retirement, leaving behind one destroyer sunk and another sinking. Abe's flagship, the battleship *Hiei,* had taken so many hits that her progress up the Slot was painfully slow. At sunrise, warplanes from Henderson Field and from Admiral Kinkaid's *Enterprise* task force hurrying up from Nouméa found her an excellent target; by evening they had sent her to the bottom.

Meanwhile Tanaka's transports and destroyers still plowed doggedly on toward Guadalcanal. On the night of the fourteenth, Japanese cruisers bombarded Henderson Field but did not knock it out: most of the planes survived to go after Tanaka and the bombardment group the next morning. A Japanese heavy cruiser was sunk and three others damaged before the Americans turned to the transports. Repeated bombing and strafing sent six to the bottom.

As darkness fell Admiral Kondo brought down his remaining battleship, *Kirishima,* and four cruisers to have another try at Henderson Field. But by now two fast, new American battleships, *Washington* and *South Dakota,* under Rear Admiral Willis A. Lee, had been detached from Admiral Kinkaid's task force and had arrived on the scene. They gave the Japanese a hot reception. Unlike most commanders in the South Pacific, Lee "knew more about radar than the radar operators." [29] He put his knowledge to good use in the night encounter with Kondo, which marked the second phase of the Naval Battle of Guadalcanal.

After a preliminary skirmish between destroyers—in which the Americans, as usual, got the worst of it—the curtain rose on one of the few battleship fights of the war. It was very different from the classic encounters anticipated by the naval war colleges. *South Dakota* suffered a power failure, became separated from *Washington,* and was exposed to the fire of the *Kirishima* and two heavy cruisers. How nearly unsinkable the new American battleships were was demonstrated when *South Dakota* survived forty-two large-calibre hits, continuing to steam at full speed. What they could *do* was demonstrated a few minutes later by *Washington,* which locked onto *Kirishima* with her radar and smothered her with nine sixteen-inch and forty five-inch shell hits in less than seven minutes. The Japanese pulled out, leaving the sinking *Kirishima* and a mortally wounded destroyer behind. Three American destroyers had been sunk and *South Dakota* had to go home for repairs, but the Japanese attempt at night bombardment had again been thwarted.

There was nothing left for Tanaka but to press on to Guadalcanal and attempt to land his troops in daylight. Four transports made it to a point near Tassafaronga, where they beached. Planes from the *Enterprise* and from Henderson Field bombed and strafed them until the decks ran with blood. Only about 2,000 Japanese soldiers and sailors got ashore. In Washington, Navy Secretary Knox called a press conference. " 'We can lick them,' " a beaming Knox told reporters; "I don't qualify that. We'll defeat them.' " [30]

Fierce fighting continued on Guadalcanal for several weeks. At the beginning of December Japanese destroyers running in supplies dealt the navy a sharp defeat in a night action called the Battle of Tassafaronga. One American cruiser was sunk and three others barely escaped destruction, all victims of the deadly Japanese torpedo. Yet Japan's hope of victory at Guadalcanal had died in the smoking hulks of Tanaka's transports. The Americans now had more than 35,000 men on Guadalcanal and close to 200 planes at Henderson Field. The outnumbered Japanese forces on the island had barely enough to eat.

On December 9 General Vandegrift turned over command of forces in the Guadalcanal and Tulagi area to Army Lieutenant General Alexander M. Patch, commander of the newly formed XIV Corps, consisting of the Second Marine Division—which had relieved the tired leathernecks of the First Marine Division—the Americal Division of the U.S. Army, and the 25th Infantry Division, which arrived at the end of December. During December Patch's soldiers and marines cleaned out Japanese positions on the high ground overlooking Henderson Field. Then, on January 10, Patch launched a major drive westward to push the Japanese off the island. With luck he hoped to crush Japanese resistance by April.

The Japanese planned differently. On December 31 the Imperial Army and Navy chiefs of staff obtained the Emperor's approval to evacuate Guadalcanal. During the first week of February, at night and in great secrecy, the Japanese evacuated almost 11,000 men. Admiral Halsey, fearing that the renewed Japanese activity presaged another offensive, deployed his forces to defend the airfield and did not interfere with the pullout. General Patch's army and marine forces pushed their way to the western end of the island on February

8 to find only empty boats and abandoned supplies. On the afternoon of February 9 Patch radioed Admiral Halsey: "Tokyo Express no longer has terminus on Guadalcanal."

● ●

Time was also running out for the Japanese forces in Papua. Originally ordered to hold their position on the southern slopes of the Owen Stanleys, General Horii's forces were subsequently brought back to Kokoda; a portion of them was sent to reinforce Buna as the situation on Guadalcanal worsened, making an American invasion of Buna appear likely.

The Australians, who were now being reinforced and resupplied regularly, pushed the Japanese back steadily, recapturing Kokoda toward the end of October. At Oivi, a little further down the trail, an Australian brigade swept around the Japanese left flank and fell on their rear. Japanese withdrawal was thrown into confusion. General Horri was killed and much food and equipment was lost before the remnants of his force finally reached Gona on the north coast of Papua, on November 7.

The Japanese had now retreated to a narrow strip of coast on which were located the three villages of Buna, Sanananda and Gona. Troops under Major General Edwin Harding, members of the American 32d Division's 126th and 128th infantry regiments, were brought to the coast from Milne Bay and Port Moresby; they were assigned the task of reducing Buna while the Australians concentrated on Gona and Sanananda. The approach to the Japanese positions led through thick jungle and swamp which were virtually impassable in places. No assault from the sea was possible because landing craft were unavailable (all were needed at Guadalcanal) and because Vice Admiral Arthur Carpender, MacArthur's naval commander, refused to risk his ships in the treacherous shoal waters off Buna where they would be within easy range of Japanese aircraft.[32]

On November 19 Harding's troops launched their first attack on Buna. They were quickly brought to a standstill by deadly Japanese machine-gun fire from a cleverly concealed network of bunkers commanding all the dry-ground approaches to the coast. Each bunker was "a fortress in miniature. Some are strengthened by great sheets of armor and by concrete . . . protected from our fire and bombs by sawn logs and filled trees which form a barrier six, ten and sometimes 15 feet thick. The logs are held in place by great metal stakes and filled in with earth in which the natural growth of the jungle has continued, providing perfect camouflage. . . . From every trench or pit or pill-box, all approaches are covered by wide fields of sweeping fire along fixed lines." [33]

The Americans made almost no progress on the nineteenth and on the twenty-first; MacArthur peremptorily ordered Harding to take Buna at all costs. Although almost half of Harding's troops had been sent to reinforce the Australians at Sanananda and most of his division supplies had been lost when trawlers bringing them from Milne Bay had been sunk by Japanese aircraft, he attempted to comply. Once again the Americans went forward into devastating crossfire from the almost invisible Japanese. The attackers had no heavy artillery, flame throwers, or tanks which might have made it possible to knock out the Japanese bunkers. Their heaviest weapons were a half-dozen light mountain guns and some 81-mm mortars. These last had only light high-explosive shells that literally bounced off the thick log walls of the bunkers. Even many of the hand grenades carried by the troops were defective.[34] The only possible method of knocking out the bunkers was "to crawl forward as close as Japanese protective fire would allow and make a sudden rush" to lob in hand grenades. Most soldiers only tried this once.

Allied aircraft, which by this time had established control of the air over Buna, might have been expected to help, but their effectiveness in close support of ground troops was near zero. MacArthur's planes bombed and strafed American troops by mistake so many times that commanders began to feel safer without air support.[35]

The fruitless attacks continued until the end of November. The Australians were no more successful at Gona and Sanananda, even when reinforced by three battalions from Harding's 32nd Division. On the day before Thanksgiving, General Blamey and Lieutenant General Edmund Herring, commander of Allied Forces in New Guinea, called on MacArthur to suggest reinforcing the Allied troops on the north coast. MacArthur proposed to bring up an additional U.S. division, the 41st, which was completing training in Australia. Blamey replied that he would rather have Australians "because he knew they would fight." To a proud leader like MacArthur, this was almost intolerable. Buna was the first real offensive undertaken by American troops under his command. To have it break down while operations on Guadalcanal went steadily forward was "a bitter pill. . . to swallow."[36]

The commander in Chief quickly ordered two of his staff officers, and then Sutherland himself, to Buna to see what the trouble was.

All reported that the troops were not fighting and that Harding and his top commanders were providing poor leadership. To this day it is hard to understand how competent observers could have concluded that the failure to reduce Buna was because " 'the Americans weren't showing the fight that they should.' " The casualties among Harding's troops were appalling. The remaining troops were short of rations, medicine, even equipment to service their rifles, and had been in action almost continuously for over a week. They lacked appropriate weapons to knock out the Japanese bunkers. General Harding had repeatedly asked for tanks and more artillery, but he had received nothing.[37] Why none of MacArthur's observers saw fit to mention these things remains a mystery.

Sutherland recommended that Harding be relieved. Lieutenant General Robert L. Eichelberger, who was training the 41st Division in Australia, was ordered to the front to take command of the 32d Division. " 'Go out there Bob, and take Buna or don't come back alive!' " was MacArthur's cheery send-off to Eichelberger as he left Port Moresby.[38]

General Eichelberger took command at a time when things were looking up for the Americans before Buna. Completion of an airstrip at Dobodura near the north New Guinea coast greatly improved the supply situation; Eichelberger was also promised the tanks and reinforcements Harding had vainly sought. Nevertheless, an all-out attack launched by Eichelberger on December 5 was stopped short with heavy casualties.

That was enough for Eichelberger. He wisely decided to refrain from any more frontal attacks and wait for his tanks. He could afford to wait because Allied planes under MacArthur's new air commander, Major General George C. Kenney, and a squadron of American motor torpedo boats ranging the north coast of New Guinea were making it increasingly costly for the Japanese to supply their forces at Buna and Gona.[39]

Meanwhile, at Gona the Australians, with the aid of fresh reinforcements and artillery shells equipped with a new delayed-action fuse, fought their way into Gona on December 9. The cost was high: more than 500 men killed. But one of the three principal Japanese strongholds had at last been reduced.

A few days later an Australian brigade and the long-awaited tanks arrived to reinforce the eastern flank of the American front at Buna, and the final push against the town opened on December 18. The Japanese resisted fiercely; Allied casualties were again heavy, but the tanks and the hard-won experience of the past weeks, plus the increasing weariness and hunger of the Japanese, made the difference. After two weeks of bloody fighting the Allies overran the last Japanese stronghold at Buna Mission on January 2.

The Australians and Americans now closed in on Sanananda, the last and most heavily defended Japanese bastion on the Papuan coast. Australian troops had been attempting to reduce Sanananda for nearly two months already, but with little success. Fresh troops brought in after the fall of Buna made little headway. Yet the Japanese situation—completely surrounded and cut off from all supplies—was now desperate. By the first week of January the defenders had eaten the last of their rice; even rifle ammunition was being strictly rationed. On January 4, the same day it decided to evacuate Guadalcanal, Imperial General Headquarters also ordered the troops at Sanananda to attempt to withdraw, either by barge or overland, to Lae and Salamaua.[40]

These orders reached the Japanese commander at Sanananda on January 13. Three days later the Americans and Australians launched the final series of attacks which brought about the fall of Sanananda on January 22. The casualties incurred in clearing out this "remnant of the enemy's forces," as one of MacArthur's communiqués called it, had been almost 3,500. That was 700 more than at Buna. The Papuan campaign had dragged on so long, MacArthur told the secretary of the Australian Defense Council, Sir Frederick Shedden, because of Australian commanders' "slowness to exploit advantages and follow up opportunities".[41]

History has not been kind to MacArthur's "striking victory" in Papua. "The only result," concluded the army's official historian, "strategically speaking, was that after six months of bitter fighting and some 8,500 casualties, including 3,000 dead, the Southwest Pacific Area was exactly where it would have been the previous July had it been able to secure the beachhead before the Japanese ever got there."[42] Others have pointed out that the Japanese entrenched at Buna and Sanananda could have been isolated and bypassed once the Allies had secured an airstrip at Dobodura.[43]

MacArthur himself never went near the front, relying on staff officers to keep him informed. His insistence on pressing forward with repeated frontal attacks by poorly supported infantry against a heavily dug-in enemy was reminiscent of the worst generalship of the First World War. It might have ended in the same futile slaughter had not the Japanese finally collapsed due to starvation.

The Guadalcanal campaign has fared better at the hands of historians.[44] It was "the first offensive," the beginning of the road back, the means of securing the line to Australia. Yet Guadalcanal had been a defensive victory, whereas most of the later land battles with Japan would be offensive in nature. The U.S. Navy still had much to learn about night fighting at sea and both the U.S. Air Force and Navy had yet to put into action a fighter to match the Zero, plane for plane.

Perhaps the most important results of both Papua and Guadalcanal were psychological. The vaunted Japanese army, which had rolled over Malaya, Hong Kong, the Philippines, and Burma, had been stopped. The Australians at Milne Bay, the Americans at the Ilu River and Bloody Ridge, had shown that Japanese attacks were not irresistible; and in the long jungle slugging matches which Papua and Guadalcanal eventually became, it was the Japanese—not the Allies—who finally gave out.

NOTES

1. Griffith, *Battle for Guadalcanal*, pp. 151–57.

2. Isely and Crowl, *U.S. Marines and Amphibious Warfare*, p. 151.

3. Lieutenant General Edwin A. Pollock, oral history interview, p. 117.

4. Quoted in Merillat, *Guadalcanal Remembered*, p. 180.

5. Miller, *Guadalcanal*, pp. 150–51; Griffith, *Battle for Guadalcanal*, pp. 152–54; Morison, *Struggle for Guadalcanal*, pp. 173–78.

6. Miller, *Guadalcanal*, p. 152.

7. Hanson W. Baldwin interview, Naval Historical Center.

8. King to Chief of Staff Army, Sub.: "Early Initiation of Limited Task Two," 15, August 1942, King Papers, Double Zero Files.

9. Morton, *Strategy and Command*, pp. 327–28.

10. Henry H. Arnold, Journal of Trip to Southwest Pacific, 16 September 1942 to 2 October 1942, Henry H. Arnold Papers, Library of Congress; Morton, *Strategy and Command*, p. 330.

11. Arnold Diaries, ibid.

12. Morton, *Strategy and Command*, pp. 352–54.

13. Craven and Cate, *Army Air Forces in World War II*, Vol. 4, *The Pacific: Guadalcanal to Saipan*, pp. 62–64; Okumiya and Hirokisho, *Zero*, pp. 157–59; "Notes on Conference at Palmyra Island 25 September 1942," copy in King Papers; Arnold, *Global Mission*, pp. 336–37.

14. Dyer, *Amphibians Came to Conquer*, Vol. 1 p. 419.

15. Griffith, *Battle for Guadalcanal*, p. 30.

16. Notes on Conference Held Aboard USS *Argonne* at Nouméa, September 28, 1942, King Papers.

17. Leighton and Coakley, *Global Logistics and Strategy, 1940–1943*, pp. 390–97, 398–403.

18. Arnold, Journal of Trip to S.W. Pacific, 16 September 1942 to 2 October 1942, Arnold Papers; Potter, *Nimitz*, p. 192; Isely and Crowl, *U.S. Marines and Amphibious Warfare*, p. 1157.

19. Hanson W. Baldwin interview.

20. Arnold, *Global Mission*, p. 340.

21. Potter, *Nimitz*, p. 197.

22. Isely and Crowl, *U.S. Marines and Amphibious Warfare*, p. 175.

23. Griffith, *Battle for Guadalcanal*, p. 164.

24. Ibid., p. 180.

25. Morton, *Stratgey and Command*, pp. 337–45.

26. Miller, *Guadalcanal*, pp. 155–57; Griffith, *Battle for Guadalcanal*, pp. 165–67.

27. Ibid., pp. 161–62; ibid., pp. 168–69.

28. Hattori, *Dai Toa Senso Zenshi*, p. 21.

29. Morison, *Struggle for Guadalcanal*, p. 270.

30. Griffith, *Battle for Guadalcanal*, p. 205.

31. *Reports of General MacArthur, Japanese Operations in the South West Pacific Area,* Vol. 2, Part 1, pp. 164–65.

32. Ibid., pp. 169–70; McCarthy, *Kokoda to Wau*, pp. 321–30.

33. Johnston, *Toughtest Fighting in the World*, p. 192.

34. Milner, *Victory in Papua*, pp. 178, 185, 375–76.

35. Ibid., pp. 180–82 and passim; Mayo, *Bloody Buna*, pp. 98–99, 117.

36. Milner, *Victory in Papua*, p. 202.

37. Ibid., pp. 196–201.

38. Robert L. Eichelberger, *Our Jungle Road to Tokyo* (New York: Viking, 1950), p. 21.

39. Samuel Eliot Morison, *Breaking the Bismarck's Barrier* (Boston: Little, Brown and Co., 1950), pp. 48–49; Craven and Cate, *Guadalcanal to Saipan*, pp. 126–28; Mayo, *Bloody Buna*, pp. 134–35.

40. Milner, *Victory in Papua*, pp. 346–47.

41. Horner, *High Command*, p. 248.

42. Milner, *Victory in Papua*, p. 378. Australian historian D. M. Horner similarly concludes: "Both MacArthur and Blamey made vital strategic miscalculations at the expense of the lives of many soldiers and the careers of subordinates, but neither would admit it." *High Command*, p. 215.

43. Mayo, *Bloody Buna*, p. 176.

44. In contrast to the numerous excellent accounts of the Guadalcanal campaign, only one book—aside from official and unit histories—has been written about the campaign in Papua.

ELEVEN

CARTWHEEL

By the time the battles in Papua and Guadalcanal reached their bloody close, American strategists were fully aware that the campaign against Rabaul—indeed any offensive in the Pacific—would be far more demanding of U.S. resources, especially ships and planes, than they had at first believed. Yet the question of allocation of resources remained to be settled. Before that could be done, however, the Allies would have to agree on a plan for victory. At the same time the end of the first phase of the Guadalcanal and Papua campaign forced the army and navy to reopen the vexed question of command in the southwestern and South Pacific.

While these questions were thrashed out, a sort of interregnum settled over American operations in the Pacific, where commanders were busy realigning and refitting their forces and integrating new units and equipment. The Japanese also attempted to shore up their defenses while launching preemptive strikes against the steadily growing Allied forces poised on the edge of their perimeter.

In the brilliant winter sunshine of Casablanca in French Morocco, Roosevelt, Churchill, and their military advisers gathered in January 1943 to plan their next moves. The Combined Chiefs held their meetings in the Anfa Hotel, a modern-looking whitewashed building overlooking the sea and crowned by a rooftop dining room appropriately dubbed "Le Restaurant Panoramique." Far below, heavily armed infantry patrolled among the sand dunes and orange groves, while fighters circled overhead. General Marshall, urged by the Quartermaster General's Department to be prepared for mosquitoes, arrived in North Africa wearing mosquito boots, mosquito gloves and a large floppy hat with a mosquito-net veil—only to be met by the ground crew wearing shorts.[1]

Posing for pictures around the conference table, the generals and admirals appeared determined and confident, but a little preoccupied. Indeed, they had much to be preoccupied about. American and British troops had landed in North Africa in November 1942, while the British Eighth Army had inflicted a decisive defeat on the German and Italian Armies at El Alamein near Alexandria, Egypt at the other end of North Africa. On Guadalcanal and in Papua, the Americans and Australians were also close to victory. But neither in Europe nor in the Pacific was a final blueprint for victory over the Axis to be discerned.

The American generals and admirals came to Casablanca still hoping to get on with preparations for their preferred approach: an attack across the Channel. They were afraid that their British counterparts would try to divert them from their intention with further adventures along the southern periphery of Europe. The Joint Chiefs wanted a larger share of the rapidly growing Allied resources of men and machines, now becoming available, for the Pacific. Early in the conference Marshall and King proposed that the Combined Chiefs agree in principle to allocate 30 percent of Allied resources to the Pacific and China, Burma, and India, which King claimed were presently receiving only about 15 percent; they wanted this question of proportion settled before discussing specific operations.[2]

Actually, the matter of allocation of resources was far more complex than King's proposal implied. In terms of army troops deployed overseas, for example, there were about 460,000 U.S. troops committed to the war against Japan as compared to only 380,000 in the war against Germany and Italy at the end of 1942, although since July the bulk of army troops and shipping had been earmarked for the Atlantic. Lend-lease supplies, on the other hand, *did* flow primarily to Europe; but against this must be weighed the great preponderance of navy resources in the Pacific.[3] Nor were all resources of equal importance. Certain items were absolutely vital to the war effort, and their availability could determine whether or not a campaign could be undertaken. In late 1942 these were such things as cargo shipping, ocean escort vessels, bombers, and landing craft.[4]

The British, in any case, were unwilling to take up King's invitation to settle the matter of resources. They artfully dodged this question while making it clear that their idea of proper strategy for the Pacific was simply to hold the Japanese at bay until victory in Europe had been won. After allowing King to " 'shoot his line about the Pacific and really get it off his chest,' " in the words of the military secretary to the British War Cabinet, they proposed to concentrate Allied efforts on the Mediterranean in the immediate future, while at the same time wearing down Germany with an all-out bomber offensive.[5.] The U.S. Chiefs of Staff retorted that Japan must be permitted no breathing spell. It would be necessary to apply constant pressure against her by continuing the limited offensives in the South and southwestern Pacific; King's naval planners were already looking towards an advance across the central Pacific along the lines of the old Orange Plan.[6]

The discussions grew heated. At one point King bluntly suggested that after the United States had fought with Britain to defeat Germany, her ally might leave America with the major burden of defeating Japan. This prompted a dramatic statement from Prime Minister Churchill that " 'when Hitler breaks down, all of the British resources and effort will be turned toward the defeat of Japan.' " He even offered to enter into a formal treaty to this effect. Roosevelt declined, saying, " 'The American people accept the word of a great English gentleman.' "[7]

In the end the Casablanca talks produced no concrete plan for the defeat of either Germany or Japan—and no ironclad commitment to devote a greater percentage of resources to the Pacific. Nevertheless, the Combined Chiefs did agree that operations in the Pacific should aim at retaining the initiative and attaining a position of readiness for the full-scale offensive against Japan to follow the defeat of Germany. This meant in effect that the Americans could go ahead with their planned moves in the Pacific.[8] As King wrote to Nimitz, the U.S. Chiefs of Staff had insisted on "recognition of the fact that there is a war going on in the Pacific and that it had to be adequately implemented even though the major operation continues in Europe." [9]

Before leaving Casablanca the president and the prime minister held a press conference. While chatting with reporters, Roosevelt declared that the Allies had resolved to aim at the "unconditional surrender" of the Axis Powers, a term first employed by General Ulysess S. Grant in the Civil War. This apparently off-the-cuff announcement had, in fact, already been approved by the British War Cabinet and the president's advisers. Although there was to be plenty of trouble later over its precise meaning and application, the phrase did serve to reassure public opinion at home and abroad that the British and Americans were "in it" together to the end.[10]

Although the Casablanca meeting gave a green light for MacArthur and Halsey to continue with operations aimed at Rabaul, there was still uncertainty about how to do it. Now that "Task One" had been completed the navy was in no hurry to turn over command of the whole show to General MacArthur, especially since Halsey would have most of the big ships of the Pacific Fleet assigned to him for the climb up the ladder of the Solomons. When on December 1, 1942, General Marshall proposed that the Joint Chiefs dispatch a message to the southwest Pacific directing the execution of Tasks Two and Three under General MacArthur's command—as provided for in the July 1942 agreement—the navy made no reply. Three weeks later Marshall submitted another proposal to "pass strategic direction" of the South Pacific Force to MacArthur. Again there was no reply, but a few days later Marshall let Admiral King's assistants know that no action would be taken on certain matters of interest to the navy, such as relieving marines in Samoa with army troops, until he, Marshall, received a reply to this recommendation of December 1.[11]

This produced an informal proposal from King's COMINCH Staff to the army that a unified command be established for the entire Pacific under the "strategic command" of the Commander in Chief, Pacific, Admiral Nimitz. The army staff replied that the most urgent problem was unity of command between the Pacific's south and southwest theaters. The question of unity of command for the entire Pacific was a far more complicated matter and would require more time.

While the chiefs sparred over the question of command, MacArthur, Halsey and Nimitz's representatives arrived in Washington to be brought up to date on Allied decisions at Casablanca and to agree on the next steps for the Pacific. Admiral Raymond Spruance represented Nimitz; General Sutherland was MacArthur's deputy; and Halsey's delegation was headed by General Millard Harmon.

At the first session of this Pacific Military Conference, attended by high-ranking officers of the Joint Staff, War and Navy Departments, Sutherland outlined MacArthur's plan for an advance on Rabaul. This was to take place in five stages. MacArthur's forces would seize airfields on the Huon Penninsula of New Guinea to provide air support for operations against New Britain Island, where Rabaul was located. Halsey's forces would capture airfields on New Georgia in the central Solomons. Next, MacArthur's forces would capture airfields in western New Britain while Halsey's men took Bougainville. Then Halsey would capture Kavieng airfield on New Ireland. Finally, the two forces would converge on Rabaul.[12] For these operations, Sutherland informed the conferees, MacArthur and Halsey would require five additional divisions and about forty-five more air groups, totalling about 1,800 planes.

The Washington brass were appalled. They had nowhere near this quantity of men and planes available for the Pacific, to say nothing of the shipping to carry it. Sutherland, never one to take pains to win friends and influence people, presented these demands in a take-it-or-leave-it manner which astounded and infuriated many of the Washington planners. Following the stunned silence provoked by Sutherland's presentation, Rear Admiral Cooke, the senior planner present, adjourned the meeting until the following day.[13]

A quick overnight check confirmed what the Washington staff already knew: the men and hardware were simply unavailable. Could the Pacific commanders make do with less? " 'No, emphatically no,' " replied Sutherland and Harmon; their outlined requirements represented " 'the absolutely essential minimum.' "[14]

A hurried series of meetings and conversations followed. The heart of the problem had to do with the Pacific commanders' request for more planes, especially long-range bombers that could reach Rabaul. On this question, the Army Air Forces, eager to get on with the big bomber offensive against Germany agreed upon at Casablanca, would not give an inch. They argued that "the heaviest possible bomber offensive against the German war effort" meant precisely that. Admiral King and his naval planners, however, pointed out that the Casablanca decisions also called for the provision of adequate forces to maintain pressure on Japan. Obviously the forces allocated so far by the War Department were not adequate. It was the old division again: between the navy, which saw the Pacific as its special war theater, and the army's air forces, which wanted to prove the efficacy of strategic bombing by knocking out the German war machine.

Significantly, however, General Kenney, MacArthur's senior Army Air Forces commander, and General Harmon, who was Halsey's, backed their chiefs against the Air Force brass in Washington. Theater loyalties and viewpoints were beginning to modify and erode the old prewar service ideologies. In part this was due simply to the military tradition of loyalty to one's chief—who also had a lot to say about one's future assignments and promotions—but it also had to do with the greater pragmatism encouraged by long months of firsthand experience in the field. As the war dragged on, the Pacific theater staffs discovered a growing community of interest and outlook as against their Washington counterparts of whatever service.[15]

In the end the Pacific commanders did get some additional aircraft and troops, but not enough to meet their requirements for an attack on Rabaul. The Joint Chiefs of Staff accordingly agreed to limit their objectives to Task Two: Halsey was to advance up the Solomons as far as Bougainville and MacArthur was to reach Cape Gloucester, at the far end of New Britain from Rabaul. The attack on Rabaul itself was postponed. Because MacArthur would not receive as many long-range bombers as he wanted, two islands in the Trobriands off the southeast coast of New Guinea, Woodlark and Kiriwina, were added to the original list of objectives as intermediate air bases.

There remained the question of unity of command in the Pacific. On this the army stood firm. All services professed to favor a single unified command. "It becomes more and more apparent that until there is one command, one plan, one thinking head, we will continue to misuse and hold idle our air force and our army," wrote General Arnold as early as September 1942.[16] Yet neither service could agree to give command to the other.

Four months of intensive debate were devoted to the question. The staffs of King and Marshall proposed mutually unacceptable plans.[17] Admiral King continued to drag his feet, insisting on receiving detailed plans from MacArthur, then proposing that the theater boundaries be adjusted again so as to place the entire Solomons chain in Halsey's theater. Marshall and the army doggedly stuck to the letter of the July 1942 agreement.[18] Although naval officers in Washington were prepared for a showdown, King appeared unwilling to damage his close and cooperative relationship with Marshall by pushing the argument to the limit.[19] The result was that the old arrangement was continued. MacArthur held overall command of Task Two while Admiral Nimitz retained control of any naval forces not specifically assigned to operations in the southwestern and South Pacific.

By the end of March 1943 the JCS finally issued the directive to MacArthur and Halsey to begin their long-planned advance on Rabaul. Halsey flew to Brisbane to confer with MacArthur. Despite their mercurial temperaments, the two immediately established a solid and cordial working relationship. They were often closeted together in MacArthur's handsome office, Halsey gesturing dramatically to emphasize a point, MacArthur pacing up and down before his large bare desk, holding his famous corncob pipe.[20]

By the end of April they had their plan. Code-named CART-WHEEL, it involved some thirteen separate, and sometimes simultaneous, operations westward along the New Guinea coast and northwestward up the ladder of the Solomons. The first phase, scheduled to begin in June, was to see the seizure of Woodlark and Kiriwina, followed by Halsey's attack on New Georgia in the Solomons. Following the occupation of Woodlark and Kiriwina, MacArthur would move on to take Salamaua, Lae and Finschhafen on the New Guinea coast. By that time New Georgia was to have been secured and Halsey would move on to the Shortland Islands and Bougainville, while MacArthur attacked Madang. The final phase of CARTWHEEL entailed a landing at Cape Gloucester by MacArthur's forces and one on the east coast of Bougainville by Halsey's.

While the Americans carried on their long debate on strategy, the Japanese had been far from idle. Following the loss of Buna and Guadalcanal they were completely on the defensive. Positions in the northern and central Solomons were strengthened and the Japanese strongholds at Wewak, Lae, Salamaua, and Madang braced for attack. From Korea and northern China, two fresh divisions were ordered to New Guinea, and Tokyo activated a new headquarters: the Eighteenth Army under Lieutenant General Adachi Hatazo to control operations.[21]

To be closer to the front, Adachi decided to shift his headquarters to Lae; he embarked from Rabaul with a convoy carrying the 51st Division to New Guinea. During its long voyage along the New Britain coast and into the Solomon Sea the convoy of eight transports and eight destroyers would be exposed to Allied air attack. To guard against this danger, almost a hundred aircraft were assigned to fly cover for the ships. Neutralization strikes were also planned against Allied air bases in New Guinea, but bad weather prevented their execution. About halfway along on its journey the convoy was spotted by American B-24 bombers.[22]

In the battles at Midway and Guadalcanal Army Air Force bombers had proven spectacularly ineffective at sinking or even hitting ships at sea. MacArthur's 5th Air Force was no better; but in August MacArthur received a new air commander, General George C. Kenney. Kenney found a dispirited and disillusioned air organization, which he quickly hauled and beat into life. Five general officers disappeared during the first two weeks, followed by a forlorn procession of colonels and majors. In their place came aggressive, canny flyers like Ennis C. Whitehead and Kenneth Walker. When Sutherland attempted to browbeat Kenney in the way he had done to so many of MacArthur's other commanders, Kenney seized a piece of blank paper from the chief of staff's desk and drew a tiny black dot in the corner. " 'The blank area represents what I know about air matters,' " growled Kenney, " 'and the dot represents what you know.' " Sutherland soon backed down and, from then on, Kenney had little trouble from the chief of staff's office in running his air force.[23]

Kenney was determined to find out why army aircraft were doing so poorly in attacking ships. He soon discovered one reason: the planes attacked from too high up. Although Arnold and the other air force leaders continued to swear by high-altitude bombing, Kenney began almost immediately to experiment with low-level antishipping strikes.[24] The B-25 medium bomber was modified to carry eight forward-firing machine guns, six one-hundred-pound bombs, and sixty small fragmentation bombs with delayed action fuses.

All through the fall and into the winter of 1942–43, Kenney's squadrons practised attacks from 150 feet up, using an old ship wrecked off Port Moresby as their target. The planes came in so low that two were hit by flying debris and another hit the old ship's mast, but by the beginning of 1943 they had become the deadliest naval weapon MacArthur possessed. By the time the convoy carrying General Adachi's troops was sighted, Kenney's flyers were itching for a fight.

As the Japanese convoy was nearing Cape Gloucester, the western tip of New Britain Island, it was attacked by two flights of high-flying B-17s, which sank a transport. A second attack—by eleven more B-17s—left another ship sinking. The following morning the convoy entered the Dampier Straight between New Guinea and New Britain, within range of Allied fighters and medium bombers. At midmorning, lookouts on the Japanese ships stared in surprise and apprehension at the black shapes of nearly a hundred Allied planes, including thirty of the modified B-25s, closing rapidly from the south.

Japanese fighters covering the convoy remained high in the sky, waiting for the usual high-level B-17 attacks, and so missed the B-25s, A-20s, and Australian Beaufighters which came in skimming the water so low and straight that the Japanese sailors thought they were being attacked by torpedo planes.[25] The Allied attackers roared over the slow-moving formation at masthead level, raining death on the crowded decks of the transports.

By the end of the day all the remaining transports and four of the eight destroyers were sunk or sinking. Allied planes and PT boats roamed the strait, shooting up survivors clinging to life rafts or debris. Since Japanese troops did not surrender, they had to be killed to prevent them from making landfall in New Guinea and possibly joining their comrades there. At least that was the reasoning. Almost 3,000 troops in all, including most of the experienced officers of the 51st Division, were lost in this Battle of the Bismarck Sea.[26]

Kenney's planes had finally achieved what General Billy Mitchell had so breezily predicted fifteen years before. They had destroyed an enemy fleet at sea unaided by naval surface forces. Yet it had required sixteen months of war experience, dearly bought air bases, specially designed equipment, painstaking training, good intelligence, and fine weather to accomplish it. No matter. The principle was established. Air power was clearly the dominant element in the southwest Pacific—but it was the kind of air power which required airfields painfully wrested from the enemy.

The Battle of the Bismarck Sea shocked Imperial General Headquarters into shifting the weight of Japanese military effort to New Guinea. Yet it was becoming increasingly difficult to shift reinforcements to that area in view of the rapidly growing threat of Allied submarines and air power. Some troops were brought in by barge at night, but this was a slow, hazardous process. The supply situation was even worse: by spring about 40 percent of Japanese front-line troops in New Guinea were suffering from disease or malnutrition.[27]

These problems were symptoms of a larger malady: the Japanese were gradually losing their ability to contest successfully for control of the air against the Allies. Not only could the United States produce far more planes than the Japanese, it could also build air bases much faster and more efficiently.[28] Moreover, Allied planes were getting better. Toward the end of the Guadalcanal campaign a new twin-engine fighter, the P-38 Lightning, had made its appearance. It possessed great range, heavy armament, and high speed. It could not beat the Zero in a dogfight—but the Lightnings seldom engaged in dogfights. They preferred to patrol at extreme altitudes and use their superior diving speed to pick off lower-flying Japanese fighters. "The peculiar sound of the P-38's twin engines soon became both familiar and bitterly hated by the Japanese all across the South Pacific." [29] Early in 1943 a second new fighter, the Chance-Vought F4U Corsair, made its appearance. Designed as a naval fighter, the early Corsair proved poorly suited to carrier operations, but from land it flew very well indeed. Heavily armed, with a powerful new engine which made it the fastest fighter in the Pacific, the Corsair soon added its contribution to Japanese woes.

In an attempt to check the erosion of Japanese air superiority in the South Pacific, Admiral Yamamoto launched a series of mass surprise air raids—the "I" operation—on Allied airfields in New Guinea and Guadalcanal. By scraping together all his available land-based air power and stripping planes from his carriers, Yamamoto put together a striking force of over 300 aircraft. Early in April he sent 224 planes against Guadalcanal and Tulagi in the largest single Japanese air attack since Pearl Harbor. A few days later almost 300 planes flew against Allied shipping in Northwest New Guinea, followed by similar attacks on Port Moresby and Milne Bay.[30]

The "I" operation was an impressive demonstration of how the Japanese might have used their advantage of interior lines to great effect against the widely separated, loosely coordinated commands of Halsey and MacArthur. Yet Yamamoto's forces, though formidable, were too small—and their efforts too brief—to achieve decisive results. Moreover, many of the pilots who flew in the "I" operation were inexperienced beginners, hastily fed in to replace the veterans lost at Midway and over Guadalcanal.[31] So the massive air raids achieved relatively little. The Allies lost only about two dozen planes, a destroyer, a corvette, two Dutch merchant ships, and an oiler. Japanese aircraft losses were at least as high as those of the Allies.[32]

Exaggerated reports by the novice pilots returned from the big raids gave Yamamoto and his staff a false impression of "I" operation's results. According to the pilots, they had sunk some twenty-five merchant ships and destroyed over a hundred planes. Yamamoto declared the operation a success: he decided to visit the flyers in southern Bougainville who had done so much damage to the Allies.

At Pearl Harbor Nimitz's cryptographers were laboring over the radio messages about the admiral's visit, which the Japanese had imprudently sent out from Rabaul. In less than a day they had broken the code. Captain Edwin T. Layton, the fleet's intelligence officer, brought the news to Admiral Nimitz. " 'Do we try to get him?' " asked Nimitz. " 'If we did, could they replace him with someone better?' " Layton shook his head. " 'All right,' " said Nimitz; " 'we'll try it.' " [33]

Yamamoto's plane, escorted by nine zeros, approached Kahili near Buin in southern Bougainville on the morning of April 18; eighteen Lightnings were waiting in ambush. There was a brief combat with the Zeros. Then four P-38s broke off, headed for the bomber carrying Yamamoto and for a second plane carrying his chief of staff. The American flight leader, Captain Thomas G. Lanphier, Jr., fired a burst with his 20-mm cannon. Yamamoto's plane burst into flames and plunged into the jungle.

On June 5 the admiral's ashes were interred in Tokyo in an impressive state funeral. Less than two weeks later the Allied offensives in the Solomons and New Guinea, which the "I" operation had vainly sought to forestall, were under way.

The Allied units moving against Japanese positions in New Guinea and the Solomons in the summer of 1943 were far more formidable than the forces which Halsey and MacArthur had commanded at Guadalcanal and Papua just six months before. They were superior not only in the number and quality of ships, planes, and men, but also in the specialized weapons they would need to do the job. The most notable of these was a whole family of amphibious craft designed to deliver men and equipment rapidly and efficiently right up to a hostile beach.

Prior to World War II, navy and Marine Corps planners had assumed that landing operations would be carried out using large transports to carry great numbers of troops and many small boats. Once the target area was reached, the troops would be transferred to the small boats for the assault. In 1941 however, the British government became interested in larger landing craft which could carry not only troops but tanks, artillery, and other heavy equipment. After Pearl Harbor, U.S. leaders quickly ordered a crash program to construct the new types of amphibious shipping proposed by the British— both for the U.S. and for the Royal navies. [34]

The largest of the new vessels was the diesel-powered Landing Ship Tank, universally called the LST, a 300-foot seagoing vessel that could carry over 2,000 tons of cargo in its cavernous interior. Its shallow draft enabled it to run right up onto or very close to a coral, sand, or mud beach, then discharge its cargo through the large doors and ramp in its bow. Its low speed and lack of maneuverability caused many sailors to declare that LST stood for "large stationary target"; Pacific commanders were soon busy adding extra antiaircraft guns to the originally scanty armament. [35] Another seagoing amphibian was the LCI (Landing Craft Infantry), considerably smaller and faster than the LST, which discharged its troops and equipment down gangways hinged to a platform on the bow "and lucky were the troops who got ashore in water less than shoulder-high." [36] The smallest of the new "beaching craft" was the LCT (Landing Craft Tank), a bargelike vessel about 120 feet long, with a bow ramp which could be lowered to discharge its cargo of medium tanks or heavy vehicles. LCTs were normally transported overseas in sections and reassembled at their destination.

Of the small landing craft carried aboard transports and cargo vessels, the most widely used was the LCVP (Landing Craft Vehicles and Personnel). It had a large bow door which could be lowered as a ramp, over which thirty-six combat troops or a single 2.5-ton truck could pass on to the beach. A truly amphibious craft, the LVT (Landing Vehicle Tracked) or AMTRAC (Amphibious Tractor)—which could climb out of the water onto land on its rubber tractor-treads—was also available, although early models were subject to frequent mechanical breakdowns. [37] By the end of June large numbers of these craft, together with transports and cargo ships escorted by warships, were on their way toward beaches in New Guinea and the Solomons.

The great preponderance of the new craft went to Admiral Halsey. MacArthur's Amphibious Force, Southwest Pacific (later the VII Amphibious Force), under the indomitable Rear Admiral Daniel "Uncle Dan" Barbey, comprised a handful of old transports and a growing number of LSTs, LCTs and LCIs, commanded by a collection of young naval reserve officers fresh out of college, many of whom had never been to sea before. (One LCT officer told Admiral Barbey that his "prior experience in leadership" had consisted solely of chairing his fraternity dance at the University of Texas. Another young ensign believed he could keep his ship out of the rays of the moon by zig-zagging.) [38]

Barbey had not only to prepare his inexperienced personnel for battle but to devise a means of making use of his meager resources in amphibious assaults. The strong naval forces available for Halsey's amphibious operations were simply unavailable in the southwest Pacific most of the time. Nor were there enough large transports to stage a conventional ship-to-shore assault, with the troops landed in small boats as at Guadalcanal. Barbey's amphibious operations relied on shore-to-shore movement of troops in LSTs and LCIs, supported by a handful of destroyers and subchasers. Gunfire support from the destroyers would be brief; the landing had to be accomplished quickly so that the vulnerable LSTs and smaller beaching craft would not be unduly exposed to Japanese air or naval counterattacks. Normally, a surprise landing on a moonless or overcast night was necessary; the ships "had to be lightly loaded and with just the right trim so they could be unloaded and away before an enemy bomber attack found them high and dry on a receding tide." [39]

Barbey did have one asset which Admiral Halsey lacked: a specially trained Army Engineer Amphibious Brigade under Brigade General William F. Heavy. The Amphibious Brigade was designed to move troops and equipment by water to a hostile shore and land them there in the face of any type of opposition. Small boat drivers, beach masters, machine gunners, shore party personnel, maintenance crews, signalmen, and quartermaster troops were all part of the single integrated team which was the Engineer Amphibious Brigade. They brought the troops and supplies to shore and organized the beachhead as a unified operation, a method far preferable to that employed in the Solomons, where Turner's sailors operated the boats but marines were responsible for unloading them. [40] Arriving in New Guinea in the spring of 1943, Heavy's Second Engineer Amphibious Brigade was to be in action almost continuously from the beginning of CARTWHEEL to MacArthur's return to the Philippines in the fall of 1944. [41] During the war, the VII Amphibious Force and the Engineer Brigade were to carry over one million Allied troops and a million tons of supplies to dozens of amphibious landings, from eastern New Guinea to the Philippines and Borneo.

• •

MacArthur's initial objective in CARTWHEEL was to occupy Woodlark and Kiriwina Islands in the Trobriands and to land troops at Nassau Bay on the coast of New Guinea near Salamaua. The landings in the Trobriands were entrusted to units of Lieutenant General Walter Krueger's newly arrived Sixth Army. The Sixth Army should have come under the operational control of General Sir Thomas Blamey, the Australian who served as Commander, Allied Land Forces in the Southwest Pacific. But for the CARTWHEEL operation MacArthur had created an independent tactical organization— "Alamo Force"—virtually identical to the Sixth Army. Since the Sixth Army thereby became a "special task force," it was under MacArthur's direct command rather than under Blamey, who now commanded little more than the Australian troops assigned to CART-WHEEL.

MacArthur failed even to consult the Australians about this bit of sleight of hand, but his action, by assigning separate tasks and command setups to the Australian and American forces involved in the operations against Rabaul probably avoided much trouble. [42] The only instance in which sizeable numbers of American troops served under Australian tactical command in the CARTWHEEL campaigns—when Colonel Archibald R. MacKechnie's 162d Infantry of the 41st Division operated with an Australian division in the Nassau Bay area—"was fraught with misunderstandings, disputes and uncooperativeness." This experience led one U.S. Army historian to conclude that "the Americans believed in Allied unity of command only if they were doing the commanding." [43]

On Woodlark, Lieutenant P. V. Mollison, a coastwatcher of the Royal Australian Navy, was awakened during the night by islanders who warned him that strange ships were standing in toward the beach. Mollison hurriedly mustered his local native militia into a skirmish line about a hundred yards from the water. They watched tensely as the first wave of invaders came ashore. Then Mollison breathed a sign of relief as he heard the unmistakable sound of American accents. [44]

The invaders were the advance party of two American regiments which occupied Woodlark and Kiriwina at the end of the month without incident. On the same day that Lieutenant Mollison welcomed the troops to Woodlark, an American battalion combat team landed unopposed at Nassau Bay and started inland. Its goal was to link up with a much larger Australian force under Major General Stanley G. Savige, near the village of Wau in the Bulolo Valley twenty-five miles southwest of Salamaua. Wau, with its valuable air strip and trails leading to the north coast, had been the target of a desperate Japanese attack at the end of January 1942. Australian troops, heavily reinforced and resupplied by the Allied air forces, stopped the attack; ever since February they had been pressing the Japanese back toward Salamaua. [45] The bloodless seizure of Nassau Bay provided a means of supplying these troops by sea and gave the Australians a staging point for further shore-to-shore movement of their New Guinea forces.

Four hundred miles away, on the other side of the Solomon Sea, Halsey's forces were also on the move toward an island called New Georgia northwest of Guadalcanal. In terrain and climate it was much like Guadalcanal; but it was far harder to approach, with a long chain of reefs, rocks, shallows, and barrier islands protecting much of the coast. The main Allied objective—the Japanese airfield at Munda Point on the southwest tip of the island—could not be approached by large vessels.

To get at Munda, Halsey's commanders planned to seize nearby Rendova Island, so close it was within artillery range of Munda, as well as protected anchorages at Segi Point, Wickham Anchorage, and Viru Harbor on the south coast of New Georgia. Rendova would be the jumping-off point for an attack on Munda. Wickham Anchorage and Viru Harbor were wanted as supply points and Segi as a fighter strip. All of these landings were unopposed, although Japanese warplanes staged several attacks on the American invasion task force. They sank the transport *McCawley,* which had served as Admiral Turner's flagship since the early days at Guadalcanal.

At nearby Munda Major General Sasaki Noboru, who had just been appointed commander of all Japanese army and navy forces on New Georgia—about 5,000 men—could see the Americans through his binoculars as they prepared to move from Rendova to the mainland. At one point Sasaki suggested that his own troops board landing craft, which would probably not be noticed among the many American craft off Rendova, and launch a surprise attack on the American positions. But he was overruled. [46] So Sasaki saved his surprises for New Georgia.

The American invaders came ashore at two widely separate points. The main landings were at Zanana beach on the south coast, about five miles from Munda. There was a landing place at Laiana Beach only two miles from Munda, but it was heavily defended. Admiral Turner and Major General John H. Hester, commander of the New Georgia occupation force, therefore opted for Zanana. This decision caused the Americans much trouble later, but it was strictly in keeping with current thinking on amphibious warfare, which held that an unopposed landing was always to be preferred. [47]

About 2,600 soldiers and marines under Colonel Harry Liversedge, USMC, was also put ashore at Rice Anchorage on the northwest coast to prevent reinforcements from nearby Kolombangara Island from reaching Munda. A Japanese squadron carrying some of those reinforcements tangled with the American task force which had just unloaded Liversedge's troops in a night battle in Kula Gulf. As in previous sea battles at night in the Solomons, the American advantage of radar was cancelled by the superior range of Japanese torpedoes. The Japanese destroyer force, encountering Admiral Walden Ainsworth's three light cruisers and four destroyers, quickly fired torpedoes and retired, sinking the light cruiser *Helena*. The Japanese lost two destroyers but delivered their reinforcements safely to Munda.[48]

A week later, on July 6, Ainsworth's task force again encountered a squadron of Japanese destroyers, led this time by the light cruiser *Jintsu,* bringing reinforcements to Kolombangara for transshipment to New Georgia. Flagship *Jintsu* was almost blown out of the water by rapid radar-directed fire from Ainsworth's three cruisers, but as the Americans pursued the retiring Japanese, they steamed right into the path of the deadly long-lance torpedoes. All three cruisers were lightly damaged; the destroyer *Gwin* was sunk.[49]

Ashore, Liversedge's men, after a nightmarish trek through rain-soaked jungle, routed the Japanese from their base at Enogai Inlet and established a road block on the main trail between Kula Gulf and Munda. Yet the Japanese continued to bring in reinforcements through Bairoko Harbor, a little west of Enogai. These made their way south to Munda, bypassing the road block.

In the south General Hester started his two regiments, the 169th and 172d Infantry of the 43rd Division, up the trail from Zanana toward Munda. They soon ran into trouble in the dense, hilly jungle. An entire battalion of the 169th was held up for two days by a single Japanese platoon dug in on the trail. At night the Japanese harassed the inexperienced soldiers with grenades and blood-chilling screams. They shouted curses in English and fired off occasional mortar rounds. The troops—mostly National Guardsmen in action for the first time—fired at shadows, imagined the Japanese to be all around them, and tossed grenades blindly into the jungle, often wounding other Americans.

After a few days the 169th and 172d finally pushed their way past the pill boxes and roadblocks to strike the main Japanese defense line on the high ground east of Munda. There they were halted. The Japanese, well dug in and camouflaged as usual, kept the Americans pinned down with well-placed mortar- and light artillery fire. To add to their troubles, Hester's troops were also beginning to run short of supplies, which had to be brought along the primitive jungle trail from Zanana, carried over the last part by hand. With this in mind, General Hester ordered the 172d to swing south and secure the beach at Laiana, much closer to Munda, where boats from Rendova could bring in supplies and reinforcements.

Its food and water almost exhausted, dogged at the rear by Japanese patrols, the 172d fought its way to Laiana, and secured it on July

13. There they were joined by a battalion of the 103d Infantry and a marine tank platoon. They resumed the advance toward Munda, making slow progress.

At this point Major General Oscar W. Griswold, commander of the XIVth Corps and Hester's immediate superior, arrived at New Georgia, took a quick look around, and reported his doubts that the 43d Division would ever take Munda. The division appeared "about to fold up." [50] Although battle casualties in the division had been rather light, a large number of men were suffering from war neurosis—what would soon become popularly known as "combat fatigue." A steady stream of hollow-eyed, muddy, bearded, exhausted men daily plodded to the rear area medical stations, where doctors puzzled over them and labeled them variously as "temporarily mentally disturbed," "physically exhausted," or as being in "psychoneurotic anxiety states." Whatever their malady, the 43d Division had a far higher percentage of them than any other unit in the Pacific, with the unfortunate 169th and 172d regiments contributing more than their share. Poor leadership, inexperience, lack of food and rest, and the nocturnal harassing tactics of the Japanese—all undoubtedly contributed to produce such alarming symptoms. After viewing these men, General Griswold urged that reinforcements be sent to New Georgia immediately.

Griswold's report affected Halsey's headquarters like an electric shock. The admiral immediately ordered two more army divisions, the 25th and the 39th, to New Georgia. He also sent his top army commander, Lieutenant General Millard F. Harmon, USAAF, up to Guadalcanal with orders to " 'take whatever steps were deemed necessary to capture Munda.' " The next day Harmon ordered Griswold to relieve General Hester as commander of the New Georgia Occupation Forces. Just at the same time, Admiral Turner departed the South Pacific to take up a new command in Admiral Nimitz's theater. He was replaced by Rear Admiral Theodore S. Wilkinson, who from then on functioned as Halsey's amphibious forces commander.

While the Americans reorganized, Sasaki prepared a counterattack. The 13th Infantry Regiment from Kolombangara, which had successfully landed at Bairoko and made its way south, was launched against the long, vulnerable, American line of communications from Zanana to the front. Simultaneously the Japanese 229th Regiment attacked the American front-line positions to keep them pinned down. A part of the 13th made it all the way to the 43d Division's command post. But they were driven off by artillery fire which the quick-thinking division artillery officer, Captain James Buhler, had directed onto the Japanese positions by field telephone. The 229th launched its own attack but made little progress. Except for giving the Americans a bad scare, Sasaki's counteroffensive was a flop.[51] In the north, Liversedge attempted to seize Bairoko, but he was eventually forced to withdraw to Enogai. The back door for Sasaki's reinforcements remained open.

By July 25 General Griswold had his reinforcements in place and was ready for another crack at the Munda airfield. In the assault on Munda Griswold's troops faced the same problems as MacArthur's had faced at Buna and Gona: well dug in, well-concealed Japanese pillboxes, often with interlocking fields of fire, manned by stubborn, fanatical fighters who seldom retreated and never surrendered. Yet unlike MacArthur's troops, the soldiers on New Georgia had the tools to deal with these obstacles: ample air and artillery support, naval gunfire from Admiral Wilkinson's destroyers, and tanks supplied by the marines. The most important new weapon was the flamethrower. Employed extensively for the first time on New Georgia, flamethrowers were large and heavy; their operators were extremely vulnerable once they exposed themselves in order to fire them, but they proved lethal against enemy pillboxes. Soldiers assaulting a pillbox were preceded by an artillery barrage and 81mm mortar fire, which ripped away the brush and foliage concealing the Japanese positions. Sometimes such barrages penetrated the pillbox or otherwise drove its occupants into the open. Then a company or platoon would provide covering fire with their rifles and grenades while another company or platoon attempted to get around the pillbox and take it from the side or rear.[52]

By early August the Japanese defenses around Munda had begun to crack. Continuous air and artillery bombardments—and inadequate medical facilities had taken a heavy toll of Sasaki's men. On July 29 Sasaki began to pull out. Leaving behind a delaying force, he withdrew most of his troops to the nearby outlying islands of Baanga, Arundel, and Kolombangara, there to await reinforcements. Troops of the 43d Division, which had begun the harrowing trek from Zanana one month before, routed the Japanese from their last defenses at Munda on the afternoon of August 5. Griswold radioed Halsey that he was now "sole owner" of the airfield, but it took two more weeks of hard fighting to mop up the forces left behind on New Georgia by General Sasaki.

Reviewing the prolonged, frustrating struggle for Munda, Major General J. Lawton Collins—a future army chief of staff—who had commanded the 25th Division on Munda, attributed many of the difficulties to Admiral Turner and his penchant for attempting to control the organization and operations of military forces ashore, a penchant which had caused considerable problems for Vandegrift and the marines in the Guadalcanal campaign. [53] One of the navy's most brillant officers, Turner "studied everything, remembered everything, interfered in everything . . . ". [54] Correspondent Robert Sherrod noted that Turner could not travel from ship to shore "without lecturing the coxswain on how to bring the boat alongside." [55]

Turner simply could not resist exercising active command over troops ashore, just as he did aboard ship. During the struggle for Guadalcanal, Turner had not only brought Vandegrift his reinforcements—a task he accomplished with skill and tenacity—but also insisted on a voice in where those reinforcements should be deployed. On two occasions he came close to landing marine reinforcements at points which would have put them in disastrous tactical positions. Throughout the first weeks of the campaign, when the marines were barely clinging to possession of Henderson Field, he urged Vandegrift to take the offensive. [56] "It wasn't the Navy that was wrong and caused trouble; it was Turner," declared one marine officer who served with him. "Turner was a martinet; very, very gifted, but he was stubborn, opinionated, conceited, thought that he could do anything better than anybody in the world. . . . I challenge anyone to name a naval officer other than Turner with whom the Marines had command difficulties. . . . by and large naval officers, they were wary of trying to run land operations, but Turner, no; because Turner knew everything!" [57]

At Munda Turner failed to utilize Griswold's XIV Corps staff to coordinate administrative and logistical arrangements; he put Hester in overall command of land operations instead of Griswold, although the former was already burdened with the 43rd Division. Liversedge was likewise saddled with command of a hybrid task force drawn from three different army regiments and a marine raider battalion. [59] Both the army and the Marines were to have more trouble with Turner in the future.

By the time General Collins's troops had completed their mopup on New Georgia, Sasaki had transferred the bulk of his troops to Kolombangara, where he waited impatiently for the reinforcements he had been promised to help retake New Georgia. The reinforcements came on the night of August 6. Four Japanese destroyers, crowded with troops for Kolombangara, entered Vella Gulf shortly before midnight. Commander Frederick Moosbrugger's Task Group 31.2 was waiting. Alerted by Allied intelligence, Moosbrugger's six destroyers had steamed rapidly up from Tulagi and were patrolling off Kolombangara on this calm moonless night. They were no scratch team, such as had often been thrown together in the past to block the Tokyo Express. Moosbrugger's own destroyer division, DESDIV 12, had trained together since 1941 and specialized in radar-controlled night torpedo attacks. All Moosbrugger's skippers were thoroughly familiar with his plans, and there were no cruisers in his task force to tie down the destroyers, as had happened in earlier Solomons battles.

The radarscope on the leading American destroyers picked up the Japanese at around 20,000 yards. Moosbrugger ordered two course changes to bring his six ships, still invisible to the Japanese, into the optimum position for firing torpedoes. At about 6,300 yards, the destroyers *Dunlop, Maury,* and *Craven* launched twenty-four torpedoes at their unsuspecting opponents. A minute later, a Japanese lookout finally spotted a shape to the southwest. Too late! The American torpedoes ripped into the advancing destroyers. *Kawakaze* blew up, sending flaming debris shooting into the sky. The *Hagikaze* and *Arashi* went dead in the water, helpless, flaming targets for the five-inch guns of the American destroyers. Only the destroyer *Shigure,* which carried no troops, escaped injury. She hastily fled north after firing her torpedoes—harmlessly—at the Americans. Over 900 soldiers and fifty tons of equipment were lost in this debacle, known as the Battle of Vella Gulf.[60]

So ended Sasaki's last hope of reconquering New Georgia. Yet he still had about 12,000 troops on Kolombangara, fighting mad and ready to make that island into another bloody Munda. Halsey knew that. He looked forward to "another slugging match" with little enthusiasm. Could Kolombangara be bypassed in favor of Vella Lavella, a little farther up the Solomons ladder? Vella Lavella had a better airfield and was closer to the ultimate objectives of Bougainville and Rabaul. But just for that reason, the Allied invaders would be exposed to heavy air attack from Japanese bases virtually next door to them. The nearest Japanese airfield on Bougainville, Ballale, was barely sixty miles away. To survive, the Americans would need speed, surprise, and a lot of air support. Halsey chose Vella Lavella.

As D-Day for Vella Lavella dawned on August 15, heavily loaded troops of the First and Second Battalions of the 35th Infantry Regiment picked their way down the landing nets of fast-destroyer transports and climbed, jumped, or fell into the small landing craft bobbing in the gentle surf. There were no Japanese on Vella Lavella except a couple of hundred ill-armed and ill-fed sailors from the destroyers sunk in Vella Gulf, so the Americans landed without difficulty. In an hour the LCIs had come up; then came the LSTs. In about twelve hours Admiral Wilkinson's amphibious forces had put ashore around 4,600 troops with fifteen days' supplies and plenty of ammunition. [61] Japanese aircraft made several attacks—but with little success.

Once Vella Lavella had been captured, Sasaki's troops on Kolombangara were of no further use in stemming the American advance but, as at Guadalcanal, most escaped to fight another day, skillfully evacuated by destroyers, barges, and landing craft under cover of darkness. When the Japanese sent a strong destroyer force to evacuate the stranded sailors on Vella Lavella, three American destroyers attempted to interfere. They sank a destroyer before being badly mauled by the deadly long-lance torpedoes of the much larger Japanese force.

While Halsey's forces pushed their way through the Solomons, MacArthur's troops were closing in on Lae and Salamaua, two coastal villages just south of New Guinea's Huon Peninsula. Lae was the real target. It had a good anchorage and an airfield; it was the key to valleys formed by the Ramu and Markham rivers. These broad, grassy lowlands ran northwest almost 400 miles and formed a natural highway to the important Japanese base at Madang on the far side of the Huon peninsula. MacArthur wanted to capture Madang in order to secure his flank in the advance against Rabaul. [62] The Salamaua attack was a diversion which, MacArthur hoped, would divert Japanese attention away from Lae and siphon off enemy strength from Lae.[63]

The campaign against Lae and Salamaua showed MacArthur and his commanders at their best. Operating in nightmarish terrain which precluded large-scale overland movements and lacking the large naval and shipping resources of Halsey's theater, they put together an innovative combination of airborne and amphibious moves which kept the Japanese confused and distracted.

First, MacArthur's engineers rapidly and secretly built a fighter strip at Tsli Tsli in a grassy inland valley west of Lae and Salamaua. Undetected by the Japanese until it was completed, the airfield was used by Kenney's fighters to escort Allied bombers on a series of major raids against the principal Japanese airbase at Wewak. Over a hundred Japanese planes were destroyed on the ground, leaving

Allied aircraft virtually unchallenged in the skies over eastern New Guinea.[64]

Next, Admiral Barbey's VII Amphibious Force and Brigadier General William F. Heavy's Second Engineer Special Brigade landed the Australian Ninth Division twenty miles east of Lae. The following day almost one hundred C-47 transport planes, escorted by nearly every fighter and bomber that could fly, carried the U.S. Army's 503d Parachute Regiment to an airborne assault on Nadzab on the north bank of the Markham River. In this first combat air assault of the Pacific war, the 503d took possession of a nearby airstrip, while Kenney's transports began ferrying in the entire Australian Seventh Division. By early September, Allied troops were closing in on Lae and Salamaua which the Japanese High Command had, by this time, decided to abandon. Salamaua fell on September 12; Lae was taken four days later.

Acting quickly to take advantage of the rapid collapse of Lae, MacArthur stepped up the timetable for the next stage in his advance. Knowing that Japanese reinforcements were on their way to his next objective—the town of Finschhafen at the tip of the Huon peninsula—he ordered Admiral Barbey to land a brigade of the Ninth Australian Division there as soon as possible. Other Australian units advanced up the Ramu and Markham Valleys to seal off the Huon Peninsula from the land side at the same time.

The Japanese did not seriously contest the Australian advance up the Markham and Ramu. But at Finschhafen they gave Brigadier General George E. Wooten's Australian veterans of North Africa plenty of trouble. Supported by units of General Heavy's amphibious engineers, the Australians captured the town after a week's hard fighting. The Japanese garrison fell back on the high ground north of the town called Satelberg, where they were reinforced by advance elements of the Japanese Twentieth Division.

General Wooten learned from a captured Japanese order that the enemy was planning to launch a combined land- and seaborne counterattack against his brigade; he passed the word to his men. Few slept that night. All along the coast eyes strained into the darkness for a sign of the expected attack. At about three in the morning, Japanese planes bombed the Finschhafen area, but they did little damage. Less than an hour later a lookout spotted four Japanese barges heading for the beach.

A steady rain fell as the barges, carrying a company of the Japanese Seventy-Ninth infantry, glided with muffled motors, toward the beach. The positions there were held by two companies of Australians and a detachment of the Engineer Special Brigade. As the barges landed, the Australians opened fire with small arms and heavy machine guns, but their heavier pieces could not be lowered enough to hit the invaders.

About fifteen yards from the barges' landing place was a camouflaged .50 calibre machine gun, manned by Private Nathan Van Noy and Corporal Stephen Popa, both of the Engineer Special Brigade. Waiting until the barges had lowered their ramps and the Japanese began to land, Van Noy and Popa suddenly opened a murderous fire on the invaders, killing many and pinning the others to the beach. The surviving Japanese tossed grenades at the machine gunners. Although both were wounded by the grenades, Van Noy and Popa managed to reload the gun and continue their unequal battle with the Japanese. Van Noy's body was later found with one leg almost blown off, his finger still on the trigger, and the last round of his ammunition fired.[65]

With growing light, the defenders quickly finished off the Japanese remnants on the beach, but this was only the beginning of the bitter struggle for Finschhafen which raged for almost a week. Strengthened by reinforcements, Wooten's men eventually beat off all attacks and then resumed the offensive. By January 1944 they had captured Sio on the far side of the Huon peninsula.

To cut off the Japanese retreat MacArthur sent General Krueger's Alamo Force to capture Saidor, far up the peninsula, in a surprise amphibious assault. The landing was successful but the Japanese, who should have been trapped between Alamo Force and the advancing Australian troops, were able to sidestep them both, escaping along inland trails to Madang and Wewak.

While the Australians were battling the Japanese on Huon peninsula, Admiral Halsey's South Pacific forces were preparing to assault their most formidable objective: the large island of Bougainville at the northern end of the Solomons chain. Bougainville would be the final link in the iron chain that the Allies were stretching around New Britain and Rabaul. With airfields on Bougainville, fighters could escort Kenney's bombers from New Guinea and Halsey's from Munda on strikes against Japan's big base at Rabaul.

The Japanese guessed that the Allies were aiming at Rabaul; they were determined to hold Bougainville as long as possible. Admiral Koga Mineichi, who had succeeded Yamamoto as commander in chief of the Combined Fleet, decided to send most of his carrier-based planes to reinforce the air defenses at Rabaul and to keep Allied assaults against that fortress at bay. [66] The Japanese called this the "RO" operation.

The carrier planes arrived at Rabaul in the midst of a heavy bombing campaign by the 5th and 13th Air Forces, intended by Kenney to "gain control of the air over New Britain, make Rabaul untenable for Japanese shipping, and set up an air blockade of all the Jap forces in that area." [67] The result was a string of fierce air battles, often involving hundreds of planes. The intensity of the struggle in the air sometimes approached that of the battles which the larger Army Air Forces in Europe were waging against the German Luftwaffe. [68] One B-24 of the 13th Air Force called *The Blessed Event* was hit by shells from Japanese fighters, knocking out the engine controls and smashing the instrument panel. The pilot, copilot, bombadier, and nose gunner were all wounded—but the *Blessed Event* pushed on to Rabaul despite further hits which killed the navigator and wounded the top turret gunner, who nevertheless continued to fire, helping to shoot down at least three Japanese planes. The *Blessed Event* headed homeward with one rudder missing and streams of gasoline pouring from more than 120 bullet- and shell holes in the wings and fuselage. Guided by its wounded pilot, the B-24 collided with a fighter while making an emergency landing; it lost one of its wheels but managed to glide to safety on its belly: one crewman was dead, one dying, and eight were wounded.[69]

Both sides claimed to have inflicted great damage on the other in the Rabaul air battles, and both overestimated their successes. Yet the Japanese suffered most. Kenney's raids failed to "make Rabaul untenable" but they did take a heavy toll of Koga's carrier planes, badly damaged Rabaul's harbors and airfields, and diverted attention from the developing Bougainville offensive.

The job of softening up Bougainville itself for invasion as well as providing air cover for the attacking forces fell to Halsey's Air Command Solomons, or "Airsols." Airsols at first sight appeared to be a solid argument for service unification. It comprised planes and squadrons from the army, navy, and Marine Corps; there were even some aircraft from the Royal New Zealand Air Force. Command rotated among the four services. Yet Airsols, headquartered at Munda, was one of the smoothest-running, hardest-hitting outfits in the Pacific. [70] As the Bougainville invasion date neared, Airsols bombers and fighters kept the five Japanese airfields on Bougainville so battered that they were virtually useless for resisting the American assault.

The campaign got under way on October 27 when New Zealand and American troops seized the small Treasury Islands just south of Bougainville. At the same time a marine parachute battalion under Lieutenant Colonel Victor H. Krulak landed from destroyer transports on Choiseul, the next large island down the Solomons chain from Bougainville. Krulak's marines raised hell all along the northern half of the island, shot up Japanese supply bases and camps, then hastily withdrew.

The Choiseul raid was a diversion for the benefit of the main Bougainville attack, which came on the first day of November. Halsey's staff had chosen Empress Augusta Bay on the west coast of Bougainville for the initial landings. This site was far from the Japanese installations on the island, but it had terrain suitable for rapid construction of an air base. Both the navy and the marines had learned a great deal about amphibious landings since Guadalcanal. At Bougainville most of the transports and cargo vessels, expertly loaded, were emptied within eight hours. Japanese opposition was light; Airsols fighters kept enemy aircraft at bay, but many landing craft were lost in the heavy surf or on the rugged shore. Fourteen thousand men of the Third Marine Division were ashore by dark.[71]

That night Vice Admiral Omori Sentaro, with four cruisers and six destroyers, attempted to duplicate Admiral Mikawa's feat at Savo Island by attacking the American landing force at Empress Augusta Bay. Army reconnaissance planes tracked Omori on his way down from Rabaul. Rear Admiral M. Stanton Merrill's Task Force 39—four new light cruisers and eight destroyers—was waiting about thirty-five miles north of the landing beaches. In the ensuing Battle of Empress Augusta Bay, fought in the early hours of November 2, Merrill skillfully maneuvered his cruisers outside of torpedo range while giving the Japanese a steady hail of six-inch shell. Omori lost the light cruiser *Sendai* and a destroyer; another destroyer was damaged.[72]

Undaunted by this failure, Admiral Koga decided to make a major effort to wipe out the American forces at Empress Augusta Bay. He ordered seven heavy cruisers, a light cruiser, and four destroyers south to Rabaul. Code-breakers at Pearl Harbor decrypted messages from Koga detailing these forces south and promptly warned Admiral Halsey.[73] The American admiral had no heavy cruisers or battleships to oppose this new Japanese threat, but he did have a carrier task force, TF 38, under Rear Admiral Frederick C. Sherman, lent by Admiral Nimitz to support the Bougainville invasion. Could the carriers be used against Rabaul? Not since the early raids of 1942 had carriers been sent against strongly defended Japanese bases; in 1943 Rabaul was far stronger than anything the Americans had taken on the year before. An estimated 150 planes were based there.

Yet Halsey had little choice. He ordered the carriers to dash in for a surprise strike against Rabaul. Airsols fighters would furnish combat air patrol. "I sincerely expected both air groups to be cut to pieces," Halsey later recalled, "and both carriers stricken if not lost. (I tried not to remember my son Bill was aboard one of them.)" [74]

Sherman's flyers did not even know where the Japanese cruisers were in Rabaul harbor, but luck was with them all the way. Rain and thick clouds hid Sherman's carriers so that Japanese scout planes mistook them for cruisers. Over Rabaul, however, the weather was fine and clear. Japanese fighters were in the air but held off attacking the Americans, expecting them to split into smaller groups when antiaircraft fire began. Sherman's pilots, however, led by Commander Howard H. Caldwell, held a tight formation until the last moment. When the confused Japanese did attack, they were too late to catch the leading bombers and torpedo planes. [75] The Japanese cruisers, which had arrived a few hours before, were caught unaware. The cruisers *Atago, Maya,* and *Mogami* all suffered damage, as did three destroyers. Only a dozen or so American planes were lost, and the carriers retired to the south unscathed.

Five days later, Halsey sent in another carrier strike. Rear Admiral Alfred E. Montgomery's Task Force 50.3, with two large and one light carrier, reinforced Sherman's task force. More Japanese ships were damaged and a destroyer was sunk, but the Japanese suffered most by attacking Montgomery's task force. Without scoring a hit, they lost thirty-five planes. Another twenty had been lost over Rabaul.[76]

As his heavy cruisers limped back to Truk or Japan for repairs, Admiral Koga counted up his losses. Only about half of his carrier aircraft were still in shape to fly. Operation RO had come to a disastrous end: Koga ordered the planes back to their ships at Truk.

The brilliance and daring of Halsey's raids on Rabaul have obscured the larger significance of this episode. Halsey's entire operation on Bougainville could be threatened by a force of only eight

Japanese cruisers because Halsey lacked large ships of his own (except the two carriers, which were in the right location largely by chance). The reason for this lack was that almost all major U.S. warships were preparing for a new offensive, soon to open in the central Pacific. The dangers of a two-pronged advance—one in the southwest and one in the central Pacific—had thus been graphically illustrated even before the latter was well under way.

Had the Japanese handled their forces more skillfully or had Sherman been less lucky, the result might well have been a disaster for the Allies: two carriers out of action and the Bougainville operation defeated. Halsey's desperate gamble was certainly justified, whatever the outcome. Yet he would not have *had* to take desperate risks if the Americans had not been trying to do two things at once. They had needlessly divided their forces in the Pacific, so that the weaker half could be menaced by a relatively small enemy force. It was not the last time that the two-pronged advance would lead the Allies close to disaster.

On Bougainville the Third Marine Division consolidated its beachhead and extended its perimeter. Reinforcements poured in as fast as the few available LSTs and destroyer transports could carry them. By the end of the third week in November there was a full army division, the 37th, ashore to back up the marines. But the Japanese also got some reinforcements ashore and there was sharp fighting along the line of the Koromokuna River, which ran inland from the beachhead, before the Japanese were finally overwhelmed by marine artillery and mortars. [77]

While Halsey's forces were consolidating their hold on Bougainville and developing airfields at Empress Augusta Bay, MacArthur's forces were preparing to assault New Britain, the island on which Rabaul itself was located. MacArthur's objectives on New Britain were Cape Gloucester at the extreme western tip of the north coast and Arawe on the western end of the south coast. Cape Gloucester commanded the Dampier Strait between the Solomon and Bismarck Seas, while Arawe was wanted as a PT-boat base.

Brigadier General Julian W. Cunningham's 112th Cavalry at first encountered little opposition when it went ashore at Arawe on December 15, 1943. Two battalions of Japanese troops, who had made their way painfully down from Rabaul by barge and jungle trail, attacked Cunningham—unsuccessfully—at the end of the month. A counterattack by the Americans in mid-January, supported by tanks and artillery, wiped out the last pockets of Japanese threatening the perimeter.

Off Cape Gloucester, troops of the First Marine Division, many of them veterans of Guadalcanal, celebrated the Christmas of 1943 by preparing for their landing at daybreak on the twenty-sixth. Landing craft from destroyer transports carried the first wave to the beaches, enveloped in drifting smoke from supporting air strikes and naval bombardment. Then came LCIs and finally LSTs. As these last craft approached the beach, they passed the returning boats of the first wave and heard the welcome news: "Landing unopposed!" [78]

Once ashore the Marines found that the weather gave them almost as much trouble as the scattered bands of Japanese who attempted to block their advance to the unfinished airfield they had come to seize. It was the height of the monsoon season, so the torrential rains kept everyone constantly wet and miserable. Giant trees, their roots rotted by excessive moisture and loosened by the shock of artillery fire, would fall without warning, sometimes crushing the unlucky men who happened to be beneath them.

The key to control of the airfield and the beaches was a 660-foot hill southeast of the airfield. The marines' route of attack on the hill lay along a long steep wooded ridge, at the top of which the Japanese were strongly entrenched. A battalion of the Seventh Marines under Lieutenant Colonel Lewis Walt—who, twenty years later, would command the Marine forces in Vietnam—managed to drag a 37-mm cannon up the jagged slopes and blast their way to the top. Then they dug in for the expected counterattack, which came early the following morning. The Japanese threw in their last fresh reserves but were unable to dislodge the marines from "Walt's Ridge." [79]

The marines pushed on to Hill 660 proper. Japanese fire down the steep slopes stopped them the first day. Then the Americans brought up tanks and mortars. Covered by their fire, the marines painfully worked their way around the hill until they found a possible route for an assault. Riflemen of the Seventh Marines drove the Japanese off the hill, some into a roadblock set up between the hill and the beach by the Seventh Marines weapons company: here the fugitives were killed or turned back. After defeating a last counterattack the next day, the weary marines, resting in the mud and rain, effectively controlled Cape Gloucester. [80]

With airfields on Bougainville and Vella Lavella, Airsols was ready to open a devastating air assault on Rabaul. By that time, however, Rabaul had ceased to be the great object of Allied campaigns in the Pacific. Other means and other goals, born in part from experience of CARTWHEEL, in part from awareness of growing American strength, had largely displaced Rabaul from center stage.

NOTES

1. Forest C. Pogue, *George C. Marshall: Organizer of Victory* (New York: Viking, 1973), p. 18.

2. Hayes, *Pearl Harbor To Trident*, pp. 348–49. The fullest treatment of the discussions of the Casablanca Conference is in Maurice Matloff, *Strategic Planning for Coalition Warfare, 1943–44* (Washington, D.C.: GPO, 1959), pp. 19–38.

3. Leighton and Coakley, *Global Logistics and Strategy*, pp. 662–63.

4. Ibid., pp. 661–62.

5. Pogue, *Organizer of Victory*, p. 19.

6. Matloff, *Strategic Planning 1943–1944*, pp. 31–33.

7. Buell, *Master of Seapower*, pp. 272–73; Leighton and Coakley, *Global Logistics and Strategy*, p. 668.

8. Hayes, *Pearl Harbor To Trident*, pp. 398–99; Matloff, *Strategic Planning 1943–1944*, pp. 36–37; Buell, *Master of Seapower*, pp. 278–79.

9. Letter, King to Nimitz, 4 February 1943, King Papers, Box 3.

10. The idea apparently originated in a subcommittee of the State Department's Advisory Committee on Postwar Policy. Roosevelt had mentioned it to the Joint Chiefs two weeks before. For a good brief discussion of the origins of the formulae, see Pogue, *Organizer of Victory*, pp. 32–34. A reliable full-length study is Raymond G. O'Conner, *Diplomacy for Victory: FDR and Unconditional Surrender* (New York: W. W. Norton, 1971).

11. "Outline History of Effort to Gain Unity of Command," Attachment to Memo for COMINCH, sub.: Effort to Gain Unity of Command in the Pacific, 20 February 1943, Double Zero Files, King Papers.

12. Hayes, *Pearl Harbor to Trident*, pp. 425; John Miller, Jr., *Cartwheel: The Reduction of Rabaul* (Washington: Office of the Chief of Military History, 1959), p. 13.

13. Miller, *Cartwheel*, p. 14; James, *Years of MacArthur*, pp. 306–7; Hayes, *Pearl Harbor to Trident*, p. 426.

14. Ibid., p. 429.

15. Ibid., pp. 430–35; Morton, *Strategy and Command*, pp. 392–93.

16. Arnold, Journal of Trip to Southwest Pacific Theater, entry for 24 September, Arnold Papers.

17. James, *Years of MacArthur*, pp. 309–10; Morton, *Strategy and Command*, pp. 361–63, 397–99; Hayes, *Pearl Harbor to Trident*, pp. 445–51.

18. "Outline History of Effort to Gain Unity of Command."

19. Admiral Richard L. Connolly interview, p. 379.

20. William F. Halsey and Joseph Bryan III, *Admiral Halsey's Story* (New York: Whittlsay House, 1947) pp. 154–55; James, *Years of MacArthur*, p. 316.

21. "History of Imperial General Headquarters, Army Section," Japanese Monograph No. 45, pp. 120–21; *Reports of General MacArthur.* Vol. 2, Part 1, pp. 171–72.

22. *Reports of General MacArthur,* Vol. 2, Part 1, pp. 201–2.

23. James, *Years of MacArthur,* pp. 200–1.

24. Arnold, Journal of Trip to Southwest Pacific, entry for 28 September 1942, Arnold Papers; Craven and Cate, *Guadalcanal to Saipan* (Chicago: Univ. of Chicago Press, 1950) pp. 140–141.

25. *Reports of General MacArthur,* Vol. 2, Part 1, p. 402; James, *Years of MacArthur,* pp. 293–94.

26. James, *Years of MacArthur,* p. 294; Craven and Cate, *Guadalcanal to Saipan,* pp. 143–46; Morison, *Breaking the Bismarck's Barrier,* pp. 58–60.

27. *Reports of General MacArthur,* Vol. 2, Part 1, pp. 205, 209–10; *8th Area Army Operations,* Vol. 4, Japanese Monograph No. 18, pp. 23–24.

28. *Reports of General MacArthur,* Vol. 2, Part 1, pp. 197–98.

29. Okumiya and Horikoshi, *Zero,* pp. 159–60.

30. Morison, *Breaking the Bismarck's Barrier,* pp. 119–26; Miller, *Cartwheel,* pp. 42–44; Morton, *Strategy and Command,* p. 413.

31. Okumiya and Horikoshi, *Zero,* pp. 174–75.

32. Miller, *Cartwheel,* pp. 43–44.

33. Potter, *Nimitz,* p. 233.

34. Daniel E. Barbey, *MacArthur's Amphibious Navy: Seventh Amphibious Force Operations 1943–1945* (Annapolis: Naval Institute Press, 1969), pp. 15–18.

35. Hough, *The Island War,* pp. 101–2.

36. Dyer, *Amphibians Came To Conquer,* Vol. 1, p. 500.

37. Hough, *The Island War,* pp. 101–2.

38. Barbey, *MacArthur's Amphibious Navy,* pp. 49, 51.

39. Ibid., pp. 42–44.

40. William F. Heavy, *Down Ramp!: The Story of the Army Amphibian Engineers* (Washington, D.C.: Infantry Journal Press, 1947), pp. 6–7, 247–48.

41. Ibid., p. 247.

42. Walter Krueger, *Fron Down Under to Nippon: The Story of the Sixth Army in World War II* (Washington: Combat Forces Press, 1953) p. 10; James, *Years of MacArthur,* pp. 312–13; David Dexter, *Australia in the War of 1939–1945,* Series 2, Vol. 6: *The New Guinea Offensives* (Canberra: Australian War Memorial, 1961), pp. 221–22.

43. Memorandum, John Miller, Jr., to Chief of Military History, 11 September 1961, Sub.: Resume of "The New Guinea Offensives," copy in Center of Military History (hereafter: CMH); Dexter, *New Guinea Offensives,* pp. 137–40, 156–58 and passim.

44. Dexter, *New Guinea Offensives,* p. 223.

45. Miller, *Cartwheel,* pp. 38–39.

46. Ibid., pp. 98–99.

47. Dyer, *Amphibians Came to Conquer*, Vol. 1, p. 591; Morison, *Breaking the Bismarck's Barrier*, pp. 155–99.

48. Morison, *Breaking the Bismarck's Barrier*, pp. 162–69; 194–97.

49. Ibid., pp. 160–67; 180–91.

50. Miller, *Cartwheel*, p. 124.

51. Ibid., pp. 135–37.

52. Ibid., pp. 160–61.

53. J. Lawton Collins, *Lightning Joe: An Autobiography* (Baton Rouge: LSU Press, 1979), p. 168.

54. Norman V. Cooper, "The Military Career of General Holland M. Smith," Ph.D. diss., University of Alabama, 1974, p. 193.

55. Sherrod, *On to Westward*, p. 250.

56. Isely and Crowl, *U.S. Marines and Amphibious War*, pp. 153–59 and passim; Millett, *Semper Fidelis*, pp. 370–71.

57. Major General Omar T. Pfeiffer, oral history interview, p. 163, Marine Corps Historical Center.

59. Morton, *Strategy and Command*, pp. 509–12; Collins, *Lightning Joe*, p. 168.

60. Morison, *Breaking the Bismarck's Barrier*, pp. 213–20; Dull, *Imperial Japanese Navy*, p. 290.

61. Miller, *Cartwheel*, pp. 178–80.

62. Ibid., p. 190; Morison, *Breaking the Bismarck's Barrier*, p. 261.

63. James, *Years of MacArthur*, p. 323.

64. Craven and Cate, *Guadalcanal to Saipan*, pp. 175–80; Miller, *Cartwheel*, pp. 198–99.

65. Dexter, *New Guinea Offensives*, pp. 529–31; Heavy, *Down Ramp!*, p. 67; Miller, *Cartwheel*, p. 219–20, Van Noy was posthumously awarded the Congressional Medal of Honor. Popa, who was wounded but survived, received a Silver Star.

66. Morton, *Strategy and Command*, pp. 547–51; Morison, *Breaking the Bismarck's Barrier*, pp. 783–86.

67. Letter, Kenney to General Henry H. Arnold, 10 October 1943. Copy in Arnold Papers.

68. Craven and Cate, *Guadalcanal to Saipan*, pp. 317–28; Morison, *Breaking the Bismarck's Barrier*, pp. 286–88; Miller, *Cartwheel*, pp. 229–232.

69. Vern Haugland, *The AAF Against Japan* (New York: Harper and Row, 1948), pp. 174–75.

70. An excellent account of the organizational development of Airsols is in Henry I. Shaw, Jr., and Douglas T. Kane, *The Isolation of Rabaul* (Washington, D.C.: G-3 Historical Branch, Headquarters, Marine Corps, 1963), pp. 456–60.

71. Shaw and Kane, *Isolation of Rabaul*, pp. 197–204.

72. Morison, *Breaking the Bismarck's Barrier*, pp. 305–22.

73. Holmes, *Double-Edged Secrets*, p. 147.

74. Halsey and Bryan, *Admiral Halsey's Story*, p. 424.

75. Belote and Belote, *Titans of the Seas* (New York: Harper & Row, 1975), pp. 191–193.

76. Morison, *Breaking the Bismarck's Barrier*, pp. 324–36; Dull, *Imperial Japanese Navy*, pp. 303–4.

77. Miller, *Cartwheel*, pp. 259–61.

78. Hough, *The Island War*, p. 155.

79. Ibid., pp. 168–169; Shaw and Kane, *Isolation of Rabaul*, pp. 381–85.

80. Shaw and Kane, *Isolation of Rabaul*, pp. 386–90.

TWELVE

The Dodging Tide

By the end of 1943 the United States had been at war with Japan for fully two years. Few if any of the great campaigns of the war (except in the Philippines) had resembled those embodied in the venerable Orange Plans, which army and navy officers had diligently studied at the war colleges. Yet the patterns and concepts of Orange were still very much alive in the minds of many officers. As early as January 1943, Admiral Ernest J. King was urging an early start to a drive across the central Pacific through the Marshalls, Truk, and the Marianas, very much along the lines of the old Orange Plan.[1] The appeal of a central Pacific drive for the navy was obvious. It was direct; it was familiar; and it offered maximum scope for employment of great fleets. For King the southwest Pacific had never been more than a part of his earlier general strategy of raiding and blocking in order to forestall the Japanese advance. Although he had pushed hard for the Guadalcanal campaign, he was now becoming dismayed at the number of ships and men required for the advance up the Solomons. His long delay on agreeing to the initiation of Tasks Two and Three may well have been due as much to these doubts as to difference over the question of command.[2] In any case, King believed that carrier task forces could not operate successfully in the narrow waters of the Solomons.[3]

At Casablanca King won grudging British consent to an American attack against the Gilbert, Marshall, and Caroline islands, to follow the projected capture of Rabaul. By February 1943 his staff was at work on plans for a drive on the Ellice and Gilbert islands, but neither of his top naval commanders, Admiral Halsey in the South Pacific or Admiral Nimitz in Hawaii, wanted to add to his own troubles by opening a whole new front in the Pacific.[4]

Nevertheless, the central Pacific route continued to look very good from Washington, if not from Nouméa or Pearl Harbor. The Joint U.S. Strategic Committee—the long-range planning organ of the Joint Chiefs—completed the first full plan for the defeat of Japan in April 1943. That defeat would have to be absolute in order to produce the unconditional surrender called for at Casablanca. Probably Japan itself would have to be invaded. Certainly, a tight blockade and intense air bombardment of the home islands would be necessary; to get at those home islands the Strategic Committee strongly favored the central Pacific route of attack.

The central Pacific was a region of a thousand tiny islands clustered in small groups extending west over 3,000 miles from the Gilberts, the easternmost chain near the equator, northwest through the Marshalls, the Carolines, and the Marianas. Against these tiny points on the map, where the Japanese could base only limited numbers of troops and airplanes, the Americans could bring to bear all the power of their rapidly growing naval and amphibious forces. If the Japanese fleet came out to challenge the advance, as it would eventually have to, so much the better. In the vast reaches of the central Pacific the U.S. Navy would be in its element, as it would never be in the narrow, treacherous waters off the Solomons and New Guinea. In addition, the coral atolls of the central Pacific offered a more salubrious area of operations than the rain-soaked malarial jungles of the South Pacific.

Yet the planners did not recommend that the South Pacific route, through the Solomons and along the New Guinea coast to the Philippines, be abandoned. Too much had already been invested in it, both militarily and politically, for that to be possible. Besides, there were many advantages to a simultaneous advance along both routes. It would keep the Japanese guessing. Nevertheless, the Strategic Committee plan emphasized the primacy of the central Pacific approach.

Future operations against Japan were divided into five broad phases. The first phase would see a simultaneous advance across the Pacific by MacArthur and Nimitz, with the main effort concentrated in the central Pacific. The second phase would entail the recapture of the Philippines, followed by the third and fourth phases—an advance to the China coast and the recapture of Hong Kong. From China, in phase five, the Allies could begin the bombing of Japan.

The Joint War Plans Committee, which succeeded the Joint Strategic Committee as the principal JCS planning group in May 1943, accepted this scheme with little change except for the addition of a sixth phase providing for the invasion of Japan. On May 8 the Joint Chiefs of Staff accepted what was now called the "Strategic Plan for the Defeat of Japan" and agreed to present it to the British chiefs at the third high-level British-American conference, to be held at Washington in May 1943.

On May 12, 1943, the giant liner *Queen Mary,* bearing Prime Minister Churchill accompanied by the British Chiefs of Staff and over one hundred other advisers and assistants, steamed into New York harbor for the series of meetings with their American counterparts known as TRIDENT. " 'I do not look forward to these meetings,' " recorded General Brooke in his diary; " 'in fact, I hate the thought of them.' " [5]

The general's mood may have been soured by his knowledge that at this conference to be held in Washington the British would enjoy no such advantages as they had at ACADIA and Casablanca. In the first place, Roosevelt was now much more in tune with his own military advisers on questions of strategy and thus less likely to be swayed by Churchill's persuasion. In the second place, the president's advisers themselves were now the beneficiaries of a rapidly maturing system of staffs and committees which provided them with the same quick, high-quality analyses and plans which the British had always enjoyed.

As the conference opened, news was received that the last Axis troops in North Africa had surrendered. Churchill and the rest of the British wanted to follow up the victory in North Africa and the invasion of Sicily, scheduled for the summer of 1943, with a full-scale effort to knock Italy out of the war. They argued that the collapse of Italy would force Germany to divert troops from other theaters and to evacuate the Balkans. Defeating Italy would also eliminate any threat from her fleet and was a necessary preliminary to a cross-channel attack on Germany.[6] U.S. strategists, led by General Marshall, pressed for an all-out assault against Germany by the spring of 1944. They feared that the Mediterranean operations favored by the British would tie up so many troops—and more important, scarce landing craft—as to make an early attack across the channel impossible.

The Pacific was America's Mediterranean. The U.S. chiefs argued that any resources which could be spared from the buildup for a channel crossing should be employed in the Pacific theater rather than against Italy. The Americans believed they had to keep the pressure on Japan lest the hardwon gains of 1942 be nullified. They came to the TRIDENT meetings determined to press for an intensified offensive in the Pacific. Admiral King outlined the U.S. Navy's plan for an advance through the central Pacific to the Marianas, from which the Allies could strike toward the Philippines or the coast of China. [7] The British chiefs worried that further American offensives in the Pacific might seriously handicap the Allied war effort against Germany.

As at Casablanca, British and American strategists eventually reached a compromise—but this was a compromise far more satisfactory to the Americans than that reached at Casablanca. In return for agreeing to go forward with plans for limited operations to eliminate Italy and for allowing the British to postpone a land campaign against the Japanese in Burma, the Americans got a firm date—May 1944—for a cross-channel attack. This operation would have "first charge" on Allied resources. The U.S. chiefs also received a go-ahead to "simultaneously . . . maintain and extend unremitting pressure against Japan with the purpose of continually reducing her military power and attaining positions from which her ultimate surrender can be forced." [8] In terms of specific operations, this meant the continuation of preparations for CARTWHEEL and the seizure of the Marshall and Caroline islands during 1943–44.

Plans for a Pacific drive now proceeded rapidly. Washington strategists soon discovered that the assault on the Marshalls could not go forward without seriously curtailing MacArthur and Halsey's operations in the South Pacific. This was because the Marshalls campaign would require both of the experienced marine divisions, together with most of their amphibious craft. That would leave MacArthur and Halsey with little offensive potential. As a compromise, the Joint Staff planners proposed that Nimitz's forces first seize the Gilbert Islands as a stepping stone to the Marshalls. That would require smaller forces and only one marine division. [9]

MacArthur objected violently, not only to losing the marine divisions but to the whole concept of a central Pacific advance. He argued that his own line of approach, through New Guinea to Mindanao in the Philippines, made full use of Australia's vast potential as a war base (something never envisioned in the Orange Plan) and that it could be supported by land-based aircraft. A central Pacific advance, on the other hand, would be nothing more than a series of " 'hazardous amphibious frontal attacks against islands of limited value' " which would have to be supported by carrier-based aircraft. [10] The southwest Pacific commander was even more appalled when he learned that Washington was considering bypassing Rabaul, merely neutralizing it by air attack and blockade in order to make available more forces for the effort in the central Pacific.

Nimitz's planners liked the Gilberts idea because those islands, unlike the Marshalls, were within range of American land-based planes. The Pacific Fleet carrier force was by now growing rapidly, but nobody was sure it was yet strong enough or experienced enough to provide the sole aerial support for an invasion. The Gilberts would also provide bases for photo reconnaissance of the Marshalls, something that could not then be done by carrier aircraft. [11] After considerable discussion and debate the Joint Chiefs accepted the Gilberts proposal. On July 20 they instructed Nimitz to capture and develop bases on Nauru and in the Gilberts, and to prepare detailed plans for the Marshalls.

As Nimitz prepared to carry out his first amphibious campaign, the army became increasingly concerned about the organization of his CINCPAC-CINCPOA command. Nimitz was not only a theater commander like MacArthur; in addition—unlike MacArthur—he was in direct command of a major component of his forces, the Pacific Fleet. His staff was actually a fleet staff with few army, marine or air officers in positions of authority. Yet in the coming campaign Nimitz would have over a hundred Air Force planes and an entire army division, as well as large numbers of marines and their supporting aircraft under his command. [12] These diverse units had vastly different logistics requirements and systems; yet Nimitz's headquarters lacked any arrangement for coordination, planning, and control of logistical matters affecting the various services. [13]

General Marshall and the Army General Staff suggested that one of Nimitz's subordinates be appointed commander of the Pacific Fleet, leaving the admiral free to concentrate on his expanded theater responsibilities; he would be aided by a theater staff drawn from all the services. But King and the navy high command were unwilling to consider such an arrangement. If the Pacific Fleet were made merely a unit under a theater commander, it would be removed from the direct control of Admiral King in his capacity as commander in chief of the U.S. Fleet. Never one to surrender power gracefully,

King stoutly resisted all talk of separating Nimitz from the fleet. But under increasing pressure from the army, King and Nimitz announced the formation of a CINCPAC joint staff in September 1943. It had four principal sections: Plans, Operations, Intelligence, and Logistics; two of the sections were headed by army officers.[14]

Nimitz also created a new operational command for the assault on the Gilberts. This was the Fifth Fleet, under Vice Admiral Raymond A. Spruance, who, following his success in the Battle of Midway, had been serving as Nimitz's chief of staff. Spruance's Fifth Fleet comprised three major components: the assault force with its transports, LSTs, cargo vessels, and supporting warships under Rear Admiral Richmond Kelly Turner; the shore-based aircraft under Rear Admiral John E. Hoover; and the fast carrier forces under Rear Admiral Charles A. Pownall.

The fast carriers were the cornerstone of the entire operation. MacArthur and Halsey's amphibious thrusts had been mainly supported by land-based aircraft; but in the Gilberts and Marshalls the carriers would be the principal source of aerial protection and attack, as well as providing direct support for amphibious assaults. Only two of the carriers which had fought in the early Pacific battles under Fletcher and Halsey were still afloat, but half a dozen new *Essex*-class carriers had arrived at Pearl Harbor by the fall of 1943. These carriers accommodated almost a hundred aircraft; they were faster and more maneuverable than their predecessors; and they were generously equipped with five-inch, 40-mm, and 20-mm antiaircraft guns.

The five-inch guns fired a new type of shell equipped with a variable time, or proximity fuse. Because even a near miss by a five-inch projectile was usually enough to destroy a plane, a tiny radio transmitter and receiver built into the warhead detonated the shell when it came close to an enemy aircraft. Armed in this fashion, and equipped with a new kind of air-search radar, the carriers were a difficult target for air attack, as Admiral Alfred Montgomery's task force had shown during its November raid on Rabaul.[15]

In addition to the *Essex*-class ships, the Pacific Fleet was receiving an equal number of *Independence*-class light carriers. These were converted cruisers of about 11,000 tons, able to carry only about half as many aircraft as the *Essex* carriers—but just as fast. Both types of carrier brought with them a new naval fighter, the F6F Hellcat. Specially modified to deal with the Zero fighter, one of which the Americans had recovered intact in the Aleutians, [16] the Hellcat could outclimb and outdive its Japanese counterpart; it was 30 miles per hour faster, more heavily armed, and much better protected. By early 1944 one type of Hellcat—the F6FSN—was also being equipped with a new lightweight airborne radar.[17]

While pilots and sailors got acquainted with their new planes and ships, strategists at CINCPAC sweated over plans for employing the new weapons to maximum advantage. The new carriers would operate in groups to take advantage of their defensive fire power and to concentrate their air strength. Sophisticated navigation radar would enable them to maintain high-speed formation in any weather.[18] During the early fall of 1943 the new carrier task forces warmed up with raids against Marcus and Wake islands, and against Tarawa in the Gilberts. As many as six carriers at a time participated in these raids, from which all returned undamaged.[19]

Yet even as the carrier was rapidly becoming the centerpiece of the war in the central Pacific, the administrative and command structure of the navy was still built around the battleship. The "gun club," or non-aviators, still dominated the top posts. In Spruance's Fifth Fleet, the chief of staff, Captain C. J. Moore, the operations officer, Captain E. P. Forrestal, and Spruance himself were all non-aviators. The sole aviator on the staff "did not have well-defined duties and rarely became involved in planning."[20] Experienced aviators and carrier commanders ground their teeth and issued dire warnings through their spokesman, Vice Admiral John H. Towers, Commander, Air Force Pacific Fleet, who was responsible for staffing and training the carrier forces. Yet it would be many months before the airmen attained the positions of influence they believed they deserved.[21]

The key officers of Admiral Turner's amphibious assault group (called V Amphibious Force) were almost as unhappy. Marine Major General Holland M. Smith, appropriately nicknamed "Howlin' Mad," was supposed to command all landing-force troops organized into the V Amphibious Corps. But he and "Terrible Turner" could not agree about where Turner's authority, as commander of the assault force (responsible for getting the troops onto the beach), ended and Smith's authority began.[22] The army, in the person of Lieutenant General Robert C. Richardson, Jr., Commanding General of U.S. Army Forces, Central Pacific, could see no good reason why the army division in Turner's force should be placed in a unit commanded by a marine.[23]

That such disputes arose was not surprising. Four different services were attempting to carry out a novel type of operation which none of them had fully anticipated before the war. Success would require an unprecedented degree of coordination and cooperation. For example, at Tarawa an Army Air Force officer, Colonel William D. Eareckson, aboard a navy ship, directed the operations of naval and Marine Corps aircraft in support of marine units ashore. [24] That kind of cooperation did not come easily.

Spruance's objectives in the Gilberts were two tiny atolls: Tarawa, at the center of the island chain, and Makin, at the extreme northwest end. Nauru, an island southwest of the Gilberts, had originally been included as a target, but a quick examination of its forbidding geography had led strategists to rule it out and substitute Makin instead. [25] The date selected for the attack was November 20, 1943.

Tarawa was far the stronger of the two bases. It had a garrison of about 5,000 troops compared to less than 800 on Makin, only about 400 of whom were trained combat troops. The Japanese had almost 200 guns for coastal defense on Tarawa, ranging from eight-inch naval rifles captured at Singapore to light machine guns. All were emplaced in strong, low-lying bunkers constructed of concrete and of coconut logs; all could be used against landing craft and for beach defense. [26] The long narrow island of Betio—only 800 yards at its widest point and two and a half miles long—was located at the southwest corner of the triangle-shaped Tarawa atoll; it held the Japanese airfield. Here the marines would make their assault.

Betio was entirely surrounded by a coral reef, a natural obstacle that spelled trouble for most types of landing craft. How deep was the water over the reef? No one knew for certain. The new amphibious tractors, the "Alligators" or LVTs, as they were usually called, could cross any reef—but they had never before been employed in a combat landing. Major General Julian Smith's Second Marine Division, which was to make the assault at Tarawa, had only about seventy-five amphibious tractors in its single amphibious tractor battalion. The division staff located fifty more tractors at San Diego and got them shipped to the central Pacific, where they arrived within hours of the invasion.[27]

Even with this reinforcement almost half of the assault waves would have to be landed in LCVPs or their equivalents. These drew at least four feet of water; no one was sure whether the water over the reef, even at high tide, would be deep enough for them to pass. The safest course was to wait a month until late December, when a full moon would bring a higher tide, but a month's delay was out of the question. Admiral King had repeatedly emphasized to

Nimitz the necessity for starting the central Pacific operation as soon as possible "so that the British could not back down on their agreements and commitments. We must be so committed in the Central Pacific," he told the CINCPAC staff, "that the British can not hedge on the recall of ships from the Atlantic." [28]

Under this sort of pressure, and worried about the speed of Japanese defensive prepations, Spruance and his commanders never considered postponing the November date. They believed that any delay would impair the momentum of the whole Pacific drive "and give the Japanese just that much longer to fortify the Marshalls." "War is a tough business," Spruance told historians after the war, "and often we gain more than we lose by pressing forward before we are entirely ready." [29]

Whether Spruance actually believed this is debatable. [30] It is certainly true that the Japanese were making frantic efforts to improve the defenses of the Marshalls; an assault launched a month or two later would have probably encountered stiffer resistance. Whether this would have entailed losses for the Americans comparable to Tarawa is more questionable. The Americans came to the Marshalls far more experienced and far better equipped for amphibious warfare than in the Gilberts. They would have had this experience and this equipment regardless of the precise amount of blood spilled at Tarawa.

The consensus among New Zealanders and Australians who had lived in the Gilberts was that five feet of water could be expected over the reef at high tide; but one old resident of Tarawa, Major Holland, who had kept the tide records for the British government, warned that the tide over the reef could be unpredictably low at this time of year. General Julian Smith, who had hunted birds in the marshes of the Chesapeake Bay, was familiar with such "neap tides." Impressed by Holland's warning, he took the old man to meet with Rear Admiral Harry W. Hill, the top navy commander for the Tarawa operation.

In a meeting with Admiral Hill's staff and the Australians and New Zealanders who were to act as pilots for the invasion, Major Holland repeated his warning. One of Hill's officers produced a chart showing that four and a half feet of water could be expected over the reef. " 'You won't have three feet!' " snapped Major Holland. [31] Admiral Hill turned to the pilots, mostly former merchant marine officers: had any of them ever been to Tarawa at a time when boats could not cross the reef at high tide? No one had. Hill was satisfied, but Holland was unimpressed. " 'You won't be able to cross that reef,' " [32] he predicted. Julian Smith grimly warned his men to be prepared to wade ashore.[33]

Admiral Turner's invasion forces for the Gilberts were divided into two groups. The northern attack force, consisting of the LSTs and transports carrying the 165th Regimental Combat Team of the 27th Division, with four battleships, four heavy cruisers, four escort carriers, and thirteen destroyers was to assault Makin; the southern attack force, with three battleships, three heavy cruisers, five escort carriers, and twenty-one destroyers would sail for Tarawa. Although Makin was less heavily defended than Tarawa, it was closer to the Japanese-held Marshalls and therefore the more likely place for any counterattack by the Japanese fleet. Hence Admiral Turner accompanied the northern attack force with his flag in the battleship *Pennsylvania.*

The southern attack force, almost a separate command, was under Rear Admiral Harry W. Hill. Hill's flagship, the battleship *Maryland,* had its communications center located on the flag bridge almost at the same level as the sixteen-inch guns. As a result, the shock of firing could knock out the delicate electronic gear and render the admiral temporarily unable to communicate with his commanders.[34] A group of four fast carrier task forces, under Rear Admiral Charles A. Pownall, provided general air protection, raided Japanese bases, and provided strikes in support of the landings.

General Smith and the marines would have liked a lengthy air and naval bombardment of Betio and a chance to position some of their artillery on neighboring islands of the atoll, but the necessity for surprise and speed meant that lengthy softening up of the objective—which would also alert the Japanese—was ruled out. The navy and marines had had plenty of experience, in the Solomons, of what happened to a task force which lingered too long near an invasion beachhead. Spruance and Turner wanted to strike hard, get the troops ashore and get out before the Japanese could react with ships, planes, and submarines. [35] As it happened, the expected enemy reaction never materialized. The Japanese carrier planes lost in the Solomons air battles and the cruisers crippled by the carrier strike on Rabaul left the Japanese fleet temporarily immobilized. But this the Americans could not know.

Just after midnight on November 20, marines and sailors in Admiral Hill's fleet began to line up for breakfast in the sweltering mess spaces of the LSTs and transports. For over a thousand marines the meal would be their last. By two o'clock lookouts on the *Maryland's* bridge could see the outline of Betio atoll by the light of the quarter moon. Air Force bombers, which had bombed Tarawa that day, had reported few signs of life and very weak antiaircraft fire. Correspondents aboard the transports speculated that Tarawa might turn out to be "another Kiska" with the Japanese already fled. "How bad do you think it will be?" newsman Robert Sherrod asked a marine sergeant. "Tougher than anyone says," was the reply.[36]

By half past four the first boatloads of marines were in the water, while amphtracs released from the LSTs sputtered and chugged toward the "Line of Departure," the point at which the waves of amphtracs and LCVPs would rendezvous and take position for their run to the beach. At 4:40, two of the Japanese eight-inch guns on Betio opened fire. The *Maryland* promptly replied with full sixteen-inch salvoes, silencing the guns and temporarily knocking out her own communications equipment.

Altogether the three battleships, four heavy cruisers, and twenty-odd destroyers of Hill's bombardment force fired a total of about 3,000 tons of shells at Tarawa in two and a half hours, interrupted for air strikes by American carrier planes. This was by far the heaviest bombardment of an invasion beach ever delivered up to that time. Yet it proved inadequate.

The low, flat Japanese pillboxes—constructed of six layers of coconut logs reinforced by sand, concrete, and steel—proved able to withstand most of the gunfire and bombing. The high-explosive shells employed by the bombarding ships usually went off before penetrating the Japanese defense works, making for an impressive explosion but doing little real damage. Smoke and dust churned up by the massive bombardment obscured the target and made accuracy impossible.[37] Still, the shelling and bombing dazed the defenders, destroyed most of their communications, and temporarily silenced some gun positions.

Even this advantage was largely lost, however, because of a mix-up in timing. Admiral Hill could not see the beaches from his flagship through the smoke and dust, so he had to estimate the time at which the first wave of landing craft would hit the beach and naval gunfire be lifted. He estimated that the landing craft would need about forty minutes to make the trip, the same time required in earlier tests. But the amphtracs took longer to get to the beach. The result was that when Admiral Hill ordered the gunfire lifted at 8:55 the tractors were not five minutes from the beach, as he believed, but fifteen to twenty-seven minutes from touchdown.[38]

Admiral Hill's radios in the *Maryland* could not reach the planes which were supposed to strafe the beaches in the last minutes, so these attacks were also delivered too early. One of these planes was able to get a radio message through to the *Maryland*, warning that the landing craft were much further from the shore than expected. Admiral Hill went into a quick huddle with General Smith. The *Maryland's* communications were down but she could still signal the need to reopen fire by opening fire herself. The problem would be to stop the firing. For that, positive communications were needed. Otherwise the ships might continue firing when their own craft were landing. Hill had no choice but to continue the cease-fire.[39] The result was that the Japanese defenders had ample time to recover from the shock of bombardment and to man their guns by the time the second and subsequent waves of landing craft reached land.

The first three waves of marines carried in amphtracs made the beach with relatively few casualties. The first unit to land was a scout sniper platoon under Lieutenant William D. Hawkins, which had the task of seizing a long pier jutting out into deep water. Landing from an LCVP at the end of the pier, Hawkins, followed by Lieutenant Alan G. Leslie with a flame thrower, advanced methodically down the narrow pier, spouting blazing death at Japanese machine-gun nests along the way.

While Hawkins dealt with the pier, the first assault waves, three reinforced rifle battalions under Colonel David M. Shoup, were coming ashore. Intense Japanese fire halted them, in most cases, less than a hundred yards from the water's edge. Just back of the beaches the Japanese had constructed a coconut-log and coral-block seawall; here most of the marines halted, pinned down under the meager cover of the wall, while deadly Japanese fire swept the area.

In the water it was worse. Succeeding waves of troops were loaded in LCVPs, which found the water much too shallow to cross the reef. The Americans had encountered what the islanders called "a dodging tide," one which ebbs and flows several times a day at unpredictable intervals and may maintain the same level for hours. A dodging tide may be abnormally high or abnormally low: on this day it was low.

Landing craft ran aground or milled about helplessly outside the reef, which was swept by crossfire from behind the beaches and from a grounded hulk northwest of the pier. At least twenty landing craft "full of dead and wounded were stuck on the reef. One large gun [ashore] was horribly accurate; several times it dropped a shell right on a landing craft just as the ramp came down, spreading a pool of blood around the boat." [40]

Amphtracs managed to off-load some of the marines, but most of them had to struggle ashore through hundreds of yards of shoulder-high water. The division reserve—a battalion of the 8th Marines—ordered ashore by General Smith, had to make their way some 700 yards through the water to the beach. Of the first wave, only 30 percent got ashore. In the second wave, less. The third wave "were practically wiped out." [41]

On shore, Colonel Shoup established his command post in the lee of a strong Japanese bunker; armed sentries guarded the entrances and vents against any Japanese who might still be inside. His radios damaged by salt water, Shoup sent Colonel Evans S. Carlson, who was along as observer, back with a message for General Smith. Shoup "proposed to stick and fight it out no matter how tough the situation became," although he had to ask for reinforcements. [42] " 'This is the damnest crap game I have ever got into,' " Shoup remarked to reporter Robert Sherrod.[43]

Aboard the *Maryland* General Smith had heard nothing from Shoup, but he knew from reports by air observers that the situation ashore was serious. A little after 11:30 he radioed Admiral Turner off Makin, requesting release of the corps reserve—three battalions of the Sixth Marine Regiment already present in transports off Tarawa. Turner gave his permission less than an hour later. That left Smith with four uncommitted battalions: the Sixth Marines plus the First Battalion of the Eighth Marines, all of them already standing by in boats at the line of departure. Smith ordered the First Battalion, Eighth Marines to land—but the message failed to get through. So the battalion spent the night in its landing craft off shore.

That night found the marines clinging to a narrow beachhead no more than 300 yards deep at any point. About 5,000 men had landed, 1,500 of them dead or wounded. A determined enemy counterattack might have swept the invaders away, but the Japanese could not counterattack. Rear Admiral Shibasaki Keiji, the island commander, was out of touch with his troops, for his communications had been destroyed in the heavy American bombardment; moreover, about half his men were already dead.

The second day began with another disaster for the marines. During the night Japanese infiltrators had reoccupied the freighter hulk and the pier as well as some disabled amphtracs. When the First Battalion, Eighth Marines finally came in to land after spending all night in their boats, they received a very hot reception. Once again boats grounded on the reef, forcing men to make their way through the water alone in the face of heavy fire. Once again the losses were heavy.

Yet the tide of battle was already turning. On the northwest tip of Tarawa a battalion under Major Michael P. Ryan, supported by gunfire from two destroyers, had fought its way across tne island, thus opening the westernmost beach for an unopposed landing. When the news of Ryan's success reached the flagship, General Smith quickly ordered a battalion of the Sixth Marines to seize the western beach. By late afternoon the First Battalion, Sixth Marines, accompanied by a platoon of light tanks, was ashore on Tarawa, intact and virtually unscathed.

While these troops were landing, Shoup's men were gradually reducing the Japanese positions to their front. Correspondent Sherrod witnessed the assault on one such position:

> A Marine jumped over the seawall and began throwing blocks of TNT into a coconut-log pillbox. . . . Two more Marines scaled the seawall, one of them carrying a twin-cylindered tank strapped to his shoulders, the other holding the nozzle of the flame thrower. As another charge of TNT boomed inside the pillbox, causing smoke and dust to billow out, a khaki-clad figure ran out the side entrance. The flame thrower, waiting for him, caught him in its withering stream of intense fire. As soon as it touched him, the Jap flared up like a piece of celluloid. He was dead instantly but the bullets in his cartridge belt exploded for a full sixty seconds after he had been charred almost to nothingness.[44]

By the end of the afternoon some of Shoup's men had fought their way to the south shore of the island. In the meantime the long-overdue high tide finally appeared. Watching the first two American jeeps roll down the pier towing 37-mm guns, Sherrod believed them "a sign of certain victory." [45]

That night Colonel Merritt A. Edson, Smith's chief of staff, came ashore to assume overall command on Tarawa, while the marines set up their own artillery on neighboring Bairiki Island to help pound the Japanese on Betio. While Edson planned the next day's attack, the Japanese radio on Betio sent out its last message: " 'Our weapons have been destroyed and from now on everyone is attempting a final charge.' "[46]

The "final charge" came the following night, after the marines had made substantial, although hard-won, gains which had pushed the opposing forces into the narrow eastern tail of the island. From there the remaining Japanese troops launched a series of heavy counterattacks against the First Battalion of the Sixth Marines. And there the last real Japanese resistance died, blown apart by marine artillery shells, grenades, and heavy machine guns. In the morning the marines counted 325 mangled Japanese bodies within a few hundred yards of their perimeter.[47] At 1:30 that afternoon General Smith announced the end of organized resistance on Tarawa.

At home in the U.S., they could not believe it. Three days of hard fighting, over 1,000 dead and 2,000 wounded—to capture an island of less than three square miles. Newspaper photos of corpses floating in the tide, or piled on the beach near wrecked and burning landing craft, made an indelible impression on an American public accustomed to viewing the war through the haze of censorship and inflated Allied claims of success.

Tarawa made an indelible impression on Pacific commanders as well. Communications were completely revamped, and amphibious task-force leaders were provided with specially fitted command ships to replace the ill-suited battleships and cruisers used previously. On gunnery ranges near Pearl Harbor, navy and marine experts painstakingly constructed exact copies of the Japanese pillboxes on Tarawa, then set out to find the best way to destroy them.[48] More amphtracs were ordered: greater speed and better protection was included; some of the new models even sported 37-mm cannon or rockets.[49]

From admirals and generals to boat drivers and platoon leaders, the men who had survived turned to analyzing in detail the mistakes at Tarawa, for mistakes there were in plenty. But it was the shallow water over the reef which had been the great killer. It was among the marines forced to wade to shore that the greatest slaughter had taken place. It was a slaughter which might have been avoided or diminished by waiting for a full moon and a higher tide.[50]

● ●

Few had expected Tarawa to be easy but Spruance and his subordinates had reason to be more optimistic about Makin. The 6,500 American assault troops of the 165th Regimental Combat Team and the 105th Infantry outnumbered the defenders at least two to one, and the Japanese had few heavy weapons. Yet Makin turned out to be as frustrating and—for the navy—as bloody as Tarawa.

The landings on the west and north shore of the island met little resistance. But from here on, progress was maddeningly slow. The troops, most of them National Guardsmen in action for the first time, allowed themselves to be pinned down by small pockets of enemy defenders and snipers, both real and imaginary. At night the green National Guardsmen were subjected to the same harassing tactics which the troops on New Georgia had found so demoralizing. The Japanese shouted curses and threats in English, threw lighted firecrackers at nearby Americans, and peppered them with grenades and sniper fire. The Americans responded with indiscriminate fire at unseen targets, thus exposing their positions and drawing accurate counterfire. Just after daybreak a trooper was seen running along the shore shouting " 'There's a hundred and fifty Japs in the trees!' " This set off "a wave of shooting 'hysteria' " which took officers many minutes to bring under control.[51]

By the second day the troops were learning to deal with snipers. Their officers had prudently persuaded them to use grenades instead of rifle fire against supposed Japanese infiltrators at night.[52] Still, the American advance was so deliberate that it took four days to clear Makin.

Casualties for the ground troops were relatively light; but the escort carrier *Liscomb Bay,* part of the naval task force which had been obliged to remain off Makin, was sunk by a submarine on the last day of the battle. There was a great loss of life. Naval officers were not slow to point out that had the army not taken so long in securing the island, the *Liscomb Bay* could have been gone before the submarine arrived.

● ●

Even as the battles on Tarawa and Makin were raging, strategists in Hawaii labored over plans for the assault on the Marshall Islands which was to follow. An attack against the Marshalls had formed part of American Pacific strategy since the prewar Orange Plan, but the question of which atolls to attack remained to be settled. Admiral Nimitz, at the suggestion of his chief planning officer, Rear Admiral Forrest Sherman, proposed to strike directly into the heart of the island group by taking Kwajalein Atoll at the geographic center of the chain.

Spruance, Turner, and Holland Smith all objected violently to this proposal. They pointed out that Kwajalein was surrounded by Japanese air bases at Wotje, Maloelap, Mille, and Jaluit, and that it was well within range of planes staging from the Marianas and Carolines. An assault force might get in all right, and even take the atoll—but it would be subject to continued violent air attacks and its line of communications would be endangered.[53] Sherman argued that the new Fast Carrier Force of the Fifth Fleet, now renamed Task Force 58, could neutralize Japanese air strength in the Marshalls before D-Day. Spruance and the others were unconvinced.

At the end of a stormy meeting on December 14, Nimitz polled his commanders. All agreed that Kwajalein was a mistake. Nimitz stuck to his guns. " 'This is it,' " he told an angry Kelly Turner. " 'If you don't want to do it, the Department will find someone else to do it. Do you want to do it or not?' " Spruance and Turner gave in.[54] At the suggestion of Carl Moore, Spruance's chief of staff, the large but lightly defended island of Majuro in the eastern Marshalls was added to the list of objectives. Its broad and deep lagoon was wanted as a safe anchorage where ships operating in the Marshalls could refuel, repair, and take on supplies.[55]

All of the principal commanders for the Marshall invasion had been at Tarawa or Makin and had absorbed their lessons well. One lesson was that future amphibious operations required more—more of everything: more preparatory naval gun fire, lasting over a period of days rather than hours; more and better amphibious craft, armed with extra armor and a 37-mm gun like the new LVT(A) tractor, or like the LCI gunboat [LCI(G)], which swapped troop-carrying space for three 40-mm guns and a bank of rockets; more and better air support, including fighter planes armed with rockets for strafing beaches.

Spruance insisted that the fast carriers of Task Force 58 strike Japanese air bases in the Marshalls well in advance of the landings and then provide continuous air cover to keep Kwajalein isolated. Battleships were to follow up the air strikes by bombarding the airfields, thus preventing them from being reinforced or repaired.[56]

While the carriers were overhauled and their crews rested and trained for these missions, land-based army Air Force and navy planes, now flying from Tarawa and Makin, began to batter the major Japanese bases in the Marshalls. Some atolls, like Mili, were attacked every day. Japanese attempts to counter these raids with assaults on the Americans in the Gilberts ran into murderous fighter patrols in daylight; their night raids did little damage.[57]

In the last days of January, the carriers reentered the battle. Task

Force 58, made up of four individual task groups totalling twelve carriers with 650 planes, eight new fast battleships, and escorting cruisers and destroyers, was now commanded by Vice Admiral Marc A. Mitscher, a veteran aviator who had commanded carriers since the early days of the war.[58] Tall, Lincolnesque, taciturn, an inspiring leader, Mitscher soon became the acknowledged master of the new carrier warfare.

Mitscher's planes swooped down upon the Marshalls like an angry cloud of hornets. One task group attacked Maloelap and the southern half of Kwajalein; one hit the northern half; another attacked Eniwetok Atoll at the extreme western end of the Marshalls. A fourth group attacked Wotje. After two days there were virtually no Japanese planes in the Marshalls still able to fly.[59]

Although deprived of air power, the Japanese at Kwajelein still possessed formidable defenses—comparable to those at Tarawa—and their garrison on Kwajalein was larger. Kwajalein was a long, crescent-shaped coral atoll, the largest in the world. The principal American objectives were the island of Kwajalein at the southern tip of the crescent and two islands, Roi and Namur, joined together by a narrow strip of land near the center of the crescent's back. Since the two objectives were forty-four miles apart, the assault on them would actually entail two separate campaigns. Admiral Turner led the operation against Kwajalein itself, while the Roi–Namur attack was conducted by a newcomer to the Pacific, Rear Admiral Richard L. Conolly, who had distinguished himself as a commander of amphibious forces in the Mediterranean.

Conolly's plan was to take the islet guarding the entrance to Kwajalein lagoon and set up artillery there. Then he would enter the lagoon and storm two of the islets on the other side, Ennubirr and Ennument, which would then serve as additional artillery platforms. The actual attack on Roi–Namur would follow the next day.

It was a complicated plan. From the first there was much delay and confusion. Both the Fourth Marine Division, which was to make the assault, and the amphibious craft that were to carry these troops were new to Pacific warfare. Amphtracs and boats became separated, failed to find the units they were to transport, or followed the wrong route. Some artillery pieces were landed hours before the crews who were to serve them. Radios failed and the lagoon soon "became the site of an amphibious traffic jam."[60] Fortunately there was little enemy resistance on any of the four islets: all fell easily to the Americans. On their own initiative a company of marines even seized a fifth islet named Ennugaret, which was the closest to Roi–Namur.[61]

Amid the confusion Conolly's warships, assisted by planes, continued to blast Roi–Namur in "a deliberate, thorough-going and destructive manner." [62] Spurred by repeated admonitions to "move in really close," Conolly's battleships closed to within 3,500 yards of the beach, while his cruisers moved in to less than 2,000 yards, earning the admiral the nickname of "Close-In Conolly." [63]

The assault against Roi–Namur saw a repeat of the previous day's alarms and confusions, but Conolly's ships and planes had done their work so well that there was little serious resistance at the beaches. On Roi, where the Japanese had their main airbase, marine medium tanks advanced so rapidly that they had to be called back so that the regimental commander could organize a coordinated attack. This drive got under way in the late afternoon and secured the island by nightfall.[64]

On Namur the marines had tougher going. A company of the Second Battalion, 24th Marines, hurling demolition charges at what they took to be a concrete bunker, instead exploded a Japanese magazine filled with torpedo warheads. A gigantic brown cloud of dust and sand shot up into the sky and seemed to cover the entire island; trunks of palm trees and fragments of concrete as large as packing cases hurtled through the air. A pilot overhead radioed that " 'the whole damn island has blown up!' " [65] The explosion left a hole the size of a large swimming pool and caused over half the casualties suffered by the marines, who completed the conquest of Namur by the next afternoon.

Forty miles to the south, the veteran Seventh Division of the army was still battling to secure Kwajalein. As at Roi–Namur, the invasion forces had seized the islets guarding the entrance to the lagoon and others as artillery bases, then entered the lagoon to attack Kwajalein itself. Richmond Kelly Turner did not receive any new nicknames at Kwajalein, but his ships blasted the Japanese from even closer ranges than "Close-In Conolly's." At one point, when Turner ordered two of his battleships to close to 2,000 yards, "the captains involved did not believe the figure and asked for clarification, so Turner subtracted 500 yards" and ordered them to open fire.[66]

The actual landings went off with the precision of a drill, for the Seventh Division had trained hard and thoroughly indeed for this operation. By nightfall the army had six reinforced battalions ashore and had reached the western end of the airfield. Advancing slowly and methodically with the help of tanks and naval gunfire from Turner's ships, the Seventh Division had cleared the island by the fourth day. That was longer than it took the marines at Roi–Namur—but in the euphoria of victory nobody was complaining. The Central Pacific Forces had seized a large atoll, as heavily defended as Tarawa, but with only a fraction of the cost in lives and in equipment. The lessons of Tarawa had been put to good use.

In addition to Kwajalein, Spruance's forces also held Majuro Atoll, which had been seized without loss a few days earlier by a small force under Rear Admiral Harry W. Hill. All this was done without committing the Central Pacific Force reserves: a regiment of marines and a regiment of army troops already embarked in transports. Flexing their muscles, Spruance and his commanders began to eye the atoll of Eniwetok at the extreme northwest end of the Marshalls, scheduled for attack about the first of May.

Spruance, Turner, Smith, and Hill put their heads together. Eniwetok appeared lightly defended now, but the Japanese were reinforcing. Why not attack immediately? Nimitz and the Joint Chiefs of Staff quickly agreed and the target date was set for February 17.[67] An assault on Eniwetok meant that Mitscher's fast carriers would have to take on one of the strongest Japanese bases in the Pacific: Truk, in the Carolines, long considered almost impregnable. Its magnificent lagoon, a principal anchorage of the Combined Fleet, was almost immune from attack by surface ships. Its four airstrips normally accommodated close to 400 planes, and Truk was close enough to Eniwetok to make any invasion attempt a nightmare.

For a carrier task force to attack such a base unaided by land-based planes or troops would have seemed near madness a year ago. Yet Mitscher, masterfully handling his carriers as a single striking unit, showed how easily it could be done. His initial attackers, all fighters, brushed aside Japanese planes attempting to intercept them. They strafed and bombed the airfields, destroying more than two-thirds of Truk's air strength. Then more fighters, along with dive-bombers and torpedo bombers, attacked ships in the lagoon.

Mitscher's planes delivered thirty strikes in all, each of them more powerful than either of the two Japanese waves at Pearl Harbor in 1941. Admiral Spruance, who had accompanied the strike force, steamed triumphantly around the island in his new flagship, *New Jersey,* accompanied by a second battleship and two cruisers, picking off small Japanese warships as they attempted to escape. Total Japanese losses in the two-day attack on Truk were two light cruisers, four

destroyers, two submarines, five auxiliaries, and twenty-four merchantmen. Mitscher's losses were about thirty planes; one carrier
was damaged. Never again would the Combined Fleet use Truk as
a major operating base.[68]

The assault on Eniwetok could now go forward with no fear of
Japanese sea- or air attack. Admiral Harry W. Hill's reserve, reinforced with supporting units from the Kwajalein operations to over
10,000 men, arrived off Eniwetok on February 17, 1944. As at Kwajalein and Roi–Namur, the Americans planned to enter the lagoon
formed by the large circular atoll and seize small islets, where they
would emplace their artillery before assaulting the three principal
islands of Engebi, Parry, and Eniwetok.

The Americans believed that Eniwetok Atoll was only lightly held
but when the troops went ashore against slight opposition on Engebi,
the first objective, Admiral Hill and his commanders got a rude
shock. From documents and prisoners captured on Engebi they
learned that there were 600 to 800 troops on Eniwetok and over
300 on Parry.[69] Admiral Hill quickly decided to beef up his attack
on Eniwetok and leave Parry until later.

Two battalions of the 106th Infantry, supported by marine tanks,
hit the beach at Eniwetok on February 19, 1944; they soon ran
into stiff opposition. The Japanese had had only a short time to bolster
the defenses of Eniwetok, and their last-minute preparations were
hindered by frequent American air strikes, which inflicted numerous
casualties and destroyed scarce supplies of food and ammunition.[70]
Yet what they built was formidable. Like the Americans, the Japanese
had profited from the experience of Tarawa and applied what they
learned to the construction of their defenses. On the lagoon side
of the atoll the defenders built a system of well-camouflaged strongpoints laid out in a spiderweb pattern. A large pillbox was at the
center of the web, surrounded by a circle of foxholes ten to fifteen
feet apart, mostly roofed over with corrugated iron and connected
with one another by trenches or tunnels. Other radial trenches and
tunnels connected the foxholes with the central bunker.[71]

In the assault on these spiderweb networks, troopers of the 106th
found themselves sniped at from both flank and rear as the Japanese
defenders rapidly shifted from one concealed foxhole to another.
It took two and a half days to clean up Eniwetok. Nearby, Parry
islet took only a day and a half—but that cost over 300 casualties.
The Japanese lost over 1,000 dead which, together with casualties

on the other islands, brought their losses at Eniwetok to more than 2,700.

The swift and relatively easy capture of the Marshalls enabled the Americans to speed up their entire effort in the Pacific. Bolder plans were conceived; timetables adjusted; troops and resources reshuffled. Already, Nimitz and Spruance were discussing an early attack on the Marianas, part of the inner ring of Japanese defenses. More important, the fighting methods which were to spell the downfall of Japan had come of age in the seas and beaches of the Gilberts and Marshalls. Those methods were the coordinated amphibious assault and fast-carrier warfare. Backed by the awesome industrial output of the United States, they were to prove unstoppable.

NOTES

1. Unless otherwise indicated, the following discussion is based on Morton, *Strategy and Command,* pp. 437–44, 447–53, 456–68.

2. I am grateful to King's biographer, Professor Robert Love of the U.S. Naval Academy, for this suggestion.

3. King, Memorandum for the President, Sub.: Building Program 1943–44, 29 May 1942, King Papers.

4. Hayes, *Pearl Harbor to Trident,* pp. 421–22; Conference Notes, COMINCH-CINCPAC Meeting, 22 February 1943, King Papers, Double Zero Files.

5. Brooke quoted in Bryant, *The Turn of the Tide,* Vol. 1, p. 500.

6. Matloff, *Strategic Planning 1943–44,* pp. 128–30.

7. Buell, *Master of Seapower,* pp. 336–38; Matloff, *Strategic Planning 1943–44,* pp. 137–38.

8. Final Report to the President and Prime Minister, 25 May 1943, CCS 242/6, JCS Records, RG 228.

9. Morton, *Strategy and Command,* pp. 465–66.

10. Grace P. Hayes, *History of the Joint Chiefs of Staff in World War II: The War Against Japan,* Vol. 2, *Advance to Victory,* p. 16. Copy in National Archives.

11. Potter, *Nimitz,* p. 243; Isely and Crowl, *U.S. Marines and Amphibious Warfare,* pp. 192–93.

12. Buell, *The Quiet Warrior,* pp. 170–71; Conference Notes, COMINCH-CINCPAC Meeting 30 July–1 August 1943, King Papers, Double Zero Files.

13. Morton, *Strategy and Command,* pp. 490–92.

14. Ibid., pp. 495–99.

15. See above, pp. 244–45.

16. See above, p. 178.

17. Reynolds, *The Fast Carriers,* pp. 56–58.

18. Ibid., pp. 54–55, 72, 75, 76.

19. Morison, *Aleutians, Gilberts, and Marshalls*, pp. 92–94; Reynolds, *The Fast Carriers*, pp. 79–88.

20. Buell, *The Quiet Warrior*, pp. 180–84.

21. Reynolds, *The Fast Carriers*, pp. 39–48; Potter, *Nimitz*, pp. 248–49, 250–51.

22. Philip A. Crowl and Edmund G. Love, *Seizure of the Gilberts and Marshalls* (Washington, D.C.: Office of the Chief of Military History, 1955), pp. 35–36; Buell, *The Quiet Warrior*, pp. 177–78.

23. Morton, *Strategy and Command*, pp. 487–96.

24. Crowl and Love, *Seizure of Gilberts and Marshalls*, pp. 36–37.

25. Buell, *The Quiet Warrior*, pp. 179–80; Potter, *Nimitz*, p. 251; Crowl and Love, *Seizure of Gilberts and Marshalls*, pp. 21–22, 26–27.

26. Isely and Crowl, *U.S. Marines and Amphibious Warfare*, pp. 212–13.

27. Ibid.; Henry I. Shaw, Jr., Bernard C. Nalty, and Edwin T. Turnbladh, *Central Pacific Drive: History of U.S. Marine Corps Operations in World War II*, Vol. 3 (Washington, D.C.: Historical Branch, G–3 Headquarters, U.S. Marine Corps, 1966), pp. 38–39.

28. Conference Notes 30 July–1 August 1943, King Papers, Double Zero Files.

29. Isely and Crowl, *U.S. Marines and Amphibious Warfare*, p. 211; Admiral Harry W. Hill interview; copy in Marine Corps Historical Center, Vol. 1, pp. 305–9.

30. Buell, *The Quiet Warrior*, pp. 205–6.

31. Lieutenant General Julian Smith oral history interview, 1973, p. 285; Marine Corps Historical Center.

32. Ibid.

33. Crowl and Love, *Seizure of Gilberts and Marshalls*, pp. 32–33. Admiral Hill later pointed out that the difference between the (high) "spring" tide and the (low) "neap" tide was only four to twelve inches. As for the "dodging" tide, it was a rare and essentially unpredictable phenomenon. Yet in the case of the landing craft used at Tarawa, even a foot of difference in the tide could be important. Furthermore, although unusual and unpredictable, dodging tides were more likely during the neap tide period. See Hill interview, Vol. 1, pp. 311, 312, 340.

34. Dyer, *Amphibians Came to Conquer*, Vol. 2, p. 611.

35. Isely and Crowl, *U.S. Marines and Amphibious Warfare*, pp. 200–2, 204–5; Harry W. Hill, interview, Vol. 1, p. 296.

36. Robert Sherrod, *Tarawa: The Story of a Battle* (New York: Duell, Sloan and Pearce, 1944, 1954), pp. 42–44; Morison, *Aleutians, Gilberts, and Marshalls*, pp. 154–55.

37. Isely and Crowl, *U.S. Marines and Amphibious Warfare*, pp. 232–33; Shaw, Nalty, and Turnbladh, *Central Pacific Drive*, pp. 55–56.

38. Isely and Crowl, *U.S. Marines and Amphibious Warfare*, pp. 228–29.

39. Harry W. Hill interview, p. 326.

40. Morison, *The Aleutians, Gilberts, and Marshalls*, p. 104.

41. Shaw, Nalty, and Turnbladh, *Central Pacific Drive*, p. 62.

42. Isely and Crowl, *U.S. Marines and Amphibious Warfare*, p. 241.

43. Sherrod, *Tarawa*, p. 164.

44. Ibid., p. 74.

45. Ibid., p. 101; see also Crowl and Love, *Seizure of Gilberts and Marshalls*, pp. 147–50.

46. Quoted in Morison, *Aleutians, Gilberts, and Marshalls*, p. 173.

47. Crowl and Love, *Seizure of Gilberts and Marshalls*, p. 154.

48. Morison, *Aleutians, Gilberts, and Marshalls*, p. 210.

49. Isely and Crowl, *U.S. Marines and Amphibious Warfare*, pp. 251–53; Shaw, Turnbladh, and Nalty, *Central Pacific Drive*, pp. 105–11.

50. Isely and Crowl, *U.S. Marines and Amphibious Warfare*, p. 235.

51. Crowl and Love, *Seizure of Gilberts and Marshalls.*, p. 108.

52. Ibid., p. 113, 117.

53. Crowl and Love, *Seizure of Gilberts and Marshalls*, pp. 168–69; Buell, *The Quiet Warrior*, p. 211.

54. Potter, *Nimitz*, p. 265.

55. Buell, *The Quiet Warrior*, p. 212.

56. Ibid., pp. 228–29, 465.

57. Morison, *Aleutians, Gilberts, and Marshalls*, pp. 213–15; Crowl and Love, *Seizure of Gilberts and Marshalls*, pp. 193–98.

58. Reynolds, *The Fast Carriers*, p. 113.

59. Morison, *Aleutians, Gilberts, and Marshalls*, pp. 218–21.

60. Shaw, Nalty, and Turnbladh, *Central Pacific Drive*, pp. 144–45.

61. Ibid., pp. 144–52; Morison, *Aleutians, Gilberts, and Marshalls*, pp. 237–40.

62. Isely and Crowl, *U.S. Marines and Amphibious Warfare*, p. 272.

63. Shaw, Nalty, and Turnbladh, *Central Pacific Drive*, p. 148; Morison, *Aleutians, Gilberts, and Marshalls*, p. 243.

64. Shaw, Nalty, and Turnbladh, *Central Pacific Drive*, pp. 164–66.

65. Ibid., pp. 170–71; Morison, *Aleutians, Gilberts, and Marshalls*, p. 248.

66. Shaw, Nalty, and Turnbladh, *Central Pacific Drive*, p. 175.

67. Crowl and Love, *Seizure of Gilberts and Marshalls*, pp. 333–38.

68. Ibid., pp. 320–31; Buell, *The Quiet Warrior*, pp. 229–35.

69. Crowl and Love, *Seizure of Gilberts and Marshalls*, p. 348; Dyer, *Amphibians Came to Conquer*, p. 836. Dyer gives the figure of 780 Japanese troops on Eniwetok; Crowl and Love say 556.

70. Crowl and Love, *Seizure of Gilberts and Marshalls*, pp. 341–343.

71. Ibid.

THIRTEEN

"They Are Waiting for Me There"

From Port Moresby, General MacArthur eyed preparations for the Central Pacific drive with growing uneasiness. Not only was he opposed to the strategy underlying the assault on the Gilberts and Marshalls, but he feared that these campaigns would divert needed resources from his own theater and relegate him to a backseat in the war.[1] In the summer of 1943 Washington strategists in the JCS Joint War Plans Committee, at work on a long-range plan and schedule for the war against Japan, were already talking of isolating Rabaul—ultimate objective of the general's CARTWHEEL operations—and then bypassing it.[2]

MacArthur hotly opposed this idea, insisting that he needed Rabaul to secure his right flank and to use as a naval base, but the Joint Chiefs were unconvinced.[3] They suspected, correctly as it turned out, that Rabaul was one of the strongest fortresses in the Pacific. After the war it was learned that the garrison there numbered almost 100,000 men, backed by tanks and artillery supplied from amply-stocked underground warehouses and repair shops. As Samuel Eliot Morison observes, "Tarawa, Iwo Jima and Okinawa would have faded to pale pink in comparison with the blood which would have flowed if the Allies had attempted an assault on fortress Rabaul."[4]

At the Quadrant Conference, held at Quebec in August 1943, the Combined Chiefs of Staff gathered at the stately Château Frontenac Hotel overlooking the St. Lawrence River to discuss the progress of their plans for an invasion of northern Europe, British proposals for Allied operations in Italy, and American plans to speed up the tempo in the Pacific. By this time Allied forces were close to victory in Sicily and there were persistent reports of Italian efforts to surrender. The British argued that now was the time to press on with operations in Italy proper to tie down German troops there. This would indirectly support OVERLORD, the cross-channel attack scheduled for May 1944. The Americans, led by General Marshall, insisted on an overriding priority for OVERLORD; they wanted no further diversions in the Mediterranean. Troops and shipping committed there would not only delay OVERLORD but would have repercussions on Pacific operations as well.[5] In a compromise worked out in two closed-door sessions, the Combined Chiefs agreed that OVERLORD would have priority for resources but that operations against Italy would go forward anyway.

For discussion of the war against Japan, the Combined Staff planners brought to Quebec an outline plan which provided for an advance across the central Pacific, coordinated with an overland drive across Southeast Asia and through China. Once ports on the China coast had been secured, long-range bombing and the blockade of Japan could begin. The plan called for capture of the Philippines, Formosa, Malaya, and the Ryukyus in 1945 and 1946, with final operations against Japan itself to commence in 1947 and continue into 1948. All this under the assumption that Germany would be defeated in 1944![6]

The Joint Chiefs of Staff were appalled at the deliberate pace of the Combined Staff planners' proposal; they insisted that a new plan be prepared to provide for the defeat of Japan within a year after the fall of Germany. Although no such document was ever approved, the Joint Chiefs did win British agreement to the principle that Japan must be defeated soon after the fighting in Europe ended.

The Joint Chiefs also presented to their British colleagues a timetable for their planned two-pronged advance in the Pacific. These drives were to be synchronized with the long-desired but still-delayed British advance in Burma. Rabaul was crossed off the list of invasion targets; its neutralization by air was to be completed by May 1944, followed by MacArthur's westward advance toward the Vogelkop peninsula of New Guinea. Meanwhile Nimitz would follow his Gilberts assault with attacks on the Marshalls, the Carolines, and the Palaus. All this was to be completed by the end of 1944. The Joint Chiefs failed to specify whether MacArthur's or Nimitz's campaigns were to receive priority, simply declaring that "due weight should be given to the fact that operations in the Central Pacific promise more rapid advance." [7]

More than a little puzzled by such circumlocutions, the British enquired whether it might not be better to limit MacArthur's operations in New Guinea to a holding mission and use the resources saved for OVERLORD. King and Marshall immediately rejected this suggestion which, while logical enough, struck at the heart of the delicate army-navy modus vivendi on Pacific strategy. Both advances were essential and mutually supporting, they declared, and in any case the forces for the Southwest Pacific operations were already in place or en route. Any surplus in that theater would have to be allocated to the central Pacific, not Europe. [8]

The British raised no more objections, though their point was well taken: the two advances could be mutually *competing* as well as mutually supporting. In critical operational situations—such as at Bougainville and later at Biak—the divided advance could lead to the edge of disaster. Even under more normal circumstances, competition for scarce resources (especially assault shipping and amphibious craft) sometimes left one theater with very meager resources to carry out its mission, particularly before an accelerated landing-craft building program began to have its effects in the fall of 1944. [9]

With Rabaul earmarked for neutralization instead of invasion, Airsols flyers began a series of systematic air attacks on the island fortress at the end of December 1943. From the newly won fields on Vella Lavella, New Georgia, and Bougainville, fighters escorted B-24 heavy- and B-25 medium bombers in raids on Rabaul airfields and supply dumps. Dive-bombers joined the assault in January, concentrating on shipping in Rabaul harbor. By the end of January few ships of any type were left around Rabaul. On February 20 all serviceable planes were withdrawn to Truk. Yet it still took more than three more months to reduce Rabaul's airfields and anti-air defenses. Its garrison and ground defense remained intact until the end of the war. [10]

In addition to the neutralization of Rabaul, the Combined Chiefs of Staff directed MacArthur to continue his advance along the north coast of New Guinea to the Vogelkop peninsula at the far western end. From there he might conceivably cross to the Philippines, but nothing was said about this at Quebec. Disappointed but undeterred,

MacArthur continued to press for a decision to occupy Mindanao and to disparage the central Pacific strategy, but to no avail.[11]

The trend of thinking in Washington was toward two mutually supporting advances across the Pacific, MacArthur's and Nimitz's, but with Nimitz's taking priority. Behind this line of thought lay not only the navy's traditional preference for a central Pacific drive such as the old Orange Plan envisioned, but also a new interest on the part of the army Air Forces. A new bomber would soon be in production—a super-bomber, the B-29.

The B-29 could carry a record bomb load over 1,500 miles to its target, then return. That was almost 500 miles further than Allied bombers then in use. Air Force planners predicted that a force of about 600 B-29s could destroy "Japanese resources to such a point that the enemy's capacity for armed resistance [will be] substantially exhausted." [12] Many of the bombers were expected to be based in China or in Eastern India, with a shuttle stop in China, but Air Force planners were also casting covetous eyes on the Mariana Islands northwest of the Marshalls and within easy bombing range of Japan.[13] Admiral King had long advocated an assault on the Marianas as the capstone of the central Pacific drive but had previously failed to interest the other service chiefs. Now, to the wry amusement of the navy, the Air Force suddenly became the most vociferous advocate of a central Pacific drive.

At the Combined Chiefs of Staff conference at Cairo, called Sextant, Allied leaders agreed upon an "Overall Plan for the Defeat of Japan," gave Nimitz the green light to move into the Marshalls in January, the Carolines and Truk in July, and the Marianas in October. MacArthur was to continue his advance along the northern New Guinea coast; nothing was said about the Philippines. The emphasis was now definitely upon the Pacific campaigns, with operations in China and Southeast Asia relegated to supporting roles. Yet the Joint Chiefs, although leaning toward the central Pacific advance, still refused to assign a clear-cut priority to either line. The "Overall Plan" provided for both offensives to proceed concurrently, with naval forces deployed "to support successive operations along each axis." When appropriate, forces might be transferred from one area to the other. Any conflicts which might arise between MacArthur and Nimitz over timing or allocation of resources were to be resolved by according " 'due weight to the fact that operations in the Central Pacific promise, at this time, a more rapid advance toward Japan and her vital lines of communications; the earlier acquisition of strategic bases closer to the Japanese homeland; and, of greatest importance, are more likely to precipitate a decisive engagement with the Japanese fleet.' "[14]

While the two-pronged advance was winning converts in Washington, the Pacific commanders still had their doubts. MacArthur's views were of course well known, but in late January 1944 he was joined by other senior officers, including Nimitz, Nimitz's deputy (Vice Admiral John H. Towers), his chief of staff (Rear Admiral Forrest Sherman), and his chief planner (Rear Admiral Charles H. McMorris), who met with South and southwest Pacific commanders at Pearl Harbor in January 1944 to discuss future operations. Few of these leaders were enthusiastic about a central Pacific drive and still fewer saw the Marianas as a desirable objective for such a drive. The islands lacked good harbors and were within range of a large number of Japanese air bases, but outside the range of U.S. land-based air support. General Kenney, who wanted B-29s for his own theater, argued that the big bombers did not need to be based in the Marianas but could operate just as well from other areas. Nimitz preferred to attack the Palaus and Truk, if necessary, rather than the Marianas, then move on the Philippines. He told the conferees he would recommend to Washington a single-pronged advance aiming at Mindanao.[15]

MacArthur was elated—and King infuriated—by the report of the conference at Pearl Harbor. In a blistering letter to Nimitz, King reminded the Commander in Chief, Pacific, that the Joint Chiefs had already decided on a central Pacific drive and that to concentrate on only the southwest Pacific would leave U.S. lines of communications vulnerable to flanking attacks from the Marianas and Carolines. Nimitz bowed to King's wishes. Preparations for the Central Pacific drive continued despite a last-ditch appeal by General Sutherland, who came to Washington in February to present MacArthur's views to the Joint Chiefs of Staff. Now MacArthur was really worried. As the campaign in the Marshalls rolled smoothly along, he probably wondered whether it might not be Nimitz rather than he who would "return" to Manila.[16]

While the southwest Pacific commander was glumly considering this possibility, his air commander, General Kenney, brought him interesting news. Kenney's pilots, who had been bombing the Admiralty Islands northwest of Rabaul since the beginning of 1944, reported little discernable enemy activity in the islands. The pilots had sighted no Japanese and the island's airfield was overgrown with grass.[17] This was an intriguing bit of intelligence because the Admiralties, with a fine, large, protected anchorage, were ideally situated to cut off Rabaul and cover the Allied advance along the New Guinea coast. They were scheduled for attack in April 1944. Could they be taken sooner? "Yes," said Kenney and Whitehead. They urged a quick strike to seize the main airfield on Los Negros Island. "No," said MacArthur's intelligence officer Brigadier General Charles A. Willoughby, who estimated that there were more than 4,000 Japanese in the Admiralties.[18] (Willoughby was correct. Captured documents later revealed that the island commander had ordered his troops to keep out of sight and not fire at American reconnaissance planes. The airstrips *were* overgrown—but only because they had not been used recently.)[19] MacArthur "listened a while, paced back and forth . . . then suddenly stopped and said: 'That will put the cork in the bottle.' "[20]

Orders were hastily despatched to General Krueger and Admiral Thomas C. Kinkaid, MacArthur's new naval commander, to prepare for an immediate reconnaissance in force of Los Negros. This would involve a squadron of the dismounted First Cavalry Division with supporting units and a navy task force under Rear Admiral Russell S. Berkey; they had only five days to get ready. Trucks with bullhorns and sirens went screaming through the streets of Brisbane, rounding up sailors on liberty from Kinkaid's flagship *Phoenix*.[21] Two days later the *Phoenix*, with General MacArthur aboard, sailed for the Admiralties, accompanied by the cruiser *Nashville* and four destroyers. Eight more destroyers and three destroyer transports under Rear Admiral William Fechteler carried about 1,000 assault troops of the First Cavalry Division, with supporting artillery and medical units under Brigadier General William C. Chase. Only destroyers and APDs (destroyer-transports) could reach Los Negros in the necessary time.

Chase's men would be attacking an objective which had originally been allotted to an entire division for assault later in the year. MacArthur knew the risks but was confident he would get his men ashore and reinforce them faster than the Japanese could react.[22] Fortunately for MacArthur and the First Cavalry the island commander, Colonel Ezaki Yoshio, had his troops deployed at the wrong side of Los Negros, defending the magnificient anchorage called Seeadler Harbor. Chase's troops, however, landed at Hyane Harbor, a smaller, crescent-shaped inlet with a short but usable beach.

Japanese shore batteries and machine guns fired at the American landing craft as they headed for the shore on the morning of February 29, but they were soon silenced by Fechteler's ships. The cavalrymen encountered little opposition at the beach. Within two hours they had captured nearby Monote Airfield. Late that afternoon MacArthur himself came ashore and inspected the beachhead—drawing occasional sniper fire—and conferring with General Chase. Apparently satisfied, MacArthur returned to the ship, leaving behind orders to "remain here and hold the airstrip at all costs." As the *Phoenix* pulled out for New Guinea, her radios crackled with orders to send reinforcements and supplies to the Admiralties as soon as possible.[23]

On Los Negros, Chase wisely decided to pull his force back into a shorter, more defensible line just east of the airstrip. That night and the next, the Japanese attacked Chase's positions. A few, using life preservers, even swam in behind the American positions. All to no avail. As his fellow officers had done at Guadalcanal, Ezaki threw away his chances in piecemeal attacks. On March 2 the first American reinforcements arrived: about 1,500 more cavalrymen complete with artillery and support units, and 400 navy Seabees.

The Seabees landed on Los Negros under intermittent machine-gun and mortar fire. They immediately began to clear and enlarge the runways at Monote. "One fifty-year-old operator drove his grader the full length of the strip three or four times, drawing sniper fire from the cocoanut grove. When he came in he said: 'I'm sure glad Mother let me come this time; you know, she wouldn't let me go to the other war!' "[24]

Ezaki's main attack was delayed until the night of March 3. By that time the Americans had had time to prepare good defensive positions covered by interlocking sectors of mortar- and artillery fire, with minefields to their front. The Japanese came on with reckless determination. Troops advanced shouting, talking, and singing, through the minefields right up to the cavalrymen's machine-gun barrels. Some troopers swore the Japanese were singing "Deep in the Heart of Texas." A few penetrated American defenses, but the attackers were too few and too scattered. By morning they all were dead.[25]

Reinforcements now poured into the Admiralties. Allied warships penetrated Seeadler harbor on March 8 while the cavalrymen continued their advance on Los Negros. On March 9 the Second Cavalry Brigade, under Brigadier General Verne D. Mudge, landed at Salami Plantation on the Seeadler side of Los Negros; on the fifteenth, Mudge's men were ferried across the harbor to attack the last Japanese strongpoint near Lorengau, a village almost directly opposite the entrance to Seeadler anchorage. With the fall of Lorengau to the

Second Cavalry on March 18, the Admiralties were securely in American hands.

MacArthur's gamble at Los Negros had paid off handsomely but it remains in retrospect an unnecessarily reckless gamble. Admiral Barbey, MacArthur's amphibious commander, pointed out many years later that Chase's men, once landed, could not have been withdrawn. "A disaster at Los Negros would have set back the Pacific campaign several months at least. The psychological effect of an American defeat on the Japanese would have been tremendous." Had the Japanese commander concentrated his forces against the beachhead during the first two nights, "there is little question that General Chase's force would have been overrun." [26] Brigadier General Clyde Eddleman, who helped plan the operation, agreed that "if we had waited a couple of weeks, we could have done it much easier." [27]

The capture of the Admiralties was intended to complete the American operations around Rabaul but someone had forgotten to tell this to the Japanese. On Bougainville, Lieutenant General Hyakutaka—he of the Guadalcanal failures—had painstakingly assembled a force of more than 15,000 men to hurl at the American airfields at Empress Augusta Bay. They were supported by the greatest concentration of artillery the Japanese had ever assembled in the Solomons. Hyakutake's aim was to penetrate the American perimeter around Empress Augusta Bay, destroy the three airfields there, and push the defenders into the sea.

Unfortunately for Hyakutake, he had underestimated the strength of the defenders—two divisions and support troops totalling almost 62,000 men under Major General Oscar Griswold—by half. Perhaps worse, his attack plans, including a diagram indicating the spot where the American surrender would be accepted, had been captured by Griswold's troops.[28]

On March 8 the Japanese opened their operations with an artillery barrage which drove most of the planes from the airfields. But their ground attack, at a steep slope called Hill 700 on the northeast side of the American perimeter, achieved only a shallow salient. Nevertheless, it took three days of nasty, close-in fighting by the 37th Division to dislodge the Japanese from this advance position. In the meantime an even tougher fight was raging at an American outpost called Hill 260, about 300 yards east of the main perimeter. Here the Japanese had seized the second of the twin peaks or "knobs"—called North Knob and South Knob—which were only about 150 yards apart. From the North Knob, still in American hands, the 182d Infantry of the Americal Division launched one attack after another on the South Knob, only to be repulsed each time. Then the Americans pulled back and blasted the South Knob with more than 10,000 rounds of artillery fire. By March 13 most of the Japanese had retreated, leaving behind 560 dead.[29]

The final Japanese thrust on March 11, near the center of the American perimeter, made only small gains. Units of the 37th Division, supported by tanks, soon restored the line. Hyakutaka pulled most of his troops off Hill 260 and Hill 700, flinging them into a final attack on March 23; but the Americans were ready and, supported by an overwhelming superiority in artillery, shattered the attack.[30]

Events on Bougainville could have little effect on the course of the Pacific War, but the impact of the Admiralties campaign was profound. With the islands in American hands, the Japanese had to evacuate their base at Madang on the north coast of Papua and move further west to Hansa Bay, Wewak, and Aitape. But MacArthur was already thinking of bypassing these formidable bastions with a 580-mile leap to Hollandia on the north coast of Netherlands New Guinea.

Washington strategists too were impressed with MacArthur's triumph in the Admiralties. At the time of that operation, Marshall had been fighting a rearguard action against the growing insistence on the part of the other services and the Joint Strategic Survey Committee (JSSC) that "the primary effort against Japan be made from the east across the central Pacific, with a view to the early seizure of the Formosa, Luzon, China coast area as a base to attack Japan." The southwest Pacific area would "support the primary effort" with whatever resources could be spared.[31] Then came word of MacArthur's stroke in the Admiralties. This was followed a few days later by the southwest Pacific commander's proposal to bypass Hansa Bay, scheduled for attack in late April, and make the 580-mile jump directly to Hollandia, thus isolating some 40,000 enemy ground forces along the New Guinea coast.

That proposal was part of a comprehensive plan, RENO IV, submitted by MacArthur and presented by Sutherland in Washington during early March. RENO IV required retention by MacArthur of most of Halsey's South Pacific forces, then about to wind up their operations, as well as the support of carrier task forces from the Central Pacific. If the plans were followed, Sutherland assured the Washington strategists, Luzon could be invaded as early as January 1945.[32] Now it was Nimitz's turn to protest. The central Pacific commander pointed out that if MacArthur's plan were followed, the central Pacific drive would lose momentum and the Marianas operations would have to be deferred into the typhoon season.

After listening to all sides, the Joint Chiefs issued a new directive to cover operations in the Pacific for the rest of 1944. MacArthur was ordered to continue his advance into western New Guinea and the islands northwest of the Vogelkop peninsula in preparation for the invasion of Mindanao, around the middle of November. At the same time, Nimitz's central Pacific forces were to neutralize Truk, occupy the Marianas in mid-June, and take the Palau Islands, about 600 miles due east of Mindanao, around the middle of September.[33] Halsey's South Pacific forces were divided between Nimitz and MacArthur, with MacArthur getting most of the army units and Nimitz receiving the bulk of the naval forces, including the large marine air squadrons.

While discussions of strategy gradually reached their climax in Washington, MacArthur's staff studied the possibilities of a strike at Hollandia. Intelligence confirmed that it was weakly defended and that the Japanese expected an attack elsewhere, probably at Wewak or Hansa Bay.[34] Yet Hollandia was barely within range of Kenney's fighters and the Japanese could defend it with planes from bases even farther away to the west. Fighter support had been shown to be essential to success in the southwest Pacific's amphibious hops. Carrier-based fighter cover was the obvious answer to this problem. It was in recognition of this that the Joint Chiefs had instructed Nimitz in their March 12 directive to cooperate with MacArthur in providing air support for the Hollandia operation.[35]

On March 25 the CINCPAC commander flew to Brisbane for the first personal meeting between the two theater commanders since the outbreak of war. Both were on their best behavior, determined to scotch the widespread gossip that they were jealous rivals who could not cooperate. The general and his entourage were on hand to greet Nimitz as he stepped from his plane. That evening MacArthur presided at a lavish banquet in the admiral's honor. Later MacArthur invited Nimitz to dinner in his suite at Lennon's Hotel. There Nimitz presented Mrs. MacArthur with several varieties of rare orchids he had brought from Hawaii; the general's young son, Arthur, with silk playsuits in Hawaiian prints.[36]

Despite the displays of genuine cordiality and good feeling, there were differences over the Hollandia plans. Nimitz refused to expose his big carriers in the dangerous waters off Dutch New Guinea for more than one day, although Admiral Kinkaid persuaded him to allow some smaller escort carriers to remain for about a week to support the assault. Kenney told the admiral not to worry. He would have all the Japanese planes in the vicinity "rubbed out" by April 5. Everyone except MacArthur looked skeptical about that—but Kenney was as good as his word.

In mid-April the attack force for Hollandia, appropriately code-named RECKLESS, sailed from the Admiralties under Lieutenant General Robert L. Eichelberger. A second task force, code-named PERSECUTION, under Brigadier General Jens A. Doe, headed for the town of Aitape in northeast New Guinea, about 125 miles east of Hollandia. Aitape, lightly defended, was wanted as a site for Allied fighters operating in support of the Hollandia landings.

Hollandia, situated on the broad waters of Humboldt Bay, would be attacked by a part of Eichelberger's task force, the 41st Division, commanded by Major General Horace H. Fuller. The other half of RECKLESS, the 24th Division, under Major General Frederick A. Irving, would land at Tanahmerah Bay, some twenty-five miles west of Humboldt Bay. Then it would push east around the rugged Cyclops Mountains, which bordered the coast between the two bays, to a flat plain between the mountains and a narrow body of water called Lake Sentani; there the Japanese had built their airfields. The 41st Division would converge at the same time on the lake and airfields by moving inland from Hollandia.

At Hollandia there were about 11,000 Japanese; only 500 of them were combat troops. The senior officer, Major General Kitazono Toyozo, had arrived from Wewak only ten days earlier. He was replaced on the day of the invasion by an air corps officer. Neither had any plan of defense—or even enough weapons to arm the garrison.[37] The Japanese Second Army, which was responsible for the defense of eastern New Guinea, had ordered reinforcements to Hollandia from General Adachi's forces at Wewak and Hansa Bay; but Adachi stalled, believing that the next Allied blow would be against Wewak.[38]

The Allies did all that they could to confirm Adachi in this belief. Heavy bombing raids and a naval bombardment were directed at Wewak. Motor torpedo boats patrolled offshore; transport planes dropped dummy parachutists near the base.[39] Eichelberger's headquarters deliberately encouraged rumors about an attack on Hansa Bay with "leaks" and gossip.[40]

The result was all that could have desired. The American invaders achieved complete surprise at Aitape and at Hollandia. Many of the Japanese garrisons fled in disorder when warships of the invasion task forces opened fire. At Humboldt Bay General Fuller's men found breakfast bowls still half full of rice and tea still brewing when they entered the Japanese installations. At Tanahmerah the first troops to land were surprised and relieved to find carefully prepared fire lanes and half-finished pillboxes where "a squad could have held up a division"—all abandoned by the enemy.[41] If the Japanese failed to make their normal stubborn defense of the beaches, the usual fierce air reaction was also absent; for Kenney's Fifth Air Force, true to his promise, had all but totally eliminated Japanese air power in Dutch New Guinea. By the 26th, all three airfields near Lake Sentani were in American hands, as was the airstrip near Aitape. The Japanese had lost more than 3,000 dead and 600 captured. Many others who fled from Hollandia—short of rations and without medical supplies—died in the jungles or ran into Allied patrols and roadblocks.[42]

While Japanese service troops fled from Hollandia in panic, other, more determined, men were pushing their way west toward the Americans at Aitape. There the 32nd Division under Major General William H. Gill had relieved General Doe's 163d Regimental Combat Team. General Adachi's Eighteenth Army, battered and short of supplies but still full of fight, was making its way from Wewak through the rain-soaked jungles toward Aitape. It took Adachi's troops—on half rations, plagued by malaria, carrying their supplies forward by hand—about a month to travel the ninety miles to the Driniumor River, the eastern anchor of General Gill's defenses, and almost another month to position themselves for attack.

In the meantime the Allies, having learned of the Japanese intentions through reconnaissance, radio intercepts, and captured documents, had reinforced Aitape to a strength of fifteen battalions of infantry and two dismounted cavalry squadrons with supporting units. Major General Charles P. Hall was commander of all these forces.

Adachi's 18th Army comprised two divisions and many smaller units, but its actual combat strength was only about 20,000—of whom not more than 8,000 were trained infantrymen. Many of the others were former service troops, artillerymen without guns, or sailors without ships. Adachi's men had only about half the ammunition they required for their small arms and almost no communications equipment.

Despite these problems the 18th Army's attack on the night of July 10, 1944, succeeded in punching a hole 1,300 yards wide in the American line on the Driniumor. Hall's troops fell back to their second delaying position on the X-ray River a few miles east. From there they launched a series of counterattacks which restored the Driniumor line by the eighteenth of July.

But Adachi was not finished. Reshuffling his forces, he began a movement around the southern end of the American line in the foothills of the Torricelli Mountains, near a village called Afua. Fierce fighting raged for more than two weeks. Afua changed hands many times as the Americans and Japanese shifted and adjusted their lines, parrying and thrusting at each other half-blindly in the rugged jungle hills. At one point a segment of the 112th Cavalry was completely cut off and surrounded by stronger Japanese forces, but it managed to hold out for four days until relief arrived.[43]

General Hall launched his own flanking movement at the end of July. Five battalions struck due east from the northern end of the Driniumor line, then swung south to roll up Adachi's supply lines and rear area units. Yet the Japanese—their food gone, their few artillery pieces destroyed, most of their battalion and company officers dead or wounded—were already withdrawing to the Dandriwad River fifteen miles away. After twenty-five days' continuous fighting, the almost leaderless Japanese regiments were down to less than a hundred men. Some battalions had been completely annihilated by American artillery and mortar fire. A total of 9,000 men were dead or missing. Adachi's 18th Army had ceased to be a serious threat to Allied operations in New Guinea.[44]

A major reason for the seizure of Hollandia was the need to provide the Allies with heavy-bomber bases to support MacArthur's drive toward the Philippines and Nimitz's operations in the Marianas and Palaus. The Allies had only two other satisfactory bases for heavy bombers in the entire southwest Pacific area: at Nadzab and in the Admiralties, and these were too far away for present purposes. Bases at Hollandia were vital, but MacArthur quickly learned that they would not be ready soon. The soil was too soft to support a heavy-bomber strip until extensive engineering work could be done. Mac-Arthur's engineers were working on this problem as well as on other projects which would convert Hollandia into a major air and naval base. In the meantime, however, other fields were needed for the bombers.[45]

MacArthur's headquarters was already planning the seizure of Japanese airfields west of Hollandia near the town of Sarmi, on the coastal island of Wakde,* and on Maffin Bay between Wakde and Sarmi. These plans were now rapidly pushed to completion. An added incentive to quick work was the fear that these fine airfield sites might soon be utilized by the Japanese in a counterattack unless the Allies moved quickly.

Even the bases in the Wakdi–Sarmi area, however, were not good enough for heavy bombers. For that MacArthur's forces would have to move on to the small island of Biak, in the Shouten island group off the northwest coast of New Guinea, about 300 miles west of Hollandia. Biak would be needed soon if the southwest Pacific bombers were to be in position to support Nimitz's moves on the Marianas and Palaus. Still, air bases in the Wakde–Sarmi area would be needed to support an attack on Biak.

On May 17 units of General Doe's 163d Regimental Combat Team, 41st Division—the same men who had taken Aitape a few weeks earlier—landed at the village of Arare on the New Guinea mainland, four and a half miles southwest of Wakde. Encountering little opposition, the troops rapidly fanned out from the beach and secured the village of Toem, directly opposite Wakde, in a few hours. Other units embarked in LCVPs headed for unoccupied Insoemanai, the small island close to Wakde, where they quickly set up heavy machine-gun and mortar positions. All day long, the big guns of supporting destroyers and General Doe's artillery on the mainland pounded Wakde. The following morning six waves of boats, carrying the First Battalion of the 163d, left Toem for Wakde.

To reach the landing beaches, the assault waves would have to make a sharp right turn around Insoemanai and run parallel to the Wakde shore for about a thousand yards. Japanese machine gunners, dug in on that parallel shore, were waiting to give the invaders a warm reception; but three rocket-firing LCI gunboats kept the Japanese positions under heavy fire and distracted their attention from

* The airfield was actually located on Insoemoar Island, one of the two which comprised the Wakde islands, but MacArthur's forces always referred to Insoemoar as Wakde.

the landing boats. The troops landed in good shape and had reached the southern end of the airfield within an hour.

It took two more days' fighting to clear the island, but even before the shooting stopped, engineers and aviation technicians were already at work rebuilding and enlarging the airfield which would soon accommodate two bomber- and two fighter groups. Two and half days after the first invaders landed on Wakde, the airfield was operational. A week later navy B-24s from Wakde made the first aerial reconnaissance of southern Mindanao in the Philippines.[46] There would be many more American planes in Philippine skies before long.

General Doe's force had now accomplished its mission. But General Krueger, Doe's superior, made the unfortunate decision to launch a drive on the town of Sarmi about sixteen miles east of Toem, Sarmi was the headquarters of the Japanese 36th Division, under Lieutenant General Tagami Hachiro. Krueger's intelligence reported Japanese preparations for an attack on the Alamo forces in the Wakde area; the advance toward Sarmi was intended to forestall it. Krueger also believed—incorrectly—that Japanese strength and defenses around Sarmi were weak. The first to learn otherwise were the men of the 158th Regimental Combat Team, which had relieved Doe's troops. At Lone Tree Hill, a 175-foot rise on the coastal plain just west of Maffin Bay, the Japanese had constructed a maze of defenses comprising caves, pillboxes, and log-and-earth dugouts covered by well-concealed 75-mm mountain guns. It was manned by tough, experienced veterans of the fighting in China who were thoroughly familiar with the terrain. From a well-camouflaged lookout post atop a giant tree on the hill, the Japanese could keep the entire area from Sarmi to Arare under observation.[47]

In four days the 158th Regimental Combat Team suffered almost 300 casualties in vain attempts to take Lone Tree Hill. The attack was resumed almost a month later by the Sixth Division, which had relieved the 158th Regimental Combat Team. At first the attackers had little success. After three days, however, a heavy bombardment by the Sixth Division's 105-mm and 155-mm howitzers and a squadron of fighters from Wakde enabled two battalions of the 20th Infantry Regiment to fight their way to the top of Lone Tree Hill. There they were soon cut off and surrounded. Yet the Americans on the hill held their ground; gradually they began to clear the Japanese from their caves and crevices, using flame throwers, hand grenades, bazookas, high explosives, and even flaming gasoline. At a cost of almost a thousand casualties, the Sixth Division captured Lone Tree

Hill; but the Japanese held out in the Sarmi area until the end of the war.[48]

While men fought and died at Lone Tree Hill, other units of Krueger's Alamo Force were waging an equally hard struggle for Biak, the ultimate objective of the Wakde–Sarmi–Toem campaign. Biak was a large island east of the Vogelkop peninsula at the western end of New Guinea. The principal town was Bosnek on the southeastern shore, from which a seven-mile coastal road led to the Japanese airstrips near Mokmer village. A group of high, steep, coral cliffs paralleled the road roughly a hundred yards inland. In these cliffs, and in others bordering the airfields, were innumerable caves where the Japanese had emplaced artillery and antiaircraft guns, automatic weapons, mortars, and observation posts. Living quarters for the 11,000-man garrison, as well as the supply dumps and communication facilities, were all located in these caves, which were ringed with pillboxes and bunkers.[49]

Biak's commander, Colonel Kuzume Naoyuki, was still hurrying to complete these defensive preparations when the American forces, built around the 41st Division (less the regimental combat team which had landed at Wakde), came ashore near Bosnek on May 27, 1944. There was little opposition at the beaches themselves. Although the leading battalion landed on the wrong beach, the Americans quickly consolidated their positions and advanced rapidly west along the coastal road toward Mokmer airfield.[50]

It was not until the lead unit, the Third Battalion, 162d Infantry, was within about 200 yards of the airfield that the Americans realized they had walked into a trap. From the caves north of the road the Japanese poured in a hail of automatic weapons fire, punctuated by the frequent, sharp cough of their mortars. A Japanese battalion counterattacked from the west, driving a wedge between the companies of the Third Battalion. By evening the Third Battalion had been forced to conduct a difficult withdrawal, covered by the Second Battalion of the 162d.

The following morning Kuzume threw in his secret weapon: tanks. In earlier island battles, it had usually been the Americans who had had the tanks. But on Biak, the Japanese had collected a number of light, nine-ton tanks armed with 37-mm guns. These tanks spearheaded a series of attacks against the now isolated Second Battalion, 162d Infantry. The Americans, however, had brought up their own tanks; the larger and more heavily armed "General Shermans." Seventy-five milimeter shells from the Shermans ripped jagged holes in their thin-skinned Japanese opponents and blew off their turrets, while the Japanese shells literally bounced off the larger American tanks. The only damage the Japanese could do was to lock the 75-mm gun of one Sherman in place with a lucky hit. Undaunted, the commander of the damaged tank backed part way into a shell hole; with the elevation thus obtained he continued to fire and score hits on the enemy.[51] Second Battalion held out through three attacks, but its position was hopeless, so it was evacuated by amtracs brought in under cover of darkness.[52]

General H. H. Fuller, commanding the 41st Division, called for more troops. He got two more battalions, which he sent on an end run over rugged native trails behind the ridge lines. Meanwhile a much stronger force, backed by artillery and air, advanced down the coastal road again. The heat and humidity were almost as much trouble as the Japanese. There were few sources of water on Biak and there was never enough to go around. "It was really a terrible operation," recalls one officer who was there. "Men had to fight in extreme heat with only one canteen of water every 24 hours."[53] "More than one American died in the night as he crawled forward to replenish his canteen" from one of the rare and precious water holes.[54]

A week of hard fighting found General Fuller's troops in possession of Mokmer airfield; but the Japanese still held the ridges overlooking it, and they were able to keep it under fire with mortars and artillery from their strongholds in the caves. In the meantime General Krueger, under pressure from MacArthur to get the Biak airfields into operation in time for the Marianas campaign, relieved General Fuller and appointed General Eichelberger commander of the American forces on Biak.[55]

The Japanese High Command was also watching events on Biak with great interest. To the Japanese navy the assault on the island was a threat which could not be ignored. Navy strategists were expecting further American advances in the central Pacific: on the Marianas, the Carolines, or the Palaus. In that event the Japanese navy would sally forth for a decisive battle, the so-called A-GO operation.[56] Yet the fleet could hardly hope to fight a successful battle with Allied airplanes on Biak threatening its flank. Japanese strategists therefore prepared a preliminary operation called "Kon" to annihilate the American forces on Biak.

Moving quickly, the Imperial Navy high command ordered about half of its land-based air strength from the central Pacific to bases in or near Western New Guinea. At the same time the navy prevailed upon the army to agree to send its Second Amphibious Brigade to Biak and assembled a strong escort to transport it there.[57]

Twenty-five hundred troops of the Amphibious Brigade sailed for Biak from Mindanao at the end of May. They were escorted by Japanese warships, including a battleship. But they were soon spotted by an American Liberator flying from Wakde, while their own reconnaissance planes incorrectly reported an American aircraft carrier and many other warships off Biak. That was enough for the Japanese, who turned back for the Philippines. In fact, the Allies had nothing stronger than a handful of cruisers and destroyers in the Biak area— and nothing bigger within hundreds of miles.[58] When the Japanese tried to send in 600 troops in six destroyers a week later, they were discovered and attacked by Kenney's B-25s from Hollandia. One destroyer was sunk; the other skirmished with U.S. destroyers off Biak, then fled.[59]

Still determined to recapture Biak, the Japanese now assembled an overwhelming force, including the giant battleships *Musashi* and *Yamato;* but just as this armada was about to set out, word was received of Spruance's advance on the Marianas. At once the Imperial Navy suspended the Biak operation and, in accordance with long-established plans, headed north for the "decisive battle" with the American fleet in the Marianas.[60]

A distinguished historian of the Pacific War has observed that the close relationship between the Japanese efforts at Biak and their reaction to the Marianas invasion was "a striking illustration of the mutual interdependence of the Allied Southwest and Central Pacific Areas."[61] It was indeed, but it was also an illustration of how the American strategy of two different drives across the Pacific under independent command might easily have led to disaster. By dividing their forces the Americans had given the Japanese an opportunity to concentrate a locally superior force against one part of their advance, something the Japanese achieved at Biak. Had Combined Fleet proceeded with the third attempt to reinforce Biak, it would have probably inflicted a serious defeat on the inferior Allied naval forces, delivered a destructive bombardment of American positions on Biak, and gotten their much-needed reinforcements ashore. Such a Japanese success might have set back the whole American timetable for the Pacific War. Yet the Japanese—true disciples of Mahan—preferred to rush off for a full-dress fleet action in the Marianas, one that would cost them dearly.

The Japanese on Biak were now doomed; but it took several weeks to secure the remaining airfields, and even longer to blast and burn the stubborn defenders out of their cave strongholds. In the meantime MacArthur, impatient with progress there and still eager to secure more airfields, ordered Krueger's Alamo Force to seize the island of Noemfoor about sixty miles west of Biak, where the Japanese had three large air bases. Krueger gave the task to Brigadier General Edwin D. Patrick's 158th Regimental Combat Team, which had fought at Lone Tree Hill.

At Noemfoor, the 158th found the going far easier, thanks to a heavy air- and naval bombardment. Between June 20 and July 1, the Allied air forces dropped over 8,000 tons of bombs on the island, leaving the surviving Japanese so stunned and dazed they offered little resistance.[62] The worst American casualties occurred among the men of the 503d Parachute Infantry Regiment, landed on the island as reinforcements. Dropped at less than 400 feet over a hard coral airfield strewn with wreckage and surrounded by trees, the paratroopers sustained almost 10 percent casualties. All the same, they went on to mop up the remaining Japanese. Airfields at Noemfoor were in operation to support the allies by the end of July.[63]

MacArthur's forces now completed their advance across Dutch New Guinea with little opposition, seizing positions for airfields on the Vogelkop peninsula near the villages of Sansapor and Mar. The final stepping stone to the Philippines was the island of Morotai in the Moluccas, which lay between the Vogelkop and Mindanao. Troops of the 31st Division landed unopposed at Morotai on September 15.

It had taken the Allied forces under MacArthur six months to retake Papua from the Japanese. Nine months had been required to cut off Rabaul and clear northeast New Guinea. Yet in less than three months, MacArthur's forces had advanced 1,400 miles from the Admiralties to the Vogelkop and north to the Moluccas.

On September 15, less than two hours after American troops had gone ashore at Morotai, MacArthur arrived to look over his most advanced outpost, only 300 miles from the Philippines. " 'He gazed out to the northwest,' " one aide recalls, " 'almost as though he could already see through the mist the rugged lines of Bataan and Corregidor. " 'They are waiting for me there,' " he said. " 'It has been a long time.' " [64]

NOTES

1. James, *Years of MacArthur*, p. 331 and passim.
2. Preparation of Plans for the Defeat of Japan, 7 July 1943, JPS 67/6; Specific

Operations in the Pacific and Far East, 6 August 1943, JCS 446. Both in RG 218.

3. James, *Years of MacArthur 1941–1945*, p. 330.

4. Morison, *Breaking the Bismarck's Barrier*, pp. 403–09.

5. Matloff, *Strategic Planning 1943–44*, pp. 220–21.

6. Appreciation and Plan for the Defeat of Japan, 18 August 1943, CCS 313, RG 218.

7. Specific Operations in the Pacific and Far East 1943–1944, 6 August 1943, JCS 446, RG 218.

8. Matloff, *Strategic Planning 1943–44*, p. 235.

9. Coakely and Leighton, *Global Logistics and Strategy*, pp. 401–3.

10. Morison, *Breaking the Bismarck's Barrier*, pp. 396–408.

11. Hayes, *Advance to Victory*, pp. 97–98; James, *Years of MacArthur*, pp. 363–65.

12. JCS Memorandum, Sub.: Air Plan for the Defeat of Japan, 20 August 1943, CCS 373.11 Japan (20 August 1943) Part 1, RG 218, National Archives.

13. Hayes, *Advance to Victory*, pp. 75, 103–8.

14. Quoted in Matloff, *Strategic Planning 1943–44*, pp. 373–78.

15. Potter, *Nimitz*, pp. 281–82.

16. James, *Years of MacArthur*, pp. 368–69.

17. Barbey, *MacArthur's Amphibious Navy*, p. 148.

18. Miller, *Cartwheel*, pp. 320–21.

19. Barbey, *MacArthur's Amphibious Navy*, p. 153.

20. James, *Years of MacArthur*, p. 380.

21. Morison, *Breaking the Bismarck's Barrier*, pp. 435–36.

22. James, *Years of MacArthur*, p. 383.

23. Ibid., pp. 384–85; Miller, *Cartwheel*, pp. 326–29; Morison, *Breaking the Bismarck's Barrier*, pp. 437–39.

24. Morison, *Breaking the Bismarck's Barrier*, p. 441.

25. Miller, *Cartwheel*, pp. 333–35.

26. Barbey, *MacArthur's Amphibious Navy*, p. 157.

27. Conversations between General Clyde D. Eddleman and Lieutenant Colonel L. G. Smith and Lieutenant Colonel M. C. Swindler, p. 26, Senior Officer Debriefing Program, U.S. Army Military History Institute.

28. Miller, *Cartwheel*, pp. 351–58; Morison, *Breaking the Bismarck's Barrier*, pp. 417–28.

29. Miller, *Cartwheel*, pp. 365–72.

30. Ibid., pp. 372–77.

31. Report by JSSC, "Strategy in the Pacific," JCS 713, 16 February 1944, CCS 381, Pacific Ocean Area (10 June 1943) Section 2, RG 218; Hayes, *Advance to Victory*, pp. 174–79.

32. Hayes, *Advance to Victory*, pp. 179–180; James, *Years of MacArthur*, p. 392.

33. Hayes, *Advance to Victory*, pp. 185–86; Robert Ross Smith, *The United States*

Army in World War II: The Approach to the Philippines (Washington: Office of the Chief of Military History, 1953), pp. 11–12.

34. MAGIC Diplomatic Summary, Japanese Army Supplement: 13 March 1944; 20 March 1944; 21 March 1944; 1 April 1944; SRH-170, RG 457.

35. James, *Years of MacArthur*, pp. 444–45; Smith, *Approach to the Philippines*, p. 20.

36. Potter, *Nimitz*, pp. 289–91; James, *Years of MacArthur*, pp. 399–402.

37. Smith, *Approach to the Philippines*, pp. 84, 96–99.

38. "History of Second Area Army," Japanese Monograph No. 31, pp. 30–46.

39. Samuel Eliot Morison, *New Guinea and the Marianas* (Boston: Little, Brown and Co., 1964), p. 66.

40. Eichelberger, *Jungle Road to Tokyo*, p. 102.

41. Ibid., pp. 106–8.

42. Smith, *Approach to the Philippines*, pp. 100–1.

43. Ibid., pp. 147–50.

44. Ibid., pp. 158–204; Hattori, "History of the Greater East Asian War," pp. 147–48.

45. Smith, *Approach to the Philippines*, pp. 207–8; Eichelberger, *Jungle Road to Tokyo*, pp. 113–14.

46. Morison, *New Guinea and the Marianas*, pp. 98–101.

47. Smith, *Approach to the Philippines*, pp. 248, 264–66.

48. Ibid., pp. 267–75.

49. Ibid., pp. 300–1; Eichelberger, *Jungle Road to Tokyo*, pp. 135–36; "North of Australia Operations Record Supplement, General Outline of Second Army Operations at Sarmi and Biak," Japanese Monograph No. 136, pp. 49–51.

50. Morison, *New Guinea and the Marianas*, pp. 110–13; "North of Australia Operations Record," p. 53.

51. Smith, *Approach to the Philippines*, p. 310; "North of Australia Operations," p. 58.

52. Morison, *New Guinea and the Marianas*, p. 115.

53. George H. Decker oral history interview, p. 22, U.S. Army Military History Research Institute.

54. Eichelberger, *Jungle Road to Tokyo*, p. 135.

55. Smith, *Approach to the Philippines*, pp. 241–45; James, *Years of MacArthur*, pp. 459–60.

56. "History of Imperial General Headquarters, Army Section," Japanese Monograph No. 45, pp. 190–91; "The A-GO Operation 1944," Japanese Monograph No. 60, pp. 16–19.

57. Smith, *Approach to the Philippines*, p. 350.

58. Ibid., pp. 352–53; Morison, *New Guinea and the Marianas*, pp. 119–20.

59. Morison, *New Guinea and the Marianas*, pp. 126–30.

60. Ibid., pp. 131–32; "North of Australia Operations Record," Japanese Monograph No. 136, pp. 64–66; "The A-GO Operation, 1944", pp. 22–23.

61. Smith, *Approach to the Philippines,* p. 362.
62. Ibid., pp. 406–11; Morison, *New Guinea and the Marianas,* pp. 136–38; James, *Years of MacArthur,* pp. 463–64.
63. Smith, *Approach to the Philippines,* pp. 411–13.
64. James, *Years of MacArthur,* p. 489.

FOURTEEN

To the Marianas

An observer of the Pacific theaters in the spring of 1944—Spruance and the largest fleet in the world about to descend on the Marianas, MacArthur preparing his move on the Philippines with five divisions and two air forces—might well wonder what had become of the "Germany First" principle of strategy adopted by the Allies before Pearl Harbor and so often reaffirmed thereafter. The principle stood unchallenged, but in terms of resource allocation the Pacific theaters had more than held their own. During the first months following Pearl Harbor, men and planes had been sent to the Pacific in greater numbers than to Europe in an effort to stem the Japanese onslaught and protect the American line of communication to Australia.[1] Once deployed there, these forces tended to stay in the Pacific.

The greater part of the U.S. Navy was also in the Pacific and had been since the beginning of the war. Its carriers and battleships would in any case have found little profitable use in Europe. The army had about an equal number of troops deployed in the Pacific and the Atlantic by the end of 1943, although most reinforcements were by that date earmarked for the European theater. In the matter of aircraft the European theater had a small edge, especially in heavy and medium bombers, but the new B-29 "super-bombers" were scheduled for deployment only to the Pacific.[2]

Transporting and supplying these vast forces was a logistical nightmare. All supplies had to move by sea, not only from the United States to the Pacific theaters but between points within the theaters. The distances involved were immense: 7,000 miles from San Francisco to Brisbane; over 6,000 miles from San Francisco to New Caledonia; 1,500 miles from Brisbane to Guadalcanal. At the end of these long lines of communication there were no modern ports like Belfast, Southampton, and Liverpool which could handle large tonnages and provide ample storage. Outside of Australia, New Zealand, and Hawaii, the port facilities of the Pacific theaters were primitive— often nonexistent. The vast area covered by MacArthur's forces in their advance across New Guinea in 1943 and 1944 contained not a single deep-water pier. All ships had to be unloaded by lighters; to MacArthur's logistics officers, it seemed to take " 'a year to get the stuff from the ships on to the shore.' " There was also a shortage of lighters. During one month in 1944 there were over 140 ships at Milne Bay waiting to be unloaded.[3]

It is hardly surprising, then, that the progress of the Pacific advances was marked by periodic shipping crises: in the fall of 1942, the fall of 1943, and the fall and winter of 1944. Such crises were caused by the unexpectedly rapid advance of American forces (in 1943 and 1944) and the tendency of area commanders to retain ships for use in their own theaters, although they should have been returned to the worldwide allied shipping pool.[4]

Almost as large a problem as shipping was the construction of bases. The entire progress of the war in the South and southwest Pacific and, to a lesser degree, the central Pacific, was keyed to the rate of development of air bases in newly captured areas from which Allied planes could neutralize and isolate Japanese targets in the next objective area. The war in the Pacific, then, was an engineer's war as well as a naval, air, and amphibious war. Yet there were never enough engineers and other service troops, and those available often lacked sufficient equipment.

Allied commanders often opted for extra combat units or supplies rather than devote precious shipping space to engineer or construction units. The result was that engineer units were brought in late, often without the heavy construction equipment needed to finish the job on time.[5] Throughout the entire war period in the Pacific, there was a shortage of engineer units and, indeed, of service and technical units of all types. "The shortage of port battalions contributed to every instance of ship congestion; the shortage of quartermaster troops to every instance of spoiled rations; that of engineer troops to every instance of failure to build airfields, roads and other facilities on time." [6]

This shortage could be traced directly to the unwillingness of theater commanders to sacrifice scarce combat troop shipping space to make room for service forces. Few generals were willing to pass up the chance of receiving an extra tank company or infantry battalion in order to get a bulk fuel storage company or an engineer maintenance unit. As a result combat troops were often pressed into service for construction and labor duty; the few trained specialists available were worked almost around the clock to meet impossible schedules. Many engineers in MacArthur's theater were employed at the front for over two years with no relief and no individual leave.[7]

In the central Pacific the problem was not only base construction but the supply and support of the gigantic, fast-moving armada of warships in Spruance's Fifth Fleet. To service Spruance's task forces operating thousands of miles from Pearl Harbor, Nimitz organized mobile supply and support bases. These mobile floating bases—composed of fuel barges, repair ships, tenders, tugs, floating docks, salvage ships, lighters, and store ships—would anchor in a protected lagoon where they were safe from submarines and usually out of range of enemy aircraft. There they would service and make minor repairs to ships of the fleet while barges, protected by destroyers, floated supplies to the combat zone.[8] To meet the voracious appetites of the warships for oil, roving fueling task groups of two or three giant tankers escorted by destroyers took station at designated fueling areas, large rectangles of ocean about twenty-five miles wide by seventy-five miles long. Men-of-war would rendezvous with the oilers and take on fuel while all ships continued to steam at eight to twelve knots.[9]

The mobile supply base "was the logistic counterpart to the aircraft carrier" and made possible the latter's slashing attacks on widely scattered enemy bases.[11] When the fleet moved to a new area of operations, so did the mobile supply squadron: it was based first at Majuro Atoll in the Marshalls, then at Eniwetok, and later at Ulithi Atoll in the Palaus.

Throughout the war the army and navy continued to maintain their own distinct supply services, even though army, navy, and marine forces often used the same equipment or supplies and shared base facilities on the same island. Measures to integrate the logistical systems were undertaken with varying degrees of success, but total unity was never even approached in either MacArthur's or Nimitz's theater.[11]

To the soldier the most obvious result of the separate army and navy supply systems was a sort of "dual standard of living," particularly in rear areas. The two services continued to adhere to their own standards of housing, feeding, and equipping their personnel— and the navy's seemed far higher than the army's. In New Caledonia for example, soldiers living in thatched huts with dirt floors enviously eyed the sturdy, dry, wooden barracks of their navy counterparts. When bases had electricity or refrigeration, the navy usually had it first. Navy mess halls appeared better built and served better food— and the sailors always seemed to have more beer.[12]

• •

One thousand miles from the mobile base at Eniwetok lay Nimitz's next objective: Saipan, in the Marianas. Saipan was one of three large islands which the Americans wanted to use as advanced naval bases. They planned a move either west to the Philippines or northwest toward the Bonins and Japan. Bases in the Marianas would also provide airfields from which the new B-29s could reach the heart of Japan. The other two islands were Tinian, a few miles south of Saipan, and Guam, the southernmost island, which had been an American possession until lost to the Japanese in 1941; they were to be taken after Saipan, which was closest to Japan.[13] In fact it was only twelve hundred miles from Tokyo—far closer to Japan than Hawaii was to California.

The Marianas were much different from the tiny, low-lying atolls which the marines had captured in the Gilberts and Marshalls. Saipan, Tinian, and Guam were large and varied land masses with everything from swamps and sugarcane fields to high, jungle-covered peaks and steep ravines. They combined all the hazards which American soldiers and marines had learned to dread in their earlier island campaigns: a fringing coral reef protecting a shallow lagoon, rugged jungle terrain, and lots of limestone and coral caves for bunkers and artillery positions.

The assault on the Marianas was entrusted to Admiral Spruance as commander of the Fifth Fleet. Under him were over 127,000 troops in the transports and landing craft of Vice Admiral Richmond Kelly Turner's Joint Expeditionary Force. They were divided into two segments. The Northern Attack Force—the 2d and 4th Marine

Divisions with the 27th Infantry Division in reserve—was to assault Saipan and, after that, Tinian. The Southern Attack Force comprised the Third Marine Division and the 1st Provisional Marine Brigade, the latter of which was earmarked for Guam after the assault on Saipan. The 77th Infantry Division in Hawaii was available as a general reserve.

Turner, who had just been promoted to Vice Admiral, had by now conducted over a half-dozen large amphibious operations. The strain was beginning to tell. " 'When I came back from the Marshalls I was dead tired,' " he later told his biographer: " 'I stayed dead tired for the rest of the war.' " [14] During the campaign he had had also sustained a back injury and had to wear a heavy brace which caused him a good deal of discomfort. Turner had begun to drink heavily and although he remained sober and alert for duty, his hangovers did nothing to improve an already irascible disposition.[15] Turner personally commanded the Northern Force, while General Holland M. Smith had charge of the ground troops organized as the V Amphibious Corps. The Southern Force was commanded by Rear Admiral Richard L. Conolly; Major General Roy S. Geiger, who had led the marine aviators at Guadalcanal, led the ground troops of the III Amphibious Corps.

Supporting the landings was Admiral Mitscher's Task Force 58, now made up of fifteen fast carriers and seven new battleships. In late February Mitscher began softening up the Marianas and nearby island chains in tandem with landbased planes from the Marshalls, Cape Gloucester, and the South Pacific. By D-Day of June 15, Japanese air power in the Marianas had been reduced to a handful of planes.

There were about 32,000 Japanese troops on Saipan—double what the Americans had expected. But the island's defenses were incomplete due to a late start and interference by American submarines which decimated many Saipan-bound convoys. Only a portion of the heavy guns and mortars were in place and, after the battle, Americans found many emplacements only just begun, bales of wire still unstrung, mines not laid, and heavy guns still on flatcars.[16] What defenses there were, however, gave the attackers plenty of trouble.

Holland Smith's plan for the Saipan campaign, suggested by his chief of staff Colonel Graves B. Erskine, called for two divisions to land abreast on a front almost two miles wide on the southwest coast near the town of Charan Kanoa. Erskine's idea was to make the landings a kind of amphibious blitzkrieg that would carry the first wave of assault troops more than a mile inland. This would be done by having the amphibian tractors carry the troops out of the water across the beach and inland to the first high ground before debarking them. A new "armored amphibian" tractor (LVTA)—which carried a 75-mm gun in a turret, together with a heavy machine gun instead of passengers—would precede the tractors and clear the way through enemy defenses which, it was expected, would already have been greatly weakened by Admiral Turner's preparatory bombardment.[17]

It was a brilliant plan. But the amphtracs and their armored cousins were simply not up to it. The thin skins of the armored amphibians were vulnerable to hits that would have bounced off a real tank, and the amphtracs had no armor at all. Nor could either vehicle easily cross landing beaches strewn with debris, tree stumps, shell holes, and ditches.[18]

They might have had an easier time had the preparatory bombardments really crippled enemy resistance, as Smith had expected. There was certainly plenty of firepower available. The seven new battleships of Admiral Mitscher's Task Force 58 bombarded Saipan two days before D-Day with over 2,400 sixteen-inch shells. Yet these valuable battleships were kept well away from possible minefields off the islands, so they delivered their fire from 10,000 yards or more. Their spotters knew little about shore bombardment: they tended to concentrate on large, but not necessarily important, targets. Thus a big, empty sugar mill at Charan Kanoa was pulverized while the low-lying pillboxes near it were left in peace.[19] The eight old battleships of Turner's force, which took over the next morning, were much better in their targeting, but they had insufficient time and ammunition to neutralize all the positions on the large island. Air strikes were not much help either,[20] although they tore up nearby airfields and kept all but a few Japanese planes away from the landing beaches.

The result was that the amphtracs and armored amphibians churning toward the beach on the morning of June 15 encountered fierce resistance. As the first waves left the line of departure, tractor drivers could see large splashes thrown up by Japanese artillery shells falling directly behind them. When the landing craft crossed the reef and entered the lagoon, the enemy unleashed a barrage of artillery, mortar, and machine-gun fire. Marines crouched low in the bobbing amphtracs, listening to the whistle of heavy shells and feeling the sickening thud and jerk produced by near misses. The amphtracs and armored amphibians answered with their 75-mm guns and automatic weapons, while planes from nearby escort carriers swooped down on the beaches like angry hawks, firing rockets and machine guns and bombing targets just beyond the beach.[21]

Despite the heavy Japanese fire, most landing craft reached land intact, although some troop-carrying amphtracs forged ahead of the slower armored amphibians, blocking the latter's field of fire. In the first twenty minutes 700 amphtracs and 8,000 troops came ashore. Casualties were heavy, especially among officers, but the use of the amphtracs made it unnecessary to wade in, thus preventing the kind of slaughter experienced at Tarawa. Few tractors could carry their passengers any significant distance inland, as Holland Smith had hoped, because of unfavorable terrain or heavy fire.

On the left, the 2d Marine Division landed too far north. A combination of a northerly current and heavy enemy fire from the south caused many amphtracs to land their troops on the wrong beaches. The 2d Battalion of the 8th Marines landed on the 3d Battalion's beach, while the 2d and 3d Battalions of the 6th Marines landed about 400 yards north of their assigned positions. This opened a dangerous gap between the 2d Marine Division and the 4th Marine Division to the south. To close this gap the 2d Division had to fight its way south as well as inland.

On the right, the 1st Battalion, 25th Marines, had the roughest time. Its beachhead was only twelve yards deep, exposed to the direct fire of at least four Japanese 75-mm guns on the high ground ahead of them. It took an air strike, naval gunfire from a battleship, and reinforcements to keep the 1st Battalion from being pushed back into the sea.[22]

Elsewhere along the shore marines consolidated their positions and evacuated their wounded. Some had to spend most of the day fighting their way to the portion of the beach where they should have landed in the first place.

By nightfall almost 20,000 men were dug in on a beachhead 1,000 yards deep, together with seven battalions of artillery and two tank battalions. Casualties were heavy and the gap between the 2nd and 4th Divisions had not been closed; but the marines were strong enough to repulse three large Japanese counterattacks, supported by tanks, against the 2nd Division during the night. Star shells from destroyers offshore silhouetted the attackers, while marine rocket launchers and light artillery stopped the thin-skinned Japanese tanks in their tracks.[23]

While the marines were digging in for the night, Lieutenant Commander Robert Risser, captain of the submarine *Flying Fish,* was peering through his periscope at a parade of Japanese battleships and carriers silouetted against the coastline of San Bernardino Strait in the Central Philippines, about 900 miles from Saipan. It was the biggest group of targets Risser had ever seen; but he knew that his first priority had to be getting word of this fleet to Spruance and CINCPAC. When darkness fell the *Flying Fish* surfaced and sent out her message: " 'The Japanese Fleet is headed for the Marianas.' " [24]

Daylight at Saipan found the marines still holding their positions and reinforcements moving toward the beach, but Spruance was worried. He now had two reports from submarines which had sighted Japanese forces coming north.[25] He sent word to two of the carrier groups of Task Force 58—which had gone on to strike the Bonin and Volcano Islands—to cut short their raids and rejoin the rest of the task force. Then he ordered Turner and Smith to meet him aboard the former's flagship *Rocky Mount*.

" 'The Japs are coming after us,' " Spruance told his two commanders. Could the transports and cargo ships move out of harm's way for awhile? "No," answered Turner, perhaps thinking of Guadalcanal. There was still a lot of tough fighting to do ashore and the troops would need more supplies and ammunition. " 'Well,' " replied Spruance, " 'I will join up with Mitscher and Task Force 58 and try to keep the Japs off your neck.' " [26]

Messages crackled from Spruance's flagship *Indianapolis* as she pulled out to join Mitscher's carriers, taking with her most of Turner's cruisers and destroyers. Carriers were to fuel and rendezvous at a point about 180 miles west of Tinian. Long-range seaplanes were ordered up from the Marshalls to begin searches to the east. The old battleships of the bombardment force would remain near Saipan with a few cruisers and destroyers to protect the beaches.[27] Air strikes were sent against Guam and Rota to neutralize any threat from that quarter.[28] From Pearl Harbor Admiral Nimitz radioed: " 'On the eve of a possible fleet action, you and the officers and men under your command have the confidence of the naval service and the country. We count on you to make the victory decisive.' " [29]

The Japanese were also thinking of decisive victory. After the carrier battles around Guadalcanal in late 1942, the Japanese navy's carrier-based air units had been dispersed to scattered land bases. Many suffered heavy losses in the air battles in the central Solomons during 1943. There was little opportunity for the air units to operate with their carriers.[30] By March 1944, when the Japanese fleet was reorganized as a carrier striking force similar to Task Force 58, its

nine aircraft carriers—many of them newly commissioned—had few
veteran pilots. The most experienced pilots in Vice Admiral Ozawa
Jisaburo's First Mobile Fleet had only six months' training. Some
had as little as two months. By contrast, even the newest American
aviators had two years' training and over 300 hours in the air.[31]
Senior Japanese air group commanders with Ozawa were, on the
average, ten years younger (and ten years less experienced) than
those who had sailed with Admiral Nagumo at Midway. In practice
bombing operations against an old battleship moving at sixteen knots
(half the speed of a modern warship), some dive-bomber squadrons
had failed to score a single hit.[32]

Nevertheless, the Japanese had big plans for their new carriers.
The navy's general scheme for blunting the American thrust in the
Pacific, Operation A-GO, anticipated a decisive air- and sea battle
in the area of the Palaus or the Western Carolines, close to Japanese
fuel supplies and within range of Japanese land-based air forces. The
land-based air power was important because the Japanese knew they
would be outnumbered by the American carriers and counted on
the island-based planes to even the odds.[33]

By mid-May the greater part of Ozawa's striking force lay at Tawi-
Tawi in the Sulu Archipelago, awaiting developments. There the
fleet was well located for a sortie to the north, east, or southeast.
Yet Tawi-Tawi was a far from ideal base. U.S. submarines constantly
harassed the fleet in the poorly protected anchorage, and lack of
an airfield prevented any effective training for the carrier groups.
For almost a month no training was accomplished. The inexperienced
pilots' level of proficiency dropped even lower. Finally Ozawa persuaded Combined Fleet Headquarters to allow him to move to the
port of Cebu in the Central Philippines, which was better suited to
training; but shortly after arriving there he received word of the
American attack on Saipan.[34]

Although A-GO called for a naval battle in the Palaus or Western
Carolines, the invasion of the Marianas was too serious to be ignored.
By stretching their fuel supplies and using unprocessed Borneo petroleum (good but highly flammable) the fleet could give battle near
the Marianas as well. On June 15 Ozawa received orders to "activate
the A-GO Operation for decisive battle."[35]

As he steamed north, Ozawa could count 222 fighters and about
200 dive- and torpedo bombers embarked in his nine carriers, compared to almost 500 fighters and over 400 dive- and torpedo bombers
in Mitscher's fifteen carriers. Still, Ozawa was confident he could

handle the Americans. His planes, owing to lack of armor and self-sealing fuel tanks, had a greater range than those of the Americans. Ozawa's planes could search as far out as 560 miles and attack at 300 miles, whereas Mitscher's could search only to about 350 and attack at 200.[36] Ozawa was also counting heavily on land-based planes at Guam, Rota, and Yap to whittle down the American Fleet. (Actually, these forces had done no damage to Task Force 58 but had instead been well worked over by Mitscher's planes.) Ozawa also expected to use Guam to rearm and refuel his own aircraft after striking the Americans. Vice Admiral Kakuta Kakuji, who commanded the land-based planes, had so misled Ozawa about his strength and the extent of his losses that Ozawa steamed into battle expecting substantial help from Guam and Tinian.[37] Finally, neither the Japanese nor the Americans realized how far the Japanese pilots had fallen below the skill and experience of their U.S. opponents.

Ozawa's search planes located Mitscher's fleet on the afternoon of June 18. Rear Admiral Obayashi Sueo, who commanded one of the carrier divisions, began to ready his planes for a strike but Ozawa ordered him to wait for morning. There were only a few hours of daylight left and the condition of the airfields at Guam, where the aircraft would have to land after dark, was unknown.[38] Had Obayashi gone ahead with his attack, he might have caught the Americans by surprise for, by the evening of the eighteenth, the exact whereabouts of the Japanese were still unknown to Spruance and Mitscher despite two days of air searches. On the other hand, the Americans would still have had some warning from radar, and an attack by only one portion of Ozawa's striking force might have been even less effective than the concentrated attacks which came later.[39]

Around midnight on the 17th, the U.S. submarine *Cavalla* had reported a Japanese task force 800 miles west-southwest of Saipan and closing. In the morning the *Cavalla* radioed again that the Japanese fleet was still on course and 100 miles closer to Saipan. Mitscher wanted to steam southwest at high speed to close on the *Cavalla*'s contact but Spruance wanted to keep Task Force 58 in position to cover Saipan against all eventualities.

From a study of other Japanese operations and captured documents, Spruance believed that the Japanese might divide their forces, using one portion as a decoy and the other portion to make an end run around Task Force 58 to get at the transports. He warned his commanders: " 'Diversionary attacks may come in from either flank or reinforcements come in from the Empire.' " Additional in-

telligence from high-frequency direction finders, which pinpointed
Ozawa's position on the night of the eighteenth, failed to dissuade
him. Mitscher again asked to head for the area of contact so as to
be in position to launch an attack in the morning, but Spruance
actually ordered the fleet to double back toward Saipan to prevent
any Japanese force from passing them in the dark. " 'Task Force
58 must cover Saipan and our forces engaged in that operation,' "
he signalled Mitscher. " 'We should . . . remain in air supporting
distance of Saipan until information of enemy requires other
action. . . .' " [40]

Neither Spruance nor his battleship commander, Rear Admiral
Willis A. Lee, wanted any possibility of a night surface engagement,
even though the American battle line was more modern and superior
in firepower to the capital ships in Ozawa's fleet. The Americans
also had the considerable advantage of radar. But Admiral Lee, who
had won the naval battle of Guadalcanal in November 1942, knew
all about radar and also about the disadvantages of fighting at night.
"He'd had a lot of experience of night attacks and most of it bad," [41]
recalled Mitscher's chief of staff. Lee's ships had spent so much time
operating as part of the carrier task groups that they had had little
opportunity to practice for night battle. So the chance for a night
engagement was reluctantly declined, much to the chagrin of many
younger officers. [42]

Ozawa had indeed divided his forces, but only for the purpose
of delivering a massive long-range attack on Mitscher's carriers. The
Japanese carriers were in two groups. A vanguard force of three
smaller carriers, with four battleships and nine heavy cruisers escorted
by eight destroyers, steamed one hundred miles ahead of the main
body. The larger group was made up of six larger carriers, a battleship, four cruisers and fifteen destroyers. This disposition allowed
the best use of the battleship and cruiser float-planes for scouting.
It employed the three smaller, less valuable, carriers as decoys of a
sort to lure attacking planes away from the bigger carriers and into
the powerful antiaircraft barrage of the battleships and cruisers in
the vanguard. [43]

But Ozawa had no intention of waiting to be attacked. A better
student of psychology than Spruance, he guessed that the latter would
probably hang back to protect Saipan, allowing the Japanese to take
full advantage of the greater striking range of their planes. [44] By
7:30 on the morning of June 19, Ozawa's scouting planes had found
the American task force and reported its position. About an hour

after receiving this report, Ozawa launched the first of four heavy raids against Mitscher's carriers.

Spruance and Mitscher were still in ignorance of Ozawa's whereabouts and Spruance was considering a strike against Guam and Rota to neutralize their airfields. A contact report by a long-range flying boat which had found the Japanese fleet an hour after midnight never reached Task Force 58.[45] Mitscher had three of his carrier groups in a north–south line twelve miles apart. The battleships, under Admiral Lee, were in a circular formation fifteen miles ahead of the carriers, while a fourth carrier task group cruised north of the battle line to provide air cover. The first wave of Japanese attackers headed for Lee's force, but many failed to get that far.

On the American carriers fighter-director officers expertly utilized radar to guide fighters intercepting the raiders. These officers were all young lieutenants and lieutenant commanders, recently recruited from civilian life and put through a rigorous selection and training process designed to identify men who could cope with the complex calculations and instant decisions required for the job. When incoming enemy planes were spotted, the fighter director had to accurately estimate their range, speed, and altitude, then choose the best type of interception tactic, taking into account such diverse factors as sun position, cloud cover, and visibility.[46] In Mitscher's flagship *Lexington,* communications technicians and the admiral's Japanese language officer huddled around a radio locked onto the voice circuit of the Japanese air coordinator, a senior squadron commander who orbited high over the task force directing the Japanese fighter groups. Within seconds after "Coordinator Joe" opened up on his radio, Mitscher's staff knew the time, direction, and strength of the enemy strikes.[47] Hellcats swarmed over the Japanese, shooting down at least two dozen. The veteran American pilots, flying superior aircraft, made it a very uneven contest: only one U.S. plane was lost to this first wave of attackers.

Those Japanese who survived the onslaught of the Hellcats ran into a blizzard of fire from Lee's battle line. Using proximity fuses, the battleships and their escorts downed a dozen more Japanese planes. Only one enemy plane scored a hit, which did some minor damage to the battleship *South Dakota.*

The second raid, with over 125 aircraft, suffered even heavier losses. Only a handful survived the gauntlet of fighters and fire from the battle line to attack Mitscher's carriers; none did any damage. The third group of attackers eluded the battle line by circling around to the north; it attacked one of the carrier task groups after fighting its way through intercepting Hellcats. Again, no carriers were hit.

The final wave of attackers became separated and attacked piecemeal during the early afternoon. Many failed to find the American task force at all and were intercepted and shot down while trying to land on Guam. In all, fewer than 100 of the 373 planes which had attacked Task Force 58 in the four mass attacks managed to return to their carriers. The Americans lost only 29 planes in the one-sided action, which one of Mitscher's pilots in *Lexington* labelled "the Great Marianas Turkey Shoot."

Some of the returning Japanese flyers found no carrier to land on. The U.S. submarines *Albacore* and *Cavalla* made contact with Ozawa's fleet and sank the carriers *Shokaku* and *Taiho*. The latter was the largest carrier in the Imperial Navy and served as Ozawa's flagship. Admiral Ozawa transferred his flag to a destroyer, then to the carrier *Zuikaku,* and carried on.

In Task Force 58 there was elation at the day's results, combined with frustration over inability to find the Japanese. As darkness fell, the Americans knew no more about the whereabouts of Ozawa's fleet than they had known that morning—and, because the U.S. carriers had been obliged to steam east into the wind to launch and recover their planes, they were still no closer to the enemy.

There were no searches that night: Mitscher's night fighters were trained only for short-range interceptions, not long-range search. But the next morning the sky was full of search planes from the American carriers.[48] Planes from *Lexington* flew as far out as 475 miles and still found nothing. Afternoon came; nerves were on edge and tempers grew short aboard the carriers. Perhaps—thought many—the Japanese had pulled out after their debacle the day before.

Then, around 4:00 P.M., a plane from the *Enterprise* sighted Ozawa's fleet about 275 miles from Task Force 58. That was a very long range. But with only three hours of daylight remaining, Mitscher could delay not a minute in launching his warplanes. Attacking at such distance, some planes would probably have insufficient fuel to return. The rest would have to land on their carriers after dark, something for which they had never trained. Mitscher consulted his operations officer, Commander W. J. Widhelm. " 'It's going to be tight,' " was Widhelm's reply.[49]

Yet there was little choice; the carriers had been steaming at high speed for the last three days and would have to fuel the next day, making further pursuit impossible. At 4:10, pilots and crews who had been on alert all afternoon received the order: "Man Aircraft!" Over two hundred planes were launched in less than twenty minutes. As the planes left their carriers, additional reports and calculations by Mitscher's staff revealed that the Japanese were sixty miles further west than had been first estimated. This unhappy news was relayed to the pilots and crews already headed for Ozawa's fleet. Pilots and crew made quick, worried calculations. It was clear that even under the best circumstances the chances of having sufficient fuel to return from this longer trip were slim indeed. "The intercom chatter, today quite subdued, died away to almost nothing as the pilots realized the import of the new position report." [50]

The Japanese carriers had been fueling when radio operators aboard one of Ozawa's cruisers picked up a radio call to Spruance indicating that the Americans had found the Japanese forces.[51] About seventy-five planes rose to meet the Americans or to clear the carriers' decks. Time was on the side of the Japanese fleet for, if they could evade their attackers for just twenty minutes, they would be lost in darkness.[52] But neither darkness nor fighters could save all the Japanese carriers from Mitscher's tired pilots. The attackers sank the carrier *Hiyo* with a well-placed torpedo, badly damaged three other carriers, and sank two of the accompanying oilers. The three other Japanese carriers escaped unhurt and the damaged ones returned to Japan for repairs. Japanese losses might have been greater had all the American torpedo planes actually been carrying torpedoes. But after the poor showing of the torpedo planes at the battles of Coral Sea and Midway, many of the *Avengers* were armed with bombs.[53]

It was pitch dark, with no moon and only occasional flashes of lightning from an approaching thunderstorm by the time the first American planes finally returned to their carriers. Standard flight operating procedure provided for carriers to display their deck landing and ramp lights for night landings even though this might reveal the ship to lurking submarines.[54] Mitscher went much further than that, ordering the carriers to flash their signal lights and point a searchlight beam straight into the sky. Cruisers and destroyers also turned on their truck lights and fired star shells to illuminate the area. To one night-fighter pilot sent aloft to guide the planes home, the scene seemed like " 'a Hollywood premier, Chinese New Year and the Fourth of July all rolled into one.' " [55] About eighty planes were lost through want of fuel or in landing accidents, but only about sixteen pilots and thirty-three crewmen were lost; the others were rescued from the water that night or the next day by patrolling warships and aircraft.

Despite the aerial victories, the Battle of the Philippine Sea, as the action of the nineteenth and twentieth of June came to be called, left a feeling of bitterness and disappointment among Spruance's commanders. That feeling was summed up by a single sentence in Mitscher's after action report: "The enemy had escaped." Captain Arleigh Burke, who drafted the report, believed that "we could have gotten the whole outfit! Nobody could have gotten away if we had done what we wanted to." [56]

Most of the controversy about the battle, which continues to the present day, centers around Spruance's decision on the night of the eighteenth to nineteenth of June: the decision to turn back toward Saipan rather than continue west. Going west would have put Mitscher's search planes within range of the Japanese fleet by morning. Defenders of Spruance argue that his decision—although based on the faulty premise that the Japanese had divided their forces for an end run around Task Force 58—in the end worked out for the best, since the last of Japan's carrier-based planes and pilots were virtually annihilated at small cost to the U.S. Any other decision might have achieved less satisfactory results.[57] On the other hand, critics of Spruance have gone so far as to suggest that he and his battleship-oriented staff, trained at the Naval War College to refight the Battle of Jutland, did just that, allowing the Japanese to escape exactly as Admiral Jellicoe allowed the Germans to slip by him in 1916.[58]

Whatever the reasons and whatever the outcome, it is hard to deny that Spruance made a mistake. As his biographer Thomas Buell suggests, he chose to risk his carriers rather than the forces off Saipan. This was a poor choice, since the loss of the carriers would ultimately have been far more disastrous for the Marianas operation than the loss of some transports.[59]

● ●

Spruance might have acted differently had he known how much the situation on Saipan had changed in the Americans' favor since he had conferred with Turner and Smith on the morning of the sixteenth. The 27th U.S. Infantry Division, Holland Smith's corps reserve, had landed on the sixteenth and seventeenth—minus one regiment which came ashore on the twentieth. On the night of the seventeenth, two

companies of the 2d Marine Division repulsed a Japanese counterattack spearheaded by over forty tanks.[60]

During the next two days, the marines and army troopers to the
south fought their way across the island, capturing the airfield and
penetrating Nafutan Point, the southern finger of the island. The
gap between the 2d and 4th Marine Divisions was closed at the
same time. By June 20, as Mitscher's aviators were delivering their
twilight attack against Ozawa's carriers, Holland Smith's forces on
Saipan had consolidated their gains. They were now moving into
position for a new advance to the north against the enemy's main
line of defense, which stretched across the center of the island from
east to west.

The two marine divisions were attacking toward the north, the
2d Marine Division on the left and the 4th on the right—or east
side—of the island, while elements of the 27th Division moved into
the Nafutan peninsula to the south, where a pocket of Japanese was
still holding out. On June 22 the marines launched their assault;
they were joined the next day by most of the 27th Division, which
Holland Smith withdrew from Nafutan and placed in the center of
the line between the two marine divisions. The 27th's line of advance
led through some of the toughest terrain on the island: a valley
flanked on both sides by high, fortified hills, sheer cliffs, and mountains, while the 2d Marine Division had the even rougher task of
fighting its way up Saipan's highest mountain, Mount Topatchau.
Such obstacles made little impression on the 2d Marine Division's
bellicose commander, Major General Thomas E. Watson, who was
once heard shouting over the field telephone in the midst of battle:
" 'There's not a goddam thing up on that hill but some Japs with
machine guns and mortars. Now get the hell up there and get
them!' " [61]

On the twenty-third of June the two marine divisions jumped off
for another attack, supported by eighteen batteries of artillery and
gunfire from Turner's ships. The 27th Division should have joined
in that attack but one of its regiments got lost on the way to the
front, became entangled with another regiment, and got the whole
division off to a late start. As the marines advanced on the right
and left, the 27th Division bogged down, unable to make headway
against the deadly fire from well-concealed Japanese mortars and
machine guns hidden in the hillside caves flanking the valley, which
the troops soon named Death Valley. After two days of fighting,

the American line of advance was bent back into a U-shape, with the 27th Division at the center of the U. The bend in the line was over 1,500 yards deep, and the flanks of the marine divisions were dangerously exposed.[62]

Meanwhile, the units of the 27th Division still on Nafutan Peninsula had made virtually no progress against the Japanese stragglers holding out there. The army's official history notes that the attack of infantry companies was frequently uncoordinated: "Units repeatedly withdrew from advanced positions to their previous night's bivouac, and repeatedly yielded ground they had gained."[63]

Worried and exasperated by these developments, Holland Smith made what was to become one of the most hotly debated decisions of the war. After consulting with Admiral Turner and Admiral Spruance, he relieved the 27th Division's commander, Major General Ralph Smith, replacing him with Major General Sanderford Jarman, who had been slated to be the commander of the Saipan garrison. Five other army generals had been relieved of division commands in the Pacific for unsatisfactory performance. In most cases, the unfortunate generals had given their superiors far less justification than had Ralph Smith. Yet this case was different: Holland Smith—a marine general—had relieved an army general.

It was a bitter moment for Holland Smith. He had been one of the Marine Corps' leading pioneers in amphibious warfare, had crusaded for better landing craft, and from 1939 until 1943 he had been in charge of amphibious training on the east coast, where both army and marine divisions had learned their amphibious skills in training centers and exercises devised by him. Saipan, however, had been his first chance to exercise independent command of a large amphibious assault. He was under no illusions about the probable consequences of his action. " 'I know I'm sticking my neck out—the National Guard will be down my throat,' " he told a war correspondent; " 'I don't care what they do to me. I'll be 63 years old next April and I'll retire anytime after that.' "[64]

The shock waves were felt all the way back to Washington. Soldiers of the 27th Division interpreted General Ralph Smith's relief as a reflection on their own combat performance—as indeed it was. Nothing is more infuriating to men who have fought a hard exhausting battle under adverse conditions, seen friends killed or wounded, and seen others make almost superhuman efforts, than to be told that some general in the rear thinks they ought to try harder. After the war members of the 27th Division, most notably the division's historian, the talented writer Edmund G. Love, hotly contested the judgment that the division had failed to measure up.[65]

Yet not only the 27th Division was involved. Army officers viewed General Ralph Smith's relief as an affront to their service and a reflection on their methods of leadership. They had long questioned the ability of marine officers to command large formations like divisions and corps, pointing out that the marines had never had such large units before World War II. Marine officers were inexperienced, they said, in the necessary command and staff work. So it was absurd to employ army divisions as part of marine-commanded amphibious corps. The army was especially concerned since future island campaigns might involve as many as five divisions.[66]

However much the army's complaints may have applied to marine officers in general, they applied not all to Holland Smith and his V Amphibious Corps staff, which had been planning and training troops for amphibious warfare since 1940. Smith himself had served on the staff of army General Hunter Liggott's I Corps in World War I. Afterward he had been on the staff of the Third Army and a member of the Army-Navy Planning Committee of the Joint Board.[67]

In a way, it was ironic that the army should feel called upon to justify the performance of the 27th Division, since it was in no way a typical army division. It was a National Guard unit, one of the few guard divisions which had escaped thorough reorganization by the War Department before being sent overseas. Almost all its regimental and battalion commanders, and most of the division staff, were New York National Guard officers and were, on the average, ten years older than their opposite numbers in the Marine Corps. A few of these National Guard officers were superb. Many were incompetent. During one landing exercise in the United States, many officers had left their men bivouacked on the beach and spent the night in a hotel, rejoining the troops in the morning. One officer served on the division staff with many of his former employees who, although they sometimes outranked him, continued to look to him for leadership. An army officer who had observed Ralph Smith and the 27th Division later remarked that Smith would have been an outstanding division commander—of any other division.[68]

As interpreted by contemporary newsmen in the U.S. favorable to the army, the Saipan controversy was caused by the refusal of an army general to recklessly sacrifice lives to a speedy advance in the manner of the Marine Corps. As portrayed by newsmen favorable to Holland Smith, the controversy was caused by the army's efforts to excuse or deny the marginal, almost craven, performance of the 27th Division.

Time has not been favorable to either version. Army and Marine Corps officers both favored speed and aggressiveness in offensive operations, or at least said that they did. This is unsurprising since both groups had been trained in the same tactics and with the same field manuals. Often they had attended the same schools and training courses.[69] Nor, in the final analysis, can the 27th Division's slow, methodical performance at Makin, Eniwetok, and Saipan be shown to be more conservative of lives than the speedier marine conquest of adjacent real estate. On Saipan the 27th Division actually had a slightly higher percentage of casualties than the 2d Marine Division while fighting on similar terrain; on Makin, the 27th Division's casualties had been extremely high in proportion to the number of Japanese engaged.[70] On the other hand, there is no reason to believe that individual soldiers or officers of the 27th Division were less brave and determined than the marines. One of the 27th's regimental commanders won the Medal of Honor on Saipan, and many other members of the unit distinguished themselves as well.[71]

Yet the division simply did not measure up as a coordinated fighting team. That General Ralph Smith's relief did little to improve its performance is true, but irrelevant. Removal of a unit commander was an accepted method of attempting to remedy a unit's deficiencies. It is hard to resist the conclusion that Holland Smith's greatest sin was that he happened to be from a different service than Ralph Smith.

While navy, army and marine officers sent blistering memos to each other, the fighting on Saipan continued. By the end of June the 27th Division had at last fought its way through Death Valley and linked up with the 2d Marine Division on its left. As the advance north continued and the island narrowed, the 2d Marine Division was pulled into reserve, leaving the 27th Division to move up the west coast of the island and the Fourth Marine Division up the east coast and the center. By July 5, when this change was completed, the principal towns and airfields were all in American hands and the Japanese had been forced back into the narrow northern tip of the island.

From there the defenders launched the greatest banzai attack of the war. Early on the morning of July 7, 3,000 screaming Japanese soldiers and sailors—some armed only with grenades or with long poles fixed with bayonets, poured through a gap in the American lines which the 27th Division's 105th Infantry Regiment had allowed to develop near the coast. The First and Second Battalions of the 105th were practically wiped out by the Japanese onslaught, which carried on to marine artillery batteries further down the coast. "When they hit us there were so many of them we couldn't shoot fast enough," recalled Technical Sergeant Frederick Stiltz of the First Battalion, 105th Infantry. "'We were shooting them at 15 or 20 yards. [Our perimenter] was about 50 yards deep and 100 yards across. Artillery was breaking them up but some of the artillery fell short and hit among us. We must have killed 300 or 400 Japs; they were piled around us.'" [72] Remnants of the two battalions of the 105th, now surrounded by Japanese, set up a hasty perimeter around the coastal village of Tanapang. The marine artillerymen, taken by surprise, snatched up carbines and pistols to fight it out with the Japanese.

The marines were soon relieved by army troops. But a regiment of the 27th, sent to relieve the two trapped battalions at Tanapang, halted for the night only a few hundred yards short of the village because their commander was concerned about Japanese to his rear. The trapped battalions were finally evacuated by destroyers and amphtracs.[73] Holland Smith, infuriated and disgusted by the 27th Division's latest failure, ordered the entire unit into reserve, vowing that he would never use it again. For their part, army generals swore that they would never again serve under Smith. Amid these mutual recriminations the battle for Saipan ended on July 9, 1944, with over 14,000 Americans killed or wounded and about 30,000 Japanese dead.

Yet the end of the battle did not complete the cycle of mass deaths on Saipan. Thousands of civilians, mostly women and children, who had fled to the northern tip of the island, chose to join the soldiers in death. They hurled themselves onto the jagged cliffs along the coastal wall of the island, waded into the surf to drown, or blew themselves up with grenades. Interpreters and captured Japanese, using loud speakers, pleaded with the Japanese to surrender. Some did; but almost two thirds of the 12,000 noncombatants chose suicide. The commander of a patrol craft said that "'the progress of his boat was slow and tedious because of the hundreds of corpses floating in the water.'" [74] A navy lieutenant saw the corpse of a nude woman who drowned while giving birth. "'The baby's head had entered this world but that was all of him.'" [75]

A Japanese sniper who had been exchanging shots with a platoon of marines spotted a Japanese couple with four children out on the rocks, unable to bring themselves to make the fatal leap. "'The

Jap sniper took aim. He drilled the man from behind, dropping him off the rocks into the sea. The second bullet hit the woman. She dragged herself about thirty feet along the rocks, then she floated out in a pool of blood. The sniper would have shot the children, but a Japanese woman ran across and carried them out of range. The sniper walked defiantly out of his cave and crumpled under a hundred American bullets.' '' [76]

With the fall of Saipan, the days of the neighboring Japanese stronghold on Tinian were numbered. Tinian was much smaller than Saipan; but it was valued for its excellent airfields and because, at only three and one-half miles' distance, it was close enough to Saipan to give plenty of trouble. For weeks Tinian had been battered by American planes and warships, supplemented by a formidable concentration of artillery on nearby Saipan. Tinian had few beaches suitable for landing craft. The best beaches were all located around the main settlement of Tinian Town, where the Japanese had their strongest defenses. Those beaches also lay beyond the range of American artillery on Saipan.

The only alternative was to use the beaches designated "White," on the north end of the island just across from Saipan. Both Holland Smith and Rear Admiral Harry W. Hill, who would command the invasion forces, favored these beaches. They were lightly defended and well within range of Saipan-based artillery. Yet the White beaches were tiny—so narrow that only four to eight amphtracs could land abreast (as compared to the ninety-six in each wave at Saipan). [77] Hill and Smith proposed to land two divisions reinforced by tanks, artillery and supplies on these beaches.

Admiral Turner firmly vetoed Hill's proposal and told him to get to work planning for a landing near Tinian Town. Hill reluctantly complied, but he ordered part of his staff to keep working on the White beaches plan.[78] Meanwhile, reconnaissance of both the White and Tinian Town beaches revealed that the latter were protected by moored mines and by artillery on the reverse slope of the cliffs above the shore. Heavy surf and strong winds prevailed during most hours of the day. The White beaches, on the other hand, had few natural or man-made obstacles.[79] Hill and Smith tried once again to change Admiral Turner's mind, but he remained obstinate. In a characteristic exchange, the admiral told General Smith that " 'you are not going to land on the White beaches; I won't land you there.' " " 'Oh yes you will,' " replied the general. " 'You'll land me any goddamned place I tell you to.' " Turner was adamant: " 'I'm telling you now it can't be done. It's absolutely impossible.' " " 'How do you know its impossible?' " asked Smith. " 'You haven't studied the beaches thoroughly. You're just so goddamned scared that some of your boats will get hurt. . . .' " [80]

Neither this exchange nor the more subtle efforts of Admiral Hill served to convince Turner, so Hill reluctantly took the matter to Admiral Spruance. Spruance liked the White beaches idea, but he was reluctant to overrule Turner, his expert on amphibious warfare. A conference with Turner and his subordinate commanders was arranged aboard the flagship. All spoke in favor of the White beaches. Spruance turned to Turner. The latter calmly announced that he favored the White beaches also.[81]

Two weeks later, on July 24, over 15,000 Marines and sailors were put ashore on the narrow White beaches, one company at a time, with little opposition. An entire regiment landed in less than three hours. On the other end of the island, opposite Tinian Town, marines in transports along with bombarding warships staged a full-dress phony landing to distract Japanese attention. The invaders achieved complete surprise; within eight days they controlled the entire island.[82]

Three days before the attack on Tinian, other marine and army troops were fighting their way ashore on Guam, the first bit of former United States territory to be retaken from the Japanese. The main American objective on Guam was Apra harbor with its anchorage and airfields. The invading forces landed on beaches five miles apart to the north and south of Apra. On the northern beaches, just southeast of the principal town of Agana, the Third Marine Division faced tough going against Japanese defenders who occupied the high ground all around the beachhead. A Japanese counterattack was beaten off the next morning. After that the marines, well supported by artillery and naval gunfire, gradually cleared the cliffs and hills.

Five days after the landing, on July 26, the Japanese delivered a carefully planned counterattack against the Third Marine Division. Small groups of Japanese infiltrated the overextended American lines, while others hurled themselves in bloody frontal attacks against the marine positions. One battalion of the 9th Marine regiment absorbed seven such frontal attacks and suffered 50 percent casualties—but the battalion held. In the rear, cooks, clerks, truck drivers, and even hospital patients repulsed the infiltrating Japanese.[83]

To the south, where the 1st Provisional Marine Brigade, reinforced by the army's 77th Division, had come ashore against stiff opposition, the Japanese launched a similar attack. They ran headfirst into the corps and division artillery. "Pack howitzers were dragged to within thirty-five yards of the infantry front lines to fire point-blank at the onrushing enemy. 'Arms and legs,' reported one observer, 'flew like snow.' " [84]

The Japanese lost about 3,500 men and up to 95 percent of their officers in the two attacks. Some hard fighting still remained, but on July 26 the defenders had been broken. In the south the first Marine Brigade drove down the Orote peninsula, which formed the southern arm of Apra's harbor. They held the airfields while the 77th Division pushed east and north from the beachhead to join up with the 3d Marine Division. Both divisions then swept north, entering Agana on the thirty-first of July.

In comparison to what had happened on Saipan, army–marine relations on Guam were almost a mutual admiration society. The 77th was an untested division, but it had been exceptionally well trained and had an aggressive, intelligent commander in the person of Major General Andrew D. Bruce. In the fighting on Guam, the 77th did more than hold their end up.

The 77th and the 3d Marine Division reached the northern end of the island on August 8. Two days later the entire place was declared "secure." For the tired soldiers and marines, the conquest of Guam held an interest lacking in other central Pacific battles for the Japanese had apparently used the island as their main liquor supply dump. "Nowhere else did troops on our side ever come on such prodigious stores as were captured there: Scotch and American whiskies, and Japanese imitations thereof, sake galore and beer in quantities. . . . Before the occupation was far along, men who would have given their all for a snort of jungle juice . . . were becoming choosy as to brands and accepting no substitutes." [85]

With the recapture of Guam the Marianas campaign drew to a close. Already engineers were busy expanding and improving the island airfields which, in a few months, would bring the new B-29s, with their cargos of fiery death, within range of Japan's poorly defended cities.

NOTES

1. Richard M. Leighton and Robert W. Coakley, *The United States Army in World War II; The War Department: Global Logistics and Strategy 1940–1943* (Washington, D.C.: Office of the Chief of Military History; 1955), p. 165.

2. Coakley and Leighton, *Global Logistics and Strategy 1943–1945*, pp. 392–94; Matloff, *Strategic Planning 1943–44*, pp. 397–400.

3. Brigadier General Harry Van Wyk quoted in James, *Years of MacArthur*, p. 353.

4. Coakley and Leighton, *Global Logistics and Strategy 1943–1945*, pp. 456–62, 469–70, 551–62.

5. Major General Hugh J. Casey, *Engineers of the Southwest Pacific 1941–1945*, Vol. 8, *Critique* (Washington, D.C.: GPO, 1950), pp. 371–72.

6. Coakley and Leighton, *Global Logistics and Strategy 1943–1945*, p. 494.

7. Casey, *Engineers of the Southwest Pacific*, pp. 371–72.

8. Rear Admiral Worrall R. Carter, USN, *Beans, Bullets, and Black Oil* (Washington, D.C.: Department of the Navy, 1953), pp. 90–103, 105–7, 138–41; Morison, *Aleutians, Gilberts, and Marshalls*, pp. 105–7.

9. Carter, *Beans, Bullets, and Black Oil*, pp. 139–40; Morison, *Aleutians, Gilberts, and Marshalls*, pp. 107–8.

10. Morison, *Aleutians, Gilberts, and Marshalls*, p. 107.

11. Coakley and Leighton, *Global Logistics and Strategy 1943–1945*, pp. 417–31, 435–52 and passim.

12. Craven and Cate, *The Pacific: Guadalcanal to Saipan* pp. 271–73; Coakley and Leighton, *Global Logistics and Strategy 1943–1945*, pp. 442–43.

13. Isely and Crowl, *U.S. Marines and Amphibious Warfare* p. 312.

14. Dyer, *Amphibians Came to Conquer*, p. 853.

15. Harry W. Hill interview, p. 571; Buell, *The Quiet Warrior*, p. 255.

16. Morison, *New Guinea and the Marianas*, pp. 163–69; Carl W. Hoffman, *Saipan: The Beginning of the End* (Washington, D.C.: Historical Division Headquarters, U.S. Marine Corps, 1950), pp. 11–13.

17. Hoffmann, *Saipan*, p. 29; Isely and Crowl, *U.S. Marines and Amphibious Warfare*, pp. 317–18, 337–38; Cooper, "Holland M. Smith" pp. 300–1; Erskine interview pp. 187–88, 335–36.

18. Philip A. Crowl, *Campaign in the Marianas* (Washington, D.C.: Office of the Chief of Military History, 1960), pp. 85–86.

19. Hoffmann, *Saipan*, pp. 36–37.

20. Ibid., p. 41; Crowl and Isely, *U.S. Marines and Amphibious Warfare*, pp. 331–32.

21. Hoffmann, *Saipan*, pp. 49–50; Morison, *New Guinea and the Marianas*, pp. 190–91.

22. Hoffmann, *Saipan*, pp. 56–57.

23. Crowl, *Campaign in the Marianas*, pp. 95–96.

24. Blair, *Silent Victory*, p. 624.

25. Morison, *New Guinea and the Marianas*, p. 241.

26. Buell, *The Quiet Warrior*, pp. 262–63.

27. Morison, *New Guinea and the Marianas*, pp. 242–43.

28. Ibid, p. 242; Buell, *The Quiet Warrior*, p. 263.

29. Buell, *The Quiet Warrior,* p. 262.

30. "The A-GO Operation, 1944," Japanese Monograph No. 60, p. 18.

31. Morison, *New Guinea and the Marianas,* p. 235.

32. Okumiya and Hirokoshi, *Zero,* pp. 236–38.

33. Ibid., pp. 216–19; "The A-GO Operation, 1944," pp. 28–33; Dull, *Imperial Japanese Navy,* pp. 315–16.

34. John Toland interview no. 2 with Captain Toshikazu Ohmae.

35. Morison, *New Guinea and the Marianas,* pp. 214–15, 232.

36. Ibid., p. 221.

37. Dull, *Imperial Japanese Navy,* pp. 317–19; Okumiya and Hirokoshi, *Zero,* pp. 232–33.

38. Morison, *New Guinea and the Marianas,* pp. 247–48, 250–54; Buell, *The Quiet Warrior,* pp. 268–74.

39. William T. Y'Blood, *Red Sun Setting: The Battle of the Philippine Sea* (Annapolis: Naval Institute, 1980), pp. 86–87.

40. Ibid., p. 90.

41. Arleigh Burke, oral history interview no. 4, pp. 315–16, U.S. Naval Historical Center.

42. Ibid.; Malcolm Muir, "Misuse of the Fast Battleship in World War II," *U.S. Naval Institute Proceedings,* February 1979, pp. 59–61.

43. Morison, *New Guinea and the Marianas,* pp. 264–65.

44. Buell, *The Quiet Warrior,* pp. 279–80.

45. Y'Blood, *Red Sun Setting,* pp. 95–99.

46. Barrett Tillman, "Coaching the Fighters," *U.S. Naval Institute Proceedings,* January 1980, pp. 41–43.

47. Morison, *New Guinea and the Marianas,* p. 274; Arleigh Burke oral history interview no. 4, pp. 320–21.

48. Reynolds, *The Fast Carriers,* p. 196.

49. Ibid; Morison, *New Guinea and the Marianas,* pp. 290–92; Arleigh Burke oral history interview no. 4, pp. 373–74.

50. Y'Blood, *Red Sun Setting,* p. 151.

51. Dull, *Imperial Japanese Navy,* p. 321.

52. Reynolds, *The Fast Carriers,* pp. 197–98.

53. Ibid., p. 199; Morison, *New Guinea and the Marianas,* p. 299.

54. Reynolds, *The Fast Carriers,* p. 201.

55. Morison, *New Guinea and the Marianas,* p. 302.

56. Arleigh Burke oral history interview no. 4, p. 326.

57. Morison, *New Guinea and the Marianas,* pp. 315–16; Potter, *Nimitz,* pp. 302–5. When Ozawa's six surviving carriers reached port, they had only thirty-five operational aircraft among them.

58. Reynolds, *The Fast Carriers,* pp. 165–66, 209–10; Weigley, *The American Way of War,* pp. 293–98. The fullest discussion may be found in Y'Blood, *Red Sun Setting,* pp. 204–11.

59. Buell, *The Quiet Warrior,* pp. 270–72, 277–78.

60. Hoffmann, *Saipan,* pp. 86–90.

61. Norman V. Cooper, "The Military Career of Lieutenant General Holland M. Smith," Ph.D. diss., University of Alabama, 1974, p. 311.

62. Crowl, *Campaign in the Marianas,* pp. 179–190.

63. Ibid., p. 161.

64. Cooper, "Holland M. Smith," p. 340.

65. Edmund G. Love, "The 27th's Battle for Saipan," *Infantry Journal* 59 (September 1946), pp. 8–17; Edmund G. Love, "Smith versus Smith," *Infantry Journal* 63 (November 1948), pp. 3–13.

66. Potter, *Nimitz,* pp. 284–85; Cooper, "Holland M. Smith," pp. 81–84.

67. Cooper, "Holland M. Smith," pp. 81–85 and passim.

68. Cooper, "Holland M. Smith", pp. 220–23; Robert Sherrod, "An Answer and Rebuttal to Smith vs. Smith: The Saipan Controversy," *Infantry Journal* 64(Janurary 1949), p. 25; "Reminiscences of Major General Wood B. Kyle," pp. 102–3, Marine Corps Oral History Collection.

69. Isely and Crowl, *U.S. Marines and Amphibious Warfare,* p. 339.

70. Ibid., p. 340; Crowl and Love, *Seizure of the Gilberts and Marshalls,* pp. 126–29; Cooper, "Holland M. Smith," pp. 231–32.

71. Crowl, *Campaign in the Marianas,* p. 192; Buell, *The Quiet Warrior,* p. 283.

72. Robert Sherrod, *On to Westward* (New York: Duell, Sloan and Pearce, 1945), p. 138.

73. Hoffman, *Saipan,* pp. 221–27; Crowl, *Campaign in the Marianas,* pp. 255–62.

74. Hoffman, *Saipan,* p. 245.

75. Toland, *The Rising Sun,* p. 517.

76. Sherrod, *On to Westward,* p. 146.

77. Morison, *New Guinea and the Marianas,* pp. 355–56.

78. Harry W. Hill interview, pp. 524–29.

79. Ibid.; Buell, *The Quiet Warrior,* pp. 293–94.

80. Cooper, "Holland M. Smith," pp. 365–66.

81. Buell, *The Quiet Warrior,* p. 294; Harry W. Hill interview, p. 534.

82. Carl W. Hoffmann, *The Seizure of Tinian* (Washington, D.C.: Historical Division, U.S. Marine Corps, 1951), pp. 64–70, 112–46; Crowl, *Campaign in the Marianas,* pp. 288–98, 301–3.

83. Crowl, *Campaign in the Marianas,* pp. 364–65; Hough, *The Island War,* pp. 273–74.

84. Crowl, *Campaign in the Marianas,* p. 365.

85. Hough, *The Island War,* p. 260.

FIFTEEN

"A Hell of a Beating"

Across the endless reaches of the Pacific, the United States confronted Japan almost unaided—and unhindered—by her European allies. Australia contributed her small navy and air force, and her not inconsiderable army, but with the collapse of ABDACOM, the overall direction of the Pacific War was firmly vested in Washington.

In Asia the situation was quite different. The fate of the great colonial empires of Britain, France, and the Netherlands waited upon the outcome of the war. The British were determined to hold India against the Japanese and to reclaim the rest of their Asian empire, lost in the first weeks of the war. The French and Dutch, although unable to participate in any important way in the war against Japan, watched nervously from the wings, constantly reminding the Allies of their rights, claims, and demands.

Above all there was China, a country which had fascinated generations of American adventurers, missionaries, journalists, and traders. Although it was the Japanese threat to Southeast Asia which immediately precipitated the final crisis leading to Pearl Harbor, most Americans believed with some justification that U.S. unwillingness to acquiesce in the Japanese conquest of China was the root cause of the war.[1]

In the next four years of war, the United States would spend millions of dollars, tie down some of its best technicians, engineers, and aviators, and exhaust the efforts of some of its most impressive public men in a vain effort to make China a major contributor to the war against Japan. Yet China remained, as it had been for many years, torn by warlordism and civil war, a country whose appalling weight of social and economic problems prevented any real effort to fight the war to a decisive end—even as the necessities of that endless war sapped all efforts to deal with those problems.

At the time of Pearl Harbor, China was already receiving weapons and equipment from the U.S. under Lend-Lease, and an American military mission had been established at Chiang Kai-shek's wartime capital, Chungking. There was also an "American Volunteer Group," composed of American aviators and technicians released from the army and navy for service in China. The first squadrons of the American Volunteer Group were just completing their training under the command of the redoubtable Colonel Claire Lee Chennault (he who had so vigorously disputed the claims of the bomber enthusiasts at the Air Corps Tactical School in the mid-thirties) when Japan attacked Pearl Harbor.[2]

Chennault's pilots flew Curtis P-40Bs, obsolescent fighters without adequate radios, gunsights, bomb racks, or auxiliary fuel tanks, but their leader knew how to get the most out of both planes and men. The AVG flyers were endlessly drilled in Chennault's system of aerial combat. Hit-and-run attacks by fast-diving pairs of P-40s enabled the Americans to minimize the superior maneuverability of their Japanese opponents and take advantage of their own fighters' superior speed, strength, and firepower.[3]

Flung into the battle for Burma early in the war, the "Flying Tigers," as newsmen soon labeled the AVG because of the large sharks' teeth painted on their planes' noses, achieved remarkable success against heavy odds. Their exploits made front-page news and Chennault, once an obscure, retired army captain, became one of the best-known American aviators in the world.

That the Flying Tigers soon became virtual folk heroes in the United States was nevertheless due less to Chennault's military achievements than to the enduring romanticism with which the American public viewed China. Generations of Christian missionaries, recently reinforced by writers like Pearl S. Buck, Hollywood, and a well-organized China lobby in the United States had accustomed Americans to think of the Chinese as " 'those millions,' " who, in the words of President Roosevelt, had " 'for four and a half years . . . withstood bombs and starvation and have whipped the invaders

time and again in spite of superior Japanese equipment and arms.' " [4]
Journalists vied with each other in describing the heroic leadership
of the generalissimo and the stoic determination of the Chinese
peasants.[5]

The reality of the war in China was far different. The Chinese
army had not fought a serious battle with the Japanese since 1938.
In the western sense it was really not an army at all, but a coalition
of warlord bands scattered over twelve "war areas" which roughly
corresponded to groupings of the old provinces of Imperial China.
Each local warlord functioned as war area commander; in this capacity
he exercised both civil and military control. Many of the warlord
armies were ill-equipped and poorly trained. They seldom fought
the Japanese, serving mainly to buttress the power of the war area
commander instead. The core of divisions directly under the control
of the generalissimo were better trained and equipped. But even
they were undermanned and lacked artillery; in most cases they were
commanded by officers chosen more for their loyalty to the generalissimo than for their military prowess.[6]

" 'The general idea in the United States that China has fought
Japan to a standstill and has had many glorious victories is a delu-
sion,' " wrote a member of the American military mission to China.
" 'Japan has generally been able to push forward any place she wanted
to. She has stopped mainly because of the fact that a certain number
of troops can safely hold only a certain number of miles of front.
. . . The will to fight an aggressive action does not yet exist in the
Chinese Army.' " [7]

Corrupt, demoralized, inefficient, and oppressive, Chiang's Kuomintang government was uninterested in "aggressive action." It was
interested in surviving the war against Japan with its armies intact,
ready to deal with the generalissimo's rivals among the warlords
and his far more dangerous enemies, the Chinese Communist forces
of Mao Tse-tung. A handful of Americans on the scene, like Ambassador Clarence Gauss, a dour New Englander with few illusions, attempted to enlighten Washington about the actual state of things,
but had no discernable impact.[8]

News of the entry of the United States into the war was greeted
with jubilation at Chiang's headquarters. "Kuomintang officials went
about congratulating each other as if a great victory had been won.
Crowds rejoiced in the streets of Chungking." [9] Like Churchill,
Chiang saw at once that American participation in the war would
ultimately seal the doom of Japan. The generalissimo lost no time
in advising his new British and American allies as to what ought

to be done. All the enemies of Japan should immediately conclude a joint military pact, agree upon a comprehensive plan for action against Japan, and establish a joint military council in Chungking under the leadership of the United States to coordinate their operations.[10]

That Chungking should become a center for determining the strategy and direction of the war with Japan was never a serious possibility. While Chiang was making his proposals, the Americans and British were reaffirming their Europe-first strategy at the ARCADIA conference, as well as frantically searching for means of shoring up the defense of Southeast Asia. China was of distinctly secondary interest for the moment.

As a sop for Chiang's prestige, the generalissimo was asked by the British and Americans to assume the position of Supreme Commander, China Theater, represented as a kind of parallel to the ABDA command of General Wavell. The China theater would include, besides China itself, such parts of Indochina and Siam as might become accessible to troops of the Associated Powers.[11] In effect Chiang was simply receiving a more grandiose label for what he was already doing, plus the right to command the handful of British and American troops in his theater.[12] The inclusion of Siam and Indochina in his area of responsibility was purely for prestige purposes. There was no possibility that Allied forces would be operating there in the near future. Yet the placing of these countries in the generalissimo's nominal sphere of operations was to cause endless trouble between the British, French, and Americans later in the war.

One country which might well have been included in Chiang's theater was Burma. Burma, with its port of Rangoon, was China's last remaining land link with the outside world. Along the so-called "Burma Road"—700 miles of primitive dirt highway connecting Chungking with Burma through the jungles and mountains of south China—flowed the lend-lease supplies and other outside aid which kept China in the war. An American lend-lease program, which had been approved in the summer of 1941, called for the shipment of military supplies sufficient to equip thirty Chinese divisions and a small air force. By the end of the year, a huge backlog of this material had accumulated in Burma. Some 79,000 tons of Chinese goods were in storage at Rangoon awaiting shipment; another 30,000 tons were at Lashio, the terminus of Burma's primitive railroad.[13]

As the danger of Japanese invasion loomed ever more threateningly, the Chinese and Americans became ever more concerned about the disposition and safety of these supplies. British commanders in

Burma were anxious to utilize a portion of this valuable equipment
for the defense of that country. The Chinese were aware of British
interest in the lend-lease materials and therefore all the more anxious
to be involved in Burma's defense.

Yet Burma was a British colony and the British adamantly objected
to putting any part of their territory under Chinese control. When
War Department planners proposed to include northeast Burma in
Chiang's theater, the British representative in the Combined Chiefs'
meeting quickly struck it out.[14] Nor were the British particularly
anxious to have Chinese help in defending Burma. Early in December, when Chiang proposed to send two Chinese armies to operate
in Burma, General Wavell, then commander in chief, India, accepted
only a small proportion of the troops offered. Wavell's ostensible
reasons were that it would be too difficult to arrange a separate
line of communications and a separate front for the Chinese. But
he had political motives as well for turning down Chiang's offer:
the British general believed that " 'it would be more desirable to
defend a part of the British Empire with Imperial troops than Chinese.' " He was also concerned about Chinese political ambitions
in Burma, fearing that the Chinese, once established in north Burma,
might be hard to dislodge.[15]

Wavell might have been more friendly to the Chinese had he
foreseen the imminent Japanese attack on Burma. But in the first
weeks of the war, the commander in chief, like many other British
and American strategists, believed that the Japanese were already
overextended and would not soon be able to spare troops for Burma.
The error in these calculations became abundantly clear on January
20, when two Japanese divisions rolled into southern Burma from
Siam, driving the Indian, British, and Burmese troops before them.

● ●

In proposing to Chiang Kai-shek that he assume command of the
China theater, the Americans and British had suggested that he establish a joint planning staff consisting of military representatives of
the British, American, Chinese, and Dutch governments. Shortly
thereafter, Stimson and Marshall decided to send a senior U.S. Army
officer to China to represent the United States on that joint staff
and to take charge of all American military and Lend-Lease activities
in China. A few days later, the Chinese government also requested
that President Roosevelt nominate a high-ranking American officer
to serve as chief of the generalissimo's joint staff.[16]

Secretary of War Stimson initially favored Lieutenant General Hugh A. Drum for this assignment. The senior general in the American army, Drum had been Pershing's chief of staff in World War I. He had been a close rival of Marshall's for the position of chief of staff in 1939 and he believed that President Roosevelt had promised him the premier field command in the event of war. Summoned to Washington on New Year's day, 1942, he quickly impressed Stimson and Marshall as more concerned with insuring that China would be a theater suitable to his great talents than with furthering the war effort.[17] That finished Drum.

General Marshall then suggested Lieutenant General Joseph W. Stilwell, a brilliant troop commander whom Marshall had selected to command the first American overseas operations in Europe. Stilwell, who had had extensive experience of China and spoke fluent Chinese, was not particularly anxious to go; but he was the natural choice for the job and, after meeting with Stimson and Marshall, he agreed to " 'go where I'm sent.' "[18]

Stilwell left Washington in early February to take up his new command in China. His instructions were " 'to increase the effectiveness of United States assistance to the Chinese government' " and to " 'assist in improving the combat efficiency of the Chinese Army.' " In addition to serving as chief of the generalissimo's joint Allied staff, Stilwell was assigned a number of other duties which supplemented and often conflicted with this function. He commanded all American forces in China, Burma, and India; he was the president's personal military representative to the generalissimo, and he controlled and supervised the disposition of American Lend-Lease aid.[19] Finally, now that the Japanese were pushing into southern Burma and the British had decided they wanted Chinese help after all, it was expected in Washington that Stilwell would probably be offered command of the Chinese troops sent to Burma.

The confusion about Stilwell's mission was a reflection of the larger American confusion about China and the role it ought to play in the war. Watching the Japanese swallow up one island after another in the Pacific and push their defensive perimeter ever further south and west during the first months of the war, many Americans agreed with the *Christian Science Monitor* that "China is the best base, both geographically and politically, for any serious offensive against Japan."[20] Secretary of War Stimson was thinking along the same lines when he told General Drum, in one of their ill-fated interviews, that China might become "a main theater of operations."[21]

Other Americans, especially air-power enthusiasts, saw China as an ideal base. From airfields in China, American planes could harrass Japanese armies, destroy Japanese shipping, sever her communications, and, with the big B-17s and even larger bombers soon to come, carry the war to the cities of Japan itself. Still other Americans were excited by China's almost limitless manpower. China's armies might be relatively ineffective now—but trained, equipped, and perhaps commanded by experienced American officers, they would be a force to be reckoned with.

Above all, American leaders were determined to treat China as a great power and an equal partner with the British and the Russians in the war against the Axis. Impressed by the suffering and sacrifices China had already sustained, they feared that she might soon collapse if not given substantial help. " 'If China goes under,' " worried Roosevelt, " 'how many divisions of [Japanese] troops do you think will be freed—to do what? Take care of Australia? Take India?' " [22] All of these ideas had their spokesmen in Chungking and Washington, and their continued vitality was to provide a large element of tension as well as confusion to Stilwell's mission.

By the time Stilwell landed in Chungking early in March, the elaborate house of cards which the Combined Chiefs of Staff had erected for Southeast Asia at the ARCADIA Conference was already crumbling. Singapore had fallen; the Japanese had occupied most of the Dutch East Indies; and the ABDA command had been dissolved.

In Burma, British, Indian, and Burmese troops briefly halted the Japanese on the Bilin River, then withdrew west toward the Sittang, a wide, swift-flowing river spanned by a single railway bridge which had been planked over for foot and motor traffic. As the retreating imperial forces slowly wound their way toward the bridge, Japanese detachments attacked their flanks and shelled the bridgehead. The British brigadier commanding the bridge area, believing that Japanese capture of the bridge was imminent, had it blown up on the night of February 23, stranding the greater part of the 17th Indian Division on the far side.[23]

Fifty miles west of the Sittang, panic and near chaos reigned in Rangoon. Shopkeepers, clerks, and minor civilian functionaries fled the city. Burma had been a British colony less than seventy years and the proud, warlike Burmese had never been exactly enchanted with British rule. They had even less liking for the Indian functionnaries, shopkeepers and technicians who followed in the imperial wake. The British had made some important concessions to Burmese demands for self-rule—but they were too little and too late to satisfy local political leaders. It was an open secret that these leaders were in contact with the Japanese; when the invasion came, some of them helped to form a "Burma Independence Army" to fight as auxiliaries to the Japanese. The Burma Independence Army was hardly a formidable force, and most of the population was apathetic rather than actively hostile; but the lack of support from the local inhabitants was enough to deprive the British of reliable intelligence, threaten their communications, and generally make life even more unpleasant for British and Indian troopers.[24]

Rangoon fell to the Japanese on March 8. The colonial government hastily moved north to the summer capital of Maymyo. Even before these disasters, the British had changed their minds about the use of Chinese troops in the defense of Burma: they now asked for all that could be spared. Three divisions of the Chinese 6th Army and elements of the 5th were moving into north Burma by the end of February.

Arriving in Chungking, Stilwell learned that Chiang did indeed intend to place him in command of the Chinese armies in Burma but the generalissimo had his own ideas about how those armies should be used. Suspicious of, and angry with the British, he had no wish to throw away his best divisions while the British escaped to India. He warned Stilwell to be cautious and to maintain a defense in depth.[25] Stilwell, who wanted to strike swiftly at the Japanese, chafed under these restrictions and finally succeeded in getting one Chinese division moved south into line with the British.

The British and Chinese now held a line across lower Burma stretching through the towns of Prome (held by the British) and Toungoo (held by the Chinese 200th Division). During late March the 200th Division conducted a stout defense of Toungoo, but Stilwell found he could not really control the other Chinese formations nominally under his command. Their leaders freely disregarded his orders, and the generalissimo insisted on sending detailed instructions to his division commanders, thus bypassing Stilwell. The American general's efforts to bring more troops to the support of the 200th Division proved fruitless: the Allies were soon obliged to abandon the Prome-Toungoo line.[26]

Disgusted, Stilwell flew to Chungking to confront the generalissimo with the demand that he either relieve him or give him real authority and freedom of action in Burma.[27] On April 1, Stilwell met with Chiang "and threw the raw meat on the floor." Chiang promised to go in person to Burma to "make it very plain to the boys that I am the boss." [28] He also reluctantly agreed to Stilwell's plan for a counterattack against the Japanese advancing toward the town of Pyinmana once the Allies had established a new line of defense.

Before the attack could be launched however, the British line on the Irrawady River to the east collapsed under renewed Japanese attacks, exposing the Chinese right flank. Stilwell sent the Chinese 38th Division to aid the British. In a three-day battle around the town of Yenangyuang, the 38th Division, together with a British armored brigade, held the Japanese long enough for the 1st Burma Division and the 17th Indian Division to escape north toward India.[29] By this time, however, the Japanese had also struck at the opposite end of the line, the part held by the Chinese 6th Army.

The outflanked 6th Army began a disorderly retreat toward Lashio, a key juncture on the Burma road. Racing north, the Japanese seized the town, thus cutting off the Chinese escape route via the Burma road. Stilwell attempted to organize an orderly withdrawal, but discipline had by now all but collapsed and Chinese commanders were unable or unwilling to follow his orders. The retreat soon became a disorderly flight.

Stilwell himself was obliged to lead his staff on a rugged overland march through 140 miles of jungle-covered mountains to India. Thanks to his resourceful leadership, Stilwell's party reached India without losing a man. But the Burma campaign had ended in utter defeat for the Allies. " 'I claim we got a hell of a beating,' " Stilwell told reporters soon after his arrival in India. " 'We got run out of Burma and it's humiliating as hell. I think we ought to find out what caused it, go back, and retake it.' "[30]

The debacle in Burma left all parties involved with a feeling of bitterness and betrayal. The Chinese blamed Stilwell for brow-beating and cajoling them into a campaign which they had all along known to be beyond their capabilities. Stilwell had his own list of reasons for defeat. These included hostile population, lack of air support, inferior equipment, inadequate transport, " 'stupid, gutless command,' " Japanese infiltration, " 'interference by CKS [Chiang Kai Shek], British mess on railroads, British defeatist attitude, vulnerable tactical situation.' "[31]

Stilwell was incensed over Chiang's interference more than anything else. Most other American observers would have emphasized "British defeatist attitude" as the prime cause of the debacle. Americans were convinced that the British defense of Burma had been halfhearted or incompetent or both. In the final weeks of the Burma campaign, correspondent Claire Booth Luce had talked with the British commander in Burma, Sir Harold Alexander, and come away convinced that " 'Sir Childe Harold Alexander has small intention of holding the dark tower he has come to if it proves too painful.' " [32]

Contempt for British military performance in Malaya and Burma reinforced the traditional American suspicion of British Imperialism. Brigadier General William Gruber, Stilwell's representative in New Delhi, wrote to General Marshall that the British were "only half-hearted in their efforts to defend Burma" because that country was not essential to the defense of India and "a strong China was not in accordance with British policy." [33]

Actually, the British attitude toward China was more sympathetic than Americans imagined. Few Britons in positions of responsibility expected to return to the good old days of Western exploitation and special privilege in China, but the British were nevertheless far from accepting the American view of China as an area of pivotal importance and a future world power.[34] Nor did they share either the exaggerated American fears of an imminent Chinese collapse or the extravagant hopes for striking a major blow at Japan from China.

If Americans were mistrustful and impatient with British policies toward China, they were even more exasperated with British actions in India. The collapse of Burma and a destructive Japanese carrier raid into the Indian Ocean in April * convinced many that India was next on the Japanese agenda of conquests. The defeat in Burma, which cut China off from all overland communications with her allies, had made India almost as important militarily to the United States as to Britain. Arms and supplies for China now had to be flown from India across the so-called "Hump" of the 15,000 foot Himalaya Mountains in rickety, overworked transport planes. The pilots flew on oxygen, dodging bad weather and Japanese fighters to bring their cargoes to Kunming in southern China.

To replace the old Burma road, the Allies had already begun planning a new overland route into China, from the town of Ledo in the Indian province of Assam, across the mountains and jungles of Burma, and then into southern China. Since the road was to be built from India, Americans believed that the British should assume major responsibility for the project, but the latter were unenthusiastic. They were not eager to build roads to the eastern frontier of their empire, which might later be utilized by unfriendly forces. Besides,

* See Chapter 7.

argued the British, the road was an engineering nightmare, a nearly impossible job, a waste of resources.[35] Ultimately it was the Americans, and Stilwell above all, who would push the road through to completion; but in 1942 Stilwell advocated a more straightforward method of supplying China: retake Burma.

Stilwell's plan, elements of which he had worked out in the final days of the Burmese debacle, called for an offensive into eastern Burma. Thirty Chinese divisions, specially reorganized and trained by American advisers in Yunnan province, known as "Y" force would undertake this thrust.[36] The western prong of the offensive would comprise three Chinese divisions then undergoing training at Ramgarh, a former prisoner-of-war camp in the province of Bihar in eastern India. Chinese units which had retreated from Burma to India comprised the nucleus of the new divisions. Others were flown in from China. Stilwell reasoned that it was easier to bring the Chinese troops to American lend-lease supplies and weapons in India than it was to bring these supplies over the Hump to China.

Transports flying food, fuel, and weapons for China returned to India packed with Chinese recruits for Ramgarh. The troops arrived without uniforms or weapons, in poor physical shape, often sick, sometimes literally naked. "For Americans," wrote correspondent Theodore White, "Ramgarh was Siberia, only one thin cut above jungle duty. . . . For the Chinese soldiers, Ramgarh was a wonderland. They were fed for the first time as much food and meat as they could stuff into their hungry bodies. . . . They practised on ranges with live shells and real bullets. . . . hospitals doctored them. . . . Between 1942 and 1944, four Chinese divisions were created and equipped here of an effectiveness never before known in Chinese history."[37] The key to Ramgarh's success was the fact that Stilwell's chief of staff, Brigadier General Haydon L. Boatner, commanded the training center and retained exclusive control of all finances, supplies, and even rations. Boatner's Chinese subordinates were obliged to "play ball" and cooperate in the American program to rehabilitate their army. Several emerged as capable commanders.[38] American and Chinese officers messed together and soon established a close if not always harmonious relationship.[39]

The airlift to China, the Ledo road, Stilwell's Burma offensive— all these depended on the continued security and viability of India. Unfortunately, as Stilwell's political advisor, John Paton Davies, quickly discovered, "both the Indians and the Indian Government were facing in the wrong direction for the war we were in."[40] Supplies for China and for the construction of the Ledo road had to travel more than a thousand miles by rail from the port of Karachi, in present-day Pakistan, via the overburdened, sometimes primitive Indian railway system, to Calcutta and Assam. Furthermore, British defenses in India were designed for a defense of the western approaches—the fabled Khyber Pass and the Northwest Frontier area—rather than the east. In the first two years of the war, more than a quarter of a million Indian troops had been sent west to the Middle East and Europe. Indian soldiers were trained and equipped for warfare in the deserts of North Africa, not the mountains and jungles of southeast Asia.[41]

Politically, both British and Indians looked westward toward Europe and the Middle East rather than toward China and Japan. At the time of Pearl Harbor, Indian nationalist leaders were far more suspicious of the government of India than of the Japanese. The viceroy of India, Lord Linlithgow, an amiable dinosaur, had alienated leaders of the Indian National Congress, the predominant nationalist organization, at the outset of the war by taking India into the conflict without even consulting any of her political leaders. The viceroy was legally correct in his action, but he acted in so arbitrary and high-handed a way that many Indian politicians were offended. National Congress leaders who held government positions at the provincial level resigned in October 1939. " 'We want to combat fascism,' " wrote Jawaharlal Nehru, " 'but we will not have war imposed on us by outside authority. We will not sacrifice to preserve old injustices or to maintain an order based on them.' "[42]

In March 1942 Churchill, under intense pressure from the United States, Chiang Kai-shek and members of his own government, announced the formation of a special mission to India to be headed by Sir Stafford Cripps. Cripps brought with him a pledge from the British government that India would be granted dominion status at the conclusion of the war. An elected constitutional convention representing British India and the princely states would draw up a basic constitution for the new dominion. Any state or province would be free to opt out of the proposed union if it so chose. Meanwhile, the viceroy's Executive Council would be enlarged; representatives of the principal political parties would be invited to join.

Congress leaders were unhappy with Cripps's "post-dated check," as Gandhi called the British offer. Its provision for the voluntary nonaccession of states and provinces seemed an open invitation to disunion and an encouragement to the followers of Muhammed Ali

Jinnah's Muslim League which favored a separate state—"Pakistan"—for Indian Muslims. Perhaps more important, the arrangements for interim collaboration between the viceroy and Indian political leaders seemed to leave all effective power, especially in regard to defense, in the viceroy's hands.

Both the government of India and the Congress regarded control of defense as a crucial issue because neither thought that the other would put up much of a fight against the Japanese. By April the Indians had learned of the British disasters in Burma and Malaya. Indian refugees fleeing Burma brought with them tales of British colonial officials forsaking their posts, panicking at the first sign of the enemy, and abandoning their Indian subordinates and retainers to their fate. "After Malaya and Burma," Nehru told an American diplomat, "there is a widespread belief in India that [the British have] no serious intention or capacity to resist a Japanese invasion." [43]

With the failure of the Cripps mission, the Indian National Congress and the government of India were obviously headed for a showdown. Mohandas K. Gandhi, for over forty years the charismatic leader of the opposition to British rule and an inspirational figure to millions, called for an immediate British withdrawal from India and nonviolent resistance to the Japanese should they attack. Most Americans were convinced that the British had done their best to give India a fair deal and blamed the Indian National Congress for the failure of the Cripps mission. They were also angered and surprised at Gandhi's public pronouncements, which seemed to suggest that India would have no trouble with Japan if the British would only clear out. [44] Gandhi also looked askance at the large number of U.S. Army Air Forces support and service troops who were rapidly arriving in India. American troops, he told Stilwell's political advisor, merely reinforced British domination of India. [45]

At the urging of Nehru and of Congress supporters in the U.S., Gandhi soon modified his stand. In his newspaper and in a letter to President Roosevelt, he promised that if India gained independence she would still permit the Allies to keep troops in India for defense against the Japanese and to support China. [46]

On July 14 the Working Committee of the National Congress adopted a resolution proposed by Gandhi. It called on the British to "quit India" immediately, but promised that Allied forces could remain. Chiang Kai-shek begged Roosevelt to intervene with the British to head off the imminent showdown; but the president merely passed Chiang's message to Churchill with the request that the prime minister suggest an appropriate reply.[57] Churchill shot back a message assuring Washington that "the Congress party in no way represents India . . . and can neither defend India nor raise a revolt." [48]

One week later the Congress party adopted the "Quit India" resolution. Early the next morning, August 9, all the top Congress leaders were summarily arrested. News of the arrests brought the revolt which Churchill had assured Roosevelt was impossible. All over India masses of Congress sympathizers, leaderless but angry and determined, rose in rebellion. Huge demonstrations, riots, and thousands of acts of sabotage occurred all over India. By the end of August over 1,000 people had been killed and 100,000 Congress sympathizers were in prison. Close to sixty battalions of the British and the Indian Army were tied down to maintain internal security.[49] An official government tally recorded more than 600 bomb explosions and nearly 500 other acts of sabotage, 200 police stations and 750 other government buildings destroyed or severely damaged between August 1942 and December 1943.[50]

The "Quit India" uprising marked the real beginning of the end of British rule in India. British officials there now recognized that the National Congress was not simply a handful of agitators and politicians, but a broadly based mass movement which—even with its leaders in jail—could count on the loyalty and active support of millions. From this point on, knowledgeable colonial officials recognized that their days in India were numbered.[51] Yet this was far from obvious to American observers in Washington and Delhi. Americans believed that by riding out the revolt the British had demonstrated that they could preserve "order" in India. (With 100,000 opponents in jail!) So long as the Japanese made no further move toward India, British control was secure.

How much India could contribute to the Allied war effort was another matter. William Phillips, a personal friend of President Roosevelt who succeeded Louis Johnson as the president's personal representative in India, advised that "unless the present atmosphere is changed for the better, we Americans will have to bear the burden of the coming campaign in this part of the world." [52]

From Phillips and Stilwell to the lowest-ranking GIs, who quipped that CBI (China-Burma-India) stood for "Confused Bastards in India," Americans who served in India were almost invariably convinced that neither the British nor the Indians cared much about fighting the Japanese. However unfair or exaggerated this belief, it was to bedevil Allied relations in that theater till the end of the war.[53]

Whatever the problems at his rear headquarters in New Delhi, Stilwell's main headache remained the war in China. In many respects he was superbly equipped for his difficult mission. An outstanding soldier with long years of experience in China, he spoke fluent Chinese and had a thorough understanding of the strengths and weaknesses of the Chinese army; he also had a genuine respect for the much-abused Chinese soldier. Yet Stilwell was also irascible, impatient, forgetful, and a sloppy administrator—with little interest in or patience for staff work, planning, or logistics.[54] A staff officer recalled that "there was a lack of coordination amongst his various headquarters which caused confusion and conflict. The general had a tendency to render important decisions to subordinate commanders on field trips without letting his staff in on the secret. . . . He detested all paper work."[55] Despite his disdain for staff work, Stilwell insisted on absolute loyalty from his staff and subordinate commanders and regarded as little more than turncoats officers who accepted or requested assignments out of his theater. He devised a special mock decoration, the "Order of the Rat" to be hung from a double cross for those officers " 'who ran out on us.' "[56] (Many of the "rats" did extremely well in other theaters, rising to the rank of general.[57])

Stilwell came away from the Burmese defeat more than ever convinced of the need for reform and reorganization of the Chinese army. This entailed "the merging of the hundreds of scattered, ill-equipped, ill-supported divisions . . . a rigid purge of inefficient high commanders and complete unity of command."[58] But Chiang Kai-shek was uninterested in this sort of reform: while it might improve the combat effectiveness of the army, it would also destroy the generalissimo's power base among those same "inefficient high commanders" whom Stilwell proposed to get rid of. What Chiang wanted from the United States was not reform but hardware: bombers, tanks, big guns, fighters, transports. Even though many of the military gadgets Chiang desired were impractical in China—few bridges in China could support the tanks he favored, for example—they would nevertheless add to his prestige without threatening his power base.

Stilwell, whose function was to approve American military aid for China, frequently opposed Chiang's requests for impressive but useless equipment or weapons. This alone would have been sufficient to put the generalissimo and his American chief of staff on a collision course, but the situation was further complicated by the fact that Chiang was not fully informed of all aspects of Stilwell's mission and responsibilities; he tended to think of him as simply a kind of American adviser whose function was to obtain for him the Lend-Lease material that he needed. The generalissimo's ignorance was assiduously buttressed by his representative in Washington, Foreign Minister T. V. Soong, who routinely edited messages from Roosevelt to Chiang, omitting portions that might displease the generalissimo.

Even Soong, however, could not keep all unpleasant news from Chiang. In June 1942 British reverses in North Africa led the Combined Chiefs of Staff to divert all aircraft en route to China to the Middle East. They did the same with the heavy bombers of General Lewis Brereton's Tenth Air Force, which had operated in support of China. The decision was made without consulting Chiang; it was left for Stilwell to convey the unwelcome news to him at Chungking.

The Generalissimo was furious, demanding to know " 'whether the Allies consider this theater necessary and will support it.' "[59] Three days later Stilwell was summoned to Chiang's headquarters and handed a virtual ultimatum for transmittal to Washington. The message contained " 'three minimum requirements for the maintenance of the China War Theater.' " These requirements, soon known simply as the Three Demands, were: three American divisions for the campaign to retake Burma; 500 planes for the air force in the China theater; and monthly deliveries of 5,000 tons of supplies over the Hump. All this to be accomplished by August.[60]

The Three Demands caused vigorous hand-wringing in Washington. Lauchlin Currie, lend-lease administrator for China, was hurriedly despatched to Chungking "to lay calm hands on the fevered brow of the Generalissimo." [61] After reciting his woes for the American visitor, Chiang told Currie that he was prepared to undertake a campaign in Burma along the lines Stilwell proposed, but only with the full participation of British troops, British naval forces sufficient to control the Bay of Bengal, and Allied air superiority over Burma. Chiang probably felt safe in making this commitment, since the British were unlikely to be able or willing to meet his conditions in the foreseeable future. The generalissimo agreed to drop his demands for American troops; in return Washington agreed to beef up air strength in the China theater and build toward a total of 100 transport planes for the Hump.[62]

Having agreed to a major offensive in Burma, Chiang subsequently devoted his energy and ingenuity to getting out of it. In this he was greatly assisted by the British. The latter at first were taken aback that the Americans should presume to propose operations to them in what was, after all, a former British colony. The Commander in Chief, India, General Sir Archibald Wavell, did not even communicate directly with Stilwell until September of 1942. By then letters and messages from Field Marshall Sir John Dill, the British Chiefs of Staff representative in Washington, had made it clear to London that American responsibilities in China and planned operations in the Pacific made the U.S. vitally interested in the reconquest of Burma.[63]

After that, Wavell and Stilwell cooperated closely on plans for the reconquest of Burma. Wavell even added American representatives to his planning staff; but by late October he was convinced that a full-scale offensive in Burma—such as Stilwell was urging for the spring and summer of 1943—would be impossible because of supply problems, the state of his troops, the monsoon weather, and unavailability of adequate naval and air support.[64] Wavell preferred instead a limited offensive which got underway toward the end of 1942; an advance down the west coast of Burma to capture the town of Akyab with its important airfields.

In Washington, the War Department and JCS took much the same view. With the struggle for Guadalcanal and the campaign in North Africa both at a critical stage, no additional resources could be spared to support even a limited campaign in Burma. In late November the War Department informed Stilwell that because of the pressing needs of other theaters, nothing could be spared for China beyond material and men which had been allotted months before.[65] "Peanut [The G-M.] and I are on a raft with one sandwich between us," wrote Stilwell to his wife; "and the rescue ship is steaming in the other direction." [66] A few weeks later, with more encouraging news coming in from the Solomons and North Africa, the JCS relented somewhat and arranged to send Stilwell additional drafts of American service troops as engineer, signal, and medical support, along with more than 60,000 tons of road-building equipment to enable the Americans to assume major responsibility for building the Ledo road. But this came too late to halt the British and Chinese drift away from the plan for a major campaign.

Seizing on British unwillingness to undertake large-scale land and sea operations in Burma, Chiang informed Washington that he was unable to go ahead with the proposed campaign in north Burma.

The Japanese were sure to fight tenaciously; the British could not control the seas; the Indian army forces Wavell proposed to use were inadequate, and China could ill afford to risk another disastrous defeat in Burma.[67]

As an alternative Chiang suggested a stepped-up air offensive based in China. Such an air offensive from China was a project close to the heart of General Chennault. He had been loudly and persistently compaigning for it for months. In October he had taken advantage of former Republican presidential candidate Wendell Wilkie's goodwill visit to press his views on Washington. Wilkie, who departed from Chungking convinced that China was a " 'warm-hearted, hospitable land filled with friends of America,' " carried with him a letter from Chennault to President Roosevelt outlining the general's plan " 'to accomplish the downfall of Japan . . . within one year.' " For this, he would require only 105 fighters, 30 medium, and 12 heavy bombers. Chennault's planes would first annihilate Japan's air force, then attack her shipping and, finally, " 'destroy the principal industrial centers of Japan.' " [68] To make possible these air operations, Chennault wanted the bulk of the tonnage being flown over the Hump alloted to him; he also desired the establishment of an independent command in China—his own.

In retrospect, Chennault's proposal to "destroy the industrial centers of Japan" with twelve heavy bombers seems almost comical. Yet in 1942 the proposal to switch the main effort in China to air warfare had solid attractions, both for Chiang and for Roosevelt. An air campaign would not risk the defeat of Chinese armies. It would not demand painful and politically dangerous "reforms" of these armies to prepare them for battle: the kinds of reforms Stilwell was always tiresomely pressing. The plan also appealed to President Roosevelt and other Americans looking for a quick, cheap, success against Japan. Stilwell and General Marshall might explain that the Hump air route could not provide the supplies needed for extensive air operations, and that the very airfields Chennault used were vulnerable to Japanese ground attack; but armchair strategists—of which there were a great many in Washington—were uninterested in these details.

Chennault continued his sales campaign. His public relations aide, Captain Joseph Alsop (promptly dubbed "Alslop" by Stilwell), wrote privately to the president's confidential adviser, Harry Hopkins, expounding on the "brilliant and easy opportunities in the air." Marine Corps Lieutenant Colonel James M. McHugh, the naval attaché in

China and an old crony of Chiang, informed navy secretary Knox on a visit to Washington that Stilwell simply did not understand air power and that the generalissimo would not be sorry to see him replaced by General Chennault.[69] McHugh's reports to Knox produced a near explosion from General Marshall, who would have liked to court-martial the colonel; but Roosevelt read McHugh's writing "with much interest." [70]

Despite the president's enthusiasm for concentrating on an air campaign in China, Washington still had plenty of interest in the recapture of Burma. General Marshall and Secretary of War Stimson continued to stand firmly behind Stilwell's projects. The navy was also vitally interested in any actions in China which would help to divert Japanese forces and attention from the Pacific.[71] Navy strategists, and Admiral King in particular, were convinced "the Japanese could not be defeated by the destruction of her [*sic*] fleet alone but that her ultimate defeat must be brought about by operations from the China coast." [72] The recapture of the China coast was therefore seen by the navy as vital to winning the war—a view which King and Nimitz would hold until the very end.

At the Casablanca Conference in January 1943, Marshall and King urged upon the British a campaign to retake Burma during the next winter. They argued that the proposed Burma operation, code-named ANAKIM, was essential to keep China fighting and ease the pressure on American forces in the Pacific. The British agreed that ANAKIM was important—but they were in no hurry about it. Their planners estimated that sufficient forces might be available toward the end of 1944!

King and Marshall were appalled at the British attitude. Never one for diplomatic subtleties, Admiral King called the British idea that nothing could be done before 1944 "fantastic," while Marshall warned that if ANAKIM were delayed, "a situation might arise in the Pacific . . . that would necessitate the United States regretfully withdrawing from commitments in the European theater." [73]

The British were still doubtful; there would not be enough landing craft by 1943, they said. Admiral King assured them that the United States would provide the landing craft from its expanding production. What about crews to man them? asked the British. The Royal Navy had no crews to spare. The landing craft could be shipped from the southwest Pacific along with their crews, King declared, and the U.S. would also provide naval cover if necessary.[74] As it turned out, the British were correct. Landing craft remained in critically short supply throughout 1943. In the face of King's implacable generosity, however, the British could only agree. Plans and preparations for launching ANAKIM in the fall of 1943, at the end of the monsoon season, would proceed; a final decision would be made by the Combined Chiefs in the summer of 1943.

NOTES

1. Herbert Feis, *The China Tangle* (New York: Athenuem Publishers, 1965), p. 3; Charles E. Neu, *The Troubled Encounter*, pp. 183–84.

2. Charles F. Romanus and Riley Sunderland, *Stilwell's Mission to China* (Washington, D.C.: GPO, 1953), pp. 17–20.

3. Claire Lee Chennault, *Way of a Fighter* (New York: G. P. Putnam's Sons, 1949) pp. 111–14; Craven and Cate, *Plans and Early Operations*, p. 490; Pappy Boyington, *Baa, Baa Black Sheep* (New York: Arno Press, 1972) pp. 35–63.

4. Barbara W. Tuchman, *Stilwell and the American Experience in China* (New York: Macmillan Publishing Co., 1971), p. 250.

5. Ibid., p. 251; Warren I. Cohen, *America's Response to China: An Interpretative History of Sino-American Relations* (New York: John Wiley and Sons, 1971), p. 143.

6. Romanus and Sunderland, *Stilwell's Mission to China*, pp. 33–35.

7. Memorandum, Lieutenant Colonel George W. Sliney to Brigadier General John Magruder, 10 December 1941: cited in Romanus and Sunderland, *Stilwell's Mission to China*, pp. 43–44.

8. Tuchman, *Stilwell*, p. 262; E. J. Kahn, *The China Hands: America's Foreign Service Officers and What Befell Them* (New York: Viking Press, 1975), pp. 64–65.

9. Tuchman, *Stilwell*, p. 233.

10. Ibid., p. 234; Romanus and Sunderland, *Stilwell's Mission to China*, pp. 50–51.

11. CNO to U.S. Naval Attaché, Chungking, 3 December 1941, reproduced in Hayes, *Pearl Harbor To Trident*, p. 102.

12. Feis, *China Tangle*, p. 123; Romanus and Sunderland, *Stilwell's Mission to China*, pp. 61–62.

13. Romanus and Sunderland, *Stilwell's Mission to China*, pp. 21–26, 45–46.

14. Hayes, *Pearl Harbor to Trident*, p. 101.

15. Ibid., p. 112; Thorne, *Allies of a Kind*, p. 187; S. Woodburn Kirby, *The War Against Japan*, Vol. 2, *India's Most Dangerous Hour* (London: HMSO, 1953), pp. 16–19.

16. Romanus and Sunderland, *Stilwell's Mission to China*, p. 66.

17. Hayes, *Pearl Harbor to Trident*, p. 103; Pogue, *Marshall: Education of a General*, pp. 344–48.

18. Pogue, *Ordeal and Hope*, pp. 356–60; Romanus and Sunderland, *Stilwell's Mission to China*, pp. 63–70.

19. Theodore H. White, ed., *The Stilwell Papers* (New York: Schocken Books,

1982), p. 19; Romanus and Sunderland, *Stilwell's Mission to China,* pp. 243–47.

20. *Christian Science Monitor,* July 25, 1942.

21. Romanus and Sunderland, *Stilwell's Mission to China,* p. 64.

22. Tuchman, *Stilwell,* p. 238.

23. Kirby, *India's Most Dangerous Hour,* pp. 63–72.

24. Ba Maw, *Breakthrough in Burma* (New Haven: Yale University Press, 1968), pp. 12–44; Thorne, *Allies of a Kind,* pp. 59–60, 205–7.

25. Tuchman, *Stilwell,* p. 266.

26. Romanus and Sunderland, *Stilwell's Mission to China,* pp. 108–9.

27. Ibid., p. 117.

28. White, ed., *The Stilwell Papers,* p. 80–81.

29. Major General Sun Li-jen, the 38th Division Commander, was a graduate of the Virginia Military Institute.

30. White, ed., *The Stilwell Papers,* p. 106.

31. Romanus and Sunderland, *Stilwell's Mission to China,* p. 148.

32. Luce quoted in Tuchman, *Stilwell,* p. 285; see also Thorne, *Allies of a Kind,* pp. 202–9.

33. Memorandum, Gruber to Chief of Staff, Sub.: Situation in the China Theater, 28 July 1942, OPD 381, Record Group 165, National Archives, Washington, D.C.

34. Thorne, *Allies of a Kind,* pp. 179–80, 184–91.

35. Romanus and Sunderland, *Stilwell's Mission to China,* p. 152.

36. Major General Hayden L. Boatner, who headed the Ramgarh training center, questions whether Stilwell actually had a firm plan upon his return from Burma. Boatner points out that Stilwell's original program for Ramgarh was considerably modified to meet practical considerations and objections by the Chinese. Boatner's marginal note on Message, Boatner to Stilwell, 11 October 1942, copy in Boatner Papers, U.S. Army Military History Research Collection. (USAMHRC)

37. White, ed., *The Stillwell Papers,* pp. 137–38.

38. Marginal note by Boatner on Message, Stilwell to Boatner, 4 October 1942, copy in Boatner Papers, USAMHRC.

39. Message, Boatner to DC/S, Re: HQ USAF CBI, New Delhi, 5 February 1943, copy in Boatner Papers, USAMHRC.

40. John Paton Davies, *Dragon by the Tail* (London: Robson Books, 1974), p. 234.

41. Philip Mason, *A Matter of Honour: An Account of the Indian Army, Its Officers and Men* (New York: Penguin Books, 1976), p. 494.

42. Sarvapalli Gopal, *Jawaharlal Nehru: A Biography* Vol. 1, *1889–1947* (Bombay: Oxford University Press, 1976), p. 251.

43. Nehru to Lampton Berry, June 23, 1942, in Jawaharlal Nehru, *A Bunch of Old Letters* (Bombay: Asia Publishers House, 1958), pp. 481–83.

44. Gopal, *Nehru,* p. 289; *Harijan,* May 3, 1942; Hess, *America Encounters India, 1941–1947* (Baltimore: John Hopkins University Press, 1971), pp. 65–66.

45. Davies, *Dragon by the Tail*, p. 238.

46. Hess, *America Encounters India*, p. 69.

47. Roosevelt to Churchill, 29 July 1942, in Francis L. Lowenheim, Harold Langeley, and Manford Jonas, eds., *Roosevelt and Churchill: Their Secret Wartime Correspondence* (New York: E. P. Dutton, 1975), pp. 229–230.

48. Ibid., Churchill to Roosevelt, 31 July 1942, p. 230.

49. Gopal, *Nehru*, p. 300; Hess, *America Encounters India*, p. 88.

50. "Statistics Connected with Congress Disturbances for Period Ending 31 December 1943," in Francis G. Hutchins, *India's Revolution: Gandhi and the Quit India Movement* (Cambridge: Harvard University Press, 1973), pp. 230–31.

51. Hutchins, *India's Revolution*, pp. 272–76.

52. Phillips to Roosevelt, April 19, 1943, *Foreign Relations of the United States, 1943*, Vol. 4, p. 217.

53. Edmond Taylor, *Richer by Asia*, 2d ed. (New York: Time Life Books, 1964), pp. 46–47.

54. Major General Haydon L. Boatner, "Barbara Tuchman's *Stilwell and the American Experience in China*, A Statement Thereon For the Record," pp. 14, 16, 18, 36.

55. Fred Eldridge, *Wrath in Burma* (New York: Doubleday and Company, 1946), p. 166.

56. Tuchman, *Stilwell*, p. 341.

57. Boatner, "Barbara Tuchman's *Stilwell*," p. 20.

58. Stilwell, "Notes for the Generalissimo," 26 May 1942, in Romanus and Sunderland, *Stilwell's Mission to China*, pp. 153–54.

59. Reproduced in Romanus and Sunderland, *Stilwell's Mission to China*, p. 171.

60. Ibid., p. 172.

61. Davies, *Tiger by the Tail*, p. 249.

62. Hayes, *Pearl Harbor to Trident*, pp. 313–14.

63. Michael Howard, *Grand Strategy*, Vol. 4, pp. 39–91.

64. White, ed., *The Stilwell Papers*, pp. 179–80; Thorne, *Allies of a Kind*, p. 225; Howard, *Grand Strategy*, Vol. 4, pp. 83–87.

65. Romanus and Sunderland, *Stilwell's Mission to China*, pp. 244–45.

66. White, ed., *The Stilwell Papers*, p. 171.

67. Hayes, *Pearl Harbor to Trident*, pp. 346–47.

68. Ibid.; Tuchman, *Stilwell*, pp. 336–37.

69. Hayes, *Pearl Harbor to Trident*, pp. 340–41; Tuchman, *Stilwell*, pp. 337–39, 358–59.

70. Tuchman, *Stilwell*, p. 389.

71. Hayes, *Pearl Harbor to Trident*, p. 322.

72. Minutes of King-Nimitz Meeting, 22 February 1943, p. 3, King Papers.

73. Hayes, *Pearl Harbor to Trident*, pp. 402–3.

74. Ibid., p. 406.

SIXTEEN

The Road to Myitkyina

No sooner had the Casablanca Conference adjourned than the ANAKIM plan began to unravel. In Delhi to confer on the project, General Arnold found Wavell's operational plan not so much a plan as "several pages of well-written paragraphs telling why the mission could not be accomplished." [1]

Moving on to Chungking, Arnold received the generalissimo's reluctant assent to the Burma operation; but what Chiang really wanted was an independent army air force for China under General Chennault, a vast increase in supplies flown over the Hump, and five hundred more planes by November. In a letter to President Roosevelt, carried to the U.S. by Arnold, the generalissimo spent one paragraph on the Burma campaign and the remainder on his demands for more air power.[2]

In Washington the generalissimo's demands found a sympathetic audience in the president and his closest adviser, Harry Hopkins. Perhaps a shift of emphasis to air operations might be more rewarding than a slow and costly ground campaign. That view appeared to be confirmed by the outcome of the limited British ground offensive in Burma, launched at the end of 1942.

To boost morale and to show that they were still in the war, the British had mounted an attack into the Arakan, the narrow coastal strip of west Burma. Their goal was to capture Akyab Island, which had airfields that would be valuable for the support of future operations against Rangoon. Holding the island would also strengthen the air defense of Calcutta.[3] The area was lightly held. British plans were to send a reinforced division down the coast, while other troops advanced by short, amphibious hooks and a commando force swung in from the east. However, landing craft were unavailable—and the commandos were needed elsewhere. So the 14th Indian Division, under Major General W. L. Lloyd, was sent down the ninety miles to Akyab, plodding through mud and rice paddies flanked by jungle covered hills.

After a slow start the advance went well—until the 14th reached the towns of Donbaik and Rathedung, only ten miles from Akyab. Here the British and Indian troops became acquainted for the first time with Japanese log and earth bunkers, already unhappily familiar to the Allied troops in Papua, and here they were held up for a month while the Japanese brought in reinforcements.[4]

Then the Japanese took their turn at counterattack, moving right across the jungle ridges which the British had thought impassable, striking at the division's rear and flank, and sending the British reeling back to the north. Now the tired, badly shaken Indian and British troops—many of them inexperienced and incompletely trained—began to crack. Many of "the troops that had been in action for the past weeks," recalled General William Slim, hastily called in to take command, "were fought out and could not be relied on to hold anything . . . [They] were untrained for the jungle and feared it more than they did the enemy."[5] By May the Anglo-Indian troops were back where they had started—exhausted, racked by malaria, with morale at an all-time low.

To this dreary tale there was one hopeful footnote. In late 1942 Wavell had formed a large commando force called the Seventy-seventh Long-Range Penetration Brigade under Brigadier Orde Wingate, a brilliant eccentric and a veteran of irregular warfare in Palestine and Ethiopia. Wingate, with his magnetic personality, ascetic appearance, and far-away expression, was part visionary, part lunatic—but all soldier. His idea was that a relatively small force working behind enemy lines could cause damage out of all proportion to its numbers, confuse and demoralize the enemy, and wreck his communications. The Long-Range Penetration Brigade would work independently, in small groups, keeping in touch by radio and receiving supplies by airdrops.[6]

Wavell had originally planned to employ Wingate's men in coordination with the Chinese offensives in north Burma planned for 1942–1943. Those offensives had long since been cancelled; there seemed little point to sending in a diversionary commando force when there was now nothing to divert the enemy from. Wingate however, argued forcefully for the mission to proceed to forestall any planned Japanese offensive and test the theory of long-range penetration.[7]

In mid-February 1943 Wingate's brigade of about 3,000 men—called "Chindits" after the griffinlike creatures which guard Burmese temples—crossed the river Chindwin and plunged into the jungle.[8] Splitting up into seven columns, the Chindits attacked Japanese outposts and cut the north-south railway in more than seventy places. For three months they eluded the Japanese, covering over 1,500 miles. But the cost was high. Only about two-thirds of the force recrossed the Chindwin in May; many of the survivors were so debilitated they could never be used in combat again. One column of 1,000 men had returned with just 260. Sick and wounded had had to be left behind.

British commanders in India, viewing Wingate's exhausted and disease-ravaged troops, were inclined to write the experiment off as another costly failure. Yet the operation caught the imagination of the world. The Japanese, heretofore regarded as invincible jungle fighters, had been bested at their own game. Wingate's Chindits had demonstrated that British and Gurkha soldiers could also live and fight in the jungle and that, if supplied by air, they could be more mobile than the Japanese.

After the humiliating defeats in Malaya, Burma, and the Arakan, the news of Wingate's raid provided a sorely needed boost to British morale and self-respect. Correspondents proclaimed him "the Clive of Burma." " 'In the welter of inefficiency and lassitude which have characterised our operations on the India front,' " wrote Prime Minister Churchill, " 'this man, his force and his achievements stand out. . . . I consider Wingate should command the Army against Burma. He is a man of genius and audacity.' " With that, the prime minister summoned Wingate to London for a personal conference.[9]

In the end however, the Chindit expedition proved most important not as a morale booster, but because it persuaded the Japanese high command to try something even crazier: a large scale invasion of India across the rugged Assam-Burma frontier to improve the Japanese hold on Burma and stave off further incursions. In the summer of 1943 planning began for an attack across the roadless mountainous frontier, an attack which would lead the Japanese to disaster.[10]

• •

Meanwhile, in Washington the argument over air power in China had swung in favor of Chennault and Chiang. Stilwell and the War

Department pointed out that any air offensive which was strong enough to really hurt the Japanese would result in a Japanese ground offensive to wipe out the airfields supporting it. That was what had happened after Doolittle's Tokyo raid, when Japanese troops had rampaged through eastern China destroying every air base in sight. Nevertheless, the president was determined to go ahead. Backing for Chennault might not produce the great results promised—but it would keep Chiang happy and demonstrate American support of China.[11]

At the president's order Chennault was given command of an independent air force, the Fourteenth, thus freeing him from serving as part of the Tenth Air Force under General Clayton Bissell, an old enemy. Some of Chennault's flyers had come to hate Bissell so much that at one air base a Chinese coolie who knew no English had been hired and carefully taught to shout "PISS ON YOU BISSELL!" at incoming Tenth Air Force planes.[12] Chennault's existing forces were also to be reinforced as quickly as feasible and to be allocated a guaranteed share of the Hump tonnage. Existing airfields were to be upgraded and new ones constructed.

All this still failed to satisfy Chennault, who complained that Stilwell was not giving him an adequate share of the Hump supplies. In April 1943 both Stilwell and Chennault were summoned to Washington for the TRIDENT meeting of the Combined Chiefs, which was to be held in May. Meeting with the president, Chennault was articulate and persuasive, while Stilwell was sullen and uncommunicative. "Vinegar Joe" disliked Roosevelt, disliked blowing his own horn—and probably felt resentful at having to explain the obvious to a rank amateur.[13]

Whatever Stilwell might have said would probably have made little difference, for both Roosevelt and Churchill had by now decided that a full-scale campaign in Burma on the lines of ANAKIM was undesirable. Roosevelt liked Chennault's ideas better, while Churchill and the British chiefs had always believed the jungles of Burma the worst place on earth to fight the Japanese. Churchill favored bypassing Burma altogether and striking into the Dutch East Indies as a step toward retaking Singapore. As for China, the best course was to expand the air route across the Hump to support Chennault's air offensive.[14]

The ANAKIM plan was thus quietly shelved and replaced by a scheme to build up the Hump route as quickly as possible. A much-abbreviated campaign into northern Burma alone was also included in Allied plans; its goal was to open a land route to China and thus shorten the flight across the Hump. Most of the anticipated increase in air tonnage was to go to Chennault, who was given an absolute claim on the first 4,700 tons flown in every month. A portion of what was left over would go to Stilwell to prepare the Chinese army for the campaign in northern Burma. Stilwell compared this arrangement to " 'trying to manure a ten-acre field with sparrow shit.' " [15]

Actually, the situation was even worse than it appeared, for the TRIDENT decisions had been based on the assumption that the Hump air route would be able to carry a greatly increased load. Seven thousand tons a month was the target set for July 1943, and 10,000 for September. To this end the engineers and construction equipment earmarked for the Ledo road were shifted to upgrading and enlarging airfields and transport aircraft was rushed to India. Yet airfield construction soon lagged behind schedule due to heavy rains, difficulties with local labor, and bottlenecks in the movement of supplies north from Calcutta to the air-base sites in remote, undeveloped Assam. By July only 4,300 tons of supplies—not 7,000—got over the Hump; only 6,700 tons arrived in September.[16] Since Chennault had absolute call on the first 4,700 tons over the Hump, little indeed would be left for upgrading the Chinese army—or anything else Stillwell might hope to accomplish.

Over the next few months Chennault's Fourteenth Air Force achieved little. His fighters inflicted heavy losses on their Japanese opponents, but they failed to achieve air superiority and were eventually driven from their advance bases in east China by unremitting Japanese air raids. Fourteenth Air Force bombers claimed to have sunk over 40,000 tons of enemy shipping during the summer of 1943, but the actual total was just a little over 3,000 tons. Many of the additional planes promised for the Fourteenth failed to arrive; those that did added to the supply problem by consuming oceans of fuel. B-24 heavy bombers could not be serviced at all in China: to attack Japanese targets they had to fly across from India carrying their own supplies, then return when these were exhausted.[17]

Meanwhile Churchill and the British chiefs, reviewing the debacle in the Arakan and the general situation in India, and anxious to show the Americans that they were committed to a real effort in East Asia, decided to propose a new Allied command for Southeast Asia.[18] General Wavell had shortly before been appointed viceroy of India; he was replaced as commander in chief, India, by General Sir Claude J. E. Auchinleck. Under the new arrangement Auchinleck would have no responsibility for operations against the Japanese in

Southeast Asia. These would be entrusted to a new supreme Allied commander, who also had a mandate to develop air and land communications with China.

The British preferred to have the new Southeast Asia command set up along the lines of Nimitz's and MacArthur's commands in the Pacific. Thus, the Allied supreme commander would receive his operational direction from the British Chiefs of Staff, while general supervision over grand strategy would be exercised by the Combined Chiefs. The Americans, however, insisted on a command similar to that of General Eisenhower in the Mediterranean whereby the Allied commander answered directly to the Combined Chiefs, and was assisted by a deputy of a different nationality.[19] The Combined Chiefs agreed upon a compromise arrangement at the QUADRANT Conference in Quebec during August 1943. The new commander was placed under the "general jurisdiction of the Combined Chiefs" on matters of strategy but retained the right of direct access to the British Chiefs of Staff. He would have an American deputy but his land, air, and naval commanders would all be British.[20]

Selection of a supreme commander caused even more trouble than defining the command. The British Chiefs of Staff nominated Air Marshall Sir Shulto Douglas. Douglas was heartily disliked by the Americans because of his habit of speaking "in derogatory terms of U.S. units and operations"—a habit which had on at least one occasion, nearly led to a fistfight.[21] Churchill then turned to consideration of a general or an admiral; he finally hit upon the idea of nominating Vice Admiral Lord Louis Mountbatten, an officer highly thought of by all American leaders.

The U.S. Chiefs at Quebec enthusiastically concurred in Mountbatten's appointment as "Supreme Allied Commander, Southeast Asia" (SACSEA). Stilwell was appointed "Deputy Supreme Allied Commander," thus adding another to his chain of confusing and overlapping responsibilities. The British Chiefs were to oversee all matters pertaining to operations, but the Combined Chiefs retained responsibility for strategy and for allocating resources between Chiang's theater and Mountbatten's. Mountbatten's Anglo-American staff included Lieutenant General R. A. Wheeler as his G-4 and administrative troubleshooter and Major General Albert C. Wedemeyer as deputy chief of staff.[22]

Mountbatten was only forty-two years old at the time of his appointment. Tall, handsome, a close relative of the royal family, he had distinguished himself as commander of a destroyer flotilla early in the war. (His exploits provided the inspiration for Noel Coward's popular movie *In Which We Serve.*) Brought to London in late 1941 as chief of Combined Operations and a member of the Chiefs of Staff Committee, he had been the youngest vice admiral in British history.[23]

A man of immense personal charm with a genius for public relations, Mountbatten was considered something of a lightweight by some of the more senior generals and admirals, who resented his swift rise to prominence. His new command was far from being the smoothly running Allied team which Eisenhower would soon command in Great Britain. American and British officers on the SEAC staff bickered endlessly over petty details, churned out endless operational plans which were subsequently cancelled, and cursed the Dalhi weather and "the Wogs." American officers proclaimed that SEAC stood for "Save England's Asiatic Colonies." [24]

Suspicion of British motives was widespread. *Life* Magazine reminded the British that "one thing we are sure we are *not* fighting for is to hold the British Empire together." [25] Stilwell's political adviser, John Paton Davies, summed up the views of many Americans when he wrote that "British policy is naturally directed toward reestablishment of imperial rule over her colonies. Our policy is to cultivate friendly and politically disinterested relations with the peoples of Asia." He warned that "our present military association with the imperialist powers has created suspicion of American motives among peoples of Southeast Asia which, if uncorrected, will impair our relations with these people for years to come." [26] The British for their part complained that the Americans could see "no role for SEAC at all except to cover General Stilwell's supply route." British strategists commented acidly on China's "inexhaustible capacity for absorbing resources without producing any concrete or timely result." [27]

Although Stilwell and Mountbatten publicly professed admiration for each other, their behind-the-scenes relations were poor, sometimes hostile. Stilwell made no secret of his contempt for the British military effort in Asia; his conduct toward his "Limey" colleagues was often tactless and rude. Admiral Mountbatten claimed after the war that he had intervened on Stilwell's behalf when the generalissimo was about to sack him after a quarrel in October 1943; contemporary records show that the SEAC commander welcomed such a move. Indeed, Mountbatten was surprised and disappointed when Chiang relented.[28]

At Cairo, in November 1943, the generalissimo met for the first and only time with Roosevelt, Churchill, and their chiefs of staff.

Publicly, the Allies hailed the meeting as demonstrating China's new status as one of the great powers; privately, Churchill and Roosevelt were exasperated by Chiang's stubborness, his seemingly erratic positions on strategy, and the spectacular incompetence of his Chinese military staff and advisers.[29] Roosevelt told Stilwell he felt " 'fed up with Chiang and his tantrums.' " According to Stilwell's chief of staff, General Frank Dorn, the president even suggested that the Americans in Chungking arrange for the Chinese leader's assasination.[30]

Mountbatten came to Cairo with an ambitious plan to retake Burma and break the blockade of China. The plan included two separate operations, code-named TARZAN and BUCCANEER. TARZAN consisted of an offensive by the American-trained Chinese divisions from India; they were to attack eastward, clearing a path for the Ledo Road and capturing the important communications center of Myitkyina in northern Burma. A much larger Chinese force in Yunnan Province called "Yoke," or "Y Force," was to advance westward into Burma to link up with the American-trained divisions. These operations had already begun when Mountbatten arrived at Cairo. The British part of TARZAN was to be a combined land and airborne offensive into the north-central area of Burma around the towns of Indaw and Katha. In conjunction with TARZAN the British would mount BUCCANEER, an amphibious operation in the Bay of Bengal to capture the Andaman Islands, which would then provide a base for future landings on the Burmese mainland and for air operations in southern Burma and in Siam. How the capture of the Andaman Islands would help retake Burma or break the blockade of China was not very clear, but Chiang had long insisted on some British naval action in the Bay of Bengal. BUCCANNEER was Mountbatten's offering, and assault shipping for the operation had already arrived in India from the Mediterranean.

All of these elaborate projects were soon reduced to little more than reams of paper. Returning to Cairo for a second round of talks after meeting with Stalin at Teheran, Churchill, Roosevelt, and their military advisers promptly scratched BUCCANEER off the list. Its assault shipping was urgently needed for the cross-channel invasion of France—OVERLORD—which the Big Three had scheduled at Teheran for May or June of 1944. Shipping was also needed for a supporting attack on southern France called ANVIL. At Teheran Stalin had promised that the Soviet Union would enter the war against Japan shortly after Germany was defeated. This pledge, Churchill argued, greatly reduced the potential importance of China in bringing about the defeat of Japan.[31]

Some American strategists disputed Churchill's conclusion. But whatever they might think, the Cairo decisions marked a real change in American military policy toward China. Those decisions foreclosed the last opportunity for a major Allied offensive in China and the last possibility that Chinese armies would play much part in bringing about Japan's surrender. A January memorandum by the Army Plans Division on the "Future Military Value of [the] China Theater" acknowledged this new state of affairs, suggesting that henceforth the main effort against Japan would be made through advances in the central and southwest Pacific. China's main contribution would be as a base for Allied air power in support of those campaigns.[32] Navy strategists still called for seizure of a port on the China coast, but it was becoming clear that such an operation would probably come only at the end of a trans-Pacific drive.

Whatever planners in Washington had in mind, Stilwell was determined to proceed with operations to open the way for the Ledo road. He had taken the cancellation of BUCCANEER calmly, never having believed much in its value anyway. But when Mountbatten's headquarters later proposed to cut short the long-projected campaign to retake north Burma and extend the Ledo Road, the American general was furious. Mountbatten's planners now favored an amphibious attack against Sumatra and Malaya in 1944–1945.[33] To sell his new position to the Combined Chiefs, Mountbatten despatched a high-level mission called AXIOM to London and Washington. Getting wind of this, Stilwell sent his own group to Washington, which presented the case for operations in Burma.

Although Stilwell was technically Mountbatten's subordinate, he despatched the counter-AXIOM mission without his superior's knowledge.[34] He then gave an off-the-record press conference in Delhi to present his views. Those views did not remain off the record for long. A few weeks later *The New Republic* reported "some Americans believe the British are subordinating military strategy to the political aim of reconstituting her colonial empire" and that "the quickest way into China is to reopen the Burma road rather go around Thailand." The article closed with a warning about the "frankly imperialistic" group surrounding Prime Minister Churchill.[35]

The British complained bitterly of "the reptilian activities of General Stilwell," while Vinegar Joe denounced the AXIOM mission's " 'fancy charts, false figures and dirty intentions.' "[36] Predictably, Mountbatten's plans appealed to London; Washington—and particularly the Joint Chiefs of Staff—staunchly backed Stilwell.[37] The result might have been the usual stalemate; but now, for the first time, developments on the battlefield, rather than at the conference table, began to exert a dominant influence on the war in Southeast Asia.

At the end of 1943, Stilwell had launched his long-planned campaign to reopen northern Burma. His objective was the town of Myitkyina and its airfield, a vital communications hub for the whole region. South of Myitkyina, the Ledo Road could hook up with existing tracks which led to the old Burma Road into South China; Hump flights could use the shorter, safer, Myitkyina route.

To carry out his mission Stilwell had the three Chinese divisions (the 22nd, 38th and 30th) he had been meticulously training at Ramgarh. The greatest Allied asset was command of the air, an essential requirement for fighting in the trackless jungles and mountains which lay between Stilwell's forces and Myitkyina. The route of advance ran through some of the worst terrain in the world—"a rat hole," in Stilwell's phrase—comprising three valleys, the Hukawng, the Mogaung, and the Irrawaddy. The valleys were an area of thick underbrush, impenetrable clumps of bamboo, and knife-edged elephant grass; and the intervening mountain ranges were worse. In such terrain troops could be resupplied only by air.

The area was held by one of Japan's best divisions, the eighteenth, which had helped conquer Burma and Singapore in 1942. Stilwell's Chinese divisions outnumbered the Japanese and were tolerably well trained and equipped, but their commanders often displayed a lack of zest for combat. Well aware of these Chinese proclivities, Stilwell acted as his own corps commander in the Burma campaign, making his headquarters near the front, threatening, goading, persuading, and even blackmailing his top Chinese officers into action.[38]

● ●

The Joint Chiefs of Staff had been so impressed by Orde Wingate, whom Churchill had brought with him to the Quebec Conference in August 1943, that they not only agreed to provide air support for a second and much larger Chindit raid into central Burma, but also to organize an American commando force to serve with it. That was the origin of the 5307th Provisional Regiment, an all-volunteer unit code-named GALAHAD. It was the first American ground combat unit assigned to the China-Burma-India theater.

The War Department intended that GALAHAD be composed of hardened jungle fighters. There were some of those, veterans of fighting in the southwest Pacific, but there was also a good sprinkling of the bored, the restless, the adventurous, and the "misfits of half a dozen divisions." [39] "We expected picked troops," wrote a medical officer with GALAHAD. "Instead, we found many chronically ill men. Many brave men came, but also numerous psychiatric problems as well as men with chronic disturbances who believed they might get treatment if they could get away from their outfits." [40] Because attacks of malaria in the Pacific "were given little more nursing care or rest than the average common cold at home," many Pacific veterans "volunteered in the hope that they would get hospital care." [41] A strong motivation for some GALAHAD volunteers was the thought that assignment to a dangerous overseas mission ought to bring them home leave. It didn't.

Shipped to India with great speed and secrecy, the 5307th began training under the tutelage of Wingate's Chindits. Stilwell, however, wished to use the unit to spearhead his campaign in Burma. Mountbatten finally agreed, as he told Stilwell's chief of staff, " 'because it seemed to mean more to Joe than the bickering was worth.' " [42] Wingate was less philosophical about the matter. He reportedly told the unit's temporary commander, Colonel Francis G. Brink: " 'Brink, you tell General Stilwell he can take his Americans and stick 'em up his ass.' " thereby impressing the colonel and his staff with his surprising command of colloquial American expressions. [43] Stillwell appointed one of his best officers, Brigadier General Frank Merrill, who had accompanied him on his famous "walk out" from Burma in 1942, to command the unit. Reporter James Shepley of *Time-Life* promptly dubbed the force "Merrill's Marauders." [44]

An even more unorthodox element of Stilwell's command were the Kachin Rangers, warlike tribesmen of north Burma who, unlike their hereditary enemies the Burmese, had sided with the Allies against Japan. Organized and trained by OSS detachment 101, squads of Kachins operated as pathfinders and scouts for the Marauders and other Allied units. [45] " 'Often, we had a Kachin patrol with us and we never, if possible, moved without Kachin guides,' " recalled an officer in the Marauders. " 'The Kachins not only knew the country and the trails but they also knew better than anyone but the Japanese where the Japanese were, and often they knew better than the higher Japanese commands.' " [46]

At the end of October 1943, elements of the Chinese 38th Division entered the Hukawng Valley of Burma. They promptly bogged down and were soon surrounded by the Japanese. Stilwell arrived at 38th Division headquarters and prodded the Chinese into action. Near the village of Yupang Ga, they won their first victory over the Japanese in Southeast Asia. It was not a very big fight, Chinese casualties were high, and most of the enemy escaped—but it convinced the Chinese soldiers that they were a match for the Japanese.[47]

Because the Japanese army in Burma was preparing for a big offensive of its own against the British in Assam, its 18th Division was obliged to go on the defensive, fighting a delaying action against the advance of Stilwell's Chinese forces. Repeatedly Stilwell sent his numerically superior forces on wide swings to envelop the 18th Division, but the slow-moving Chinese could never quite close the trap. One Chinese regiment spent a week in what it called "preparations for attack."[48] In February Stilwell determined to use the GALAHAD force, which had now joined him in Burma, to establish a block right across the Japanese line of withdrawal, trapping them between the Americans and the advancing Chinese.

The 18th Division commander, Lieutenant General Tanaka Shimishi, guessed what was happening. He decided to capitalize on the slowness of the Chinese to throw his entire force against the Marauders, who had established their block at the little settlement of Walawbun. He was confident of destroying the Marauders before the lethargic Chinese units could close up to help.

Dug in along a river, the Nampyek Nha, just east of Walawbun, the Marauders repulsed the Japanese attacks. Tanaka soon found himself in serious trouble. A force of Chinese tanks—the First Provisional Tank Group, commanded by U.S. Army Colonel Rothwell H. Brown—had advanced rapidly from the north, cut between two of Tanaka's regiments and began to fire on his division headquarters. Thoroughly shaken, the Japanese commander decided to give up his attempt to destroy the GALAHAD force. Instead he sought to move his division south to safety.[49] In the confused fighting which followed, the Japanese lost heavily but still made good their escape.

Stilwell had once again failed to trap the 18th Division. But the Japanese had suffered another defeat: they lost over 800 men to the Marauders alone. General Merrill told his tired but exultant commandos: " 'Between us and the Chinese, we forced the Japanese to withdraw farther in the last three days than they have in the last three months of fighting.' "[50]

Encouraged by these results, Stilwell resolved to send the Marauders on another long, enveloping swing to cut off the Japanese retreat to Kamaing, the central position in the Mogaung Valley, while the Chinese forces continued to attack from the front. Two battalions of Merrill's troops pushed their way south through the jungle to Inkangahtawng, about twenty miles above Kamaing, where they set up a block. The Japanese counterattacked so strongly that Merrill, concerned that his battalions might be decimated by the time the slow-moving Chinese came up, decided to pull his battalions out of Inkangahtawng into the surrounding hills.

Now the Japanese tried an envelopment of their own, sending a force north to attack the flank of the main Chinese drive. Learning of this move, Stilwell's headquarters ordered Merrill to take his men to the village of Nhpum Ga and cut the trail which the Japanese flankers would have to follow.[51] For the already tired Marauders, the move to Nhpum Ga meant another exhausting trek through the jungles of north Burma; it also meant that they would have to conduct a static defense instead of the fast-moving, slashing attacks for which they were best suited.

At Nhpum Ga, Merrill placed one battalion on a hilltop near the village and another at Hsamshingyang three miles away to protect the airstrip, which was the Marauders' only means of supply and communication with the outside world. Merrill's men had barely time to dig in at Nhpum Ga when the Japanese came at them in force. There followed one of the toughest fights of the campaign, with the Marauders battling both to hold the village and to keep open the trail from the airstrip. During the first few days the Japanese pounded the Americans mercilessly with artillery and mortar fire. The attacking Japanese cut the trail from Hsamsingyang airstrip and captured the defenders' water hole.

Allied aircraft dropped enough water for the beleaguered Marauders to hold on. Gradually the two battalions narrowed the gap between them on the road between Nhpum Ga and Hsamsingyang, while the Japanese exhausted themselves in fruitless assaults. One night Sergeant Roy Matsumoto, GALAHAD's Nisei interpreter, overheard Japanese conversations indicating that the enemy planned to attack a small salient of the American perimeter. Warned by Matsumoto, the defenders withdrew from their salient and booby-trapped the abandoned foxholes. When the Japanese attacked they were met by a wall of fire from the waiting Americans. They dove into the foxholes for cover, only to set off the booby traps. At the height of the confusion, Matsumoto yelled "Charge!" in Japanese at the top of his lungs, bringing a supporting Japanese platoon to disaster as well.[52] Early in April the Japanese abandoned their fruitless siege of Nhpum Ga and melted away into the jungle.

The GALAHAD survivors had been through two arduous jungle campaigns. Their ranks had been thinned by casualties and disease.

The Army K-ration supplied to the Marauders as a routine diet was designed only for short-term combat situations and did not provide the necessary calories for an active adult.[53] Among Merrill's men the average weight loss was over twenty pounds—and these men were already lean and hardened by arduous marching. According to the usual rules for jungle commando groups, the Marauders should have been relieved. But Stilwell had one more mission for them: the capture of Myitkyina, the great prize and objective of the campaign in northern Burma.[54]

General Merrill had suffered a debilitating heart attack during the siege of Nhpum Ga. The Marauders, now down to somewhat less than half their original strength, were commanded by Lieutenant Colonel Charles N. Hunter. Stilwell's force, however, had been reinforced by two fresh Chinese divisions flown into north Burma; the remaining GALAHAD combat teams were also reinforced by Chinese units. Stilwell's command included as well the five brigades of Wingate's Chindits. They had been inserted deep into central Burma to operate against Japanese lines of communication and prevent attacks on Stilwell's flank. That March, Wingate himself had been killed in a plane crash. The Chindits, who had now been in the jungle for over four months, were in even worse shape than the Marauders.

Stilwell knew the Marauders were near the end of their endurance, but he was planning a bold strike across the mountains to seize Myitkyina airstrip. For that task he would need a force he could count on to obey orders; only GALAHAD was available. So the hungry, tired Marauders, weak with disease, set out on their final mission. They crossed the 6,000-foot Kuman Mountains on an end run to Myitkyina, accompanied by about 4,000 Chinese troops and several hundred Kachin Rangers. Less than three weeks later they emerged at Myitkyina and seized the airfield with little difficulty from the surprised handful of Japanese defenders.

Stilwell was exultant. " 'WILL THIS BURN UP THE LIMEYS,' " he wrote in his diary. Churchill cabled Mountbatten demanding to know how " 'the Americans, by a brilliant feat of arms, have landed us in Myitkyina.' "[55]

Then things began to go wrong. Allied intelligence underestimated the number of Japanese in Myitkyina. The Allied forces at Myitkyina, expecting to receive food, ammunition, and reinforcements on the first planes landing there, found that they carried an antiaircraft battery and aviation engineers instead. The Japanese rushed reinforcements to Myitkyina town; attempts by Chinese units to take the place ended in fiasco. The monsoon rains set in and the attempt to take Myitkyina settled into a long siege, reminiscent of Buna and Gona.

The Marauders, thoroughly "shot," in Stilwell's words, were being evacuated at the rate of seventy-five to a hundred a day. Their commander noted that as one company trudged onto the airstrip, " 'hardly a man could walk normally for fatigue, sores and skin diseases." One platoon suffered so severely from dysentery that the men had cut away the seat of their trousers so as not to be hampered in combat.[56] Many believed the widely repeated reports that Stilwell had promised the unit would immediately be evacuated to rest camps in India upon the successful seizure of the Myitkyina airfield.[57] Instead of being relieved they went directly into the battle for Myitkyina, along with American engineer units pulled off their construction assignments on the Ledo Road and "any other American who could carry a rifle." At one point Stilwell ordered GALAHAD personnel in hospitals—evacuated for fatigue and disease—back to the front.

Stilwell had little choice. He had repeatedly demanded that the British keep the tired Chindits, with their hundreds of sick and wounded, in the field; he was constantly pressuring Chiang for more Chinese units to commit to the campaign. Under these circumstances the American general could hardly afford to place himself in a position where he appeared to be overly sparing of his own troops. "While Americans were in the battle, the expenditure of Chinese troops at Myitkyina could not be challenged. And while he continued to fight at Myitkyina, the need for the British below Mogaung could be demonstrated." [58] Yet Stilwell made things worse than necessary by his inadequate support for the Marauders, both physically and psychologically. Up to the battle for Myitkyina, "no member of GALAHAD had received a combat decoration, no member had received a promotion, a candy bar, a bag of peanuts, an issue of cigarettes, a can of beer, a bottle of whiskey, or a pat on the back by anyone." [59]

Had the Japanese made a determined counterattack at Myitkyina, they might have swept the Chinese-American forces from the airfield. Fortunately, they overestimated the strength of besieging forces. Meanwhile the Chinese, in an unexpected display of skill and determination, had dealt their old antagonist, the 18th Division, a shattering blow, capturing Kamaing and driving the Japanese from the Mogaung Valley. This cut off one source of supply and reinforcement for the defenders at Myitkyina. By the end of May, the Japanese were entirely isolated from the outside world. Yet they fought on throughout the rain-soaked summer, while the Allied lines closed ever tighter around them.

Myitkyina fell on August 3, 1944. The cost was high but the rewards were substantial. A way had been opened for the Ledo Road. Engineers, laborers, technicians, and construction crews, following closely on the heels of the combat troops, were already clearing ground for the highway, gas stations, supply points, and motor shops along the route of the Ledo Road; they were building pipelines to carry aviation gas and motor fuel directly from India to China. Even before the fall of Myitkyina town, the Hump air transports, using the shorter, safer route via the Myitkyina airstrip, had increased the tonnage delivered to China from 13,700 tons in May to 25,000 tons in July.[60]

While Japanese, Chinese, and Americans stubbornly fought it out in the sodden mud of Myitkyina, the decisive battle of the war for Southeast Asia was reaching its bloody climax hundreds of miles to the southwest around the towns of Imphal and Kohima on the Indo-Burmese border. Here the Japanese had launched their long-planned offensive, aimed at cutting off the British army in Burma and severing the line of communications through Assam which supported both Stilwell's army and the China air supply route over the Hump.

At first all went well for the Japanese. They followed their usual tactic of infiltrating around and behind British units, cutting them off from support, and forcing them to retreat. Yet the British now controlled the air and were able to shift men and supplies rapidly to threatened areas. At one point an entire division, complete with artillery and mules, was airlifted in eleven days.

Although badly outnumbered and cut off by the Japanese, the British and Indian troops at Kohima held out stubbornly until, just as the garrison appeared about to fall, a relief column spearheaded by the First Punjabi Regiment broke through with reinforcements and supplies. Further south, much larger British and Japanese forces were battling it out on the Imphal plain. The struggle developed into a bloody contest of attrition which the Japanese later compared to Verdun in the First World War.[61] The British, abundantly supplied by air, gradually wrested the initiative from the Japanese, who had long since outrun their supply lines. By early July the emaciated survivors of the Japanese Fifteenth Army were withdrawing back across the Chindwin River into Burma.

Less than half of the Japanese soldiers who had set out for Imphal and Kohima returned. The Japanese military hold on Burma had been dealt a shattering blow and the way lay open for a British counterstrike to drive them from the country.

NOTES

1. Arnold, *Global Mission,* p. 407.

2. Arnold, *Global Mission,* pp. 421–27; Romanus and Sunderland, *Stilwell's Mission to China,* pp. 275–77.

3. Kirby, *India's Most Dangerous Hour,* pp. 249–50; Field Marshal The Viscount Slim, *Defeat Into Victory* (New York: David McKay Co., 1961) p. 123.

4. Kirby, *India's Most Dangerous Hour,* pp. 263–69; Slim, *Defeat Into Victory,* pp. 124–25.

5. Slim, *Defeat Into Victory,* p. 132.

6. Christopher Sykes, *Orde Wingate* (Cleveland: World Publishing, 1959), p. 368.

7. Ibid., pp. 384–86; Kirby, *India's Most Dangerous Hour,* pp. 309–10.

8. Actually "Chinthe." The name "Chindits" was the result of Wingate's misunderstanding his interpreter. Sykes, *Orde Wingate,* pp. 442–43.

9. Sykes, *Orde Wingate,* p. 445.

10. Kirby, *India's Most Dangerous Hour,* pp. 328–29.

11. Letter, Roosevelt to Marshall, March 8, 1943; Memorandum, Marshall for President, Sub.: Your Note to Me of March 8. Both in CSA 381 China (3–16–43), RC 165; Tuchman, *Stilwell,* pp. 360–61.

12. Edward J. Harris, "War Wasn't All Hell," *E-CBI Roundup,* March 1977.

13. Tuchman, *Stilwell.*

14. Romanus and Sunderland, *Stilwell's Mission to China,* pp. 330–31; Howard, *Grand Strategy* IV, pp. 399–405.

15. Theodore H. White, *In Search of History* (New York: Warner Books, 1978), p. 142.

16. Coakley and Leighton, *Global Logistics and Strategy 1943–1945,* p. 504; Craven and Cate, *Guadalcanal to Saipan,* pp. 444–45.

17. Romanus and Sunderland, *Stilwell's Mission to China,* pp. 336–39, 345–47.

18. John J. Sbrega, "Anglo-American Relations and the Selection of Mountbatten as Supreme Allied Commander Southeast Asia," *Military Affairs,* 46 (October 1982), p. 139.

19. John Ehrman, *Grand Strategy,* Vol. 5 (London: HMSO, 1956), pp. 139–45.

20. Sbrega, "Selection of Mountbatten," p. 144.

21. Ibid., p. 142.

22. Thorne, *Allies of a Kind,* pp. 297–300.

23. John Terraine, *The Life and Times of Lord Mountbatten* (London: Hutchinson, 1968), pp. 60–101 and passim.

24. Thorne, *Allies of a Kind,* pp. 337–39.

25. "Open Letter To The People of England," *Life,* October 12, 1942.

26. "American Psy war in CBI Theater," enclosure by Davies to Lieutenant Colonel P. Pennoyer, 24 April 1944, ABC 040.9 OWI, ABC Files, RG 165.

27. J. C. Sterndale-Bennet to Major General L. C. Hollis, 24 October 1944, F5893/50/G, PO 371/41746, Public Record Office.

28. Thorne, *Allies of a Kind,* p. 337.

29. Tuchman, *Stilwell,* pp. 403–6. Michael Schaller, *The U.S. Crusade in China 1938–45* (New York: Columbia University Press, 1979), p. 151.

30. Schaller, *U.S. Crusade in China,* pp. 152–53.

31. Ehrman, *Grand Strategy V,* pp. 216–223; Charles F. Romanus and Riley Sunderland, *Stilwell's Command Problems* (Washington, D.C.: The Chief of Military History, 1956), pp. 63–71; Leighton and Coakley, *Global Logistics and Strategy 1943–1945,* pp. 284–94, 515–17.

32. Memorandum, Chief Strategy and Policy Group, OPD, for A Chief of Staff OPD, 8 January 1944, Sub.: Future Military Value of China Theater, OPD 201, Record Group 165.

33. Hayes, *History of the Joint Chiefs of Staff in World War II: The War Against Japan,* Vol. 2, *The Advance to Victory,* pp. 202–3.

34. Boatner, "Barbara Tuchman's *Stilwell,*" pp. 32–35.

35. "Far East Muddle," *The New Republic,* March 13, 1944. The British Embassy in Washington credited the views in the article to "emissaries of Stilwell." AN126/181/45 FO 371/3861, Foreign Office Records.

36. Anthony Eden to Churchill, February 29, 1944, F993, PM/44/122, Public Record Office; Tuchman, *Stillwell,* pp. 429–30.

37. Tuchman, *Stilwell,* pp 419–23.

38. Romanus and Sunderland, *Stilwell's Command Problems,* pp. 124–35 and passim.

39. Charlton Ogburn, *The Marauders* (New York: Harper and Row, 1959) pp. 31–34.

40. James H. Stone, ed., *Crisis Fleeting* (Washington, D.C.: Office of the Surgeon General, 1969), p. 303.

41. Ibid., p. 301.

42. Boatner, "Barbara Tuchman's *Stilwell,*" p. 42.

43. Charles N. Hunter, *Galahad* (San Antonio: Naylor, 1963), p. 10.

44. Ibid., pp. 69–70; Tuchman, *Stilwell,* p. 425.

45. See Chapter 20.

46. Ogburn, *The Marauders,* p. 105.

47. Romanus and Sunderland, *Stilwell's Command Problems,* pp. 124–25.

48. Ibid., pp. 134–46.

49. Romanus and Sunderland, *Stilwell's Command Problems,* pp. 151–58.

50. Ogburn, *The Marauders,* p. 134.

51. Romanus and Sunderland, *Stilwell's Command Problems,* pp. 181–82.

52. Ibid., p. 190–191.

53. Hunter, *Galahad,* pp. 16–17.

54. The British estimated three months as the maximum time one of their long-range penetration groups could remain in the jungle.

55. Tuchman, *Stilwell,* p. 448.

56. Romanus and Sunderland, *Stilwell's Command Problems,* p. 230; Military Intelli-

gence Division, War Department, *Merrill's Marauders* (Washington, D.C.: Office of Chief of Military History, 1945), pp. 112–13.

57. James Stone, ed., *Crisis Fleeting* (Washington, D.C.: GPO, 1969), pp. 339–341.

58. Stone, *Crisis Fleeting,* p. 361. Even Lieutenant Colonel Charles N. Hunter, in his highly critical book on the Myitkyina campaign, conceded that Stilwell's decision to hold GALAHAD at Myitkyina "was forced on him by circumstances." *Galahad,* p. 172.

59. Hunter, *Galahad,* p. 130.

60. Romanus and Sunderland, *Stilwell's Command Problems,* pp. 14-15, 139-41, 154.

61. E. D. Smith, *The Battle for Burma* (New York: Holmes and Meier Publishers, 1979), p. 115.

SEVENTEEN

Ichigo

While the Allies were achieving their hard-won successes in Burma and India, the military and political situation in China continued to deteriorate. Beginning in April 1944 a series of powerful Japanese attacks, striking deep into the heart of China, threatened to bring about the collapse of the Nationalist war effort and the loss of the entire theater to the Japanese. The Japanese offensives, which they called *"Ichigo,"* were intended to stop 14th Air Force attacks on their supply lines by depriving Chennault of his air bases in eastern China. *Ichigo* was also directed against the more serious threat of raids by the new American superbombers, the B-29s, which had recently begun operations against Japan and Manchuria from bases in China.[1]

Ichigo opened with a drive into Honan province in the region between the Yangtze and Yellow rivers. The Chinese defenders of Honan, estimated by the Americans to number at least thirty-four divisions, simply melted away as the Japanese advanced. An American intelligence officer reported Japanese forces moving " 'virtually at will. The Chinese have shown only slight evidence of either plan or capability to hamper Japanese movement or regain lost territory.' "[2] Japanese units numbering a few hundred seized positions held by thousands of Chinese. While their troops fled, Chinese officers used the military trucks assigned to their units to move their families, household furniture, and other valuables out of danger.[3]

In June the Japanese turned their columns south to capture the two communication centers of Changsha and Heng Yang in Hunan Province. At Changsha, the Chinese Fourth Army abandoned the city without a fight and marched off to the southwest. Heng Yang was a different story. There, determined Chinese troops of the Tenth Army under Major General Fong Hsien-Chueh, skillfully supported by Chennault's flyers, held the Japanese at bay for over six weeks.

Had the Chinese forces in other parts of Hunan fought as well as those at Heng Yang, they might have pinched off the long, vulnerable Japanese supply lines and relieved the siege. But the Chinese armies suffered from the same old problems of divided command, incompetence, insubordination, and corruption which had plagued Stilwell's forces in the first Burma campaign. The generals commanding in Hunan were old enemies of Chiang. Neither side trusted the other. "Chungking breathed down the neck of the field commanders," reported American correspondent Theodore White; "Chungking decided when and how and where the action of the day should take place. Reinforcements were fed piecemeal in nibbling assaults. . . . It was as if Eisenhower, in fighting the Battle of the Bulge, had had to argue with Marshall for weeks over each move he wanted to make in the field." [4]

The generalissimo was reluctant to send military equipment to potential political rivals. What American aid was available was often wasted—as when U.S. advisers discovered that Chinese artillery commanders, fearing the consequences if they lost their fine new American howitzers, left most of them miles behind the front.[5]

Heng Yang fell on August 8, opening the road to the 14th Air Force's bases at Kweilin and Liuchow. Chennault frantically called for more supplies and equipment, suggesting that material stockpiled for B-29 operations be diverted to him. Learning of Japanese plans for *Ichigo* in April, he had exasperated Stilwell by urging the generalissimo to withdraw troops from the Salween front to reinforce central and eastern China.

Stilwell viewed the Japanese advance as the inevitable result of Chennault and Chiang's mistaken emphasis on air power at the expense of an effective Chinese army. Chennault had repeatedly assured the generalissimo that his 14th Air Force could stop an invasion. Now, with the invasion at hand, Stilwell believed Chennault was trying to " 'duck the consequences of having sold the wrong bill of goods.' " [6] Furious at Chennault's attempt to interfere with the

Salween operations, Stilwell asked Washington to relieve the 14th Air Force commander. The War Department refused, pointing out that to remove Chennault at the height of the East China crisis would leave Stilwell with the burden of blame for any subsequent losses of territory. In spite of his misgivings, Stilwell scraped together additional Hump tonnage for the 14th Air Force; he even asked Washington for release of the B-29 supplies, a request promptly denied by Marshall and Arnold.[6]

As the Japanese rolled on, Washington leaders became increasingly alarmed and impatient with Chiang and his henchmen. The romantic view of China so popular in Washington during 1941 and 1942 was now out of fashion. American leaders were paying increasing attention to reports from American foreign service officers in China, which told of the progressive demoralization and disintegration of Chiang's regime under the double burdens of continuing war and rampant inflation.[7]

If the political future of China appeared bleak, the immediate military situation appeared catastrophic: the Joint Chiefs of Staff, at the suggestion of General Marshall, warned the president that disaster threatened in China. Only if General Stilwell were placed in complete command of the Chinese armies and war effort could the situation be salvaged. Roosevelt, who by this point retained few illusions about Chiang's leadership, responded with a sharply worded message to the generalissimo on July 6, 1944, pointing to the seriousness of the situation and calling upon the Chinese leader to delegate to Stilwell, now promoted to full general, the power to coordinate and direct all Allied forces in China, "including the Communist forces." [8]

Chiang had not the slightest intention of allowing Stilwell or any other foreigner to command his troops, upset the delicate balance of forces between the generalissimo and the war-lord generals, unleash the Communists in the north, or cause him to lose face before his own people. Yet he also realized that an outright refusal at this point might jeopardize his chances for continued American military and economic support. The Joint Chiefs of Staff were already grumbling loudly about the cargo planes "wasted" flying the Hump, planes which could better be employed in France or Italy.[9]

So the generalissimo stalled. He still had powerful friends in Washington and he knew that the president was preoccupied with many other matters. Replying to Roosevelt's message, he agreed in principle to place Stilwell in command but cautioned that the measure could not be carried out in haste; he asked that the president despatch a high-level emissary to act as his personal representative in "adjusting" the relationship between himself and the American general.

Chiang's reply had the effect he desired. It bought time. It was almost two months before the president's personal representative, Major General Patrick J. Hurley, a flamboyant Oklahoma lawyer who had been secretary of war under Hoover, arrived in Chungking. As Hurley began his talks with Chiang regarding Stilwell's future role, a new military crisis loomed.

In April 1944, after incessant prodding by Stilwell and a threatened cutoff of Lend-Lease by Washington, Chiang had reluctantly committed his American-equipped forces in Yunnan, known as the Y-Force, to cross the Salween River. These troops were to attack into Burma in support of Stilwell's drive on Myitkyina; they were also to assist in clearing the last section of the Burma Road. Now Chiang, frightened by the rapid advance of the Japanese in East China, began to talk of pulling the Y-Force back across the Salween to protect Kunming. At that moment the Y-Force, after hard fighting, was on the verge of capturing the last Japanese strongholds on the Ledo Road. To pull it out now struck Stilwell as insane. When the generalissimo insisted, Stilwell radioed General Marshall that Chiang was about to " 'throw away the results of all our labors' " to break the blockade of China. He pointed out that Chiang had utterly failed to send reinforcements or even replacements to the Y-Force, so that its actual strength was now less than 15,000 men.[10]

The response to Stilwell's message was a 600-word note drafted by Marshall for the president's signature. The note called upon him to place Stilwell in command at once and reinforce the Y-Force, warning that " 'all your and our efforts to save China [would] be lost by further delays.' "

Delighted by this virtual ultimatum to the exasperating Chinese leader, Stilwell quickly had a Chinese translation prepared and personally took it to the generalissimo's residence. There Chiang was in conference with Hurley and several high-ranking Chinese generals when an orderly entered and announced that General Stilwell had arrived and wished to speak to Hurley. On the veranda outside, Stilwell showed Hurley the president's note. Hurley was aghast; he suggested that Stilwell let him tone it down a bit. Stilwell refused.[11] There had been too much of this paraphrasing and toning-down already in past Washington communications.[12]

Returning to the conference room with Hurley, Stilwell told the generalissimo that he had a message from the president and " 'handed this bundle of paprika to the Peanut.' " [13] Reading the note, the generalissimo appeared to Hurley like a man who " 'had been hit in the solar plexus.' " But Chiang betrayed no emotion, remarking simply, " 'I understand.' " Then, after a short silence, he adjourned the meeting.[14]

Privately, the generalissimo was furious. He resolved to get rid of his troublesome American military adviser and to call Washington's bluff. Using Hurley as a channel to convey his displeasure to Roosevelt, he demanded Stilwell's recall. He was still prepared to place his armies under American direction, he said, but not under Stilwell.

Chiang and his supporters were betting that the president, busy with many even more urgent war situations, would be unwilling to force a showdown with China, especially since Roosevelt had been assured by Hurley that the root problem was simply a personality conflict between the generalissimo and Stilwell. In any case, with the Marianas bomber bases now a reality and MacArthur's forces about to land on Leyte, China appeared far less important to Allied success than it had in 1942. Stalin's promise at the Teheran Conference to enter the war against Japan when Germany was defeated had greatly eased American worries about the large Japanese armies in China and Manchuria.[15] As General Merrill put it, "all [U.S.] plans for operations against the Japanese assume that China does nothing but contain some Japanese. We do not desire to get mixed up on the Continent with large U.S. forces." [16] In a message to Chiang on October 18 Roosevelt announced that Stilwell would be recalled immediately.

The president had declined to nominate another American officer to command the Chinese armies, either because he thought the military situation in eastern China was past saving or because he had learned by now that such a post would carry no real power. Major General Albert C. Wedemeyer, who had built a solid reputation as a planner in the War Department General Staff's Operations Division and as chief of staff to Mountbatten, was named to replace Stilwell. Wedemeyer thus became the generalissimo's chief of staff and senior American military adviser. The old China-Burma-India theater was split in two. India, Burma, Siam, Malaya, and Sumatra now constituted a new India-Burma theater under Lieutenant General Daniel I. Sultan, a veteran engineer who had been Stilwell's deputy theater commander.

Ironically, Stilwell left the Far East just at the moment when his strenuous efforts to break the blockade of China were at last bearing fruit. The capture of Myitkyina had enabled the air transports carrying supplies to China to fly the safer, shorter, southern route to Kunming. Delivery rates soared. In all of 1942 the transports had brought a scant 3,700 tons to China. For 1943 the figure was 61,000 tons; and at the time of Stilwell's departure, the figure stood at over 30,000 tons for a single month.[17] At the Indian end of the air line, in remote Assam province, American railwaymen and engineers had transformed the primitive railways, roads, and bridges of that province into an efficient transportation network able to handle over 125,000 tons a month.

Most spectacular of all, the Ledo Road, dubbed "the Stilwell Road" by Chiang and "Pick's Pike" by local G.I.s—after Major General Lewis A. Pick, who commanded construction operations—was nearing completion. Under the indomitable Pick, American engineers and Indian, Chinese, and Assamese laborers had pushed the road through steep gorges, across towering mountains and flooded streams, and through a sea of mud, until it was within sight of the old Burma Road. In the fall of 1944 Stilwell's old Ramgarh-trained Chinese divisions, who had fought in the Myitkyina campaign, reinforced by a British division and new GALAHAD-type American brigade called MARS Force, all under General Sultan, had fought their way across north Burma. There they linked up with the battered Chinese Y-Force, which had resumed its advance after fighting off a Japanese counteroffensive in September.[18] On January 12 the first convoy to Kunming departed from Ledo; on February 4 the long line of trucks and prime movers, decorated with small Chinese and American flags, rolled through the pagoda-like West Gate of Kunming, led by General Pick, standing erect in his jeep while crowds lined the streets, firecrackers exploded, and bands played. The $150 million road was at last completed. Paralleling the road ran two pipelines, constructed with similar pain and hardship. Through the pipelines flowed a steady supply of aviation gasoline for the B-29s and for Chennault's 14th Air Force, as well as fuel for the trucks making the return trip to India.

While the Ledo Road promised better times for the future, the immediate military situation in China remained bleak. In the same week that Stilwell had been relieved, the Japanese resumed their advance in eastern China. Ten days after Wedemeyer's arrival they captured the key cities of Kweilin and Liuchow, with their surrounding air bases. The Chinese defenders abandoned the cities on the approach of the Japanese, apparently unconcerned about a "categorical assurance which Chiang had given Wedemeyer that they would hold out for two months." [19] The Japanese now threatened Kweiyang; from there they could easily turn against Chungking or—even worse—against Kunming, the terminus of China's painfully constructed lifeline to India.

Panic reigned in Chungking. Rumors were rampant. Wedemeyer described the generalissimo and his adherents as "impotent and confounded." Chinese government officials inquired at the American embassy about evacuating their families by air. [20]

Desperate to shore up the defenses of Kunming and the Chinese capital, Wedemeyer endorsed a decision by Chiang to transfer his two Myitkyina-experienced divisions, the 22d and the 38th, currently fighting under Sultan's command in Burma, back to China. In addition, Wedemeyer requested the transfer to China of two groups of transport aircraft then supporting Allied operations under Mountbatten in Burma. Mountbatten, whose forces were beginning the decisive phase in their pursuit of the Japanese falling back from defeat at Imphal, strenuously objected to losing almost half of his airlift capacity to Wedemeyer. British officers at SEAC headquarters and in London acidly pointed out that it was the United States which had long pushed for an offensive to liberate Burma. Now that the British had one underway, the Americans proposed to let the air out of its tires. Some British officials even expressed the view that the transfer of troops and aircraft was intended not so much to deal with the eastern China offensive as to ensure that SEAC would play no major role in the defeat of Japan. [21]

Despite the howls from Ceylon and London, the Combined Chiefs of Staff agreed to the transfer of forces to China. [22] Yet by the time the troops arrived, the need for them had passed. The Japanese, having achieved all the objectives of *Ichigo,* were now shivering in the winter cold at the end of a long and precarious supply line. They were worried as well by the growing threat to the China coast posed by American success in the Philippines. Consequently, they halted their advance. That was fortunate for Wedemeyer because, aside from the two Burma divisions, he had been able to move few Chinese forces into position against the enemy. Although Chiang had agreed that Kunming was vital and must be defended, the American general soon discovered that the Koumintang generals were actually moving divisions out of that area to protect themselves and their families in Chungking. An engaging and tactful man who, upon his arrival, hoped to substitute "honey" for "vinegar" in his relations with the generalissimo, Wedemeyer was soon sending messages about Chinese vacillation, inefficiency, and duplicity which must have reminded the War Department of Stilwell.[23]

Far away in central Burma, Lieutenant General William Slim, commanding the 14th Army, the main British force pursuing the retiring Japanese, got his first inkling of the transfer of troops and planes to China. He was awakened one morning by the roar of aircraft engines. Scores of transport planes previously alloted to his army were taking off for China, leaving the supplies they had been scheduled to deliver to his units in the field scattered over the airstrip.[24] The British general's comments on this occasion have not been preserved. But they must have been pungent, for his troops, having pursued the Japanese right through the monsoon and pushed them back beyond the Chindwin River and across the Schwebo Plain, were about to attempt the crossing of the Irrawaddy, which the Japanese had made their new main line of defense.

In addition to a large edge in armor, the British commander was counting on absolute Allied supremacy in the air. Southeast Asia Command had well over 1,800 operational aircraft, while the Japanese had only a few dozen fighters and perhaps a score of other planes.[25] The ability to move and supply troops by air was a priceless asset. That fact explains the heated arguments by SEAC and China theater commanders over the allocation of transports. In road-poor, rain-sodden Burma, a squadron of transport planes corresponded in value to an aircraft carrier or an amphibious task force in the Pacific.

Undeterred by the loss of part of his air support and a numerically superior enemy on the opposite bank, Slim continued his plans for forcing the Irrawaddy River. One of the 14th Army's two corps, the XXXIII, would cross the river north and west of the key town of Mandalay. Elaborate deception measures were carried out, including the establishment of a dummy corps headquarters, to convince the Japanese that this was the main British effort. As the Japanese rushed reinforcements to this sector, Slim's other corps, the IV, which had secretly been moving far to the south, would cross the river near the town of Pakokhu and race for the major Japanese communication and supply center at Meiktila, south of Mandalay.[26]

Slim's plan succeeded perfectly. General Kimura Hoyotaro, the Japanese commander in Burma, rushed reinforcements northwest to contain the bridgeheads of the XXXIII Corps. Meanwhile, the IV Corps, crossing the Irrawaddy near Pakokhu and the ancient Burmese capital of Pagan, fought its way into Meiktila. The Japanese counterattacked savagely. At one point they had the town cut off; but the British flew in reinforcements and reopened communications. Meanwhile, XXXIII Corps broke out from its bridgeheads and swept down on Mandalay, capturing the city and the old summer capital of Maymyo (from which the British had ignominiously fled in 1942). By late March 1945 the British had inflicted another shattering defeat on the Japanese and now stood astride the main road and rail net of Burma.

General Slim had intended to push on to Rangoon, but the fierce Japanese resistance around Meiktila retarded his timetable. Now there were only about six weeks left before the monsoon rains turned the area into a sea of mud which would swallow the tanks and trucks of Slim's IV Corps, the unit which was to make the dash for Rangoon. To get to Rangoon in time, the corps' worn-out and obsolescent tanks and armored cars would have to cover an average of eight to ten miles a day—against enemy opposition. Slim was confident that his men could do it. But to preclude a suicidal last-ditch stand by the Japanese at Rangoon—which would leave his army stalled outside the city during the monsoon—he asked SEAC to dust off one of its countless plans for an amphibious assault on Rangoon and put it into effect, using troops from the Arakan.[27]

In the midst of frantic preparations for the drive on Rangoon came news that Wedemeyer and Chiang wanted to withdraw the remaining Chinese divisions and the MARS Force to China. There they would form the nucleus of a retrained and reequipped Chinese army which Wedemeyer was preparing for a drive to the China coast.[28] Slim thought he could probably spare the troops, but he objected violently to the diversion of the transport planes needed to move them. A direct appeal from Prime Minister Churchill to General Marshall brought a limited concession from the Joint Chiefs. Mountbatten and Slim could keep the transport planes until they had captured Rangoon. But they had to do this before the monsoon began: when the rains came the planes would go, whether Slim's troops were in Rangoon or not.[29]

Now the capture of the Burmese capital became more vital than ever. General Slim put his troops on half rations to make more space for fuel and ammunition, and exhorted his tank commanders to squeeze a few more miles out of their dying vehicles. " 'I told them that when I gave the word for the dash on Rangoon, every tank they had must be a starter and that every tank that crossed the starting line must pass the post in Rangoon. After that they could push them into the sea if they wanted!' " [30.] By the end of May the British and Indian forces had reached Pegu, only forty miles from Rangoon. Then the rains came—two weeks early.

The rain slowed, but did not stop, the British drive: on May 2 the amphibious forces brought from the Arakan landed south of Rangoon and pushed their way north. That same day a pilot flying over Rangoon in support of the landings noticed a large sign on the roof of a prisoner-of-war compound: "JAPS GONE." The following morning, beneath a heavy downpour, troops of the amphibious force plodded into the city.[31] The reconquest of Burma by land—a feat which British leaders from Churchill to the lowest echelon officers of Mountbatten's staff had repeatedly declared to be impractical, if not impossible—had now been accomplished . . . principally by British and Commonwealth troops.

●   ●

While SEAC forces were defeating the Japanese in Burma, Wedemeyer was attempting to build an effective Chinese army to wrest the initiative from the enemy in his theater. His first step was to establish an organization to provide American advisers for Chinese units in the field. This organization called the "Chinese Combat Command," was headed by Major General Robert B. McClure. It supplied American liaison officers and NCOs to the thirty-six Chinese divisions which Wedemeyer's staff had earmarked for training and equipping with U.S. supplies and weapons. The American liaison detachments would advise Chinese officers on training, operations, and supply procedures. To ensure that their advice was followed, the Americans relied on the carrot of American arms, equipment, and rations—and on the stick of denying them. Wedemeyer also established a training center at Kunming to supervise and advise the various schools and training programs of the Chinese army.

Surveying the Chinese system of conscripting and caring for soldiers, many of Wedemeyer's liaison teams wondered whether the average Chinese recruit could stay alive long enough to benefit from training. The conscripts' rations were so meager and passed through so many hands that a new soldier stood a good chance of dying of disease and starvation before he reached his first post. " 'As they march along to the training camps they turn into skeletons; they develop signs of beriberi, their legs swell, their bellies protrude, their arms and thighs get thin,' " wrote an American officer.

At a replacement depot inspected by an American ration purchasing commission, 100 percent of the recruits were suffering from malnutrition, tuberculosis, beriberi, and other diseases. "The seriously sick replacements had to cook for themselves in kitchens which were immediately adjacent to latrines. The dead were lying next to the barely living and left there at times for several days." Dead conscripts had a special value in China since, as long as a soldier's death went unreported, his commanding officer continued to receive his pay and rations.[32]

Wedemeyer observed that many of the Chinese formations—like the 13th Army, whose troops were "unable to make even a short hike without men falling out wholesale and many dying of starvation"—seemed " 'ready for a general hospital rather than the General Reserve.' "[33] Using U.S. purchasing commissions, mess officers, supply officers, and nutrition experts, Wedemeyer's men made heroic efforts to improve the soldiers' basic diet. They made scarcely a dent in the monolith of Chinese army corruption and indifference, but they did produce a core of physically fit, healthy soldiers for the divisions which were to form the core of Wedemeyer's striking force.

As the new programs got underway, Wedemeyer gradually replaced many of Stilwell's old staff and commanders with new men. The most prominent change was the relief of General Chennault. With the Burma campaign drawing to a close, the India-based Tenth Air Force was scheduled to send some of its aircraft home and transfer the remainder to China. To command the Tenth and Fourteenth air forces in China, Wedemeyer established a new headquarters: "Army Air Forces, China Theater." Chennault might logically have been selected for this new post, but the crusty old fighter had by now accumulated even more enemies in high places than had Stilwell. Arnold and the Army Air Forces establishment had always viewed him with suspicion; General Marshall and the War Department remembered the many problems he had created for them with his end runs to the president and the generalissimo. Chennault's fate was sealed when Roosevelt died in April 1945. Arnold and Marshall notified Wedemeyer that the 14th Air Force commander was to be eased out: Lieutenant General George E. Stratemeyer, who had been serving as Allied air commander in SEAC, was to be appointed as the head of Army Air Forces, China Theater.[34]

Thus, just a few weeks before the final victory, Chennault—bitter, disappointed, and in poor health—left China for the U.S. and retirement.[35] His airmen had not brought Japan to her knees, as he had rashly promised in 1942; but on more than one occasion his pilots, with their courage and brilliant improvisation, had been all that stood in the way of utter defeat for the Chinese forces.

The object of all Wedemeyer's programs and alterations was to lay the groundwork for an offensive in the summer of 1945. The Chinese divisions would recapture lost ground in the Liuchow-Nanning area and then drive on to capture a port in southeast China, probably Canton or Hong Kong. Wedemeyer believed that if it succeeded, such an offensive would tie down Japanese troops who might otherwise be sent back to defend Japan. Once a port was captured the increased flow of supplies—plus the confidence and experience gained in the offensive—would enable Chinese armies to undertake a general campaign to wipe out all Japanese forces on the Asiatic mainland. Wedemeyer's proposals seemed especially desirable in early 1945, when many American strategists expected that the Japanese, even with the home islands overrun, might make a final stand at strongholds in China and Manchuria.

In preparing his offensive, Wedemeyer—like Stilwell before him—cast interested glances at the Chinese Communist forces far to the northeast. Ever since the start of the disastrous *Ichigo* offensive, American leaders had been considering ways of establishing contact with the Communists at their base areas in Shantung, Hopei, and Shansi. Rumors and scattered news reports, always second- or thirdhand, credited the Chinese Communists with a formidable military potential and with waging a determined, aggressive guerrilla war against the Japanese.

Like the Nationalists, the Communists had taken some hard knocks from the Japanese. In August 1940 they had rashly launched a general attack against Japanese communications throughout northern China, called "the Hundred Regiments Offensive." It cost the Communists heavy casualties, and the Japanese struck back with a devastating counterattack in 1941.[36] That same year Nationalist and Communist troops clashed in the so-called New Fourth Army Incident. The Communists lost an additional 5,000 men, including the New Fourth Army's high command. This marked the end of any real cooperation between the two rival political factions.[37]

Yet the Communists profited from their mistakes. Under the leadership of Mao Tse-tung (who blamed the setbacks on his rivals, whom he then purged), the Communists concentrated on guerrilla warfare by small, widely dispersed units; their strategy emphasized the impor-tance of building a solid base of support among the peasants by living among them and sharing their burdens and hardships.[38] As Japanese units were gradually withdrawn from northern China to meet the Allied attacks in the Pacific, the Communists stepped up their guerrilla attacks. The *Ichigo* offensive brought them still more opportunities. By the fall of 1944 the Communists controlled large portions of four provinces. Their base areas were established in terri-tory supposedly held by the Japanese but where the latter were too weak or too thinly spread to exercise any real control.

At the start of the *Ichigo* attacks, Vice President Henry Wallace, on a special visit to Chungking, had urged that the Communists and Nationalists attempt to settle their differences in the face of the common danger and that an American military mission be allowed to visit the Communist base areas in the north.[39] Chiang reluctantly agreed. The so-called "Dixie Mission," composed of a small group of American soldiers and foreign service officers under Colonel David Barrett, arrived at Yenan in July 1944.

The men of the Dixie Mission were favorably impressed by the Communist display of energy and aggressiveness. Communist leaders like Chu Teh, Chou En-lai, and Mao Tse-tung—with their informality, homely manner and apparent frankness—struck the Americans as a favorable contrast to the traditionalism and ritual formality of Koum-intang leaders in Chungking.[40] Discussions were held; plans were made by Wedemeyer's headquarters and the OSS for military cooper-ation between the Americans and Communists, and for the Commu-nist forces to receive lend-lease military supplies and American mili-tary instructors. (The OSS had, in fact, already begun some elementary small-arms and demolition training for Communist soldiers.[41]) All these projects came to nought, however, because of the strong opposition of General Hurley who, shortly after Stilwell's recall, had replaced Clarence Gauss as U.S. ambassador to China. Hurley was in the midst of tortuous and ultimately futile negotiations to persuade the Chinese Communists to enter a coalition government under Chiang's leadership; he wanted to use access to military assis-tance as a bargaining tool.[42]

An immense amount of ink has since been spilled over whether this inconclusive Yenan episode represented a "lost opportunity" for the United States to reach a lasting understanding with the Chinese Communists or, conversely, a "sell-out" of Chiang Kai-shek to the "Reds." The latter view is no longer fashionable. Nor is it supported by the facts. But during the McCarthy era of the early 1950s, it was widely accepted, resulting in grievous and unjustified harm to the careers of many Americans who had been associated with the Dixie Mission.[43] Whatever its significance in the cold war, however, the mission had no influence on the outcome of the war with Japan.

Throughout the remainder of 1944 and into 1945, Wedemeyer pushed his preparations for a drive to the China coast. The first phase of the campaign, now called CABONADO, got underway in late July 1945. But time had run out. Just as the initial attacks got underway, news arrived of the Japanese surrender. The war with Japan had ended; the war for China was about to begin.

In the end, the war in China contributed little toward the final defeat of Japan, and it is tempting but futile to speculate about what might have happened had the U.S. not made such strenuous efforts to keep China in the war. Tempting because it is apparent that the scarce resources expended in the China theater, especially transport planes and pilots, could have been put to better use in Europe and might have helped to shorten the war there. Futile because it would have been psychologically and politically impossible for the United States, having become involved in war with Japan largely due to support for China, to abandon her ally once hostilities began. It would also have been impossible for the U.S. to turn its back on China because even the most farsighted American strategists sincerely believed until well into 1943 that operations from China would be vital to defeat Japan.

For the colonial powers and the Chinese, the war had both run on too long and ended too quickly. It had lasted long enough for the subject peoples of Southeast Asia to inhale some of the heady fumes of self-government, however limited, under the "Co-Prosperity Sphere." During the war they had seen the British and other Europeans vanquished by an Asian army and navy. Moreover, many Asians had received arms and military training under Japanese rule. That in the end many turned these arms against Japan did not mean that they would now lay them down for the benefit of their old rulers. And the war had ended too soon for the Europeans to properly reconquer their colonies—as they had long hoped and planned to do.

The British, it is true, had won a decisive victory in Burma and were about to attack Malaya when the war ended. A British official historian has observed: "The fact that British forces returned to Britain's colonies as victorious liberators accounts to a great extent for the difference between the post-war histories of Burma and Malaya and those of other European Powers with colonies in the Far East." [44] Perhaps. But it was the war itself which made the early and complete independence of these colonies inevitable.

In China, the long years of war and grinding inflation had sapped the morale and integrity of Nationalist officials to the extent that Chiang's government was actually more unpopular on the eve of victory in 1945 than it had been on the edge of defeat in 1941. And the war had ended too soon for Nationalist forces to benefit much from the program of advice and training instituted by Wedemeyer.

NOTES

1. See Chapter 21; Romanus and Sunderland, *Stilwell's Command Problems*, p. 316.

2. Ibid., p. 327; W.F. Craven and James L. Cate, *The Pacific: Matterhorn to Nagasaki* (Chicago: University of Chicago Press, 1953), pp. 222–23.

3. Theodore H. White and Annalee Jacoby, *Thunder Out of China* (New York: William Sloane, 1946) p. 178.

4. Ibid., pp. 186, 189.

5. Romanus and Sunderland, *Stilwell's Command Problems*, pp. 403–5, 408 and passim.

6. Ibid., pp. 314–15, 326–27, 364–65, 369.

7. Tuchman, *Stilwell*, pp. 455–57.

8. Romanus and Sunderland, *Stilwell's Command Problems*, pp. 379–84.

9. Ibid., pp. 379, 454.

10. Ibid., p. 435; White, ed., *The Stilwell Papers*, pp. 329–31.

11. Romanus and Sunderland, *Stilwell's Command Problems*, pp. 445–46.

12. Tuchman, *Stilwell*, pp. 493–94.

13. Ibid., p. 494.

14. Feis, *The China Tangle*, p. 191.

15. Romanus and Sunderland, *Time Runs Out in CBI*, pp. 4–5.

16. Memorandum, Merrill to Stilwell, Sub.: Matters Discussed in Washington, 3 October 1944, R.G. 332.

17. Romanus and Sunderland, *Stilwell's Command Problems*, pp. 112, 472.

18. Romanus and Sunderland, *Time Runs Out in CBI*, pp. 98–138.

19. Ibid., pp. 53–54, 56.

20. Message, Wedemeyer to Marshall for JCS, 4 December 1944, General Wedemeyer Data Book, Item 6, copy in Center of Military History; White and Jacoby, *Thunder Out of China*, pp. 194–95.

21. Romanus and Sunderland, *Time Runs Out in CBI*, pp. 143–44; British reaction to Wedemeyer's proposals may be found in Message, Political Adviser SEAC to F.O. December 14, 1944, with comment by Foreign Office and Memoran-

dum, J.C. Sterndale-Bennett to Major General L. C. Hollis, December 24, 1944; both in F 5893G FO 371/41746, Public Records Office.

22. Romanus and Sunderland, *Time Runs Out in CBI*, pp. 145–46; a newly trained Chinese division, the fourteenth, was, however, substituted for the veteran fifty-sixth.

23. Ibid., pp. 52, 150–52, 165–66.

24. Slim, *Defeat Into Victory*, p. 329.

25. John Ehrman, *Grand Strategy*, Vol. 6, *October 1944–August 1945* (London: HMSO, 1956), p. 174.

26. Slim, *Defeat Into Victory*, pp. 326–328; Ehrman, *Grand Strategy 1944–1945*, pp. 177–178.

27. Slim, *Defeat Into Victory*, pp. 395–97; S. Woodburn Kirby, *The War Against Japan*, Vol. 5, *The Surrender of Japan* (London: HMSO, 1969), pp. 2–3.

28. Romanus and Sunderland, *Time Runs Out in CBI*, pp. 223–26.

29. Winston Churchill, *Triumph and Tragedy*, p. 327; Ehrman, *Grand Strategy, 1944–1945*, pp. 195–97.

30. Slim, *Defeat Into Victory*, pp. 418–19.

31. Kirby, *The Surrender of Japan*, p. 420.

32. Romanus and Sunderland, *Time Runs Out in CBI*, p. 242, 370.

33. Ibid., p. 245; Albert C. Wedemeyer, *Wedemeyer Reports!* (New York: Henry Holt, 1958), p. 33.

34. Craven and Cate, *Matterhorn to Nagasaki*, pp. 269–72; Romanus and Sunderland, *Time Runs Out in CBI*, pp. 342–44, 357–59.

35. Romanus and Sunderland, *Time Runs Out in CBI*, pp. 358–59; Claire L. Chennault, *Way of a Fighter* (New York: Duel Sloan, 1949), p. 365.

36. William Whitson, *The Chinese High Command: A History of Communist Military Politics, 1927–1971* (New York: Praeger, 1973), pp. 70–74.

37. White and Jacoby, *Thunder Out of China*, pp. 75–77; Tang Tsou, *America's Failure in China* (Chicago: University of Chicago Press, 1963), p. 13.

38. James Reardon-Anderson, *Yenan and the Great Powers: The Origins of Chinese Communist Foreign Policy 1944–1946* (New York: Columbia University Press, 1980), pp. 13–17.

39. Michael Schaller, *U.S. Crusade in China* (New York: Columbia University Press, 1979), pp. 160–67.

40. Kenneth E. Shewmaker, *Americans and Chinese Communists 1927–1945: A Persuading Encounter* (Ithaca: Cornell University Press, 1971), pp. 299–300.

41. Romanus and Sunderland, *Time Runs Out in CBI*, pp. 73–75, 251–52; Schaller, *U.S. Crusade in China*, pp. 187–88.

42. Schaller, *U.S. Crusade in China*, pp. 191–222, and Tang Tsou, *America's Failure in China*, pp. 177–94 treat these negotiations in detail.

43. The literature on this episode is large. On the "sell-out" side are John T. Flynn, *While You Slept: Our Tragedy in Asia and Who Made It* (New York: 1951) and Freda Utley, *The China Story* (Chicago: Regnery, 1951). Tang Tsou, *America's Failure in China* is the most scholarly and sophisticated presentation

of the thesis that members of the mission were duped and misled by the Communists because of their lack of familiarity with Communist ideology and methods. On the "lost opportunity" side, see the works by Schaller and Reardon-Anderson cited earlier. A sane and balanced assessment is Kenneth E. Shewmaker, *Americans and Chinese Communists: A Persuading Encounter,* also cited above.

44. Kirby, *The Surrender of Japan,* p. 429.

EIGHTEEN

Strangers in Strange Lands

Approximately a million and a quarter American men and women served in the Pacific and other Asian theaters between 1941 and 1945; from India to Hawaii, from Alaska to New Zealand, the zones of operations embraced one third of the globe. Men worked, fought, and died in terrain as diverse as the icy, fog-bound Aleutians and the beautiful islands of Polynesia, but the war against Japan was conducted mainly in the tropics, that jungle-covered zone of the earth where rain is plentiful, heat and sweat constant, mud, insects, and decay universal.

The tropics were the happy hunting grounds of disease-bearing insects and malignant microorganisms. Poor sanitation and unhygienic living conditions invariably brought dysentery and typhoid fever. One type of insect brought dengue, another a lymphatic disease called filariasis, still another bubonic plague, still another scrub typhus. There were a dozen different varieties of malaria-carrying mosquitos.[1]

In this inhospitable environment the American serviceman—and woman—spent one, two, or often three years. For a few they were years of high adventure, of great danger and great achievement. A seaman who had joined the USS *Enterprise* in 1942, for example, and stayed in the ship until 1945, would have fought through most of the major naval actions of the Pacific War. For the vast majority, however, the war was not an adventure; it was more likely a time of loneliness, physical discomfort, boredom, and fatigue—punctuated by occasional action and danger.

Of the army and air force troops serving in the Pacific, approximately 40 percent of the officers and 33 percent of the enlisted men spent some time in combat. Another 19 percent of the officers and enlisted men had been under fire, while 40- and 45 percent, respectively, saw no action at all.[2] Combat in the Pacific was usually, but not always, characterized by short periods of intense fighting followed by long intervals of waiting. One army division which spent nineteen months in the Pacific had thirty-one days in combat. Another, which had been there for twenty-seven months, saw fifty-five days in combat.[3] By contrast, American troops in the European theater often spent months on the battle line.

In most other respects the combat soldier and marine in the Pacific had a tougher time than his counterpart in Europe. He was likely to have spent a longer time overseas and his rear base was often in an area as hot, primitive, and unhealthy as the battlefield itself. In two divisions studied by army psychologists in the spring of 1944, 66 percent and 41 percent of the infantrymen had been sent to a malaria treatment center at least once.[4]

As in all modern wars, the infantryman bore a disproportionate share of the risks. In U.S. Army divisions, infantry units constituted less than 70 percent of unit strength but suffered over 90 percent of the casualties. If a division remained in combat more than three months, the laws of probability suggested that every one of its 132 second lieutenants would be killed or wounded.[5]

If he were wounded, the World War II soldier, marine, or airman had a better chance of survival than ever before, thanks to the availability of new sulfa drugs, penicillin, blood plasma, and such innovations as air evacuation.[6] A wounded man's first stop was usually a battalion aid-station located only a hundred yards or less from the front. Here, in dugouts roofed by shelter tents, former Japanese buildings, or native huts, he would receive emergency medical treatment. More serious cases, if they were in condition to be moved, were transported back to a collecting- or clearing station where they were treated and prepared for evacuation. On most of the battlefronts in New Guinea and on the Pacific islands assaulted by MacArthur's and Nimitz's forces, large hospitals were lacking, at least during the active phase of the fighting; often, even field hospitals were unavailable.[7] The small portable surgical hospital, located less than

1,200 yards behind the lines, was introduced in the Buna-Gona campaign. This innovation proved a great success. Though labelled "surgical hospitals," they could be adapted for almost any purpose and could function even under the most adverse conditions.[8]

Still, evacuation—either by land or by sea—continued to play an important part in medical operations throughout the war. Air evacuation had previously been considered impractical, but the installation of removable litter supports in cargo planes made it possible to evacuate hundreds of patients a day from the battlefields of the Pacific islands, New Guinea, the Philippines, China, and Burma. Air evacuation was actually more efficient than any other method—fourteen C-54s could lift as many patients in a month as six 500-bed hospital ships—and the death rate was less than seven out of every hundred patients.[9] On islands beyond the range of land-based air, the traditional hospital ships or, more commonly, landing craft converted to hospital ships—continued to serve.

Aboard the converted LST type of hospital vessel, wounded men were passed in over the ramp onto the tank deck, which had been converted to accommodate a receiving room, sterilizer room, and operating room, as well as a seventy-eight-bed ward with two dozen toilets and wash basins. Conversion of LSTs to hospital ships was at first disapproved by the Navy Department but Admiral Barbey, MacArthur's amphibious force commander, who had already gone ahead with conversions, placed the negative reply in "those files most likely to be lost in combat."[10]

Whether by land, sea, or air, the wounded GIs journey was seldom a comfortable one. In the tangled jungles of New Guinea and the Solomons, for example, ambulances were of little use. Normally the first stage of evacuation was by hand-carried stretcher. On Guadalcanal, these stretcher journeys were often of considerable length and had to be made during the steaming daylight hours, for at night there was danger of mistaking a stretcher party for Japanese infiltrators. Sometimes stretchers had to be passed on steel cables or ropes across impassable ravines; "in one instance, a Stokes litter was reinforced by planks, attached to a rope, and slid down a long muddy slope impassable due to rain. At the bottom of the grade, the patient was transferred and the litter was then pulled [back] up the slope."[11] Even longer stretcher journeys—often days in length—were common during the fighting in New Guinea. To add to the excitement, both Japanese and American soldiers cheerfully shot at enemy stretcher parties whenever they had the chance.[12] In some sea evacuations, the wounded might also spend hours in bobbing amphibious tractors or LCVPs awaiting transfer to hospital ships or transports.

Wounds and death in battle were hazards faced by a minority of servicemen who saw combat. Less dramatic but far more common were the hardships of boredom, isolation, and loneliness. These were enemies faced by almost every soldier, sailor, or marine: at times they could seem more terrible than combat. "Day after day, week after week, my only companion on the long night shifts was the wind," recalled one G.I. stationed at a remote weather station in the Aleutians. " 'There were times when I had to smother an impulse to stand in its full blast and scream.' "[13] On one South Pacific island, the rats alone "were enough to provoke a man beyond provocation. . . . They marched in armies on the top of tents, their feet rat-tat-tating like drum beats on the taut canvas. Bored with their drill, they would slide down the side of the tent ropes to the ground, screeching in a high static-like pitch.' "[14]

Men stationed in remote parts of India, China, Burma, New Guinea, or the South Pacific had virtually no recreational facilities at all during most of their tours. The First Marine Division's training area, at Pavuvu in the Russell Islands, lacked any type of showers or bathing facilities for many weeks after the marines arrived. "Whenever the rains came at Pavuvu, men scrambled for their tents, where they hastily slipped out of dungarees and shoes and hurried out into the rain naked, cake of soap in hand. . . . The rains were so fickle that some were always caught fully lathered after the fall stopped.[15] At advance bases in New Guinea, living conditions were so primitive that the "head" at a naval station at Finschhafen, equipped with mahogany seats and good screening, became a sort of showpiece." "It was duly commissioned. It was so cozy it became a sort of clubhouse and flew its own pennant." [16]

In the India-Burma theater, supply officers excluded all Special Services supplies from most ships and planes; as a result, few American newspapers and magazines were available during most of 1942. In one command the only periodicals available were some issues of the 1924 *Saturday Evening Post* donated by a missionary.[17] In India a tube of Colgate toothpaste sold for $5.00, cigarettes for $2.50 a pack, and matches for $.10 a box.[18]

Even at comparatively civilized bases in Fiji and New Caledonia, most servicemen lived in floorless tents, without screens or electric lighting. Food on all Pacific islands came mainly from cans. Items such as canned fruit juice were scarce; fresh fruit was rare. Vitamin

C was provided by such unappealing items as "synthetic lemon." Fresh meat was almost nonexistent in most areas. Some units subsisted for up to two months on C rations. "Outbreaks of diarrhea and gastritis were weekly occurrences." [19] A marine recalled that "in the two years from the time it left Melbourne until it reached China, except aboard ship, the [First Marine] Division was not served fresh eggs five times." [20]

During combat the soldier or marine's only home was his foxhole. "Some outfits lived in hole after hole for as long as seventy days in succession." [21] Even after a combat operation was completed, living conditions were seldom much better. "It is fruitless and unrewarding business," wrote the historian of the First Marine Division, " 'trying to tell a civilian or a soldier who served in another theater about how rigorous and dispiriting were the periods, not in combat but between combat, in the Pacific . . . how little there was to help a man turn his back on his last meeting with the enemy and gird himself for the next.' " [22]

One of the few genuinely popular diversions available to most servicemen was movies. No matter how badly mutilated from repeated screenings, films enjoyed a universal popularity. For many men they were the only novelty in a long, tedious routine, a link—however tenuous and fanciful—with the richer, happier, world back home. Aboard naval amphibious craft in the southwest Pacific, ships had to be kept dark to frustrate night bombing attacks. Films were shown below deck in the cramped spaces and sweltering heat. "Even so, the audience stayed to the end to watch and suffer." [23]

One group of servicemen had more than the usual problems of boredom, isolation, loneliness, and danger. These were the Black GIs serving in army, navy, and Marine Corps units throughout the Pacific and Asia. Blacks had a long and honorable record of service in American wars. But by the eve of World War II, there were fewer than 4,000 American Negroes in the armed services—less than there had been in 1900. Even the famous old outfits like the army's Ninth and Tenth Cavalry had been reduced to service as truck drivers, orderlies, cooks, and grooms. The Marine Corps had no Black personnel at all; the navy had none outside the stewards branch. [24] This was the result of a tradition of racism and discrimination stretching back to the turn of the century. According to widespread opinion in the military, Blacks made only mediocre soldiers, took longer to train, and could perform at all well only if led by white officers. [25]

Even after the rapid expansion of the armed forces beginning in 1940, the services tried to avoid accepting large numbers of Negro recruits. The Selective Service Act forbade "discrimination against any person on account of race or color," but allowed the army and navy the final say about whom they would accept. The operation of the system was so discriminatory in practice that large numbers of white fathers and married men were inducted from districts which still had many eligible single Blacks. This situation, combined with a rising need for military manpower and tireless agitation by Black newspapers and civic leaders, finally had its effect: by late 1942 draft calls for Blacks were stepped up, and the navy and Marine Corps began accepting limited numbers of them.

The navy and the marines contemplated the influx of Negro servicemen with a mixture of bewilderment, consternation, and anxiety. To most white officers, Blacks were as mysterious and unpredictable as the inhabitants of a Tibetan monastery. Their previous contacts with Negroes had usually been confined to hotel porters, waiters, laundresses, and servants. "There is always one top Negro who is the boss," one navy "expert" advised commanders at a conference on handling Negro personnel. "We got one from the Hampton Institute who is a great big six-foot six-inch fellow. . . . This head man was advised to caution his men when they arrived to be quiet and modest, not to be too forward nor put themselves out in front and not to be conspicuous. . . . They were told not to get in any arguments with white people or talk back since it was accepted as a basic fact that no trouble could start without words being first passed." [26]

Over a million Black men and women ultimately served in the armed forces. Branches and specialties like the WACs, the Coast Guard, the Seabees, Officer Candidate Schools and the Red Cross were opened to Blacks. There were Black officers, Black combat pilots, even a Black general. Yet much of this was window dressing. Wartime magazines and newspapers featured pictures of Black fighter aces and Black radar technicians, but the vast majority of Negro servicemen spent their tours in so-called service units, performing hard manual labor such as road building, stevedoring, and laundering. Despite promising experiments, rigid segregation remained the rule—from the induction station to the combat zone. Most Black units had at least some white officers but few, if any, white units included Black officers.

Blacks assigned to engineer and quartermaster units served almost everywhere in the Pacific and Far East. One engineer aviation battalion, the 810th, arrived in Australia early in 1942 with the first large convoy of American troops and served in Nouméa, Guadalcanal, Espiritu Santo, Biak, and the Philippines without a single day in rest camp. The men finally arrived home four months after the war ended. Another battalion, the 811th, traded rounds with Japanese snipers while laying out B-29 runways on Iwo Jima.[27] Black soldiers also provided 60 percent of the army troops who carved the Ledo Road out of the jungles and mountains of Assam and Burma.

The army's only Black combat units to see action in the Pacific were elements of the 93d Division, which fought on Bougainville and later served on Morotai, in the Moluccas and on Saipan. The 24th Infantry of that division did such an outstanding job in mopping-up operations on Saipan that the War Department's inspector general singled them out for special praise: these men were collectively awarded the Combat Infantryman's Badge and an additional battle star for their theater service ribbon.[28] Yet it was a Black sister unit, the 25th Regimental Combat Team, which received most attention.

On Bougainville in April 1944, Company K of the 25th was on its first patrol when a platoon encountered a Japanese machine-gun position. The inexperienced troopers became confused; platoons began firing on each other. One of the platoon sergeants panicked and fled, and the entire company withdrew in disorder, ignoring pleas from the company commander to hold their position and cease fire. Ten men were killed and twenty wounded in this fiasco; the dead were left behind—along with a radio, a mortar, and several small arms.[29]

Although an inglorious episode, the Company K incident was no worse—and in some respects not so bad—as many other experiences of green troops in the South Pacific. Yet such was the climate of opinion at the time, so deep were the prejudices and doubts about Negro combat troops, that the incident became a cause célèbre. Stories circulated that the entire 25th Regimental Combat Team had broken and run or that its men "wouldn't fight—couldn't get them out of the caves to fight." Many Blacks believed that the company had been deliberately thrown into combat without adequate training and that the company commander, who was white, deserted his men under fire and fled to the rear.[30] Later in the war the 25th conducted many successful patrols, including one which resulted in the capture of one of the highest-ranking Japanese officers on the island of Morotai. Nevertheless, it was the story of Company K that was repeated, often in distorted form, and remembered.

While the 25th's record in action continued to be debated, other Black combat units saw no action at all. After arduous and lengthy training in the United States, many Blacks found themselves performing manual labor or guard duties once they arrived in the Pacific. In part this was due to the chronic shortage of service troops in all overseas theaters—but Black leaders also suspected, with good reason, that the large number of Negro units converted to labor service was due to white stereotyping of the Negro as timid, untrainable, and useful only for manual labor.[31]

In the Marine Corps, the policy of assigning a large proportion of Blacks to service units had an especially ironic result. The Marine Corps had initially organized its Black recruits into defense battalions, like the unit which had fought so valiantly at Wake Island in 1941. The defense battalion appeared to be an organization well suited to the needs of a segregated Marine Corps: it was a small, almost self-contained, unit employing a wide variety of weapons and utilizing a large number of different specialties, from radar technicians to machine gunners. But by the time these Black defense battalions were trained, organized, and ready for action, the war in the Pacific had progressed to the point where purely defensive outfits were no longer needed. So the Black defense battalions, trained for combat, spent their time in garrison duties.

In contrast, Black marine ammunition- and depot companies, that is, labor troops, were in the thick of the fighting in the central Pacific, from Saipan to Iwo Jima. The reason was that such companies served in assault landings as part of the shore parties. Earlier experience with amphibious landings had shown that specially trained, experienced troops were needed to perform the difficult task of moving supplies and ammunition quickly from the landing craft to the troops in action further inland. As a result, specialized beach- and shore units were organized for the assault on the Marianas and for subsequent invasions.

The beach party was the navy half of these operations. It consisted of teams from each transport, assigned to such functions as erecting beach markers, planting buoys, directing traffic, or setting up radio communications.[32] The marines provided the shore party, which unloaded the beaching craft—often under intense enemy artillery fire—rushed the ammunition to the front, and carried back the wounded. On Peleliu, Black marines of the shore party worked all day under fire as stretcher bearers; then "about sunset on any afternoon, small knots of them could be seen trudging forward from their rear areas behind a sergeant or corporal to do their bit in the front lines." [33]

" 'The Negro Marines are no longer on trial,' " announced Marine Corps Commandant A. A. Vandegrift after the assault on Saipan. "They are Marines, period.' " [34] Yet despite such ringing affirmations, it was not until the 1950s that Blacks would be accepted on anything like an equal basis in the Marine Corps and the other services.

Overseas, Blacks often encountered much the same type of discrimination they had known in "the good old U.S.A." British officials worried about the possibility that the appearance of Black soldiers—well-fed, well-educated, and well-paid—in their colonial possessions might give dangerous ideas to their own subject populations. Australia, with its "white Australia" policy, protested against receiving Negro troops, which eventually constituted over 8 percent of MacArthur's forces there and in New Guinea. [35]

The editor of the *Fiji Times and Herald* wrote an editorial deploring the assignment of Black U.S. Army logistical troops to his colony. He worried that the "natives" would be hopelessly spoiled by the high wages they were paid by Black GIs to perform laundry services. The American consul general, in forwarding the editorial to Washington, explained that "custom rather than ordinances govern the relationship between European and native races here and if these [Negro] troops were accorded European privileges, dissatisfaction would result. The colony's racial situation, already complicated with Fijians, Indians, Chinese, and half-castes, if aggravated might well become a major problem." [36] Similarly, army commanders in New Caledonia advised that, while combat troops were urgently needed, a Black cavalry regiment which the War Department proposed to ship was not wanted because " 'French control of local natives was delicate enough not to aggravate it further by the presence of additional Negro troops.' " [37]

Still, the Black GI overseas probably encountered more prejudice from his white fellow countryman than from the local population. When it was proposed to send Black marines to American Samoa, Marine Corps General C. F. B. Price warned of the danger of contact between Blacks and the "primitively romantic" Polynesian women. Mixture of the Polynesian with the white race and the Chinese had produced desirable results, said Price, but the union of Blacks and Polynesians had to be guarded against. He recommended stationing Black troops " 'in Micronesia where they can do no racial harm.' " [38]

In India and Australia white soldiers warned local women to stay away from Blacks, whom they described as having tails and carrying loathsome diseases. In Sydney, girls who dared to attend Black social functions at the Booker T. Washington Leave Center were sometimes beaten up as they departed. One woman was given a severe tongue-lashing by an American officer for presuming to take two Black GIs shopping in some local stores.[39] Discrimination against Black GIs in Sydney became so blatant and ugly during 1942 that Australians themselves began to protest. That May, the Australian army minister wrote General MacArthur about reports from New South Wales which described how a gang of newly arrived American white soldiers had stopped an army truck full of Black GIs and forced the troops to dismount amid jeers and name-calling. A fight subsequently developed, after which Black troops were confined to camp and Black MPs disarmed. Most of the popular music and dance halls in Sydney were declared off-limits to Negroes. The general secretary of the Australian Labor Party urged MacArthur to "eliminate this unjust discrimination before it leads to serious clashes."[40] MacArthur loftily assured the Australians that

> there is absolutely no discrimination against colored troops. . . . Without knowing anything of the circumstances, I will venture the opinion that any friction that may have arisen was based not upon racial lines but upon individual deportment and incidents of conduct. Even if the incident you speak of occurred exactly as you have surmised, it would still represent merely an isolated case of inefficiency and officiousness on the part of some subordinate commander which will be promptly corrected. You may rest completely assured that so far as I am concerned, there is no differentiation whatsoever in the treatment of soldiers.[41]

One of the most volatile racial situations in the Pacific theaters developed on Guam late in the war. On that recently recaptured island, which was being rapidly coverted into a major headquarters and supply base, friction developed between white marines and Black sailors from the naval supply depot. The trouble grew out of fights between marines and sailors over relations with local women in the town of Agana.

While fights between marines and sailors were far from rare, the trouble on Guam soon took on racial overtones. Marines in trucks or jeeps roared by the supply company camps, yelling racial insults and threats; they were met with showers of rocks from the sailors.[42] The situation was made worse by a lack of experienced leadership and effective discipline. All of the supply depot company's officers were inexperienced young white ensigns and lieutenants, junior grade, and the units lacked experienced petty officers of either race. The military police and shore patrol on the island was exclusively white. Their approach to their duties is well illustrated by the testimony of one MP sergeant before a navy court of inquiry:

> QUESTION: "Sergeant, did I understand you to use the terms "nigger" and "jigaboo" in the court here?"
> ANSWER: "Yes, Sir."
> QUESTION: "Do you use these terms when speaking to, or in the presence of, colored personnel?"
> ANSWER: "No, Sir. I use "colored man", Sir."
> QUESTION: "Are those terms frequently used by members of the military police in talking with colored personnel?"
> ANSWER: "In talking to a colored man, no, Sir." [43]

In the face of repeated threats from white marines, the sailors began to arm themselves illicitly with rifles and knives. The marines, of course, had ready access to weapons. The spark which touched off the final explosion was the shooting of a Black sailor by a white sailor in Agana on the night of December 24. That same night, shots were fired into one of the supply company camps. Groups of Black sailors commandeered trucks and attempted to drive to Agana but were stopped by military police. A riot and more shootings followed.

The full story of the circumstances surrounding the riot on Guam will probably never be known. Most of the Blacks involved refused to testify before the all-white Navy Court of Inquiry. Even a visit by the executive secretary of the NAACP, Walter White, failed to persuade them to come forward.[44] The court found that while there was "an unfortunate tendency on the part of comparatively very few white service personnel to indulge in the use of slighting and insulting terms and acts of personal aggression applied to individuals of the Negro race on the island . . . there is no organized or concerted racial prejudice or discrimination existing in the armed services on the island of Guam." On the other hand, the court found a "comparatively much more widespread tendency among a high percentage of Negro troops to magnify and accentuate the racial prejudice of the few white service individuals, to seek personal and unlawful redress [and] to foster groundless rumors of racial discrimination." [45]

Given the service attitudes and assumptions of the time, the court's conclusions are not particularly surprising. It was almost a decade before military leaders—and American society as a whole—recognized that a segregated navy, one which shrugged off the constant use of racial epithets as an inevitable minor irritation of life was, in itself, evidence of "organized and concerted racial prejudice."

However difficult their position, Black soldiers were hardly a novelty in the army. Women were another matter. They had been involved in American wars since the Revolution; some had even received awards for bravery. But until World War I, women had been rigorously excluded from serving in uniform as part of the regular armed forces.

During the First World War, the navy had enlisted women to serve as clerks (yeomen) in the navy and marines, but this experiment was hastily discontinued at the conclusion of the war. At the beginning of 1941 the only military organizations in the United States which accepted women were the army and navy Nurse corps. The nurses wore uniforms and were under military control, but they lacked military rank, equal pay, retirement privileges, and veterans rights. In short, they were considered simply as a kind of auxiliary.[46]

With the outbreak of World War II and the passage of the Selective Service Act in the United States, there were demands from women's groups and other citizens that women be permitted to serve in the armed forces. Both Eleanor Roosevelt and Congresswoman Edith Nourse Rogers called for the establishment of some type of military organization for women. During the summer of 1941 the War Department began planning for a women's force " 'so that when it is forced upon us, as it undoubtedly will, we shall be able to run it our way.' " [47]

The War Department's "way" was to establish a "Women's Army Auxiliary Corps." The key word was "Auxiliary," for the women's corps was to be *in* the army but not *of* it. "Auxiliary" status meant that the women GIs would have pay and benefits inferior to those of their male counterparts. It was not until late in 1943 that the "WAACs" became "WACs" with full army status, equivalent ranks, and equal pay.

Legislation to create an army and navy women's force finally passed Congress in the spring of 1942, despite the misgivings of congressmen who wondered who would now be left to "do the cooking, the washing, the mending, the humble homey tasks to which every woman has devoted herself?" [48] Mrs. Oveta Culp Hobby, a prominent businesswoman and civic leader from Texas, was appointed director of the new corps. The first 440 officer candidates were chosen from more than 30,000 applicants with something of the same care which was later devoted to the selection of the first astronauts. They reported to Fort Des Moines, Iowa, an abandoned cavalry post, in July 1942.

During the next year the corps expanded rapidly. By November 1942 the first WAACs were en route overseas in answer to an urgent call from General Eisenhower for skilled typists and telephone operators to serve in North Africa. By this time, the Women's Army Auxiliary Corps had expanded to three training centers, nine service companies, and twenty-seven Aircraft Warning Units. The War Department was beginning to talk about recruiting a million WAACs.

The navy's turn came a few weeks later with the creation of the WAVES (Women Accepted for Volunteer Emergency Service) under Wellesley College's former president Mildred McAfee. Over 80,000 women eventually served in the navy, marines and Coast Guard, but federal law prohibited them from serving outside the continental United States or aboard combatant ships or aircraft.[49] In late 1944 that restriction was eased somewhat to allow WAVES to serve in Alaska, Hawaii, and the Caribbean. All the same, Admiral Nimitz refused to allow women at his headquarters: it was not until CINC-PAC headquarters moved to Guam at the beginning of 1945 that WAVES were finally assigned to Pearl Harbor.[50]

The unprecedented spectacle of large numbers of women in uniform, many of them serving in or near the combat zones, gave rise to amazement and disapproval among the more conservative male soldiers and civilians. An Arkansas radio evangelist told his listeners that WAAC recruits were paraded naked before their male officers. At Daytona Beach, Florida, where there was a WAAC training center, local citizens reported that these women "were touring in groups, seizing and raping sailors and coastguardsmen."[51] Large numbers of WAAC's were reported as being returned home from overseas pregnant: it was widely believed that "WAAC's were really taken into service to take care of the sex problems of soldiers."[52]

War Department authorities pointed out in vain that illicit pregnancy among WAAC's was almost unknown, and that their venereal disease rate was lower than in any known civilian community. The colorful stories continued to circulate throughout the war years. One war correspondent drily noted that if even some of the devoutly believed stories of WAAC promiscuity were true, each of the 200-odd women serving in North Africa in 1943 must have been shipped home pregnant several times.

In the war against Japan the largest number of women—about 5,500—served in the southwest Pacific theater. Here MacArthur's forces, which had become dependent for administrative support on locally recruited Australian civilians, suddenly found themselves shorthanded when American units moved west and north into New Guinea and the Philippines, where civilians could not go. An urgent call went out for all the WAACs that could be spared. In May 1944 the first shipment of 640 WAACs arrived in Sydney, soon to move north to New Guinea.

Employment of WAACs in MacArthur's theater got off to a shaky start because of MacArthur's chief of staff's maneuvers to have his Australian girl friend, who doubled as his secretary, commissioned in the WAACs. Sutherland, by insisting that MacArthur himself desired the commissioning of the lady and two other Australian secretaries, was able to push the case through. He did so over the heated objections of Colonel Hobby, who pointed out that all WAAC officers had been selected from the ranks.

When General MacArthur eventually learned of Sutherland's machinations, and was further informed that the woman in question might be sued for divorce, "the lady was sent back to Australia with all the suddenness of the circus man shot from a cannon." [53] Yet the damage had been done. Army officers, both male and female, were infuriated. All the old stories that WAACs were simply officers' concubines were dusted off and took on a new lease on life. Examination of soldiers' mail from the southwest Pacific in the month before the first WAACs arrived "showed that 90 percent of the comments about all WAACs were unfavorable, many obscene." [54]

Undaunted, WAAC technicians, secretaries, radio operators, postal workers, supply clerks, and mechanics took up their duties in remote New Guinea and the Philippines. At most bases the WAACs lived in guarded, barbed-wire compounds which they could leave only in groups escorted by armed guards. Such precautions were thought necessary to protect them from the thousands of sex-starved GIs nearby. Off-duty activities were limited to unit parties and other group entertainment. Even attendance at movies required a formation and a guard, and all women were required to be back in quarters by midnight. [55]

At Hollandia, army and air force WAACs lived in wooden-floored tents pitched in ankle-deep mud, an elysian field for mosquitoes. At Leyte the first WAACs landed at Tacloban—on an airfield which was then being strafed by Japanese planes. The women spent their first three months working long night hours in lantern-lit tents, frequently interrupted by air raids. In Manila, they lived on K rations, dodged Japanese snipers, and took turns washing up out of their helmets.

"We began to see a steady influx of WAC's, female nurses and Red Cross workers," recalled Rear Admiral Daniel E. Barbey. "All tried to be helpful but, on the whole, they were a nuisance. . . . If we had been given the chance, we would have shipped them home." [56] Most of Barbey's colleagues disagreed. Favorable comment on women's services, as measured by remarks in mail from soldiers in the Southwest Pacific Area, rose from less than 15 percent in August 1944 to over 50 percent by March of 1945; by the end of the war over 70 percent spoke highly of them.

● ●

For one group of Americans the war was an unrelieved nightmare. They were the 20,000-odd soldiers, sailors, airmen, and marines captured by the Japanese at the surrender of the Philippines. Of these unlucky men, less than 60 percent survived Japanese imprisonment to return home in 1945.[57] Some perished at the outset of their captivity on the notorious Bataan Death March—a ghastly, forced-march evacuation of troops who had surrendered in southern Bataan, to clear the way for the final Japanese drive on Corregidor. Over 600 Americans and 5–10,000 Filipinos perished on this trek from the town of Balanga, halfway up the peninsula, to their final internment at the former Philippine Army post of Camp O'Donnell, sixty-five miles north. Sixteen thousand more Americans and Filipinos died in the first few weeks at the camp.[58]

The deaths were due in part to the poor condition of the American and Filipino prisoners, who were already weak and diseased from hard fighting, lack of proper food, exposure to malaria, dysentery, beriberi, and other diseases. In part the blame rests on poor planning and organization by the Japanese commanders, who were preoccupied with preparing the attack on Corregidor and had badly underestimated the number of Allied soldiers on Bataan. They also failed to realize how near to starvation and how racked by disease these soldiers were. As a result, the Japanese expected the prisoners to march much farther and faster than was possible for the sick, hungry, and exhausted men who had fallen into their hands.

Yet a large proportion of the Death March suffering was due to the deliberate thoughtlessness and cruelty of the Japanese. Dozens of men were bayoneted to death; many were clubbed or buried alive when they failed to keep up with their fellows, or when they fell out from exhaustion or in search of water. Private Leon Beck recalled: " 'They'd halt us in front of these big artesian wells. . . . There were hundreds of these wells all over Bataan. They'd halt us intentionally in front of these wells so we could see the water and they wouldn't let us have any. Anyone who would make a break for water would be shot or bayoneted. Then they were left there. Finally, it got so bad further along the road that you never got away from the stench of death. There were bodies laying [*sic*] all along the road in various degrees of decomposition—swollen, burst open, maggots crawling by the thousands—black featureless corpses. And they stank!' " [59] Japanese columns passing the long lines of prisoners would casually loot them of personal belongings or beat them with bamboo sticks. Toothbrushes, fountain pens, rings, and soap— all were confiscated in repeated "searches" of the prisoners. An officer who refused to surrender his wedding ring had his finger hacked off by a Japanese guard's bolo knife.[60]

Amidst the constant beatings and harassment, Captain Sidney Stewart achieved a small revenge. A Japanese soldier seized his bottle of sleeping pills. " '*Yoroshi?*' " he asked: " 'are they all right?' "— " 'Yes,' " replied Stewart, " 'very good.' " The Japanese swallowed two handfuls, which killed him in a matter of minutes.[61]

The worst single incident on the march occurred on April 12 near Balanga where the Japanese, for reasons that have never been explained, massacred almost 400 Filipino officers and NCOs of the 91st Division, hacking them to pieces with their swords.[62]

There were no other mass executions—but everywhere men were beaten, bayoneted, shot, or beheaded—either for minor infractions or simply at the whim of their captors. " 'One of these Jap soldiers . . . grabbed this sick guy by the arm and guided him to the middle of the road. Then he just flipped him out across the road. The guy hit the cobblestones about five feet in front of a tank and the tank pulled on across him. Well, it killed him quick. There must have been ten tanks in that column and every one of them came up there right across the body. When the last tank left there was no way you could tell there'd even been a man there. But his uniform was embedded in the cobblestone.' " [63]

Japanese treatment of the Bataan prisoners was inconsistent. Some rode to Camp O'Donnell in trucks and were relatively well treated; others suffered every mile of the way. Some Japanese guards allowed their prisoners to accept food and water from Filipino civilians who lined the route of march; others ruthlessly drove the civilians back

with rifle butts and bayonets. At San Fernando, many were kicked
and herded into boxcars with the doors sealed for the four-hour
ride north. Many prisoners fainted in the suffocating heat, which
was made even more unbearable by the stench of feces from those
suffering from dysentery. The sides of the metal boxcars grew so
hot in the sun that they burned the skin of anyone who touched
them.[64]

No word about the fate of the Bataan captives reached the United
States until the summer of 1943, when three American officers, William
E. Dyess, Melvin H. McCoy, and Steve H. Mellnik escaped
from a Mindanao prison camp and managed to make their way to
Australia, aided by Filipino guerrillas. Dyess was an air force officer
who had made the march all the way from the tip of the Bataan
peninsula to Camp O'Donnell. He had witnessed some of the worst
Japanese atrocities, all of which he recounted to MacArthur and his
horrified staff. For a time, Washington delayed publishing Dyess's
report for fear of Japanese reprisals against American POWs. But
by early 1944 newspapers were given the go-ahead to publish the
whole story of the Death March.

The story created a sensation in the United States. Senator Bennett
Champ Clark called on the air forces to bomb Japan out of existence
and expressed the hope that the emperor would be hanged at the
end of the war. There was a dramatic rise in the sale of war bonds.
One observer commented that if all the indignation in Washington
could have been transformed into immediate military effort, the war
would have ended in short order.[65]

Survivors of the Death March, as well as other Allied prisoners
in Japanese camps and prisons scattered from Singapore to Manchuria
had a long ordeal before them. The Japanese military code forbade
surrender under any circumstances, so the Japanese tended to regard
prisoners of war as disgraced, cowardly criminals, scarcely human.
Guarding these prisoners was almost as dishonorable as being one.
Consequently, the Japanese tended to assign misfits, troublemakers,
alcoholics, and even the insane to prison-camp duty.[66] The Japanese
claimed to abide by the Geneva Convention rules for the treatment
of prisoners of war. But few, if any, of these rules were ever followed
in practice. The International Red Cross was never permitted to
visit camps in the Philippines; rarely were visits allowed elsewhere.
Red Cross parcels were seldom distributed. Even POW mail was
frequently delayed—or never delivered.[67]

Conditions differed considerably from one prison camp to another.

But in most camps the prisoners faced a daily struggle for survival. The death rate in the camps was lower than on the Death March but dysentery, diet deficiencies, malaria, heat, and overwork still took a heavy toll. Camp diet usually consisted of a cup of cooked rice served three times daily, along with a bowl of watery soup. The prisoners' main source of protein was the Japanese *miso* or soybean paste, which occasionally accompanied these dishes.[68]

In many camps American doctors and corpsmen were permitted to practice. They could even set up rudimentary hospitals, but they had few medicines and little equipment. The infrequent arrival of Red Cross packages, and the smuggling, stealing, or bartering of food and medicine by courageous prisoners and Filipino civilians nevertheless kept the hospitals operating and saved many patients from death. In one camp the Americans discovered that their jailers had a high regard for American pills and medicines, and proceeded to manufacture bogus sulfa tablets out of flour or plaster of paris. The Japanese appeared to be quite happy with these—they did not detect the hoax until 1945.[69]

Camp discipline was strict. Ferocious punishments were meted out for the slightest offenses. In some cases prisoners forced to work on prison farms were shot for concealing a potato.[70] Death was the most frequent punishment for attempting to escape. In some camps, men were divided into "shooting squads" of ten or twenty each, all of whom would be killed if any member escaped.[71] Despite such penalties, escape was not uncommon, often aided by Filipino guerrillas.

Beatings and other forms of corporal punishment were the norm.[72] Such measures were also common in the Japanese army; they may not have been viewed as particularly cruel or malicious. " 'Sure the Japs beat you with baseball bats,' " observed one former POW, " 'but they beat each other with baseball bats too.' "[73] Few other Americans were so sanguine about these matters.

Some of the more fortunate prisoners encountered Japanese who were neither sadistic nor unreasonable. " 'I will never love Japs,' " recalled one ex-POW, " 'but this one *gunso* I admire. He was a good soldier. In all the time he was our boss, he never ever mistreated a prisoner. . . . Basically, we were his slaves, but he never took advantage of the fact. He treated us as men.' "[74]

As the war progressed, more and more prisoners were moved north from the Philippines to northern China, Taiwan, or Japan. Under the best of circumstances, these journeys through waters patrolled by American planes and submarines were highly uncomfortable and dangerous. At worst, the voyages exceeded the horrors of the Death March.

'When it was nearly full, guards came down and with whips began beating us farther back into the ship's hold until it looked as if no more men could get in. . . . Yet, more and more were coming. The ceiling were low, only about five feet high, but we were made to stand . . . we were crammed so tightly that if a man fainted he could not fall to the floor. He would be packed between them. . . . The men began screaming and fighting. They tore at each other, they fought and pushed. Their screams of terror and their laughter were terrible things. Suddenly, there was more room. The fainting and the dead were sliding down until men littered the floor underneath our feet. We had more room to move in. But under our feet were the bodies of men.' [75]

For the POWs who survived such ordeals, there were still the American submarines. Japanese prison ships carried no special markings to distinguish them from ordinary shipping. During the autumn of 1944 over 4,000 Allied prisoners were killed or drowned aboard ships sunk by U.S. submarines. Sometimes, as in the case of the *Shinyo Maru,* a handful of prisoners survived and were rescued by the Allies; others were less fortunate. [76]

For those American prisoners still in the Philippines, liberation came early in 1945 as MacArthur's forces reoccupied the islands. Other prisoners—in remote camps in Japan or Manchuria—were not released until late September. Nine years later a survey found that of the men who had fought in the Bataan campaign, only one out of seven was still alive in 1954. [77]

•   •

Whether in the South Pacific, the mountains of south China, or the parched, brown plains of India, thousands of servicemen encountered societies and countries they had heard of before only in the pages of their grammar-school geography books. Everywhere in Asia and the Pacific, Americans found unfamiliar cultures and strange peoples, and everywhere—in small ways and in large—the GIs left their mark. In remote parts of New Guinea and the New Hebrides, they inspired bizarre "cargo cults" among the local inhabitants, some of which have continued into the present day. In Australia, at least 15,000 women married American servicemen. Several thousand emigrated to America, inspiring fears that the island continent, with only 7 million inhabitants, was being depopulated. In India GIs introduced the dill pickle to Calcutta restaurants and taught their Indian bearers to act as fielders and shortstops in scratch games of baseball.[78] In China their presence fueled the already roaring black market and inflation and, for good or ill, gave millions of Chinese a chance to observe large groups of Americans at close hand. What they saw aroused both their admiration and their contempt.[79] In all places where American GIs worked, fought, and died, societies and economies were mightily affected—and sometimes changed. Of these societies Australia and India represent extremes in their reactions to the GIs—and in the GIs' reaction to them.

The country which American servicemen approached with fewest misgivings was Australia. Superficially, it seemed much like the U.S.—even if somewhat behind the times. The people there spoke English, drank beer, and rode in buses and trams. The Americans who arrived "Down Under" during 1942 and the early months of 1943 received a hero's welcome from the harried Australians. Their own forces were scattered from North Africa to Singapore—with few experienced troops left at home to meet the Japanese threat. Men of the First Marine Division, arriving in Melbourne from Guadalcanal, were hailed as "the Saviors of Australia" by local citizens.[80] "Every household in Australia put a pot of tea on the fire and sent the younger children to catch a yank." [81] A lady bus conductor paid the fares for thirty-three GIs who had no Australian coins. Newspapers published American baseball scores and Melbourne hostesses exchanged recipes for American dishes. The Yanks in turn introduced Australians to the wonders of chewing gum and Coca-Cola.

American servicemen were quickly adopted by Australian families; many developed lasting friendships. For more than a year after the First Marine Division left Melbourne, "the volume of its mail to and from that city exceeded the volume to the United States." [82] Most Americans were "pleased with Australian beer, flattered by Australian hospitality, approving of Australian weather, and delighted with Australian women"—whom they pronounced less "stuck-up" than American girls.[83] They were less enthralled by Australia's strong labor unions, which they viewed as greedy and indifferent to the war's demands. They were also a bit put off by what they took to be the slow pace of life down under. A greater irritant was the strict enforcement of Sunday blue laws in all parts of Australia, laws which prohibited even the showing of movies on the Sabbath. Most American servicemen worked every day *but* Sunday and found it extremely frustrating to wander aimlessly through the virtually deserted business districts of Australian towns on their day off. Army posts, however, organized their own Sunday entertainment, and eventually the blue laws were relaxed in many towns, much to the chagrin of the Australian clergy.[84]

As time passed, Australians other than clergymen became disenchanted with the American servicemen. As one local poet declared:

> They saved us from the Japs
> > Perhaps
> > > But at the moment the place is too Yankful
> > > For us to be sufficiently thankful.[85]

As in other parts of the world, local citizens in Australia were resentful of the relatively high pay of American soldiers, they deplored the tendency of some to throw their money around. Far more annoying was the spectacle of Australian girls, even including the wives of absent soldiers, associating with American servicemen.[86] "The present decay of morals and the menace of social disease accompanying it are unprecedented in the history of Queensland," wrote one indignant Australian cleric; "For several months now many girls associating with Allied soldiers have shown a spirit of greed and selfishness that does little credit to Australian womanhood." [87] The brutal murder of three Australian women by Private Edward Leonski, a psychopath stationed near Melbourne, seemed to confirm the worst fears about Yankee behavior. Leonski was tried and hanged, but a generation of Australians acquainted with the United States chiefly through Hollywood gangster movies wondered how many other Al Capone types might be wearing American uniforms.

Yet relations between American GIs and Australian women were neither as racy as veterans later recalled nor as sordid as contemporary critics claimed. After the first few weeks, recalls one veteran, most GIs " 'had chosen their favorite girls and begun to 'go steady'.' " Their money was running out, liberty hours were stricter, and through a combination of necessity and desire they spent quiet evenings at their girls' houses and took longer and more frequent walks in the parks and on the beaches. There were many engagements and a few marriages. Some men even rented apartments where, as one of them put it, there was a small kitchenette " 'for tea brewing.' " [88]

Problems arose mainly when Australian army units returned on furlough to areas where the Yanks had already laid claim to most of the available feminine company. In November 1944 American and Australian troops clashed in a three-hour free-for-all melee with Australian civilians cheerfully joining in. The immediate targets of Australian wrath were American military police, who had a well-earned reputation for arbitrariness and brutality. More than two dozen Americans, mostly MPs, were injured, and at least one Australian was killed in the riot.[89] An official Australian inquiry blamed heavy drinking, resentment of American pay and amenities, and the ever-present rivalries over women for the explosion.[90]

Yet such violent incidents were few. Although Australians continued to grumble over the degradation of their manners and morals, and Yanks never stopped cursing the slow-moving Aussies, the two managed to end the war in cautious, if no longer cordial, concord. An adaptation of the popular song "Thanks for the Memories" by two Australian Red Cross women appropriately summed up the experience of many GIs in Australia:

Thanks for the memory
  Of troops who'd been in strife,
    Kids who enjoyed life,
      Of love affairs,
        And foolish cares,
          And photos of your wife. . . .[91]

Whatever peculiarities and inconvenience the GI may have found in Australia paled beside the utter alienness of China and India. Nothing in the average American's education or experience prepared him for the reality of Asia: for the heat, filth, and poverty, the "staggering slowness and human toil and people who did not speak English and who did not have the sense to jump smartly out of the way when a jeep came tearing by. The American could feel like a man from Mars in lands of water buffalo, wooden plows and ox carts."[92] "The rains have been very heavy the last few days," wrote one GI from India to his sweetheart, "and the smell is worse than usual. To me that is the outstanding thing in India—the smell."[93]

If the American soldier in Australia appeared somewhat better paid and equipped than his local counterpart, in India he was a virtual millionnaire. British colonials watched in alarm and disbelief as even the lowliest American private equipped himself with personal servants, cook, bearer (valet), cleaner, usurping what had previously been the prerogative of British officers. No British or Indian army private could afford to hire servants, but American troops could and did. *Life* magazine reported that the servant of an important English official had recently deserted his employer and had since been discovered happily valeting nine black American enlisted men in a quartermaster outfit: they paid him twice his old salary.[94] The four hundred WAACs stationed in Calcutta had seventy-three servants who made beds, shined shoes, washed clothes, and polished the furniture.[95]

American living quarters were spartan and primitive by U.S. standards. But to Indian eyes the well-built barracks or Quonset huts, with their beds, fans, mosquito nets, mess halls, recreation areas— even pianos—were unbelievably luxurious.[96] GIs spent their money not only on servants but on jewelry, rugs, taxis, liquor, and women; even snake charmers and fortune tellers shared in the largesse.

Although Americans were stationed all over northern India, the hub of activity was in the east, around the sprawling, teeming, city of Calcutta. Calcutta was headquarters for various supply and service commands supporting air operations against Burma and across the Hump to China. It was a rear-area headquarters for the engineer and service units at work on the Ledo Road, as well as for Stilwell's Chinese forces training at Ramgarh.[97] It was also the principal leave and recreation area for thousands of other troops stationed in the wilds of Assam and Burma—on the rare occasions when they were able to obtain some time off.

Yet Calcutta was about as suitable for a leave and recreation center as Brooklyn for a ski resort. The city was overcrowded, teeming with refugees, unhealthy, and plagued with periodic food shortages. In 1944 these chronic shortages developed into one of the most horrible famines of the century. In some respects, nevertheless, the city rose to the challenge. All varieties of black-market liquor were readily available. Drugs were reported so plentiful that the U.S. commissioner of narcotics darkly predicted a wholesale increase in drug addiction in the U.S. after the war because many GIs would undoubtedly become addicts in India.[98] An estimated 40,000 prostitutes regularly plied their trade in Calcutta: and every pony-cart or rickshaw driver could supply a woman upon request.[99]

Officers on leave found Calcutta generally tolerable, dining at Firpo's and other fashionable restaurants while thousands of Indians slowly died of malnutrition less than a block away. For enlisted men however, Calcutta was a less satisfactory place to vacation. For a time it had no recreational facilities at all for any but officers and senior non-commissioned officers.[100] Black soldiers of all ranks found it a frustrating place. Most recreational facilities were strictly segregated; in one instance, an American general ordered the Red Cross to cancel a dance to be held for Negro GIs who had just come to town after months in the jungle at work on the Burma Road. The general had learned that some white women planned to attend.[101] White soldiers explained to their Anglo-Indian girl friends that the Negroes were a kind of American coolie; they were dangerous brutes, best left alone. The Blacks attempted to explain to these Eurasian girls that in the U.S., they too would be treated as "Niggers." Such efforts at persuasion met with indifferent success.[102]

A fortunate minority of American servicemen could have their leave not in Calcutta but in a cool, clean, British "hill station." The stations were mountain towns which had been used by the British and their families to escape the intense heat of the plains during the summer months. These neat little towns, often resembling European villages, had good restaurants, hotels, cinemas, shops, nightclubs, swimming pools, and libraries. To GIs plucked out of the jungles of Burma for rest and recuperation they appeared to be veritable paradises.[103]

British residents watched the influx of American servicemen into the hill stations with mingled incredulity and horror. " 'We shall all have to get used to walking,' " says an English matron in Paul Scott's novel, *The Towers of Silence*. " 'The cost of a tonga up the hill to the club, should one manage to find one not already loaded with G.I.'s, will be quite beyond our pockets. On second thought,' " she went on, "one would probably stop going to the club because it would be crowded with American officers . . . and perhaps with top sergeants, whatever species they were. If the cinema was any guide, even sergeants in the American Army seemed to get saluted and to call officers by their Christian names; so they would all be at the bar with their hands in their pockets, their bottoms out of their shiny trousers, bringing in Eurasian girls, getting drunk and busting up the place.' " [104]

Despite their disdain for GIs, British colonials did take a wry delight in the fact that the American servicemen generally appeared to adopt attitudes and practices toward Indians similar to their own. Foreign service officer John Davies observed that "American troops arrive in India with a kind of happy-go-lucky friendly attitude toward the people and the country, and speedily become annoyed at being swindled by their apparently servile servants. They end up very shortly by cordially disliking both Indians and British." [105] Correspondent Harold Isaacs observed that many Americans in India "gradually adopted the British habit of frigid distance and superiority enforced with abuse" in their dealings with Indians. "The general attitude of Americans in India is that of intense dislike for the Indians," noted the British Foreign Office, "and a feeling of thankfulness that the British and not Americans have to rule and cope with India." [106]

Perhaps, but not all Americans in India shed their anticolonial beliefs so easily. "Those of us who have been to Britain's colonial empire know their methods of dealing with those who dare demand freedom," wrote a veteran of the CBI Theater shortly after the war.[107] Nor did all GIs view the Indians as contemptible coolies. The Indian clerks employed by one American supply battalion, recalled a veteran, "spoke English with a precision that shamed or amused the American officers and enlisted men who supervised their work." [108] "These people had been getting along alright without us for so many generations," observed marine aviator Gregory Boyington, "before the land became infested with G.I.'s who wantonly tossed their money about." [109]

Australia and India were part of the British Empire-Commonwealth. But American soldiers and sailors also garrisoned islands of the South Pacific which had been part of the French Empire before the war. New Caledonia was one such area: a vital steppingstone on the long road from the Pacific Coast to Australia, and a staging point for operations. American forces under Major General Alexander Patch began arriving in the colony in March 1942. At one time there were as many as 118,000 American military personnel in the islands.

In addition to the usual problems which the presence of such large numbers of GIs produced, American leaders in New Caledonia had also to cope with local political problems which rivaled those of China in byzantine complexity. A few months after the defeat of France in 1940, the people of New Caledonia overthrew their Vichyite colonial government and aligned themselves with the Free French government of General Charles de Gaulle in London. At the time of General Patch's arrival from the United States, the de Gaulle government was still struggling to obtain American recognition as the sole spokesman for France, and many Gaullists were suspicious and uneasy about the presence of American troops in their colonies.

This was especially true of Rear Admiral Georges Thierry d'Argenlieu, the French high commissioner for the Pacific. Vainglorious, tactless, narrow-minded, and devious, d'Argenlieu would later play a major role in bringing about postwar conflict in French Indochina.

His conviction that New Caledonia must be "saved" from the Americans was readily accepted by de Gaulle—who was himself more than a little paranoid toward Americans.

D'Argenlieu's relations with Patch would probably have been difficult under the best of circumstances, but they were made worse by the poor arrangements for liaison between the two leaders. General Patch's "liaison officer" with d'Argenlieu's headquarters was a young naval reserve lieutenant with an excellent command of French but without any military background. The American lieutenant and the French admiral took an instant dislike to each other, and little use was ever made of this channel of communication. General Patch also had a French liaison officer attached to his headquarters but this gentleman—an outspoken supporter of one of d'Argenlieu's chief political rivals in the colony—was not only useless for liaison but a political embarrassment as well.

Events came to a head in May of 1942 with a demonstration by the New Caledonians against d'Argenlieu and his mission, whose members had thoroughly alienated the local population by their highhanded methods and their ill-concealed contempt for local views and customs. D'Argenlieu responded by arresting the popular local governor and four other New Caledonian leaders. This further angered the local population, which declared a general strike. A revolt of the local colonial militia soon followed. D'Argenlieu called upon General Patch to use his troops to "maintain order," but the American prudently refrained from intervening in support of a government which had proven itself so unpopular. It was only after d'Argenlieu was ousted by the local leaders that Patch intervened to ensure the safety of the admiral and his staff and persuade the militia to return to its barracks.[110]

D'Argenlieu departed for London soon after, having received de Gaulle's commendation for "defending French interests in the Pacific." Patch's civil affairs duties were assumed by the more diplomatic Admiral Ghormley, but French suspicion of the American presence in New Caledonia and petty squabbling between American commanders and French colonial officials continued throughout the war.

Whatever GIs may have thought about the various peoples of Asia and the Pacific who were their sometimes reluctant hosts and allies, there was unanimity of opinion regarding the character of their enemy, the Japanese. "During World War II," John Blum has observed, "Americans at home had little trouble hating their enemies."[111] Indeed, in all their wars the people of the United States had demonstrated an impressive capacity for righteous anger at the citizens of whatever foreign nation had the bad luck to be their opponents. Yet all the ill will ever directed at "the bloody Redcoats," "the cruel Spaniard," or even "the beastly Hun" paled in comparison to the unbridled fear, hatred, and distrust which most Americans felt toward the Japanese.

The "treacherous" Japanese attack on Pearl Harbor and their sweeping victories early in the war, together with the long tradition of American racial prejudice, ignorance, and misinformation about Asians, combined to produce a virulent hatred of the Japanese and a public attitude which viewed them as separate from, and more heinous than, any of America's other real or imagined enemies. Advertising surveys conducted for War Bond sales drives revealed that Americans tended to view the Japanese as "ungodly, subhuman, beastly, sneaky, and treacherous." [112] An Office of War Information study of Hollywood wartime films found that German soldiers were depicted in war movies as efficient, disciplined, and patriotic, if misguided; that Italian soldiers hardly figured at all; but that Japanese soldiers were depicted as universally cruel and ruthless. "Japanese were short, thin and wore spectacles. They were tough, but devoid of scruples." Japanese soldiers revealed loathsome buck-toothed grins as they cheerily bayoneted helpless prisoners, strafed fleeing civilians, or sniped at soldiers from the rear.[113]

Even supposed "experts" on Japan reinforced the public's stereotypes. Anthropologist Ruth Benedict, in a widely read book on the Japanese, *The Chrysanthemum and the Sword,* explained the Japanese attack on the United States as the result of pathological aspects of the Japanese national character, while psychological warfare expert John M. Maki described the Japanese as "mired in political medievalism." [114] American psychologists and anthropologists believed that the perverse and aggressive behavior of the Japanese could be explained by "harsh toilet training practices and an emphasis on shame rather than guilt." (It was only after the war that American social scientists discovered that many of the Japanese child-rearing practices on which they had based their "analyses" had never existed.) [115]

Early in the war, in what one authority has called "the most blatant mass violation of civil liberties in American history," [116] American citizens of Japanese descent and Japanese resident aliens, most of whom had lived in the U.S. for many years, were forcibly removed from their homes on the West Coast and evacuated to large internment camps in the desolate interior of California, Nevada, and Utah. All were forced to abandon their homes, farms, and businesses to the doubtful care of the Federal Reserve Bank—or to liquidate their property at a severe loss.

The citizenry of California and the other West Coast states, whose bigotry toward the Japanese had long been part of their way of life, saw their fears and suspicions amply reinforced by the nervous and indecisive leadership of Lieutenant General John L. Dewitt, the head of the Western Defense Command.[117] California newspapers carried headlines such as: JAP BOATS FLASH MESSAGES ASHORE; JAP AND CAMERA HELD IN BAY CITY; and even CAPS ON JAPANESE TOMATO PLANTS POINT TO AIR BASE.[118] At a meeting of California law enforcement officials in January 1942, the Los Angeles district attorney "asserted that the U.S. Supreme Court was packed with leftist and other extreme advocates of civil liberty and that it was time for the people of California to disregard the law if necessary to secure their protection. . . . One high official was heard to state that he favored shooting on sight all Japanese residents of the State." [119]

A nationally syndicated newspaper columnist, Henry MacLemore, urged the government to "Herd 'em up, pack 'em off . . . let 'em be pinched hungry and dead up against it." [120] During the next three years the Federal Government went far toward fulfilling MacLemore's prescription.

The American serviceman's image of the Japanese enemy faithfully mirrored those at home, often with added intensity. Correspondent Robert Sherrod reported that one renowned marine commander "hated Japs as only men who have met them in combat hate them. Whenever during his hour-long lecture . . . he used the phrase "killing Japs" or "knocking off Japs," his eyes seemed to light up and he smiled faintly." [121] One veteran of Guadalcanal wrote that "Though the Japanese possessed considerable cleverness, he could not be classified as an intellectual. He was more of an animal. He could live on a handful of rice." [122] In polling soldiers, army psychologists discovered that 38 to 48 percent indicated agreement with the statement: "I would really like to kill a Japanese soldier," whereas only 5 to 9 percent indicated agreement with the same statement applied to a German soldier.[123]

The distinction between the Japanese and other more "normal" enemies was one frequently made by American servicemen: "Killing a Japanese was like killing a rattlesnake," recalled one Marine general.

"I didn't always have that feeling in Europe about some poor German family man but I felt with a Jap it was like killing a rattlesnake." [124] In the European theater, 54 percent of combat infantrymen interviewed said that seeing Axis POWs had given them the feeling "they are men just like us; it's too bad we have to be fighting them." In contrast, only 20 percent had such a reaction in the Pacific after seeing Japanese prisoners; 42 percent "felt all the more like killing them." Only 18 percent felt more like killing the German POWs. [125] "In the last war, I looked at dead Germans and I thought about their wives and children," one general told a reporter; "these [Japanese] bastards, that doesn't even occur." [126]

Halsey's chief of staff, Rear Admiral Robert B. Carney, told reporters that in his opinion, "it would seem to be an unnecessary refinement to worry too much about" the sinking of Japanese hospital ships. "[They] have undoubtedly been used for illegal purposes and they are caring for Nips, which we failed to kill in the first attempt. Every one who is restored to duty potentially costs the lives of many of our people." [127]

One reason for the American fighting man's loathing of the Japanese was the latter's apparent fanaticism and indifference to death. In the closing months of the war, the kamikaze attacks appeared to provide the most spectacular proof of these traits; but long before those attacks, the U.S. serviceman had become well acquainted with his Japanese opponent's willingness to fight to the death. Veteran correspondent Robert Sherrod noted that less than 5 percent of the Japanese fighting forces had ever surrendered during any one battle. Usually, it was closer to 1 percent. [128] "The Japanese seem to get a grotesque pleasure from self-destruction, from planned death, whether by their own hand or by the hand of others," wrote one veteran of Guadalcanal. [129] At a conference among high-level American naval commanders in May 1943, the minutes record that: " 'All agree the only way to beat the Japs is to kill them all. They will not surrender and our troops are taking no chances and are killing them anyway.' " [130]

There is some reason to doubt that the conduct of U.S. servicemen toward their Japanese opponents was as bellicose and ruthless as their rhetoric. General Holland Smith, who had loudly proclaimed to reporters that he felt no pity for dead Japanese, actually took time in the midst of a critical phase of operations on Saipan to ensure that Japanese POWs were protected from sunstroke and had adequate food and water. [131] Army opinion surveys showed that the high degree of hatred toward the Japanese expressed by soldiers in training dropped off drastically once the men were in combat. American soldiers in the Pacific remained more hostile toward the Japanese than their counterparts were toward the Germans, "but the men fighting the Japanese were strikingly less vindictive toward the Japanese than were either soldiers in training in the United States or soldiers fighting the Germans in Europe." [132]

Nevertheless, at least a few American fighting men appear to have acted on their conviction that the Japanese were not really human. In October 1943 Marshall radioed MacArthur of his deep "concern over current reports of atrocities committed by American soldiers." A story in the newspapers told how a soldier had "made himself a string of beads from the teeth of Japanese soldiers." Another reported how a soldier had recently returned from the southwest Pacific theater with photos showing various steps "in the cooking and scraping of the heads of Japanese to prepare the skulls for souvenirs." [133]

While relatively few servicemen indulged in such activities, there can be little doubt that the general image of the Japanese as treacherous, implacable fanatics contributed to the style of warfare which the U.S. waged against its enemy. A close student of the strategic bombing campaigns against Germany and Japan cites "one of the highest ranking air commanders of the war" as privately confirming "that there existed 'a basic distinction in our thinking between the Germans and Japanese.'" [134] It was a distinction that was to have tragic consequences.

NOTES

1. Mary Ellen Condon, *U.S. Army Medical Service in the War Against Japan 1941–1945,* unpubl. MS. U.S. Army Center of Military History, p. 4.

2. Samuel A. Stouffer et al., *Studies in Social Psychology in World War II: Vol. 2, Combat and Its Aftermath,* p. 163.

3. Stouffer et al., *Combat and Its Aftermath,* p. 88.

4. Ibid., p. 69.

5. Ibid., p. 102.

6. Vern Haugland, *The AAF Against Japan* (New York: Harper, 1948), pp. 340–41.

7. Donald W. Mitchell, "The U.S. Army Medical Service in the War Against Japan," unpublished MS, U.S. Army Center of Military History, pp. 155–68, 181–89.

8. Ibid., p. 32.

9. Haugland, *The AAF Against Japan,* pp. 331–33.

10. Barbey, *MacArthur's Amphibious Navy*, p. 3.

11. Mitchell, "The U.S. Army Medical Service," p. 153.

12. Ibid., p. 152.

13. Haugland, *The AAF Against Japan*, p. 341.

14. McMillan, *The Old Breed*, p. 230.

15. Ibid., p. 231.

16. Barbey, *MacArthur's Amphibious Navy*, pp. 141–42.

17. "Army Service Forces Activities in the Supply of the CBI Theater," unpublished MS, copy in Army Center of Military History, p. 130.

18. Letter, Sergeant George Bartholomae to Annette Cragster, 14 July 1943, George Bartholomae Papers, USAMHRC.

19. Stone, ed., *Crisis Fleeting*, p. 302.

20. McMillan, *The Old Breed*, p. 235.

21. Stone, ed., *Crisis Fleeting*, pp. 302–3.

22. McMillan, *The Old Breed*, p. 228.

23. Barbey, *MacArthur's Amphibious Navy*, p. 134.

24. Jack D. Foner, *Blacks and the Military in American History* (New York: Praeger Publishers, 1974), pp. 130–32.

25. Ibid., pp. 148–49; Ulysses Lee, *The Employment of Negro Troops* (Washington, D.C.: Office of Chief of Military History, 1966), pp. 14–15, 33–35.

26. Memorandum, Chief of Naval Personnel to all Sea Frontier Commands, All Naval Districts, etc., Sub.: "Negro Personnel—Confidential Report of Conference with regard to the Handling of." Pers-1013-MK, Bu Pers Records, Naval Historical Center.

27. Lee, *Employment of Negro Troops*, pp. 598–99.

28. Memorandum for DCS, Sub: Exemplary Conduct of the 24th Infantry Regiment at Saipan 14 May 1945, in Morris J. MacGregor and Bernard C. Nalty, eds., *Blacks in the United States Armed Forces: Basic Documents* (Wilmington: Scholarly Resources, 1977) pp. 494–95.

29. Lee, *Employment of Negro Troops*, pp. 506–9.

30. Ibid., pp. 511–12.

31. Ibid., p. 527.

32. Harry W. Hill interview, USMC Oral History Collection, p. 564.

33. Hough, *The Island War*, p. 312.

34. "The Negro in the Marine Corps," unpublished MS, 1949(?), p. 9, U.S. Marine Corps Historical Center.

35. James, *Years of MacArthur*, pp. 257–58.

36. American Consul General, Nadi, to Dept. of State, 3 February 1943, 846K.20/3, National Archives RG 57.

37. Ulysses Lee, *Employment of Negro Troops* (Washington, D.C.: GPO, 1965), p. 446.

38. Morris MacGregor, *The Integration of the Armed Forces PD*, p. 92.

39. John Hammond Moore, *Down Under War: Aussie and Yank 1944–1945* (Queensland: 1980), pp. 292–93.

40. Letter, H. B. Chandler to Hon. F. M. Forde, Minister for the Army, 21 May 1942; enclosure to Forde to MacArthur, 25 May 1942, Richard K. Sutherland Papers, National Archives.

41. Letter, MacArthur to H. B. Chandler, 28 May 1942, Richard K. Sutherland Papers, National Archives.

42. Information on the Guam incident is taken from "Record of Proceedings of a Court of Inquiry, Naval Supply Depot, Guam, Marianna Islands, . . . to inquire into the Unlawful Assembly and Riot . . . at Naval Supply Depot," 30 December 1944, copy in Naval Historical Center.

43. Ibid., p. 35.

44. Ibid., p. 1265; White's memoirs are strangely silent on the subject of the Guam riot.

45. Ibid., p. 1265.

46. Except where noted, the discussion below is based on Mattie E. Treadwell, *The Women's Army Corps* (Washington, D.C.: Office of the Chief of Military History, 1954), pp. 3–70.

47. Treadwell, *Women's Army Corps,* p. 17.

48. *Congressional Record* 88, No. 55, March 17, 1942.

49. Susan H. Godson, "The Waves in World War II," *Naval Institute Proceedings* 107 (December 1981), pp. 46–49.

50. Potter, *Nimitz,* p. 287.

51. Treadwell, *Women's Army Corps,* p. 209. This rumor proved utterly false, doubtless to the disappointment of many navy and Coast Guard sailors.

52. Treadwell, *Women's Army Corps,* p. 207.

53. James, *Years of MacArthur,* pp. 597–98.

54. Treadwell, *Women's Army Corps,* p. 414.

55. Ibid., pp. 420–33.

56. Barbey, *MacArthur's Amphibious Navy,* p. 236.

57. William C. Braly, *The Hard Way Home* (Washington: Infantry Journal Press, 1947), p. 31.

58. Stanley L. Falk, *Bataan: The March of Death* (New York: W. W. Norton and Co., 1962), p. 199.

59. Donald Knox, *Death March: The Survivors of Bataan* (New York: Harcourt Brace Jovanovich, 1981), pp. 133–34.

60. Ibid., pp. 127–29.

61. Sidney Stewart, *Give Us This Day* (New York: W. W. Norton and Co., 1956), pp. 72–73.

62. Falk, *Bataan,* pp. 103–9.

63. Knox, *Death March,* p. 121.

64. Falk, *Bataan,* pp. 185–87.

65. Ibid., pp. 205–11.

66. Stewart, *Give Us This Day,* pp. 83–84; Mitchell, "The U.S. Army Medical Service," p. 34.

67. Mitchell, "The U.S. Army Medical Service," p. 37.

68. Braly, *The Hard Way Home,* pp. 50–51; John S. Coleman, *Bataan and Beyond: Memories of An American POW* (College Station, Texas: A & M Press, 1978), pp. 177–79.

69. Lieutenant Colonel Willard H. Waterous, "Statement of Experiences and Observations Concerning Bataan Campaign and Fall of Philippines," copy in U.S. Army Center of Military History, p. 177.

70. Braly, *The Hard Way Home,* pp. 64–65; Coleman, *Bataan and Beyond,* p. 178.

71. Melvyn H. McCoy and S. M. Mellnik, *Ten Escape From Tojo* (New York: Farrar and Rhinehart, 1944), p. 49: Knox, *Death March,* pp. 179–80, 182, 184.

72. Stewart, *Give Us This Day,* p. 96.

73. *Washington Post,* October 8, 1980.

74. Knox, *Death March,* pp. 193–94.

75. Stewart, *Give Us This Day,* pp. 157–62.

76. Blair, *Silent Victory,* pp. 682–84, 712–13, 244–45.

77. Mitchell, "The U.S. Army Medical Service," p. 60.

78. "Dear Mom, I Got a Valet," *Life,* November 30, 1942; the dill pickle was, according to one account, introduced by a bomber pilot from Brooklyn who persuaded a local restauranteur to produce the first batch. I am grateful to my late uncle, Sergeant Arthur Spector, U.S. Army Air Forces, for this story.

79. Harold R. Isaacs, *No Peace for Asia,* (Cambridge: MIT Press, 1967), p. 33.

80. McMillan, *The Old Breed,* p. 147.

81. Moore, *Down Under War,* p. 122.

82. McMillan, *The Old Breed,* p. 148.

83. Moore, *Down Under War,* p. 128.

84. Ibid., pp. 144–47.

85. Ibid.

86. James, *Years of MacArthur,* p. 254.

87. Moore, *Down Under War,* p. 311.

88. McMillan, *The Old Breed,* pp. 151–55.

89. Moore, *Down Under War,* pp. 303–309.

90. Dudley McCarthy, *Southwest Pacific Area: First Year* (Canberra: Australian War Memorial, 1959), pp. 625–26.

91. McMillan, *The Old Breed,* p. 154.

92. Isaacs, *No Peace for Asia,* p. 9.

93. Letter, Sergeant George Bartholomae to Annette Cragster, 14 July 1943, George Bartholomae Papers, U.S. Army Military History Research Institute.

94. "Dear Mom, I Got A Valet," *Life,* November 30, 1942.

95. Treadwell, *The Women's Army Corps,* pp. 466–467.

96. "Ram Ram Jad Jao: Yanks in India Master Lingo and Learn to Get Along," *Newsweek,* January 4, 1943. As late as 1978, the Quonset huts built in 1943 to house non-commissioned officers in Delhi were still in use by the Indian armed forces—as housing for senior officers!

97. See Chapters 15–17.

98. Memorandum, HQ Army Service Forces to CG U.S. Army Forces, CBI, 16 August 1944, Sub.: An Investigation of Drug Addiction, Record Group 332.

99. "History of Services of Supply, India-Burma Theater," Appendix 21: Provost Marshall, 25 October 1940–20 May 1945, Record Group 337.

100. Nevin Wetzel, "A Place Called Ramgarh," *Ex-CBI Roundup,* December 1978, p. 13.

101. "China Notes," n.d., 1943, Evic Sevareid Papers, Library of Congress.

102. Isaacs, *No Peace For Asia,* p. 12.

103. A good account of the establishment and operation of one of these hill station rest camps is Robert E. Henry, "A Soldier's Saga" *Ex-CBI Roundup,* December 1977, pp. 10–16.

104. Paul Scott, *The Towers of Silence* (New York: Avon Books, 1979), pp. 348–49.

105. British Embassy, Chungking to Foreign Office, Sub: Conversation between Mr. John Paton Davies, Sir George Sansom and Mr. P. H. Gore-Booth, F4688, October 3, 1944, FO371/41746, Foreign Office Records.

106. Isaacs, *No Peace for Asia,* p. 11; "Report on Public Relations and Conditions in India and SEAC," enclosure by British Embassy Washington to Foreign Office, F4872, October 11, 1944 FO371/41746, Foreign Office Records.

107. Quoted in Taraknath Das, "Britain Must Stop Her Anti-Indian Propaganda in the United States," *Bombay Chronicle Weekly,* March 10, 1946.

108. Robert Hullihan, "The Christmas Spy," *Ex-CBI Roundup,* December 1978.

109. Gregory Boyington, *Baa Baa Black Sheep* (New York: Putnam, 1958), pp. 67–68.

110. The foregoing is based primarily upon an untitled 1945 report on civil affairs in New Caledonia; copy in General Board Records Box 73, Naval Historical Center.

111. John M. Blum, *V Was for Victory: Politics and American Culture During World War II* (New York: Harcourt Brace Jovanovich, 1976), p. 45.

112. Ibid., p. 20.

113. Gregory D. Black and Clayton R. Koppes, "OWI Goes to the Movies: The Bureau of Intelligence's Criticism of Hollywood 1942–1943," *Prologue,* Spring 1974, pp. 53–54.

114. Richard H. Minear, "Cross-Cultural Perception and World War II: American Japanists of the 1940's and their Images of Japan," *International Studies Quarterly,* 24 (December 1980), pp. 562, 564 and passim; Sheila K. Johnson, *American Attitudes Toward Japan* (Washington, D.C.: AEI, 1975) pp. 3–9.

115. Johnson, *American Attitudes Toward Japan,* p. 5.

116. Blum, *V Was for Victory,* p. 155.

117. The literature on the Japanese evacuation is immense. A few of the most important works are Martin Grodzins, *Americans Betrayed* (Chicago: University of Chicago Press, 1949); Jacobus ten Broek, Edward N. Barnhart, and Floyd Matson, *Prejudice, War and the Constitution* (Berkeley: University of California Press, 1954); Stetson Conn, "Japanese Evacuation from the West Coast" in

Stetson Conn, Rose C. Engelman, and Byron Fairchild, eds., *The Western Hemisphere Guarding the United States and Its Outposts* (Washington: GPO, 1964); Audrie Girdner and Anne Loftis, *The Great Betrayal* (New York: Macmillan, 1969); and Roger Daniels, *Concentration Camps U.S.A.* (New York, 1971). A good bibliographic essay is Howard Sugimoto, "A Bibliographic Essay on the Wartime Evacuation of the Japanese from the West Coast Areas" in Hilary Conroy and T. S. Miyakawa, eds., *East Across the Pacific* (Santa Barbara: ABC–Clio, 1972). A fine memoir is Jeanne Wakatsuki Houston and James Houston, *Farewell to Manzanar* (Boston: Houghton Mifflin, 1973).

118. Roger V. Daniels, *The Decision to Relocate the Japanese Americans* (Philadelphia: Lippincott, 1975) p. 12.

119. Ibid., p. 40.

120. Blum, *V Was for Victory*, p. 158.

121. Sherrod, *Tarawa*, p. 24.

122. T. Grady Gallant, *On Valor's Side* (New York: Doubleday and Co., 1963) p. 288.

123. Stouffer et al., *Combat and Its Aftermath*, p. 34.

124. Lemuel C. Shepherd, oral history interview, p. 242, U.S. Marine Corps Historical Center.

125. Stouffer et al., *Combat and Its Aftermath*, p. 161.

126. Cooper, "Holland M. Smith," p. 240.

127. Denis Warner and Peggy Warner, *The Sacred Warriors: Japan's Suicide Legions* (New York: Van Nostrand, 1982), pp. 35–36. Carney's contention that the Japanese hospital ships carried contraband was borne out when U.S. destroyers stopped the hospital ship *Tachibana Maru* in August 1945 and discovered 1,500 able-bodied combatants as well as a large quantity of weapons.

128. Sherrod, *On to Westward*, p. 15.

129. Gallant, *On Valor's Side*, p. 288.

130. Buell, *Master of Seapower*, p. 357.

131. Cooper, "Holland M. Smith, " p. 313.

132. Stouffer et al., *Combat and Its Aftermath*, p. 157.

133. Message, Marshall to MacArthur, WAR 8640, 1 October 1943, copy in Richard K. Sutherland Papers.

134. David MacIsaac, *Strategic Bombing in World War II: The Strategic Bombing Survey* (New York: Garland, 1976) pp. 203–4.

Admiral Nimitz (right) confers with Admiral Spruance on Kwajalein during the Marshalls campaign. *U.S. Navy*

Troops of the 7th Division attack a Japanese blockhouse on Kwajalein with flame thrower. Flame throwers proved one of the most effective weapons against block houses and pillboxes, though they needed to be used at close range and their operators were extremely vulnerable to enemy fire. *U.S. Army*

Marine armored amphibious vehicles on the beach at Saipan. These "Amtracs" were superior landing craft but were unable to function as light tanks as called for in Holland Smith's plan.
U.S. Marine Corps

Marines move through the flaming streets of Garapan in Saipan. Unlike the tiny atolls of the Gilberts and Marshalls, Saipan was a relatively large island and its conquest involved two full marine divisions plus an army division.
U.S. Army

Two Marines display U.S. flag recaptured on Guam. Marine on right is future Marine Corps Commandant Louis Wilson. Except for uninhabited Attu and Kiska, Guam was the first former U.S. territory recaptured from the Japanese. *U.S. Marine Corps*

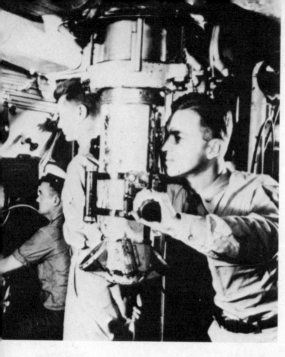

Submarine skipper directs a periscope depth attack in the crowded conning tower of a fleet type submarine. Cryptographers provided submarines many opportunities to intercept Japanese shipping but defective torpedoes often nullified this advantage. *U.S. Navy*

Three-inch deck gun of submarine *U.S.S. Silversides* fires on a Japanese picket boat. Crewman at far left is about to pass another round to the gun crew. All ammunition had to be hauled by hand from below. *U.S. Navy*

Twenty-millimeter guns of destroyer *Thorn* in action at Leyte Gulf. Leyte Gulf was the largest naval engagement in history and resulted in the destruction of most of the remaining Japanese fleet. *U.S. Navy*

Smoke and flames errupt from the hangar deck of *U.S.S. Suwanee* following a suicide crash by a Zero which penetrated the escort carrier's flight deck during the Battle of Leyte Gulf. In less than three hours the fires had been put out, the flight deck repaired, and air operations resumed.
U.S. Navy

MacArthur enroute to Tacloban, Leyte, for liberation ceremonies, aboard a P.T. boat—the same type of craft in which he had made his famous escape from Corregidor in 1942. On MacArthur's right is *PT-525*'s skipper, Lt. Alexander Wells. On his left are General Walter Krueger (next to machine guns) and Commander Selmon S. Bowling, Commander of 7th Fleet PT boats.
U.S. Navy

An aerial photo reveals the devastation in Manila following the bloody battle for control of the city between MacArthur's forces and the Japanese in 1944. Of Allied cities, only Warsaw suffered greater damage than Manila in World War II. *U.S. Army*

WACs arriving in Australia, May 1944. The women soldiers arrived under a cloud, caused by General Sutherland's machinations to have his secretary, and reputed mistress, commissioned as a WAC officer. The largest number of WACs stationed overseas served in the southwest Pacific. *U.S. Army*

Crewmen aboard an Army Air Force C-47 prepare to drop supplies to Merrill's Marauders during Stilwell's campaign in North Burma. Pvt. Robert L. Crane braces against bulkhead ready to "kick out" crate of supplies while crew chief Sgt. Donald R. Ross and Pfc. Charles E. Banks watch for pilot's signal. Air resupply was essential to Stilwell and Slim's operations in Burma. *U.S. Army*

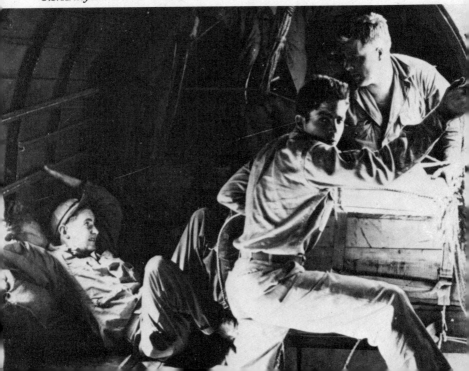

WACs in CBI theater pose at entrance to the gardens of the Taj Mahal. India was a major supply and staging area for U.S. forces flying the hump to China and building the Ledo Road. *U.S. Army*

Brigadier General Frank D. Merrill (left) talks with General Stilwell during the campaign for Myitkyina. Merrill's GALAHAD task force, popularly known as Merrill's Marauders, the only U.S. ground combat unit in the theater, played a decisive role in the defeat of the Japanese in Stilwell's Burma campaign, 1943-1944. *U.S. Army*

NINETEEN

Where Is Task Force 34?

In the late afternoon of July 26, 1944, the cruiser *Baltimore*, flying the presidential flag, eased alongside a pier at Pearl Harbor. In the brilliant sunlight a row of admirals from Nimitz's headquarters, resplendent in white mess uniforms, waited to board the ship. At their head was Nimitz's chief of staff, Admiral Charles H. McMorris. "Right face!" ordered McMorris—and two of the admirals promptly faced left, much to the delight of the *Baltimore*'s sailors. Seldom had they witnessed such a graphic confirmation of their private views on the competence of "the top brass."

The president had come to Pearl Harbor to confer with these brass hats, and with others from the southwest Pacific, about important decisions on future strategy for the Pacific. Roosevelt had just been renominated for a fourth term; there were those who believed his dramatic visit to Hawaii, unaccompanied by any of the Joint Chiefs except Leahy, was simply a political stunt. This was certainly the opinion of Douglas MacArthur. Not above a little grandstanding himself, the general arranged to arrive at the dock about a half hour after the president, riding in "the longest open car" ever seen in the islands, and preceded by a screaming motorcycle escort. "The car travelled some distance around the open space and stopped at the gangplank. When the applause died down the general strode rapidly up the gangplank all alone" pausing when halfway up to acknowledge the plaudits of the crowd.[1]

Despite such playing to the galleries, Roosevelt, MacArthur, and Nimitz had matters of great moment to discuss. By July of 1944 the war against the Axis was going well, almost unbelievably well. The great Anglo-American invasion of Europe on June 6, 1944 had succeeded; more than a million Allied soldiers were in France; General Omar Bradley had just launched his decisive breakout from Normandy. In the Pacific MacArthur and Nimitz were battering at the inner ring of Japan's defenses from their newly acquired strongholds in the Marianas and Western New Guinea. The question was where to go next.

The old Strategic Plan for the Defeat of Japan, approved by the Joint Chiefs in the spring of 1943, aimed at securing control of the South China coast, Luzon, and Formosa. That would make it possible to seize and develop air bases in China to bombard Japan and cut its line of supplies. Now, flushed with recent successes, some Washington strategists wanted to bypass Luzon and strike directly for Formosa or even the main islands of Japan.[2]

Admiral Nimitz was willing to consider bypassing Luzon provided other bases could be seized in the Philippines, but that was as far as he would go in meeting the audacious suggestions from Washington. MacArthur was livid at talk of leaving any part of his beloved islands under the Japanese heel. At Pearl Harbor he held forth in vivid and dramatic style to the president on the moral and strategic reasons for proceeding with the conquest of Luzon. " 'Give me an aspirin,' " ordered the president after three hours of the general's oratory. " 'In fact, give me another aspirin to take in the morning. In all my life nobody has ever talked to me the way MacArthur did.' "[3]

MacArthur's admirers claim that at the Pearl Harbor meetings he converted the president to the strategy of striking at Luzon before, or instead of, Formosa.[4] D. Clayton James, in his distinguished biography, suggests that the general and the president may have struck an informal deal at the conference: Roosevelt would use his influence in favor of Luzon rather than Formosa and the general would boost the president's reelection campaign by reporting on how well the war was going in his theater.[5]

Whatever the case, the question of future strategy remained far from settled, for the Formosa approach had an advocate as powerful as General MacArthur: Admiral Ernest J. King. Throughout the summer and autumn of 1944 King continued to argue, with his usual force, that Formosa be captured first. In this he was joined by most high-ranking Washington officers—with the notable exceptions of Admiral Leahy and Lieutenant General Brehon B. Somervell, the army's chief logistician. Most Pacific commanders tended to support MacArthur's advocacy of Luzon.[6]

Three developments finally settled the question. Admiral Halsey's fast carrier task forces, raiding the southern Philippines and neighboring island groups during September, reported them to be only lightly defended. Halsey radioed a message to Nimitz urging that the previously planned deliberate approach to the Philippines by way of Yap, the Palau, and Talaud island chains be cancelled. He asked that even the invasion of Mindanao, the southernmost island in the Philippines, be called off; instead he wanted the Pacific forces to move directly against the more northern island of Leyte.

Nimitz approved Halsey's suggestions (except for cancelling the attack on the Palaus) and sent them along to the Joint Chiefs of Staff, who were then gathered at Quebec for the Anglo-American strategy conference called OCTAGON. The chiefs radioed the proposed change in schedule to MacArthur for his comments. The southwest Pacific commander was at that time aboard a cruiser accompanying one of his invasion forces and consequently maintaining radio silence. But his chief of staff, General Sutherland, knew how valuable an advance in the timetable for the Philippines could prove in MacArthur's battle with King. Sutherland radioed an approval in MacArthur's name, although his intelligence officers were well aware that Japanese strength in the Philippines was far stronger than Halsey supposed.[7]

Sutherland's message reached the Joint Chiefs at a formal dinner with Canadian officers. The Americans excused themselves, held a hurried consultation, decided to go ahead with the cancellation of all preliminary operations except the Palaus, and set the new date— for Leyte—as October 20.[8]

From that point on, events conspired to make a decision in favor of Luzon rather than Formosa all but inevitable. First, MacArthur informed the Joint Chiefs that the new invasion date for Leyte would enable him to invade Luzon two months ahead of schedule, on December 20, 1944. Formosa could not possibly be invaded so soon. Then Washington planners discovered that the manpower needs for a campaign against Formosa far exceeded the number of troops actually available in the Pacific. The most glaring deficiency was in the category of service troops. Nimitz alone would require between 90,000 to 200,000 for a campaign against Formosa. To obtain that many new service troops, Nimitz would have to wait until the war in Europe was over.[9] Finally, bad news arrived from China: Major Japanese offensives overran most of the air bases in east China— bases from which the Joint Chiefs had planned to launch their aerial bombardment of Japan. The loss of these airfields rendered the seizure of a port on the China coast less than urgent. In any case, the Air Forces had long since begun to look to the Marianas as the principal base for their B-29s.

These developments convinced everybody but King, who made a final attempt to block a decision for Luzon by objecting that a Luzon campaign would tie up the navy's fast carrier forces for six weeks, an unacceptably long time. MacArthur shrewdly countered by pointing out that Formosa would tie the carriers up even longer. Finally, on October 3, the CNO gave in. The Joint Chiefs directed MacArthur to invade Luzon on December 3; Nimitz was to support him with the Third Fleet.

• •

While the Joint Chiefs debated about Luzon, the one operation they had failed to cancel, and upon which Nimitz had insisted—the assault on the Palaus—went forward as scheduled. It turned into one of the toughest, bloodiest operations of the war. The island of Peleliu, which contained the principal airfield, was the main target. One marine officer recalled that the First Marine Division commander, Major General William H. Rupertus, "was very, very optimistic" about his troops' ability to capture the island quickly. His instructions to his regimental commanders predicted "a quickie, probably faster than Tarawa. As a result, some newspaper correspondents left because after what he told them, they said 'what's the use of sticking around?'." [10]

The Americans had little information about the terrain on Peleliu except some inadequate aerial photos. As a result they failed to recognize its potential for defense. The northern peninsula of the small island was a series of jagged coral ridge lines, honeycombed with natural caves which the Japanese had improved into almost impregnable fortresses. Blast walls of reinforced concrete or oil drums filled with coral protected the entrances to the caves, which often faced each other from the sheer walls of twisting gorges, and were thus mutually supporting. In the larger cave fortresses, the Japanese had installed electric lighting, ventilating systems, stairs, telephones, and radio communications. One large cave was discovered "to have nine staggered levels and so many entrances that it was all but impossible to count them." [11]

Protected by these caves, the Japanese defenders suffered little from the American preinvasion shellings and bombings, and were able to give the men of the First Marine Division a hot reception when they landed on September 15. Yet the worst fighting was to come after the marines had secured their main objective, the airfield, but still had to dig the Japanese out of their coral strongholds, a task which took until late November.

In heat that rose to 115 degrees, with water strictly rationed, the marines, later joined by elements of the army's 81st Division, grimly set about clearing the cave pockets, crags, and ravines. "The terrain was abominable," recalled one marine; "it was the worst terrain I've ever encountered. It was as though several submerged reefs had been forced up out of the water with their jagged edges making several ridges that were up to two or three hundred feet high. The sharp coral could cut the shoes and clothing of the Marines. The island had been mined for phosphate and so there were many tunnels running through those ridges. So a situation actually existed where the Marines would . . . be in possession of the ground and the Japanese would be underneath them and there would be no way to get at them. . . ." [12] Artillery and air support were of little use; flamethrowers, demolition charges, and handgrenades were the best weapons—along with luck. Late September brought heavy rain and gales of near-typhoon force; the island was declared secure on September 30—and still the fighting went on.

Altogether, the assault on Peleliu cost the U.S. well over 1,000 killed and 5,000 wounded to capture an island base which proved, at best, of only marginal importance to the Allies' Pacific advance.[13] With the aid of hindsight, it was clear that Nimitz would have done well to cancel the Palaus operation along with all the others. Admiral Halsey had suggested that course but Nimitz, with little accurate intelligence about the islands, believed they would be necessary as staging areas for the Leyte operations.

Although American leaders had taken four months to make up their minds to attack the Philippines, Japanese strategists had expected such an attack almost since the fall of the Marianas. In the early days following that defeat, some strategists had estimated that the Americans might next strike at the Ryukyus or Okinawa. To be on the safe side, however, they prepared four operational plans called the *Sho,* or Victory, plans: *Sho*-1 for a defense of the Philippines,

Sho-2 for the Kuriles and Ryukyus, *Sho*-3 for southern and central Japan, and *Sho*-4 for northern Japan and the Kurile Islands.[14]

If the battle was to be in the Philippines, as the Japanese expected, they planned to conserve their air and naval forces until the actual invasion and then launch them at the invaders in an allout attack. Ashore, the defenders would make no attempt to hold beachhead defensive positions under the kind of devastating naval bombardments the Americans had delivered in the Marianas. Instead, the Japanese army would establish a defense-in-depth far enough inland to escape the deadly naval guns, and await opportunities for successful counterattack. The Japanese land and sea-based air forces would also be husbanded until the critical moment, then launched against the invaders when they had actually begun their landings.

Japanese strategists would have preferred to keep the fleet concentrated in home waters, ready to strike in any direction where danger threatened. Yet American submarines had done such an effective job of cutting Japan's oil supplies from Southeast Asia that most of the Imperial Navy's heavy warships had to be based at Lingga Roads, near Singapore, close to their fuel supplies. Admiral Ozawa remained in home waters with those carriers which had survived the Philippine Sea battle, training replacement pilots and awaiting the arrival of new aircraft. With him was a small covering force of cruisers and destroyers under Vice Admiral Shima Kiyohide. When Ozawa had completed his replacement program, probably in November, he was to join the rest of the fleet in the south. In the meantime the battleships and cruisers at Lingga had the latest radar installed and practised evasive maneuver against air attack. Extra antiaircraft guns were crammed into any available space. The fleet knew that in the next battle there would probably be no friendly air cover.[15]

The Americans were also readying their forces for battle. General MacArthur, Commander, Southwest Pacific Area, commanded the Leyte invasion forces. They were embarked in the transports, and protected by the warships, of Vice Admiral Thomas C. Kinkaid, commander of the Seventh Fleet. Troops of General Walter Krueger's Sixth Army provided the ground forces for the attack. The covering force for the invasion, the Third Fleet, was not under MacArthur's command but was part of Admiral Nimitz's Pacific Fleet.

The Third Fleet was identical to Spruance's Fifth Fleet except that, since the summer of 1944, Halsey and his staff had alternated with Spruance and his staff in heading it. While one admiral and his team commanded the fleet at sea, the others rested and planned the next operations. The arrangement had been designed to utilize Halsey's unique talents as a leader by providing him with an active command after the South Pacific had become a secondary theater.[16]

Spruance and Halsey were very different commanders. As Nimitz observed, "Halsey was a sailor's admiral and Spruance was an admiral's admiral." Halsey was impulsive, colorful, a risk-taker. To sailors and public alike, he was a hero and an inspiring leader. Spruance was aloof, cautious, brilliant, and methodical. " 'When you moved into Admiral Spruance's command from Admiral Halsey's,' " recalled an officer who had served under both, " 'you moved from an area in which you never knew what you were going to do in the next five minutes or how you were going to do it, because the printed instructions were never up to date. . . . He [Halsey] never did things the same way twice. When you moved into Admiral Spruance's command, the printed instructions were up to date and you did things in accordance with them.' " [17]

The Third/Fifth Fleet was by this time a completely air-oriented naval force. It could operate at sea for weeks at a time, thanks to improvements in the navy's oceangoing supply system. An armada of thirty-four oilers plus aviation store ships, ammunition ships, and refrigerator ships kept the fighting vessels supplied and fueled, while specially assigned escort carriers brought in replacement aircraft.[18]

Although promotion of aviators to flag rank was still slower than the airmen felt it should be, the influence of the aviator had increased enormously since the early months of the war, when carrier task forces had been commanded by nonflying admirals of the old school. Now almost all carrier task force commanders were qualified aviators. Since late 1942 about 70 percent of the captains promoted to rear admiral had been aviators.[19] What was more, Admiral King had directed that in carrier task groups, the carrier admiral would always be in tactical command regardless of whether he was senior to the other admirals in the task group commanding the cruiser or battleship screen.

Beginning in January 1944 King also decreed that fleet- or task-force commanders had to have an aviator as chief of staff unless they were aviators themselves, and non-aviators as chief of staff if they were. Ironically, it was an aviator, Admiral Mitscher, who complained loudest about this rule; for a while he gave his new chief of staff, the famed destroyer tactician Arleigh Burke, a very tough time.[20] Admiral Spruance also lost his capable chief of staff, Captain Charles J. Moore, under this arrangement.

Since September the Third Fleet had been carrying out heavy attacks against Japanese air bases in the Philippines and against nearby bases from which the Philippines could be supported. On September 9 and 10 they raided Mindanao, on the twelfth they hit the Visayas, and on the twenty-first and twenty-second they assaulted Luzon. The Japanese, according to plan, held their aircraft in reserve and did not strongly contest the raids, but many of their aircraft were destroyed on the ground and the overall damage to Japanese installations was severe. These were the attacks which had prompted Halsey to suggest stepping up the timetable for the Philippines.

When the Third Fleet returned on October 10 to raid Luzon, the Ryukyus, Okinawa, and Formosa, the Japanese struck back. It was, as Admiral Halsey put it, a "knock-down drag-out fight between carrier air and shore-based air." In ten days of intense combat, the Japanese flung everything they had at the attackers. Their successes, however, were minimal.

The Japanese pilots who rose to meet the Americans bore only a superficial resemblance to the implacable air aces who had ravaged Pearl Harbor and the Indian Ocean. These aviators were new recruits, some of whom had never even flown in formation before. Many had learned all they knew about aerial combat by watching training films. They were no match for Halsey's veterans.

Admiral Fukudome, who commanded both army and navy air forces on Okinawa, knew his pilots were far too green to press home a daylight attack against the Third Fleet carriers. But he was confident that they could at least hold their own in combat over their own airfields. Fukudome's confidence evaporated rapidly as he watched his planes fall in flames after futile attacks on the American raiders. It seemed to the admiral that "our fighters were nothing but so many eggs thrown at the stone wall of the indomitable enemy formation." [21] The defenders lost over 500 planes; much shipping was sunk and the base facilities wrecked. American losses were less than 100 planes; two cruisers, *Canberra* and *Houston,* were badly damaged by torpedo bombers.

The two cruisers fell victim to planes of Admiral Fukudome's Typhoon Attack Force, a special army- and navy strike force trained to attack during bad weather or at night. These pilots, while more successful than their comrades in fighters, were almost as inexperienced. Few, especially among the army aviators, could tell a transport from a battleship. [22]

Inexperienced and overexcited, they claimed to have inflicted heavy losses on the Third Fleet. "A near miss became a hit; a hit became a fatal blow. . . . Sometimes the bursting of a bomb or the flare of antiaircraft fire was mistaken for a shipboard explosion. A fire in the darkness which suddenly disappeared was seen as a vessel sunk beneath the waves." [23] Imperial General Headquarters issued a communique announcing the sinking of eleven carriers and two battleships by the intrepid flyers. Once the reports were broadcast over Radio Tokyo, the total had risen to nineteen carriers along with several battleships, cruisers, and destroyers. The Emperor issued a special rescript to commemorate the "Victory of Taiwan," and celebrations were held throughout Japan.[24]

Halsey, hearing the triumphant announcements from Tokyo, decided to take advantage of Japanese delusions by stationing one of his carrier groups between Japan and the crippled cruisers, which were slowly retiring under tow, hoping that the cripples would act as bait to draw out the Japanese fleet. "Don't Worry!" Halsey cheerily signaled Rear Admiral L. T. Du Bose, who commanded the damaged ships and their screen—which Third Fleet wits promptly christened "Bait Div. 1." *

The Japanese, swallowing the bait, despatched Vice Admiral Shima's cruiser-destroyer force from the Inland Sea to finish off what they thought to be the battered remnants of the Third Fleet. Fortunately for Shima, scouting aircraft the next day got a good look at the disconcertingly large numbers of American carriers still afloat and intact. After they relayed this information to Imperial General Headquarters, Shima prudently retired. Halsey sardonically announced that: " 'All Third Fleet Ships Recently Reported Sunk by Radio Tokyo Have Been Salvaged and Are Retiring At High Speed Toward The Japanese Fleet.' " [25]

The chimerical victory of Taiwan had important consequences. Although Japanese losses in land-based aircraft were rapidly replaced, losses among Ozawa's remaining carrier air crews, who had been unwisely flung into the battle off Formosa, could not be made good. The Japanese carriers faced the coming confrontation with the American invasion forces stripped of their best offensive weapons.

The Japanese army faced the invasion with fewer anxieties. No naval officer at Imperial General Headquarters bothered to tell his army counterpart that the American losses off Formosa were probably greatly exaggerated. Army strategists had planned to fight only hold-

---

* A pun on the usual Navy abbreviation "Bat div." for "battleship division."

ing actions on most of the Philippine Islands and make an all-out
stand on Luzon, which had the best supply system and was big enough
for a defense-in-depth to be effective. Now, however, after the supposed grave losses to the American fleet, the invading forces were
expected to be much weaker. Perhaps the invasion could be contained. With the loss of so many American carriers and planes, Leyte
or other outlying islands could be reinforced without danger of inter-
diction by air. On October 18, as the American invasion fleets closed
in on the Philippines, Army Section of Imperial General Headquarters decided to fight the decisive battle on Leyte.

● ●

There is a photograph of part of the Leyte invasion fleet at anchor
at Hollandia in early October 1944, probably taken from a low-
flying aircraft. Even across the gap of forty years and through the
obscurity of the print, it is an impressive sight. Ships stretch to the
horizon like small black islands on the flat, calm sea. They fill the
whole ocean. Nothing but ships and white cumulus clouds can be
seen receding off into the grey distance. "Welcome to Our City"
was what Kinkaid signalled MacArthur as the cruiser *Nashville,* with
the southwest Pacific commander aboard, joined the invasion fleet.
Four hundred seventy-one ships sailed from Hollandia, another 267
from Manus in the Admiralties; together they carried over 160,000
troops with their equipment and supplies. Battleships, cruisers, escort
carriers, and destroyers from Kinkaid's Seventh Fleet provided the
escort for the invasion convoys, while Halsey's Third Fleet fast-carrier
task forces ranged the waters north and east of the Philippines, delivering their deadly air strikes against targets on Luzon.

Neither Halsey nor Kinkaid expected the Japanese fleet to make
a fight for Leyte since the impending invasions of Luzon and Mindoro
would put the Americans in a far more vulnerable spot—inside the
South China Sea, with their ships' backs to Japanese air bases in
China, Formosa, Okinawa, and Indochina. The southwest Pacific intelligence summary and the Seventh Fleet's operations plans minimized
the possibility of a naval battle at Leyte.[26] Halsey felt so confident
the Japanese were not coming out that he sent one of his four carrier
task groups, TG 38.1 under Vice Admiral John S. McCain, back
to the fleet's operating base at Ulithi for rest and replenishment.

Still, some members of Admiral Barbey's VII Amphibious Force,
which would be transporting the invasion troops, felt uneasy when
they learned that the battleships supporting the assault would carry

only 25 percent armor-piercing ammunition (the kind suitable for fighting other ships) in their magazines. That was only about twenty-five rounds per gun. Barbey's staff appealed to Seventh Fleet headquarters about this, but without success.[27]

Just after midnight on October 20, 1944, the invasion convoys began entering the channel leading to Leyte Gulf and the invasion beaches on the northeast coast of the island. Troops of the Sixth Ranger Battalion had seized the small islands of Suluan, Dinagat, and Homonhon at the entrance to the gulf a few days before: As their ships swept by in the predawn darkness sailors could see the navigation lights placed there by the rangers. The sun rose over heavy clouds to the east as the invading forces headed for their beachheads. Rear Admiral Daniel Barbey's Northern Attack Force made for San Pablo Bay off the town of Tacloban, and Vice Admiral Theodore Wilkinson's Southern Attack Force steamed toward the town of Dulag, about fifteen miles to the south of Tacloban. From the bridge of the *Nashville* General MacArthur could see Tacloban, where he had spent his first tour of duty as a young second lieutenant, fresh from West Point, forty-one years before.

Around six-thirty the battleships, cruisers, and destroyers opened fire. Seen from Admiral Barbey's flagship, the southwest horizon appeared a solid ring of flashes. To the west, dust, smoke, and flames obscured the view of the beach.[28] Four divisions—Major General Verne D. Mudge's First Cavalry Division, Major General F. A. Irving's 24th Infantry Division, Major General A. V. Arnold's Seventh Division and Major General James L. Bradley's 96th Infantry Division—were landed simultaneously at 10:00 A.M. The troops encountered scattered opposition as they came ashore and more as they moved inland, but by evening the Americans were well dug in along the eastern shore of Leyte. The First Cavalry stood on the outskirts of Tacloban, holding the airfield and the high ground surrounding it, while to the south the Seventh Division had captured Dulag and was moving on the nearby airstrip.

At one o'clock that afternoon, while the fighting still raged, MacArthur left the *Nashville* in company with the new President of the Philippines, Sergio Osmeña, and headed for Red Beach, where the 24th Division was making its way inland. Mortar- and small-arms fire could be heard as the landing craft approached the shore; a large LCM was burning on the beach. MacArthur's boat drew too much water to land, and one of his aides radioed the navy beachmaster for a smaller craft to take the general—resplendent in

freshly pressed khakhis, field marshall's cap, and sunglasses—
ashore. " 'Let 'em walk!' " snapped the harried Navy beachmaster,
who was struggling to unload hundreds of boats under intermittent
sniper fire.

Down came the ramp and out stepped MacArthur and his party
into the knee-deep water—and into one of the most famous photos
of the war. Pictures and newsreels of the general wading ashore
wearing his best man-of-destiny expression became so famous that
MacArthur's detractors later charged that the whole event had been
staged.

A few yards from the beach, correspondent Jan Valtin observed
that troops nearby were frantically donning their shirts as a small
group of men crossed the beach; " 'then you notice that one of the
group, the leader, wears no helmet. He wears a cap and he is smoking
a corncob pipe. He walks along as if the nearest Jap snipers were
on Saturn instead of in the palm tops a few hundred yards away.' " [29]

After a brief inspection of the beachhead, MacArthur stepped up
to a radio transmitter mounted on a weapons carrier and spoke into
the microphone: "People of the Philippines, I have returned! By
the grace of Almighty God, our forces stand again on Philippine
soil."

During the next two days the Americans steadily expanded their
beachhead. Advance elements of the First Cavalry Division entered
Tacloban on the afternoon of the twenty-first. To the south, the
Ninety-sixth and Seventh Divisions slogged through the swamps and
mud toward the airstrips of the southern Leyte valley west of Dulag.
On October twenty-third, a second ceremony was held on the steps
of the capitol building in Tacloban, where MacArthur and Osmeña
announced President Roosevelt's restoration of civil government to
the Philippines. A bugler sounded colors and, as an honor guard
of First Cavalry troops stood at attention, the American and Philippine
Commonwealth flags were hoisted at opposite ends of the building.

Far out at sea, other flags were flying from the signal halyards of
Admiral Halsey's flagship, *New Jersey*. A large Japanese fleet had
been sighted, headed for Leyte.

To Admiral Toyoda, commander in chief of the Combined Fleet,
there had been no question of waiting for a better opportunity. The
fleet would fight for Leyte, for once the U.S. gained a lodgement
anywhere in the Philippines, it could completely cut the navy's lifeline to its fuel sources in the south. [30] Toyoda's battle plan was designed to allow the Japanese fleet to make optimum use of its single

remaining asset: the largely undiminished power of its battleline and heavy cruisers. Combined Fleet's aircraft carriers were virtually help-less, with few planes and fewer pilots, but of the ten battleships with which Japan had entered the war, seven were still undamaged, while two of the gigantic *Yamato*-type battleships had since joined the fleet. There were also more than a dozen of the fine heavy cruisers which had borne the brunt of the fighting in the South Pacific.

The details of the plan called *Sho*-1 were very complicated but their essential aim was to use the nearly empty carriers to decoy Halsey's Third Fleet to the north, away from the Leyte beaches. Meanwhile, two task forces of battleships and cruisers would steam north from Linga. After threading their way through the central Philippines—one by Surigao Strait, the other by San Bernardino Strait—they would converge on the American transports and shipping in Leyte Gulf. The two striking forces were to emerge into Leyte waters at roughly the same time: a difficult feat of coordination in-deed.

Vice Admiral Nishimura Shoji commanded the Surigao Strait Force; it included the battleships *Fuso* and *Yamashiro,* a heavy cruiser, and four destroyers. Vice Admiral Shima's cruiser-destroyer force was supposed to steam down from the Inland Sea to join Nishimura, but the two never made contact and entered the strait separately. A far more powerful force, under Vice Admiral Kurita Takeo, was assigned to the San Bernardino Strait approach. Kurita's formation included the super-battleships *Yamato* and *Musashi,* three older battle-ships, ten heavy cruisers, two light cruisers, and more than a dozen destroyers. It was Kurita's force which the U.S. submarines *Darter* and *Dace* sighted off the southern entrance to Palawan Passage north-east of Borneo, a little after one o'clock on the morning of October 23.

The two subs radioed word of their contact to Seventh Fleet, then attacked the Japanese ships, which were steaming north at only sixteen knots to conserve fuel. The heavy cruiser *Atago,* Kurita's flagship, was torn apart by four torpedoes from the *Darter,* which also put two more into the heavy cruiser *Takao,* sending her limping back to Borneo for repairs. Meanwhile the *Dace* attacked the *Maya:* it blew up in less than four minutes after being hit by four torpedoes. Badly shaken, Admiral Kurita and his staff transferred to the *Yamato* and continued north.

All day on the twenty-third, Halsey's Third Fleet task groups took on fuel and ammunition from their supply flotilla; then they moved west toward the Philippines to launch searches the following morning. But Japanese land-based planes from Luzon were looking for Halsey: on the morning of the twenty-fourth, a few minutes after American search planes made contact with Kurita's force, by now south of Mindoro, three waves of Japanese fighters, bombers and torpedo bombers struck Admiral Frederick C. Sherman's Task Group Three.

Sherman's Hellcats were waiting: they took a heavy toll of the attackers. A single pilot, Commander David McCampbell, of the *Essex,* accounted for at least nine enemy planes, an all-time record, for carrier-borne fighters. McCampbell's flight of seven fighters picked away at the Japanese formation, taking advantage of the Hellcat's superior speed and high altitude performance to dive out of the sun at groups of stragglers.[31] Few of the Japanese attackers survived the relentless Hellcats; one that did, however, hit the carrier *Princeton* with a bomb, starting fires which ignited the gasoline and torpedoes of some planes on the hangar deck.

All morning and into the afternoon, firefighting crews battled to save the *Princeton,* while destroyers took off the rest of the crew and the cruiser *Birmingham* attempted to take the damaged ship in tow. Around three-thirty a tremendous explosion in the torpedo stowage area blew the carrier's flight deck into the air and sent deadly metal debris flying everywhere. Jagged bits of steel, gun barrels, and steel plates rained down on the *Birmingham.* Casualties were heavy on both ships, and the *Princeton* had to be scuttled. Meanwhile, Rear Admiral Bogan's carrier Task Group Four, unmolested by Japanese air attacks—which had concentrated exclusively on Sherman—launched his own strikes at Kurita's fleet.

On the bridge of the *Yamato,* now in the brilliant blue waters of the Sibuyan Sea, Admiral Kurita anxiously scanned the horizon. He knew that American carrier planes would find him soon. Where was the land-based fighter cover allocated to his force in the *Sho*-1 plan? After a time, a handful of planes arrived and took station over the fleet—all that remained from the morning battles with Sherman's task group. Most land-based planes were far away, attacking the American carriers. Admiral Fukudome, who commanded these aircraft, considered this to be more effective support of Kurita than providing fighter cover.[32]

Then at 10:30, a swarm of black spots appeared out of the east: American planes from Admiral Bogan's carriers. A strike from Sherman's carriers, which had been delayed by the Japanese air attacks, followed later. All that day, the American carrier aircraft worked over Kurita's task force, concentrating on the giant *Musashi,* the biggest target any of the pilots had ever seen. The augmented antiaircraft batteries on the Japanese men-of-war put up an impressive display but failed to do much damage to the attackers. By evening the *Musashi* was a wreck: hit by nineteen torpedoes and almost as many bombs, all power gone, badly flooded forward, her bow nearly under water. At 7:35 that night, one of the greatest battleships in the world rolled over slowly to port and sank, taking along about half her crew of 2,300.[33]

Battleships *Yamato, Nagato* and *Haruna,* and light cruiser *Yahagi* also received some damage; the heavy cruiser *Myoko* had to turn back to Brunei for repairs. Nevertheless, most of Kurita's force was still intact. But he was of no mind to sail into the narrow waters of San Bernardino Strait as American air attacks became heavier all the time. The admiral had heard nothing from Ozawa's carrier group or Nishimura's southern fleet; he could only assume that these forces had failed in their mission or been destroyed. At three in the afternoon Kurita signalled Combined Fleet that he was reversing course to get beyond range of Halsey's implacable carrier planes and await developments.[34]

Although Kurita could not know it, his order came at the moment when the *Sho* plan was on the verge of success. Far to the north Admiral Ozawa, his four carriers, *Zuikaku, Chitose, Chiyoda,* and *Zuiho,* left with only about 110 planes after the slaughter of the Formosa air battles, was doing his best to act as bait for the Third Fleet. That morning he had flung his few remaining planes at Admiral Sherman's task group to support the Luzon-based fighters, but the expected massive counterblow from the American carriers never came. In desperation, Ozawa ordered the *Ise* and *Hyuga,* two peculiar battleships which had been fitted with flight decks aft, to run south with some destroyers and engage the enemy. It was this force that was finally sighted by American search planes around four in the afternoon. An hour later, other searchers finally spotted Ozawa's carriers.

To Admiral Halsey and his staff in *New Jersey,* this was the news they had been waiting for. Nishimura's southern force had been discovered early that morning and Kurita's San Bernardino force had been under attack all afternoon, but the whereabouts of the Japanese carriers were, in Admiral Halsey's words, " 'the one piece missing in the puzzle.' "[35] He knew there had to be carriers around; the Japanese would not risk an operation as large as this was shaping up to be without them. Some of the planes which attacked Sherman had been reported as carrier types. Now, at last, came the sighting report.

How many Japanese carriers were there? The pilots' estimate, as reported by Admiral Mitscher, was one small and two large carriers, four battleships or heavy cruisers, eight other cruisers, and nine destroyers.[36] The mistake in number of aircraft carriers was unimportant, but the miscount of battleships was to have grave consequences. Instead of only *Ise* and *Hyuga,* which had had four of their twelve big guns removed after the Battle of Midway to accommodate a flight deck and were therefore weaker than any of their American counterparts, the pilots' reports suggested there might be as many as four powerful battleships with Ozawa.

Halsey and Kinkaid now knew the location of all three Japanese striking forces. Kurita's retreat had been reported. Nishimura's task force had been attacked by planes from Vice Admiral Ralph E. Davison's Carrier Task Group Four that morning. But these strikes had had little effect; Nishimura was still coming on. Ever since noon, Kinkaid's Seventh Fleet had been preparing to give him a hot reception.

That left the two fleets of Kurita and Ozawa. Until Ozawa's carriers were sighted, Halsey had been preparing for a fight with Kurita, should he change course and come through San Bernardino. That afternoon Halsey had transmitted a battle plan to Mitscher and his task-group commanders. He announced that four battleships, two heavy- and three light cruisers, and fourteen destroyers would be pulled out of the carrier formations to form a new Task Force 34, commanded by Vice Admiral Willis A. Lee. The new unit would take on any heavy surface forces that might be encountered. A later despatch advised that the task force would be formed when directed by Admiral Halsey.

Halsey's message was intended for his own commanders, but copies were sent for the information of CINCPAC in Hawaii and of Admiral King in Washington. Admiral Kinkaid was not an addressee, but his communicators intercepted the plan and showed it to him. Kinkaid was pleased with the news. The plan was "exactly what I would do." [37] Now the Seventh Fleet could concentrate on Surigao Strait, confident that Halsey's Task Force 34 was guarding San Bernardino.

That was the way Admiral Kinkaid interpreted the message and that was the way it was read in Honolulu and Washington. Everyone assumed that Task Force 34 had actually been formed. This conclusion seemed to be confirmed by a message Kinkaid received from Halsey around eight that night. The message read: " 'Central Force [Kurita] heavily damaged according to strike reports. Am proceeding north with three groups to attack carrier forces at dawn.' " [38] Since the Third Fleet had three carrier task groups, Admiral Kinkaid interpreted this message to mean that Halsey was going north with his three carrier groups, but leaving Task Force 34—the *fourth* group—behind to watch San Bernardino Strait.[39]

But Task Force 34 was not at San Bernardino Strait. In fact it had never been formed. Its battleships and cruisers were with Halsey's carriers, proceeding north at a leisurely sixteen knots. Meanwhile Kurita, spurred on by urgings from Combined Fleet, had turned his force around, passed through San Bernardino Strait around midnight, and turned south for Leyte Gulf.

Halsey's decision was based partly on reports by Mitscher's carrier pilots, who claimed far more damage to Kurita's fleet than they had actually inflicted, but he had other reasons as well. The Third Fleet commander and his staff were well aware of the criticism which had been leveled at Admiral Spruance for allowing the Japanese Fleet to "escape" at the Battle of the Philippine Sea.[40] Mitscher's chief of staff, the outspoken Arleigh Burke, had even sent a copy of his critique of Spruance's operations to his friend Rear Admiral Robert B. Carney, Halsey's chief of staff. As Burke observed, Halsey "didn't want any damn super-cautious business tied to him. . . ." [41] Nimitz's orders to Halsey included the sentence: " 'In case opportunity for destruction of major portion of the enemy fleet is offered, or can be created, such destruction becomes the primary task.' " [42]

Well, this was such an opportunity; Kurita's battered force might or might not wend its way through San Bernardino Strait, but here to the north was a new, unhurt, and apparently more dangerous force, one which included all the enemy carriers. It was this northern force which Halsey decided to destroy. To ensure that destruction would be complete, he would strike the northern force with all the strength of the Third Fleet, leaving nothing behind.

Task Force 34 would not wallow around off San Bernardino, a target for Japanese air strikes; it would accompany Mitscher's carriers on their run north. The big-gun ships of Task Force 34 would attack ahead of the carriers, which would "launch air strikes over the heads of the battleships like long-range artillery, then send in the surface force like infantry to mop up cripples and stragglers and slug it out with the enemy's heavy ships." [43] With the Third Fleet's massive superiority in battleships and carriers, the enemy would be annihilated.

Far to the south, meanwhile, Admiral Kinkaid prepared to take on Admiral Nishimura's southern force, confident that "Task Force 34" was guarding his northern flank. All of Kinkaid's big-gun ships and most of his destroyers under Rear Admiral Jesse B. Oldendorf were stationed near the entrance to Surigao Strait. Surigao, where Ferdinand Magellan had first sailed into the Philippines in 1521, was only about twelve miles wide at its southern mouth between Leyte and the Panaon Islands on the west and Dinagat and Mindanao on the east. Here Oldendorf had deployed six old battleships—all but one of which had been salvaged from the wreckage of Pearl Harbor—four heavy cruisers, four light cruisers, and about thirty destroyers. Back and forth across the northern end of the strait the battleships steamed in stately procession, cruisers and destroyers ahead and on either flank. It was a formation that Admiral Togo or Jellicoe or Sheer would have easily recognized and approved.

Far out in the Mindanao Sea, almost sixty miles from the lower entrance to the strait, however, another American fleet waited, one that would have seemed quite strange to the shades of those elder admirals. The ships in question were the Seventh Fleet's thirty-nine motor torpedo ("PT") boats under Lieutenant Commander R. A. Leeson. The diminutive PT boats were among the most glamorous craft in the navy. Commanded by young Reserve officers—many of them former yachtsmen, such as Lieutenant (j.g.) John F. Kennedy—they enjoyed a well-established reputation for feats of derring-do, a reputation enhanced by the well-publicized escape of General MacArthur from Corregidor aboard a PT boat in 1942.

It is unlikely that MacArthur knew about Oldendorf's disposition for battle; but if he did, he may have thought it fitting that the same craft which had carried him on his harrowing retreat from the Philippines should now be the first warships to engage the Japanese fleet upon his return. When Kinkaid first sent out his call for PT boats, only about twenty reported "ready for operations," but as word spread that the Japanese fleet was on its way, other boats "stirred around and got their engines put together so we ended up with 39 of the available 45." [44] All were on station before dark with orders to search for the enemy, report him when sighted, and attack independently.

A half hour before midnight, the first group of three PT boats sighted Nishimura's task force: four destroyers in the van, followed by the battleships *Yamashiro* and *Fuso,* with the cruiser *Mogami* in the rear.[45] Repeated attacks by the PTs failed even to slow down Nishimura. They scored no hits with their torpedoes and suffered considerable damage from Japanese fire; but their sighting reports were of considerable help to Oldendorf, who sent his destroyers into action.

And now a more deadly force greeted Nishimura as he made his way north. Destroyers of Captain Jesse B. Coward's Destroyer Squadron 54, racing down both sides of the strait, put a torpedo into the battleship *Fuso,* sank the destroyers *Yamagumo* and *Michishio,* and damaged the destroyer *Asagumo.* The last destroyer attack—by nine ships under Captain Roland Smoot—torpedoed the battleship *Yamashiro.* Oldendorf's battleships and cruisers had by this time opened fire on the Japanese column, now reduced to only three ships. Battleships, cruisers, and light cruisers alike poured a hail of armor-piercing shell into the hapless Japanese.

Oldendorf's aged battlewagons had done what every admiral dreamed of. They had "capped the 'T' " on the enemy. More precisely, they had put up the cross of the "T" and the Japanese had steamed into it.[46] It was all over in less than fifteen minutes. Of Nishimura's fleet, only *Mogami* and the destroyer *Shigure* managed to escape the deathtrap of Surigao Strait, and the *Mogami* was later finished off by air attack. Oldendorf lost no ships, although the destroyer *Albert W. Grant* was severely damaged when she got caught in a crossfire between the Japanese and American ships.

As she limped down the strait, the *Shigure* passed Admiral Shima's force, still trying to catch up with Nishimura. Shima had already had a brush with the PT boats, one of which had put a torpedo into light cruiser *Abukuma.* Now, a few minutes after passing the *Shigure,* Shima's flagship, the cruiser *Nachi,* collided with the crippled *Mogami.* That was enough for Shima: he beat a hasty retreat, harassed after daybreak by American planes.

Well satisfied with the night's work, Kinkaid held a final meeting of his staff early on the morning of October 25. As the meeting broke up, Kinkaid turned to his chief of staff, Captain Richard H. Cruzen. " 'Now Dick, is there anything we haven't done?' " " 'Admiral, I can think of only one thing,' " answered Cruzen. " 'We have never directly asked Halsey if TF 34 is guarding San Bernardino Strait.' " " 'Well, let's ask him,' " Kinkaid replied. At 4:12 he radioed Halsey: " 'IS TF34 GUARDING SAN BERNARDINO STRAIT?' "

Because of unaccountable delays, the message was received by

the *New Jersey* only at 7:00 A.M. It was not until then that Kinkaid
received the disquieting reply: " 'NEGATIVE. TF34 IS WITH ME
PURSUING ENEMY CARRIER FORCE.' " [47] Twenty minutes later
came another message, this time from the small escort carriers and
destroyers supporting the landing forces in Leyte Gulf. They were
under attack by Kurita's battleships and cruisers.

• •

After his pounding on the twenty-fourth, Kurita was amazed and
relieved to find his passage through San Bernardino unimpeded.
Expecting to fight their way out, his men were even more elated
to find only open water awaiting them as they emerged into the
Philippine Sea and swept down the east coast of Samar toward Leyte
Gulf. About half an hour after sunrise, lookouts aboard the flagship
Yamato sighted two masts to the southeast.[48]

The masts belonged to ships of Rear Admiral Clifton T. Sprague's
"Taffy 3," one of three groups of escort carriers under Rear Admiral
T. L. Sprague (no relation) supporting the operations of MacArthur's
troops ashore. Sprague's escort carriers (actually converted merchant
ships with a flight deck added) had been built to provide antisubmarine protection to convoys in the Atlantic. In the Pacific they were
also employed to beef up the close-in air support for amphibious
operations.

Sprague's five carriers were too slow to outrun even a battleship;
they had no armor and only a single five-inch gun. Their pilots were
trained solely for antisubmarine work and for the support of land
operations. With the carriers were three destroyers and four destroyer
escorts.

No one in Taffy 3 or the other two escort carrier units ever expected to fight a naval battle against the main Japanese fleet, yet
Admiral Clifton Sprague reacted as if he had been rehearsing the
situation for weeks. He changed course so as to open the range
but still keep near enough to the wind to launch planes, ordered
all ships to make smoke, and rapidly flew off all his remaining planes
to attack the enemy. A fantastic running battle now ensued between
Sprague's fleeing carriers and Kurita's fleet. The Japanese commander
believed he was engaging Halsey's big fleet carriers and other heavy
ships. Excitedly, he ordered "General Attack!" which sent his battleships, cruisers, and destroyers racing in pell-mell to attack the American carriers. It was almost as if, having finally achieved their objective,
the Japanese had gone to pieces.

Even at that, the slow "baby flattops" could not long have escaped annihilation, were it not for good luck and the courageous improvisation of Sprague's sailors and aviators. Planes from the carriers made repeated vicious, slashing attacks on the Japanese battleships and cruisers. Many planes were armed only with small, general-purpose bombs that could not penetrate warship armor. Others had no bombs at all, but made repeated "dry runs" to distract the attacking warships and cause them to change course. Fortunately, bombers from Rear Admiral Felix Stump's Taffy Two, just south of Sprague's group, had been properly armed with torpedoes. These planes soon entered the battle, inflicting heavy damage on Kurita's cruisers and helping to send three of them to the bottom.

Now chasing salvoes, now dodging into a friendly rain squall, Sprague's carriers fought to delay the inevitable. As the pursuers closed in, Sprague ordered his destroyers and destroyer escorts to deliver a torpedo attack. Three times the handful of destroyers and destroyer escorts dashed out of the smoke screen to engage whole columns of battleships and cruisers. Two of the destroyers and one destroyer escort were sunk, but their attacks distracted and disorganized the Japanese pursuit. Battleship *Yamato* steamed so far north to avoid torpedo tracks that she took herself completely out of the battle. A Japanese destroyer squadron was so badgered by the damaged destroyer *Johnston* that they fired torpedoes prematurely at long range.[49] An Avenger torpedo plane from carrier *St. Louis* actually managed to explode one of the torpedoes in the water by strafing; another was picked off by a five-inch gun from the same ship.[50]

Far to the north Admiral Halsey was receiving frantic calls for help from both the Spragues and Admiral Kinkaid. All through the previous night, as the Third Fleet steamed north, Halsey's officers had experienced growing doubts about the wisdom of leaving San Bernardino Strait. Late on the evening of the twenty-fourth, scouting planes from the carrier *Independence,* which carried aircraft equipped for night operations, reported that Kurita had turned around and was making for San Bernardino Strait again. Yet when Rear Admiral Gerald Bogan passed this information on to Halsey's flagship by voice radio, he was answered by the impatient voice of a staff officer who gruffly replied: "Yes, yes, we have that information." Admiral Lee twice signalled Halsey that he was certain Kurita was coming through San Bernardino Strait but received only a "Roger" in reply.[51] Aboard Mitscher's flagship *Lexington,* the staff held the same view as Lee, but was unable to convince Mitscher he should appeal to Halsey for a change of plans.[52]

When the frantic messages from the south began to come in,

Mitscher's planes were already in the air attacking Ozawa's decoy ships. The carriers *Chitose* and *Zuikaku* and the destroyer *Akitsuki* were already sinking as Mitscher's bombers and torpedo planes, unhindered by defending fighters, leisurely worked over the Japanese task force.[53]

Halsey still refused to turn south to get Kurita. Task Force 34 had finally been formed but Halsey wanted its battleships to polish off Ozawa's damaged ships. He continued north; but he did order Vice Admiral John S. McCain's Task Group One, which had been heading for Ulithi to rest and rearm, to go to the aid of the escort carriers. McCain had already been recalled to the Philippines but would require more than two hours to get within range of Kurita.

Although Halsey refused to be swayed by Kinkaid's alarms, they were producing vigorous handwringing in Pearl Harbor and Washington. More than an hour had already passed. The Third Fleet commander had failed to indicate what he would do to help the beleaguered escort carriers other than despatching McCain's far-distant task group to the scene. Admiral Nimitz made it a rule to avoid interference with his commanders in battle, but his concern was now so great that at 9:45 A.M., Philippine time, he sent a message to Halsey asking: " 'Where is Task Force 34?' " Nimitz was fairly certain by then that the task force must still be with Halsey: he intended the message as a gentle nudge to send TF34 south. A yeoman, detecting a certain note of emphasis in his boss's voice, added a "Repeat" after the words "where is." The complete message read: " 'TURKEY TROTS TO WATER RR FROM CINCPAC ACTION COM THIRD FLEET INFO COMINCH CTF SEVENTY-SEVEN X WHERE IS RPT WHERE IS TASK FORCE THIRTY FOUR RR THE WORLD WONDERS.' "

The opening phrase, "Turkey Trots to Water," and the closing one, "The World Wonders," were "padding"—that is, irrelevant phrases added to encrypted messages to make them harder for enemy code-breakers to crack. However, in the case of Nimitz's message, the *New Jersey*'s communicatiors guessed that "The World Wonders" might possibly be part of the real message. So it was that at 10:00 A.M. Halsey was handed what was to become one of the most famous and controversial messages of the war. What the Admiral saw was: " 'Where is, Repeat, Where is, Task Force 34, The World Wonders!' "[54]

Halsey was infuriated at the supposed insult. He was not to know until much later that the phrasing was a mistake, but he continued north for an additional hour before finally pulling out Task Force 34 and one of the carrier task groups, sending them south to help the Seventh Fleet. Kinkaid had long since ordered some of his old battleships, which had fought at Surigao Strait, to head north for Leyte Gulf; but they were over three hours away, and many were short of ammunition.

In the escort carrier task groups the situation was rapidly going from very bad to desperate. Sprague's carriers were being steadily herded in toward Leyte Gulf to the southwest. The carrier *Gambier Bay* was on fire and sinking, and Admiral Stump's middle group of escort carriers was now coming within range of Kurita's battlewagons. Then, around nine-thirty that morning, the incredible happened: the enemy cruisers and destroyers flanking Sprague's carriers abruptly turned northward and retired. " 'G-dammit, boys, they're gettin away!' " yelled a signalman on Admiral Clifton Sprague's flagship *Fanshaw Bay.* The admiral, who had expected "at best to be swimming by this time," could not believe it.[55]

It was true. Kurita was by this time so rattled and tired he believed that the carriers were outrunning him. He had still heard nothing from Ozawa, whose messages that the *Sho* Plan had succeeded never reached him, but he knew that Nishimura had been destroyed in Surigao Strait. His force was by now scattered over miles of ocean and more carriers had just been sighted. (These were Stump's force, identified like Sprague's by the Japanese as large fleet carriers.) Kinkaid's calls for battleships and cruisers, broadcast in plain English, had been read aboard *Yamato* and made Kurita wonder what additional forces might be closing in on him.[56]

The Japanese commander therefore decided to break off action and at least give his scattered force a chance to reform. After milling about for more than two hours, rounding up stragglers and cripples and fighting off more air attacks, he signalled Tokyo at 12:30 that he was heading north for San Bernardino Strait.[57]

Meanwhile, McCain's task group had been rushing toward Leyte Gulf at high speed. To avoid slowing the task force, McCain ordered the carriers to recover combat air patrol and scouts by speeding up to thirty-three knots, thus forging ahead of the fleet, which was steaming downwind. Then the carriers made a quick countermarch through the formation, recovering their planes in the process.[58] At a range of almost 340 miles, McCain launched a heavy strike. It did little damage, but it may have reinforced Kurita's determination to retire.

To the north, Halsey was slowed by the need to fuel his escorting destroyers. In the late afternoon he formed a smaller task group of the two fastest battleships, three light cruisers, and eight destroyers. Then he rushed down toward San Bernardino Strait—too late to catch Kurita. Ozawa, too, was retiring: he had lost all four of his carriers but accomplished his mission of decoying the Third Fleet.

However, the Battle of Leyte Gulf was not yet ended, for the Japanese still had one further weapon remaining: a suicide-attack unit known as the kamikaze. Kamikaze means "divine wind," and refers to the typhoon which shattered the great invasion fleet of Emperor Kublai Khan in the thirteenth century. The original Japanese name for the suicide units was *"Shimpu,"* a more dignified reading of the characters for "divine wind." Throughout the war they were referred to by the Japanese as *Shimpu* units. Yet they have been remembered by the more daredevil connotation, kamikaze.[59]

The first suicide-attack units were the brainchild of Vice Admiral Onishi Takijiro, commander of the First Air Fleet, who had concluded that Japan was now so outnumbered and outclassed in the air that conventional air attacks stood little chance of success.[60] The only hope was to turn the planes into human missiles by crash-diving them into the American men-of-war.

Although organized suicide attacks had never been employed on a large scale by the Japanese navy before, the advantages of such a method of warfare now appeared increasingly attractive. A suicide dive could be performed by even an inexperienced pilot, flying almost any kind of aircraft—and a crash-dive was hard to stop. The attacking plane had to be completely destroyed, not simply damaged, by antiaircraft fire. Japanese military leaders also believed that the inspiring example of sacrifice provided by the suicide pilots would bolster morale at home and unnerve the enemy. The Japanese spirit (*Yamatodamashii*) would triumph over the material superiority of the Americans.[61]

Onishi had hoped to coordinate the first kamikaze attacks closely with the sortie by the Combined Fleet under the *Sho* Plan. But such coordination proved impossible, so the first suicide missions were not flown until near the conclusion of Admiral Kurita's indecisive encounter with the American escort carriers off Samar.[62]

The target of these first attacks was the southernmost group of escort carriers under Rear Admiral Thomas L. Sprague. The kamikazes approached in groups of three escorted by other fighters and an evaluation plane.[63] One kamikaze dove on the carrier *Santee*, crashing through the flight deck and starting fires below. Another hit the carrier *Suwanee* forward of the after elevator, tearing a ten-foot hole in her flight deck.

Further north another group of planes attacked Rear Admiral Clifton Sprague's group, which had just escaped Kurita's guns. The carrier *St. Lo* was fatally damaged by a kamikaze which crashed through her flight deck, igniting the bombs and torpedoes below. The ship blew up and sank a half hour later.

It was a bloody introduction to a kind of war that would become wearisomely familiar to sailors in the closing months of the Pacific War. As Onishi had hoped, the fantastic suicide tactics surprised and dismayed the Americans.[64] Still, the new weapon did not slow them down and, as one recent student has suggested, the picture of fanaticism and contempt for life conveyed by kamikaze tactics may have contributed to American willingness to employ the atomic bomb as an alternative to confronting an entire nation of kamikazes in an invasion of Japan itself.[65]

To the American sailors and airmen who were on the receiving end of these relentless tactics of self-destruction, the kamikazes seemed motivated by a kind of supreme fanaticism. They appeared to be a sort of super-samurai who believed that in dying for the Emperor, they would achieve immortality in some heroes' paradise. In fact, most kamikaze pilots were not professional warriors but recent university students or graduates who were not particularly religious and had no expectation of a blissful or heroic afterlife. They were motivated by the traditional Japanese feeling of *"on,"* or obligation and gratitude toward their family and country, and by the traditional Japanese admiration for noble death in a worthy if hopeless cause.[66]

With the kamikaze attacks the bloody three-day naval battle for Leyte Gulf drew to a close. It was the greatest naval encounter in world history and the last real fleet action of World War II. It was a smashing defeat for the Japanese: they lost three battleships, all four of their carriers, six cruisers, and more than a dozen destroyers. Yet the *Sho* Plan had succeeded! Halsey had been lured away to the north; Kurita had fought his way to within sight of victory before throwing it all away in a fit of nerves, confusion, or bad judgment.

On the American side, most criticism centered on Halsey for leaving San Bernardino Strait unguarded and then failing to respond immediately to Kinkaid's calls for help. In his defense, Halsey cited his orders to make the Japanese fleet his main objective. He never conceded that Ozawa's carriers were a decoy and contended that Kurita's force had been so damaged by air attack that it could safely be left to Kinkaid.[67] The arguments continued for years but even at the time, it was evident to all observers, including Nimitz and King, that Halsey had made a serious error in judgment. Another officer might have been relieved under such circumstances—but Nimitz knew that Halsey was still the navy's most inspiring leader, so he kept his post.[68]

For the sailors off Leyte, the kamikazes were an ominous preview of times to come. For the soldiers ashore, the reconquest of the Philippines had barely begun. The road was to be long and hard.

NOTES

1. Samuel I. Rosenman, *Working With Roosevelt* (New York: Random House, 1952), pp. 456–57; Potter, *Nimitz*, p. 316.

2. Robert Ross Smith, "Luzon Versus Formosa," in Kent Roberts Greenfield, ed., *Command Decisions* (Washington: Office of Chief of Military History, 1960), pp. 463–65; Matloff, *Strategic Planning 1943–44*, pp. 480–83.

3. William Manchester, *American Caesar: Douglas MacArthur* (Boston: Little Brown, 1978), p. 369.

4. Courtney Whitney, *MacArthur: His Rendevous With Destiny* (New York: Knopf, 1956), p. 125; Gunther, *The Riddle of MacArthur*, pp. 9–10; Eichelberger, *Our Jungle Road to Tokyo*, pp. 165–66.

5. James, *Years of MacArthur*, pp. 533–34.

6. Smith, "Luzon versus Formosa," pp. 464–69.

7. M. Hamlin Cannon, *Leyte. The Return to the Philippines* (Washington, D.C.: Office of Chief of Military History, 1954), pp. 8–9; James, *Years of MacArthur*, p. 538.

8. Arnold, *Global Mission*, pp. 527–28.

9. Smith, "Luzon versus Formosa," pp. 471–72.

10. Major General Oliver P. Smith oral history interview, p. 124, Marine Corps Historical Center. Smith was assistant division commander of the First Marine Division.

11. Hough, *The Island War*, pp. 307–8.

12. Silverthorne, oral history interview, pp. 318–19.

13. Isely and Crowl, *U.S. Marines and Amphibious Warfare*, pp. 393–422; Samuel Eliot Morison, *Leyte* (Boston: Little, Brown, and Company, 1963), pp. 36–43. The best account is Frank O. Hough, *The Assault on Peleliu* (Washington, D.C.: Historical Division, Headquarters Marine Corps, 1950). A vivid eyewitness narrative is George P. Hunt, *Coral Comes High* (New York: Harper, 1946).

14. "History of Imperial General Headquarters, Army Section," Japanese Monograph No. 34, p. 131; Fukudome Shigeru, "The Battle off Formosa," in *The Japanese Navy in World War II* (Annapolis: U.S. Naval Institute, 1969), p. 100.

15. Koyomagi Tomiji, "The Battle of Leyte Gulf," in *The Japanese Navy in World War II* (Annapolis: Naval Institute Press, 1968), p. 108.

16. Memorandum, King to Secretary of the Navy, 3 June 1944, Ernest J. King Papers, Box 4.

17. Vice Admiral George C. Dyer quoted in E. B. Potter, "The Command Personality," *U.S. Naval Institute Proceedings,* January 1969, p. 25.

18. Morison, *Leyte,* pp. 75–80.

19. Buell, *Master of Sea Power,* pp 317.

20. Arleigh Burke, "Admiral Marc Mitscher: A Naval Aviator," *U.S. Naval Institute Proceedings,* April 1975, pp. 57–58.

21. Fukudome, "The Battle off Formosa," pp. 103–4.

22. Ibid.

23. Stanley Falk, *Decision at Leyte* (New York: W. W. Norton and Co., 1966), p. 60.

24. Morison, *Leyte,* p. 93.

25. Halsey and Bryan, *Admiral Halsey's Story,* pp. 207–8.

26. Reynolds, *The Fast Carriers,* p. 255; oral history memoir of Rear Admiral Charles Adair, 1975, pp. 400–1, Naval Historical Center.

27. Adair interview, p. 401.

28. MacArthur, *Reminiscences,* pp. 214–15; "Extract from Journal of Capt. Raymond Tarbuck U.S.N.," reproduced in Barbey, *MacArthur's Amphibious Navy,* pp. 244–48.

29. Cited in James, *Years of MacArthur,* p. 556.

30. Morison, *Leyte,* p. 167; James A. Field, *The Japanese at Leyte Gulf* (Princeton: Princeton University Press, 1947), p. 11.

31. C. Vann Woodward, *The Battle for Leyte Gulf* (New York: Macmillan Co., 1947), p. 55.

32. Morison, *Leyte,* p. 187.

33. Field, *Japanese at Leyte,* p. 69.

34. Koyomagi, "Battle of Leyte Gulf," p. 111.

35. Woodward, *Battle for Leyte Gulf,* p. 64.

36. Ibid., pp. 71–73.

37. Admiral Thomas C. Kinkaid oral history interview, Vol. 3, p. 317, U.S. Naval Historical Center.

38. Morison, *Leyte,* p. 296.

39. "Special Notes by Admiral Thomas C. Kinkaid" to "The Greatest Sea Fight" in Hanson W. Baldwin, *Battles Lost and Won* (New York: Harper and Row, 1966), p. 476.

40. Holmes, *Double-Edged Secrets,* pp. 192–93; Arleigh Burke oral history interview no. 4, p. 330.

41. Burke, ibid., pp. 329–30.

42. Morison, *Leyte,* p. 58.

43. Woodward, *Battle for Leyte Gulf,* p. 135.

44. Kinkaid oral history interview Vol. 3, p. 318.

45. Field, *Japanese at Leyte,* pp. 84–85.

46. Kinkaid oral history interview, Vol. 3, pp. 311–12. "Crossing the T" normally referred to a situation in which two battle lines steam parallel; the battle line with superior speed uses this advantage to cross ahead of the other.

47. Ibid., pp 370–71.

48. Field, *Japanese at Leyte,* pp. 98–100.

49. Morison, *Leyte,* pp. 255–73.

50. Ibid., p. 273.

51. Ibid., p. 195.

52. Ibid., p. 196; Burke interview no. 3, p. 133.

53. The dozen-odd defensive fighters left to Ozawa did no damage and were picked off by Mitscher's first attack wave.

54. Potter, *Nimitz,* pp. 338–40.

55. Morison, *Leyte,* p. 288.

56. Ibid., p. 298; Field, *Japanese at Leyte,* pp. 121–25. Kinkaid, after the war, wryly dismissed speculation that he had sent the messages in clear simply to scare Kurita. Kinkaid interview Vol. 3, pp. 338, 441.

57. Woodward, *Battle for Leyte Gulf.*

58. Thach interview no. 4, pp. 381–83.

59. Ivan Morris, *The Nobility of Failure: Tragic Heroes in the History of Japan* (New York: Holt, Rhinebart and Winston, 1975), pp. 288–89.

60. Inoguchi Rikihei and Nakajima Tadashi, "The Kamikaze Attack Corps," in *The Japanese Navy in World War II,* pp. 120–21.

61. Morris, *The Nobility of Failure,* p. 285.

62. Inogushi and Nakajima, "The Kamikaze Attack Corps," p. 123.

63. Inoguchi Rikihei and Nakajima Tadashi, *The Divine Wind: Japan's Kamikaze Force in World War II,* trans. Roger Pineau (New York: Ballantine, 1958), p. 119.

64. Kinkaid interview Vol. 2, p. 344.

65. Morris, *The Nobility of Failure,* pp. 329–30.

66. Ibid., pp. 305–20.

67. "Special Notes by Fleet Admiral William F. Halsey U.S.N. (Ret)" in Baldwin, *Battles Lost and Won,* pp. 481–87; Message, Commander Third Fleet to CINC-PAC, 25 October 1944, copy in King Papers.

68. Potter, *Nimitz,* pp. 344–45.

TWENTY

Behind the Lines

Intelligence played an important, sometimes vital, role in the war against Japan. Yet intelligence as it was conceived in the popular imagination—as an activity involving spies, double agents, secret reconnaissance, and the other ingredients of countless movies and thrillers—played a subordinate role to newer sources and methods spawned by the sophisticated technology of the twentieth century. Agents, saboteurs, commandos, and guerrillas there were in plenty, but the key figures of World War II intelligence were seldom mysterious agents lurking in the back streets of Tokyo or Singapore. More often it was hollow-eyed, unshaven cryptologists or photo-reconnaissance analysts deep in a basement or windowless room, surrounded by the clack of IBM sorters and tabulator machines or the stench of darkroom chemicals—it was men (and women) of this sort who were the intelligence aces of World War II. Far from the fighting fronts, in Pearl Harbor, Melbourne, New Delhi, and Washington, small groups of seldom-seen, overburdened, relentlessly driven men and women labored over the greatest intelligence feat of the war: the recovery, decryption, and analysis of Japanese coded messages.

The attack on Japanese military codes was part of a larger enterprise called communications intelligence. The widespread use of wireless telegraph or radio by armed forces and their governments, which began in the years just before World War I, provided new opportunities for gaining reliable and important information by eavesdropping on the messages or "traffic" which military units exchanged with each other. Of course, these messages were almost always coded and encyphered so as to make them unreadable to anyone not possessing the proper code books or encoding machines.

Cryptologists—or "codebreakers"—spent months, often years, trying to "break" a cypher or code. Yet even if one could not read the messages, it was possible to gain a great deal of valuable information from studying the frequency, quantity, origin, addressees, and other characteristics of radio messages. This process was known as radio traffic analysis; it frequently allowed American and Japanese intelligence officers to pinpoint the strength, location and destination of their opponent's forces.[1]

Beginning in the 1920s, the U.S. army and navy had begun to employ a system of cryptanalysis and traffic analysis. This involved the establishment of a system of intercept stations using sophisticated radio direction-finding and communications equipment and an organization of code-breakers to work over the intercepted messages. The army's codemaking and codebreaking organization was the Signal Intelligence Service, established in 1929 and headed by the brilliant Colonel William F. Friedman. It was Friedman who led the team which had broken the high-level Japanese diplomatic code called "Purple"—by building a duplicate of the Japanese code machine. In a display of interservice cooperation rare for those times the navy had supplied money and information on other Japanese codes and taken over all other decoding work to free the army team for its attack on Purple.[2] In the six months before Pearl Harbor, over 7,000 Japanese messages had been intercepted, decrypted, and translated—an average of almost 300 per week.[3]

American code-breakers' mastery of the Purple code was so complete that top American leaders appear to have considered sending out a bogus message as a deception measure. George Linn, a senior Navy codebreaker, recalled that early on the afternoon of December 7, "G-2 came in and motioned me to one side. I was floored when he asked me if we could encrypt a message in purple."

Linn thought for a moment then replied that such an operation was possible but would take time and was sure to be discovered by the Japanese in the end. "Years of work will go down the drain," he warned, once the Japanese caught on and began to reevaluate their crypto system. After some time, Linn received word that the bogus message plan was off.[4] For a few hours on the day of the Pearl Harbor attack, the United States had come close to losing a weapon far more important than any of the battleships sunk by the Japanese.

In a less spectacular manner the army's 2d Signal Service Company, under an equally dedicated officer, Major (later Lt. Col.) Joseph R. Sherr), had also begun to carry out important radio-intelligence work from its base in the Philippines. Originally established to intercept and forward Japanese diplomatic messages to Washington, the 2d Signal Service Company also exchanged raw and processed radio intelligence with navy codebreakers on Corregidor. Beginning in the summer of 1941, copies of these intercepts were delivered regularly to MacArthur's chief of staff, General Sutherland; those of special interest were taken directly to the commanding general.[5] MacArthur thus enjoyed the advantage, unavailable to his counterparts in Hawaii, of firsthand access to the fruits of American code-breaking.

Following the attack on the Philippines, the army code-breakers concentrated on traffic analysis of Japanese air units. In addition, they were able to intercept and translate some of the large number of messages which Japanese pilots transmitted "in clear." Within a few days, the 2d Signal Service Company were able to pinpoint the Japanese radio nets in Formosa and the southern Philippines. By monitoring the nets they could determine when Japanese air attacks were on their way. Unfortunately, their warnings were often ignored by the Army Air Forces commanders, who were generally unfamiliar with signal intelligence.[6]

The codebreakers, however, had implicit faith in their system. "When the sensitivity control [on our receiver] read 'zero' and the signals could be heard out in the yard," recalled one codebreaker, "someone would alert the guard. As soon as the guard heard motors and saw specks in the sky, he would bang the side of the building with his rifle butt. The door would fly open and erupt operators who hit the ground a-running for the shelter. I have made the hundred-yard dash over broken ground and through the weeds in what the boys swore was much less than ten seconds."[7]

Ironically, the Signal Service Company achieved one of its greatest tactical successes after MacArthur's air force had been almost wiped out by Japanese air attacks. Early in March 1942 an American observation plane, escorted by MacArthur's four remaining P-40 fighters, was returning to Bataan when they were spotted by a Japanese reconnaissance plane. Army code-breakers on Corregidor picked up conversations between the reconnaissance plane and its base, including the information that six Japanese fighters had been despatched to polish off the P-40s. This was relayed to the American fighters, who concealed themselves behind a nearby mountain and waited for the Japanese. "The enemy fighters split formation, three coming down the China Sea side and three coming down the Manila Bay side of Bataan. When they arrived, two P-40's jumped each formation. The three Japs who came down the China Sea side were down in the water in nine minutes. . . . The three Japs who came down the Manila Bay side lasted about fifteen minutes . . . one of our planes pulled up behind the Japs and with two short bursts within ten seconds he shot down two planes. . . ." [8] In addition to this small success, radio intercepts also made possible the destruction of three Japanese landing barges during the Battle of the Points.

But these achievements could have no effect on the losing battle for Bataan. The army codebreakers were evacuated to Corregidor, where they continued to make good progress on mapping Japanese radio nets and decrypting intercepted messages. Moved to Australia shortly before Wainwright's surrender, the 2d Signal Service Company formed the core of the American component of MacArthur's cryptographic operation in the southwest Pacific theater.

The navy's cryptanalytic and traffic analysis organization was the Communications Security Unit, or OP-20-G, under Commander Laurence F. Safford, who had headed the navy's communications intelligence efforts since 1924. In that year, Safford took charge of what was then known as the "research desk" of the Code and Signal Section in the Office of the Chief of Naval Operations. By 1925 radio surveillance units were established at Guam and the commander in chief of the Asiatic Fleet assumed responsibility for the collection of radio intelligence on the Japanese. Intercept stations were set up at Shanghai and Peking and aboard ships at sea. By the end of the 1920s navy radio intelligence activities in the Far East were concentrated in the Philippines, where codebreakers were reporting good progress in solving some of the Japanese naval codes.[9] During the late 1930s the Philippine codebreakers published a weekly "Summary of Radio Intelligence," which reported on information gained concerning Japanese naval and air activities.[10]

By 1941 the Philippine branch had become one of two major communications intelligence centers operated by OP-20-G in the Pacific. The second was at Pearl Harbor. Supporting them both was a widespread network of outlying stations which intercepted the raw messages and forwarded them to OP-20-G for analysis. The navy cryptanalysts concentrated their efforts on Japanese naval codes. The two which received most attention were JN-25, the standard operational naval code, and a special high-level code called the Japanese Flag Officer's Code. The Flag Officer's Code was reserved for only the most important command messages. Since it was seldom used, the codebreakers lacked a sufficient volume of messages to work on and consequently never cracked it. Good progress was made with the widely employed JN-25 code, but a few days before the Pearl Harbor attack, the code was suddenly changed.[11]

At the beginning of the war therefore, despite the brilliant codebreaking feats of the past, the navy was unable to read any of the major Japanese military codes. All navy efforts were thrown into breaking down the new standard five-digit code introduced in December 1941, but OP-20-G and its field stations were seriously handicapped by lack of trained personnel and equipment. In addition, officers with a knowledge of Japanese were rare. In more than two decades, the U.S. Navy had managed to produce only about 40 competent Japanese-language officers, and many of these men were in jobs unrelated to codebreaking. The codebreaking unit in Hawaii was so shorthanded it was reinforced by musicians from the band of the crippled battleship *California*. They proved to be such able natural cryptanalysts that Naval Intelligence began to pay special attention to recruiting men with musical backgrounds.[12]

The most experienced and talented codebreakers were at Pearl Harbor in the communications intelligence unit later known as the Fleet Radio Unit, Pacific ("FRUPAC"), commanded by Commander Joseph J. Rochefort.[13] Together with the codebreakers of OP-20-G and the Philippine station ("Station Cast," soon evacuated to Australia), they worked mind-numbing hours in stale, windowless rooms, surrounded by IBM machines and piles of paper. Rochefort felt a large measure of personal blame for the fact that Pearl Harbor had been taken by surprise; he drove himself and his men unsparingly.

By March 1942 portions of the new Japanese main naval code could be read, as could the Japanese weather-forecasting cypher and a minor code used in the mandated islands. This progress in cryptanalysis, plus information gained through traffic analysis and direction finding enabled Rochefort and his codebreakers to identify Port Moresby as the objective of an upcoming Japanese operation called "MO," involving two carriers from Admiral Nagumo's striking force as well as other naval and land-based air units.[14] Nimitz's forces were duly alerted. The ensuing Battle of the Coral Sea early in May generated a still larger volume of radio traffic, highly useful to the codebreakers. Not all messages were intercepted, and not all intercepted messages could be read even in part, but by spring the codemakers had made gigantic strides. They were aided by the fact that Japan's far-flung operations during the early months of the war had greatly complicated her communications security problems. By April 1942 there were so many different garrisons, task forces, commands, and other organizations in the various parts of Japan's newly won empire that distributing code- and cypher books for a major code change became a formidable task. Such changes were often delayed; units that had failed to receive new code books had to continue using older codes—some of which could be read by the Americans. This situation continued throughout the war—an immense help to American cryptanalysts.

In the spring of 1942, long-overdue changes in the Japanese main naval code were not carried out until the end of May. By that point American codebreakers had pieced together almost the whole of Yamamoto's operation plan for Midway, including identification of the Aleutians as diversionary targets and the date and position from which the Japanese would launch their attacks.[15]

Codebreaking did not assure the American victory at Midway but it made victory possible. Midway was the greatest single success produced by intelligence in the war with Japan, but it was far from typical. Cryptanalysts did not often acquire information which enabled commanders to shape an entire operation on sure knowledge of the enemy's strategy and plans. Far more typical was information gleaned about the enemy's order of battle, the state of his supplies, the readiness of his forces, the location of units, the sailing of a convoy—day-to-day details which, when pieced together over days and weeks, gave American leaders an important, sometimes decisive, edge.

The treatment of Commander Rochefort and his men by the navy and by the country to which they had rendered such outstanding service was shabby and disgraceful. After the Midway victory, Rochefort had become involved, or perhaps was merely the victim of, a bureaucratic power struggle between the Office of Naval Intelligence and the Office of Naval Communications. Both wanted control of OP-20-G and its field operations in Hawaii and Australia. Eventually, the Office of Naval Communications won out, much to the chagrin of Rochefort, who railed against the leadership of the Office of Naval Communications and talked of FRUPAC's "seceding" from it.[16]

Following on this development came a strong recommendation

from Nimitz and Admiral Worth Bagley, commandant of the 14th Naval District, that Rochefort and other Hawaii codebreakers receive decorations for their part in the Midway victory. These recommendations were received with great resentment in Washington. The Office of Naval Communications, Rochefort recalled, "had taken the position that the solving of the key message at the Battle of Midway had been a joint, a team effort by NEGAT (OP-20-G), HYPO (Hawaii) and CAST, and that no single person deserved credit. In reality, the NEGAT people had taken most of the credit themselves. They had convinced Admiral King that they had done the bulk of the work." [17]

None of the principal officers involved in the codebreaking effort in Pearl Harbor before Midway ever achieved flag rank. Rochefort himself was relieved of command of the communications intelligence unit the following October and ordered to sea. Admiral King subsequently turned down Nimitz's suggestion that Rochefort be awarded the Distinguished Service Medal. Several years after the war Nimitz tried again, writing a long letter to the secretary of the navy outlining Rochefort's services and recommending him for the Distinguished Service Medal. His letter was returned with a note by the assistant secretary of the navy explaining that the time for consideration of World War II awards had passed and could not be reopened.[18]

From the codebreakers' point of view, American intelligence at Midway was almost too successful. Word of the American intelligence triumph soon began to seep into the press. The British, who earlier in the war had broken the major German codes, often employed the expedient of giving credit to scouting planes and submarines for naval successes actually achieved through the help of cryptanalysis. Whenever British forces enjoyed such successes, the government always hastened to have stories planted in the press lauding the excellent scouting of the Royal Navy and Royal Air Force.[19]

The U.S. Navy was less fortunate. Shortly after the Battle of Midway the *Chicago Tribune* published a front page story headlined "NAVY HAD WORD OF JAP PLAN TO STRIKE AT SEA," which declared that the U.S. Navy had known in advance the strength and disposition of the Japanese forces. The article went on to describe these in detail, even citing the names of major warships in the Japanese task forces. The source of the story was *Tribune* correspondent Stanley Johnston, who, contrary to security regulations, had been shown a copy of Yamamoto's decyphered operations order by a naval officer friend.

Yet this was not the end of the security leaks. The nationally known radio news analyst, Walter Winchell, mentioned in at least two broadcasts that the navy had advance knowledge of the whereabouts of the Japanese fleet.[20] Winchell's source was unknown but the navy insisted on prosecuting Johnston and the *Tribune* for espionage.[21] The Justice Department reluctantly undertook the prosecution but the case came to nothing when a navy expert witness refused to tell a grand jury *why* the enemy could benefit from the information in the article.[22] Meanwhile, a freshman Congressman, Elmer J. Holland, took it upon himself to denounce the *Tribune* on the floor of the House. In the course of his speech he declared that: " 'Somehow our Navy had secured and broken the secret code of the Japanese Navy.' "[23]

Navy codebreakers were beside themselves. They were certain that the Japanese were making drastic changes in their code and cypher system, and strenuous efforts to improve their communications security—even to the extent of encyphering radio call signs—all as a result of the *Tribune* leak.[24] No post-war evidence has ever been put forward to suggest that the Japanese learned of the *Tribune* article, but for whatever reason, the task of the cryptographers after Midway became much more difficult. The Japanese changed their codes on June 1 and then changed them again in August, just as the cryptanalysts were beginning to make some progress.[25] Cryptanalytic solutions which earlier in the war could be achieved by a few experts using relatively simple means now required close teamwork by large numbers of codebreakers and complex calculating and tabulating machinery. Yet the frequent code changes were causing the Japanese problems as well, for some of their more remote units in the Pacific could not be supplied with current code books and cyphers on time, and had to employ minor or superseded codes which American cryptanalysts could read.

Before the end of 1942, the codebreakers, aided by Japanese code books captured in the Solomons, were again reading large parts of the principal Japanese navy code. A few months later they achieved another important breakthrough in decrypting the code employed by the Japanese to transmit orders to their supply and merchant ship convoys and escorts.

Codebreaking had played an important part in American submarine operations since the beginning of the war, but with the breaking of the convoy code, Pacific Fleet submarine operations were closely integrated with the flow of decrypted information furnished by Nimitz's codebreakers. A direct-line telephone was installed between the Pacific Fleet's submarine operations office and the communications intelligence organization. Submarines could now be routed directly to potential targets, eliminating the need for long, fuel-consuming searches.[26]

Yet as in the Battle of Midway, such information only made success possible; it did not ensure it. During the year 1943, codebreakers directed patrolling submarines to a total of over 800 potential targets. Of these, 445 were not even sighted, either because the submarines contacted were pursuing other targets, were unable to reach the desired area, or were in the area but could see no targets. Of the 350-odd Japanese ships sighted, only about one-third were actually attacked. Thirty-three of these were sunk, fifty-six damaged, and thirty-one were either not hit or sustained no important damage. Two hundred thirty-four ships were left unmolested, usually because the attacking sub was engaging other targets or was in an unfavorable position.[27] The overall value of communications intelligence to submarine operations in the Pacific is hard to assess, because during the brief periods when the codebreakers were unable to read the convoy code due to a change in the cypher, submarine sinkings of Japanese ships were almost as high as when cryptgraphic information was available. However, many submarine skippers attributed these successes, in part, to knowledge about Japanese routes and operational procedures they had gained through earlier intercepts supplied by the codebreakers.[28]

In the struggle for Guadalcanal, cryptanalysis played at best a secondary role to other types of intelligence. For most of that time the Japanese codes were unreadable, but during January 1943, when the codes could again be read, decrypted Japanese messages and traffic analysis enabled the navy to intercept and turn back three runs of the Tokyo Express. In late January Allied forces learned through communications intelligence of scheduled supply runs by Japanese submarines. One of these, "I-1", was intercepted and sunk by the New Zealand corvettes *Kiwi* and *Moa* near Guadalcanal, yielding the code books which proved so valuable in future cryptanalytic efforts.[29]

In April 1943 radio traffic analysts and cryptanalysts at Pearl Harbor, closely monitoring Japanese radio communications at Rabaul, were able to piece together the itinerary for Admiral Yamamoto's ill-fated inspection visit to the Northern Solomons. The result was the skillful, minutely timed interception of his plane over Buin by

American fighters. This striking success gave Nimitz's codebreakers days of anxiety again, lest the Japanese draw the obvious conclusion that their codes were being read.[30]

Although the achievements of Nimitz's codebreakers were probably the most spectacular, the cryptanalysis effort in the war with Japan was a worldwide one. In Washington the navy's OP-20-G and the army's Signal Security Agency continued to work on high-level Japanese army and navy codes. In New Delhi and London British and American cryptanalysts also tackled the Japanese codes.[31] Both the army and the navy codebreaking establishments expanded greatly in the months following Pearl Harbor. In June of 1942, the army, the navy, and the Federal Bureau of Investigation agreed on a division of cryptanalytical work. The army assumed full responsibility for the production of intelligence from diplomatic traffic—that is, the "MAGIC" intercepts—while the FBI and navy undertook the work on traffic sent by clandestine radio transmitters. The navy's share of the clandestine work was in turn assumed by a Coast Guard communications intelligence unit which had been operating under OP-20-G's direction. This left navy codebreakers free to concentrate all their efforts on Japanese naval traffic. The following month this arrangement was officially approved by the president, who issued a directive specifically confirming all cryptanalytic work to the three agencies. (The Federal Communications Agency, however, continued to monitor foreign radio broadcasts and work on the detection of unlicensed radio transmitters.[32])

OP-20-G expanded rapidly; by February 1943 it had outgrown its quarters in the temporary Navy Department building complex on Constitution Avenue and moved to the Mount Vernon Seminary, five miles from downtown Washington. Here, in a former private school for girls, over 1,100 men and women worked on the complex problems associated with codebreaking. By the end of the war, there were over 5,000 persons so employed.[33]

In addition to its Washington unit, the navy continued to operate two field processing centers, at Pearl Harbor and in Australia. The Australian center, originally called FRUMEL (Fleet Radio Unit, Melbourne), had as its nucleus the U.S. Navy's communications intelligence personnel from the Philippines who had been evacuated by submarine to Java and then to Australia shortly before the fall of Corregidor. This group joined with a Royal Australian Navy cryptanalytic unit housed in Victoria Barracks in Melbourne.[34] Together with other Australian and British codebreakers, they constituted a combined U.S.-Australian naval unit under the commander in chief of the Seventh Fleet.[35] FRUMEL was under the control of the Chief of Naval Operations, not directly under MacArthur: his G-2, General Willoughby, later complained that FRUMEL failed to supply MacArthur's headquarters with timely intelligence because it was answerable only to Washington, "is not bound by any local responsibilities, forwards what they select and when it suits them." Still, MacArthur was more than a little to blame for this state of affairs since he had rigidly excluded naval intelligence personnel from his own codebreaking agency, called Central Bureau.[36]

In any case, historians have recently presented convincing evidence that, whatever the formal arrangements might have been, MacArthur was receiving the results of naval codebreaking efforts undertaken not only in Melbourne, but also at Pearl Harbor. This was arranged by General Sutherland, who met daily with the naval intelligence liaison officer from the Seventh Fleet, Captain A. H. McCollum, to receive the latest intercepts.[37] Captain J. R. Fife apparently performed the same function with regard to diplomatic intercepts received by FRUMEL.[38]

The army's Signal Intelligence Service underwent an expansion similar to OP-20-G. It, too, outgrew its Washington headquarters and moved across the Potomac River to Arlington Hall—another former girls' school, but in the Virginia suburbs. Unlike OP-20-G, which was ultimately subject to the director of Naval Communications, the army's codebreaking activity remained under Army Intelligence as "Special Branch, Military Intelligence Service." Its head was the formidable Colonel Alfred McCormick, a former New York lawyer and a confidant of Secretary Stimson. Special Branch produced a daily MAGIC Summary which provided high-level leaders with a synopsis of the most important diplomatic intercepts as well as supplements relating to the Japanese army and navy.[39]

In the Southwest Pacific Area MacArthur had inherited the small army communications intelligence unit, 2d Signal Service Company, under Lieutenant Colonel J. R. Sherr. In April 1942 Sherr's unit was combined with the Australian army's Special Wireless Group, which had seen service in North Africa and the Middle East, and some Royal Australian Air Force Personnel, forming the "Central Bureau" under the general direction of MacArthur's Chief Signal Officer, Major General Spencer B. Akin.[40]

Initially, Central Bureau concentrated its efforts on radio traffic analysis and on breaking lower-grade Japanese cyphers. Later it progressed to solution and translation of higher-level Japanese army codes.[41] Like other parts of MacArthur's headquarters organization, Central Bureau grew rapidly. By late 1943 it employed over a thousand men and women drawn from the Australian, American, British, and Canadian armed forces. By the end of the war its strength was over 4,000 men and women, with detachments in all parts of the southwest Pacific theater.[42] Through its liaison with the Australians and British, Central Bureau had access to British decrypts of German messages which the British called ULTRA, and also to the highly successful British codebreaking activities in India, where cryptanalysts had made significant progress in breaking Japanese army traffic.[43]

Typically for the southwest Pacific, the hand of General Sutherland and MacArthur's GHQ lay heavily on Central Bureau's efforts. Sutherland and Akin blocked most attempts by the bureau to coordinate its work more closely with codebreaking operations in other theaters and in Washington. Even liaison with other parts of MacArthur's GHQ were rigidly restricted by General Akin.[44]

Central Bureau's intelligence gave MacArthur valuable, sometimes vital, intelligence in his long road back to the Philippines. During the Hollandia-Aitape campaign, it provided a steady stream of information on enemy strengths and dispositions, the state of Japanese supplies—even the complete defense plan for the Madang Wewak Hansa Bay area. This intelligence enabled MacArthur to plan his bold leap to Hollandia in confidence that the enemy would indeed be taken unaware. When the Japanese counterattacked along the Driniumor River in July, the Allies already had the complete plan of attack for Adachi's 20th and 41st divisions: they had been decrypted and made available to American commanders two weeks before the Japanese offensive.[45]

Central Bureau performed a similar service for the American forces on Bougainville in March 1944. It intercepted a message to Tokyo from the Japanese 17th Army on March 19, reporting plans for an attack on American forces at Cape Torokina three days later. The message was translated by mid-afternoon on the twenty-first and transmitted immediately to Torokina.[46]

Despite such successes, U.S. Army intelligence experts rated Central Bureau far below the organizations in Hawaii and Washington in efficiency and value of its output. An intelligence officer with MacArthur's Far East air forces reported that their primary source of tactical intelligence for air operations were navy decoded messages, with Washington decrypts a secondary source and Central Bureau a "relatively minor" third.[47] Another officer observed that " 'MacArthur has been oversold by his subordinates on the quality of production of his theater agency, Central Bureau. . . . Tactically, the Navy is incomparably superior to Army production.'" During the final year of the war, southwest Pacific ground and air units depended upon their own mobile Signal Radio Intelligence companies or squadrons for most of the information they obtained through codebreaking.[48]

A continuing headache for Allied codebreakers was the problem of safeguarding the intelligence they obtained through cryptanalysis—above all, safeguarding the fact that the Japanese codes were being read. Next to the atomic bomb, this was probably the most important secret of the Pacific War. How to safeguard this secret while making use of the intelligence obtained was a vexing problem for all commanders. King and Nimitz oscillated between daring and extreme caution in their handling of decrypts. In their cautious phase, even submarine war diaries and patrol reports were censored so as to contain no reference to this special intelligence.[49] In Task Force 58, not even Admiral Mitscher's chief of staff was authorized to see cryptographic information.[50]

The worst security conditions probably prevailed at MacArthur's headquarters during the reconquest of the Philippines. Army intelligence officers bemoaned the fact that the southwest Pacific commander's staff offices had no adequate safes and that his subordinates insisted on passing ULTRA information over the telephones, although these were almost certainly being tapped.[51] Eventually the army established a system of Special Security Officers with responsibility for receiving, safeguarding, and disseminating ULTRA intelligence—a successful arrangement which remained in effect through the end of the war.

● ●

Codebreaking was only one part of the vast and complicated Allied intelligence effort in the war against Japan. Each theater was organized differently for intelligence purposes. In Nimitz's Pacific Ocean Areas, the creation of a joint staff led to establishment of the Joint Intelligence Center, Pacific Ocean Areas under Brigadier General Joseph J. Twitty. The Joint Intelligence Center was responsible for interpretation of aerial photographs, translation of captured documents, and interrogation of prisoners. It provided whatever was needed in the way of maps, charts, and terrain models. It also published a classified "Weekly Intelligence Bulletin."

During the early months of the war there was little for the translators and interrogators to do, but as the campaigns in the central Pacific progressed, a huge tide of captured documents flooded the Joint Intelligence Center. Fifty tons of documents were received from Saipan alone. By 1944 the Joint Center employed more than 200 translators, most of them young naval reserve officers especially recruited for their language proficiency.[52]

The codebreaking group, now officially titled Fleet Radio Unit, Pacific, remained outside the Joint Intelligence Center under the Pacific Fleet's communications officer. The link between the Fleet Radio Unit and the Joint Center was the latter's Estimates Section, headed by Captain W. J. Holmes, USN. Housed in the same building as the Fleet Radio Unit, the Estimates Section received all decrypted messages from OP-20-G, Fleet Radio Unit, and other naval cryptographic centers, then processed the information for dissemination to CINCPAC commands.[53]

In MacArthur's southwest Pacific theater all intelligence activities came under the direction of his G-2 section head, Major General Willoughby. G-2 exercised broad authority over a wide variety of intelligence agencies. The Allied Intelligence Bureau (AIB) was principally concerned with the secret collection of intelligence in enemy-held areas, mainly by means of agents on the ground reporting by radio or courier. AIB was responsible for coordinating and supporting the clandestine activities of various British, American, Dutch, and Australian intelligence units in its theater. These included sabotage, espionage, commando operations, and assistance to guerrilla resistance movements.[54]

Probably the single most valuable operation run by the Allied Intelligence Bureau was the coastwatcher service. Developed by the Royal Australian Navy after World War I as a network of observers to keep an eye on the continent's vast unguarded coast, the organization gradually expanded into the Solomons, New Guinea, and the Bismarcks during the 1930s. The watchers selected were mainly planters, missionaries, or government officers in the remote villages, plantations, and mines of New Guinea and the southwest Pacific. The watchers were supplied with special battery-powered "teleradios" which could stand up to tropical heat and damp. They had a range of 400 miles for voice transmissions and 600 miles if telegraphic keys were used. Unfortunately, the radios were heavy—very heavy, requiring up to sixteen porters to transport them from place to place.[55]

The coastwatchers and their chief, Lieutenant Commander Eric

A. Feldt, RAN, were taken over by the Allied Intelligence Bureau in 1942. By this time a good part of the Solomons had been occupied by the Japanese. Some of the coastwatchers had remained behind in Japanese-held territory, helped by friendly local inhabitants; others had been shipped in by submarine or plane. In the Solomons campaign the coastwatchers attained near-legendary status among American fighting men for their accurate and timely intelligence. Their reports of Japanese ship or aircraft movements repeatedly saved Allied forces at Guadalcanal from disaster.

Constantly on the move, with little or no means of defense, and totally dependent on the goodwill of their local guides and assistants, the coastwatchers managed to keep MacArthur and Halsey well informed. They used a network of hidden radio stations, stretching south from Bougainville through the central Solomons to Guadalcanal and to Port Moresby in New Guinea. To give them some protection under international law, the civilian coastwatchers were inducted en masse into the Australian army and navy. Unfortunately, this distinction availed them little if they fell into Japanese hands.

In addition to their intelligence work, coastwatchers aided in the rescue of over a hundred U.S. aviators.[56] It was an Australian coastwatcher from Kolombangara, Arthur Reginald Evans, who arranged the rescue of Lieutenant (j.g.) John F. Kennedy and his crew from the sunken PT-109 in August 1943. Like the exploits of the cryptographers, those of the coastwatchers were never mentioned in the press: the successes to which they contributed were all credited to skillful tactics or good scouting.

A second important agency in southwest Pacific intelligence work was the Allied Translator and Interpreter Section (ATIS) which was responsible for the translation of captured documents and the interrogation of prisoners. Called by General Willoughby "possibly the most important single intelligence agency of the war," [57] ATIS drew heavily on the Nisei—Americans of Japanese descent, many of whose relatives were languishing in internment camps in the United States.[58] ATIS translators and interpreter teams accompanied combat units in the field, sharing the hazards of battle but also the special hazard, for the Nisei, of capture by the enemy which would have meant slow death for themselves and cruel reprisals against any relatives still living in Japan.[59]

The Allied Geographical Section, a third agency in Willoughby's empire, had a vast amount of work to accomplish. Many parts of New Guinea and the southwest Pacific islands were completely unmapped or poorly mapped at best. The Geographical Section was responsible for collecting, collating, checking and integrating all types of geographical information useful for military operations. It disseminated this information in the form of terrain studies, special reports, and over 100,000 pocket-size handbooks issued to amphibious assault troop commanders.[60]

As the war progressed, all these organizations expanded rapidly, ultimately employing hundreds of officers and enlisted men and spawning new subagencies. Some attained a semi-independent status within the theater, although all were ultimately responsible to MacArthur. The southwest Pacific commander had little use for any organization in his theater, combatant or otherwise, which was not under his control.

If MacArthur succeeded in keeping the strings of control over most intelligence activities in his hands, Allied commanders in China and Southeast Asia often appeared not even to know where the strings were. The most active and ubiquitous U.S. intelligence agency in China and Southeast Asia was one which had been resolutely excluded by Nimitz and MacArthur from their theaters in the Pacific. This was the Office of Strategic Services, headed by William J. Donovan, a New York lawyer and politician who had had a distinguished military career in World War I, winning the Medal of Honor as a battalion commander with the famous "Fighting Sixty-ninth" Regiment of the New York National Guard.[61]

Donovan had returned from two special missions to Europe in 1940 convinced that the Axis powers were far ahead of the United States in espionage and unconventional warfare, and with a vision of intelligence as part of an integrated package of what he called "psychological warfare." Intelligence penetration of an enemy country was to serve as only the first step in psychological warfare. After the intelligence was analysed and processed, it would be utilized for propaganda to weaken the enemy's will to resist. Then would come special operations in the form of sabotage and subversion, to be followed by commando raids and guerrilla uprisings so that the enemy's territory would be thoroughly softened up for later conventional attack.[62]

In July of 1941 Donovan was appointed Coordinator of Information by President Roosevelt. In this capacity Donovan was responsible for coordinating and analysing the flow of intelligence from abroad, and for conducting overseas propaganda. But the marriage of intelligence with propaganda proved an unhappy one; the more so because the heads of the foreign information programs, Archibald MacLeish and Robert E. Sherwood, had very different ideas from Donovan about the methods and uses of propaganda.[63]

In June 1942 the Coordinator of Information became head of the Office of Strategic Services under the jurisdiction of the Joint Chiefs of Staff. The foreign information activities of the old COI were divorced to form a new organization, the Office of War Information. Yet this change in organizational arrangements made life no easier for Donovan's group, which was soon known simply by its initials, OSS. The new organization was regarded with suspicion by the State Department, the FBI, the army's Military Intelligence Service and the navy's Office of Naval Intelligence.[64] Old-line military intelligence officers had trouble taking Donovan's heterogeneous collection of Wall Street lawyers, college professors, Hollywood stunt men, and European émigrés seriously. When the newspapers learned of the number of bluebloods and Ivy Leaguers like David Bruce, William H. Vanderbilt, Kermit Roosevelt, and Lester Armour enrolled in its ranks, they promptly dubbed it "Oh So Social." [65] Donovan's unorthodox organization proved its worth in the North African invasion, however, and in December 1942, the OSS was given a broad charter by the Joint Chiefs of Staff to act as their agency for sabotage, espionage, and psychological and guerrilla warfare.[66]

Just as in Washington, the OSS got off to an uncertain start in the Far East. During the earlier period of the war, it formed part of a combined Chinese-American intelligence and guerrilla warfare unit called the Sino-American Co-Operative Organization ("SACO"). The other American participant in SACO was the U.S. Navy Group China commanded by Captain (later Rear Admiral) Milton E. Miles. Miles was a close friend and confidant of General Tai Li, the Chinese spymaster who headed Chiang Kai-shek's Bureau of Investigation and Statistics, the espionage and counterintelligence organization which formed the Chinese half of SACO.

Tai Li, "the Chinese Himmler," as one OSS report described him, controlled a huge espionage organization in both free and occupied China. His agents, thugs, and assassins were daring, ruthless, and effective in eliminating enemies of the Chiang Kai-shek regime— but only secondarily interested in hard intelligence and operations against the Japanese. Tai Li was himself almost pathologically hostile and suspicious of foreigners (Miles and his staff excepted) and had none of the veneer of pious boyscoutism which so endeared Chinese like Madame Chiang and Ambassador T. V. Soong to Americans.

He was widely accused of being an assasin, narcotics smuggler, black-mailer, and torturer.[67]

Yet Miles and Tai Li got on famously. To the American, he was a "liberal democratic individual" who "only established concentration camps that were fully legal, and the money he used to run his organization was all borrowed from savings banks, and he loved his mother and supported education for women." [68]

Miles had been sent to China a few months after Pearl Harbor, when that country still loomed large in American strategy. His secret verbal orders from Admiral King were to do all that he could to prepare for an American landing on the coast of China and, in the meantime, to gather intelligence and harass the Japanese.[69] Miles held the post of U.S. naval observer in China, loosely attached to the embassy at Chungking. In fact his organization was virtually independent, reporting only to King and the Joint Chiefs; it was supplied by the navy and guaranteed a fixed amount of the precious tonnage flown over the Hump.

Miles shared his supplies with Tai Li in exchange for the latter's cooperation in establishing training centers for training and equipping Chinese to act as guerrillas against the Japanese.[70] By the war's end SACO was operating ten guerrilla training camps, where navy instructors and OSS technicians introduced students to the fine points of demolitions, communications, close combat, and guerrilla tactics. The guerrillas, organized in "columns" of about 1,000 men with a handful of American advisers, ranged from the China coast to the borders of Mongolia, ambushing and harassing Japanese convoys, raiding supply dumps—and frequently shooting it out with Chinese Communist military units. Miles and Tai Li also operated a network of coast-watchers and weather stations to supply information to U.S. Navy units in the Pacific.[71]

In his memoirs, published many years after the war, Miles claimed that his guerrillas did enormous damage to the Japanese. A recent student has suggested rather that "SACO's essential policy had been to prepare the KMT for civil war." [72] It is true that Miles naïvely swallowed the Koumintang's anti-Communist platitudes and was not averse to seeing his guerrillas save a little of their ammunition to use against "the political explosion of the Yenan Reds." [73] Yet Miles was first and foremost concerned with winning the fight against the Japanese, just as were the Americans who favored closer ties with Yenan.

OSS association with Miles was a marriage of convenience. Seeking a foothold for his organization in China, Donovan had signed an agreement with Miles at the beginning of 1943. It named Miles chief of OSS activities in China. The OSS thus became a subordinate part of SACO: OSS specialists served as instructors at guerrilla training centers and as technical advisers for special operations. But OSS officers were soon complaining that Miles's efforts to stay in the good graces of the Chinese were slowing the training program. They wanted to use SACO's Hump supplies and weapons as bargaining chips to induce Tai Li to move faster on projects desired by the U.S. More importantly, they argued that the U.S. must have the ability to acquire and evaluate intelligence in China independently. Miles was content to rely on Tai Li's service for intelligence—which the OSS described as meager and obsolete.[74] As a loyal servant of Chiang, Tai Li naturally had an interest in ensuring that the U.S. knew as little as possible about matters discreditable to the Koumintang regime.

After a year of increasingly acrimonious "cooperation" between OSS, Tai Li and the navy in SACO, Donovan found a new haven for his organization in General Chennault's 14th Air Force. Chennault was badly in need of good tactical intelligence for his air operations; he also wanted some means of recovering airmen shot down over enemy-controlled territory. In April 1943 the OSS activated a new unit, the 5329th Air and Ground Forces Resources and Technical Staff, or AGFRTS, as a component of the 14th Air Force. The arrangement proved mutually satisfactory to both the airmen and the OSS. AGFRTS expanded rapidly; given a relatively free hand, it was able to expand its intelligence-collection activities, set up new networks behind enemy lines and in neighboring Japanese-controlled Indochina, and conduct "black propaganda" operations. All this in addition to supplying Chennault with abundant and accurate target data and an efficient pilot-rescue service.

The final OSS bureaucratic triumph in China came in February 1945, when the China theater headquarters was reorganized at General Wedemeyer's direction. The OSS was recognized as an independent agency under the theater commander, charged with coordination of all U.S. covert operations in China. Yet it was easier to reorganize on paper than in real life: the SACO-OSS feud continued to the end of the war.

If the intelligence picture in China was confused, that in India and Southeast Asia was even more so. During the first two years of the war, the army's G-2 had maintained a small observer group at the headquarters of the Commander in Chief, India. OSS personnel had cooperated with the British in counterintelligence operations on the subcontinent. But by far the largest undertaking by the U.S. in Southeast Asia during this time was OSS detachment 101's operations in Japanese-occupied Burma.[75]

The OSS commander involved was Major Carl Eifler, a 250-pound giant of a man who had been a border patrol officer in peacetime. " 'After an exchange of salutes, he offered his hand," recalled a recruit about his first meeting with Eifler. "He proceeded to crack every joint, smiling all the time. . . . The next thing, as if it were entirely habitual, he took a stiletto-type dagger and drove it a good two or three inches into the top of his desk. He looked pleased.' " [76]

Detachment 101 had originally been intended to operate in China, but the stolid opposition of General Tai Li and Vinegar Joe's low opinion of covert operations had prevented that. Instead, Stilwell assigned the unit to carry out guerrilla warfare from India into Burma. " 'All I want to hear from you are booms from the Burma jungle,' " he told Eifler.[77]

That was the beginning of one of the most successful guerrilla operations of the war. Detachment 101 operated all over northern Burma. Its mainstay was the support of thousands of Kachin tribesmen—small, wiry, dark-skinned men who lived near the upper Irrawaddy River. Their traditional enemies, the Shans and Burmese, were allied with the Japanese. This made the Kachins natural partners for the British and Americans; since they were also fierce fighters, masters of the hills and jungle, Eifler's men quickly molded them into a formidable military force.

The detachment's Kachin groups pinpointed targets in the thick jungle for the Tenth Air Force, harassed Japanese patrols, performed mayhem against enemy rail lines and bridges, and reported on troop movements. During the campaign for Myitkyina in 1943–1944, Kachin rangers fought in support of Merrill's Marauders and acted as guides and scouts; they cleared trails, built bamboo bridges, located water holes, and selected areas for planes to drop supplies. By late 1944 Detachment 101 had a strength of 566 Americans and almost 10,000 Kachin tribesmen. By war's end, they had inflicted an estimated 5,500 casualties on the enemy and rescued over 200 Allied airmen. Only 15 Americans and less than 200 rangers were killed in action.[78]

Other American efforts to organize guerrilla warfare in Japanese-controlled Southeast Asia met with varying degrees of success. In countries which had long been under the yoke of European colonialism, organization of effective underground resistance was difficult, sometimes impossible.

The Japanese came to Southeast Asia fully prepared to exploit the growing nationalism and desire for independence of subject peoples. Their propaganda message spoke of "Asia for the Asians," of a "Greater East Asia Co-Prosperity Sphere" from which outsiders would be expelled so that the region's resources could be developed under Japan's benevolent economic and political leadership. The Japanese carefully tailored their message to each country. They appealed as fellow Buddhists to the Burmese and Thais. In Indonesia they supported Islam against the infidel Dutch and the hated Chinese merchants. In all cases there were vague promises of self-government and eventual independence.[79]

In Burma, Indonesia, and Malaya, nationalist leaders initially cooperated with the Japanese. The Philippines and Burma were granted "independence" in 1943. Subhas Chandra Bose—a former rival of Nehru for leadership of the Congress Party who believed that only military force could free India—set up a "Provisional Government of Free India," later renamed simply *Azad Hind* ("Free India"). Bose recruited a considerable number of British Indian Army prisoners of war in Southeast Asia into his Indian National Army. The Burmese and Indonesians were also encouraged to form auxiliary military forces to serve alongside the Japanese.

Prime Minister Tojo invited Bose, Ba Maw of Burma, Jose Laurel of the Philippines, and other Asian leaders to Tokyo in November 1943 for a Greater East Asia Conference. There the delegates drank toasts to Asian solidarity, pledged themselves to fight for the recovery of Asia for the Asiatics, and swore to " 'push aside the artificial barriers which Western intruders have set up between us.' "[80]

This talk of Asia for the Asiatics was highly disquieting to American and British leaders. State Department officials worried (and continued to worry after the war) that a strong pan-Asian movement would prove hostile to Western—and particularly to U.S.—interests in Asia. For this reason they believed it vital to keep China in the war on the Allied side and urged the British to satisfy the demands of Indian nationalists.[81] If China and India could be kept firmly in the Allied camp, they would give the lie to Japanese pretensions of leading a united Asian crusade against Western dominance.

These apprehensions ultimately proved exaggerated. No pan-Asian movement emerged from World War II. Asian nationalists who had at first cooperated with the Japanese grew ever more disenchanted as the Japanese war effort placed increasingly heavy strains on their countries' economies. In addition, the arrogant, sometimes brutal behavior of the Japanese military alienated their people.[82] By the last months of the war, most of the Japanese-trained armies of Asia had turned their guns against their tutors.[83] In Burma and Siam, these forces actively cooperated with the Allies.

However, support of or acquiescence in the Japanese military occupation by many of the peoples of Southeast Asia posed a formidable barrier to clandestine operations by the Allies until the last year of the war. Efforts by Dutch and Australian agents of MacArthur's Allied Intelligence Bureau to operate in Java were generally unsuccessful because the local Indonesians refused cooperation and frequently betrayed Allied agents to the Japanese.[84] Attempts by OSS units to penetrate Sumatra met a similar fate. One "high caliber" Indonesian agent intended for Palembang was arrested almost as soon as he landed.[85]

An Allied Intelligence Bureau attempt to penetrate the former Portuguese colony of Timor, east of Java, which had fallen to the Japanese in 1942, had disastrous consequences. A Portuguese-Australian team of about thirty-four men was captured there by the Japanese in September 1943. The Japanese subsequently used the party's radio to open communications with Australia and transmit false information. AIB remained blissfully unaware of the fate of the party until the end of the war; two subsequent parties sent out to join them fell easily into the hands of the Japanese.[86]

Clandestine operations in Southeast Asia were most successful in the Philippines, where most of the population had fought loyally and gallantly alongside the Americans in MacArthur's ill-fated defense of Bataan and Corregidor. Heavy-handed Japanese attempts to appeal to Filipino feelings of "oriental solidarity" grated on many Filipinos, who prided themselves on their western culture as well as on their oriental heritage.[87] Mistreatment of Filipino and American prisoners of war and detainees aroused anger and indignation. The presence of Philippine Commonwealth President Manuel Quezon and Vice President Sergio Osmeña in Washington gave the lie to claims by various collaborationist governments established by the Japanese that they commanded the allegiance of the Filipino people.[88]

Yet Filipino opposition to the Japanese did not arise simply as a response to errors or abuses on the part of the occupation authorities. As one historian observes: "The universality of the [guerrilla] movements and the mass participation in them was tangible proof that the initial decision to fight against the Japanese and for the Americans was a commitment of the people. Filipinos continued to fight as staunchly after the formal surrender as before. The nation felt itself part of the frontline.'' [89]

The guerrilla movements were of various types. Some were headed by former American and Filipino officers of Wainwright's command. For example, there was Colonel Russell W. Volckmann, who commanded a force of several thousand guerrillas in Northern Luzon. Colonel Macario Peralta on Panay and Colonel Ruperto Kangleon on Leyte led similar groups, as did Colonel Wendell W. Fertig on Mindanao, whose command eventually grew to almost 40,000 men. Fertig's inspired leadership made possible a brief alliance between the traditionally hostile Moro and Christian populations of Mindanao in the common cause of fighting the hated Japanese. [90]

Also active against the Japanese were the 30,000 guerrillas in the left-wing *Hukbalahap* movement, or the Huks, as they were popularly known. Led by veteran Communist Luis Taruc, they eventually controlled large areas of central Luzon. A considerable problem for the Japanese, they were to prove an even bigger headache to the conservative postwar governments of the Philippines. Outright banditry also flourished in the disorganized, war-ravaged provinces of the islands. Many cutthroat bands of outlaws and looters also took on the mantle of resistance fighters.

The guerrilla movement in the Philippines, which at its height may have involved some 200,000 fighters and many more supporters and collaborators, never effectively challenged Japanese military supremacy, but it undermined Japan's civil control, kept resistance morale high, and provided invaluable intelligence to the Allies.

MacArthur's headquarters in Australia was at first unaware of guerrilla resistance in the islands until escapees from the islands reached Australia in the spring of 1942 with reports of large guerrilla groups on Luzon and elsewhere. [92] Soon after, radio contact was established with Colonel Fertig and other guerrilla leaders. During late 1942 submarines carried small parties of Allied Intelligence Bureau agents with supplies, radios, and code books to make contact with guerrilla leaders in person.

By the spring of 1943 a new Philippine Regional Subsection, under Colonel (later Brigadier General) Courtney Whitney, had been set up at MacArthur's headquarters to support and coordinate guerrilla activities. A regular flow of weapons, supplies, agents, and radios was despatched to the islands by submarine. The submarines also carried matchboxes, mirrors, and cigarette packs stamped with the famous phrase, "I SHALL RETURN—MacArthur," a slogan devised by Whitney to bolster Filipino morale.[93]

Aside from the Philippines, where a majority of the population actively opposed the Japanese, clandestine operations in Southeast Asia were most successful where a reluctant government had been forced into collaboration with the Japanese. This was the case in Siam and, until March 1945, in French Indochina. In Siam, the government of Marshall Phibul Songkram, aware that it could expect no assistance from the British or Americans, had surrendered to the Japanese in December 1941 after only a few hours of resistance. A few weeks later Siam signed a treaty of alliance with Japan; in January she declared war on the United States and Britain. The Siamese minister in Washington, M. R. Seni Pramaj, refused to deliver the declaration of war to the State Department, publicly declaring that it was illegal and did not represent the will of the Thai people; in Bangkok, Phibul's chief rival in the cabinet, Pridi Phanomyong, went into hiding to avoid the signing the document.[94]

Almost immediately, Siamese leaders began to organize resistance to Japan. Pridi became the driving force behind these activities at home, while in the U.S. the legation and minister Seni Pramaj urged Siamese students in America to volunteer for service against the Japanese. Seni also assisted the Office of War Information in preparing propaganda broadcasts to Southeast Asia.

The United States and Britain differed in their attitudes toward Siam. Washington ignored the declaration of war and insisted upon treating her as a friendly country occupied by the Japanese, but the British were angered by Siamese collaboration with the Axis, which permitted the use of their territory to attack Malaya and Burma, while the Siamese proceeded to annex territory in British Malaya and Burma. London considered such actions a betrayal and insisted that, after Allied victory, the Thais "would have to work their passage home." [95]

Despite these differences, both the American OSS and the British SOE availed themselves of the opportunity to utilize Thai nationals to penetrate Southeast Asia. Intelligence from Siam was urgently needed to support Allied military operations in Burma, to locate profitable bombing targets, and to acquire information on the location and condition of POWs in Southeast Asia.[96]

Initial OSS efforts to infiltrate its Thai agents into the country from southern China were frustrated by Tai Li; it was not until the spring of 1944 that Thai agents of the OSS and SOE, equipped with radios, were successfully parachuted into Siam from India.[97] In the meantime, Pridi's resistance group had established contact with the Allies in China and arranged for cooperation. By this point, most of the key figures in the Siamese government, including the regent, the chief of police, the minister of foreign affairs, and senior naval officers, were all supporting the resistance movement. With the resignation of Phibul in the summer of 1944, senior army leaders also joined the conspiracy.[98]

From the end of 1944 on, both the OSS and SOE cooperated actively with the Thais to train and supply guerrilla forces for future operations and to provide intelligence for the Allies. Such intelligence proved extremely valuable. Not only did it include information on Japanese activities in Southeast Asia but, through their embassy in Tokyo, the Thai underground leaders were able to supply information on political and economic conditions in Japan as well as reports on the effectiveness of American air raids.[99] Planning for the initial B-29 strike against Japan was, in fact, based on information supplied by the Thai underground.[100]

Resistance activities paid rich dividends to the Thais also, for their help to the Allies strengthened their claim to be treated as an independent state rather than as a Japanese puppet: thus the United States was better able to blunt British demands for punitive action against the kingdom at war's end.

In many respects French Indochina was in a position similar to that of Thailand. A reluctant French colonial government, under Admiral Jean Decoux, had been forced to acquiesce in Japanese occupation of the country in return for the continuation of formal French control of the civil administration. President Roosevelt and some of the State Department's Far East experts hoped to see French rule in Indochina replaced by a United Nations' trusteeship following the end of the war. In the meantime they wished to have as little as possible to do with the Decoux government, which they rightly suspected of fascist leanings.[101]

Yet intelligence on Indochina was almost as important to the Allied war effort as intelligence from Thailand. Information was required on likely targets for American aerial attacks from China, on weather, on air defenses, and on Japanese troop movements. Information on troop movements was of special significance because the shifting of Japanese forces in or out of Indochina could affect the military situation in southern China.

As early as 1943, Miles' Navy Group had taken steps to establish an intelligence network within Indochina, headed by Commander Robert Meynier, an anti-Vichy, anti-Gaullist French naval officer whom Miles had spirited out of North Africa. Meynier's wife was Vietnamese; she had important connections among the mandarins of northern and central Vietnam. The other members of Meynier's group had good contacts among French officials in Vietnam. He succeeded in establishing a network of agents inside Vietnam, many of them operating from inside the French intelligence office, the *Deuxième Bureau*. They supplied Miles with information on fortifications, troop movements, bombing targets, and local political developments.[102]

Complementing Miles' efforts was an organization known as the GBT group, so called from the first letter of the last names of its organizers: Laurance Gordon, a Canadian formerly employed by the Cal-Texaco Oil Company; Harry Bernard, a British tobacco merchant; and Frank Tan, a Chinese-American businessman. The original purpose of the GBT group was to look after British and American property in Vietnam, but it soon expanded to include espionage activity. From an outpost near the Chinese-Vietnamese border GBT directed a network of couriers and clandestine radio transmitters throughout Vietnam. By 1944 it had become the most widely used and reliable source of intelligence on Indochina and had throughly infiltrated the French colonial government and armed forces.[103]

That government had itself become progressively cooler toward the Japanese. The liberation of France and American victories in the Pacific during 1944 had brought about a dramatic change in outlook among the French colonials. Old feuds between Vichyites and Gaullists were put aside as attempts were made to establish contact with the new French government of General Charles de Gaulle in Paris.[104] Preparations for an underground resistance, similar to the *Maquis* in metropolitan France, were begun with the help of specially trained French officers and agents parachuted into Indochina by SOE along with arms, communications equipment, and demolition gear.[105]

It seemed to be Siam all over again so far as Allied intelligence prospects were concerned. Then, in March 1945, the situation changed with dramatic suddenness. The Japanese, well aware of

French plans for resistance, deposed the Decoux Government in a surprise coup and disarmed or annihilated the French armed forces except those in the north, who were able to make a fighting retreat to China.[106]

After the Japanese coup, the old sources of intelligence for the Allies promptly evaporated. Moreover, French agents sent into Vietnam from China were promptly apprehended by the Japanese or had to beat a hasty retreat. The Vietnamese were proving as hostile to the French as the Indonesians had been to the Dutch. Their hostility made French clandestine activities after the March coup all but impossible.

However, unlike the Indonesians, Vietnamese nationalists did not side with the Japanese. Under the leadership of Ho Chi Minh, a veteran Communist revolutionary, Vietnamese guerrillas in northern Vietnam eventually reached a working arrangement with the OSS to provide U.S. forces in China with intelligence and with assistance in rescuing Allied pilots shot down over Indochina. In return, Ho's resistance group—the Viet Minh—received communications equipment, small arms, medical supplies, and, eventually, OSS instructors to train them for guerrilla warfare against the Japanese.[107] This arrangement worked well enough during the war. But it became a subject for bitter recrimination by the French, who tended to blame American support of the Viet Minh for all their postwar troubles in Indochina.

Real or imagined differences among the Allies over Asian policy also complicated the tasks of intelligence and special warfare officers. In the newly created Southeast Asia Command, the British and Americans suspected political motives behind all intelligence projects. Each wished to act independently of the other, even in the same area of operations. Thus, British and American agents were parachuted into opposite ends of Siam at the same time without either knowing of the existence of the other; and the OSS operated its own liaison detachments to the Chinese guerrillas of the People's Anti-Japanese Army in the highlands of Malaya.[108]

The situation with regard to Indochina was further complicated by the fact that the two theater commanders, Wedemeyer and Mountbatten, both believed that country lay within the legitimate boundaries of their command. At one point in 1944, after the British and French had refused to tell Wedemeyer the details of their clandestine operations in Indochina, he closed Kunming airport to SEAC planes flying in support of those operations. The British nevertheless continued to carry out operations from eastern India, and in January 1945 fighters of the 14th Air Force mistook three British bombers on an intelligence mission for Japanese planes and shot them down. The Royal Air Force liaison officer with the 14th Air Force had not been informed of the mission "due to the political situation." [109]

This obscure disaster served to highlight a fundamental fact affecting all Allied intelligence in the war against Japan—namely, that intelligence had political as well as technical and military dimensions. Intelligence in the Pacific War was an immense and complicated undertaking, ranging from arcane feats of cryptography to dramatic commando raids; yet whatever their nature, these projects were most successful where bureaucratic and political rivalries were held to a minimum—and least successful where they were given free rein.

NOTES

1. Holmes, *Double-Edged Secrets*, p. 18; Blair, *Silent Victory*, p. 42.

2. Ladislas Farago, *The Broken Seal* (New York: Random House, 1967), pp. 97–99; the literature on Friedman and the Purple code is extensive: See especially Ronald W. Clark, *The Man Who Broke Purple* (London: Weidenfeld and Nicholson, 1977); Kahn, *The Codebreakers;* Lewin, *The American Magic*, pp. 36–47; and Friedman's own account: "A Brief History of the Signal Intelligence Service," SRH-024, RG 457.

3. Memorandum for Colonel Carter W. Clarke, 15 April 1943, Sub.: Origin, Functions and Problems of the Special Branch, MIS, SRH-116, RG 457.

4. "Information from Captain George W. Linn, USNR," SRH-081, RG 457.

5. "Reminiscences of Lieutenant Colonel Howard W. Brown, 4 August 1945," SRH-045, RG 457.

6. Ibid., pp. 18, 23–24.

7. Ibid., p. 24.

8. Ibid., p. 39.

9. "U.S. Naval Pre-World War II Radio Intelligence in the Philippine Islands," pp. 1–3, 12, SRH-180, RG 457.

10. Ibid., pp. 29–30.

11. Blair, *Silent Victory*, pp. 52–53; Holmes, *Double-Edged Secrets*, pp. 45–47, 53.

12. Blair, *Silent Victory*, p. 94.

13. Prior to the fall of 1943, Rochefort's group was known by a variety of other cover names, of which the most common was "Combat Intelligence Unit."

14. "The Role of Radio Intelligence in the American-Japanese Naval War," Vol. 1, SRH-012, Records of the National Security Agency, National Archives RG 457; Lewin, *The American Magic*, pp. 91–92.

15. Holmes, *Double-Edged Secrets*, pp. 88–96; Lewin, *The American Magic*, pp. 89, 104–9.

16. Blair, *Silent Victory,* pp. 236–37; Rochefort's oral history memoirs, which might well shed light on this episode, are still classified (as of 1983). However, Blair apparently interviewed Rochefort or was given access to the interview.

17. Ibid., p. 238.

18. Holmes, *Double-Edged Secrets,* pp. 116–17; Potter, *Nimitz,* p. 104.

19. "The Role of Radio Intelligence in the American-Japanese Naval War," Vol. 2, SRH-012, Records of the National Security Agency, National Archives RG 457.

20. "Need for New Legislation Against Unauthorized Disclosures of Communications Intelligence Activities," 9 June 1944, RG 457.

21. "Midway Despatch Under Inquiry," *Newsweek,* August 31, 1942.

22. *Washington Post,* November 11, 1942.

23. Blair, *Silent Victory,* p. 235.

24. "New Legislation Against Unauthorized Disclosures."

25. Holmes, *Double-Edged Secrets,* pp. 108, 118.

26. Ibid., pp. 126–29; "The Role of Communications Intelligence in Submarine Warfare in the Pacific, January 1943 to October 1943, Vol. 1; Contributions to the Operations of the U.S. Submarine Force, Pacific Fleet," pp. iv–v, SRH-011, RG 457.

27. "Communications Intelligence in Submarine Warfare," p. ix.

28. Ibid., pp. iv–v.

29. "Radio Intelligence in World War II: Tactical Operations in Pacific Ocean Areas," pp. 1–5, SRH-036, RG 457.

30. Holmes, *Double-Edged Secrets,* pp. 135–36.

31. "Radio Intelligence in World War II," pp. 3–6; Holmes, *Double-Edged Secrets,* pp. 124–25.

32. "Communication Intelligence Organization," SRH-197, pp. 2–3, RG 457.

33. Ibid., p. 6. A fine memoir concerning the work of OP-20-G is Edward Van Der Rhoer, *Deadly Magic* (New York: Charles Scribner's Sons, 1978).

34. "Evacuation of USN COMINT Personnel from Corregidor in WWII," SRH-207, RG 457.

35. "Communication Intelligence Organization," SRH-197, RG 457; Desmond J. Ball, "Allied Intelligence Cooperation Involving Australia During World War II," *Australian Outlook* 32 (December 1978), p. 302.

36. Affidavit by Major General Charles A. Willouby, May 8, 1945, *Pearl Harbor Attack,* Part 35, p. 87; Alexander S. Cochrane, Jr., "MacArthur, ULTRA and the Pacific War 1942–44," unpublished paper, March 1982.

37. Cochrane, "MacArthur, ULTRA and the Pacific War." Captain McCollum appeared to confirm this surmise during discussion of Cochrane's paper at the American Historical Association meeting of 1981.

38. D. M. Horner, "Special Intelligence in the Southwest Pacific Area in World War II," *Australian Outlook* 32 (December 1978), p. 317.

39. "Origin, Function and Problems of the Special Branch, MIS," SRH-116, RG 457.

40. Memorandum for the Special Security Officer, MIS, 20 December 1945, Sub.: Report of Major John R. Thompson, Deputy Special Security Representative, SWPA, in "Reports by U.S. Army ULTRA Representatives in SWPA, POA and CBI," SRH-032, RG 457.

41. Ibid.; "A Brief History of the G-2 Section, SWPA and Affiliated Units," pp. 66–67, GHQ, Far East Command, Military Intelligence Section 1948, copy in Center of Military History.

42. Memorandum for the Special Security Officer, MIS, 20 December 1945, Sub.: Report of Major John R. Thompson.

43. Horner, "Special Intelligence in the Southwest Pacific," p. 321; Memorandum for Brigadier General Clarke and Colonel McCormack, 9 April 1945, Sub.: Activities of Dr. Marshall Stone, SRH-196, RG 457.

44. Memorandum for Special Security Officer, MIS, December 20, 1945, Sub.: Report of Major John R. Thompson.

45. "Intelligence Derived from ULTRA," 21 December 1944, attachment to Memorandam First Lieutenant Richard A. Grodin to Colonel Sinkov, Sub.: Messages of Operational Importance Published by Central Bureau Since December 1944," 24 June 1945, SRH-059, RG 457.

46. Ibid.

47. History of Special Security Office with Far East Air Forces, 24 Oct 44–2 Sept 45, in "Reports by U.S. Army ULTRA Representatives."

48. Major John H. Gunn, Memorandam for Special Security Officer, 23 October 1945, no subject, in ibid.

49. "Role of Communications Intelligence in Submarine Warfare," p. x.

50. Arleigh Burke interview no. 4, p. 281.

51. Memorandum, Major John H. Gunn to Special Security Officer, MIS, 23 October 1945, in "Reports of U.S. Army ULTRA Representatives," pp. 25–27; Memorandam for Brigadier General Carter W. Clarke, no date, Sub.: Report of Captain James C. Sergeant; History of Special Security Office, HQ, Sixth Army. Both in "Reports by U.S. Army ULTRA Representatives to the Field Commands."

52. Holmes, *Double-Edged Secrets,* pp. 167–68.

53. Special Security Officers Attached to CINCPOA; in "Reports by U.S. Army ULTRA Representatives to the Field Commands."

54. "A Brief History of the G-2 Section, GHQ SWPA," pp. 37–38; James, *Years of MacArthur 1941–1945,* pp. 178–79; Allison Ind, *Allied Intelligence Bureau: Our Secret Weapon in the War Against Japan* (New York: McKay, 1955), p. 9.

55. Eric Feldt, *The Coastwatchers* (New York: Oxford University Press, 1946), pp. 4–11; Walter Lord, *Lonely Vigil: Coastwatchers of the Solomons,* pp. 6–7.

56. Lord, *Lonely Vigil,* p. 245.

57. "Brief History of G-2 Section, GHQ SWPA," p. 63.

58. The reminiscences of Nisei translators and interpreters have been collected in Joseph D. Harrington, *Yankee Samurai* (Detroit: Pettigrew, 1979).

59. "Brief History of G-2 Section, GHQ SWPA," pp. 63–64; Sidney F. Mashbir, *I Was an American Spy* (New York: Vantage Press, 1953), pp. 242–44.

60. "Brief History of G-2 Section, GHQ SWAP," pp. 59–63.

61. Corey Ford, *Donovan of OSS* (Boston: Little, Brown and Company, 1970), pp. 33–50.

62. Kermit Roosevelt, *War Report of the OSS* (New York: Walker, 1976), pp. 15–16.

63. Ibid., p. 10; Allan M. Winkler, *The Politics of Propaganda: The Office of War Information 1942–1945* (New Haven: Yale University Press, 1978), pp. 18–19 and passim.

64. Roosevelt, *War Report of OSS,* pp. 24–26.

65. Ibid., pp. 99–102; Ford, *Donovan of OSS,* pp. 132–34.

66. Roosevelt, *War Report of OSS,* pp. 99–105.

67. Kermit Roosevelt, *The Overseas Targets: War Report of the OSS, Vol. 2* (New York: Walker, 1976), pp. 416–17; R. Harris Smith, *OSS: The Secret History of America's First Central Intelligence Agency* (Berkely: University of California Press, 1972), p. 245.

68. Schaller, *U.S. Crusade in China,* p. 243.

69. Memorandum by Miles, August 1945 cited in Schaller, *U.S. Crusade in China,* p. 241.

70. Milton E. Miles, *A Different Kind of War* (New York: Doubleday and Co., 1967), p. 18.

71. Miles, *A Different Kind of War,* pp. 149–51, 227–29, 247–48, and passim.

72. Miles, *A Different Kind of War,* pp. 346–47; Schaller, *The U.S. Crusade in China,* p. 250.

73. Miles, *A Different Kind of War,* pp. 402–4. On the other hand, this anti-communist rhetoric may have been added during the "ghosting" of Miles's posthumous memoirs.

74. Roosevelt, *The Overseas Targets,* pp. 421–22.

75. Report by the Joint Staff Planners, Sub.: OSS Organization in India, JCS 261/1, 6 May 1943, CCS196/1, RG 228.

76. Peers and Brelis, *Behind the Burma Road,* p. 39.

77. Richard Dunlop, *Behind Japanese Lines: With the OSS in Burma* (Chicago: Rand McNally and Co., 1979), p. 109.

78. Roosevelt, *The Overseas Targets,* pp. 371–73, 384–91.

79. John F. Cady, *Southeast Asia* (New York: McGraw Hill, 1964), pp. 565, 568; Harry J. Benda, *The Crescent and the Rising Sun* (The Hague: W. Van Hoeve, 1958), pp. 61–86; Ba Maw, *Breakthrough in Burma,* in W. L. Holland ed., *Asian Nationalism and the West* (New York: Macmillan, 1953); Joyer Lebra, *Japanese-Trained Armies in Southeast Asia* (New York: Columbia, 1977).

80. Toland, *The Rising Sun,* pp. 457–59; "Japanese-Burmese Relations," 9 May 1945, SRH-074, RG 457.

81. Thorne, *Allies of a Kind,* pp. 7–9, 358–59 and passim; Letter, Arthur Denning to Foreign Office, No. 148, 16 September 1944, W0203/5621 Foreign Office Records, Public Record Office.

82. The best account of Southeast Asia under Japanese occupation is John Bastin

and Harry J. Benda, *History of Modern Southeast Asia* (Englewood Cliffs: Prentice-Hall, 1968), pp. 124–150. See also the important collection of essays edited by Alfred W. McCoy, *Southeast Asia under Japanese Occupation* (New Haven: Yale University Press, 1980).

83. Lebra, *Japanese-Trained Armies in Southeast Asia.*

84. "Operations of the Allied Intelligence Bureau GHQ SWPA," pp. 23–25, 43–44, 75, Historical Manuscripts Collection, Center of Military History.

85. Roosevelt, *The Overseas Targets,* pp. 405–406.

86. "Operations of the Allied Intelligence Bureau, GHQ, SWPA," pp. 73–74.

87. David J. Steinberg, *Philippine Collaboration in World War II* (Ann Arbor: University of Michigan Press, 1967), pp. 48–49.

88. Ibid., pp. 54–56, 67 and passim; Bastin and Benda, *Modern Southeast Asia,* pp. 137–39.

89. Steinberg, *Philippine Collaboration,* p. 57.

90. Fertig's experiences are recounted in John Keats, *They Fought Alone* (Philadelphia: Lippincott, 1963); see also Russell W. Volckmann, *We Remained* (New York: Norton, 1954).

91. Bastin and Benda, *Modern Southeast Asia,* p. 138.

92. "Operations of the Allied Intelligence Bureau, GHQ SWPA," pp. 24–25; Ind, *Allied Intelligence Bureau,* pp. 115–16.

93. James, *Years of MacArthur;* GHQ U.S. Army Forces Pacific: The Intelligence Series: Vol 1, "The Guerrilla Resistance Movement in the Philippines," Vol. 2, "Intelligence Activities in the Philippines During the Japanese Occupation," both in Historical MSS File, Center of Military History.

94. John B. Haseman, *The Thai Resistance Movement During the Second World War* (Northern Illinois University Center for Southeast Asian Studies: Special Report No. 17, 1978), pp. 17–19.

95. Proposed Declaration by the British Government in Regard to Thailand, *Foreign Relations of the United States 1944,* Vol. 5, p. 1312. Extensive documentation on U.S.-British relations regarding Thailand may be found in this volume, pp. 1311–1320, and in *Foreign Relations of the United States 1945,* Vol. 6, pp. 1240–1279. See also Thorne, *Allies of a Kind,* pp. 460–62 and passim, and Nicholas Tarling, "Atonement Before Absolution: British Policy Towards Thailand in the Second World War," *Proceedings of the Seventh IAHA Conference* (Bangkok, 1979), Vol. 2, pp. 1433–1505. Tarling suggests that the British pursued a divided and inconsistent policy until it was too late for them to hope to influence events.

96. Nichol Smith and Blake Clark, *Into Siam, Underground Kingdom* (New York: Bobbs Merrill, 1945), pp. 16–17.

97. Haseman, *Thai Resistance Movement,* pp. 42–44, 72–84.

98. Roosevelt, *The Overseas Targets,* p. 408.

99. Haseman, *Thai Resistance Movement,* p. 91.

100. Ibid., p. xv.

101. Christopher Thorne, "Indochina and Anglo-American Relations 1942–1945," *Pacific Historical Review,* 45 (February 1976); Gary Hess, "Franklin Roosevelt

and Indochina," *Journal of American History* 59 (1972); Memorandum by President Roosevelt to Secretary of State, 16 October 1944, *Foreign Relations of the United States 1944,* Vol 3, p. 777; Ronald Spector, *Advice and Support: The Early Years: 1941–1960* [The U.S. Army in Vietnam] (Washington: G.P.O., 1983), pp. 21–29.

102. "Report on Activities of SACO Directed Toward Indochina," Milton E. Miles Papers, Office of Naval History, Washington, D.C.

103. General Wedemeyer's Data Book Section 20; Letter, Wedemeyer to Major General Claire E. Chennault, 27 December 1944, both in Wedemeyer Files RG 407; Organizational Report, 5329th Air Ground Forces Resources Technical Staff, August-September 1944, 30 September 1944, pp. 13–15; 14th Air Force Records, Albert F. Simpson Historical Center, Maxwell Air Force Base, Alabama.

104. "Conditions in French Indochina," OSS R & A Report 0016, 15 October 1944. Copy in G-2 I.D. Files, National Archives, RG 319.

105. Force 136 Future Plans, 16 November 1944, Force 136 Future Plans for French Indochina, 28 October 1944, both in W0203.4331, Public Records Office.

106. Lieutenant Colonel Sakai Tatek, "French Indochina Operations Record," Japanese Monograph No. 25, pp. 22, 24–29; Joseph Buttinger, *Vietnam: A Dragon Embattled* (New York: Praeger, 1967) pp. 216–22.

107. Smith, *OSS,* pp. 328–30; Charles Fenn, *Ho Chi Minh* (London: Studio Vista, 1973), pp. 74–83; Memorandum, Major Allison K. Thomas to Chief S.O. Br. OSS/CT, Sub.: Report of Mission Deer, 17 September 1945 in *Hearings on Causes, Origins, and Lessons of the Vietnam War,* 92d Congress Senate, 2d Session, p. 255. These operations are discussed in more detail in Spector, *The Early Years,* pp. 39–43.

108. Roosevelt, *The Overseas Targets,* pp. 393–94, 396–97, 406; Chief Political Adviser to Foreign Office, 8 February 1945, W0203/5561, Extract from Report of Lieutenant Colonel Carver, W0203/5210, both in SEAC Records, Public Record Office; Romanus and Sunderland, *Time Runs Out in CBI,* pp. 259–60; Haseman, *Thai Resistance Movement,* p. 78.

109. Note on Loss of Three Liberator Aircraft of No. 358 Squadron, Night of January 22/23, 1945, W0203/4331, SEAC Records, Public Record Office.

TWENTY-ONE

The War of Attrition

By early 1945 the forces of Nimitz and MacArthur were closing in on the outer defences of Japan itself. Plans went forward for the final attack on the home islands, but whether the invasion of Japan would be necessary depended in the end on the capabilities of two weapons which had figured little in earlier planning: the submarine and the long-range bomber.

● ●

In 1920 Admiral (then Captain) Thomas C. Hart delivered a lecture on submarines at the Naval War College. Hart had commanded a contingent of American submarines in European waters during World War I; he was considered one of the navy's leading experts on the subject. " 'I shall pass over the inhumane features of German submarine warfare because their ways were characteristic of the race,' " observed Hart. " 'Any nation that attempts commerce destruction by submarines will tend toward certain of the same practices that the Germans arrived at; how far it will go depends on its racial characteristics and, very likely, by how hard it is pressed.' " [1]

In 1941, the United States felt itself to be very hard pressed. A few hours after the Pearl Harbor attack, Washington instructed naval commanders in the Pacific: " 'Execute Unrestricted Air and Submarine Warfare Against Japan.' " [2] Twenty-five years after entering the First World War, in large part because of Germany's policy of unrestricted submarine warfare, the United States had itself adopted that same policy.

Not only did this order break with long-standing American attitudes toward war at sea: it also repudiated the international agreement signed by Britain, the United States, and Japan at the London disarmament conference of 1930. That agreement specified that a submarine "may not sink, or render incapable of navigation, a merchant vessel without having first placed passengers, crew and ship's papers in a place of safety. For this purpose the ship's boats are not regarded as a place of safety unless the safety of the passengers and crew is assured in the existing sea and weather conditions. . ." These provisions were incorporated into the "Tentative Instructions for the Navy of the United States Governing Maritime and Aerial Warfare," the navy's list of do's and don'ts for its commanders at sea.

In the spring of 1941, however, some naval strategists proposed an important change in these instructions. To solve the problems in their annual war game against Japan the staff and students at the Naval War College recommended that the United States consider declaring areas in waters of the Far East as "war zones which all merchant ships would enter at their peril." They pointed out that the Germans in the Atlantic, and the British and Italians in the Mediterranean, were in effect already conducting unrestricted submarine warfare: any other use of submarines and aircraft by the United States in a war with Japan would be impractical and unrealistic.[3]

The General Board of the navy categorically rejected the college's recommendations in a letter to the secretary of the navy. The General Board pointed out that "war zones" had no standing in international law and that the United States would be surrendering a long-defended position on this issue were it to tell its commanders to establish such zones.[4]

Even as the General Board was rebutting the arguments for such war zones, however, plans to establish them in case of hostilities were being incorporated into U.S. plans. Rainbow 3 and Rainbow 5 authorized fleet commanders to establish strategic zones or areas from which commercial planes and merchant shipping would be excluded. " 'The purpose of such an arrangement,' " as the Navy Department candidly explained to the British Admiralty, would be "to wage unrestricted warfare not only by submarines but also by aircraft.' " Such a course of action " 'need not necessarily depend on prior similar action in that area . . . by an enemy of the United States.' "[5]

As commander of the Asiatic Fleet, Thomas C. Hart—the same who had delivered the 1920 lecture referring to German inhumanity in submarine warfare—was painfully aware in 1941 that the most powerful part of his striking force in the Far East was the new fleet submarines his fleet had recently received. He repeatedly called the attention of the Navy Department to what might be accomplished if his force were authorized to wage unrestricted submarine warfare.[6] In November 1941 Admiral Harold Stark informed Hart that in the event of war with Japan, he could expect instructions granting him such authority for warfare against Axis shipping.[7]

In the weeks before Pearl Harbor, British, Dutch, and American naval commanders in east Asia incorporated provisions for "strategic zones"—in which merchant ships could be sunk at sight—into their plans for coordinated defense.[8] Yet the president had still not approved the shift to unrestricted submarine warfare. Nor were submarine commanders at Hawaii and in the Far East informed of the contemplated change in their mission.

That was how matters stood on December 7, 1941, when word of the Pearl Harbor attack was received in Washington. That afternoon Admiral Stark telephoned the White House to report on the Japanese attack. Roosevelt instructed him to place the agreed plans for war with Japan into effect. Stark then read to the president a telegram to Pacific commanders instructing them to commence unrestricted submarine warfare. The president's comments have not been preserved—but it would be surprising if, in the aftermath of the Japanese attack, he needed any persuading. The message was sent shortly before six that evening.[9]

The fleet, however, was largely unprepared to wage such warfare. Neither the Japanese nor the American navy expected to imitate the German submarine war against commerce. Instead, submariners on both sides attempted to find a role for themselves in the prevailing prewar strategy which looked forward to decisive clashes between the main battle fleets. Japanese and American strategists envisioned their submarines mainly as scouts and ambushers serving the main fleet: subs would lie in wait across the enemy's route of advance or outside his bases, picking off heavy ships as they passed. Then, in a fleet action, they would act as underwater destroyers, attacking the enemy's battle line from below.[10]

Large warships were considered the submarines' proper quarry. In the First World War German submarines had sunk ten capital ships and eighteen cruisers. More modern submarines were expected to do even better. The Japanese navy carried the emphasis on attacking big ships to the point of specifying the number of torpedoes to be fired at various targets. (Merchant ships and destroyers rated only one.) [11]

Submarine operations with the fleet called for boats with a large cruising radius and a relatively high speed—seventeen knots sustained surface speed was needed to keep up with the battle line. Such craft were a long time in development, mainly due to the lack of a suitably powerful and reliable engine. However, by 1941 the U.S. Navy had developed a type of submarine which could more than meet such requirements. The latest—the *Tambor* class—displaced about 1,500 tons with a top speed of close to twenty-one knots and a range of about 10,000 miles; such submarines could crash-dive to periscope depth in thirty-five seconds; they were relatively handy and quiet, once they were submerged. With their light-weight sturdy hulls, large torpedo capacity, and excellent habitability, they were the finest submarines in the world.[12]

The Japanese navy was not so well endowed. Their submarines were larger than their American counterparts and carried heavier deck armament, but Japanese long-range submarines—the *I-class*— were crowded, difficult to handle when submerged, took a long time to dive, and had the fatal flaw of being very noisy below the surface. Until very late in the war they also lacked radar.[13]

The personnel of both the Japanese and American submarine service were elite groups, all of them volunteers, specially selected and trained for the arduous and hazardous duty of extended undersea patrols. The *Tambor* class "fleet" subs and their successors were far more habitable than any previous submarines. They even included such amenities as air conditioning; yet they were still austere and hazardous war machines. Close to eighty men lived for weeks in conditions so cramped as to border on the claustrophobic. Over half the crew had their sleeping quarters in a room smaller than a good-sized kitchen. Other crewmen, in the forward and aft torpedo rooms, shared their bunks with these deadly projectiles. The officers' wardroom, about the size of a restaurant booth, was luxurious compared to the crew's mess, where the men ate in shifts. Yet the food was traditionally excellent, the discipline easy, and a strong *esprit* made submariners a proud, close-knit navy elite. All U.S. skippers were graduates of Annapolis; the quality of U.S. enlisted personnel was so high that almost 50 percent of the initial enlisted force had become officers by the end of the war.[14]

U.S. submarine commanders were a handpicked, highly qualified group, at least by peacetime standards. But the test of war was to show that some could not measure up to the immense new burdens of wartime command. All services have officers of poor or indifferent ability, but capable subordinates and superiors can often carry them along and compensate for their shortcomings. This was not so in the case of submarines, where the success—and even the survival— of the ship often rested solely on the judgment, skill, and nerve of the skipper. Submarines usually operated alone; the commander decided whether to attack, how to attack, and then himself directed the attack from his periscope. In addition, he had to deal with the myriad mechanical and administrative problems of running a war-ship—details which multiplied greatly in wartime.

Almost 30 percent of all submarine commanders were relieved for unfitness, or lack of results, during 1942. About 14 percent were removed for these reasons during 1943 and 1944.[15] This high turn-over rate forced the navy to promote ever-younger men to command. By the close of the war, officers who had left the naval academy less than seven years ago were commanding submarines on war patrols in the Pacific. Such a development was viewed with grave misgivings by many senior admirals, who looked upon age and experience as an indispensable prerequisite for command. Even more distasteful to many of them was the idea of giving command to a reservist, no matter how well qualified: although the shortage of effective submarine skippers remained an acute problem throughout the war, only seven reservists ever attained combat commands in submarines.[16]

One reason so many of the older submarine skippers failed to measure up may have been the prewar doctrine and training of sub-mariners: it emphasized extreme caution in attacks on the heavily defended capital ships and carriers which were presumed to be the most suitable targets for submarines. Experience in prewar maneuvers and exercises had given the navy a greatly exaggerated idea of the effectiveness of aircraft and destroyers equipped with sonar in hunting down submarines. In the excellent sound conditions and calm seas of the target-practice areas, patrolling aircraft were frequently able to spot submarines at periscope depth; destroyers were often able to detect attacking submarines under similar conditions. Commanders whose submarines were caught in this fashion received a severe dress-ing-down: navy doctrine cautioned against making attacks from peri-scope depth if the sea was calm or the target was screened by aircraft or destroyers. An attack from 100 feet or more, using sonar to locate the target, was recommended instead. Such a "sound attack" was considered far safer than one utilizing the periscope; it was also, as wartime experience would prove, completely impractical. Although navy doctrine left the choice of sound or periscope attack to the "experienced judgement" of the submarine skipper, in practice the more conservative "sound attack" was emphasized. The navy was aware that the Germans were achieving good results with nightime surface attacks. But night battle practice was hazardous for submarines, so it was only in the last few months of peace that the navy began to experiment with this type of operation.[17]

The war opened with resounding failures by both the U.S. and Japanese submarine forces. Americans were shocked by the failure of their submarines to interfere seriously with the Japanese invasion of the Philippines. "We had the greatest concentration of submarines in the world there," recalled correspondent Hanson Baldwin, "but we didn't do a thing!" [18]

Japanese submarines did almost as poorly at Pearl Harbor, where the midget submarines failed to do any damage and almost gave away the surprise. Larger Japanese submarines, lurking in Hawaiian waters, failed to sink or even sight any American warships, while I-70 was sunk by carrier planes from the USS *Enterprise.* Three other Japanese submarines, returning from patrols off California, chatted so often by radio that communications intelligence experts were able to plot their course and place the submarine *Gudgeon* in their path. *Gudgeon* sank I-173—the first Japanese warship a U.S. submarine sent to the bottom.

Successes such as this were few for American submarines during the first year of the war. After the dissolution of the ABDA command, U.S. subs operated principally out of Pearl Harbor and from bases in Australia. Torpedoes were in short supply: skippers were cautioned not to "waste" them by firing large spreads at unimportant targets. Prewar submarine doctrine had discussed the concentration of submarine patrols in narrow shipping lanes, where they would have the most targets. All the same, no coordinated overall strategy for sub deployments was worked out by submarine force commanders, whether in Australia or Hawaii.[19] In those early days, submarine admirals thought in terms of tonnage sunk rather than what kind of tonnage had gone down. Little thought was given to concentrating on priority targets like tankers.[20] During 1942 U.S. submarines sank 180 Japanese ships—for a total of about 725,000 tons. Japan was able to replace all but 90,000 tons by new construction, and she actually increased her tonnage in tankers. Imports of raw materials from Southeast Asia to the home islands remained unimpaired. Submarines devoted much effort to attempted ambushes of large Japanese warships, utilizing information provided by the codebreakers, but results were nil. Japanese carrier forces were well screened; they operated at high speed, making them a difficult quarry for a slow-moving submerged submarine.[21] About two-dozen successful contacts with battleships or carriers were made acting on intercepts, but none resulted in sinkings.

Despite the lack of appropriate strategy and doctrine, U.S. submarines would undoubtedly have been far more successful had it not been for a still more serious handicap: defective torpedoes. The latest torpedo carried by American submarines, the Mark-14, was equipped with a magnetic exploder, a device designed to be triggered by the changes which a steel-hulled ship caused in the earth's magnetic field. Exploding under the keel, rather than directly against the armored side of a warship (as old-style "contact" torpedoes did), the Mark-14 would cause a far more powerful explosion. The Mark-14 was a marvel of sophisticated engineering; each one cost $10,000. Because this torpedo was so expensive, the Bureau of Ordnance, which had designed and built the Mark-14, never tested it with a live warhead. Instead the bureau used exercise warheads filled with water. A generation of submariners grew up without ever having seen— or heard—a torpedo explode.[22]

Besides depriving sailors of the pleasure of hearing explosions, the lack of realism in peacetime exercises had a more serious consequence. Fatal defects in the operation of the Mark-14 torpedo remained unknown. The first of these defects—discovered by frustrated submariners at war—was the Mark-14's habit of running deeper than its setting. If a skipper set his torpedoes to run at, say, ten feet, they might actually run at twenty or twenty-five feet, passing harmlessly under the target.

Rear Admiral Charles A. Lockwood, who commanded the submarine force operating from Fremantle, Australia, decided to run tests on the Mark-14; he soon discovered the trouble. The Bureau of Ordnance, however, at first loftily ignored the reports of Lockwood's tests and refused to run any tests of its own. Under pressure from Admiral King, himself an ex-submariner, the bureau did finally run tests—which confirmed that the Mark-14 depth-control mechanism was defective.[23]

Yet even after the faulty depth mechanism had been discovered in August 1942, submarine commanders continued to experience premature explosions and duds when firing their torpedoes in action.

Many skippers began to suspect that not only the depth mechanism in the Mark-14, but the magnetic- and contact exploders as well were defective. The problem with the magnetic exploder stemmed from the fact that the magnetic field of a ship varied in shape according to the position of the ship on the earth's surface. Near the equator, the magnetic field of a ship was shaped quite differently from a ship in the waters off New England, where the Mark-14 had been developed.

The problem with the contact exploder was less esoteric. The firing-pin mechanism didn't work. When a torpedo hit something, the impact released a spring which pushed the firing-pin between a pair of guides and into the fulminate cap. With the Mark-14 however, a direct, head-on hit often caused the firing-pin to jam against the guides.[24] It was not until September 1943 that the last of the defects in the Mark-14 torpedo was finally eliminated. The magnetic exploder was deactivated and a new, stronger, lighter, metal firing-pin was devised by Nimitz's ordnance experts at Pearl Harbor and at last fitted to the Mark-14. After twenty-one months of war, U.S. submarines finally had an effective weapon.[25]

Other favorable developments also increased the deadliness of the U.S. submarine force. Codebreakers at Pearl Harbor were now reading the Japanese code used to transmit the schedule and routing of merchant marine convoys. American submarines could be sent directly into the path of the slow-moving Japanese convoys, eliminating the need for long, fuel-consuming searches in the vast Pacific.[26] Beginning late in 1943, submarine admirals at Pearl Harbor and Australia began experimenting with "wolf-pack tactics," in which a number of submarines combined to deliver a coordinated attack on an enemy convoy. Finally, substantial numbers of new submarines and new torpedoes had begun to arrive in the Pacific, remedying the worrisome shortages which had made some submarine commanders opt for conservative tactics. By July 1944 there were about a hundred American subs operating from Pearl Harbor and forty more from Australia. They carried a new type of electrical torpedo, the Mark-17, which left no wake, in addition to the old, now reliable, Mark-14.[27]

The Japanese navy was singularly unprepared to deal either defensively or offensively with the deadly onslaught of the U.S. submarine, which began in earnest toward the end of 1943. Prewar Japanese plans had estimated that transport of petroleum and food supplies to the home islands would not be much of a problem.[28] Japanese strategists expected to lose about 800,000 tons of shipping the first year of the war but then expected a sharp drop in the rate of losses.[29] The Japanese thought that American submarines were inferior to theirs and that American sailors were too soft and luxury-loving to stand the rigors of undersea warfare. The indifferent success of the U.S. submarine effort during the early months of the war, together with evidence of American torpedo failures, served to reinforce this false sense of security.[30]

Japanese complacency rapidly dissipated as sinkings by U.S. submarines mounted. Already by the middle of 1943, these losses were a serious problem. More numerous U.S. submarines operating from advanced bases in New Guinea, the Admiralties and the Marianas sank more than 600 Japanese ships during 1944, for a total of about 2.7 million tons—more than the 2.2 million tons sunk during 1941, 1942, and 1943 combined. About half of Japan's merchant fleet, including replacements, and about two-thirds of her tanker fleet had been destroyed by the end of 1944. The flow of oil from the East Indies was almost completely cut and general bulk imports fell by close to 40 percent.[31]

The Japanese were slow to react to this growing crisis. At the beginning of the war the Imperial Navy had no units assigned exclusively to antisubmarine warfare. Combined Fleet admirals demanded the best destroyers for duty with the combat forces. The first two escort groups, formed in April 1942 to protect communications to Singapore and to Truk, had only a handful of old destroyers. In November 1943 a Grand Escort Command Headquarters was established to coordinate and direct protection of all overseas shipping, but the Combined Fleet continued to get the best escort vessels and the Grand Escort Command received only older ships.[32]

A few Japanese naval officers pressed for a counteroffensive against U.S. merchant shipping. Beginning in the summer of 1942, plans were drawn up for an unrestricted submarine campaign along the lines of the German U-boat effort; but by the autumn of 1942, Japanese submarines which might have been employed against U.S. shipping were being diverted in large numbers to carrying supplies for beleaguered Japanese garrisons in the Pacific. Japanese submarine commanders protested this dangerous and unrewarding assignment but the Navy High Command, unimpressed by the I-boats' performance in the first year of the war, were more willing to assign subs than the more highly valued destroyers to supply and reinforcement duties.[33] The navy even laid down a new type of cargo-carrying submarine. Many Japanese submarines also fell victim to American men-of-war coached on to their locations by code intercepts.

The U.S. submarine offensive against Japan was one of the decisive elements in ensuring the empire's defeat. A force comprising less than 2 percent of U.S. Navy personnel had accounted for 55 percent of Japan's losses at sea. U.S. submarines sank over 1,300 Japanese ships including a battleship, eight aircraft carriers, and eleven cruisers in the course of the war.[34]

The cost was high. About 22 percent of U.S. submariners who made war patrols in World War II failed to return—the highest casualty rate for any branch of service. For the Japanese, the cost in lives was higher still. About 16,000 merchant seamen were killed as a result of submarine attacks and some 53,000 were wounded.[35] The number of civilians, including women and children, who lost their lives in merchant- and passenger ship sinkings has not been calculated.

● ●

Just as Americans before World War II had condemned unrestricted submarine warfare, so had they condemned, perhaps more strongly, the indiscriminate bombing of civilians. George Fielding Elliott and R. Ernest Dupuy, two respected American writers on military affairs in the 1930s, predicted that no "country will consider it worthwhile to start so dreadful and unpredictable a cycle of slaughter." [36] When the Axis powers did, in fact, adopt such a course, the American reaction was one of outrage and anger. Accounts of Japanese bombing and machine-gunnings of Chinese civilians from the air appeared in all American newspapers. Secretary of State Hull condemned "the large number of instances" in which the Japanese had resorted to aerial slaughter "at places near which there were no military establishments or organizations." The secretary particularly denounced "the use of incendiary bombs which inevitably and ruthlessly jeopardize non-military persons and property." [37]

Condemnation of Japanese conduct in China gradually grew into a desire for retaliation. As early as 1940, American leaders were toying with schemes to enable China to hit back at her tormentors. In December of that year, Treasury Secretary Henry Morgenthau worked out a project with Chinese Ambassador T.V. Soong to transfer heavy bombers to China with the understanding that they would be used to bomb Tokyo and other Japanese cities. "I am convinced that overnight it would change the whole picture in the Far East," wrote Morgenthau in his diary; "Soong is convinced that it would have a very decided effect on the Japanese population. . . ."[38]

Hull, who had already suggested that American planes from the Aleutians overfly Japan as a demonstration, readily accepted the plan; Morgenthau presented it to the president at a meeting with Stimson and Knox on December 19, 1940. Roosevelt was "delighted" and told Morgenthau to go ahead.[39] However, General Marshall promptly threw cold water on the whole scheme, pointing out that there was an acute shortage of both B-17s and trained crews to fly them, that maintenance of the aircraft in China would be impossible, and that the Chinese had already suffered heavy losses in trying to operate Martin B-10 bombers against the Japanese.[40] Morgenthau's plan was promptly scaled down to the Flying Tiger project.

Yet Roosevelt and his advisers never lost their desire to hit back directly at Japan—a desire much inflamed by Pearl Harbor and early American setbacks in the Pacific. In addition to the Doolittle raid, various other schemes were examined and then laid aside for lack of resources. Finally, in 1943 a weapon was at hand: the B-29 heavy bomber.

The B-29 was a revolutionary advance over its predecessors. It was twice as heavy as the B-17 and could carry a 20,000-pound bomb load 7,000 miles. Yet its new, very powerful, lightweight engines gave it a speed 30 percent higher than the older bomber. Intended to operate at high altitudes, the B-29 had pressurized crew spaces in the front and rear of the plane, connected by a long tube just wide enough for an airman to crawl through. A new centralized fire-control system designed by General Electric enabled any gunner to take control of any of the plane's five power-driven turrets, while a small, automatic, onboard computer helped to aim the guns.[41]

Before the B-29 had made its first test flight in September 1942, the Army Air Forces had ordered 250 planes from the Boeing Company, which built an entire new plant to produce only the new bomber. A crash program was begun to produce the "superfortress." The program almost came to a screeching halt in February 1943, when one of the two prototype B-29s, which had performed well in earlier tests, crashed near Seattle, Washington, killing Boeing's chief test pilot and his entire crew. The cause of the crash was traced to a fault in the engines, and development continued. Although design and production of the B-29 had been unusually rapid by all previous standards, the first planes delivered to the air force in early 1944 were still too late to be used against Germany as originally planned. But with her great range and defensive power, the new bomber appeared the ideal weapon to strike at the Japanese home islands.

At the beginning of 1944, China was the only Allied territory from which the B-29s could reach Japan. General George C. Kenney urged the air force high command to forget China and send the big bombers to the southwest Pacific, where they could operate from Australia against Japanese petroleum facilities in the East Indies.[42] But there were powerful political and psychological reasons to choose China as a base. In addition to the old desire to hit back at the Japanese homeland, there was a widespread belief among air force strategists that the targets offered in Manchuria and Japan (coke and steel, harbors and aircraft assembly plants) were of greater immediate importance in crippling Japan's war effort.[43] Finally, the government of Chiang Kai-shek had been disappointed so many times in its expectations of the Allies, had seen so many promises evaporate, that arrival of the superbombers in China was looked upon by Washington planners as a vital boost to Chinese morale.

So it was that in April 1944, the Joint Chiefs formally approved a plan, code-named MATTERHORN, for sustained bombing of Japan by B-29s based in China. By that time the first B-29s were already arriving in Karachi and Calcutta on the last leg of their journey to China. There, in the area around the Szechuan city of Chengtu, 300,000 Chinese laborers worked day and night to build airfields for the giant planes. Workers were drafted wholesale by the Szechuan government to work on the project, every one hundred households being required to furnish fifty laborers.

An American correspondent rhapsodized that the Chengtu airfields were a monument to the "goodwill" of the "nameless little people" of China, who constructed them largely by primitive hand labor.[44] Whether "the nameless little people" felt much goodwill toward a project which tore them from their villages during the lunar New Year holiday, put them to work under armed guards, and paid them barely enough to buy their own food, is debatable. But politicians and contractors in Chungking must have been pleased: for the Chinese government, in the time-honored way, proceeded to fleece the War Department by insisting that the U.S. pay for the airfields at the rate of one dollar to twenty Chinese yuan, instead of the actual free-market rate of one dollar to one hundred yuan.[45]

The Joint Chiefs of Staff created an entirely new organization, the 20th Air Force to direct the operations of the B-29s. The 20th operated directly under the Commanding General, Army Air Forces: "Hap" Arnold acted as executive agent for the Chiefs. The 20th Air Force was independent of theater or area commanders, though the latter were responsible for providing logistical support and base defenses. The theater commanders could, however, utilize the B-29s for their own operations in an emergency. This arrangement meant that, in addition to his demanding duties as head of the Army Air Forces and member of the Joint Chiefs, Arnold would be commanding a bomber force in combat operations.

The overall headquarters for MATTERHORN was the Twentieth Bomber Command. The B-29s themselves were organized into squadrons of seven planes each, four squadrons comprising a group, and four groups a wing. The bombers had a crew of eleven, five officers and six enlisted men. Most of the enlisted men doubled as gunners; all bomber squadrons had mechanics assigned as part of their regular organization.

After a "warm-up" attack on railway yards at Bangkok, the Twentieth Bomber Command launched its first strike against Japan on June 14, 1944. More than sixty bombers attacked the large iron- and steel works at Yawata on the island of Kyushu, which produced about a quarter of the empire's rolled steel. The city was completely blacked out and few bombs hit the steel complex, but the psychological results were considerable. In Washington the House and Senate halted their deliberations to hear the announcement of the bombing raid; Major General Kenneth B. Wolfe, commander of the new force, proclaimed the impending destruction of Japan's industries.

From Washington, Arnold called on Wolfe for more strikes to keep up the pressure on Japan. But the Twentieth Bomber Command was almost literally out of gas. The B-29s, like Chennault's B-24s, had to fly in their own fuel over the Hump from India, a process one commander likened to "getting money in the bank and having our spree." In addition, the big bombers still suffered from plenty of mechanical defects, which kept a significant percentage of them grounded. When Wolfe tried to explain these facts to Arnold and urged him to cut back on his ambitious schedule, the air force chief relieved him, replacing him with Major General Curtis E. LeMay, who had commanded B-17s in Europe.

While the bomber command waited for LeMay to arrive it made further raids on Manchuria and Japan, as well as a long-range raid, staged through Ceylon, on the Japanese oil refineries at Palembang in the Netherlands East Indies. All achieved meager results. However, Japanese aerial counterattacks against the Chengtu bases were even less effective.

A veteran of air combat in Europe, LeMay "was a big, husky, healthy, rather stocky, full-faced man, thirty-nine years old, from Columbus, Ohio. He apparently couldn't make himself heard even in a small room except when you bent all your ears in his direction, and when you did, he appeared to evade your attempt to hear him. He did this by interposing a cigar or pipe among words which were trying to escape through teeth which had obviously been pried open only with an effort, an effort with which the speaker had no real sympathy." [46]

LeMay immediately introduced changes to improve the performance of aircraft and crews. He scheduled practice missions against poorly defended targets to improve the accuracy of radar bombing. He also increased the size of the basic bomber formation. In spite of all efforts, however, the Twentieth was never successful in seriously damaging Japan's war effort. The planes flew about two sorties a month per plane—only about half of which were against Japanese industrial targets. Little real damage was done to production in the home islands, and the damage to industrial targets in Manchuria, while far more severe, was unimportant because Japan's shipping losses had by that time deprived her of the ability to carry Manchurian products to her own factories. [47]

One of the command's most spectacular successes came in a raid on Singapore when two B-29s—part of a fifty-three-plane strike—wrecked the King George VI Graving Dock, the largest drydock at Singapore, with pinpoint hits. This was the sort of unerring accuracy advocates of precision bombing were always talking about. Ironically, Southeast Asia Command subsequently deleted the Singapore dry docks from its target list because the British expected to recapture Malaya in the near future and wanted the docks intact. [48] The B-29s attacked Hankow in support of Chinese efforts to stem the Japanese offensives in November and December of 1944; they bombed Formosa in support of MacArthur's Leyte operations.

The Hankow mission was the first mass B-29 attack to employ incendiaries, a weapon Chennault had long advocated as most appropriate for strategic bombing in the Far East. [49] By 1944 a much more effective incendiary bomb had been developed by U.S. scientists and the Army's Chemical Warfare Service. The most advanced type of incendiary, the M-69, was a six-pound projectile filled with a slow-burning, gelatinous kind of gasoline called napalm. When set aflame, napalm flowed like a river—incinerating everything in its path. Upon impact, a mechanism in the M-69 threw out masses of napalm in all directions.

In the Hankow raid, smoke from the first group of incendiaries obscured the city, so that only about 40 percent of the bombs dropped were on target. Nonetheless, most of Hankow's docks and warehouses were destroyed by the raiders. The Twentieth Bomber Command's intelligence officer estimated that the 38 percent of the bombs which struck home had destroyed almost half the target area. Less happily, many of the other bombs had fallen on Chinese civilians.[50]

The Hankow raid was a kind of swan song for the B-29s flying from China. By the time of the Hankow attack in December 1944, other B-29 groups were operating from the Marianas bases, which could accommodate many more aircraft and did not suffer from the problems in logistics and defensibility which plagued the Chengtu bases. Chiang Kai-shek, Stilwell, and Chennault had long since begun to look askance at the considerable proportion of Hump tonnage (close to 15 percent) consumed each month by the B-29s. Chennault desperately wanted this tonnage for his 14th Air Force to help hold southwest China against continuing Japanese attacks. General Wedemayer, who had replaced Stilwell in October 1944, backed him up, as did Ambassador Hurley.[51] The B-29s were transferred in late January 1945 to bases in eastern India from which they operated in support of Southeast Asia Command, attacking Japanese-held ports and shipping. Thence they finally moved to the Marianas in February and March.

While B-29 operations in China and Southeast Asia were winding down, another, larger, B-29 force, the Twenty-first Bomber Command, was gearing up for operations from Saipan, Tinian, and Guam. These bombing operations were viewed by navy leaders with a mixture of skepticism and uneasiness. The B-29s would be flying from islands under navy control, islands which the navy, marines, and army had wrested from the Japanese in an arduous land-, sea-, and air campaign. "The interests of the AAF and the Navy clash seriously in the Central Pacific campaign," noted a member of Admiral King's staff. "The danger is obvious of our amphibious campaign being turned into one that is auxiliary support to permit the AAF to get into position to win the war." Some navy planners questioned whether Japan's defeat could be advanced by the B-29 campaign and predicted that "the results of the very long-range bombing will not be commensurate with the effort expended; the Marianas VLR

operations can be treated as a sideshow of the stunt category . . ." [52]
Given such views, both Arnold and King were well aware that more
was riding on the B-29 campaign than simply crippling Japanese
production.

To head the new bomber command, Arnold had appointed Brigadier General Haywood S. Hansell, a veteran of air combat in Europe
and one of the foremost strategists in the Army Air Forces. Hansell
had, since the 1930s, been a strong advocate of sustained precision
bombing by large formations of heavy bombers operating at high
altitudes, a method of warfare he now intended to wage against
Japan.[53]

After practice bombings against Japanese island bases in the Pacific,
Hansell despatched his B-29s against Tokyo in the first of a sustained
series of raids on Japan aimed at crippling aircraft production in
the home islands. In almost all these raids, Hansell's bombers encountered high winds and clouds over the target; this frequently threw
off their aim or forced them to bomb by radar. "We were up about
as high as you could go," recalled one crew member; "practically
in a stall at 30,000 feet. We never saw it [our target] we were
going so fast downwind there was no way the bombardier could
get on that bomb sight, look through it, and synchronize everything."
When one squadron attempted to attack upwind, "the damn target
backed right off the radar; we were going backward over ground." [54]

Some damage was done to aircraft production facilities, but on
the whole the raids were a failure. Only about half of the bombers
hit their primary target. Hansell's flyers were plagued with many
of the same troubles as those operating from China: mechanical defects, inadequate maintenance facilities, inexperience, and long over-
water flights which consumed much of their fuel and left little margin
to compensate for navigational errors or unforeseen headwinds.

Major General Curtis LeMay relieved Hansell in January 1945.
Ironically, this happened just as Hansell's bombers were achieving
one of their rare successes by virtually crippling the Akashi works
of the Kawasaki Aircraft Industries Company near Kobe, forcing
the shutdown of the entire factory complex.[55] But achievements like
that were rare—and LeMay did little better than Hansell. Bomber
losses, light at first, were beginning to mount, totaling almost 6 percent of the force during January. As many bombers were lost to
operational problems as to Japanese fighters or antiaircraft guns.

One way to reduce operational losses was to reduce the hazards
of the flight from the Marianas to Japan by seizing an intermediate

airbase where B-29s could refuel or make emergency landings. The leading candidate was Iwo Jima, a tiny piece of volcanic rock almost midway between Saipan and Tokyo. Japanese aircraft operating from that island could strike Saipan, Tinian, or Guam as well as harass B-29s en route to Japan. To avoid the neighborhood of Iwo, the big bombers were obliged to fly a long, dog-leg course which complicated navigation, consumed precious fuel, and reduced the bomb load they could carry. Even with the dog-leg course, the B-29s were easily picked up on Iwo Jima's radar, which provided the home islands with ample warning of impending raids.[56] Spruance and other naval strategists had also been eying Iwo Jima for some time as a base for projecting land-based air power into the Ryukyu and the Japanese home islands to augment the carriers' striking power.[57]

The important strategic decisions reached by the Joint Chiefs of Staff in the fall of 1944 not only settled the question of Luzon versus Formosa in favor of the former. They also led to a directive to Nimitz to occupy "one or more positions in the Nanpo Shoto," the long chain of islands extending 750 miles southward from central Japan. Iwo Jima was the only island of this group which possessed both passable landing beaches and suitable terrain for airfield construction.[58] Aside from these two qualities, the place had little to recommend it. Roughly 4½-miles long by 2½-miles wide, it was shaped like a lopsided pear and covered with fine brown volcanic ash. At the south end of the island rose Mt. Suribachi, a live but dormant volcano. With Suribachi as the stem, the "pear" gradually widened and the ground rose steadily in uneven terraces and plateaus. There was a broad tableland in the center upon which the Japanese had constructed two airstrips and begun a third.

Iwo's volcanic ash soil had one virtue: when mixed with cement it could be converted into a superior type of concrete.[59] Ever since June of 1944, the Japanese had been anticipating an American assault on the island and Iwo's commander, Lieutenant General Kuribayashi Tadamichi, was determined to make good use of this asset. He promptly scrapped plans by his predecessor to meet the invasion at the water's edge and began preparations for a prolonged defense of the entire island. Kuribayashi knew that he could expect no help from the fleet nor from navy or army air forces. When the Americans struck, only those forces and weapons already on the island would be available to him and they would have to hold to the last man. Of the ultimate outcome he had no illusions: upon leaving home he had left behind the samurai sword which had been in his family for generations, along with the saber presented to him by the Emperor upon his graduation from the staff college.[60]

All civilians on the island were evacuated to Japan in July 1944. In their place came reinforcements from Japan and other Pacific garrisons, bringing the total strength of army and navy forces on the island to 21,000 men.[61] With the troops came mining engineers to draw plans for the extensive underground fortifications which soon dotted the island.

Over 361 artillery pieces, 65 mortars, 33 large naval guns, and close to 100 large-caliber antiaircraft guns disappeared into reinforced concrete bunkers, blockhouses, or improved natural caves—redoubts which made the formidable Japanese installations on Peleliu look almost primitive by comparison. Miles of tunnels linked the subterranean command posts, ammunition dumps, and living quarters with one another and with the blockhouses which protruded slightly above ground. General Kuribayashi's own command post in the northern part of the island was located in a cave 75 feet underground, one of several linked by over 500 feet of tunnels. Like all underground installations on Iwo, this complex featured multiple entrances and exits, stairwells, and interconnecting passages.

From there Kuribayashi would direct his defense of Iwo Jima, a defense which was to have no do-or-die stands on the beaches, no reckless banzai charges, not even a large-scale counterattack—simply a stubborn, sustained defense designed to inflict maximum casualties and wear down the invader. Kuribayashi's artillery would not expose their positions by engaging in fruitless duels with the American fire support vessels, but would husband their full strength to unleash upon the invading troops ashore. On the walls of pillboxes and bunkers Kuribayashi had posted copies of the "Courageous Battle Vow" which pledged the defenders to "kill ten of the enemy before dying." [62]

The full extent of Japanese defensive effort on Iwo Jima was unknown to the Americans but enough information was available to make commanders uneasy. Documents captured on Saipan and Tinian, and aerial photographs of the island suggested that Iwo would be a difficult target indeed. Almost everything about the topography of the island favored the defense and the small size of the place left little room for offensive maneuvers.

The largest force of U.S. Marines ever assembled under one command was earmarked for the assault on Iwo Jima. The Third, Fourth and Fifth Marine divisions were organized into the V Amphibious

Corps under Major General Harry Schmidt. The Third and Fourth divisions had seen action in the Marianas, while the Fifth was a new division, but fleshed out with experienced officers and NCOs and veterans of marine raider and parachute battalions. Vice Admiral Richmond Kelly Turner again commanded the amphibious forces afloat, but he delegated most of his tactical and planning responsibilities to his two subordinates, Rear Admiral Harry W. Hill, who commanded the transports, cargo ships, and landing craft, and Rear Admiral W. H. P. Blandy, who had charge of minesweeping, reconnaissance, naval gunfire, and air support.

Schmidt's planners did not like the look of Iwo Jima: they called for ten days of preliminary bombardment by the Navy's warships before the first marine set foot ashore. Only naval gunfire could do the job of stripping away camouflage and demolishing the Japanese concrete bunkers and pillboxes. The marines knew that naval gunfire could never knock out all the defense works—but the more it did destroy, the better.

Unfortunately for the marines, Iwo Jima had to compete for resources with other important operations in the Pacific. MacArthur's forces were heavily engaged in the Philippines and required the continued support of the navy, while the projected invasion of Okinawa would also require all-out naval support. Finally, Spruance was planning a large-scale carrier raid against Tokyo and adjacent areas to coincide with the prelanding bombardment of Iwo.

More ships and more ammunition would have been available had not Spruance scheduled his raid on Japan for the same time as the attack on Iwo Jima. Although the ostensible reason for Spruance's move was to neutralize possible Japanese aerial opposition to the Iwo Jima landings, the operation soon took on a life of its own. Spruance and his staff were eager to try a carrier attack against Japanese aircraft factories that the B-29s of the Twentieth Air Force had been bombing with only indifferent success. The admiral believed that it was time to "stop fighting the products of the Jap aircraft factories on the perimeter and take our carrier air into the center to knock out the factories themselves. We cannot afford to await the outcome of bombing with 'precision instruments' from 30,000 feet, often enough through solid overcast." [63] In retrospect, it is hard to see how bombing aircraft plants in Japan could have had an immediate effect on the situation at Iwo Jima, and it is hard to escape the conclusion that the navy was eager to have a go at upstaging the Army Air Forces—even at the expense of some fire support for the marines.

With all these commitments in mind Spruance, in overall command of the Iwo operation, cut the marines' request down to three days of naval bombardment. He acted with the concurrence of Turner, who argued that his forces lacked the ships and ammunition for a sustained bombardment of ten days. Instead Turner proposed three days of intensive bombardment which, he said, would drop as many projectiles on the island as the marines had requested for the entire ten days. The marines replied that it was not the sheer tonnage of ammunition expended which counted, but the length of time allowed for deliberate, point-blank fire by heavy naval guns.

Spruance either failed to understand the marines' arguments or was unimpressed by them. He told Schmidt to expect three days of naval gunfire. The admiral added that the steady bombing of Iwo Jima by the air force, which had begun some six months before, ought to be worth at least the equivalent of one day's naval bombardment. (It was only after the war that military historians, analyzing the results of air force strikes, were to conclude that their chief effect had been to drive the Japanese deeper underground.) As a belated concession to the marines, Spruance did authorize a fourth day of bombardment if, after the first three days, commanders on the scene believed it necessary.[64]

• •

At dawn on February 16, 1945, General Kurabayashi's men looked out of their bunkers and observation posts to find Iwo ringed with warships. As the morning grew lighter, minesweepers threaded their way through the inshore waters to clear a path for the larger warships, while destroyers and destroyer-transports formed a screen on the seaward side of the invasion fleet. Some of the warships in Admiral Blandy's bombardment force were older than most of the men who sailed in them. There was the battleship *New York,* which had sailed with the British Grand Fleet in the First World War, and the *Arkansas,* completed in 1912, the oldest U.S. battleship still in commission.

Admiral Blandy commanded from a well-equipped headquarters and communications ship. Aboard this flagship were special staffs to correlate reports from spotting planes, keep track of targets, interpret aerial photographs, and estimate damage. Pilots specially trained in spotting for naval gunfire accompanied the fleet in the escort carrier *Wake Island.* The entire island had been mapped out in numbered squares, with each square assigned to a different warship and known targets marked and numbered. There were over 700 of these suspected targets, each entered in a card index aboard Blandy's flagship.

At the end of the first day's bombardment, less than two dozen of those targets had been destroyed. Low ceiling and frequent rain squalls hampered visibility and limited the battleships and cruisers to only intermittent firing. " 'By dispensation of Heaven,' " wrote one of Iwo's defenders, " 'the characteristic mist of this island caused the sky to overcast.' " [65]

The next day dawned clear with good visibility and Blandy's ships closed to 3,000 yards. Japanese gunners mistook a group of rocket-firing LCIs for the first wave of a landing force; when they opened fire, they revealed their gun positions to the bombardment ships—which promptly went to work on them. The LCIs suffered heavy casualties but the Japanese suffered more, for their powerful batteries flanking the landing beaches and in casemates at the foot of Mt. Suribachi were prematurely revealed to the Americans, who damaged them badly. Firing on the LCIs was the only serious error made by the Japanese during the battle.

That night, as Radio Tokyo congratulated the Iwo Jima defenders on their repulse of the American "invasion," a worried group gathered aboard Admiral Blandy's flagship. The duel with the Japanese batteries that afternoon had demonstrated with brutal clarity how formidable the island's defenses were and how little damage had been done by the first two days' bombardment. Now only one day of naval gunfire remained before the scheduled assault.

How to make best use of that last previous day was the subject of intense discussion on the flagship. Lieutenant Colonel Donald M. Weller, the marines' naval gunfire expert, urged Blandy to forget about artillery, blockhouses, and pillboxes inland and to concentrate all fire on positions which could threaten the landing beaches. This was what the marines had wanted all along. After some further discussion, the navy agreed.[66]

Sunday, February 18th, dawned gray and rainy. Four of the five battleships in the bombardment group concentrated their fire on enemy batteries flanking the beaches or on the beaches themselves. The ships received permission to fire all their remaining ammunition except that needed for D-Day.

At ranges of less than a mile and a half, the battleships proved highly effective, destroying more than two-thirds of the guns and blockhouses in their target areas near the beaches. The heavy fire also stripped away much camouflage: aerial photographs in the late afternoon revealed still more targets to Blandy's staff. For the last three hours of the day, the bombardment was even more deadly.

Navy and air force planes also pounded the island, but were far less effective.[67]

Blandy radioed his report to Admiral Turner that evening. The day's results had been good but there were still many enemy installations undamaged, and Blandy's warships had not expended all their pre-D-Day ammunition. However, a landing appeared possible in the morning as scheduled.[68] Turner decided to go ahead, basing his decision mainly on the weather, which was predicted as fair for the nineteenth, but poor for the following day. Had the marines not landed on the nineteenth, the assault would probably have had to be postponed until the twenty-first.

And many marines would soon wish that it had been. For it is clear in retrospect that two additional days of naval gunfire would have been immensely helpful and, in all probability, would have shortened the fighting ashore.[69] As it was, the marines went ashore with many of the island's defenses, especially those away from the beaches, intact. No other island in the Pacific had been assaulted with so many of its defenses unscathed.[70] Samuel Eliot Morison has observed that regardless of the length of naval bombardment, it "could not reach underground into the maze of caves and tunnels" carefully prepared by the Japanese.[71] That is true enough, but there were plenty of targets on Iwo which the battleships and cruisers *could* reach and whose locations were known; they were left intact because of the brevity of the bombardment.

Aboard the transports and LSTs, the marines, mercifully ignorant of the state of the island's defenses, ate an early breakfast of steak and eggs in the predawn darkness. Each marine was carrying at least fifty pounds of equipment and most carried seventy-five to a hundred pounds. Learning from past experience, the marines had beefed up their assault units with demolition squads equipped with flamethrowers, rocket-firing "bazookas," and explosive charges. This added greatly to marine firepower but also increased the load which many leathernecks had to carry in the landing.

At 6:45 A.M. Blandy's ships, reinforced by battleships and cruisers of Task Force 58 just returned from their raid on Japan, opened the heaviest naval bombardment of the Pacific War. The landings themselves were carried out with the precision of a parade. The first landing craft crossed the line of departure at 8:30 while naval shells ripped overhead and aircraft swooped down to deliver a final attack on beach positions. The leading assault wave—consisting of armored amphibious tractors, supported on their flanks by rocket-firing LCI gunboats—touched down precisely on time, followed at two-minute intervals by the second and third waves with troop carrying amphtracs.

Leaping from their landing craft, the Marines found themselves sinking to their ankles in the soft volcanic ash. A steep fifteen-foot terrace directly behind the beach blocked fields of fire for the armored amphibians and slowed the advance to a crawl. Some of the amphibians managed to climb the terrace and push beyond it, while behind them successive waves of marines continued to land. The landing beaches stretched north and eastward about 3,500 yards from the base of Mt. Suribachi. The Fifth Marine Division was to land on the southernmost beaches and drive across the narrow neck of the island while elements of one regiment, the 28th Marines, would capture Suribachi.[72] The Fourth Marine Division would land to the northeast and drive for the southernmost Japanese airstrip, "Airfield No. 1," then turn to the north.

For the first few minutes following the initial landings, Japanese fire was light and intermittent, but it increased steadily in volume and accuracy until the entire beach area, as well as the reserve waves of troops and equipment still on the water, came under intense bombardment. Huge 320-mm. Japanese mortars lobbed 700-pound shells at the hapless invaders; less spectacular but equally deadly artillery, machine guns, and lighter mortars added to the carnage. The edge of the beach was littered with burning or wrecked landing craft, while further inland tanks and jeeps lay mired in the volcanic ash. "Wounded men were arriving on the beach by the dozen where they were not much better off than they had been at the front. . . . The first two boats bringing in badly needed litters were blown out of the water. Casualties were being hit again as they lay helpless under blankets awaiting evacuation."[73] Neither the casualties nor anyone else on that hellish beach could find any protection from the intense rain of shells. Seabees, doctors, shore parties, ammunition handlers, and boat crews were often subject to heavier fire than the assault troops themselves. Despite all, the marines had some 30,000 men ashore by the end of the first day, along with artillery, tanks, and supplies. Some units had reached their initial objectives, albeit at the cost of heavy casualties.

That night the Americans braced for a large-scale Japanese counterattack—but none came. Instead, the rain of shells and bullets from unseen Japanese positions continued unabated. Two casualty stations on the beach received direct hits and many of the patients were killed. Dawn of the second day revealed the bodies of the dead scattered about the beach. "They died with the greatest possible violence. Nowhere in the Pacific have I seen such badly mangled bodies," wrote Robert Sherrod, who had been at Tarawa. "Many were cut squarely in half. Legs and arms lay 50 feet away from any body." [74]

At first light the 28th Marines commenced their attack on Suribachi, while the other forces on Iwo wheeled to the right, beginning the main advance northeastward up the island. The approaches to Suribachi were honeycombed with caves, pillboxes, and bunkers. From the top of the mountain, Japanese observers could direct artillery onto any element of the attacking marine forces. On the first day of the attack, a tank company found that there was no spot where they could halt even to take on fuel and ammunition without drawing Japanese mortar fire.[75]

The Marines advanced by yards. Infantrymen, machinegunners, and tanks and halftracks would keep a pillbox under fire while a flamethrower team worked its way forward to spray lethal bursts at the apertures or cave mouths. Flamethrowers were so heavily used that a shortage of flamethrower fuel developed.[76]

After three days of hard fighting, a patrol from E Company of the Second Battalion, 28th Marines, under Lieutenant Harold G. Schrier, picked its way cautiously to the crater atop Suribachi and raised a small American flag on a twenty-foot length of pipe. Though small, the flag was visible from everywhere on the beach and at sea. Tired Marines wept, cheered, and slapped each other on the back while out at sea, ships sounded their whistles and horns. Watching from the beach, Secretary of the Navy James V. Forrestal, who had been present in Turner's flagship throughout the operation, turned to General Holland Smith and remarked: "Holland, the raising of that flag on Suribachi means a Marine Corps for the next 500 years." [77]

Near the summit of Suribachi, Associated Press photographer Joe Rosenthal learned that the marines were preparing to raise a larger flag obtained from an LST and keep the original as a souvenir. Piling up some stones to give him more height, Rosenthal hastily sighted his camera and clicked one shot. The photograph was sent off to Guam that evening along with seventeen others he had taken that day.[78] Rosenthal was unaware that he had just taken the most famous photograph of the Pacific war and one of the best known war photos of all time. Reproduced thousands of times, it won a Pulitzer prize for Rosenthal and inspired the giant bronze monument to the Marine Corps by Felix de Weldon near Arlington Cemetery.

Suribachi's fall marked only the beginning of the fight for Iwo Jima. The rest was less dramatic but even more bloody as the marines advanced north into the island's most rugged terrain, which concealed the bulk of Kuribayashi's man-made defenses. Reinforced by two regiments of the Third Marine Division, the men of the Fourth and Fifth Divisions began to push their way north against the Japanese main defensive lines.

Their advances measured in yards, the marines slowly fought their way through terrain appropriately nicknamed "Bloody Gorge" and "Meat Grinder," and dozens of other deadly ridges, ravines, and caves. Behind them Seabees and Marine Corps engineers were already at work reconstructing and enlarging captured airfields to accommodate fighters and B-29s. By the time fighting finally ceased at the end of March, the marines had lost 6,821 men killed and close to 20,000 wounded. Nineteen of the twenty-four original battalion commanders who had landed with their men were killed or wounded. In one battalion of the 25th Marines, fewer than 150 of 900 men survived unhurt.[79] The 21,000 Japanese defenders died almost to a man. Only a few hundred, mostly wounded, survived to become prisoners. They had conducted the stoutest defense of the Pacific War; for the first time in the island campaign, the Japanese had inflicted greater casualties on the invaders than they had suffered themselves.

Iwo Jima never became the major offensive base envisioned by Spruance. Nor was it much needed as a base for fighter escorts, because Japanese air strength in the home islands was decreasing rapidly and the B-29s were turning to night raids. The island was mainly used as an intermediate landing point, particularly for B-29s suffering damage or low on fuel. By the end of the war the bombers had made about 2,400 emergency landings on Iwo Jima, leading some writers to claim that taking into account the eleven-man crews, the island airstrips saved about 20,000 airmen.[80] Of course, such a figure assumes that none of the bombers in distress would have reached the Marianas and that if forced down at sea, the crews would not have been rescued—an obvious exaggeration.

Whatever the exact figure, it is probably true that the airmen saved exceeded the number of marines killed in taking the island and, since Japan surrendered a few months after the Iwo battle, this seems a persuasive calculus. Yet had the war gone as expected, with an invasion of Japan necessary in early 1946, the wholesale sacrifice of three well-trained and expert assault divisions simply to secure emergency landing fields might have loomed as a gross strategic error.

Twenty-seven Marines and naval medical corpsmen won the Medal of Honor at Iwo Jima, many posthumously. "Among the Americans who served on Iwo Island," wrote Admiral Nimitz, "uncommon valor was a common virtue." A wounded marine added a pithier comment: "I hope to God that we don't have to go on any more of those screwy islands." [81]

● ●

By early 1945, all but the truest of the true-believers in the air force high command had been forced to the reluctant conclusion that daylight precision bombing, even with so superb an instrument as the B-29, was proving relatively ineffective for the defeat of Japan. Other means would have to be tried.

Air Force strategists began to consider the use of incendiaries once again. Japanese cities had long been known to be exceptionally vulnerable to fire. Admiral Yamamoto himself had repeatedly expressed his fear of air raids on Japan. "Japanese cities, being made of wood and paper, would burn very easily," he told a group of officers in 1939. "The Army talks big, but if war came and there were large-scale air raids, there's no telling what would happen." [82]

As far back as 1919, a marine officer who had served in Japan told the General Board of proposals for large high-speed cruisers built especially to carry a large number of seaplanes, which would drop incendiary bombs on Japan.[83] In prewar staff conversations British officers had emphasized the vulnerability of Japanese cities to strikes by American carrier planes. In February 1943 intelligence analysts in Washington had suggested that mass air attacks on Japanese urban areas, using incendiaries, could have an important effect on war production. Later studies confirmed these conclusions, and tests conducted on model Japanese buildings at the Army's Dugway Proving Ground in Utah suggested that Japanese cities, in which factories and mills were frequently surrounded by crowded, highly inflammable wooden residences, would prove highly vulnerable to incendiary attack.[84]

The results of the Twentieth Bomber Command raid on Hankow offered practical proof of what could be done; but trials of incendiary bombing by the Twenty-first Bomber Command against the city of

Nagoya in central Honshu had been inconclusive. Then, on February 4, LeMay's bombers struck at Kobe, Japan's sixth largest city and most important port, using only incendiaries dropped from high altitudes. The results were encouraging; five of the twelve principal factories were damaged and one of the two largest shipyards had to reduce production by half.

A second high-altitude incendiary raid on February 25 followed, this time against Tokyo. By the time of the Tokyo raid, LeMay had over two hundred B-29s available, having been reinforced by two more bomber wings earlier in the year. The Tokyo raid's results were even more impressive than those at Kobe: 28,000 structures were destroyed and about a square mile of the city was leveled.

Reviewing the results of this raid against the meager achievements of the daylight precision-bombing campaign, and faced with the prospect of even poorer weather in the coming months, LeMay decided on a change of tactics. Accepting poor weather and thus poor visual conditions as unavoidable, he decided to rely on area attacks. For area attacks, incendiaries had been shown to be far more effective than high explosives. Yet incendiaries were not very accurate and they would be even less accurate when dropped from high altitudes by bombers battling the strong winds over Japan.

Bringing the bombers down to low altitudes would increase accuracy, cut down on the wind problem and allow the planes to carry a heavy bomb load. Low altitudes would also expose the bombers to far greater danger from enemy flak but LeMay, who had seen plenty of German flak over Europe, was confident that the risk was bearable. He also knew that the Japanese had few night fighters; and those were not very effective.[86] Early in March, one of LeMay's group commanders volunteered to take his B-29 on a test run over Tokyo at night at low altitude. The plane returned unscathed. "I think we can do it," growled LeMay, clamping down more tightly on his pipe.[87]

On March 8 LeMay issued new orders for his command. Three hundred thirty-four bombers, armed only with incendiaries, would strike Tokyo at night from altitudes as low as 4,900 feet. Even the machine-gun ammunition would be removed to enable the planes to carry heavier bomb loads. The target was a rectangular area of the Japanese capital more than four times as densely populated as the average American city.

Weather over Tokyo was unusually good and LeMay's new tactics took the Japanese defenders by surprise. The planes bombed individually in a wide, loose formation. Soon a large section of the target zone was in flames, the fires fanned by a moderately heavy wind. Almost sixteen square miles of the city were burnt out, including 18 percent of the industrial area. Some 267,000 buildings were destroyed. It was the most destructive single bombing raid in history—more destructive than the Moscow fire of 1812, the great Chicago fire of 1871, or the San Francisco earthquake.[88]

The Japanese were ill prepared to counter this new onslaught. The lack of success of the Nagoya incendiary raid had given them false confidence in their ability to cope with raids of that type. Their fire departments were poorly trained and organized, while the "firefighting equipment in common use would, in large part, have been shunned by small-town volunteer fire departments in the United States."[89] Conflagrations soon raged out of control. Entire blockfronts burst into flame. Water boiled in the canals. Great clouds of smoke and soot filled the night sky. Thousands perished in the fires. Charred bodies were later found by officials piled on bridges, roads, and by canals. Altogether, more than 83,000 people died in the flaming holocaust; another 41,000 were injured.

The Tokyo raid of March 9 set the pattern for American strategic bombing for the remainder of the war. By early June, the six most important industrial cities (Tokyo, Nagoya, Kobe, Osaka, Yokohama, and Kawasaki) had been devastated. Over 40 percent of the total urban area of these cities had been gutted; millions had been rendered homeless. LeMay next turned to the destruction of Japan's smaller cities. His bomber force, now almost 600 strong, ranged over Japan almost at will, visiting destruction on half a hundred smaller cities and manufacturing centers.

Almost as destructive was an aerial mining campaign unleashed by the 20th Air Force in March. The Allied submarine and air campaign had forced the Japanese to funnel most of their shipping through the Inland Sea and coastal waters. LeMay's bombers, trained and equipped by Navy mine experts, aimed their efforts at Shimonoseki Strait, the narrow neck of water separating the southwest tip of Honshu from Kyushu. The mines sank a number of ships and paralyzed traffic in the Inland Sea. At the large port of Kobe, shipping had declined from 320,000 tons in March to 44,000 in July.[90]

So confident was LeMay of his mastery of the situation that his bombers adopted the practice of dropping leaflets to warn the population to evacuate a specific list of cities marked for bombing. Although LeMay's "warnings" were viewed primarily as psychological warfare by the AAF, they may also have served to assuage a lingering feeling of uneasiness among Americans about the new form which the air war had assumed. Few Americans doubted that Japan "had it coming," that she herself had begun this sort of business with her bombing of Chinese cities in 1937 and her "sneak attack" on Pearl Harbor, and even fewer doubted that the all-out B-29 bombings would soon cripple Japanese industry and shorten the war. And yet, some bomber crews flying through the dense clouds of smoke and ash, smelling the smell of burning cities, whose flames were visible to aviators from a distance of over 150 miles, probably realized that this was something new, something more terrible than even the normal awfulness of war. Machines of war had achieved the power to match natural catastrophes in destructiveness and, as in natural disasters, neither the young nor the very old, the innocent or the helpless, were spared.

NOTES

1. Thomas C. Hart, "Submarines," Naval War College Lecture, 20 December 1920, Naval War College Historical Collection, RG 14.

2. In addition to specific documents cited below, information for this section was obtained from Samuel Flagg Bemis, "Submarine Warfare in the Strategy of American Defense and Diplomacy 1915–1945," unpublished Ms, Naval Historical Center.

3. Letter, President of Naval War College to Chief of Naval Operations, 20 March 1941, Serial 6838, General Board No. 425, General Board Records.

4. Letter, Chairman, General Board to Secretary of the Navy, enclosure to Memorandum, "Are We Ready, 3," General Board 425, 14 June 1941, Records of General Board.

5. Letter, Commander L. R. McDowell to the Joint Secretaries to British Joint Staff Mission, 20 October 1941, OP-12-V05 Serial 011312–82, Flag Screener's Files, Naval Historical Center.

6. Ibid.

7. CNO to Commander in Chief, Asiatic Fleet, 26 November 1941, CNO despatch file, Naval Historical Center.

8. "Combat Zone," Extract from PLENAP "A" of 10 July 1941, U.S.-U.K.-Dutch Conversations (Singapore), SPO, Series 7, Naval Historical Center.

9. Bemis, "Submarine Warfare," p. 32.

10. Blair, Silent Victory, pp. 26–27, 45–46; W. J. Holmes, *Undersea Victory, The Influence of Submarine Operations in the Pacific* (New York: Doubleday and Co.,

1966), p. 46; Hashimoto Mochitsura, *Sunk* (New York: Avon Books, 1954), p. 49; Memorandum, Director, Fleet Maintenance Division to Director, War Plans Division, Sub.: Employment of Submarines—Orange War, 25 April 1936, OP23C-10, Naval Historical Center.

11. Hashimoto, *Sunk*, p. 50.

12. Blair, *Silent Victory*, pp. 46, 58.

13. Holmes, *Undersea Victory*, p. 44; Edward L. Beach, "Introduction" to Hashimoto, *Sunk*, p. 17.

14. Holmes, *Undersea Victory*, p. 37.

15. Blair, *Silent Victory*, pp. 87–89, 93, 176–78, 523, 793.

16. Ibid., p. 793.

17. The foregoing discussion is based primarily on "Employment of Submarines," Staff Presentation, U.S. Naval War College, 21 August 1941, in Strategic Plans Division Records Series 2, Naval War College Materials on Employment of Submarines, U.S. Naval Historical Center; Holmes, *Undersea Victory*, pp. 47–48; and Blair, *Silent Victory*, pp. 45–46.

18. Hanson W. Baldwin interview p. 334, Naval Historical Center.

19. "Employment of Submarines"; Blair, *Silent Victory*, pp. 314, 331, 333–35.

20. Blair, *Silent Victory*, p. 331.

21. Holmes, *Double-Edged Secrets*, pp. 128, 334.

22. Holmes, *Undersea Victory*, p. 43.

23. Blair, *Silent Victory*, pp. 252–54.

24. Potter, *Nimitz*, pp. 231–32.

25. Blair, *Silent Victory*, pp. 410–11.

26. Holmes, *Double-Edged Secrets*, pp. 126–29; "Role of Communications Intelligence in Submarine Warfare in the Pacific, Jan. 1943 to Oct. 1943," Vol. 1, pp. iv-v, SRH 011, RG J, 457.

27. Blair, *Silent Victory*, p. 668.

28. Saburo Ienaga, *The Pacific War: World War II and the Japanese 1931–1945* (New York: Random House, 1978), p. 140.

29. Holmes, *Undersea Victory*, p. 192.

30. Toland interview with Captain Atsushi Oi, 12 June 1969, Toland Interview Collection; Hashimoto, *Sunk*, pp. 158–60.

31. Blair, *Silent Victory*, p. 792.

32. Atsushi Oi, "Why Japan's Anti-Submarine Warfare Failed," *U.S. Naval Institute Proceedings* 78 (June 1952), pp. 588, 593–97 and passim.

33. Carl Boyd, "The Japanese Submarine Force and the Legacy of Strategic and Operational Doctrine Developed Between the Wars," in Larry H. Addington et al., eds., *Selected Papers From the Citadel Conference on War and Diplomacy* (Charleston: Citadel Foundation, 1978), pp. 29–31.

34. Blair, *Silent Victory*, pp. 851–53.

35. Ibid., pp. 851–52.

36. George Fielding Eliot and R. Ernest Dupuy, *If War Comes* (New York: Macmillan and Co., 1937), p. 62.

37. Carl Berger, *B-29: The Superfortress* (New York: Ballantine Books, 1970), p. 37.

38. John Morton Blum, ed., *From the Morgenthau Diaries: Years of Urgency 1938–1941* (Boston: Houghton Mifflin Co., 1965), p. 366.

39. Ibid., pp. 367–68.

40. Romanus and Sunderland, *Stilwell's Mission to China,* pp. 12–13.

41. Berger, *B-29: The Superfortress,* pp. 29–53; Wilbur H. Morrison, *Point of No Return: The Story of the 20th Air Force* (New York: Times Books, 1979), pp. 24–27.

42. W. F. Craven and J. L. Cate, *Army Air Forces in World War II,* Vol. 5, *The Pacific: Matterhorn to Nagasaki* (Chicago: University of Chicago Press, 1953), p. 12; Stanley L. Falk, "General Kenney, the Indirect Approach, and the B-29s," *Aerospace Historian* 27 (September 1981), pp. 152–53.

43. Craven and Cate, *Matterhorn to Nagasaki,* pp. 27–30, 93, 99 and passim.

44. *New York Times,* June 17, 1944.

45. Craven and Cate, *Matterhorn to Nagasaki,* pp. 68–70; Tuchman, *Stilwell,* p. 456.

46. St. Clair McKelway, "A Reporter with the B-29s," *New Yorker,* June 16, 1945, p. 32.

47. Craven and Cate, *Matterhorn to Nagasaki,* pp. 170–71.

48. Ibid., pp. 156, 160.

49. Berger, *B-29: The Superfortress,* p. 97.

50. Craven and Cate, *Matterhorn to Nagasaki,* pp. 143–44.

51. Romanus and Sunderland, *Time Runs Out in CBI,* p. 161.

52. Captain A. K. Doyle, Memorandum for Admiral Duncan, Sub.: Press Release for VLR Operations from Marianas, 20 May 1944, COMINCH File, King Papers.

53. Message, Hansell to Arnold, 21 December 1944; Letter, Hansell to Lieutenant General Barney E. Giles, 27 March 1945. Both in Arnold Papers.

54. "Interview of Gen. David A. Berchinal," 11 April 1975, p. 60, USAF Oral History Program, copy in Office of Chief of Air Force History, Washington, D.C.

55. Craven and Cate, *Matterhorn to Nagasaki,* pp. 565–66.

56. Ibid., p. 586.

57. Buell, *The Quiet Warrior,* pp. 306–7.

58. Samuel Eliot Morrison, *Victory in the Pacific 1945* (Boston: Little, Brown and Co., 1975), p. 5.

59. George W. Garand and Truman R. Strobridge, *History of U.S. Marine Corps Operations in World War II,* Vol. 4, *Western Pacific Operations* (Washington, D.C.: U.S. Marine Corps, 1971), p. 455.

60. Richard F. Newcomb, *Iwo Jima* (New York: Holt, Rinehart and Winston, 1965), p. 8.

61. The exact strength of the Iwo garrison is unknown. The total above is based on information supplied by the War History Office of the Japanese Defense Agency to the U.S. Marine Corps, Historical Division. See Garand and Strobridge, *Western Pacific Operations*, p. 458.

62. Ibid., pp. 453–60.

63. Letter, Spruance to Rear Admiral John H. Hoover, 30 November 1944; cited in Buell, *The Quiet Warrior*, pp. 318–19.

64. Isely and Crowl, *U.S. Marines and Amphibious Warfare*, 439–44; Buell, *The Quiet Warrior*, pp. 316–18; Garard and Strobridge, *Western Pacific Operations*, pp. 487–92.

65. Quoted in Isely and Crowl, *U.S. Marines and Amphibious Warfare*, p. 464.

66. Ibid., p. 470; Newcomb, *Iwo Jima*, p. 83.

67. Isely and Crowl, *U.S. Marines and Amphibious Warfare*, pp. 470–71; Garand and Strobridge, *Western Pacific Operations*, pp. 499–500.

68. Whitman S. Bartley, *Iwo Jima: Amphibious Epic* (Washington, U.S. Marine Corps, 1954), p. 49.

69. Isely and Crowl, *U.S. Marines and Amphibious Warfare*, pp. 474–75.

70. Ibid., p. 465; Garand and Strobridge, *Western Pacific Operations*, p. 716.

71. Morison, *Victory in the Pacific*, p. 73.

72. A vivid account of the 28th Marines' experiences on Iwo Jima may be found in Richard Wheeler, *Iwo* (New York: Lippincott, 1980), pp. 51–57, 87–94, 155–64 and passim.

73. Howard M. Cannon, *The Spearhead: The World War II History of the Fifth Marine Division* (Washington, D.C.: Infantry Journal Press), p. 53.

74. Sherrod, *On to Westward*, pp. 136–137.

75. Garand and Strobridge, *Western Pacific Operations*, p. 531.

76. Ibid., pp. 532–33.

77. Ibid., p. 542.

78. Slightly different accounts of the famous flag raising may be found in Newcomb, *Iwo Jima*, pp. 165–70 and Richard Wheeler, *Iwo*, pp. 157–63.

79. Millett, *Semper Fidelis*, p. 430.

80. Craven and Cate, *Matterhorn to Nagasaki*, pp. 597–98; Smith and Finch, *Coral and Brass*, p. 241.

81. John P. Marquand, "Iwo Jima Before H-Hour," cited in Morrison, *Victory in the Pacific*, p. 33.

82. Agawa, *The Reluctant Admiral*, p. 127.

83. Testimony of Major W. L. Redles, 1 October 1919, *Hearings Before the General Board 1919*, Vol. 4, p. 1098, Naval Historical Center.

84. Marder, *Old Friends, New Enemies*, p. 70; *U.S. Strategic Bombing Survey: Effects of Strategic Bombing on Japan's War Economy*, Appendix "A" (Washington, D.C.: G.P.O., 1946); pp. 78–79; Craven and Cate, *Matterhorn to Nagasaki*, p. 610.

85. Craven and Cate, *Matterhorn to Nagasaki*, p. 569–70.

86. Ibid., pp. 614–15.

87. "Interview of Gen. David A. Berchinal," p. 65.

88. Ibid., p. 616–17.

89. *U.S. Strategic Bombing Survey: Final Report Covering Air Raid Protection and Allied Subjects in Japan* (Washington, D.C.: G.P.O., 1947), p. 8.

90. Craven and Cate, *Matterhorn to Nagasaki*, pp. 662–73.

TWENTY-TWO

From Leyte to Luzon

A t Leyte, the Japanese had lost the largest naval battle in history. Decisive victory in a naval battle was supposed to enable the victor to "control the seas," to cut off the enemy's seaborne supplies and reinforcements, and ensure the arrival of one's own. That was what strategists in both the U.S. and Japan had long believed. Yet the "seas" around Leyte were far from being under American control.

From Cebu, from Mindanao, from Panay and, above all, from Luzon, Japanese convoys threaded their way through the narrow, treacherous waters of the Philippine archipelago, carrying reinforcements to the port of Ormoc on the west coast of Leyte. Nine major convoys and many smaller shipments of troops and equipment by barge and coastal craft sailed for Leyte in the six weeks following the Battle of Leyte Gulf. On the day of the American invasion Japanese strength on Leyte had comprised a single division, the 16th, which totalled about 20,000 men, counting its attached units. By mid-November two more divisions—the 26th and the crack 1st Division—plus elements of the 30th and 102d Divisions, with several other units and supporting equipment, had arrived at Ormoc: Japanese strength stood at approximately 55,000 men. Ten thousand more would arrive by early December.[1]

The reason for the Japanese success in running reinforcements lay in the relative weakness of American air power in the Philippines.

American escort carriers off Leyte were in poor shape after their battering in the battle off Samar and due to the incessant kamikaze attacks. Halsey's big carriers were low on fuel and supplies; moreover, they were needed for urgent missions against the home islands and in support of the invasion of Iwo Jima. Naval air support at Leyte would have to be supplemented as quickly as possible by land-based planes of General Ennis Whitehead's Fifth Air Force. But the primitive dirt landing strips on Leyte required major construction work before they could accommodate large numbers of American planes. This construction work soon turned into a nightmare in the incessant monsoon rain of October. The four captured Japanese airstrips at Bayug, Buri, Dulag, and San Pablo were turned into seas of mud by monsoon downpours often exceeding an inch a day. All but Dulag were eventually abandoned; army engineers, often working up to their knees in water and muck, began construction for new airfields in areas with better surfaces and drainage. After considerable effort a small airstrip was opened at Tacloban on October 27. It accommodated a few dozen P-38 fighters—but it would still be many days before adequate numbers of planes could be based on Leyte.

In the meantime, the Japanese were able to bring in their own planes from Formosa and Japan. The Japanese army and navy committed planes to the Leyte battle on a scale unprecedented since the early battles in the Solomons; while they failed to win control of the air, they nevertheless vigorously contested for it until almost the end of the campaign.[2]

To meet the Japanese air threat and help cut the flow of seaborne reinforcements to Ormoc, General MacArthur asked that Halsey resume fast-carrier operations in support of his forces on Leyte.[3] Nimitz agreed to MacArthur's request, so Halsey's carrier task groups, after fueling at Ulithi, returned to Philippine waters. There they launched heavy attacks. An air strike by three of Halsey's task groups in November had already destroyed an entire Japanese convoy carrying 10,000 reinforcements to Ormoc.[4] American land-based air attacks began to take a heavier toll of Ormoc-bound shipping at the same time but, as at Guadalcanal, the Americans never completely cut off the flow of enemy men and supplies.

From Manila, General Yamashita watched the reinforcements depart on their perilous journeys to Leyte with growing reluctance. He had never favored the decision to make Leyte the scene of decisive battle. As late as November he attempted to dissuade Field Marshall Terauchi from stripping Luzon of any more troops—troops that could be more usefully employed to meet the inevitable American invasion of that island. Terauchi was unconvinced. He promised Yamashita more troops for Luzon but refused to stop the convoys to Leyte.[5]

In the south Lieutenant General Suzuki Sasaki, commanding the 35th Army, which was responsible for Luzon's defense, knew nothing of Yamashita's misgivings. Suzuki's officers believed that the Battle of Leyte Gulf had been a victory for the Imperial Navy, and that the Japanese now controlled the sea and air in that area. Suzuki's chief of staff enthusiastically discussed plans to seize MacArthur and demand the surrender of the entire American army.[6]

MacArthur's generals were also optimistic. The U.S. Army combat forces on Leyte—General Krueger's Sixth Army—were twice the size of Suzuki's army. They were organized in two corps: Major General Frank C. Sibert's X Corps, consisting of the First Cavalry and 24th Infantry divisions, and Major General John R. Hodge's XXIV Corps, comprising the Seventh and 96th Infantry divisions. Two more divisions, the 32d and 77th, were available in reserve but were not yet on Leyte.

At first all went well. Striking out from their beachheads, XXIV Corps troops pushed into the mountains of southern Leyte, capturing the important town of Dagami at the end of October after a hard fight. One battalion of the Seventh Division also made its way south along the coast to Abuyog and then, meeting no opposition, drove clear across the island—along trails the Japanese had believed impassable—to Baybay on the west coast. Meanwhile Sibert's corps closed in on the key crossroads town of Carigara on the north coast of Leyte.

The enemy also wanted Carigara: as a jumping-off point for an attack across the Leyte Valley which would push the Americans back into the sea. Therefore the Japanese began moving reinforcements in that direction from Ormoc. But the Americans moved faster. On November 2, troops of the First Cavalry and the 24th Division took the town. General Suzuki, who had just moved his headquarters to Leyte from Cebu, decided to make a stand west of the town in the rugged mountains which stood astride the American route to Ormoc.

Had General Krueger moved swiftly to seize these heights before the Japanese forces, which Suzuki was pushing north from Ormoc, arrived in strength, he would probably have shortened the entire Leyte campaign by many days. But Krueger's troops were spread thin and he was worried about a Japanese seaborne attack in the area of Carigara Bay. Adopting a cautious course, Krueger ordered

General Sibert to postpone his drive south until the X Corps could deploy its forces and dig in along the beaches at Carigara.

Four decades later, Krueger's disastrous decision to delay the push into the mountains west of Carigara in favor of beach defense remains a mystery. It might be thought that something in the intelligence reports based upon intercepted and decrypted Japanese messages might have prompted Krueger's decision. Yet an examination of intercepted messages available to the Americans reveals no such basis for the general's decision. Intercepts did give American leaders a clear picture of the Japanese operations to reinforce Ormoc by sea—but none of these messages suggested that Japanese seaborne forces were bound for any destination other than Ormoc.[7] Indeed, it would appear that Krueger and his staff, rather than basing their estimates on cryptographic intelligence, disregarded it in favor of their own surmises.

The Japanese were meanwhile digging in along the mountain approaches to Ormoc. This area was held by troops of the elite First Division, recently arrived in the Philippines from Shanghai. In the few days' grace given them by Krueger's decision to deploy along Carigara Bay, they turned the convoluted ridges, steep slopes, and rocky crevices west of Carigara into a veritable fortress. As they had done elsewhere, the Japanese made full use of the naturally rugged terrain, dug themselves in deeply, and made excellent use of camouflage. Reverse slopes were skilfully utilized for defense and mutual support. Guns and automatic weapons were emplaced where they were easy to conceal, even when this meant sacrificing fields of fire; ridge lines were honeycombed with hidden trenches and "spider holes" which would sometimes remain undiscovered even after repeated sweeps of the area by U.S. troops.[8]

On November fifth a regiment of the 24th Division of Sibert's corps began an attack on the hilly mass southwest of Carigara. The troops soon named it "Breakneck Ridge." Hurled against the well-entrenched Japanese, the assault quickly bogged down. The struggle for Breakneck Ridge developed into the bloodiest fighting of the Leyte campaign. The Japanese defenders were now equal in number to their attackers; the Americans' only edge lay in their greatly superior artillery. Both sides suffered from shortages of supplies. The Japanese supply situation became desperate after two battalions of the U.S. 24th Division made their way through unoccupied high ground to the east and by sea to the west, setting up a blocking position on Kilay Ridge. From there they looked down on the Ormoc road, severing the Japanese line of communication to their supply base.

Nevertheless, the stubborn defenders of Breakneck Ridge hung on. Krueger sent additional troops of the Seventh Division across southern Leyte to Baybay; these began attacking toward Ormoc from the south, while the 96th moved in from the east. The 32d Division, newly arrived in Leyte, was sent forward to relieve the exhausted 24th Division at Breakneck Ridge.

Yet what Krueger really desired was an amphibious end run around the bloody mountain battlefields north and south of Ormoc to land troops right at the town's doorstep. MacArthur had done this sort of thing often enough in his advance through New Guinea. Now, however, there was insufficient assault shipping available to carry out a division-size landing, and Admiral Kinkaid was unenthusiastic about exposing his ships to kamikazes in the narrow waters of Ormoc Bay.

Then, at the end of November—two weeks after Krueger had originally proposed his amphibious venture—General MacArthur decided to postpone by ten days the scheduled invasion of Mindoro, the island just south of Luzon. That postponement freed the shipping and naval support which had previously been unavailable. Rear Admiral Arthur D. Struble's Amphibious Group 9 loaded the newly arrived 77th Division at Dulag on December 6. Troops and ships headed for Ormoc Bay.

Meanwhile, the Japanese had been planning their own new offensive on Leyte. The object of these Japanese operations was recapture of the Leyte airstrips. First would come an airborne assault on the three American airstrips around Burauen, carried out by the Second Parachute Brigade, which had recently arrived in the Philippines. An attack the next day by the Japanese 16th and 26th divisions would link up with the paratroopers and secure the airfields. The plan was called the *Wa* Operation.

Almost from the first, things began to go wrong for Operation *Wa*. The airfields which were the object of their attack had already been largely abandoned by the Americans as unusable, and most air operations had shifted elsewhere. A pre-attack raid by airborne commandos—assigned to put the American airfields at Burauen out of action—ended in complete failure when three of the four transport planes carrying the commandos missed the airfields and crash-landed near the beach at Dulag. The fourth plane reached Buri airstrip, but was shot down by antiaircraft fire; all aboard were lost. In the mangled wreckage, the Americans found documents outlining the entire *Wa* Operation.

General Krueger's headquarters warned Sixth Army units to be on the alert for further airborne attacks but most commanders around Burauen concluded that the raid had simply been a suicide mission.[9] They were totally surprised, therefore, when elements of the Japanese 16th Division burst from the jungle around Buri airstrip and crashed through the bivouac areas where American engineer and supply troops were billeted, tossing grenades into tents and bayoneting men in their beds.

The 16th Division's attack was to have been coordinated with other attacks by the 26th Division and airdrops by Japanese paratroopers, supported by fighters and bombers. Word of a last-minute postponement of the attack, however, failed to reach the 16th Division: it attacked a good twelve hours earlier than the paratroopers, who dropped on Buri and San Pablo airstrips on the evening of December 6.

Perfect confusion reigned at those two fields as Japanese paratroopers raced up and down, shooting wildly, firing off flares, and shouting English phrases such as " "Hello, Hello, where are your machine guns?' " and " 'Surrender, Surrender! Everything is resistless!' " [10] The Americans at the strip, mainly supply and service troops, were in an even greater state of confusion, "firing at everything that moves" and probably inflicting as many casualties on friendly troops as on the Japanese.[11]

By morning two U.S. infantry battalions despatched by Krueger had reached the airfields and began to clear the Japanese from their positions there. The Japanese, well supplied with captured American arms and ammunition seized in their initial attack, resisted fiercely; but by December 10 all had been driven off or killed.

En route to their ill-fated attack on Burauen, the Japanese paratroop transports had flown over Admiral Struble's task force, which carried Major General Andrew D. Bruce's 77th Division to Ormoc. Bruce's men went ashore unopposed on the morning of December 7 near the tiny village of Deposito. From there—three miles south of Ormoc—they advanced rapidly inland.

At sea, Admiral Struble's task force came under heavy air attacks, resulting in the loss of a destroyer and a destroyer-escort. But the Japanese fared far worse that day, for one of their convoys carrying troops to Ormoc was hit by waves of Army Air Force and Marine Corps planes, which forced them to seek shelter in San Isidro harbor at the northwest tip of Leyte. The convoy troops never reached Ormoc.[12]

Ashore, the Japanese rushed reinforcements overland to Ormoc, but they could not match Bruce in infantry strength or firepower. On the morning of December 10, preceded by an intense bombardment by artillery, rocket-firing landing craft, and mortars, two regiments of the 77th Division fought their way into Ormoc. That evening General Bruce radioed generals Hodges and Krueger: " 'Have rolled two sevens in Ormoc.' " The Japanese on Leyte were now divided and isolated, cut off from reinforcements. Fighting would continue for several more weeks, but the real contest for Leyte was over.

For MacArthur, the Leyte campaign had proven unexpectedly long and difficult, and the island's usefulness as an air base had been woefully overrated. Yet the Japanese decision to make Leyte the scene of the "decisive battle" had cost them their fleet and most of their remaining airpower; it doomed the remaining Japanese forces in the Philippines—now isolated, unsupported, and drained by the Leyte campaign—to certain defeat.

As the unexpectedly long and frustrating campaign on Leyte drew to a close, MacArthur still lacked sufficient air power to support his cherished plan for an attack on Luzon. Airfield construction on Leyte was well under way but still behind schedule. Even when the new strips were finished, MacArthur would not have enough land-based air within range of Luzon, Formosa, and other Japanese air bases to support his operations north of Leyte. He would still have to rely on naval air support from Kinkaid's escort carriers (borrowed from Nimitz), and from the big carriers of Halsey's Task Force 38. But Halsey's ships needed replenishment and repairs after their extended operations in support of the Leyte campaign. This meant a postponement of the move north. Weather and tide conditions also mandated a delay, so the Luzon invasion, originally scheduled for December 20, was now set for January 9.[13]

MacArthur's plans called for the invasion of Mindoro, just south of Luzon. The airfields there would provide land-based air to support the other Luzon operations and to protect the ships bringing supplies to the invasion forces. But who would provide the air support needed to take Mindoro? The only available source was the embattled group of escort carriers which had already taken so many hard knocks off Leyte. Six of these CVEs, along with three battleships, half a dozen cruisers, and other smaller warships formed the Mindoro invasion support force. Transports and escorts sailed from Leyte on December 13.[14]

Two days later the landing force came ashore on Mindoro. The weather was good and the few surprised Japanese on the island offered virtually no opposition. One veteran combat engineer observing the landings remarked that the " 'operation was just a maneuver for shore party units." ' [15] It was more than a maneuver, however, for the ships of the invasion fleet, which were heavily attacked by Japanese kamikazes. The flagship *Nashville* was hit by a suicide dive-bomber on the thirteenth and lost over 130 men killed and 190 wounded, including Brigadier General William C. Dunkel, commander of the landing force. Later air attacks by kamikazes fatally damaged two LSTs and disabled several other ships.

American and Australian engineers were already working furiously on Mindoro to prepare airfields for the planes which would support the Luzon invasion. One airfield for fighters was completed in five days; a second was ready in thirteen days—one week ahead of schedule.[16] From these Mindoro bases, Army Air Force fighters and bombers could support the Luzon invasion forces, attack the kamikazes in their lairs, and strike Japanese ships in transit to and from Formosa and Japan.

MacArthur's initial objective on Luzon had long been decided. Lingayen Gulf, about halfway up the western coast of the rectangular island, had excellent landing beaches and afforded easy access to the best rail and road network in the Philippines—a network running south through the central plains to Manila, with its important harbor facilities. In addition, the region provided adequate maneuvering room for the large forces MacArthur intended to employ on Luzon. Two armies—comprising ten divisions, five regimental combat teams, and numerous supporting units—would ultimately see action on Luzon. This made the campaign by far the largest of the Pacific: more U.S. troops were engaged than had been employed in North Africa, Italy, or southern France.[17]

In Manila, General Yamashita was also giving thought to the impending struggle for Luzon. Now that the futile battles on Leyte had, as he had predicted, absorbed his best troops and air support, Yamashita believed that the only realistic approach was to fight an extended delaying action in the Philippines: to occupy as many enemy forces as possible for as long as possible. Unlike MacArthur, he intended to defend neither Bataan nor Manila. Instead, he withdrew the bulk of his troops to three mountain strongholds, from which he could conduct a prolonged defense and inflict heavy casualties on Allied forces attempting to reduce them. The strongest and most important of the three positions comprised all of Luzon north and east of Lingayan Gulf (the gulf itself Yamashita did not intend to defend) and included the fertile Cagayan Valley, which he hoped would serve as a secure source of food for his troops. Yamashita's forces in this sector were called the "*Shobu* Group" and were under his direct command. A much smaller command, the "*Kembu* Group," occupied the mountains to the west of the central plains and the important complex of air bases at Clark Field. *Kembu* Group's principal mission was to deny use of those airfields to the Americans and to threaten the right flank of the American advance on Manila. The third command, the "*Shimbu* Group," was concentrated in the mountains east of Manila, where it could control the source of the capital's vital water supplies.[18]

On January 2 Rear Admiral Jesse B. Oldendorf's bombardment and support force of escort carriers, battleships, cruisers and destroyers, sailed from Leyte Gulf. Two days later the transports and amphibious craft of the invasion force and their escorts followed. The Japanese had only about 200 aircraft fit to fly, but they managed to make the voyage of the invasion fleet a harrowing ordeal. Fortunately for the troops crowded aboard the transports and LSTs, Oldendorf's warships in the van got most attention. The escort carrier *Ommaney Bay* was sunk when a kamikaze crashed through her flight deck and started fires raging in the engine room and on the hangar deck. The following day kamikazes damaged a destroyer, two heavy cruisers, and the escort carrier *Manila Bay.*

Yet the worst attacks were still to come. As the ships entered Lingayen Gulf and began their preliminary bombardment and minesweeping, kamikazes appeared in successive waves. Many were intercepted by the fleet's combat air patrol of screening fighters; others were destroyed by antiaircraft fire—but some got through. The kamikazes had improved their tactics and technique since their debut at Leyte Gulf. They flew low along the nape of the hills and valleys surrounding Lingayen Gulf to avoid radar detection and to maneuver radically to throw off antiaircraft fire and cause confusion as to which ship they were aiming at.[19] Battleships *New Mexico* and *California,* cruisers *Louisville, Columbia,* and *Australia,* and a number of smaller ships were damaged, and destroyer-escort *Long* was sunk.[20]

Altogether, Admiral Oldendorf had twenty-five ships sunk or damaged in the Lingayen invasion operations. The CVEs of Oldendorf's force were not equipped to intercept enemy planes and interdict airfields as Mitcher's big fleet carriers had done at the Philippine Sea and at Leyte Gulf. Oldendorf warned MacArthur and Kinkaid that his carriers, with their relatively small number of older fighters, could not cope with continuing large-scale kamikaze attacks unaided by Halsey's Third Fleet and Allied air forces, and that if the kamikazes went to work on the transports, disaster might result.[21]

Fortunately for the Americans, the Japanese were running short of planes. The attacks of the next few days were on a smaller scale, but several more ships suffered damage in the course of the week. Japanese planes had sunk twenty-four U.S. ships and damaged sixty-seven others in all, but with that they had shot their bolt: few enemy planes appeared over Luzon to challenge MacArthur's troops.

In contrast to the ordeal approaching Lingayen Gulf, the invasion itself was a walkover: the Japanese made no attempt to defend the Lingayen beaches. In a few days General Krueger's Sixth Army had close to 175,000 men ashore, firmly established along a twenty-mile beachhead. The left flank of the beachhead was held by the I Corps. Its mission was to protect the flanks and rear of the XIV Corps on the right, while the latter drove south for Clark Field and Manila. The I Corps's principal objective was to drive north and east, seizing the junction of Routes Three and Eleven, where the road leading from the coastal town of Damortis met the two-lane asphalt highway leading northeast to the mountain town of Baguio.

I Corps wished to seize the road juncture primarily to forestall any threat of counterattack against the beachhead and the rear of XIV Corps. To reach the junction, however, the troops had to pass through forbidding mountain country. The Japanese, as usual, had made good use of the terrain to construct strong defenses based on mutually supporting caves and tunnels. Their artillery, mortars, and machine guns, well concealed in the caves on the high ground, dominated the Damortis road, making it unusable by U.S. forces. Heavy fighting soon developed; the advance on the 3–11 road junction slowed to a crawl.

Meanwhile, XIV Corps, probing south through the open, flat farmland in its sector, had encountered little opposition. Its route to Manila appeared wide open.[22] General Krueger, however, was disinclined to begin his advance on Manila until the First Corps had seized its objective and secured his left flank.[23]

MacArthur had other ideas. He urged Krueger to push on toward Manila immediately. The SWPA commander had few worries about a Japanese counterattack on the Sixth Army's rear but he was concerned about seizing the all-weather airfields of the Clark Air Base complex and the port facilities of Manila. Although his G-2, Major General Charles Willoughby, had grossly underestimated the strength of the Japanese forces on Luzon, MacArthur nevertheless guessed correctly that the Japanese would not make a major stand in the central plains.[24] He therefore directed the XIV Corps to drive on south without delay—an order the still reluctant General Krueger attributed to MacArthur's desire to be in Manila by his birthday, January 26.

On January 18, then, XIV corps began its drive south, although its left flank was virtually unprotected. The advance went well: little opposition was encountered, in fact supply problems slowed the units down more than did the Japanese. By January 23 the corps had reached the forward defenses of the *Kembu* Group defending Clark Field.

Taking position in the rugged hills overlooking the airbase complex and the north-south road, the *Kembu* Group fought a stubborn, yard-by-yard battle against the advancing Americans.[25] It took more than a week to clear the area of the Japanese.

By February 2 XIV Corps—minus the 40th Division, which stayed behind to occupy the Clark Field area—was back on the road to Manila. But progress was still too slow for MacArthur. On January thirtieth he made an inspection by jeep of the 37th Division's operations as that unit advanced south from the town of San Fernando, south of Clark Field, toward Calumpit. Returning to his headquarters, he despatched a message to Krueger deploring "the noticeable lack of drive and aggressive initiative today in the movement toward Calumpit." [26] Visiting the First Cavalry Division, which had just arrived on Luzon to reinforce XIV Corps, MacArthur urged its commander, Major General Verne D. Mudge, to " 'Go to Manila, Go around the Nips, Bounce off the Nips, but go to Manila.' " [27] Mudge's unit, smaller and lighter than an infantry division, was ideally suited to such a mission. Mudge formed two motorized squadrons or "Flying Columns" under Brigadier General William C. Chase. Each was composed of a cavalry squadron, a company of tanks, a 105-mm howitzer battery, and enough trucks and tanks to carry all the troops. Mudge instructed them to dash south for Manila, leaving the remainder of the division to follow later and mop up.

In addition to the 37th and the First Cavalry, still another American unit entered what was rapidly shaping up as a race for Manila. On

January 31 two regiments of the 11th Airborne Division, part of Lieutenant General Robert L. Eichelberger's Eighth Army, landed at Nasugbu on the southwest coast of Luzon, about 45 miles southwest of Manila. Seizing an important bridge before the surprised Japanese could destroy it, the airborne troops raced northwest along Route Seventeen toward Manila. Joined by its third regiment, the 511th Parachute, which dropped on the area by air, the Eleventh continued its advance. A battalion of the 511th sped north along the concrete-paved highway through towns and barrios lined with cheering Filipinos.

At the small town of Imus, Japanese defenders in an old stone building blocked the battalion's route to the only remaining bridge across the Imus River. When the paratroopers' light 75-mm howitzers failed to penetrate the thick walls of the old building, Technical Sergeant Robert C. Steel climbed to the top of the building, battered a hole in the roof and poured in gasoline, followed by a white phosphorus hand grenade. As the Japanese sought to escape the flaming building, they were shot down by Steele's men. The 511th pushed on north and west until on February 4, they were halted at the Paranague River, just four miles from Manila. They had run up against a line of camouflaged steel and concrete pillboxes—the main Japanese defense line south of the city.

The race for Manila was now between the 37th Division and the First Cavalry Division. At the start, on January 30, the 37th had been much closer to the city than the First Cavalry; but the infantry division was slowed down by unbridged and unfordable streams where it had to halt and either ferry its artillery and tanks across the water or wait for engineers to throw up bridges. The First Cavalry was more fortunate in finding bridges and fordable streams on its route; its two Flying Columns tried to beat each other to the capital, at times reaching speeds of almost fifty miles an hour along the primitive gravel roads.

Near the town of Talipapa a few miles northeast of Manila, a Japanese convoy carrying troops and supplies was about to enter the main road from the east just as the Second Squadron of the Fifth Cavalry Regiment came roaring down from the north. Troopers aboard the leading American vehicles brazenly waved the enemy trucks to a halt—and the astonished Japanese complied. Then, as each of the Fifth Cavalry's vehicles sped by, they unleashed a burst of fire at the confused Japanese, leaving four trucks in flames behind them as they raced on toward Manila. It was, an army historian later observed, one of the few instances in which a squadron of army vehicles had executed the classic naval maneuver of crossing the T! [28]

The final barrier to Manila was the steep gorge of the Tuliahan River just north of the city. Here the Japanese had prepared the only remaining bridge for demolition when a squadron of the 8th Cavalry Regiment arrived. The Japanese opened fire from the far end of the bridge and lit the long fuse leading to a large dynamite charge. Ignoring the Japanese fire, Navy Lieutenant James P. Sutton, a demolitions expert attached to the First Cavalry, dashed onto the bridge and cut the burning fuse.

By evening of that same day, February 3, the 8th Cavalry's Flying Column was passing through the northern suburbs of Manila. As darkness fell, a tank of the 8th Cavalry's attached 44th Tank Battalion burst through the gates of the wall of Santo Tomas University, where close to 4,000 Allied civilian prisoners of war had been interned. Japanese prison guards were quickly routed and most of the prisoners liberated.[29] The First Cavalry Division had won the race to Manila.

In contrast to the swiftness of the American advance on the capital, wresting the city from the Japanese proved a long and bloody ordeal. Manila was one of the largest cities of Southeast Asia, with a population of over 800,000. Its large public buildings—constructed of reinforced concrete designed to resist earthquakes—and its old Spanish stone fortifications presented numerous strong defensive positions for the Japanese.

Nevertheless, General Yamashita originally had no intention of holding the city. He could not feed the capital's hundreds of thousands of civilians, nor adequately defend the vast perimeter of the flat metropolitan area; moreover, the city's many wooden structures and thatched-roof houses made it highly flammable.[30] Yamashita instructed General Yokoyama Shizuo, the *Shimbu* Group Commander, to destroy the bridges over the Pasig River separating northern Manila from the southern part of the city, to blow up other key installations, and then evacuate the city. Rear Admiral Iwabachi Sanji, who commanded the naval forces in the Manila area, was determined to fight for Manila, however, and General Yokoyama soon discovered that under the peculiar command and control arrangements of the Japanese army and navy, he could do little to get Iwabachi to do otherwise. Making the best of a bad situation, Yokoyama added the remaining army troops in the capital—about three battalions—to Iwabuchi's naval detachments of some 16,000 men. Few of the admiral's sailors had had any training or experience as infantry but they were well supplied with automatic weapons, converted antiaircraft guns, and naval cannon salvaged from damaged ships in the harbor.

As units of the First Cavalry and the 37th Division closed in on the city, Iwabachi's forces withdrew across the Pasig River, destroying as much as they could of the military facilities and supplies in the port area, as well as the Pasig bridges. Flames from these demolitions spread to the highly flammable dwellings of the heavily populated residential areas, and American troops spent much of the next two days battling the fires.

Meanwhile, MacArthur's headquarters issued a communiqué announcing the imminent recapture of Manila, and his staff began planning a grand victory parade through the streets of Manila.[31] The battle for the capital had barely begun, however: for as they pushed into the city south of the Pasig River, MacArthur's troops encountered stubborn resistance from Iwabachi's sailors. The Eleventh Airborne, moving up from the south, was even more heavily engaged.

Fighting raged in the city for almost a month. It was often block-by-block, building-by-building. The Americans quickly learned what infantrymen fighting in cities have always learned: that the surest way into a building is often through the top. Small assault squads worked their way from roof to roof, then chopped their way into the top floor and fought their way down, making liberal use of grenades, flamethrowers and demolitions.

MacArthur forbade air attacks in support of his troops in order to avoid civilian casualties. Nevertheless, civilians died in large numbers from the heavy use of artillery by both sides. Japanese fighting men added to the carnage by murdering, raping, beating, or burning hapless Filipino civilians caught within their lines. About 100,000 Filipino civilians died in the battle for Manila—almost six times the number of soldiers killed on both sides.[32] On March 3 General Griswold reported that the last resistance had ceased, and Manila's residents attempted to resume their normal lives in the devastated city. Of all Allied cities, only Warsaw suffered greater damage during the war than Manila.

While XIV Corps had been advancing on Manila, I Corps had eliminated the threat to the Sixth Army's rear and flanks. It had also captured the key town of San Jose, gateway to *Shobu* Group's mountain strongholds in the north, wiping out much of Yamashita's remaining armor in the process.

A third American task force, XI Corps—consisting of the 38th

Division and a Regimental Combat Team under Lieutenant General Charles P. Hall—had meanwhile landed unopposed on the Zambales coast. Its mission was to seal off Bataan and recapture Corregidor in order to secure control of Manila's harbor. Hall's troops easily captured Olongapo on Subic Bay, site of the long-planned but never established U.S. fleet base, then started eastward along the base of the Bataan peninsula. At "Zig Zag Pass" along Route Seven they ran into a network of Japanese foxholes, pillboxes, and trenches, well concealed by the heavily jungled terrain.

At first, underestimating the strength of the Japanese defenses, the corps committed units piecemeal to the attack on Zig Zag. As a result the Americans suffered heavy losses with little to show for them. One regiment lost so many of its key officers and NCOs that it had to be withdrawn from the battle. Hall relieved the 38th Division's commander and replaced him with General Chase, who had led the First Cavalry's drive on Manila, but the change made little difference at first. It was only after Chase was able to muster additional forces, and after air support from a newly completed airstrip became available that the 38th Division was able to clear Zig Zag.

In contrast to the bloody struggle at Zig Zag Pass, the XI Corps encountered little trouble in regaining the rest of Bataan. The 1,400 Japanese on the peninsula offered only scattered resistance as one of Hall's regiments drove down the east coast while another made an amphibious landing against slight opposition at Mariveles, at the southwest tip. By late February Bataan was securely in American hands again.

Corregidor fell to a combined airborne and amphibious assault spearheaded by the 503d Regimental Combat Team. The tadpole-shaped island was barely long enough to make a paratroop drop feasible. American commanders anticipated heavy casualties in landing an entire regiment on a sloping plot of ground barely 350 yards long by 200 yards wide, but the surprise value of a combined airborne and seaborne attack seemed worth the risk.

Following a heavy air- and naval bombardment, troops of the Third Battalion of the 503d began dropping on what, in prewar days, had been the island's golf course and parade ground. Less than an hour later the first wave of amphibious assault troops hit the southern beaches near the foot of Malinta Hill. Surprise was complete. The Americans quickly established themselves ashore and turned to rooting out the Japanese from the network of American-built tunnels on the island fortress. The end came on the morning of February

26: the remaining Japanese defenders, either by accident or design, set off the tons of ammunition and explosives which they had stored in the tunnels. Scores of Americans and hundreds of Japanese were killed by flying debris, buried in rock slides, or hurled bodily off the island as Corregidor erupted in mighty explosions. On March 2, 1944, in front of the gutted, blackened barracks, on topside General MacArthur raised the American flag on a "shell- and bomb-scarred ship's mast with rigging and ladders still hanging from its yard arm." [33]

Even while fighting still raged in Manila, MacArthur had issued orders to General Eichelberger's Eighth Army to begin the liberation of all the remaining islands of the archipelago. Although the Joint Chiefs of Staff had issued no directive to the southwest Pacific commander to seize these outlying islands (in fact, they had indicated to their British counterparts that these areas would be left to the Filipino guerrillas), MacArthur had intended since September 1944 to reconquer the entire archipelago.[34]

Seizure of these islands was of little importance for the overall defeat of Japan. MacArthur's plans contemplated an attack on Borneo by Australian forces, so the conquest of Palawan Island and the Zamboanga peninsula at the southwest corner of Mindanao, and perhaps some of the islands in the Sulu archipelago, could be justified to provide air bases to cover the Australian operations. Yet by 1945, Japan had been effectively cut off from the rich oil resources of Borneo by the destruction of her navy and by the depredations of American submarines. So the attacks on Borneo were themselves of dubious worth except to recover British and Dutch colonial real estate.

The remaining islands of the Philippines, including Mindanao east of the Zamboanga peninsula, were of no strategic value whatsoever. Moreover, operations in the southern islands would leave fewer troops to deploy against the still-formidable forces of General Yamashita in the mountain fortresses of Luzon. The southern campaign was all the more wasteful because MacArthur assigned five full divisions to liberate these weakly held islands, leaving Krueger's Sixth Army badly depleted.

MacArthur's motives for embarking upon this militarily pointless campaign must remain a matter of conjecture. D. Clayton James speculates that the southwest Pacific commander was influenced by a mixture of personal, humanitarian, political, and strategic motives. There were certainly compelling humanitarian reasons—in view of

the Japanese treatment of civilians and POWs during the battle for
Manila—for wishing to liberate as many Filipinos as possible and
as soon as possible. MacArthur had recently learned of a Japanese
massacre of 140 American and Filipino prisoners on the island of
Palawan; he may well have feared more of the same as the Japanese
came closer to final defeat.[35] Still, civilian populations in occupied
countries all over Europe had been exposed to the same hazards
and worse at the hands of the Nazis by Allied decisions to concentrate
on the military defeat of Germany rather than liberation of territory
per se.

MacArthur's other motives for launching the southern campaign
are less laudatory. He undoubtedly wished to be remembered as
the liberator of all the islands and to fully redeem his pledge that
he would return. In addition, he could not be unaware that the
employment of the Eighth Army, the 11th Air Force, and a significant
part of the Seventh Fleet in operations in the southern archipelago
would preclude the transfer of these valuable assets from MacArthur's
empire to Nimitz's theater.[36]

Whatever the motives for them, Eichelberger's operations in the
south were executed with a skill and dash which—MacArthur later
declared—reminded him of Stonewall Jackson.[37] If Eichelberger was
Stonewall Jackson, Kinkaid and Barbey of the Seventh Fleet and
Lieutenant General Paul B. Wurtsmith of the 13th Air Force were
his Julian Ewell and Jubal A. Early. They were ably assisted by marine
flyers, whom Admiral Halsey had first lent to MacArthur during
the Leyte campaign, and by the webfooted soldiers of the Engineer
Special Brigades.

American ships and planes roamed the archipelago unchallenged
by the Japanese, protecting and convoying units of Eichelberger's
amphibious army to landing beaches on Palawan, Zamboanga, Panay,
Mindanao, and Cebu. In all, the Eighth Army conducted fourteen
major and twenty-four minor amphibious landings in forty-four
days.[38] The Japanese failed to put up a strong defense at the beaches;
they usually withdrew to inland strongpoints, harried by local Filipino
guerrilla units as they went. Although Japanese resistance continued
in parts of the islands until the end of the war, the airfields, principal
towns, and roads were all in Allied hands, and civil government
had been reestablished by June.

In contrast to the southern archipelago, there was little dash or
drama about the campaign for northern Luzon. With the possible
exception of General Kurabayashi on Iwo Jima, Yamashita was the

most able Japanese general the Americans had to face in the Pacific; he fought one of the shrewdest delaying campaigns of the war.[39]

The Sixth Army's first task after the fall of Manila was to clear southern Luzon and push back the *Shimbu* Group astride the city's water supply northwest of the capital. While units of the First Cavalry and the 158th Infantry cleared the long, narrow Bihol peninsula which pointed southeast toward Samar, XIV Corps troops moved into the Marikina Valley to secure the Wawa and Ipo dams, which were thought to be the key to control of Manila's water supply. The battle for Wawa Dam developed into a bitter two-month struggle; it was not until the fight was nearing its end that MacArthur's headquarters learned that the dam was no longer used, and that the more distant Ipo Dam was the source of the city's water.

Fortunately, Ipo Dam proved easier to capture—thanks to heavy attacks by Fifth Air Force fighter-bombers utilizing napalm, and to aggressive assistance from a Filipino guerrilla regiment which fought its way to the dam on the same day as the Americans. The campaign for the dams finished the *Shimbu* Group, which withdrew deep into the Sierra Madre mountains to fight a steadily losing battle with starvation, disease, and guerrillas until the end of the war.

While Griswold's corps had been dealing with the *Shimbu* Group, General Swift's I Corps had been fighting a grinding battle against the *Shobu* Group, which outnumbered his force almost two to one. Swift's corps had been badly depleted by MacArthur's reinforcements to Eichelberger, and a lack of warships and transports made an amphibious end run out of the question. Yamashita's mountain defenses were centered on a triangle whose apexes were formed by the towns of Baguio, Bontoc, and Bambang. Yamashita's goal was to delay the Americans as long as possible. By withdrawing forces for the Eighth Army's strategically useless operations, MacArthur obligingly played into his hands.[40]

General Krueger planned to make his main effort against the town of Bambang. But the first American success was actually scored against Baguio, Yamashita's mountain headquarters and the former summer capital of the Philippines. The 33rd Division, assigned to probe the approaches to Baguio, had found the best road, Route Eleven, to be heavily defended, so it made little progress there. Other 33rd Division units, however, moving north and east from the coastal town of Caba, encountered surprisingly little resistance. When his troops secured the town of Bauang further up the coast, then turned inland and took Naguilian, Major General Percy Clarkson, the division commander, began calling loudly for permission to make a dash west from those towns along Route Nine, coming down on Baguio from the northeast.

While Swift and Krueger considered Clarkson's request, the 33d continued its advance along Route 9; in a week it was halfway to Baguio, probing the main Japanese defense line near the town of Sablan. By then Krueger had secured an additional division, the 37th, from Manila mop-up duties; he immediately sent it north to backstop the 33d in the drive on Baguio. Allied air attacks and guerrilla forrays had by that time made a shambles of Yamashita's supply lines, and his front-line troops around Baguio were on the verge of starvation. At the end of March, two weeks before the start of the American drive, the Japanese commander had ordered Japanese civilians and the Filipino puppet government to evacuate Baguio; he himself decamped for the Bambang front several days later. The remaining defenders made their last stand at the Irisan Gorge, where Route 9 crossed the Irisan River about three miles from Baguio. Here they held out for six days, but were eventually driven from the ridges around the gorge. They withdrew to join the other Japanese troops leaving Baguio.

Yamashita had lost one of the three legs of his defense triangle, but the Americans achieved no rapid successes against the other two. Right up to the end of the war, men of the Sixth Army battered against the Japanese mountain defenses on the road to Bambang. One division, the 32d—which had also seen heavy fighting on Leyte— was worn away on the Villa Verde trail approach to Bambang. The Japanese were pushed slowly back and suffered heavy casualties in battle, still more from disease and starvation. At the end of the war they were still holding out through the torrential rains of the Philippine summer in the rugged valley of the Asin River, in north central Luzon.

One of MacArthur's biographers, William Manchester, recently characterized the general's campaign on Luzon as "the achievements of a great strategist," and speculated about "what would have happened had MacArthur, not Mark Clark, been the U.S. Commander in Italy." [41] Manchester was thinking of MacArthur's advance on Manila and his swift reconquest of the southern Philippines. The fighting in northern Luzon, however, took place in terrain and circumstances quite similar to those of Italy—and the results were the same. MacArthur's forces in northern Luzon—like those of Clark in Italy— were committed to slow, bloody slugging matches against a well-entrenched enemy who took every advantage of the mountain terrain to fight a superb delaying action. Ironically, it was MacArthur's "brilliant" campaigns in other parts of the Philippines which drained men from the northern Luzon campaign and guaranteed this result.

NOTES

1. M. Hamlin Cannon, *Leyte: The Return to the Philippines* (Washington, D.C.: Office of the Chief of Military History, 1954), pp. 99–102; Falk, *Decision at Leyte*, pp. 221–24.

2. Falk, *Decision at Leyte*, p. 225; Morison, *Leyte*, pp. 344–46, 349–50.

3. James, *Years of MacArthur*, p. 569; Morison, *Leyte*, p. 354.

4. Morison, *Leyte*, pp. 352–53.

5. Falk, *Decision at Leyte*, pp. 221, 255–56.

6. Tomochika Yashiharu, "The True Facts of the Leyte Campaign," December 1946, pp. 12–13, copy in CMH.

7. MAGIC Far East Summaries—Japanese Army Supplement: 25–27 October 1944, SRS-226; 29 October 1944, STS-224; 4 November 1944, SRS-231: RG 457.

8. Cannon, *Leyte*, pp. 211, 251–53.

9. Ibid., p. 298; Falk, *Decision at Leyte*, p. 274.

10. Falk, *Decision at Leyte*, p. 282.

11. Cannon, *Leyte*, pp. 300–3.

12. Morison, *Leyte*, pp. 379–84.

13. Morison, *The Liberation of the Philippines*, pp. 6–9; Robert Ross Smith, *Triumph in the Philippines*, (Washington, D.C.: Office of Chief of Military History, 1963), pp. 22–25, 34–35.

14. Morison, *Liberation of the Philippines*, pp. 9–11, 23.

15. Smith, *Triumph in the Philippines*, p. 48.

16. Ibid., p. 49.

17. Ibid., p. 30.

18. "14th Area Army Operations on Luzon," Japanese Monograph No. 8, pp. 4–28, 39–40: copy in CMH.

19. Smith, *Triumph in the Philippines*, p. 61.

20. Morison, *Liberation of the Philippines*, pp. 104–6.

21. Ibid.; Smith, *Triumph in the Philippines*, pp. 64–65.

22. Except where noted, the following is based on Smith, *Triumph in the Philippines*, chapters 6, 8, and 9.

23. Krueger, *From Down Under to Nippon*, p. 227.

24. Willoughby's estimate was no worse than the army's Military Intelligence Service (MIS) in Washington, which based its count on intelligence intercepts. MIS also failed to identify four of the nine Japanese divisions on Luzon. However,

Washington intelligence analysts, like MacArthur and Willoughby, correctly surmised that Yamashita would fight a withdrawing action. MAGIC Far East Summary, 20 December 1944, SRS-275; 13 January 1945, SRS-297; 19 January 1945, SRS-305: RG 457.

25. Smith, *Triumph in the Philippines,* p. 175.

26. James, *Years of MacArthur,* pp. 627–28.

27. Ibid., p. 632.

28. Smith, *Triumph in the Philippines,* pp. 218–19.

29. A few guards, led by the camp commander, took some of the prisoners hostage; they did not release them until allowed to withdraw with their weapons.

30. "14th Area Army Operations," Japanese Monograph No. 125, pp. 4–6, 8–9.

31. James, *Years of MacArthur,* pp. 637–40.

32. Ibid., p. 644.

33. Harold Templeman, *The Return to Corregidor* (New York: Strand, 1945), pp. 20–21.

34. James, *Years of MacArthur,* p. 737; Morison, *Liberation of the Philippines,* pp. 213–14.

35. James, *Years of MacArthur,* pp. 737–39. Both James and Manchester believe that Washington's failure to challenge—or even question—MacArthur's unilateral action in the southern Philippines without JCS approval laid the foundation for MacArthur's later "insolence toward his superiors in Washington" during the Korean conflict. James, *Years of MacArthur,* p. 738; Manchester, *American Caesar,* pp. 478–80.

36. James, *Years of MacArthur,* p. 739.

37. Frazier Hunt, *The Untold Story of Douglas MacArthur* (New York: Devin-Adair, 1954), p. 382.

38. Eichelberger, *Our Jungle Road to Tokyo,* p. 200. Comprehensive accounts of the campaign in the southern Philippines may be found in Morison, *The Liberation of the Philippines,* pp. 215–51 and Smith, *Triumph in the Philippines,* pp. 583–648.

39. Smith, *Triumph in the Philippines,* p. 579.

40. Ibid., pp. 456–59.

41. Manchester, *American Caesar,* p. 411.

TWENTY THREE

"I Am Become Death, Shatterer of Worlds"

April 1, 1945, was a brilliantly clear day in the East China Sea. Over 1,200 ships, carrying more than 180,000 marines and soldiers, converged on the sixty-mile long, banana-shaped island of Okinawa, 350 miles southwest of Japan. They were supported by more than forty large- and small carriers, eighteen battleships and close to two hundred destroyers. It was Easter Sunday, D-Day for the American attack, the final step in the strategic program adopted by the Joint Chiefs of Staff the previous October: a program which had sent MacArthur's forces to Luzon and Nimitz's forces to Iwo Jima—and now to Okinawa.[1]

On the doorstep of Japan—and almost as close to Formosa and the coast of China—Okinawa could provide sites for air bases and fleet anchorage, while the island itself was to serve as the staging area for invasion of Japan proper. That final campaign was already being planned in Hawaii, Manila, and Washington.

Spruance and Turner commanded the seaborne phase of the invasion which rivaled the Allied invasion of Normandy in size. The newly formed Tenth Army, under Lieutenant General Simon Bolivar Buckner—he who had held the thankless command in the Aleutians—would land two army and two marine divisions on the west-central beaches near Hagushi village. Another marine division, the Second, would counterfeit a landing on the southeast coast as a diversion, then join the main attack. Standing by in reserve were two more army divisions, one already afloat off Okinawa, the other on alert in the South Pacific. From Leyte, from garrisons in the central Pacific, and from as far away as Seattle, over 400 assault ships would carry the American troops to the small, mountainous island which had been a vassal kingdom of both Japan and China since the Middle Ages, and legally a part of the Japanese Empire since 1879.

While Spruance and Buckner were assembling these vast forces, Lieutenant General Ushijima, commanding the Japanese 32d Army responsible for the defense of Okinawa, was losing one of his most experienced divisions, the Ninth, which Imperial General Headquarters had decided to send to reinforce the Philippines in December. Ushijima knew that he had too few troops to defend the beaches of Okinawa against the massive American invasion force. Besides, bitter experience had taught the Japanese how difficult it could be to stop an amphibious invasion backed by an overwhelming weight of air attack and naval gunfire. Ushijima also expected that kamikaze aircraft, then being assembled in unprecedented numbers for the battle of Okinawa, would so damage the American fleet supporting the landings that the American troops ashore would be deprived of most of their usual air- and naval gunfire support. A decisive battle could be joined once the troops on the beach had thus been isolated.

So General Ushijima's forces would not try to defend the beaches; they would not even defend the important airfields at Kadena and Yontan. Instead, the 32d Army would establish a system of strong concentric defensive perimeters, centered on the ancient castle town of Shuri in the south-central portion of the island.[2]

Japanese defenses were anchored in the natural and artificial caves which dotted the mountainous regions around Shuri. Caves served as hospitals, barracks, or command posts. They were connected by tunnels to artillery- and machine-gun positions which dominated the surrounding terrain. A single 2,500 by 4,500-yard sector of the Japanese defensive perimeter was later discovered to include caves and bunkers containing sixteen grenade launchers, eighty-three light- and forty-one heavy machine guns, seven 47-mm antitank guns, six field guns, two mortars, and two 70-mm howitzers.[3] From these formidable defensive positions the Japanese could deny the Americans control of the important southern half of the island with its airfields, the port town of Naha, and the potential fleet anchorage of Nakagusuku Bay.

Ushijima's plan worked well. The American invasion forces, landing along a seven-mile front on the Hagushi beaches, encountered only light opposition. By evening there were over 50,000 troops ashore. Major General Roy Geiger's III Amphibious Corps, comprising the First and Sixth Marine divisions, landed at the northern end of the beaches, while Major General John R. Hodge's XXIV Corps—two army divisions, the Seventh and the 96th—landed to the south. All of these units had seen fighting elsewhere in the Pacific, and the men were relieved and surprised to find the landings practically unopposed: " 'I've already lived longer than I thought I would,' " declared an infantryman of the Seventh Division.[4]

In contrast to Saipan, army-marine relations at the command level here were smooth and cooperative. Buckner and his senior marine subordinate, General Geiger, respected each other's abilities. "There was never any friction. General Buckner was a field soldier [like General Geiger]. He too would visit the front lines on frequent occasions. So he and General Geiger got along very well."[5]

As American troops fanned out to the north and south, crossing the island and easily capturing the two airfields, even seasoned veterans began to feel an unwonted optimism. "I may be crazy but it looks like the Japanese have quit the war, at least in this sector," Turner radioed to Admiral Nimitz. To which CINCPAC replied: "Delete all after 'crazy.' "[6]

Events soon proved Nimitz correct. Toward the end of the first week, troops of the 96th Division struck the first of the three main defensive lines on the Kakazu Ridge, near the town of Machinato, north of Naha. Although they did not know it, the Americans had reached the outermost and strongest ring of Ushijima's defensive lines. The honeymoon period was over.

For the next two weeks, three full U.S. Army divisions battered at the Japanese defenses on Kakazu Ridge. During the first few days, battalion after battalion of the 96th Division pushed its way up the steep slopes—only to be pinned down, then forced to retreat by intense enemy fire from concealed machine guns and from artillery sighted on the reverse slopes. In one company of eighty-nine men which attacked the ridge on April 9, only three returned unwounded.[7] On April 12 the Japanese launched a counterattack, but were thrown back. Two companies of Japanese infantry attacking in the 96th Division sector were repulsed by Staff Sergeant Beauford T. Anderson, who ordered his mortar section to shelter in a tomb. The unit then began tossing mortar shells in football fashion at the advancing Japanese after releasing the safety- and setback pins by slamming the rounds against a rock.[8] On April twenty-fourth, battered by unrelenting American attacks, the Japanese finally withdrew from Kakazu.

As the Americans moved toward the enemy's main defensive lines around Shuri, the 77th Division—fresh from a short but bloody conquest of Ie Shima island and its airstrip just off the northwest coast of Okinawa—replaced the weary 96th Division, while the First Marine Division relieved the 27th Division. Some of Buckner's commanders hoped that he would use the 77th and the marines for an amphibious hook around the rear of the Shuri defenses—landing these troops on the beaches near Minatoga in the southeast where the fake landing of April 1 had been staged. Major General Bruce, the 77th's commander—whose division had captured Ormoc on Leyte with an amphibious sweep—strongly urged such a move. But General Buckner believed that opening another drive from the south would overtax his supply system, particularly since kamikazes had recently sent two of his ammunition ships to the bottom. In retrospect it is clear that Buckner ought to have given more consideration to an amphibious attack. His supply problems were real enough—and a force landed at Minatoga might have simply bogged down—but in view of the way the campaign for Shuri developed, the proposed Minatoga landings would seem to have been a very worthwhile risk.[9]

Just as the Americans were completing their new dispositions, the Japanese launched another counterattack, far stronger than the first. Small amphibious units in landing craft and canoes preceded the main offensive. They attempted landings behind the American lines on the eastern and western coasts, but the Japanese were easily detected and destroyed—one force while still afloat, the other at the water's edge. Then, behind a heavy artillery barrage and sporadic attacks by Japanese aircraft, three Japanese regiments assailed the Seventh and 77th divisions—only to be driven back with losses of between five- and six thousand men.[10] American casualties totalled just over 700. With almost nothing to show for their efforts, the Japanese had lost some of their most experienced troops and much of their artillery. Yet the Shuri defenses were still formidable and much hard fighting lay ahead.

While soldiers and marines fought their way through the deadly gorges, draws, and ridges of southern Okinawa, sailors offshore were fighting an equally hard and wearing battle. The Japanese had long planned to meet the Okinawa invasion with massive air attacks—emphasizing kamikaze aircraft concentrated in the home islands and Formosa. By the invasion date they had assembled some 700 combat

aircraft. That was far short of the 2,000 they had planned for their
air offensive (called "*ten-Go,*")—but still enough to pose a formidable
menace.[11] During preliminary air raids against Kyushu in March,
Spruance had already seen four large carriers badly damaged by
Japanese air attacks. One of them, the *Franklin,* had been hit by
two bombs, which set off a chain of explosions among her heavily
armed aircraft on deck. The *Franklin* suffered close to a thousand
casualties, and "the appearance of her flight deck was graphically
compared to that of a half-eaten shredded-wheat biscuit," but she
came home under her own power—the most heavily damaged carrier
to be saved. And these attacks were only a preview of what was to
come.[12]

In the central Pacific campaigns, American carrier task forces had
usually neutralized all Japanese air bases within striking distance of
the objectives before D-Day. Okinawa, however, was out of range
of American air bases, but well within range of Japanese airstrips
on Japan and Formosa. The Japanese airfields were too numerous
to knock out; their aircraft were well dispersed and concealed. The
American fleet would thus have to remain off Okinawa as long as
necessary to shield the landing forces and to provide air- and gunfire
support. Until the airfields on Okinawa could be put into operation,
carriers would have to supply all aerial protection for the fleet and
for the troops ashore.

Japanese air attacks began in earnest on the afternoon of April
6; they continued through the next day, when 700 planes, half of
them kamikazes, struck at the American fleet in successive waves.
Large numbers were shot down by the combat air patrol and antiaircraft guns, but those planes that got through did a lot of damage.
Three destroyer-type ships, an LST, and the two ammunition ships—
which General Buckner would sorely miss later—were sunk. Ten
other ships, mostly destroyers, were seriously damaged.[13]

That was only the beginning. Between April 6 and June 22, there
was a total of ten mass attacks by 50 to 300 aircraft against the
fleet off Okinawa. The fleet's anchorage among the islands of the
Kerama group, twenty miles southwest of Okinawa, which had been
seized by the 77th Division at Adm. Turner's insistence on March
26, began to fill up with mangled, blackened ships. Spruance's own
flagship *New Mexico* spent two weeks there repairing damage after
a kamikaze crashed into her on May 12.[14]

Hardest hit were the destroyers and smaller vessels assigned to
radar picket duty, disposed around the fleet like irregular spokes

on a wheel at varying distances of fifty miles or less. Their task was to give early warning of air attacks and to vector patrolling fighters so they could intercept the attackers. At one station, during early May, four out of six vessels—including two destroyers—were sunk in a single day, with the loss of close to 100 men. The destroyer *Laffey* was attacked in mid-April by more than twenty planes. Her gunners shot down nine of them—but six others crashed into the ship, and she was hit by four bombs and near misses. With the rudder jammed, fires blazing, three after-crew compartments flooded, mainmast and yardarm shot away, the *Laffey* continued to steam and fire back at her attackers. In the ship's wardroom, surgeon Mathew Driscoll was wounded in the hand by bomb fragments but continued to treat the sixty wounded men, working with his remaining good hand while verbally directing his assistants in aiding the other wounded.[15]

Ships like *Laffey* and *Franklin* survived due to the courage and skill of their crews, but also due to the navy's farsighted decision in late 1942 to begin an intensive program of training in firefighting techniques for all sailors and to develop new and improved firefighting equipment. Sparked by two navy lieutenants, Harold J. Burke and Thomas A. Kilduff, former professional firefighters from New York and Boston, the navy established schools for this purpose at every continental naval base. There, damage-control parties were trained and sailors familiarized with the fundamentals of firefighting. What marksmanship training was to the army, firefighting and damage-control drills became to the navy. Navy warships received new damage-control equipment: mobile gasoline-operated pumps, portable steel-cutting outfits, rescue- and breathing gear, and foam-generating fire mains which could operate even when a ship's power was knocked out.[16]

Day after day, week after week, the Japanese onslaught continued. The radar picket destroyers continued to bear the brunt of these enemy attacks. After a particularly grueling battle, sailors on one destroyer "set up a huge arrow-shaped sign pointing rearward and reading 'Carriers this way.'"[17] Carriers and other large warships suffered also from the unremitting suicide attacks, however. With fewer large carriers operational than at the Battle of the Philippine Sea, Spruance had reason to feel grateful for the presence of Task Force 57, a British Royal Navy fleet under Vice Admiral Sir Bernard Rawlings. Task Force 57 included four fast carriers, two modern battleships, five cruisers, fifteen destroyers, and its own supply and service squadron. Task Force 57 had the mission of neutralizing the airfields in the southern Ryukyus and portions of Formosa.[18] That mission brought the British their share of attention from kamikazes—but the British carriers, whose design sacrificed plane-carrying capacity for armored hangars and flight decks, proved far better able to stand up to suicide crashes than the thin-skinned American carriers.

As an integral part of the kamikaze attacks, the Imperial Navy planned a sortie by the giant battleship *Yamato,* which had survived the battles at Leyte more or less intact. She formed the nucleus of a "Surface Special Attack Force" which also included the new light cruiser *Yahagi* and eight destroyers. Her mission was to break through to the American fleet off Okinawa, do as much damage as possible and then beach herself on the shores of the island and use her huge eighteen-inch guns to support the defenders. The ships carried only enough fuel for a one-way trip. Many of the ships' captains questioned the wisdom of a dash on Okinawa: they contended that the *Yamato* and *Yahagi,* with their destroyers, would do much better as raiders—but their protests were disregarded.[19]

The *Yamato* and her consorts sailed from the Inland Sea on the afternoon of April 6. Almost immediately they were spotted by lurking U.S. submarines, which alerted Admiral Mitscher and Task Force 58. Search planes from the task force and from the Kerama Islands found the *Yamato* flotilla the following morning. Under Rear Admiral Morton L. Deyo, a string of six old battleships with escorting cruisers and destroyers sortied from Okinawa to intercept, but they were unneeded. Beginning shortly after noon on the seventh, wave after wave of planes from carriers of Task Force 58—close to 300 in all—struck the *Yamato* formation. Deprived of all air cover for the sake of the kamikaze attacks, with her half-trained gunners unable to make effective use of her formidable antiaircraft battery, *Yamato* was a sitting duck for American bombers and torpedo planes, which sent her to the bottom along with *Yahagi* and four destroyers. Most of the crews, totaling about 3,600 men, perished.

Although the loss of the *Yamato* is invariably referred to by historians as marking "the end of the Imperial Navy," [20] it was not. A Japanese heavy cruiser and destroyer fought a surface battle with five Royal Navy destroyers more than a month after the *Yamato's* last sortie and a handful of Imperial Navy cruisers, battleships, and carriers remained afloat in various states of readiness until the Japanese surrender. Yet these ships—crippled by lack of fuel and sometimes by lack of trained specialists—remained incapable of offensive action; they were merely targets for American air attacks.

As the kamikaze battles continued, the nerves of sailors with the Fifth Fleet began to wear thin. Endless alerts, lack of sleep, the possibility of sudden, fiery death at any hour—all this began to take its psychological toll. In some cases, crews were so keyed up that they learned to listen for the telltale click and static of the ships' loudspeakers being activated—they were already running for their battle stations by the time "General Quarters" was sounded.[21] American communications intelligence enabled the American commanders to anticipate the larger air attacks, and at first crews were alerted accordingly. "But this practice," recalled one correspondent, "had to be stopped. The strain of waiting, the anticipated terror, made vivid from past experience, sent some men into hysteria, insanity, breakdown." [22]

Nimitz and Spruance were also becoming increasingly concerned. Nimitz insisted that LeMay's Mariana-based B-29s strike the Kyushu air bases of the kamikazes. LeMay demurred, pointing out that heavy bombers could not be effective against the well-concealed, well-dispersed Japanese planes on Kyushu. But Nimitz was adamant. He invoked his authority as theater commander to divert the B-29s from their strategic bombing mission. LeMay complained to Arnold that Nimitz was hampering the war effort; Admiral King, in turn, suggested that if the Army Air Forces were not willing to pitch in against the kamikazes, the navy might decide to cease supplying the big bombers in the Marianas. B-29 raids on Kyushu continued, but they could not stop the kamikaze raids. Attacks by MacArthur's Fifth Air Force against Formosa were of even less help from the navy point of vew.[23]

Spruance was also mightily unhappy with the slow progress of the army on Okinawa. " 'I doubt if the Army's slow, methodical method of fighting really saves any lives in the long run,' " he wrote to his former chief of staff. " 'It merely spreads the casualties over a longer period. The longer period greatly increases the naval casualties when Jap air attacks on ships is a continuing factor. . . . There are times when I get impatient for some of Holland Smith's drive.' " [24]

Yet lack of "drive" was not the problem on Okinawa. There was no way—save perhaps for the abortive landing in the south—that any general, whether army or marine, could have significantly speeded up the fighting on Okinawa. The Japanese had to be blasted out of their superb defensive positions yard by bloody yard. "The Japanese did a magnificent job of withdrawing and fighting a delaying action; that was all that was left to them and they did that beautifully," recalls one marine commander. "We poured a tremendous amount

of metal in on those positions. Not only from artillery but from
ships at sea. It seemed nothing could possibly be living in that churning mass where the shells were falling and roaring but when we
next advanced, Japs would still be there, even madder than they
had been before." [25]

In the Okinawa fighting, Americans relied heavily on tank infantry
teams to reduce the deeply dug-in enemy. Tanks provided a powerful,
accurate, direct-fire weapon—those mounting flame throwers were
especially effective—but they were vulnerable to Japanese assault
squads armed with explosive charges. So the tanks required infantry
support to deal with this threat.[26] Infantrymen were fond of pointing
out to the tankers that, while the tank crews were protected by several
inches of armor plate, the foot soldiers were protected by a khaki
shirt.[27]

It was not until June 21 that organized resistance on Okinawa
ended. By that time, the fighting had claimed the lives of some 7,000
U.S. soldiers and marines—including General Buckner, who was
killed in the closing days of the battle. Navy casualties in the protracted sea-air battle offshore were also heavy. Close to 5,000 sailors
died and 5,000 more were wounded, a total far exceeding the losses
suffered in any previous U.S. naval campaign. Seventy thousand Japanese died on Okinawa, along with at least 80,000 Okinawans, most
of them civilians.[28]

● ●

The battle for Okinawa had ended in another overwhelming American victory. An entire Japanese army had been destroyed, together
with hundreds of planes and the greatest battleship of the Imperial
Navy. Yet few Americans who took part in the campaign felt any
sense of exaltation when it was over. The general feeling was one
of anxiety and dread before the tasks that lay ahead. If the capture
of a base in the Ryukus had been this bad, what would the assault
on Japan itself be like?

In Washington, Tokyo, Manila, and Guam, Japanese and American
planners were already studying that question. The final attack on
Japan proper would at last bring the forces of Nimitz and MacArthur
together: a reshuffling of commands could no longer be avoided.
The army had always been dissatisfied with an arrangement whereby
Nimitz's navy-dominated headquarters controlled several army divisions, while MacArthur normally controlled only insignificant naval
forces. Nimitz was not only a theater commander, but doubled as

the head of all naval forces in the Pacific; it seemed only right, there-fore, that MacArthur should command all army forces.[30] In addition, army logisticians had always been unhappy with Nimitz's supply sys-tem: they viewed it as wasteful and geared primarily to the needs of the navy. They suspected that this navy control of Pacific logistics was responsible for the bitterly resented "higher standard of living" of navy forces in the central Pacific.[29]

While army and navy officers in Washington still paid lip service to the ideal of a unified command in the Pacific, all realized by now that the services were unlikely ever to agree on such an arrange-ment. Instead, General Marshall proposed to the Joint Chiefs that MacArthur command all army forces and bases in the Pacific, while all naval resources would be under Nimitz. King and his naval advis-ers strongly objected to the proposed new arrangement, but in the end the army got most of what it wanted. A JCS directive at the beginning of April designated MacArthur as "Commander in Chief, U.S. Army Forces, Pacific" (CINCAFPAC), with authority over all army forces there except those in Hawaii and the southeast Pacific. Nimitz, as CINCPAC, was to command all naval forces except those in the southeast. The Twentieth Air Force continued under the Joint Chiefs of Staff; in June it became a part of the Strategic Air Force under General Carl A. Spaatz, which was also to include the famous Eighth Air Force, soon to be redeployed from Europe.

Beside supplying military planners with a new set of unwieldy acronyms, the revised command setup had little impact on the actual conduct of the Pacific War. MacArthur's and Nimitz's combat forces were fully committed to active operations; it would be many weeks before they could be sorted out and redistributed. Untangling the complex of bases, shipping, supply and service forces would take even longer—and promised to be a major headache for all con-cerned.[30]

In their April directive on command changes, the Joint Chiefs of Staff had also instructed Nimitz and MacArthur to make plans and preparations for an attack on Japan. But here again there were impor-tant differences between the army and the navy. Navy strategists still favored the seizure of positions on the south China coast, from which the aerial bombardment and blockade of the Japanese home islands could be carried on with greater intensity. Spruance, King, and navy planners in Washington were confident that such pressure would bring about Japan's collapse—without an invasion.[31] Army strategists, however, pointed out that blockade and bombardment could drag on for years; moreover, operations on the China coast would not necessarily be less costly in casualties than an invasion of Japan. MacArthur shared these views. He urged an early assault on Kyushu, the southernmost island of Japan, to be followed by an invasion of the main island of Honshu.[32] He pointed out that reliance on bombardment alone to achieve a Japanese surrender would be least costly in casualties—if it succeeded. Yet there was no guarantee of success. On the contrary: air bombardment alone had failed to bring about the defeat of Germany, which had been subjected to a more intensive bombing campaign than could be mounted against Japan.[33]

Admiral King was unconvinced by these arguments. He pointed out the great advantages which the Japanese army would enjoy in a battle for the home islands. These included ample room for maneuver, thorough familiarity with the terrain, and proximity to sources of supply. When Nimitz joined MacArthur in recommending an invasion of Kyushu, however, King agreed.

Still to be worked out between MacArthur and Nimitz was the division of responsibility for the invasion. After a good deal of bickering between army and navy at the Washington level, the Joint Chiefs met in closed session on May 25. At that time they agreed on a directive to the two commanders. MacArthur was charged [in paragraph 1b(1)] with primary responsibility for the conduct of the Kyushu operation, "including, in case of exigencies . . . the actual amphibious assault through the appropriate naval commander." Nimitz had "responsibility for the conduct of naval and amphibious phases [subject to paragraph 1b(1) above]."[34] How (and whether) this arrangement would have worked in practice is an intriguing question.

MacArthur's subordinates had meanwhile been preparing a plan for the actual invasion of Japan; it was labelled DOWNFALL. DOWNFALL was divided into two main operations: OLYMPIC, the assault on Kyushu, scheduled for autumn of 1945, and CORONET, the invasion of the main island of Honshu, scheduled for March of 1946. General Walter Krueger's Sixth Army, winding up its arduous operations in northern Luzon, was charged with the planning and execution of OLYMPIC. For this task the Sixth Army would have a total of eleven U.S. Army and three Marine divisions—some 650,000 ground troops, staging from as far away as Hawaii. Three corps, of three divisions each, would land at separate points in southern Kyushu while a fourth corps (the XI) of two divisions would make a diversionary move off Shikoku. Only the southern third of

Kyushu, demarcated by a diagonal line drawn from Tsuno on the east coast to Sendai on the west, was to be occupied. Here the Allies could develop the airfields and staging areas required for the final assault on Honshu.[35]

In a meeting with President Truman on June 18, the Joint Chiefs of Staff presented their recommendation that American forces land on Kyushu in November. No other operation promised more decisive results; no other would so clearly indicate to the Japanese how firmly resolved the U.S. was to bring about their complete surrender. Casualties would probably be high—but no higher than might be incurred in attacking an alternate target such as Korea or Formosa. The president was concerned about this question of casualties. He "hoped that there was a possibility of preventing an Okinawa from one end of Japan to the other." Admiral Leahy recalled that troops on Okinawa had suffered about 35 percent casualties, and that this was a reasonable estimate for Kyushu.[36] With 767,000 men scheduled to participate in the campaign, this would mean around 268,000 dead and wounded.

On Kyushu, the Japanese waited. Okinawa—although a complete American victory—had the paradoxical effect of discouraging the Americans while inspiring the Japanese. Imperial Navy strategists, reviewing the damage, real and imagined, which the kamikazes had inflicted on American shipping, estimated that 30 to 50 percent of the American invasion fleet could be put out of action prior to landing.[37] Several thousand planes had been carefully husbanded awaiting the approach of the American attack on the home islands. Japanese army planners were also encouraged by thoughts of the battle for Okinawa, where less than three divisions, cut off from all support and subject to naval gunfire, had nonetheless held out for over a hundred days against an American force more than twice as strong. They expected the battle for Kyushu "to be fought under conditions incomparably more advantageous to the Japanese."[38]

Much of Kyushu was mountainous, rugged country, the same sort of excellent defensive terrain the Japanese had turned to such good advantage on Luzon and Okinawa. Fourteen Japanese divisions and five independent brigades were deployed there—almost equal in total manpower to Krueger's entire invasion force. The Japanese plan was to hold the beaches at all costs. The Kyushu coast was well suited to the use of enfilade fire; heavy artillery, well-concealed in caves, had been emplaced to cover the approaches to all important beaches.[39]

From past experience, the Japanese had come to consider American tanks, especially those equipped with flamethrowers, as the most serious threat to their defenses. Although the Japanese, fighting in their homeland, would be free to employ their own armored forces, their tanks were decidedly inferior: even their best antitank guns were effective against American M-4 tanks only at close ranges. To make up these deficiencies, large numbers of men in each unit, as well as civilian volunteers, were assigned to make "close-quarter attacks" against tanks, utilizing special explosives which burned their way through armor, called shaped charges, various types of "Molotov cocktail"—and even explosive charges strapped to the backs of the assaulting soldier.

Japanese staff officers maintained that "all able-bodied Japanese, regardless of sex, should be called upon to engage in battle. . . . Each citizen was to be prepared to sacrifice his life in suicide attacks on enemy armored forces." Imperial General Headquarters hoped that children, the aged, and the infirm would not be drawn into the battle—but there were "insurmountable obstacles" to their evacuation from the probable combat areas.[40]

Army and navy planners in Washington suspected that the conquest of Kyushu and Honshu would be bloody: bloody beyond comparison even with earlier Pacific campaigns. An army study of September 1944 had concluded that an invasion of Japan would be more difficult and dangerous than the Normandy invasion.[41] "We must be prepared to accept heavy casualties whenever we invade Japan," warned Admiral Nimitz. "Our previous successes against ill-fed and poorly supplied units, cut down by our overpowering naval and air action, should not be used as sole basis of estimating the type of resistance we will meet in the Japanese homeland where the enemy lines of communication will be short and enemy supplies more adequate."[42]

Since the beginning of the war, few American GIs—except the severely wounded or those with exceptional skills or assignments—had been brought home from the Pacific. A regular rotation policy for ground troops was not even begun until 1944 and even then only a trickle of men met the rather stringent qualifications.[43] American servicemen in the Pacific experienced a sense of hopelessness and despair at the prospect of apparently endless combat duty. " 'A man feels he is drowned at times,' " wrote one GI. " 'He feels [that] as long as he is able to keep going he will be kept over here until he is a physical wreck or his body is buried with four or five more in some dark jungle or scattered over the ground by artillery shells or bombs.' " " 'Take it from the voice of experience,' " warned one combat veteran; " 'if my company makes one more invasion you had better tell the medical corps to be sure and have 42 straightjackets for there are only 42 of us left.' " [44] An army public opinion poll showed that 66 percent of the soldiers in the southwest Pacific believed that after a man had been overseas eighteen months, he had done his full share and deserved to go home. [45]

In addition to the men already in the Pacific, thousands who had seen long and arduous combat in the European theater would have to be moved to the Pacific for the assault on Japan. General Marshall warned that "war weariness in the United States may demand the return home of those who have fought long and well in the European war regardless of the effect of such a return on the prosecution of the Japanese war." [46] Some military officials wondered whether Japan might somehow be induced to surrender *before* the scheduled invasion.

The chief obstacle to an early Japanese surrender was seen by many U.S. leaders as the "Unconditional Surrender" formula announced at Casablanca. Opponents of this sweeping declaration pointed out that it was likely to make the Japanese fight all the harder. This was particularly true because the demand for unconditional surrender contained no guarantee that the Emperor and the Imperial system—towards which all Japanese leaders felt their strongest loyalties—would be retained. Indeed, many wartime Allied statements and news accounts strongly implied that the Americans were determined to do away with the imperial system.

Japanese fears about the Emperor were amply justified. Among many American leaders, as well as in the popular mind, the Emperor was seen as "the source and symbol of the Japanese militarism they hated and feared." A Gallup poll taken in June 1945 indicated that 33 percent of all Americans wanted the Emperor executed as a war criminal. Eleven percent wanted him imprisoned. Nine percent wished to see Hirohito exiled, while only 7 percent favored his retention, even in a puppet role. [47]

Despite popular vindictiveness towards the Emperor, however, State Department experts on Japan, as early as the autumn of 1943, had recommended retention of the imperial system. They argued that within a democratic constitutional framework, the Emperor could provide a valuable element of stability in the reform of postwar Japan. [48] A few months later, military members of the special interdepartmental committee established to aid the State Department in postwar planning proposed that the Emperor be allowed to remain in office following the surrender, subject to the control of U.S. occupation forces.[49]

Meeting with Roosevelt at Malta in February 1945, Churchill also suggested that some "mitigation" of the unconditional surrender formula might be a means of shortening the war.[50] Army Chief of Staff Marshall and Admiral Leahy also favored modifying the doctrine to allow for retention of the Emperor. Yet many other high-ranking American officials—including presidential adviser Harry Hopkins, Archibald MacLeish, then an assistant secretary of state, and Dean Acheson, also an assistant secretary—opposed any change in the surrender terms.[51]

To resolve this dilemma, President Truman established a high-level committee—composed of Stimson, Navy Secretary James Forrestal, and Under-Secretary of State Joseph C. Grew—to study the problem of securing a Japanese surrender. The committee recommended the retention of the Emperor. It produced a draft surrender demand which, while providing for the complete surrender and disarmament of all Japanese forces and the occupation of Japan by the Allies, nevertheless held out the promise that a postwar Japanese government "may include a constitutional monarchy under the present dynasty if it be shown to complete satisfaction of the world that such a government shall never again aspire to aggression." [52]

President Truman took the proposed draft with him when he travelled to Potsdam in July to meet Stalin and Churchill. With him went the newly appointed Secretary of State James F. Byrnes. A longtime leader in Congress, Byrnes was convinced that a retreat from unconditional surrender could have devastating political consequences for the president, since the vast majority of the public was still opposed to retention of the Emperor. At Byrnes's urging, Truman agreed to a rewording of the surrender demand.[53] The "Potsdam Declaration," as it came to be called, issued on July 26, closely followed the wording of the committee draft but made no mention, however, of the Emperor, and merely promised the establishment "in accordance with the freely expressed will of the Japanese people, of a peacefully inclined and responsible government." [54]

This ambiguous phrase met the concerns of men like Byrnes and MacLeish, who feared that public opinion would not tolerate an explicit guarantee to retain the Emperor. At the same time, advocates of such a guarantee—officials like Stimson, Grew, and Forrestal—could hope that Japanese leaders might read between the lines and realize that the Japanese could " 'freely express their will' " by retaining the imperial institution.[55] As Stimson saw it, they were appealing to "the large submerged class in Japan who do not favor the present war, to arouse them" and "develop any possible influences they might have . . . . [56]

The "large submerged class"—in reality a small coterie of the Japanese elite—was already fully aroused to the dangers of continuing the war. Developing their influence was a more difficult matter. Although a few Japanese leaders, notably Foreign Minister Togo Shigenori and the late Admiral Yamamoto, had always doubted that Japan could be successful in a war with the U.S., the search for peace on the part of the Japanese began only with the collapse of the Tojo Government following the invasion of the Marianas in July 1944. Tojo's Government was succeeded by a cabinet headed by retired General Koiso Kuniaki and retired Admiral Yonai Mitsumasa as deputy premier and navy minister.

The Koiso cabinet contained a number of men like Yonai who favored an early end to the war. They formed a tacit alliance with a small group of elder statesmen or *"jushin"* (former prime ministers who served as extraconstitutional advisers to the Emperor) like Konoye Fumimaro and Okada Kasuke, and also with the Lord Privy Seal, Marquis Kido Koichi, the Emperor's closest political adviser.[57] In spite of all their efforts, these men achieved little. Open advocacy of peace could not be thought of. Japan was a police state; the military high command was still determined to fight to the end. Any sign of public dissent from the military's position brought with it the certainty of arrest or assassination.[58]

Although Koiso was privately pessimistic about the course of the war, he believed he had no choice but to back the military in its demand for one more chance to improve Japan's bargaining position through a decisive military success; simultaneously he sought the Soviet Union's aid in securing a favorable peace settlement from the Allies. Defeats in the Philippines ended hopes for a military success and the Soviet Union rebuffed Japanese attempts to open discussions on a general settlement of the war. April 1945 brought the invasion of Okinawa and the resignation of the Koiso Cabinet. At the same time the Soviet Union announced that it would not renew its four year old neutrality pact with Japan.

The new prime minister was retired Admiral Suzuki Kantaro, a man who had barely escaped death at the hands of assassins in 1937. He chose as his foreign minister Togo Shigenori, the most outspoken critic of the war and the military among senior Japanese statesmen. Yet Suzuki's own views on ending the war were far from clear. After the war he recalled that he had endeavored from the beginning to carry out the Emperor's desire to see the war ended. His public pronouncements, however, spoke only of fighting to the bitter end. Perhaps, as one astute observer has suggested, it was only after he assumed office that the old admiral came gradually to understand and acknowledge the necessity of ending the war.[59]

The Suzuki government continued the Koiso government's efforts to induce the Soviet Union to mediate the conflict on terms favorable to Japan. For such mediation, the Japanese were prepared to offer substantial territorial and economic concessions in the Far East, concessions probably exceeding those which the Soviets received at Yalta. Yet there was virtually no chance of a Soviet acceptance of Japan's offers—not with Japan on the verge of defeat.

While plans for an approach to Russia proceeded, the military prepared for still another "decisive" battle. This time the struggle in the home islands, where they were confident they would win enough success on the battlefield to open peace negotiations on more favorable terms. At a Conference in the Imperial Presence on June 8, the Suzuki cabinet resolved to "prosecute the war to the bitter end." [60]

The Emperor and Kido were both profoundly disturbed and disappointed by the "bitter-end" spirit of the conference. Kido was by now convinced that only the Emperor's personal intervention could alter the course of events. The Emperor had recently received frank reports on the hopeless military situation from Admiral Hasegawa Kiyoshi and from General Umezu Hoshijiro, who had just returned from inspection tours of the home islands and Manchuria.[61]

On June 22, after confidential discussions between Suzuki, Togo, Yonai, and Marquis Kido, the Emperor summoned the prime minister, foreign minister, and the military heads to an imperial conference. Here, for the first time during the war, the Emperor took the initiative, strongly urging the government and high command to make all possible efforts to end the war by diplomatic means. The psychological impact of the Emperor's intervention had the desired effect: even the war minister and the army chief of staff reluctantly agreed they should attempt to end the war by negotiation. Yet the new policy resulted merely in the intensification of Japan's futile efforts to persuade the Soviets to mediate on her behalf—efforts which wasted valuable time and fed Japanese delusions.

Codebreakers intercepted and made available to American leaders translations and analyses of the message traffic between Foreign Minister Togo and Japan's ambassador to Moscow, Sato Naotake.[62] This fact has led some historians to argue that the American leaders should have realized that Japan was anxious to end the war. Yet the messages also revealed that Japan was determined to fight on to the end rather than accept unconditional surrender. Thus, an intelligence analysis based on "MAGIC" intercepts, completed less than a week before the bombing of Hiroshima, observed that while Japan was ready to conclude peace "on the basis of the Atlantic Charter," she was "still balking at the term unconditional surrender" and "still determined to exploit fully the possible advantage of making peace first with Russia."[63] Secretary of the Navy Forrestal noted after reading the intercepts that the Japanese cabinet appeared to have decided "that the war must be fought with all the vigor and bitterness of which the nation is capable so long as the only alternative is unconditional surrender."[64]

Receipt of the Potsdam Declaration failed to shake Japanese hopes for Soviet aid. Foreign Minister Togo found the declaration encouraging. He and his foreign office advisers realized that the proclamation in fact spelled out the "conditions" of the "unconditional" surrender and that these conditions were probably the best which Japan could hope to obtain. In addition, the foreign minister hoped that Japan might obtain a favorable interpretation of those conditions through Soviet mediation.[65]

Togo succeeded in persuading his colleagues on the Supreme Council for the Direction of the War that Japan should make no immediate answer to the Potsdam Declaration, concentrating instead on obtaining Soviet help. Yet the terms of the proclamation could not be kept from the public—if for no other reason than that Allied planes were dropping thousands of Japanese translations of the document on the country. The cabinet agreed that the newspapers should be allowed to publish a censored version of the declaration and that the government should make no official response. In a meeting with reporters two days after receipt of the declaration, however, Premier Suzuki observed that the Potsdam Declaration was "of no great value" to the government. This, following upon newspaper reports that the cabinet had decided to treat the proclamation "with silent contempt," led Allied leaders to conclude that Japan had in effect haughtily rejected their terms.[66]

Togo and the foreign office were distressed that what they had intended as a "wait and see" policy had been undermined by these statements, but they still hoped for some favorable development in their approaches to the Soviets. Yet a new and awesome factor was about to enter the calculations of the peace advocates.

• •

In 1944 agents of the military intelligence division of the War Department visited the editorial offices of *Astounding,* a popular American science-fiction magazine, to investigate the background of a recent story by author Cleve Cartmill. The story was entitled "Deadline" and dealt with the development of an atomic bomb.[67] What Cartmill and his readers could not know was that the United States was even then working in conditions of utmost secrecy, at desperate speed, and at the cost of over $600 million a year to translate science fiction into reality.

The development of the atomic bomb was made possible, and perhaps inevitable, by revolutionary advances in physics in the late 1930s. The discovery that the nucleus of the uranium atom could be split, and made to yield energy far greater than that released by ordinary chemical action—a process called fission—and that this process could theoretically become self-sustaining through the freeing of neutrons in the uranium nucleus—a so-called chain reaction—had led scientists and science writers to speculate about the possibility of producing a powerful new explosive by this means. Yet the scientific and technical obstacles to producing a practical atomic explosive device appeared so numerous and difficult that few knowledgeable authorities expected to see such a development in the near future.[68]

The outbreak of war in Europe, however, led to renewed consideration of an atomic weapon, especially on the part of those European émigré scientists driven from their homelands by the fascists, many of whom had settled in the United States. These men were well aware of progress in the study of nuclear physics recently made in Germany, where physicists Otto Hahn and Fritz Strassmann had led the way in the discovery of nuclear fission. The émigré scientists suspected (correctly) that the Nazis, utilizing Germany's unparalleled scientific resources, would undertake to produce an atomic explosive.

In October 1939 two of these physicists, Eugene Wigner and Leo Szilard, persuaded the world-renowned scientist Albert Einstein to sign a letter to President Roosevelt. In his letter, Einstein called attention to the possibility of producing uranium bombs—and to the strong probability that the Germans were already working to produce one.[69] The president responded to Einstein's letter by establishing an ad hoc scientific panel, "the Uranium Committee," to study the military implications of nuclear physics. Little progress was made, however, until the summer of 1941. At that time secret reports were received from scientists in Britain—where research was also under way—which made it appear that a practical atomic explosive could be produced before the war was over.

In July 1941 the president's top scientific adviser, Vannevar Bush, reported that an atomic explosive appeared feasible; should one be perfected, "its use might be determining." [70] Now began an all-out race to produce an atomic weapon—ahead of the Germans, who were perceived to have a two-year head start—and in time to be used during the war. A director of the research program, Nobel Prize winner Arthur H. Compton, outlined the time schedule for the project in January 1942:

—By July 1942, to determine whether a chain reaction was possible.
—By January 1943, to achieve the first (controlled) chain reaction.
—By January 1944, to extract the first element 94 from uranium.
—By January 1945, to have a bomb.[71]

The obstacles were immense, the remaining problems formidable, the project itself quickly grew into the largest and most expensive weapons research-and-development operation of the war. Immense industrial plants had to be erected to produce U-235, a rare uranium isotope, and plutonium, a synthetic element, both of which had previously been available only in microscopic quantities. Over 120,000 people, working at thirty-seven different facilities in nineteen states and in Canada, were employed in the project at a cost of more than $2 billion dollars. Out of thirty-three nuclear physicists characterized by the government's Office of Scientific Research and Development as "leaders in the field," twenty were employed on the project, as were large numbers of the country's most talented chemists, metallurgists, mathematicians, and engineers.[72]

At one point Under Secretary of War Robert P. Patterson—concerned that the size, cost, and secrecy of the "Manhattan" project might invite Congressional inquiries and charges of waste—asked the experienced consulting engineer Michael J. Madigan to inspect the project's vast plants and report. " 'Judge,' " declared Madigan upon the conclusion of his inspection tour, " 'I have been all around and seen everything and I am here to tell you that you have nothing to worry about at all—nothing to worry about. If this thing works, they won't investigate anything and if it doesn't work—if it doesn't work—they won't investigate anything else. Alongside of this, everything else that we have done will seem a sensible procedure.' " [73]

In the early morning hours of July 16, 1945, the first atomic bomb was successfully detonated at a remote section of Alamogordo Air Force Base in the New Mexico desert. One observer, sixty miles from the explosion, saw "a blinding flash of light that lighted the entire northwestern sky. In the center of the flash there appeared to be a huge billow of smoke. . . . As the first flash died, there arose in the approximate center of where the original flash had occurred an enormous ball of what appeared to be fire and closely resembled a rising sun . . ." [74] Watching the test from 10,000 yards away was scientist J. Robert Oppenheimer whose team had designed and built the bomb at Los Alamos. The awesome spectacle reminded Oppenheimer, who had studied Sanskrit at Harvard, of some lines from the Bhagavad Gita: "If the radiance of a thousand suns were to burst at once into the sky, that would be like the splendor of the Mighty One. . . . I am become Death, Shatterer of Worlds." [75] The American scientists had won their race with the Germans. Indeed, it had been hardly a race at all. The Germans had not even succeeded in producing a self-sustained chain reaction. In fact, they had abandoned hope of producing a bomb for use in the war. [76]

By this time Roosevelt was dead. His successor. Harry S Truman, received the news of the successful test at Potsdam, where he was meeting with Stalin and Churchill in the last of the great wartime summits. According to Churchill's recollection, the president, who was having increasing difficulties with the Soviets over Eastern Europe, was tremendously buoyed up by the news of the successful test " 'and stood up to the Russians in a most emphatic and decisive manner.' " [77]

Ever since Pearl Harbor American leaders had considered the entry of Russia into the Pacific War an important goal. During the first desperate weeks of the war, Russian entry had been ardently hoped for as a means of taking the pressure off hard-pressed Allied forces in the Philippines and Malaya. Yet the Soviets made it clear that their own critical battle against Germany made it impossible for them to enter the Far Eastern war in the near future. [78] American strategists continued to discuss measures to be taken should Russia be forced into the war by a Japanese attack, but it was not until the Teheran conference and Stalin's famous promise to enter the war against Japan that Americans received any clear indication of

Russian intentions. By that time, the Joint Chiefs of Staff had concluded, correctly, that Russia would enter the war for her own ends at a time most advantageous to herself.[79]

Still, Russian entry into the war would have many advantages to the U.S.—provided that the Russians were on the offensive and not surprised by a Japanese attack. As the Joint Chiefs began to consider the necessity of invading Japan, they recognized that "a Russian drive into Manchuria coincident or prior to our invasion of Kyushu would prevent any appreciable movement of Japanese forces southward into Korea and North China and necessitate the retention of all Japanese forces on the Asiatic mainland."[80] Also, the Soviet Union might agree to allow American bombers to operate from their territory against Japan's home islands.

At Yalta the British and Americans had agreed to Russian desires for restoration of her special rights in Manchuria, the return of the southern half of Sakhalin Island, and the annexation of the Kurile Islands as the price for Soviet entry into the war. By that point American military leaders had concluded that the entry of Russia was not absolutely essential to defeat Japan, although it was still desirable. They also recognized that " 'the concessions to Russia on Far Eastern Matters made at Yalta are generally matters which are within the military power of Russia to obtain regardless of U.S. military action short of war.' "[81]

With the atomic bomb a reality, the participation of the Soviets in the war against Japan now appeared unnecessary, if not actually undesirable. Ever since Yalta some American leaders had had doubts about the value of Soviet participation, and now General Marshall again advised the president that the Soviets were not really needed.[82] Yet whatever U.S. leaders might think, the Russians could not be kept out. The Soviets had notified the Japanese in April that their neutrality pact was at an end. At Potsdam the Soviet chief of staff, General Alexsey Antonov, informed the Allied strategists that the Russians would be ready to move by mid-August.[83] Marshall himself pointed out that Russia would march into Manchuria when she was ready, regardless of what the U.S. did.

As the conference drew to a close, Truman casually mentioned to Stalin "that we had a new weapon of unusual destructive force." The Soviet leader replied almost as casually that "he was glad to hear it and hoped we would make good use of it against the Japanese."[84] Stalin could afford to be offhanded, since the Soviets already knew most of the essential facts about the bomb's development. The exiled German physicist Klaus Fuchs, a naturalized British citizen who was a member of the British scientific team at Los Alamos, had kept Russian agents well informed about the design of the plutonium bomb. Earlier he had supplied them with information about British and American research on the production of U-235. American spies—including David Greenglass, a young GI technician at Los Alamos—had supplied other helpful details.[85]

• •

As early as September 1944 Roosevelt and Churchill had agreed that when an atomic bomb was finally ready, "it might perhaps, after due consideration, be used against the Japanese." [86] In Washington, a committee of scientists and Army Air Force officers had been at work since April selecting a suitable target. In mid-June, the Secretary of War's top scientific advisers reluctantly concluded that they could "propose no technical demonstration of the bomb likely to bring an end to the war . . . no acceptable alternative to direct military use." [87]

A specially selected Air Force unit of B-29s, the 509th Composite Group, had been training through the winter and spring under conditions of great secrecy to deliver the new weapon. By late July the 509th had been making practice runs over Japan from Tinian for some months, dropping simulated atomic bombs. The Japanese had become accustomed to seeing small formations of B-29s which did little damage and could be safely ignored.[88] Also by July, the target committee in Washington had drawn up its list of cities and settled on a schedule for the atomic attack. With Japan's apparent rejection of the Potsdam Declaration, the president and his advisers saw no reason to refrain from going ahead.

Although Truman would insist to the end of his life that he had "never had any doubt" and felt no guilt or regret over that decision, the recent discovery of his private papers has provided a different picture. "It was a terrible decision," he confided in a letter to his sister.[89] In his private journal he mused that "even if the Japs are savages, ruthless, merciless and fanatic, we as the leader of the world for the common welfare cannot drop this terrible bomb on the old capital or the new [Tokyo]." [90]

At the insistence of Truman and Stimson, the historic old Japanese capital of Kyoto was deleted from the list of targets, although Army Air Force planners had considered it the most suitable from the technical and military points of view. Much has been written about

Stimson's humanitarian instincts in preserving for Japan and for mankind one of its most important artistic and cultural treasures.[91] Less sentimental investigators have suggested that Stimson's and Truman's motives were largely pragmatic rather than humanitarian, arising from the fear that the wholesale destruction of Japan's historic, cultural, and religious center would harden Japanese hostility to the United States and possibly drive them into the arms of the Russians.[92]

But if Kyoto was to be spared, other Japanese cities would not be so lucky. There was never any doubt that the bomb would be used. Years of American talk about the Japanese as savage fanatics who cared nothing about human life had prepared the way for such a decision. The "sneak attack" on Pearl Harbor, accounts of Japanese atrocities in prisoner of war camps and in occupied Asia, the kamikazes, and the bloody last-ditch resistance on Iwo Jima and Okinawa had confirmed and hardened these beliefs. "When you deal with a beast you have to treat him as a beast," wrote Truman a few days after Nagasaki.[93]

On August 6, 1945, three B-29s appeared over Hiroshima, Japan just after eight in the morning. The lead bomber, *Enola Gay,* piloted by Colonel Paul Tibbets, commander of the 509th Composite Group, carried an atomic bomb; the two escorting bombers, cameras and scientific instruments. The city of Hiroshima, eighth largest in Japan, was clearly visible at 31,600 feet to the *Enola Gay*'s bombardier, Major Thomas Ferebee, as he took control of the aircraft for the final minutes of the bomb run. At 8:15 A.M., the *Enola Gay*'s bombbay doors swung open. As the bomb was released, Tibbets banked sharply right away from the target. Forty-five seconds later, most of Hiroshima disappeared in a searing flash of heat and light. Close to 100,000 people died instantly. Thousands more died later of burns, shock or radiation poisoning. A carefully prepared White House statement released a few hours later announced the existence of the terrible new weapon and warned that if the Japanese did not now surrender, "they may expect a rain of ruin from the air, the like of which has never been seen on this earth."[94] Two days after the Hiroshima bombing, Russia declared war on Japan. That same evening, a second B-29 left Tinian with a second atomic bomb. A few hours later Nagasaki lay in ruins: a further 35,000 people had perished.

Just a few hours before the bomb fell on Nagasaki, the Supreme Council for the Direction of the War had convened at Togo's urging to discuss acceptance of the Potsdam Declaration. Arguments continued for hours, but even the grim news of Nagasaki and Hiroshima did not induce the military representatives to agree that the war should be ended—at least not on the basis of the Potsdam conditions alone.

At this critical juncture the Emperor once again intervened. Meeting with the Supreme Council late on the evening of August 9, His Majesty expressed his desire that Japan accept the Potsdam terms with the sole reservation that the imperial institution be preserved. The following day, August 10, the Japanese government announced its acceptance of the Potsdam Declaration with the proviso that " 'it does not compromise any demand which prejudices the prerogatives of His Majesty as a Sovereign Ruler.' " [95]

Meeting with Stimson, Forrestal, Byrnes, and other advisers at the White House, President Truman discussed the unexpected Japanese offer. The president pointed out that of the 170 telegrams received at the White House during the past twenty-four hours, 153 had urged the harshest surrender terms for Japan. One congressman demanded that the U.S. " 'let the Japs know unqualifiedly what unconditional surrender means. Let the dirty rats squeal.' " Secretary Byrnes agreed with that sentiment, if not with the language; he saw no reason for the U.S. to soften the terms agreed at Potsdam.

Stimson pointed out, however, that retention of the Emperor was the only hope of saving "us from a score of bloody Iwo Jimas and Okinawas." [96] The Emperor was the only source of authority able to compel the Japanese armies in Manchuria, China, and Southeast Asia to lay down their arms. He warned that the longer the war lasted, the more say the Soviets would have in the final outcome, now that they had entered the conflict.

As a compromise, Byrnes drafted a reply which declared that:

> From the moment of surrender, the authority of the Emperor and the Japanese Government to rule the State shall be subject to the Supreme Commander of the Allied powers who will take such steps as he deems proper to effectuate the surrender terms.

Byrnes's message repeated the assurance of the Potsdam Declaration that "the ultimate form of the Government of Japan shall be established by the freely expressed will of the Japanese people." [97] With British, Chinese, and Russian agreement quickly obtained, the note was despatched to Switzerland for delivery to the Japanese. While awaiting a reply, Truman directed that the air and naval attacks against Japan be continued with the proviso that no more atomic bombs be dropped—although more would soon be ready.[98]

Tokyo's receipt of the Byrnes note precipitated another crisis in Japanese councils of state. The military were for outright rejection on the grounds that the note did not guarantee the preservation of the national polity. Togo and the Foreign Office urged acceptance; Prime Minister Suzuki vacillated. For three days Japanese leaders argued fruitlessly. Then, on the fourteenth, American planes showered Tokyo with propaganda leaflets in Japanese which gave the full text of the Japanese government's surrender offer of the tenth and Byrnes' August 11 reply.

Fearing that news of these negotiations would touch off outbreaks among the army and navy, Marquis Kido urged the Emperor to summon another Imperial Conference to end the deadlock. The Emperor readily agreed. Before a stunned and saddened meeting of the cabinet he announced his desire that his ministers " 'bow to my wishes and accept the Allied reply forthwith. In order that the people may know of my decision, I request you to prepare at once an imperial rescript that I may broadcast to the nation.' " [99] The Emperor's decision to broadcast to the nation—a drastic and unprecedented step—was designed to forestall any attempt by right-wing fanatics and the military to interfere with the termination of the war. Without this, such groups might stage a coup, or claim that surrender was not truly in accordance with the will of the Emperor.

That this precaution was amply justified was demonstrated on the evening of August 14, when a group of fanatical army officers took control of the Imperial Guards Division in Tokyo, assassinated its commander, and broke into the palace grounds and NHK radio in search of the recordings the Emperor had made earlier that day bearing his surrender message. They failed to find them, and the revolt collapsed when senior officers refused to join the rebels and brought in loyal troops to clear the palace. During the next few days, Kido, Suzuki, and other leaders of the government all narrowly escaped assassination. General Anami Korechika, the war minister who had opposed surrender to the bitter end, but who had taken no part in the attempted coup, committed suicide on the fourteenth so as to be spared hearing the Emperor's proclamation and to atone for the army's defeats.[100]

Well aware of the danger from fanatics, Japanese leaders took further precautions. Two separate imperial rescripts were issued to the armed forces ordering them to lay down their arms. Members of the imperial family were despatched to overseas garrisons to persuade military commanders to comply. A new government, headed by Prince Higashikuni, the younger brother of the Emperor, assumed office on August 15, thus removing the prime minister as a target for superpatriot assassins.

● ●

Historians have long been preoccupied by the vexing question of Japan's surrender in World War II. Could a surrender have come sooner? If so, when? Was Japan's prolonged resistance the result of mistakes and missed opportunities on the part of the United States or of the suicidal stubbornness of Japan's militarist rulers? What role was played by the two atomic bombs? Might their use have been avoided? Would one have sufficed? [101]

Many historians argue that the bomb was not really needed to bring about the surrender of Japan. That island empire, these critics argue, was so crippled by the cumulative effects of American blockade and bombing that, as Lisle Rose has declared, "she simply could not have continued the war beyond mid-autumn." [102] Rose attributed the decision to use the bomb to the U.S. Government's "refusal to rise above wartime emotionalism and the momentum of unrestrained militarism to consider realistically or humanely the plight of Japan." [103] Other critics of the decision have argued that Truman and his advisers, well aware that Japan was defeated anyway, nevertheless insisted on the atomic attacks in order to coerce the Soviets by a massive demonstration of America's new power. [104]

Yet it was not only academic critics of America's cold war policies who questioned the atomic bomb decision. The notion that the war could have been won by conventional air- and sea power—without either an invasion or a revolutionary new weapon—had an obvious appeal to many navy and air force leaders, many of whom voiced such views after the war. [105] Whether Japan would have been eventually forced to surrender by sheer exhaustion can never be proved or disproved conclusively. Yet it is hard to see how a long-continued aerial bombardment of Japan would have cost fewer lives than the two atomic bombs.

Other writers have conceded the need for an atomic attack: they argue that it provided the necessary shock which finally galvanized the peace faction among Japanese leaders to take action and the Emperor decisively to intervene in the peace process. Yet, they argue that a *second* atomic attack was probably unnecessary and, in any case, came too soon on the heels of the first to allow the Japanese government sufficient time to reach a decision.[106]

All the same, none of the critics of the atomic bomb decisions has been able to demonstrate how the Japanese high command might have been induced to surrender without the *combined* shock of Russia's entry into the war and the use of *two* atomic bombs. The most careful and authoritative study of Japan's decision to surrender notes that "although the atomic attack on Hiroshima had made it impossible for anyone present to continue to deny the urgency of Japan's situation, it apparently had not made a deep enough impression on the chiefs of staff and the War Minister as to make them willing to cast their lot outright for a termination of the war."[107] Some Japanese leaders were already speculating that perhaps the Americans had but one bomb or that a defense could be quickly improvised.[108]

There is another perspective as well. To the infrantrymen and marines preparing for the assault on Japan, to the sailors who had undergone the weeks of kamikaze attacks off Okinawa, the atomic bombs seemed not the first chapter of a catastrophe for mankind, the dawn of a new age of terror, the first gun of the cold war but, in Churchill's words, a "miracle of deliverance." " 'I was a 21-year-old second lieutenant leading a rifle platoon," wrote one veteran three and a half decades later; " 'although still officially in one piece, I had already been wounded in the leg and back severely enough to be adjudged, after the war, 40 percent disabled. But even if my legs buckled whenever I jumped out of the back of a truck, my condition was held to be satisfactory for whatever lay ahead. When the bombs dropped and news began to circulate that "Operation Olympic" would not, after all, take place, that we would not be obliged to run up the beaches near Tokyo assault-firing while being mortared and shelled, for all the fake manliness of our façades, we cried with relief and joy. We were going to live. We were going to grow up to adulthood after all."[109]

● ●

On September 2, 1945, General Douglas MacArthur, newly appointed Supreme Commander, Allied Powers in Japan, stood before an old mess table aboard the battleship *Missouri* at anchor in Tokyo Bay. There he accepted the formal surrender of the Japanese government representatives. After the last of the Japanese and Allied representatives had signed the instrument of surrender, MacArthur stepped forward and intoned these final words: "Let us pray that peace be now restored to the world and that God will preserve it always."

The American war with Japan had ended.

• •

So the United States had done the impossible. It had waged war simultaneously on two fronts, separated by thousands of miles, and had prevailed. There had been able leaders and superior strategists on both sides, as well as dedication, bravery, and perseverance. Yet in the end, it was superior American industrial power and organizational ability which had succeeded—as Admiral Yamamoto had foreseen. In the Battle of the Philippine Sea, for example, Japan's strategy had been largely successful. But the Japanese had suffered a devastating defeat because of the superior training, experience, equipment, and numbers of the Americans.

Because of its material superiority, the United States could afford such expensive—and occasionally dangerous—luxuries as divided command and the lack of an overall strategy in its war against Japan. The Japanese, for their part, were content to remain on the defensive after the summer of 1942 and allow their American opponents to get on-the-job training.

Both Japanese and Americans paid a price for the tradition of separateness and rivalry among their respective armed services. The Americans, to a greater extent than the Japanese, did go far toward achieving interservice coordination and cooperation, particularly at the operational level. Yet for the United States, the record of the Pacific War is not so much a story of how the services forgot their differences but rather of the ingenuity displayed by service leaders in devising courses of action which allowed them to get on with the war without having to settle those differences.

For the American people, the aftermath of the war was disappointing. The American monopoly of the atomic bomb was shortlived. The existence of the new weapon led only to greater insecurity. China, upon which so many extravagant hopes had been lavished, emerged from civil war as a Communist state, bitterly hostile to the U.S., while the breakup of the former Japanese and European empires in Asia led to new wars and upheavals. In the cold afterlight of the 1950s, more than a few writers suggested that the U.S. had made an error in destroying the military power of Japan. Such action, they argued, resulted only in laying Asia open to the expansion of communism.

From a more distant perspective the picture appears more sanguine. The United States acquired a strong democratic ally in the new Japan which emerged from the wreckage of war. The existence of three great powers in East Asia, China, Japan, and the Soviet Union, has surely made that region more safe and stable than the older system in which Japan, the Soviet Union, and the European powers struggled for supremacy in a weak and divided China. Similarly, few would wish to trade the vibrant, rapidly growing new nations of Asia—like Singapore, Taiwan, India, and Malaysia—for the stagnant, impoverished, and exploited colonies of the 1930s. The existence of the strong and stable independent nations of Asia is perhaps the most important and lasting legacy bequeathed by the men and women who perished in the American-Japanese war.

NOTES

1. Basic treatments of the Okinawa campaign include Roy E. Appleman, James M. Burns, Russell A. Gugeler, and John Stevens, *Okinawa: The Last Battle* (Washington, D.C.: Historical Division Department of the Army, 1948); Bemis M. Frank and Henry I. Shaw, Jr., *Victory and Occupation* (Washington, D.C.: G-3 Division Headquarters, U.S. Marine Corps, 1968), pp. 31–397; Samuel Eliot Morison, *Victory in the Pacific 1945* (Boston: Little, Brown and Co., 1960), pp. 79–285. An excellent general history based on extensive research is James and William Belote, *Typhoon of Steel: The Battle for Okinawa* (New York: Harper and Row, 1970).

2. Appleman et al., *Okinawa*, pp. 91–96.

3. The most complete description of Japanese defensive preparations is in Frank and Shaw, *Victory and Occupation*, pp. 40–55.

4. Baldwin, *Battles Lost and Won*, p. 370.

5. Lieutenant General Silverthorne interview, p. 339.

6. Potter, *Nimitz*, p. 372.

7. Belote and Belote, *Typhoon of Steel*, pp. 128–29.

8. Ibid., p. 138.

9. Ibid., pp. 212–13; Appleman et al., *Okinawa*, pp. 260–264. Buckner's marine generals were also divided on this question. General Lemuel C. Shephard told the Belotes he had suggested several times to Buckner that he land the Second Marine Division, which had enough organic logistical support to sustain operations for at least thirty days, on the Minatogawa beaches. Belote and Belote, *Typhoon of Steel*, p. 214. On the other hand, General Merwin Silverthorne observes that, "The logistic considerations, once the Second Division got inland, to establish another whole line of communication, if you will, up to the front lines from the beaches would have magnified the task out of proportion to any tactical advantage. . . . I don't think pressure there would

have caused any difference in the final outcome. . . ." Lieutenant General Merwin Silverthorne interview, p. 353.

10. Frank and Shaw, *Victory and Occupation,* p. 213 gives a figure of 6,200 Japanese killed; Belote and Belote, p. 233, say about 5,000.

11. Rear Admiral Yokoi Toshiyuki, "Kamikazes and the Okinawa Campaign," *U.S. Naval Institute Proceedings,* 80, p. 505–8.

12. Morison, *Victory in the Pacific,* pp. 182–97.

13. Ibid.

14. Buell, *The Quiet Warrior,* pp. 358–59.

15. Belote and Belote, *Typhoon of Steel,* pp. 167–70; Morison, *Victory in the Pacific,* pp. 233–36

16. Morison, *Victory in the Pacific,* pp. 98–99.

17. Belote and Belote, *Typhoon of Steel,* p. 147.

18. For accounts of Task Force Fifty-seven operations, see Morison, *Victory in the Pacific,* pp. 102–7, 211–14, 249–65, and Rear Admiral Sir Bruce Fraser, "The Contributions of the British Pacific Fleet to the Assault on Okinawa, 1945," *London Gazette Supplements 1946–1951* Vol. 2 and S. W. Roskill, *The War at Sea,* Vol. 3, Part 2, pp. 431–501.

19. Dull, *Imperial Japanese Navy,* p. 346. Useful accounts from the Japanese perspective are Ito Masanori, *The End of the Imperial Japanese Navy* (New York: W. W. Norton and Co., 1962), and Yoshida Mitsuru, "The End of the Yamato," *U.S. Naval Institute Proceedings,* 68 (February 1952), pp. 117–30.

20. Cf. Dull, *Imperial Japanese Navy,* p. 347.

21. Private communication to the author by officer who served in the USS *New Mexico.*

22. Baldwin, *Battles Lost and Won,* p. 377.

23. Potter, *Nimitz,* pp. 371–72.

24. Buell, *The Quiet Warrior,* pp. 356–57.

25. Major General Wilburt S. Brown oral history interview, Marine Corps Historical Center, pp. 214–15.

26. Isely and Crowl, *U.S. Marines and Amphibious Warfare,* pp. 575–76.

27. Major General Brown interview, p. 217.

28. Belote and Belote, *Typhoon of Steel,* pp. 310–11.

29. Coakley and Leighton, *Global Logistics and Strategy, 1943–1945,* pp. 579–80.

30. Ibid; James, *Years of MacArthur,* pp. 724–28; Potter, *Nimitz,* pp. 379–80.

31. Potter, *Nimitz,* p. 381; Buell, *The Quiet Warrior,* pp. 364–66; Morgan, "Planning the Defeat of Japan," pp. 153–54.

32. Morgan, "Planning the Defeat of Japan," pp. 153–57; Message, MacArthur to Marshall, 20 April 1945, CM-IN-19089, OPD Files, RG 165.

33. *Reports of General MacArthur. The Campaigns of MacArthur in the Pacific,* Vol. 1, p. 398.

34. JCS to MacArthur, Nimitz, and Arnold, 25 May 1945, CM-IN.987938, OPD Files, RG 165.

35. Details of Planning for OLYMPIC may be found in *Reports of General MacAr-*

thur, Vol. 1, Chapter 13, "Sixth Army Occupation of Japan," 8th Information and Historical Service, Section I, MS copy in CMH; General Headquarters U.S. Army Forces Pacific, "DOWNFALL Strategic Plan," copy in CMH; and Message, CINCAFPAC to WARCOS, 9 August 1945, copy in Sutherland Papers.

36. Minutes, JCS Meeting with President, 18 June 1945, RG 165.

37. *Reports of General MacArthur: Japanese Operations in the Southwest Pacific Area,* Vol. 2, Part 2, p. 653.

38. Ibid., p. 657.

39. Ibid., "Sixth Army Occupation of Japan," pp. 4–6.

40. *Reports of General MacArthur: Japanese Operations,* Vol. 2, Part 2, p. 612.

41. Cline, *Washington Command Post,* pp. 340–49.

42. Message, Nimitz to King, 28 April 1945, King Papers, Double Zero Files.

43. Stouffer et al., *Combat and Its Aftermath,* pp. 89–90, 457–59.

44. Ibid., p. 90.

45. Stouffer et al., *The American Soldier: Adjustment During Army Life,* pp. 186–87.

46. JCS 1340, 9 May 1945, CCS 387 Japan, Records of Joint Chiefs of Staff, RG 218.

47. Barton J. Bernstein, "The Perils and Politics of Surrender: Ending the War with Japan and Avoiding the Third Atomic Bomb," *Pacific Historical Review,* February 1977, p. 5.

48. Akira Iriye, *Power and Culture: The Japanese-American War 1941–1945* (Cambridge: Harvard University Press, 1981), pp. 149–52.

49. Brian L. Villa, "The U.S. Army, Unconditional Surrender and the Potsdam Proclamation," *Journal of American History* 63 (June 1976), p. 75.

50. Ibid., p. 78.

51. Ibid., pp. 80–84.

52. Draft proclamation, June 29, 1945; copy in OPD 387.4, RG 165.

53. Villa, "The U.S. Army," p. 89; Iriye, *Power and Culture,* p. 256. Byrnes's view of general U.S. opinion was correct. Army polling of soldiers, however, revealed that few fighting men cared whether the Emperor remained or not so long as surrender could be quickly achieved. Villa, "The U.S. Army," p. 84.

54. Iriye, *Power and Culture,* pp. 253–62.

55. Ibid., p. 263.

56. Rose, *Dubious Victory,* p. 225; Bernstein, "Perils and Politics," p. 25.

57. Robert J. C. Butow, *Japan's Decision to Surrender* (Stanford: Stanford University Press, 1954), pp. 17–42.

58. In April 1945, 400 people were arrested by order of the war minister on suspicion of "harboring end-the-war sentiments." Butow, *Japan's Decision to Surrender,* p. 75.

59. Butow, *Japan's Decision to Surrender,* pp. 69–72.

60. Ibid., p. 100.

61. *Reports of General MacArthur: Japanese Operations in the Southwest Pacific Area*, Vol. 2, Part 2, p. 694.

62. "Russo Japanese Relations, July 21–27, 1945," August 2, 1945, SRH-086 and "MAGIC Diplomatic Extracts, July 1945," SRS-040, both in RG 457.

63. "Russo Japanese Relations, July 21–27, 1945," August 2, 1945, p. 21, SRH-086, RG 457.

64. Walter Millis, ed., *The Forrestal Diaries* (New York: Viking, 1951); For a differing view, see Iriye, *Power and Culture*, pp. 259–260.

65. *Reports of General MacArthur: Japanese Operations* pp. 700–1; Butow, *Japan's Decision to Surrender*, p. 143.

66. Butow, *Japan's Decision to Surrender*, pp. 146–49.

67. Brian W. Aldiss, *Billion Year Spree: The True History of Science Fiction* (New York: Schocken Books, 1974), p. 233.

68. Martin J. Sherwin, *A World Destroyed: The Atomic Bomb and the Grand Alliance* (New York: Vintage Books, 1977), pp. 17–18.

69. Richard G. Hewlett and Oscar E. Anderson, Jr., *The New World 1939–1946* (University Park, Pa.: Pennsylvania State University Press, 1962), pp. 17–19.

70. Sherwin, *A World Destroyed*, p. 37.

71. Hewlett and Anderson, *The New World*, pp. 54–55.

72. Sherwin, *A World Destroyed*, p. 42.

73. William L. Laurence, *Dawn Over Zero: The Story of the Atomic Bomb* (New York: Alfred A. Knopf, 1946), pp. 92–93.

74. Memorandum, Major General Leslie Graves to Secretary of War, July 18, 1945, Sub.: The Test, Special Interest to General Graves: TS Files, Manhattan Engineer, District Records, National Archives.

75. Lansing Lamont, *Day of Trinity* (New York: Atheneum Publishers, 1965), p. 235.

76. Laurence, *Dawn Over Zero*, pp. 113–15; Leslie R. Groves, *Now It Can Be Told: The Story of the Manhattan Project* (New York: Harper and Row, 1962), pp. 244–46.

77. Quoted in Sherwin, *A World Destroyed*, p. 224. Lisle A. Rose, however, argues that however exhilirated the Americans may have felt, the news had little practical effect on their negotiating position: *Dubious Victory*, pp. 309–22.

78. U.S. Dept. of Defense, *Entry of the Soviet Union Into the War Against Japan: Military Plans 1941–1945* (Washington: GPO, 1955), pp. 1–5; Matloff and Snell, *Strategic Planning for Coalition Warfare 1941–1942*, pp. 84–87.

79. JCS Memorandum, Sub.: Estimate of Enemy Situation 1943–1944, Pacific-Far East Area, 6 August 1943, CCS 300, RG 228.

80. Report by the Joint Plans Committee, Sub.: Operations Against Japan Subsequent to Formosa, 30 June 1944, JCS 924, RG 228.

81. Letter, Stimson to Acting Secretary of State, May 21, 1945, cited in *Entry of the Soviet Union Into the War*, p. 70.

82. Sherwin, *A World Destroyed*, pp. 226–27; Hayes, *The Advance to Victory*, pp. 398–99; Leahy, *I Was There*, p. 419.

83. Millis, ed., *The Forrestal Diaries*, p. 11.

84. *Memoirs of Harry S Truman: Years of Decisions* (Garden City, N.Y.: Doubleday, 1955), pp. 322–23.

85. Lamont, *Day of Trinity*, pp. 65–66, 272–78, 280–83.

86. Hewlett and Anderson, *The New World*, p. 327.

87. Ibid., pp. 358, 365; Sherwin, *A World Destroyed*, p. 214.

88. Laurence, *Dawn Over Zero*, pp. 200–1.

89. Margaret Truman, *Harry S Truman* (New York: Morrow, 1972), p. 6.; *Memoirs of Harry S Truman*, Vol. 1, *Years of Decisions*, p. 419.

90. Robert H. Ferrell, ed., *Off The Record: The Private Papers of Harry S Truman* (New York: Norton, 1980), p. 55.

91. Otis Cary, "Mr. Stimson's Pet City—The Sparing of Kyoto, 1945." Cited in Asada Sadao, "Japanese Perceptions of the A-Bomb Decision, 1945–1980," in Joe C. Dixon, ed., *The American Military and the Far East* (Washington, D.C.: GPO, 1980), p. 212.

92. Ibid.

93. Barton J. Bernstein, "Roosevelt, Truman and the Atomic Bomb 1941–1945: A Reinterpretation," *Political Science Quarterly* 90 (1975), p. 61.

94. Laurence, *Dawn Over Zero*, pp. 224.

95. Bernstein, "Perils and Politics of Surrender," p. 5.

96. Ibid.

97. Byrnes to Swiss Chargé d'Arraires, August 11, 1945, *Foreign Relations of the United States, 1945*, Vol. 6, p. 632

98. Marshall to Groves, 10 August 1945, Manhattan Engineers, District TS Files, 5. RG 77.

99. Butow, *Japan's Decision to Surrender*, p. 208; a slightly different version of the Emperor's remarks is in Toland, *The Rising Sun*, p. 937.

100. Butow, ibid., p. 219.

101. A good survey of the debate may be found in Barton J. Bernstein, "The Atomic Bomb and American Foreign Policy 1941–1945: An Historiographical Survey," *Peace and Change* (Spring 1974). Bernstein's own views may be found in his "Roosevelt, Truman and the Atomic Bomb: A Reinterpretation," *Political Science Quarterly* 90 (1975). An excellent discussion of Japanese attitudes about, and historical interpretations of, the atomic bomb is Asada Sadao's, "Japanese Perceptions of the A-Bomb Decision, 1945–1980," in Joe C. Dixon, ed., *The American Military and the Far East* (Washington, D.C.: GPO, 1980), pp. 199–217. Asada notes that there are "striking differences between Japanese and American perceptions of the A-Bomb decision" and that the Japanese "feel that for the mistake of starting the Pacific War they have already taken their punishment and are thus absolved while the American side remains unrepentant for the atomic holocaust. In Japanese consciousness, moreover, Pearl Harbor and Hiroshima belong to totally different categories—in terms of sheer

number of casualties, the nature of human suffering and symbolic significance for the future of mankind." (pp. 200, 206–207.)

102. Rose, *Dubious Victory,* pp. 365–66.

103. Ibid.

104. Athan Theoharis, *The Yalta Myths* (Columbia, Mo.: University of Missouri Press, 1970), pp. 114–29, 154–79; Gar Alperowitz, *Atomic Diplomacy: Hiroshima and Potsdam* (New York: Vintage, 1967) pp. 237–39, 241; Charles L. Mee, *Meeting at Potsdam* (New York: Evans, 1975), pp. 238–39, 288–89; P. M. S. Blackett, *Fear War and the Bomb* (New York: Whittlesey House, 1949), p. 139.

105. See for example Potter, *Nimitz,* p. 400.

106. Sherwin, *A World Destroyed,* p. 237; Barton J. Bernstein, "Doomsday II," *New York Times Magazine,* July 27, 1975.

107. Butow, *Japan's Decision to Surrender,* p. 163.

108. Ibid., pp. 152, 163.

109. Paul Fussell, " 'Thank God for the Atomic Bomb,' " *Washington Post,* August 23, 1981.

Bibliographic Note

In the discussion which follows, only those sources which were of most importance in the preparation of this book have been cited. Some of the more specialized records, books and articles, are discussed in the relevant chapter footnotes. The inclusion or absence of a particular source is not intended as a reflection on its overall value to students of the Second World War but only its relevance to the present undertaking. Those in need of a more extensive discussion of the literature should consult the relevant bibliographic essays in Robin Higham ed., *A Guide to the Sources of United States Military History* (Hamden: Archon Books, 1975, 1981), the excellent bibliographic essay prepared by Dean C. Allard for the published edition of Grace P. Hayes, *The History of the Joint Chiefs of Staff in World War II: The War Against Japan* (Annapolis: U.S. Naval Institute, 1982), or Janet Ziegler's comprehensive *World War II: Books in English, 1945–1965* (Stanford: Hoover Institution Press, 1971).

OFFICIAL RECORDS

Almost all important U.S. military records relating to the War with Japan have been declassified and are principally found in two major repositories: The Modern Military Records Branch, National Archives, and the U.S. Naval Historical Center, both in Washington D.C. Those utilized in this study include *Record Group 218,* Records of the Joint and Combined Chiefs of Staff; *Record Group 165,* Records of the War Department, General and Special Staffs; *Record Group 457,* comprising records relating to all phases of communications intelligence in World War II, recently turned over to the National Archives by the National Security Agency; other records utilized include the Records of China Theater at the National Archives annex at Suitland, Maryland; the Papers of Admiral Ernest J. King, together with a broader collection of his office files known as the Double Zero files, in the Operational Archives of the Naval Historical Center, Washington, D.C.; and the records of the Navy's War Plans Division and the General Board, also found in the Operational Archives.

British records consulted include Foreign Office Records relating to the Far East in *FO 371* and the Records of Southeast Asia Command in War Office Records *WO 203*, all in the Public Record Office, London. On British records the researcher may consult Public Record Office Handbook 15, *The Second World War: A Guide to Documents in the Public Record Office* (London: HMSO, 1972).

PERSONAL PAPERS

Personal papers collections which proved most important for this study include the papers of Henry H. Arnold, in the Library of Congress; Richard K. Sutherland and Charles A. Willoughby, in the National Archives; General Haydon Boatner in the U.S. Army Center of Military History, and the Milton E. Miles papers in the Naval Historical Center, as well as the Ernest J. King Papers referred to above.

ORAL HISTORIES

The oral history "memoirs" of American leaders in the War with Japan provide an invaluable supplement and corrective to the official record. Those consulted for this study include the *Charles Adair, Hanson W. Baldwin, Arleigh Burke, Richard L. Connelly, Harry W. Hill* and *Thomas C. Kinkaid* interviews in the U.S. Naval Historical center; the *George H. Decker, Clyde D. Eddleman* and *Robert H. Wood* interviews at the U.S. Army Military History Institute, Carlisle, Pa.; the *David A. Berchinal* interview in the Office of the Chief of Air Force History, Washington, D.C.; and the *Wilbert H. Brown, Clifton B. Cates, Graves B. Erskine, Omar T. Pfeiffer, Edwin Pollock, Merwin H. Silverthorne* and *Oliver P. Smith* interviews in the U.S. Marine Corps Historical Center, Washington, D.C. Through the kindness of John Toland, I was also able to use notes and summaries of inteviews conducted by him for his book *The Rising Sun.*

MEMOIRS AND AUTOBIOGRAPHIES

Almost all high-ranking American leaders in the War with Japan have written their memoirs (or had them written for them). A conspicuous exception was Admiral Chester W. Nimitz, but the fine biography by E. B. Potter more than fills the gap. The most important memoirs from the point of view of the present work were Ernest J. King and Walter Whitehill, *Fleet Admiral King: A Naval Record* (New York: W. W. Norton, 1952); General H. H. Arnold, *Global Mission* (New York: Harper & Brothers, 1949); Henry L. Stimson and McGeorge Bundy, *On Active Service in Peace and War* (New York: Harper & Brothers, 1948); William F. Halsey and Joseph Bryan, *Admiral Halsey's Story* (New York: Whittlesey House, 1947); William Slim, *Defeat Into Victory* (London: Weidenfield & Nicholson, 1960); Holland M. Smith and Percy Finch, *Coral and Brass* (New York: Scribners, 1949); Robert L. Eichelberger, *Our Jungle Road to Tokyo* (New York: Viking, 1950); Walter Krueger, *From Down Under to Nippon* (Washington: Combat Forces Press, 1953); Albert C. Wedemeyer, *Wedemeyer Reports!* (New York: Holt, 1958); and Daniel E. Barbey, *MacArthur's Amphibious Navy* (Annapolis: Naval Institute, 1969). Portions of General Stilwell's journals and letters edited by Theodore H. White—*The Stilwell Papers* (New York: William Sloane Associations, 1948)—might also be included in this category.

While the memoirs of the top commanders provide some useful information, none are as enlightening—or interesting—as those by men who occupied less exalted positions. Among the best of these memoirs are Charlton Ogburn, Jr., *The Marauders* (New York: Harper, 1959); W. J. Holmes, *Double-Edged Secrets* (Annapolis: Naval

Institute, 1979); and the World War II portions of Theodore H. White's *In Search of History* (New York: Harper and Row, 1978). By far the most useful Japanese first-hand accounts available in English are Masataka Okumiya and Jiro Horikoshi, *Zero* (New York: E. P. Dutton, 1956), and Mitsuo Fuchida and Masatake Okumiya, *Midway* (Annapolis: Naval Institute, 1955).

OFFICIAL HISTORIES

Although written over twenty-five years ago, the official histories published by the U.S. Army and Navy, and to a lesser degree those of the Air Force and Marine Corps, remain the basic source for the history of military operations in the War with Japan. Indeed, in some cases they are the *only* source since many battles and campaigns of the Pacific War have not received subsequent serious treatment by historians. The best known and most readable is Samuel Eliot Morison, *History of United States Naval Operations in World War II*, XV vols. (Boston: Little Brown and Co., 1947–62). All but three of Morison's volumes deal with the War Against Japan. Strong on action, they tend to slight or ignore matters of organization, logistics, intelligence, and command and control. Far more detailed is *The U.S. Army in World War II* series (Washington: Office of the Chief of Military History, 1944–1981), with its many subseries totalling over seventy-five volumes. Of the many books in the series which bear on the War with Japan, the following were most useful in the preparation of this study: Louis Morton, *Strategy and Command: The First Two Years,* and his earlier book, *The Fall of the Philippines;* Robert Ross Smith on MacArthur's campaigns in New Guinea and Luzon—*The Approach to the Philippines,* and *Triumph in the Philippines;* Philip A. Crowl, *Campaign in the Marianas;* Samuel Milner, *Victory in Papua;* John Miller, Jr., *Cartwheel: The Reduction of Rabaul;* Maurice Matloff and Edwin M. Snell, *Strategic Planning for Coalition Warfare 1941–1942;* and Maurice Matloff, *Strategic Planning for Coalition Warfare 1943–1944*. In a class by themselves are the magnificent trilogy by Charles F. Romanus and Riley Sunderland—*Stilwell's Mission to China, Stilwell's Command Problems,* and *Time Runs Out in CBI*—which remain the starting point for any serious research on wartime China, and the unique volumes by Robert W. Coakley and Richard M. Leighton, *Global Logistics and Strategy 1940–1943* and *Global Logistics and Strategy 1943–1945*. Of the specialized studies, Mattie E. Treadwell's *The Women's Army Corps* has not been superseded, despite the recent vogue of "women's histories," while Ulysses Lee's *The Employment of Negro Troops* and the more recent volume by Morris J. MacGregor, Jr., *Integration of the Armed Forces 1940–1965* (Defense Studies Series) (Washington: U.S. Army Center of Military History, 1981) have not even been approached in depth and comprehensiveness by other works.

Three of the seven volumes in Wesley F. Craven and James L. Cate, eds., *The Army Air Forces in World War II* (Chicago: University of Chicago Press, 1948–58), deal in whole or in part with the War against Japan: *Plans and Early Operations, January 1939 to August 1942; The Pacific: Guadalcanal to Saipan, August 1942 to July 1944;* and *The Pacific: Matterhorn to Nagasaki, June 1944 to August 1945*. Although of uneven quality and published before all the records were available to their authors, they remain an indispensable source.

Marine Corps Official Histories of World War II perforce deal entirely with the War against Japan. In addition to the many fine monographs such as those by Robert D. Heinl: *The Defense of Wake* (Washington: Historical Section, U.S. Marine Corps, 1947), and Carl W. Hoffmann, *Saipan: The Beginning of the End* (Washington: Historical Division, U.S. Marine Corps, 1950), the five volumes in the *History of U.S. Marine Corps Operations in World War II* (Washington: Historical Branch G-3 U.S. Marine Corps, 1958–68) contain a wealth of detailed information. More analytical and an indispensable source for understanding the Central Pacific campaigns is Jeter A. Isely and Philip A. Crowl's semi-official study, *The U.S. Marines and Amphibious War* (Princeton: Princeton University Press, 1951). Although not published until nearly thirty years after its completion, Grace P. Hayes, *The Joint Chiefs of Staff and the War Against Japan* (Annapolis: U.S. Naval Institute Press, 1982), the best study of high-level strategy in the war, has been extensively mined by serious scholars since it was declassified in 1971. Also declassified but never published were U.S. Naval War College analyses of selected naval campaigns in World War II, consulted by the author at the Naval Historical Center. Another recently declassified study, Kermit Roosevelt, *War Report of the OSS: Vol. II: The Overseas Targets* (New York: Walker, 1976), was useful for its capsule accounts of Allied intelligence operations in China and Southeast Asia.

Of the official histories published by the British and Australians, the following were used most extensively in preparation of this work. In the British series, *History of the Second World War: United Kingdom Military Series* (London: HMSO, 1956–1969): Michael Howard, *Grand Strategy, Vol IV;* John Ehrman, *Grand Strategy, Vols. V and VI;* S. W. Roskill, *The War at Sea, Vol. II: The Period of Balance;* S. Woodburn Kirby, *The War Against Japan, Vol. II: India's Most Dangerous Hour;* and *The War Against Japan: Vol. V: The Surrender of Japan.*

Of the Australian volumes, *Australia in the War of 1939–1945,* 21 vols. (Canberra: Australian War Memorial, 1952–1968), the most useful were Dudley McCarthy, *Southwest Pacific Area, the First Year: Kokoda to Wau;* David Dexter, *The New Guinea Offensives,* and Paul Hasluck, *The Government and the People, 1942–1945.*

None of the Japanese official histories have been translated into English. However, Paul Dull, a Japanese linguist, has used these histories, as well as other Japanese records, to reconstruct some of the naval engagements from the Japanese perspective in *A Battle History of the Imperial Japanese Navy* (Annapolis: Naval Institute Press, 1978). Selected translations from the official Japanese series on the origins of the Pacific War have been translated and published under the general editorship of James W. Morley. The two volumes which have so far appeared are: *Deterrent Diplomacy: Japan, Germany and the USSR* (New York: Columbia University Press, 1976) and *The Fateful Choice: Japan's Negotiations with the United States 1941* (New York: Columbia University Press, 1980).

At the conclusion of World War II, former officers of the Japanese Armed Forces prepared a series of monographs on various aspects of Japanese strategy and operations for the use of General MacArthur's G-2 Far East Command. English translations of all of these monographs are on file in the U.S. Army Center of Military History. The same authors who prepared the monographs also wrote a history entitled *Japanese Operations in the Southwest Pacific Area,* which forms the second volume of the two-volume, four-book series, *The Reports of General MacArthur* (Washington: GPO, 1966). One of the authors of the monographs, Hattori Takushiro, went on to write a long history: *The Complete History of the Greater East Asia War,* 4 vols. (Tokyo: Masu Publishing Co., 1953). A manuscript English translation is on file in the U.S. Army Center of Military History.

BIOGRAPHIES

During the last decade, much of the significant scholarship on the War with Japan has appeared in the form of biographies. Leading the list are the magisterial studies by D. Clayton James, *The Years of MacArthur,* 2 vols. (New York: Houghton Mifflin, 1972, 1975) and Forrest C. Pogue, *George C. Marshall,* 3 vols. (New York: Viking, 1964–1973). Two other studies present differing perspectives on MacArthur: William Manchester's *American Ceasar: Douglas MacArthur 1880–1964* (Boston: Little

Brown, 1978) and Carol M. Petillo, *Douglas MacArthur: The Philippine Years* (Bloomington: Indiana University Press, 1981). On the Navy side, Thomas E. Buell's *The Quiet Warrior: A Biography of Admiral Raymond Spruance* (Boston: Little Brown, 1974), and his *Master of Seapower: A Biography of Admiral Ernest J. King* (Boston: Little Brown, 1980), and E. B. Potter, *Nimitz* (Annapolis: U.S. Naval Institute Press, 1976) are essential for an understanding of the Navy's role in the Pacific War. Other fine naval biographies include James R. Leutze, *A Different Kind of Victory: A Biography of Admiral Thomas C. Hart* (Annapolis: Naval Institute, 1981) and Agawa Hiroyuki, *The Reluctant Admiral: Yamamoto and the Imperial Navy* (Tokyo: Kodansha International, 1979). Far too long but nevertheless highly useful is V. Adm. George C. Dyer, *The Amphibians Came to Conquer: The Story of Admiral Richmond Kelly Turner,* 2 vols. (Washington: Dept. of the Navy, 1969). Marine Corps Generals have not received the treatment accorded their Army and Navy peers, but researchers should not neglect the unpublished dissertation by Norman V. Cooper, "The Military Career of General Holland M. Smith" (University of Alabama, 1974). American commanders in CBI have been uniformly neglected except for Stilwell, who was the subject of Barbara Tuchman's bestseller, *Stilwell and the American Experience in China* (New York: Macmillan, 1970). William J. Donovan, the flamboyant head of the OSS, is the subject of a recent biography by Anthony Cave Brown, *The Last Hero: Wild Bill Donovan* (New York: Times, 1982), which, however, appeared too late to be used in this study.

Although published over twenty years ago, Robert J. C. Butow's *Tojo and the Coming of the War* (Princeton: Princeton University Press, 1961) remains indispensable, as does Robert E. Sherwood's even older *Roosevelt and Hopkins* (New York: Harper & Brothers, 1948).

SOME SIGNIFICANT SECONDARY WORKS

The tendency of historians to concentrate their attention on the origins and conclusion of a war holds true for the War With Japan. Among the many notable recent contributions to the extensive literature on the origins of the Pacific War are Stephen E. Pelz, *Race to Pearl Harbor* (Cambridge: Harvard University, 1974); Arthur Marder, *Old Friends, New Enemies* (New York: Oxford University Press, 1981); James R. Leutze, *Bargaining For Supremacy* (Chapel Hill: University of North Carolina Press, 1977); and the outstanding collection of papers edited by Dorothy Borg and Shumpai Okamoto, *Pearl Harbor As History: Japanese-American Relations 1931-1941* (New York: Columbia University Press, 1973). Gordon W. Prange's massive *At Dawn We Slept* (New York: McGraw-Hill, 1981) would, one would expect, be the last word on the Pearl Harbor attack; however, John Toland's *Infamy: Pearl Harbor and Its Aftermath* (Garden City, N.Y.: Doubleday, 1982) has already registered a dissenting opinion.

A landmark study of the political and diplomatic dimensions of the Pacific War is Christopher Thorne's massive *Allies of A Kind: The United States, Britain and The War Against Japan* (London: Hamish Hamilton, 1978). Robert Dallek's *Franklin Roosevelt and American Foreign Policy 1932-1945* (New York: Oxford University Press, 1979) is a fine synthesis of much of the recent scholarship on American foreign relations during the war. Akira Iriye's *Power and Culture* (Cambridge: Harvard University Press, 1981) is an impressive study of changing American and Japanese perceptions of their war aims and of each other which, however, in this author's view, seriously understates or neglects the degrees of hatred and fanaticism which animated top leaders of both sides.

Military operations of the war have received less attention but books such as John B. Lundstrom, *The First South Pacific Campaign: Pacific Fleet Strategy December*

1941–June 1942 (Annapolis: Naval Institute Press, 1976); Clay Blair, Jr., *Silent Victory: The U.S. Submarine War Against Japan* (Philadelphia: J. B. Lippincott, 1975); Clark G. Reynolds, *The Fast Carriers: The Forging of An Air Navy* (New York: McGraw Hill, 1968); William T. Y'Blood, *Red Sun Setting: The Battle of the Philippine Sea* (Annapolis: Naval Institute, 1980); Stanley L. Falk, *Decision at Leyte* (New York: W. W. Norton, 1966); and the two books by James H. Belote and William M. Belote, *Titans of the Seas: The Development and Operations of American Carrier Task Forces During World War II* (New York: Harper and Row, 1975) and *Typhoon of Steel: The Battle for Okinawa* (New York: Harper and Row, 1969), show what can be done and, in the case of Lundstrom and Blair, move far beyond the conventional accounts to break new ground and introduce new interpretations.

The opening of the communications intelligence records of World War II will doubtless lead to many new books and studies; an early effort in this direction is Ronald Lewin's *The American Magic: Codes, Ciphers and the Defeat of Japan* (New York: Farrar Straus and Giroux, 1982). Jeffrey M. Dorwart's *Conflict of Duty: The U.S. Navy's Intelligence Dilemma 1919–1945* (Annapolis: Naval Institute, 1983) appeared too late to be utilized for this work, as did Thomas Troy's important study: *Donovan and the CIA: A History of the Establishment of the Central Intelligence Agency* (Frederick, Md.: Alatheia Books, 1983).

Index

ABOUT THE AUTHOR

RONALD H. SPECTOR graduated from Johns Hopkins University and received his Ph.D. from Yale University. He served with the U.S. Marines in Vietnam and was a Senior Fulbright scholar in India during 1977 and 1978. Now a major in the Marine Corps Reserve, Spector was recently ordered to active duty to prepare a study of the Grenada operation. He has served as a Historian at the U.S. Army Center of Military History and presently teaches history at the University of Alabama. A frequent contributor to scholarly journals, Spector is the author of three books: *Admiral of the New Empire: The Life and Career of George Dewey; Professors of War: The Naval College and the Development of the Naval Profession;* and *Advice and Support: The Early Years, 1941– 1960 The U.S. Army in Vietnam, Volume 1.*